The Disability Studies Reader

Second Edition

The Disability Studies Reader

Second Edition

Edited by Lennard J. Davis

Routledge
Taylor & Francis Group
New York   London

Routledge is an imprint of the
Taylor & Francis Group, an informa business

Routledge
Taylor & Francis Group
270 Madison Avenue
New York, NY 10016

Routledge
Taylor & Francis Group
2 Park Square
Milton Park, Abingdon
Oxon OX14 4RN

Printed in the United States of America on acid-free paper
10 9 8 7 6 5 4 3 2 1

International Standard Book Number-10: 0-415-95334-0 (Softcover) 0-415-95333-2 (Hardcover)
International Standard Book Number-13: 978-0-415-95334-4 (Softcover) 978-0-415-95333-7 (Hardcover)

Library of Congress Cataloging-in-Publication Data

The disability studies reader / edited by Lennard J. Davis. -- 2nd ed.
    p. cm.
  ISBN 0-415-95333-2 (hardback : alk. paper) -- ISBN 0-415-95334-0 (pbk. : alk. paper)
  1. People with disabilities. 2. Sociology of disability. 3. Disability studies.   I. Davis, Lennard J.,
1949-   .

HV1568.D5696 2006
362.4--dc22

2006007500

Visit the Taylor & Francis Web site at
http://www.taylorandfrancis.com

and the Routledge Web site at
http://www.routledge-ny.com

Contents

*N = new
otherwise, originally in v1*

Acknowledgments

Chapter 1 reprinted by permission of Lennard J. Davis, *Enforcing Normalcy: Disability, Deafness, and the Body:* pp. 23–72, New York and London: Verso. Copyright © 1995 by Verso.

Chapter 3 reprinted with permission of The Johns Hopkins University Press from Douglas Baynton, "A Silent Exile on this Earth" in *American Quarterly* 44:2 (1992), 216-243, © The American Studies Association.

Chapter 4 reprinted by permission of the publisher and the author David Serlin, *Replaceable You: Engineering the Body in Postwar America,* pp. 21–56, Chicago: University of Chicago Press. Copyright © 2004 by The University of Chicago Press.

Chapter 5 reprinted by permission of the University of Minnesota Press from James C. Wilson, "(Re)Writing the Genetic Body-Text: Disability, Textuality, and the Human Genome Project," in *Cultural Critique* 50 (Winter 2002), pp. 23–39. Copyright © 2002 by Regents of the University of Minnesota.

Chapter 6 reprinted with permission of Taylor & Francis Group, from Harlan Lane, "Constructions of Deafness" in *Disability and Society* 10:2 (1995): pp 171–189. Copyright ©1995 by Taylor & Francis Group.

Chapter 7 reprinted from Ruth Hubbard, *The Politics of Women's Biology.* Copyright © 1990 by Rutgers, the State University. Reprinted by permission of Rutgers University Press.

Chapter 8 reprinted from Martha Saxton, *Abortion Wars: A Half Century of Struggle, 1950–2000,* Berkeley, California: University of California Press, 1998, pp. 374–393. Copyright © 1998 by the Regents of the University of California.

Chapter 10 reprinted with the permission of Simon & Schuster Adult Publishing Group, from *Stigma* by Erving Goffman. Copyright © 1963, Prentice Hall Inc; copyright renewed © 1991 by Simon & Schuster, Inc.

Chapter 11 reprinted by permission of Plenum Publishing Corporation from Lerita M. Coleman, "Stigma: An Enigma Demystified" in S. Ainlay, G. Becker, and L.M. Coleman, Eds., *A Multidisciplinary View of Stigma:* pp. 211–234. New York: Plenum. Copyright © 1986 by Plenum Publishing Corporation.

Chapter 12 excerpt from AIDS AND ITS METAPHORS by Susan Sontag. Copyright © 1988, 1989 by Susan Sontag. Reprinted by permission of Farrar, Straus, and Giroux, LLC.

Chapter 13 reprinted by permission of the author and the publisher from Simi Linton, *Claiming Disability: Knowledge and Identity* (New York and London: New York University Press, 1998), pp. 8–33. Copyright © 1998 by New York University Press.

Chapter 14 reprinted by permission of the author and publisher from Tobin Siebers, "In Theory: From Social Constructionism to Realism of the Body," *American Literary History* 13:4, 2001, pp. 737–754. Copyright © 2001 by Oxford University Press.

Chapter 15 revised and reprinted by permission of Florida State University, from "On the Government of Disability" by Shelley Tremain from Embodied Values: Philosophy and Disabilities, a special issue of *Social Theory and Practice* 27 (4), October 2001, pp. 617–636. Copyright © 2001 by Florida State University Press.

Chapter 17 reprinted by permission of the authors and publisher from David Mitchell and Sharon Snyder, *Narrative Prosthesis: Disability and the Dependencies of Discourse* (Ann Arbor: The University of Michigan Press, 2001), pp. 47–63. Copyright © 2001 by University of Michigan Press.

Chapter 18 reprinted by permission of the publisher from James I. Charlton, *Nothing About Us Without Us: Disability Oppression and Empowerment* (Berkeley, California: University of California Press, 1998), pp. 21–36. Copyright © 1998 by the Regents of the University of California.

Chapter 19 reprinted by permission of the author and publisher from *Bending Over Backwards: Disability, Dismodernism, and Other Difficult Positions* (New York: New York University Press, 2002), pp. 9–32. Copyright © 2002 by New York University Press.

Chapter 20 reprinted by permission of the author from "Towards a Feminist Theory of Disability" in *Hypatia* 4:2 (Summer 1989), pp. 104–122. Copyright 1989 by Susan Wendell.

Chapter 21 reprinted by permission of the author and publisher from Rosemarie Garland-Thomson, "Integrating Disability, Transforming Feminist Theory," *NWSA Journal* 14:3 (2002), pp. 1–32. Copyright © 2002 by Indiana University Press.

Chapter 23 reprinted with revised title by permission of the author and publisher from Anna Mollow, " 'When *Black* Women Start Going on Prozac…': The Politics of Race, Gender, and Mental Illness in Meri Nana-Ama Danquah's *Willow Weep for Me*," *MELUS* Vol. 31, 2006.

Chapter 24 reprinted by permission of the author and publisher from Robert McRuer, "Compulsory Able-Bodiedness and Queer/Disabled Existence," Brenda Jo Brueggemann, Sharon L. Snyder, and Rosemarie Garland-Thomson, *Disability Studies: Enabling the Humanities* (New York: Modern Langauge Association, 2002), pp. 88–100.

Chapter 25 "The Vulnerable Articulate: James Gillingham, Amiee Mullins, and Matthew Barney," by Marquard Smith, reprinted with permission of The MIT Press, from *The Prosthetic Impulse: From a Posthuman Present to a Biocultural Future*. Copyright © 2005 by The MIT Press.

Chapter 26 reprinted by permission of the publisher from Brenda Brueggeman, *Lend Me Your Ear: The Rhetorical Construction of Deafness* (Washington, D.C.: Gallaudet University Press, 1999), pp. 81–99. Copyright © 1999 by Gallaudet University.

Chapter 27 reprinted by permission of the authors and publisher from Carol Padden and Tom Humphries, *Deaf in America: Voices from a Culture* (Cambridge, Massachusetts: Harvard University Press, 1988), pp. 39–55. Copyright © 1988 by the President and Fellows of Harvard College.

Chapter 30 reprinted by permission of David Hevey from David Hevey, *The Creatures Time Forgot: Photography and Disability Imagery* (New York and London: Routledge), pp. 53–74. Copyright © 1992 by David Hevey.

Chapter 31 reprinted by permission of the author from *Bodyscape: Art, Modernity and the Ideal Figure* (London and New York: Routledge), pp. 37–57. Copyright © 1995 by Nicholas Mirzoeff.

Chapter 32 revised and reprinted by permission of the author and publisher from "Blindness and Visual Culture: An Eye-Witness Account," *Journal of Visual Culture* 4:2 (2005), pp. 179–190. Copyright © 2005 by Sage Publications Ltd.

Chapter 33 revised and reprinted by permission of the Modern Language Association of America from G. Thomas Couser, "Disability, Life Narrative, and Representation," *PMLA* (2005): 602–606.

Chapter 37 reprinted with the permission of the publisher from Emmanuelle Laborit, *Cry of the Gull* (Washington, D.C.: Gallaudet University Press, 1998), pp. 4–36. Copyright © 1998 by Gallaudet University Press.

Preface to the Second Edition

When I wrote the introduction to the *Disability Studies Reader* about ten years ago, I was announcing the appearance of a new field of study. I dourly noted that "it has been virtually impossible to have a person teaching about disability within the humanities. No announcements of jobs in the area of disability studies yet appear in the professional journals of English, history or philosophy." I rued the difficulty of doing research on disability studies noting, "If one looks up 'disability' or 'disability studies' in a database or library catalogue, one will find slim pickings...."

It is gratifying to note that after less than a decade, all that has changed. Disability studies is taught throughout the United States, the United Kingdom, and the world. Each year there are more and more disability studies degree-granting programs in the United States, the United Kingdom, Australia, and Canada. And disability courses are taught in departments throughout the university. The efforts of many scholars and activists have come to fruition in the birth of a fully legitimate area of study and discussion.

But just because disability studies is on the map doesn't mean that it is easy to find. We should not downplay the fact that disabilities are still often forgotten when the litany of race, class, gender, sexual orientation, and so on are articulated. Most people still give me puzzled looks when I tell them that I teach disability studies in a way that they don't when I mention feminist studies or race and ethnic studies—or even queer studies. That means there is a lot more education and outreach that needs to be done.

Ten years ago we were trying to articulate the central concerns and definitions in the field of disability studies. This was part of what I'd call a first-wave approach to the subject. That first-wave involved foundational ideas, assembling a coherent identity for a wide range of impairments, and pushing for respect, recognition, and research. I would say that this phase of the knowledge production and group solidification has been largely accomplished. We know more about disability; we have a strong sense of identity; and we are well on the way to recovering history, literature, and art that was lost in the able-bodied march of time.

Now we confront the second-wave of disability studies. In this era, the foundational "truths" come under new scrutiny. A second-wave of scholars, many of them younger, is coming into the field with the safety and security of having a field to enter, having an identity to discuss, and having a body of knowledge with which to deal. But there will always be contradictions and disparities in any field of investigation. The second-wavers will ask questions and make new assertions about the "truths" of the field. We can see this questioning already occurring in the areas of identity formation, the differences (rather than the similarities) between impairments, the seeming incompatibility between models (notably those of the United Kingdom and the United States), questions about the relation of theory to praxis, and the role of the intellectual vis à vis the activist. There are further questions about who has the right to articulate, represent, and lead disability studies and organizations. Among the paramount issues is a questioning of the biases, prejudices, and ideology of disability studies toward minorities, ethnicities, and racialized groups. Linked to all this is questioning whether one can actually have a monolithic view of disability or whether the varieties and peculiarities of impairments, beliefs, ideologies and so on can be completely represented by a singular model. Debates are now developing over notions of cure, genetic testing and prenatal technologies, cochlear implants, abortion, and end-of-life issues. It is still very possible to articulate what disabilities studies is and does, and who is a person with disabilities, but it is equally possible to interrogate the presumptions and presuppositions that go along with those definitions. In many ways, disability studies, like other area studies, is dealing with and processing the complexities of postmodern theory and its assumptions.

Revising the *Disability Studies Reader* was an exciting project for exactly those reasons I've given above. I've had to think through the changing issues and theoretical frameworks, trying to guess what kinds of works should be added. I consulted members of the disability community online and in person, and I received many helpful suggestions. Of course, it is inevitable that I've missed great essays or important areas of interest. Editing a reader is a doubtful enterprise in which you have to combine the ability to assess the past, look at the present, and think about the future. As they say, the more things change, the more they stay the same. In that spirit, the second edition has retained many early essays but added or replaced a substantial number. New topics of interest include cognitive and affective disabilities, queerness, race, theory, globalization, sexualities, memoir, genetics, prosthetics, and Foucault.

As I wrote ten years ago, "This reader is only a beginning, the thin edge of a wedge which will change" the way we think. Now in its second incarnation, the book is able to present a thicker edge, but there is still a lot more wedging to go.

I would like to give particular thanks to my research assistant Alice Haisman who helped me at every stage of the way. Without her support, the second edition would have taken much longer to get into your hands. I would also like to thank David McBride, Stephanie Drew, and Brendan O'Neill at Routledge. And finally, I'd like to thank my many colleagues and students in the disability community who are constantly teaching me new things to think and new ways to think them.

Introduction

This reader is one of the first devoted to disability studies. But it will not be the last. Disability studies is a field of study whose time has come. For centuries, people with disabilities have been an oppressed and repressed group. People with disabilities have been isolated, incarcerated, observed, written about, operated on, instructed, implanted, regulated, treated, institutionalized, and controlled to a degree probably unequal to that experienced by any other minority group. As 15 percent of the population, people with disabilities make up the largest physical minority within the United States. One would never know this to be the case by looking at the literature on minorities and discrimination.

Now the impetus to recognize the level of oppression, both overt and by marginalization, is being organized by people with disabilities and other interested parties. The exciting thing about disability studies is that it is both an academic field of inquiry and an area of political activity. The act of assembling a body of knowledge owned by the disability community as opposed to one written about that community by "normals" is part of an ongoing process that includes political actions involving the classroom, the workplace, the courts, the legislature, the media, and so on.

So, this volume appears at the moment that disability, always an actively repressed *memento mori* for the fate of the normal body, gains a new, nonmedicalized, and positive legitimacy both as an academic discipline and as an area of political struggle. As with any new discourse, disability studies must claim space in a contested area, trace its continuities and discontinuities, argue for its existence, and justify its assertions.

To do this, the case must be made clear that studies about disability have not had historically the visibility of studies about race, class, or gender for complex as well as simple reasons. The simple reason is the general pervasiveness of discrimination and prejudice against people with disabilities leading to their marginalization as well as the marginalization of the study of disability. Progressives in and out of academia may pride themselves on being sensitive to race or gender, but they have been "ableist" in dealing with the issue of disability. While race, for example, has become in the past twenty years a more than acceptable modality from which to theorize in the classroom and in print, a discourse, a critique, and a political struggle, disability has continued to be relegated to hospital hallways, physical therapy tables, and remedial classrooms. The civil rights movement, a long history of discussion of the issues around slavery, the attention demanded by the "problem" of inner cities, and governmental discrimination have created a consciousness among progressives that legitimizes ethnicity as a topic for cultural study. It is possible to have a Henry Louis Gates or a bell hooks in a literature faculty, but it has been virtually impossible to have a person teaching about disability within the humanities. No announcements of jobs in the area of disability studies yet appear in the professional journals of English, history, or philosophy. In other words, disability has been seen as eccentric, therapeutically oriented, out-of-the-mainstream, and certainly not representative of the human condition—not as race, class, or gender seem representative of that condition.

But, how strange this assumption. What is more representative of the human condition than the body and its vicissitudes? If the population of people with disabilities is between thirty-five and forty-three million, then this group is the largest physical minority in the United States. Put another way, there are more people with disabilities than there are African Americans or Latinos.[1] But why have the disabled been rendered more invisible than other groups? Why are not issues about perception, mobility, accessibility, distribution of bio-resources, physical space, difference not seen as central to the human condition? Is there not something to be gained by all people from exploring the ways that the body in its variations is metaphorized, disbursed, promulgated, commodified, cathected, and de-cathected, normalized, abnormalized, formed, and deformed? In other words, is it not time for disability studies to emerge as an aspect of cultural studies, studies in discrimination and oppression, postmodern analyses of the body and bio-power?

The first assumption that has to be countered in arguing for disability studies is that the "normal" or "able" person is already fully up to speed on the subject. My experience is that while most "normals" think they understand the issue of disability, they in fact do not. When it comes to disability, "normal"[2] people are quite willing to volunteer solutions, present anecdotes, recall from a vast array of films instances they take for fact. No one would dare to make such a leap into Heideggerian philosophy for example or the art of the Renaissance. But disability seems so obvious—a missing limb, blindness, deafness. What could be simpler to understand? One simply has to imagine the loss of the limb, the absent sense, and one is half-way there. Just the addition of a liberal dose of sympathy and pity along with a generous acceptance of ramps and voice-synthesized computers allows the average person to speak with knowledge on the subject.

But disability studies, like any other discourse, requires a base of knowledge and a familiarity with discursive terms and methodologies, as well as, most often, some personal involvement. The apparent ease of intuitive knowledge is really another aspect of discrimination against people with disabilities. How could there be anything complex, intellectually interesting, or politically relevant about a missing limb or a chronic impairment? Pity or empathy do not lend themselves to philosophy, philology, or theoretical considerations in general.

But, far from pity or empathy, people working in the field of disability are articulating and theorizing a political, social, and ideological critique. The work contained in this reader, only a sampling of the many articles and books published on the subject, is representative of this growing specialization as it spans the human sciences—literary studies, art history, anthropology, sociology, post-colonial studies, theory, feminist studies, and so on. But be aware: This book is not a collection of articles about how people *feel* about disability; nor is it designed to "sensitize" normal readers to the issue of disability; nor is it a collection of pieces focusing on the theme of disability in literature, film, or television. Rather, this is a reader that places disability in a political, social, and cultural context, that theorizes and historicizes deafness or blindness or disability in similarly complex ways to the way race, class, and gender have been theorized.

It is not as if disability studies has simply appeared out of someone's head at this historical moment. It would be more appropriate to say that disability studies has been in the making for many years, but, like people with disabilities, has only recently recognized itself as a political, discursive entity. Indeed, like the appearance of African-American studies following rapidly on the heels of the civil rights movement, there is a reciprocal connection between political praxis by people with disabilities and the formation of a discursive category of disability studies. That is, there have been people with disabilities throughout history, but it has only been in the last twenty years that one-armed people, quadriplegics, the blind, people with chronic diseases, and so on, have seen themselves as a single, allied, united physical minority.[3] Linked to this political movement, which is detailed in Joseph Shapiro's *No Pity,* David Hevey's *Creatures Time Forgot,* and Oliver Sacks' *Seeing Voices,* among other works, has been the political victory of the passage of the Americans with Disabilities Act (ADA) of 1990, which guarantees the civil rights of people with disabilities.[4]

Disability studies, as did cultural studies, unites a variety of ongoing work. That this work was largely hidden from view is a telling fact. If one looks up "disability" or "disability studies" in a database or library catalogue, one will find slim pickings, particularly if the areas of medical treatment, hospital or institutional management, and out-patient treatment are eliminated. The reason for this dearth of reference is complex. First, there is the historical absence of a discursive category. When I tried to locate a copy of my recent book *Enforcing Normalcy: Disability, Deafness, and the Body* in a university bookstore, I was told to look under "self help." Currently, there is no area in a bookstore where works on disability studies can be placed. This absence of a discursive category was more tellingly revealed at a meeting of the Committee on Academics with Disabilities at the Modern Language Association headquarters. A bibliographer of the *MLA Bibliography* informed the committee that there was almost no way of retrieving articles or books on the cultural history of disability since proper categories did not exist. For example, an article on "crippled saints" could not be searched by computer because the word "crippled" was disallowed by MLA regulations as constituting discriminatory language. The bibliographer therefore filed the article under "saints" thus rendering it unretrievable by anyone with an interest in disability.[5] Further, until now, American Sign Language was listed in the database as an "invented language" along with the language of the Klingons of *Star Trek*. Thanks to the efforts of activists, this categorization will no longer be the case and American sign language will be listed as a legitimate language. This absence of a discursive category is as much as function of discrimination and marginalization as anything else. If one had tried to find the category "composers, female" in music history thirty years ago, there would have been no such category. The category of "African-American literature" would not have existed. In the late 1990s disability studies has been "disappeared." As of 1997, the MLA is redressing this absence in its database.

The absence of categories is only one reason that disability studies has been suppressed. The second reason is the erasure of disability as a category when other "stronger" categories are present. So, unless a writer, artist, or filmmaker is known for his or her disability, as was Beethoven or Helen Keller, he is not thought of as a person with disabilities. Therefore, the work is not included in any canon of cultural production. How outrageous this is can be understood if we made the analogy with the suppression of the gender, color, race, ethnicity, or nationality of a writer. How many people realize that included in the category of people with disabilities are: John Milton, Sir Joshua Reynolds, Alexander Pope, Harriet Martineau, John Keats, George Gordon Byron, Toulouse-Lautrec, James Joyce, Virginia Woolf, James Thurber, Dorothea Lange, José Luis Borges, John Ford, Raoul Walsh, André de Toth, Nicholas Ray, Tay Garnett, William Wyler, Chuck Close, and many others? Moreover, the work of many talented writers, artists, photographers and so on who were disabled have had their work minimalized or suppressed in the same way that people of color or women have experienced. The recovery of this work is only now beginning.[6]

The work of many scholars who have investigated aspects of the body is now being reassembled into the field of disability studies. So for example, Sander Gilman's work on disease, David Rothman on asylums, Erving Goffman on stigma, Leslie Fieldler on freaks, Susan Sontag on the metaphors of illness, Mikhail Bakhtin on the grotesque, followed by postmodern work like Michel Foucault on disease, mental illness, and sexuality, Jacques Derrida on blindness, Kaja Silverman on deformity in film, Judith Butler and Susan Bordo on anorexia—all of these works might not have been seen as existing under the rubric of disability studies, but as the field evolves, it recuperates and includes this earlier work as a retrospectively organized set of originating documents much in the way that structuralism turned back to the work of Saussure or that Marx relied on Hegel.

While this historical reserve of writings on disease, the body, freakishness and so on exists, the work of a newer generation of writers and scholars looks toward feminist, Marxist, postmodern, and cultural studies models for understanding the relation between the body and power. This next generation of writing tends to be created from within the boundaries of disability. While many earlier writers had an anthropological approach, with the weakness and imperial quality of anthropological work, others wrote from the perspective of "having" a disability. That type of work tended to be written so that "normal" people might know what it is like to be blind, crippled, deaf, and so on. The danger of that kind of project is that it is embarked on with the aim of evoking "sympathy" or "understanding." The dialectical relation of power involved in such a transaction ultimately ends up having the writing be *for* the "normal." The inappropriateness of such "sensitizing" work can be seen in works written, for example, to whites explaining what it is like to be black or to men explaining what it is like to be female. Disability studies, for the most part, shuns this unequal power transaction in favor of advocacy, investigation, inquiry, archeology, genealogy, dialectic, and deconstruction. The model of a sovereign subject revealing or reveling in that subjectivity is put into question.

In this anthology, scholars discuss the construction of disability in ancient Greece, in the English Renaissance and Enlightenment, in nineteenth-century France, as well as the creation of the concept of "normalcy" in nineteenth- and twentieth-century Europe and America. This work is reflective of the new historical revisionism allowed by the introduction of the concept of disability into practices of Marxist, feminist, queer, ethnic, postcolonial, and postmodern criticism. Previous work on the body can now be amplified and expanded. In addition, works that theorize disability and Deafness look at the notion of difference as an opportunity to defamiliarize received truths about culture and the body. I have also reprinted some fiction and poetry. This literary work is not here to "sensitize" readers but to explore the richness of experience and creativity offered by the opportunity of disability. The writers are aggressive about their insight, not defensive. They have a constitutive experience of disability and use that knowledge within their aesthetic ability. But these works should not be ghettoized as "disability literature" any more than T. S. Eliot should be used as an example of able-bodied writing.

In assembling this reader, I have selected only some material and some representative impairments, but much more work is being done and needs to be done in this major project of reconceiving history through the lens of disability studies. Many will find their impairments missing. I can only plead limited resources, limited space, and probably limited imagination.

A fair number of articles deal with deafness. The reason for this focus is twofold: (1) personal interest, and (2) the rather large body of historical materials on the history of deafness. My apologies to whomever does not find this field of inquiry interesting. This reader is only a beginning, the thin edge of a wedge which will change the normative way we conceive of the world, of literature, of cultural production, of voice, of sight, of language. In its broadest application, disability studies aims to challenge the received in its most simple form—the body—and in its most complex form—the construction of the body. Since we can no longer essentialize the body, we can no longer essentialize its differences, its eccentricities, its transgressions. Perhaps disability studies will lead to some grand unified theory of the body, pulling together the differences implied in gender, nationality, ethnicity, race, and sexual preferences. Then, rather than the marginalized being in the wheelchair or using sign language, the person with disabilities will become the ultimate example, the universal image, the modality through whose knowing the postmodern subject can theorize and act.

Notes

1. African Americans make up 11.8 percent of the U. S. population. Latinos comprise 9.5 percent, and Asians are 3.1 percent of the general population (U. S. Census Bureau statistics cited in the *New York Times* (March 25, 1996; A15).
2. I will refrain from putting "normal" in quotation marks henceforth, but I do so as long as readers will recall that I am always using this term with the complex set of ironies and historic specificities the term carries. I will assume, perhaps problematically, an agreement on the fact that not one of us is, or can be, normal, nor can anyone describe what a normal person is.
3. I have deliberately left the Deaf off of this list. (I use the capitalized term to indicate the culturally Deaf, as opposed to the simple fact of physical deafness.) The reason is that many Deaf do not consider themselves people with disabilities but rather members of a linguistic minority. The Deaf argue that their difference is actually a communication difference—they speak sign language—and that their problems do not exist in a Deaf, signing community, whereas a group of legless people will not transcend their motor impairments when they become part of a legless community. The argument is a serious one and, although I personally feel that the Deaf have much to gain by joining forces with people with disabilities, I honor the Deaf argument in this reader. See Harlan Lane's article "Construction of Deafness" (in this volume).
4. This victory is in some sense a pyrrhic one since the letter of law is easier to manifest than the spirit, and so the number of people with disabilities who are unemployed, for example, remains as high if not higher than before the Act was passed. (*New York Times* October 23, 1994 A: 22). In addition, the Act has no enforcement mechanism or agency, so it relies on individuals bringing lawsuits on their own—a method that for most people with disabilities is not a practical remedy. Most recently, the budget and tax cuts of 1994–96 have sliced dramatically into entitlements for special education, home-care, and many of the other programs that people with disabilities rely on to provide access and support.
5. The MLA is now beginning to redress this problem. Presumably, other databases and catalogues will follow suit.
6. Work that does this recovery includes Nicholas Mirzoeff, *Silent Poetry: Deafness, Sign, and Visual Culture in Modern France*, Martin Nordern, *Cinema of Isolation*: *A History of Physical Disability in the Movies*, and various articles and books by John S. Schuchman.

Part I

Historical Perspectives

1

Constructing Normalcy

The Bell Curve, the Novel, and the Invention of the Disabled Body in the Nineteenth Century

Lennard J. Davis

If such a thing as a psycho-analysis of today's prototypical culture were possible...such an investigation would needs show the sickness proper to the time to consist precisely in normality.

—Theodore Adorno, *Minima Moralia*

We live in a world of norms. Each of us endeavors to be normal or else deliberately tries to avoid that state. We consider what the average person does, thinks, earns, or consumes. We rank our intelligence, our cholesterol level, our weight, height, sex drive, bodily dimensions along some conceptual line from subnormal to above-average. We consume a minimum daily balance of vitamins and nutrients based on what an average human should consume. Our children are ranked in school and tested to determine where they fit into a normal curve of learning, of intelligence. Doctors measure and weigh them to see if they are above or below average on the height and weight curves. There is probably no area of contemporary life in which some idea of a norm, mean, or average has not been calculated.

To understand the disabled body, one must return to the concept of the norm, the normal body. So much of writing about disability has focused on the disabled person as the object of study, just as the study of race has focused on the person of color. But as with recent scholarship on race, which has turned its attention to whiteness, I would like to focus not so much on the construction of disability as on the construction of normalcy. I do this because the "problem" is not the person with disabilities; the problem is the way that normalcy is constructed to create the "problem" of the disabled person.

A common assumption would be that some concept of the norm must have always existed. After all, people seem to have an inherent desire to compare themselves to others. But the idea of a norm is less a condition of human nature than it is a feature of a certain kind of society. Recent work on the ancient Greeks, on preindustrial Europe, and on tribal peoples, for example, shows that disability was once regarded very differently from the way it is now. As we will see, the social process of disabling arrived with industrialization and with the set of practices and discourses that are linked to late eighteenth- and nineteenth-century notions of nationality, race, gender, criminality, sexual orientation, and so on.

I begin with the rather remarkable fact that the constellation of words describing this concept "normal," "normalcy," "normality," "norm," "average," "abnormal"—all entered the European languages rather late in human history. The word "normal" as "constituting, conforming to, not deviating or different from, the common type or standard, regular, usual" only enters the English language around 1840. (Previously, the word had meant "perpendicular"; the carpenter's square, called a "norm," provided the root meaning.) Likewise, the word "norm," in the modern sense, has only been in use since around 1855, and "normality" and "normalcy" appeared in 1849 and 1857, respectively. If the lexicographical information is relevant, it is possible to date the coming into consciousness in English of an idea of "the norm" over the period 1840–1860.

If we rethink our assumptions about the universality of the concept of the norm, what we might arrive at is the concept that preceded it: that of the "ideal," a word we find dating from the seventeenth century. Without making too simplistic a division in the historical chronotope, one can nevertheless try to imagine a world in which the hegemony of normalcy does not exist. Rather, what we have is the ideal body, as exemplified in the tradition of nude Venuses, for example. This idea presents a mytho-poetic body that is linked to that of the gods (in traditions in which the god's body is visualized). This divine body, then, this ideal body, is not attainable by a human. The notion of an ideal implies that, in this case, the human body as visualized in art or imagination must be composed from the ideal parts of living models. These models individually can never embody the ideal since an ideal, by definition, can never be found in this world. When ideal human bodies occur, they do so in mythology. So Venus or Helen of Troy, for example, would be the embodiment of female physical beauty.

The painting by François-André Vincent *Zeuxis Choosing as Models the Most Beautiful Girls of the Town of Crotona* (1789, Museum de Louvre, Paris) shows the Greek artist, as we are told by Pliny, lining up all the beautiful women of Crotona in order to select in each her ideal feature or body part and combine these into the ideal figure of Aphrodite, herself an ideal of beauty. One young woman provides a face and another her breasts. Classical painting and sculpture tend to idealize the body, evening out any particularity. The central point here is that in a culture with an ideal form of the body, all members of the population are below the ideal. No one young lady of Crotona can be the ideal. By definition, one can never have an ideal body. There is in such societies no demand that populations have bodies that conform to the ideal.

By contrast, the *grotesque* as a visual form was inversely related to the concept of the ideal and its corollary that all bodies are in some sense disabled. In that mode, the grotesque is a signifier of the people, of common life. As Bakhtin, Stallybrass and White, and others have shown, the use of the grotesque had a life-affirming transgressive quality in its inversion of the political hierarchy. However, the grotesque was not equivalent to the disabled, since, for example, it is impossible to think of people with disabilities now being used as architectural decorations as the grotesque were on the façades of cathedrals throughout Europe. The grotesque permeated culture and signified common humanity, whereas the disabled body, a later concept, was formulated as by definition excluded from culture, society, the norm.

If the concept of the norm or average enters European culture, or at least the European languages, only in the nineteenth century, one has to ask what is the cause of this conceptualization? One of the logical places to turn in trying to understand concepts like "norm" and "average" is that branch of knowledge known as statistics. Statistics begins in the early modern period as "political arithme-tic"—a use of data for "promotion of sound, well-informed state policy" (Porter 1986, 18). The word *statistik* was first used in 1749 by Gottfried Achen-wall, in the context of compiling information about the state. The concept migrated somewhat from the state to the body when Bisset Hawkins defined medical statistics in 1829 as "the application of numbers to illustrate the natural history of health and disease" (cited in Porter, 1986, 24). In France, statistics were mainly used in the area of public health in the early nineteenth century. The connection between the body and industry is tellingly revealed in the fact that the leading members of the first British statistical societies formed in the 1830s and 1840s were industrialists or had close ties to industry (ibid., 32).

It was the French statistician Adolphe Quetelet (1796–1847) who contributed the most to a general-ized notion of the normal as an imperative. He noticed that the "law of error," used by astronomers to locate a star by plotting all the sightings and then averaging the errors, could be equally applied to the distribution of human features such as height and weight. He then took a further step of formulating the concept of "l'homme moyen" or the average man. Quetelet maintained that this abstract human was the average of all human attributes in a given country. For the average man, Quetelet wrote in 1835, "all things will occur in conformity with the mean results obtained for a society. If one seeks to establish, in some way, the basis of a social physics, it is he whom one should consider . . ." (cited in ibid., 53). Quetelet's average man was a combination of *l'homme moyen physique and l'homme moyen morale*, both a physically average and a morally average construct.

The social implications of this idea are central. In formulating the idea of *l'homme moyen*, Quetelet is also providing a justification for *les classes moyens*. With bourgeois hegemony comes scientific justification for moderation and middle-class ideology. The average man, the body of the man in the middle, becomes the exemplar of the middle way of life. Quetelet was apparently influenced by the philosopher Victor Cousin in developing an analogy between the notion of an average man and the *juste milieu*. This term was associated with Louis Philippe's July monarchy—a concept that melded bourgeois hegemony with the constitutional monarchy and celebrated moderation and middleness (ibid., 101). In England too, the middle class as the middle way or mean had been searching for a scientific justification. The statement in *Robinson Crusoe* in which Robinson's father extols middle-class life as a kind of norm is a good example of this ideology:

> the middle Station had the fewest Disasters, and was not expos'd to so many Vicissitudes as the higher or lower Part of Mankind; nay, they were not subjected to so many Distempers and Uneasiness either of Body or Mind, as those were who, by vicious Living, Luxury and Extravagancies on one Hand, or by hard Labour, Want of Necessaries, and mean or insufficient Diet on the other Hand, bring Distempers upon themselves by the natural consequences of their Way of Living; That the middle Station of Life was calculated for all kinds of Vertues and all kinds of Enjoyments; that Peace and Plenty were the Hand-maids of a middle Fortune; that Temperance, Moderation, Quietness, Health, Society, all agreeable Diversions, and all desirable Pleasures, were the Blessings attending the middle Station of Life. (Defoe 1975, 6)

Statements of ideology of this kind saw the bourgeoisie as rationally placed in the mean position in the great order of things. This ideology can be seen as developing the kind of science that would then justify the notion of a norm.[1]

With such thinking, the average then becomes paradoxically a kind of ideal, a position devoutly to be wished. As Quetelet wrote, "an individual who epitomized in himself, at a given time, all the qualities of the average man, would represent at once all the greatness, beauty and goodness of that being" (cited in Porter 1986, 102). Such an average person might indeed be a literary character like Robinson Crusoe. Furthermore, one must observe that Quetelet meant this hegemony of the middle to apply not only to moral qualities but to the body as well. He wrote: "deviations more or less great from the mean have constituted [for artists] ugliness in body as well as vice in morals and a state of sickness with regard to the constitution" (ibid., 103). Here Zeuxis's notion of physical beauty as an exceptional ideal becomes transformed into beauty as the average.

Quetelet foresaw a kind of Utopia of the norm associated with progress, just as Marx foresaw a Utopia of the norm in so far as wealth and production is concerned.

> one of the principal acts of civilization is to compress more and more the limits within which the different elements relative to man oscillate. The more that enlightenment is propagated, the more will deviations from the mean diminish.... The perfectibility of the human species is derived as a necessary consequence of all our investigations. Defects and monstrosities disappear more and more from the body. (ibid., 104)

This concept of the average, as applied to the concept of the human, was used not only by statisticians but even by the likes of Marx. Marx actually cites Quetelet's notion of the average man in a discussion of the labor theory of value. We can see in retrospect that one of the most powerful ideas of Marx—the notion of labor value or average wages—in many ways is based on the idea of the worker constructed as an average worker. As Marx writes:

> Any average magnitude, however, is merely the average of a number of separate magnitudes all of one kind, but differing as to quantity. In every industry, each individual labourer, be he Peter or Paul, differs from the average labourer. These individual differences, or "errors" as they are called in mathematics, compensate one another and vanish, whenever a certain minimum number of workmen are employed together. (Marx 1970, 323)

So for Marx one can divide the collective work day of a large number of workers and come up with "one day of average social labor" (ibid., 323). As Quetelet had come up with an average man, so Marx postulates an average worker, and from that draws conclusions about the relationship between an average and the extremes of wealth and poverty that are found in society. Thus Marx develops his crucial concept of "abstract labor."

We tend not to thing of progressives like Marx as tied up with a movement led by businessmen, but it is equally true that Marx is unimaginable without a tendency to contemplate average humans and think about their abstract relation to work, wages, and so on. In this sense, Marx is very much in step with the movement of normalizing the body and the individual. In addition, Marxist thought encourages us toward an enforcing of normalcy in the sense that the deviations in society, in terms of the distribution of wealth for example, must be minimized.

The concept of a norm, unlike that of an ideal, implies that the majority of the population must or should somehow be part of the norm. The norm pins down that majority of the population that falls under the arch of the standard bell-shaped curve. This curve, the graph of an exponential function, that was known variously as the astronomer's "error law," the "normal distribution," the "Gaussian density function," or simply "the bell curve," became in its own way a symbol of the tyranny of the norm. Any bell curve will always have at its extremities those characteristics that deviate from the norm. So, with the concept of the norm comes the concept of deviations or extremes. When we think of bodies, in a society where the concept of the norm is operative, then people with disabilities will be thought of as deviants. This, as we have seen, is in contrast to societies with the concept of an ideal, in which all people have a non-ideal status.[2]

In England, there was an official and unofficial burst of interest in statistics during the 1830s. A statistical office was set up at the Board of Trade in 1832, and the General Register Office was created in 1837 to collect vital statistics. All of this interest in numbers concerning the state was a consequence of the Reform Act of 1832, the Factory Act of 1833, and the Poor Law of 1834. The country was being monitored and the poor were being surveiled. Private groups followed, and in 1833 a statistical section of the British Association for the Advancement of Science was formed in which Quetelet as well as Malthus participated. In the following year Malthus, Charles Babbage, and others founded the Statistical Society of London. The Royal London Statistical Society was founded in 1835.

The use of statistics began an important movement, and there is a telling connection for the purposes of this book between the founders of statistics and their larger intentions. The rather amazing fact is that almost all the early statisticians had one thing in common: they were eugenicists. The same is true of key figures in the movement: Sir Francis Galton, Karl Pearson, and R. A. Fisher.[3] While this coincidence seems almost too striking to be true, we must remember that there is a real connection between figuring the statistical measure of humans and then hoping to improve humans so that deviations from the norm diminish—as someone like Quetelet had suggested. Statistics is bound up with eugenics because the central insight of statistics is the idea that a population can be normed. An important consequence of the idea of the norm is that it divides the total population into standard and nonstandard subpopulations. The next step in conceiving of the population as norm and non-norm is for the state to attempt to norm the nonstandard—the aim of eugenics. Of course such an activity is profoundly paradoxical since the inviolable rule of statistics is that all phenomena will always conform to a bell curve. So norming the non-normal is an activity as problematic as untying the Gordian knot.

MacKenzie asserts that it is not so much that Galton's statistics made possible eugenics but rather that "the needs of eugenics in large part determined the content of Galton's statistical theory" (1981, 52). In any case, a symbiotic relationship exists between statistical science and eugenic concerns. Both bring into society the concept of a norm, particularly a normal body, and thus in effect create the concept of the disabled body.

It is also worth noting the interesting triangulation of eugenicist interests. On the one hand Sir Francis Galton was cousin to Charles Darwin, whose notion of the evolutionary advantage of the fittest lays the foundation for eugenics and also for the idea of a perfectible body undergoing progressive improvement. As one scholar has put it, "Eugenics was in reality applied biology based on the central biological theory of the day, namely the Darwinian theory of evolution" (Farrall 1985, 55). Darwin's ideas serve to place disabled people along the wayside as evolutionary defectives to be surpassed by natural selection. So, eugenics became obsessed with the elimination of "defectives," a category which included the "feebleminded," the deaf, the blind, the physically defective, and so on.

In a related discourse, Galton created the modern system of fingerprinting for personal identification. Galton's interest came out of a desire to show that certain physical traits could be inherited. As he wrote:

> one of the inducements to making these inquiries into personal identification has been to discover independent features suitable for hereditary investigation.... it is not improbable, and worth taking pains to inquire whether each person may not carry visibly about his body undeniable evidence of his parentage and near kinships. (cited in MacKenzie 1981, 65)

Fingerprinting was seen as a physical mark of parentage, a kind of serial number written on the body. But further, one can say that the notion of fingerprinting pushes forward the idea that the human body is standardized and contains a serial number, as it were, embedded in its corporeality. (Later technological innovations will reveal this fingerprint to be embedded at the genetic level.) Thus the body has an identity that coincides with its essence and cannot be altered by moral, artistic, or human will. This indelibility of corporeal identity only furthers the mark placed on the body by other physical qualities—intelligence, height, reaction time. By this logic, the person enters into an identical relationship with the body, the body forms the identity, and the identity is unchangeable and indelible as one's place on the normal curve. For our purposes, then, this fingerprinting of the body means that the marks of physical difference become synonymous with the identity of the person.

Finally, Galton is linked to that major figure connected with the discourse of disability in the nineteenth century—Alexander Graham Bell. In 1883, the same year that the term "eugenics" was coined by Galton, Bell delivered his eugenicist speech *Memoir upon the Formation of a Deaf Variety of the Human Race*, warning of the "tendency among deaf-mutes to select deaf-mutes as their partners in marriage" (1969, 19) with the dire consequence that a race of deaf people might be created. This echoing of Dr. Frankenstein's fear that his monster might mate and produce a race of monsters emphasizes the terror with which the "normal" beholds the differently abled.[4] Noting how the various interests come together in Galton, we can see evolution, fingerprinting, and the attempt to control the reproductive rights of the deaf as all pointing to a conception of the body as perfectible but only when subject to the necessary control of the eugenicists. The identity of people becomes defined by irrepressible identificatory physical qualities that can be measured. Deviance from the norm can be identified and indeed criminalized, particularly in the sense that fingerprints came to be associated with identifying deviants who wished to hide their identities.

Galton made significant changes in statistical theory that created the concept of the norm. He took what had been called "error theory," a technique by which astronomers attempted to show that one could locate a star by taking into account the variety of sightings. The sightings, all of which could not be correct, if plotted would fall into a bell curve, with most sightings falling into the center, that is to say, the correct location of the star. The errors would fall to the sides of the bell curve. Galton's contribution to statistics was to change the name of the curve from "the law of frequency of error" or "error curve," the term used by Quetelet, to the "normal distribution" curve.

The significance of these changes relates directly to Galton's eugenicist interests. In an "error curve" the extremes of the curve are the most mistaken in accuracy. But if one is looking at human traits, then the extremes, particularly what Galton saw as positive extremes—tallness, high intelligence, ambitiousness, strength, fertility—would have to be seen as errors. Rather than "errors" Galton wanted to think of the extremes as distributions of a trait. As MacKenzie notes:

Thus there was a gradual transition from use of the term "probable error" to the term "standard deviation" (which is free of the implication that a deviation is in any sense an error), and from the term "law of error" to the term "normal distribution." (1981, 59)

But even without the idea of error, Galton still faced the problem that in a normal distribution curve that graphed height, for example, both tallness and shortness would be seen as extremes in a continuum where average stature would be the norm. The problem for Galton was that, given his desire to perfect the human race, or at least its British segment, tallness was preferable to shortness. How could both extremes be considered equally deviant from the norm? So Galton substituted the idea of ranking for the concept of averaging. That is, he changed the way one might look at the curve from one that used the mean to one that used the median—a significant change in thinking eugenically.

If a strait, say intelligence, is considered by its average, then the majority of people would determine what intelligence should be—and intelligence would be defined by the mediocre middle. Galton, wanting to avoid the middling of desired traits, would prefer to think of intelligence in ranked order. Although high intelligence in a normal distribution would simply be an extreme, under a ranked system it would become the highest ranked trait. Galton divided his curve into quartiles, so that he was able to emphasize ranked orders of intelligence, as we would say that someone was in the first quartile in intelligence (low intelligence) or the fourth quartile (high intelligence). Galton's work led directly to current "intelligence quotient" (IQ) and scholastic achievement tests. In fact, Galton revised Gauss's bell curve to show the superiority of the desired trait (for example, high intelligence). He created what he called an "ogive," which is arranged in quartiles with an ascending curve that features the desired trait as "higher" than the undesirable deviation. As Stigler notes:

If a hundred individuals' talents were ordered, each could be assigned the numerical value corresponding to its percentile in the curve of "deviations from an average": the middlemost (or median) talent had value 0 (representing mediocrity), an individual at the upper quartile was assigned the value 1 (representing one probable error above mediocrity), and so on. (1986, 271)

What these revisions by Galton signify is an attempt to redefine the concept of the "ideal" in relation to the general population. First, the application of the idea of a norm to the human body creates the idea of deviance or a "deviant" body. Second, the idea of a norm pushes the normal variation of the body through a stricter template guiding the way the body "should" be. Third, the revision of the "normal curve of distribution" into quartiles, ranked in order, and so on, creates a new kind of "ideal." This statistical ideal is unlike the classical ideal which contains no imperative to be the ideal. The new ideal of ranked order is powered by the imperative of the norm, and then is supplemented by the notion of progress, human perfectibility, and the elimination of deviance, to create a dominating, hegemonic vision of what the human body should be.

While we tend to associate eugenics with a Nazi-like racial supremacy, it is important to realize that eugenics was not the trade of a fringe group of rightwing, fascist maniacs. Rather, it became the common practice of many, if not most, European and American citizens. When Marx used Quetelet's idea of the average in his formulation of average wage and abstract labor, socialists as well as others embraced eugenic claims, seeing in the perfectibility of the human body a Utopian hope for social improvement. Once people allowed that there were norms and ranks in human physiology, then the idea that we might want to, for example, increase the intelligence of humans, or decrease birth defects, did not seem so farfetched. These ideas were widely influential: in the ensuing years the leaders of the socialist Fabian Society, including Beatrice and Sidney Webb, George Bernard Shaw and H. G. Wells, were among the eugenicists (MacKenzie, 1981, 34). The influence of eugenicist ideas persisted well into the twentieth century, so that someone like Emma Goldman could write that unless birth control was encouraged, the state would "legally encourage the increase of paupers, syphilitics, epileptics, dipsomaniacs, cripples, criminals, and degenerates" (Kevles 1985, 90).

The problem for people with disabilities was that eugenicists tended to group together all allegedly "undesirable" traits. So, for example, criminals, the poor, and people with disabilities might be mentioned in the same breath. Take Karl Pearson, a leading figure in the eugenics movement, who defined the "unfit" as follows: "the habitual criminal, the professional tramp, the tuberculous, the insane, the mentally defective, the alcoholic, the diseased from birth or from excess" (cited in Kevles 1985, 33). In 1911, Pearson headed the Department of Applied Statistics, which included the Galton and Biometric Laboratories at University College in London. This department gathered eugenic information on the inheritance of physical and mental traits including "scientific, commercial, and legal ability, but also hermaphroditism, hemophilia, cleft palate, harelip, tuberculosis, diabetes, deaf-mutism, polydactyly (more than five fingers) or brachydactyly (stub fingers), insanity, and mental deficiency" (ibid., 38–9). Here again one sees a strange selection of disabilities merged with other types of human variations. All of these deviations from the norm were regarded in the long run as contributing to the disease of the nation. As one official in the Eugenics Record Office asserted:

> the calculus of correlations is the sole rational and effective method for attacking…what makes for, and what mars national fitness.…The only way to keep a nation strong mentally and physically is to see that each new generation is derived chiefly from the fitter members of the generation before. (ibid., 39–40).

The emphasis on nation and national fitness obviously plays into the metaphor of the body. If individual citizens are not fit, if they do not fit into the nation, then the national body will not be fit. Of course, such arguments are based on a false notion of the body politic—as if a hunchbacked citizenry would make a hunchbacked nation. Nevertheless, the eugenic notion that individual variations would accumulate into a composite national identity was a powerful one. This belief combined with an industrial mentality that saw workers as interchangeable and therefore sought to create a universal worker whose physical characteristics would be uniform, as would the result of their labors—a uniform product.

One of the central foci of eugenics was what was broadly called "feeble-mindedness." [5] This term included low intelligence, mental illness, and even "pauperism," since low income was equated with "relative inefficiency" (ibid., 46).[6] Likewise, certain ethnic groups were associated with feeblemindedness and pauperism. Charles Davenport, an American eugenicist, thought that the influx of European immigrants would make the American population "darker in pigmentation, smaller in stature…more given to crimes of larceny, assault, murder, rape, and sex-immorality" (cited in ibid., 48). In his research, Davenport scrutinized the records of "prisons, hospitals, almshouses, and institutions for the mentally deficient, the deaf, the blind, and the insane" (ibid., 55).

The loose association between what we would now call disability and criminal activity, mental incompetence, sexual license, and so on established a legacy that people with disabilities are still having trouble living down. This equation was so strong that an American journalist writing in the early twentieth century could celebrate "the inspiring, the wonderful, message of the new heredity" as opposed to the sorrow of bearing children who were "diseased or crippled or depraved" (ibid., 67). The conflation of disability with depravity expressed itself in the formulation "defective class." As the president of the University of Wisconsin declared after World War One, "we know enough about eugenics so that if the knowledge were applied, the defective classes would disappear within a generation" (ibid., 68). And it must be reiterated that the eugenics movement was not stocked with eccentrics. Davenport was funded by Averell Harriman's sister Mary Harriman, as well as John D. Rockefeller, Prime Ministers A. J. Balfour, Neville chamberlain, and Winston Churchill, President Theodore Roosevelt, H. G. Wells, John Maynard Keynes, and H. J. Laski, among many others, were members of eugenicist organizations. Francis Galton was knighted in 1909 for his work, and in 1910 he received the Copley Medal, the Royal Society's highest honor. A Galton Society met regularly in the American Museum of Natural History in New York City. In 1911 the Oxford University Union moved approval of the main principles behind eugenics by a vote of almost two to one. In Kansas, the 1920 state fair held a contest for "fitter families" based on their eugenic family histories, administered intelligence tests, medical examinations, and venereal disease tests. A brochure for the contest noted about the awards, "this trophy and medal are worth more than livestock sweepstakes.... For health is wealth and a sound mind in a sound body is the most priceless of human possessions" (ibid., 62).

In England, bills were introduced in Parliament to control mentally disabled people, and in 1933 the prestigious scientific magazine *Nature* approved the Nazis' proposal of a bill for "the avoidance of inherited diseases in posterity" by sterilizing the disabled. The magazine editorial said "the Bill, as it reads, will command the appreciative attention of all who are interested in the controlled and deliberate improvement of human stock." The list of disabilities for which sterilization would be appropriate were "congenital feeblemindedness, manic depressive insanity, schizophrenia, hereditary epilepsy, hereditary St Vitus's dance, hereditary blindness and deafness, hereditary bodily malformation and habitual alcoholism" (cited in MacKenzie 1981, 44). We have largely forgotten that what Hitler did in developing a hideous policy of eugenics was just to implement the theories of the British and American eugenicists. Hitler's statement in *Mein Kampf* that "the struggle for the daily livelihood [between species] leaves behind, in the ruck, everything that is weak or diseased or wavering" (cited in Blacker 1952, 143) is not qualitatively different from any of the many similar statements we have seen before. And even the conclusions Hitler draws are not very different from those of the likes of Galton, Bell, and others.

> In this matter, the State must assert itself as the trustee of a millennial future.... In order to fulfill this duty in a practical manner, the State will have to avail itself of modern medical discoveries. It must proclaim as unfit for procreation all those who are afflicted with some visible hereditary disease or are the carriers of it; and practical measures must be adopted to have such people rendered sterile. (cited in Blacker 1952, 144)

One might want to add here a set of speculations about Sigmund Freud. His work was made especially possible by the idea of the normal. It shows us that sexuality, long relegated to the trash heap of human instincts, was in fact normal and that perversion was simply a displacement of "normal" sexual interest. Dreams which behave in a manner unknown or only exceptionally permissible in normal mental life" (Freud 1977, 297) are seen as actually normal and "the dreams of neurotics do not differ in any important respect from those of normal people" (ibid., 456). In fact, it is hard to imagine the existence of psychoanalysis without the concept of normalcy. Indeed, one of the core principles behind psychoanalysis was that we each start out with normal psychosexual development and neurotics become abnormal through a problem in that normal development. As Freud put it: "if the *vita sexualis* is normal, there can be no neurosis" (ibid., 386). Psychoanalysis can correct that mistake and bring patients back to their normal selves. Although I cannot go into a close analysis of Freud's work here, it is instructive to think of the ways in which Freud is producing a eugenics of the mind—creating the concepts of normal sexuality, normal function, and then contrasting them with the perverse, abnormal, pathological, and even criminal. Indeed, one of the major critiques of Freud's work now centers on his assumption about what constitutes normal sexuality and sexual development for women and men.

The first depiction in literature of an attempt to norm an individual member of the population occurred in the 1850s during the development of the idea of the normal body. In Flaubert's *Madame Bovary*, Charles Bovary is influenced by Homais, the self-serving pharmacist, and Emma to perform a trendy operation that would correct the club foot of Hippolyte, the stableboy of the local inn. This corrective operation is seen as "new" and related to "progress" (Flaubert 1965, 125). Hippolyte is assailed with reasons why he should alter his foot. He is told, it "must considerably interfere with the proper performance of your work" (ibid., 126). And in addition to redefining him in terms of his ability to carry out work, Homais adds: "Think what would have happened if you had been called into the army, and had to fight under our national banner!" (ibid., 126). So national interests and again productivity are emphasized. But Hippolyte has been doing fine in his job as stableboy; his disability has not interfered with his performance in the community under traditional standards. In fact, Hippolyte seems to use his club foot to his advantage, as the narrator notes:

But on the equine foot, wide indeed as a horse's hoof, with is horny skin, and large toes, whose black nails resembled the nails of a horse shoe, the cripple ran about like a deer from morn till night. He was constantly to be seen on the Square, jumping round the carts, thrusting his limping foot forwards. He seemed even stronger on that leg than the other. By dint of hard service it had acquired, as it were, moral qualities of patience and energy; and when he was given some heavy work to do, he would support himself on it in preference to the sound one. (ibid., 126)

Hippolyte's disability is in fact an ability, one which he relies on, and from which he gets extra horse-power, as it were. But although Hippolyte is more than capable, the operation must be performed to bring him back to the human and away from the equine, which the first syllable of his name suggests. To have a disability is to be an animal, to be part of the Other.

A newspaper article appears after the operation's apparent initial success, praising the spirit of progress. The article envisages Hippolyte's welcome back into the human community.

Everything tends to show that his convalescence will be brief; and who knows if, at our next village festivity we shall not see our good Hippolyte appear in the midst of a bacchic dance, surrounded by a group of gay companions... (ibid., 128)

The article goes on to proclaim, "Hasn't the time come to cry out that the blind shall see, the deaf hear, the lame walk?" The imperative is clear: science will eradicate disability. However, by a touch of Flaubertian irony, Hippolyte's leg becomes gangrenous and has to be amputated. The older doctor who performs the operation lectures Charles about his attempt to norm this individual.

This is what you get from listening to the fads from Paris!... We are practitioners; we cure people, and we wouldn't dream of operating on someone who is in perfect health. Straighten club feet! As if one could straighten club feet indeed! It is as if one wished to make a hunchback straight! (ibid., 131)

While Flaubert's work illustrates some of the points I have been making, it is important that we do no simply think of the novel as merely an example of how an historical development lodges within a particular text. Rather, I think there is a larger claim to be made about novels and norms.

While Flaubert may parody current ideas about normalcy in medicine, there is another sense in which the novel as a form promotes and symbolically produces normative structures. Indeed, the whole focus of *Madame Bovary* is on Emma's abnormality and Flaubert's abhorrence of normal life. If we accept that novels are a social practice that arose as part of the project of middle-class hegemony,[7] then we can see that the plot and character development of novels tend to pull toward the normative. For example, most characters in nineteenth-century novels are somewhat ordinary people who are put in abnormal circumstances, as opposed to the heroic characters who represent the ideal in earlier forms such as the epic.

If disability appears in a novel, it is rarely centrally represented. It is unusual for a main character to be a person with disabilities, although minor characters, like Tiny Tim, can be deformed in ways that arouse pity. In the case of Esther Summerson, who is scarred by smallpox, her scars are made virtually to disappear through the agency of love. On the other hand, as sufficient research has shown, more often than not villains tend to be physically abnormal: scarred, deformed, or mutilated.[8]

I am not saying simply that novels embody the prejudices of society toward people with disabilities. That is clearly a truism. Rather, I am asserting that the very structures on which the novel rests tend to be normative, ideologically emphasizing the universal quality of the central character whose normativity encourages us to identify with him or her.[9] Furthermore, the novel's goal is to reproduce, on some level, the semiologically normative signs surrounding the reader, that paradoxically help the reader to read those signs in the world as well as the text. Thus the middleness of life, the middleness of the material world, the middleness of the normal body, the middleness of a sexually gendered, ethnically middle world is created in symbolic form and then reproduced symbolically. This normativity in narrative will by definition create the abnormal, the Other, the disabled, the native, the colonized subject, and so on.

Even on the level of plot, one can see the implication of eugenic notions of normativity. The parentage of characters in novels plays a crucial role. Rather than being self-creating beings, characters in novels have deep biological debts to their forebears, even if the characters are orphans—or perhaps especially if they are orphans. The great Heliodoric plots of romance, in which lower-class characters are found actually to be noble, take a new turn in the novel. While nobility may be less important, characters nevertheless inherit bourgeois respectability, moral rectitude, and eventually money and position through their genetic connection. In the novelistic world of nature versus nurture, nature almost always wins out. Thus Oliver Twist will naturally bear the banner of bourgeois morality and linguistic normativity, even though he grows up in the workhouse. Oliver will always be normal, even in abnormal circumstances.[10]

A further development in the novel can be seen in Zola's works. Before Zola, for example in the work of Balzac, the author attempted to show how the inherently good character of a protagonist was affected by the material world. Thus we read of the journey of the soul, of everyman or everywoman, through a trying and corrupting world. But Zola's theory of the novel depends on the idea of inherited traits and biological determinism. As Zola wrote in *The Experimental Novel*:

> Determinism dominates everything. It is scientific investigation, it is experimental reasoning, which combats one by one the hypotheses of the idealists, and which replaces purely imaginary novels by novels of observation and experimentation. (1964, 18)

In this view, the author is a kind of scientist watching how humans, with their naturally inherited dispositions, interact with each other. As Zola wrote, his intention in the Rougon-Macquart series was to show how heredity would influence a family "making superhuman efforts but always failing because of its own nature and the influences upon it" (Zola 1993, viii). This series would be a study of the "singular effect of heredity" (ibid.). Zola mentions the work of Darwin and links his own novels to notions of how inherited traits interact in particular environments over time and to generalizations about human behavior:

> And this is what constitutes the experimental novel: to possess a knowledge of the mechanism of the phenomena inherent in man, to show the machinery of his intellectual and sensory manifestations, under the influence of heredity and environment, such as physiology shall give them to us. (Zola 1964, 21)

Clearly stating his debt to science, Zola says that "the experimental novel is a consequence of the scientific evolution of the century" (ibid., 23). The older novel, according to Zola, is composed of imaginary adventures while the new novel is "a report, nothing more" (ibid., 124). In being a report, the new novel rejects idealized characters in favor of the norm.

> These young girls so pure, these young men so loyal, represented to us in certain novels, do not belong to the earth.... We tell everything, we do not make a choice, neither do we idealize. (ibid., 127)

Zola's characters belong to "the earth." This commitment constitutes Zola's new realism, one based on the norm, the average, the inherited.

My point is that a disabilities studies consciousness can alter the way we see not just novels that have main characters who are disabled but any novel. In thinking through the issue of disability, I have come to see that almost any literary work will have some reference to the abnormal, to disability, and so on. I would explain this phenomenon as a result of the hegemony of normalcy. This normalcy must constantly be enforced in public venues (like the novel), must always be creating and bolstering its image by processing, comparing, constructing, deconstructing images of normalcy and the abnormal. In fact, once one begins to notice, there really is a rare novel that does not have some characters with disabilities—characters who are lame, tubercular, dying of AIDS, chronically ill, depressed, mentally ill, and so on.

Let me take the example of some novels by Joseph Conrad. I pick Conrad not because he is especially representative, but just because I happen to be teaching a course on Conrad. Although he is not remembered in any sense as a writer on disability, Conrad is a good test case, as it turns out, because he wrote during a period when eugenics had permeated British society and when Freud had begun to write about normal and abnormal psychology. Conrad, too, was somewhat influenced by Zola, particularly in *The Secret Agent*.

The first thing I noticed about Conrad's work is that metaphors of disability abound. Each book has numerous instances of phrases like the following selections from *Lord Jim*:

> a dance of lame, blind, mute thoughts—a whirl of awful cripples.
> (Conrad 1986, 114)
> [he] comported himself in that clatter as though he had been stone-deaf.
> (ibid., 183)
> there was nothing of the cripple about him. (ibid., 234)
> Her broken figure hovered in crippled little jumps... (ibid., 263)
> he was made blind and deaf and without pity... (ibid., 300)
> a blind belief in the righteousness of his will against all mankind... (ibid., 317)
> They were erring men whom suffering had made blind to right and wrong. (ibid., 333)
> you dismal cripples, you... (ibid., 340)
> unmoved like a deaf man... (ibid., 319)

These references are almost like tics, appearing at regular intervals. They tend to focus on deafness, blindness, dumbness, and lameness, and they tend to use these metaphors to represent limitations on normal morals, ethics, and of course language. While it is entirely possible to maintain that these figures of speech are hardly more than mere linguistic convention, I would argue that the very regularity of these occurrences speaks to a reflexive patrolling function in which the author continuously checks and notes instances of normalcy and instances of disability—right down to the linguistic level.

Conrad's emphasis on exotic locations can also be seen as related to the issue of normalcy. Indeed the whole conception of imperialism on which writers like Conrad depend is largely based on notions of race and ethnicity that are intricately tied up with eugenics, statistical proofs of intelligence, ability, and so on. And these in turn are part of the hegemony of normalcy. Conrad's exotic settings are highlighted in his novels for their deviance from European conceptions. The protagonists are skewed from European standards of normal behavior specifically because they have traveled from Europe to, for example, the South Seas or the Belgian Congo. And Conrad focuses on those characters who, because they are influenced by these abnormal environments, lose their "singleness of purpose" (which he frequently defines as an English trait) and on those who do not.

The use of phrenology, too, is linked to the patrolling of normalcy, through the construction of character. So, in *Heart of Darkness* for example, when Marlow is about to leave for Africa a doctor measures the dimensions of his skull to enable him to discern if any quantitative changes subsequently occur as a result of the colonial encounter. So many of the characters in novels are formed from the ableist cultural repertoire of normalized head, face, and body features that characteristically signify personal qualities. Thus in *The Secret Agent*, the corpulent, lazy body of Verloc indicates his moral sleaziness, and Stevie's large ears and head shape are explicitly seen by Ossipon as characteristic of degeneracy and criminality as described in the theories of the nineteenth-century eugenic phrenologist Cesare Lombroso.

Stevie Conrad's most obviously disabled character, is a kind of center or focus of *The Secret Agent*. In a Zolaesque moment of insight, Ossipon sees Stevie's degeneracy as linked to his sister Winnie:

> he gazed scientifically at that woman, the sister of a degenerate, a degenerate herself—of a murdering type. He gazed at her and invoked Lombroso.... He gazed scientifically. He gazed at her cheeks, at her nose, at her eyes, at her ears... Bad!... Fatal! (Conrad 1968, 269)

This eugenic gaze that scrutinizes Winnie and Stevie is really only a recapitulation of the novelistic gaze that sees meaning in normative and nonnormative features. In fact, every member of the Verloc family has something "wrong" with them, including Winnie's mother who has trouble walking on her edematous legs. The moral turpitude and physical grimness of London is embodied in Verloc's inner circle. Michaelis, too, is obese and "wheezed as if deadened and oppressed by the layer of fat on his chest" (ibid., 73). Karl Yundt is toothless, gouty, and walks with a cane. Ossipon is racially abnormal having "crinkly yellow hair…a flattened nose and prominent mouth cast in the rough mould of the Negro type…[and] almond-shaped eyes [that] leered languidly over high cheek-bones" (ibid., 75)—all features indicating African and Asian qualities, particularly the cunning, opiated glance.

Stevie, the metaphoric central figure and sacrificial victim of the novel, is mentally delayed. His mental slowness becomes a metaphor for his radical innocence and childlike revulsion from cruelty. He is also, in his endless drawing of circles, seen as invoking "the symbolism of a mad art attempting the inconceivable" (ibid., 76). In this sense, his vision of the world is allied with that of Conrad, who himself could easily be described as embarked on the same project. Stevie is literally taken apart, not only by Ossipon's gaze and by that of the novelist, but centrally by the bungled explosion. His fragmented body[11] becomes a kind of symbol of the fragmentation that Conrad emphasizes throughout his opus and that the Professor recommends in his high-tech view of anarchism as based on the power of explosion and conflagration. Stevie becomes sensitized to the exploitation of workers by his encountering a coachman with a prosthetic hook for an arm, whose whipping of his horse causes Stevie anguish. The prosthetic arm appears sinister at first, particularly as a metonymic agent of the action of whipping. But the one-armed man explains: "This ain't an easy world…'Ard on 'osses, but dam' sight 'arder on poor chaps like me." He wheezed just audibly" (ibid., 165). Stevie's radical innocence is most fittingly convinced by the man's appeal to class solidarity, so Stevie ultimately is blown up for the sins of all.

In *Under Western Eyes*, the issue of normalcy is first signaled in the author's Introduction. Conrad apologizes for Razumov's being "slightly abnormal" and explains away this deviation by citing a kind of personal sensitivity as well as a Russian temperament. In addition, Conrad says that although his characters may seem odd, "nobody is exhibited as a monster here" (Conrad 1957, 51). The mention of exhibition of monsters immediately alerts us to the issue of nineteenth-century freak shows and raises the point that by depicting "abnormal" people, the author might see his own work as a kind of display of freaks.[12] Finally, Conrad makes the point that all these "abnormal" characters "are not the product of the exceptional but of the general—of the normality of their place, and time, and race" (ibid., 51). The conjunction of race and normality also alerts us to eugenic aims. What Conrad can be seen as apologizing for is the normalizing (and abnormalizing) role of the novel that must take a group of nationals (Russians) and make them into the abnormal, non-European, nonnormal Other. Interestingly, Conrad refers to anarchists and autocrats both as "imbecile." The use of this word made current by eugenic testing also shows us how pervasive is the hegemony of normalcy.

Razumov's abnormality is referred to by the narrator, at one point, as being seen by a man looking at a mirror "formulating to himself reassuring excuses for his appearance marked by the taint of some insidious hereditary disease" (ibid., 220). What makes Razumov into the cipher he is to all concerned is his lack of a recognizable identity aside from his being a Russian. So when he arrives in Geneva, Razumov says to Peter Ivanovitch, the radical political philosopher, that he will never be "a mere blind tool" simply to be used (ibid., 231). His refusal to be a "blind tool" ends up, ironically, in Razumov being made deaf by Necator, who deliberately bursts his eardrums with blows to the head. The world becomes for Razumov "perfectly silent—soundless as shadows" (ibid., 339) and "a world of mutes. Silent men, moving, unheard …" (ibid., 340). For both Conrad and Razumov, deafness is the end of language, the end of discourse, the ultimate punishment that makes all the rest of the characters appear as if their words were useless anyway. As Necator says, "He shall never be any use as spy on any one. He won't talk, because he will never hear anything in his life—not a thing" (ibid., 341). After Razumov walks into the street and is run over by a car, he is described as "a hopeless cripple, and stone deaf with that" (ibid., 343). He dies from his disabilities, as if life were in fact impossible to survive under those conditions. Miss Haldin, in contrast, gains her meaning in life from these events and says, "my eyes are open at last and my hands are free now" (ibid., 345). These sets of arrangements play an intimate part in the novel and show that disability looms before the writer as a *memento mori*. Normality has to protect itself by looking into the maw of disability and then recovering from that glance.

I am not claiming that this reading of some texts by Conrad is brilliant or definitive. But I do want to show that even in texts that do not appear to be about disability, the issue of normalcy is fully deployed. One can find in almost any novel, I would argue, a kind of surveying of the terrain of the body, an attention to difference—physical, mental, and national. This activity of consolidating the hegemony of normalcy is one that needs more attention, in addition to the kinds of work that have been done in locating the thematics of disability in literature.

What I have tried to show here is that the very term that permeates our contemporary life—the normal—is a configuration that arises in a particular historical moment. It is part of a notion of progress, of industrialization, and of ideological consolidation of the power of the bourgeoisie. The implications of the hegemony of normalcy are profound and extend into the very heart of cultural production. The novel form, that proliferator of ideology, is intricately connected with concepts of the norm. From the typicality of the central character, to the normalizing devices of plot to bring deviant characters back into the norms of society, to the normalizing coda of endings, the nineteenth- and twentieth-century novel promulgates and disburses notions of normalcy and by extension makes of physical differences ideological differences. Characters with disabilities are always marked with ideological meaning, as are moments of disease or accident that transform such characters. One of the tasks for a developing consciousness of disability issues is the attempt, then, to reverse the hegemony of the normal and to institute alternative ways of thinking about the abnormal.

Notes

1. This thinking obviously is still alive and well. During the U. S. Presidential election of 1994, Newt Gingrich accused President Clinton of being "the enemy of normal Americans." When asked at a later date to clarify what he meant, he said his meaning was that "normal" meant "middle class." (*New York Times*, November 14, 1994, A17)

2. One wants to make sure that Aristotle's idea of the mean is not confused with the norm. The Aristotelian mean is a kind of fictional construct. Aristotle advocates that in choosing between personal traits, one should tend to chose between the extremes. He does not however think of the population as falling generally into that mean. The mean, for Aristotle, is more of heuristic device to assist in moral and ethical choices. In the sense of being a middle term or a middle way, it carries more of a spacial sense than does the term "average" or "norm."

3. This rather remarkable confluence between eugenics and statistics has been pointed out by Donald A. MacKenzie, but I do not believe his observations have had the impact they should.

4. See my *Enforcing Disability* Chapter Six for more on the novel *Frankenstein* and its relation to notions of disability.

5. Many twentieth century prejudices against the learning disabled come from this period. The founder of the intelligence test still in use, Alfred Binet, was a Galton acolyte. The American psychologist Henry H. Goddard used Binet's tests in America and turned the numbers into categories—"idiots" being those whose mental age was one or two, "imbeciles" ranged in mental age from three to seven. Goddard invented the term "moron" (which he took from the Greek for "dull" or "stupid") for those between eight and twelve. Pejorative terms like "moron" or "retarded" have by now found their way into common usage. (Kevles, 78) And even the term "mongoloid idiot" to describe a person with Down's syndrome was used as recently as 1970s not as a pejorative term but in medical texts as a diagnosis. [see Michael Bérubé's fascinating article "Life As We Know It" for more on this phenomenon of labelling.]

6. If this argument sounds strangely familiar, it is being repeated and promulgated in the neo-conservative book *The Bell Curve* which claims that poverty and intelligence are linked through inherited characteristics.

7. This assumption is based on my previous works—*Factual Fictions: Origins of the English Novel and Resisting Novels: Fiction and Ideology*—as well as the cumulative body of writing about the relationship between capitalism, material life, culture, and fiction. The work of Raymond Wiliams, Terry Eagleton, Nancy Armstrong, Mary Poovey, John Bender, Michael McKeon, and others points in similar directions.

8. The issue of people with disabilities in literature is a well-documented one and is one I want generally to avoid in this work. Excellent books abound on the subject, including Alan Gartner and Tom Joe, eds., *Images of the Disabled, Disabling Images* (New York: Praeger, 1987) and the work of Deborah Kent including "In Search of a Heroine: Images of Women with Disabilities in Fiction and Drama" in Michelle Fine and Adrienne Asch, eds. *Women with Disabilities: Essays in Psychology, Culture, and Politics* (Philadelphia: Temple University Press, 1988).

9. And if the main character has a major disability, then we are encouraged to identify with that character's ability to overcome their disability.

10. The genealogical family line is both hereditary and financial in the bourgeois novel. The role of the family is defined by Jürgen Habermas thus: "as a genealogical link it [the family] guaranteed a continuity of personnel that consisted materially in the accumulation of capital and was anchored in the absence of legal restrictions concerning the inheritance of property." (47) The fact that the biological connectedness and the financial connectedness are conflated in the novel only furthers the point that normality is an enforced condition that upholds the totality of the bourgeois system.

11. I deal with the Lacanian idea of the *corps morcelé* in Chapter 6 of *Enforcing Normalcy*. In that section I show the relation between the fragmented body and the response to disability. Here, let me just say that Stevie's turning into a fragmented body makes sense given the fear "normal" observers have that if they allow a concept of disability to associate with their bodies, they will lose control of their normalcy and their bodies will fall apart.

12. See Chapter 4 of *Enforcing Normalcy* for more on the relation of freak shows to nationalism, colonialism, and disability. See also Rosemarie Garland Thompson's *Freakery: Cultural Spectacles of the Extraordinary Body* (New York: NYU Press, 1996).

Works Cited

Bell, Alexander Graham. 1969. *Memoir upon the Formation of a Deaf Variety of the Human Race*. Washington, DC: Alexander Graham Bell Association for the Deaf.

Blacker, C. P. 1952. *Eugenics: Galton and After*. Cambridge, Mass.: Harvard University Press.

Conrad, Joseph. 1924. "An Outpost of Progress." In *Tales of Unrest*. Garden City: Doubleday, Page & Company.

———. 1990 [1968]. *The Secret Agent*. London: Penguin.

———. 1989 [1957]. *Under Western Eyes*. London: Penguin.

———. 1924. *Youth*. Garden City: Doubleday, Page & Company.

———. 1986. *Lord Jim*. London: Penguin.

Defoe, Daniel. 1975. *Robinson Crusoe*. New York: Norton.

Farrall, Lyndsay Andrew. 1985. *The Origin and Growth of the English Eugenics Movement 1865–1925*. New York: Garland.

Flaubert, Gustave. 1965. *Madam Bovary*. Trans. Paul de Man. New York: Norton.

Freud, Sigmund. 1977. *Introductory Lectures on Psychoanalysis*. Trans. James Strachey. New York: Norton.

Kevles, Daniel J. 1985. *In the Name of Eugenics: Genetics and the Uses of Human* Heredity. New York: Alfred A. Knopf.

MacKenzie, Donald. A. 1981. *Statistics in Britain, 1865–1930*. Edinburgh: Edinburgh University Press.

Marx, Karl. 1970. *Capital*. Vol. 1. Trans. Samuel Moore and Edward Aveling. New York: International Publishers.

Porter, Theodore M. 1986. *The Rise of Statistical Thinking 1820–1900*. Princeton: Princeton University Press.

Stallybass, Peter and Allon White. 1987. *The Politics of Transgression*. Ithaca, NY: Cornell University Press.

Stigler, Stephen M. 1986. *The History of Statistics: The Measurement of Uncertainty before 1900*. Cambridge, Mass.: Harvard University Press.

Zola, Emile. 1964. *The Experimental Novel and Other Essays*. Trans Belle M. Sherman. New York: Haskel House.

———. 1993. *The Masterpiece*. Trans. Thomas Walton. London: Oxford University Press.

2

Deaf and Dumb in Ancient Greece[1]

M. Lynn Rose

Just as the nature of traditional scholarship rendered women in the ancient world inconsequential and invisible—save a few, remarkable ladies—people with disabilities have been all but invisible, save a handful of blind prophets. Beyond simply cataloguing disabled people, one must ask what constituted "ability" and "disability" for any given culture. At the heart of disability studies is a recognition that disability is a cultural construction; that is, that "'disability' has no inherent meaning."[2] It is not appropriate to investigate the phenomenon of disability in ancient societies from the perspective of a medical model,[3] whereby people are deemed inherently able-bodied or disabled according to medical definition and categorization. Rather, if disability is viewed as "relational and not inherent in the individual,"[4] the risk is much lower of contaminating the ancient evidence with modern cultural assumptions. The Greeks perceived deafness as an intellectual impairment because of the difficulty in verbal communication that accompanies deafness. The obsolete expression "deaf and dumb" is an apt description of the way in which a deaf person was perceived in ancient Greece.

The surviving ancient Greek material that mentions or depicts deafness is meager. While it does not allow a reconstruction of everyday life for deaf and hearing-impaired people, it does allow an investigation into the environment in which deaf people lived. This discussion of deafness in the ancient Greek world begins with a survey of the etiology of deafness, which suggests that the causes of deafness in the modern world existed in the ancient world. An examination of the term "deaf" (κωφός) reveals both that the term was flexible in its range of meanings, and that deafness was inextricably intertwined in Greek thought with an impairment of verbal communication. Next, I discuss the Greek medical understanding of deafness, as well as medical and nonmedical treatments for deafness in terms of how they illuminate Greek attitudes toward deaf people. Finally, while attitudinal subtleties are lost, we can determine broad cultural assumptions that shaped the realities of hearing-impaired people.

The only significant instance of a deaf person's appearance in the surviving Greek literature is Herodotus' tale (1.34; 1.38; 1.85) of Croesus' anonymous deaf son.[5] Herodotus tells us that Croesus, the king of Lydia and richest man in the world, had two sons. Atys, the elder, was brave and skilled, but died as a youth. The other son, whose name we never learn, was worthless to Croesus because he was deaf and mute. When Croesus has failed at his plans to conquer the Persians and is about to die at the hands of his captors, his son regains his voice at the last minute in order to save his father from the pyre.[6] One deaf boy is hardly representative of the portion of the population that was hearing-impaired, as the following etiological survey will show.

In the United States today, there are about twenty-two million hearing-impaired people; of these, two million are profoundly deaf (unable to hear anything) or severely deaf (unable to hear much).[7] Hearing impairment results from three major factors that are not necessarily exclusive: environmental, hereditary, and old age.

Environmental causes include noise-induced, accidental, toxic, and viral. Noise-induced deafness is primarily a phenomenon of the modern industrial world, though stonemasons, for example, may have been subject to hearing-loss in the ancient world.[8] Permanent deafness resulting from toxicity is also a phenomenon of the modern world.[9] Deafness from accident, such as a blow to the ear, must have resulted from time to time.[10] Viruses, too, were very much part of the ancient world. Of the six main viruses that can cause deafness today—chickenpox, common cold viruses, influenza, measles, mumps, and poliomyelitis—there is evidence for five in ancient Greece.[11] There is also evidence for the presence of bacterial meningitis, whose classic complication is hearing loss.[12] In modern, developed countries, preventative medicine reduces the incidence and severity of these viruses, but in the ancient world, as in third-world countries today, these viruses must have taken their toll.[13]

There is no reason to rule out hereditary deafness in the ancient world, and there is some conjectural evidence for the results of in-breeding, although not specifically for deafness.[14] Plutarch (*Moralia* 616 b) and Strabo (*Geography* 10.5.9), for example, observe the prevalence of premature baldness on Myconos. It is not surprising that island communities would have their own genetic peculiarities. Genetic phenomena such as the present-day prevalence of female muteness on Amorgos and Donussa would have been common in ancient Greece.[15] In addition to inbreeding, other hereditary factors would have produced deafness. Some families simply have a genetic background that favors deafness.[16] Furthermore, a chromosomal aberration can produce deafness, with or without a hereditary factor.[17]

Hearing loss is expected in elderly people in the modern world. Today, almost thirty percent of people sixty-five to seventy-four years old and almost fifty percent of those seventy to seventy-nine years old have some hearing loss; in other words, one third of those over sixty-five years old have clinically abnormal hearing.[18] Fewer people, of course, attained old age in the ancient world.[19] There is no reason to suppose that hearing loss would be less a part of old age in the ancient world than it is today;[20] if the incidence was similar, one Greek in three, sixty-five years or older, would have suffered some degree of hearing loss.

Finally, in addition to the three factors above, any condition that manifested in muteness would not have been differentiated from deafness.[21] Muteness can result from faulty information processing brought on by forms of autism, learning disabilities, and mental illness.[22]

Although Herodotus' fanciful tale of two sons and a kingdom does not represent the proportion of deaf people in the ancient world, it is useful in that it coincidentally illustrates two important ancient Greek assumptions about deaf people. First, and crucial to our understanding of the Greek concept of deafness: deafness went hand-in-hand with muteness. The Lydian boy's deafness was the sole reason for his worthlessness not because he could not hear, but because he could not speak.[23] In this case, the word "deaf" (κωφός) encompassed both conditions; a deaf person was voiceless by nature, mute in the sense that the sea or the earth is mute, "stone deaf."[24]

The second and related assumption seen in Herodotus' tale is that muteness indicated diminished worth. Croesus' deaf son was incapacitated (διέφθαρτο)[25] by his condition (Herodotus, 1.34), and it could not be clearer that the sole reason for the boy's uselessness was his deaf-muteness alone; in all other respects, he was acceptable (τᾱμὲν λλα ἐπιεικῆς, ἄφωοςδέ) (Herodotus, 1.85).[26] Croesus literally discounts his deaf son (οὐκεῖναί μοι λογίξομαι) (Herodotus, 1.38).[27] A deaf male child was perhaps as "worthless" as a girl. Deafness certainly indicated worthlessness in the political sphere; this was so taken for granted that Herodotus uses it as a literary device: when Croesus' son finds his voice, Herodotus has created the irony that Croesus gained an heir when he lost his kingship.[28]

A survey of the use of the word "deaf" (κωφός) shows that the term had a much wider range of meaning than the English term. Deafness and speechlessness were intertwined from the earliest appearance of the word "deaf" (κωφός), and the term does not always refer to a person's speech or hearing. In the *Iliad* (11.390), the term describes the bluntness of a weapon; the silence of an unbroken wave (14.16); and the muteness of the earth (24.54). This basic use of the word continues through the Archaic poets; for example, Alcman refers to a mute (κωφόν) wave.[29]

Even when the term describes deafness as a human characteristic, it implies a range of conditions that include an overall inability to communicate verbally. The first surviving use of "deaf" (κωφός) that probably describes human beings appears in Aeschylus (*Libation Bearers* 881), though "My cry is to the deaf" (κωφοῖς) could refer to anything that does not, or cannot, hear. There is a similar use

(*Seven Against Thebes* 202) when Eteocles asks the chorus of Theban women if he speaks to the deaf (κωφῇ).

The term unmistakably refers to a specific human sensory condition in the Hippocratic Corpus, and it appears abundantly there.[30] It is in the Hippocratic Corpus, too, that the term first refers to a class of people.[31] There are two references to deaf people as a distinct group,[32] although most of the references are to deafness as a temporary condition, a symptom of another condition, or a diagnostic tool. Hippocratic writers rarely mention permanent deafness, as opposed to the temporary conditions such as "night deafness" that frequently accompanies other ailments.[33] Deafness is mentioned in passing as a possible complication for the mother during childbirth, and muteness as a potential problem in the case of female hysteria.[34] The author of *Internal Affections* (18.24) warns that deafness may result from a botched cauterization of one of the main veins in the body.[35] In short, throughout the Hippocratic Corpus, deafness is seen more as a valuable diagnostic tool than as a physical infirmity in itself.[36]

There is not much surviving mention of medical treatment for deafness in the Classical period. Hippocratic theory becomes Hellenistic practice in the writings of Celsus, who lived about six centuries after the earliest Hippocratic writers. In Celsus' writings, we see specific medical treatments for hearing impairment that are based on Hippocratic theory.[37] For example, there is a connection throughout the Hippocratic Corpus between bilious bowels and deafness.[38] Celsus (2.8.19) takes this connection another step in his recommendation to balance the humors by producing a bilious stool. Other remedies for ear ailments and dull hearing include shaving the head, if the head is considered too heavy (6.7.7 b), and flushing the ear with various juices (6.7.8 a).[39] Some of the more drastic treatments suggest to the modern reader that hearing impairments might have been aggravated or even caused by medical treatment, such as when a probe with turpentine-soaked wool is inserted into the ear canal and twisted around (6.7.9 a).[40]

While the surviving medical literature of the Classical period does not include treatments for deafness, we do find reports of cures for deafness in the nonmedical literature. For example, psychological trauma instantly restored Croesus' son's capacity to speak (Herodotus, 1.85),[41] and a fourth century B. C. inscription at Epidaurus testifies to a spontaneous cure of muteness (ἄφωνος).[42]

Deafness is not a common ailment among the surviving testimonies of Asclepiadic cures, but the paucity of written remains does not necessarily indicate that the Greeks did not seek cures for it. Because it is an abstract characteristic, deafness is not easily depicted, and, like headache, is difficult to interpret in representation.[43] Clay representations of human ears were prominent among the offerings of body parts at the healing temples, and many survive. They may or may not represent thank offerings or pleas for cures of deafness.[44] The ear was, obviously, connected with hearing and thus communication and—in ancient thought—intelligence. By extension, the ear was for Aristotle (*History of Animals* 1.11.492 a) also indicative of personality.[45] Similarly, Athenaeus (12.516 b) tells us that when Midas became deaf (κεκωφημένον) through his stupidity, he received the ears of an ass to match his "dumbness."

Because deafness and muteness were intertwined, models of mouths or complete heads are just as likely as ears to have represented deafness.[46] But the ear was, certainly, the most obvious channel of hearing, listening, and understanding, and this is why it was important to have the ear of the god from whom one sought a favor. If one's prayer was heard, it was granted.[47] Having the god's ear was taken literally: some temples included depictions of gods' ears into which the suppliant could speak.[48]

Against this background, it is possible to reconstruct generally some of the realities of deaf people's lives in the ancient Greek world. I will discuss people with mild hearing impairments, followed by those people who were more severely deaf but who still spoke, and, finally, people who were prelingually deaf.

People with partial hearing loss outnumber people with severe or profound deafness in the modern world, and there is no reason to think that the situation would be different in the ancient world. Partial loss of hearing, because of the difficulty in verbal communication it brought on, implied partial loss of wit. Perhaps Aristophanes (*Knights* 43) used a hearing impairment as a comic vehicle: Demosthenes describes his master as a bit hard of hearing (ὑπόκωφων), quick-tempered, and country-minded.[49] As in the modern world, old people were expected to become slightly deaf (ὑπόκωφος). Slight deafness was the "old man's forfeit," along with a decrease in sight, wit, and memory (Xenophon, *Memorabilia* 4.7.8).[50] Old men and deafness were so intertwined that it is difficult to separate deafness from old age as the butt of the joke in Attic comedy.[51] Aristophanes' Acharnian men (*Acharnians* 681) contrast the city's brash and forensically skilled youth with their own deafness. The deafness here is literal but it reveals layers of symbolism in the conflict of generations. A diminished ability to communicate by speech accompanies hearing loss; the assumption of faulty thought accompanies this diminished ability to communicate easily; the picture of dull-witted old age results.[52]

What this picture of diminished intellect meant in the everyday life of someone with a mild hearing impairment is impossible to determine in any detail. Hard-of-hearing old men, though portrayed comically, are never portrayed—at least in the surviving material—as "worthless." In fact, an important measure of a Greek man's worth was his participation in the army or, at Athens, in the navy. Old men were not excluded from the hoplite forces. All citizens, regardless of age or physical fitness, were included in the military.[53] Of these old men, a significant proportion—upwards of thirty percent, we have noted—must have been hearing-impaired. This could have worked to their advantage in the noisy confusion of Greek combat, where panic could quickly scatter the phalanx.[54]

As scant as the information is for deaf and hearing-impaired men, there is even less information about women.[55] An epigram from the first century A. D. describes a very deaf old woman (δύσκωφον γραῖαν) who, when asked to bring cheeses (τυφός) brings grains of wheat (πῦρός) instead.[56] While the epigram, on its own, tells us little about deaf women, it does further illustrate the perceived connection between deafness and impaired communication.[57]

The degree of one's hearing loss never appears to be an important issue; what mattered to the Greeks was one's ability to speak.[58] Even profoundly deaf people who learn spoken language before losing their hearing do not necessarily lose their capacity to speak. When Pseudo-Aristotle (*Problems* 14.962 b) asks why deaf people talk through their noses, he refers to people who remember how to speak, but who do not remember how to regulate their voices.[59] Being able to speak intelligibly, even if imperfectly, separated the "dumb" from those who merely had variations of speech, though the philosophical line was thin.[60] Pseudo-Aristotle (*Problems* 10.40.895 a) compares speech disorders with muteness: he asks why man is the only animal that stammers, and asks in answer if it is because only man suffers from muteness (ἔνεον) and stammering is a form of muteness. The ancient literature is full of references to people who lisped, stuttered, stammered, or mumbled. Their speech was ridiculed (Plutarch, *Demosthenes* 4.4) or admired (Plutarch, *Alcibiades* 1.4), but there is nothing to indicate the degree of derision seen in the story of Croesus' son.[61]

Some deaf people did not learn spoken language. About one in 1000 people in the world today are congenitally deaf[62] and there is no reason to believe that the proportion was much different in the ancient world.[63] In the absence of modern educational methods, one must hear spoken language in order to learn to speak it.[64] People in the ancient world who became deaf *in utero* or before learning to speak were necessarily mute.[65]

Of course, prelingually deaf people who could not talk communicated in other ways;[66] speech is only part of the method by which even people with full hearing transmit information.[67] Deaf children who are not taught a signed language naturally learn a system of gestures.[68] An example from the modern world demonstrates how this might have played out in daily life in ancient Greece. Harlan Lane observed families in Burundi, Africa, where many deaf people are without the means to learn true signed language.[69] A mother describes gestural communication with her profoundly deaf daughter:

> She uses little gestures with me that I understand, that her sisters and brothers understand. . . . We don't have conversations, because that's impossible with a deaf person, but when I want her to go fetch water, I can take the jug that she always uses, show it to her, and point my finger in the direction of the well, and she knows that I need some water.[70]

While all language involves gesture,[71] a system of gestures does not necessarily comprise a language.[72] Conditions for a true, signed language would have been present only in areas in which deaf people interacted.[73] Furthermore, any such area would have to include adults who could teach sign language, and an ongoing need to use the language.[74] Highly populated urban areas such as Athens and, especially, island communities that had a high incidence of deafness due to genetics may have included generations of deaf people who used sign language.[75]

There is no proof of the presence, or the absence, of ancient Greek sign language.[76] Someone signing language looks like someone gesturing.[77] The handful of references to the gestures used by deaf people[78] is inconclusive. A Greek would not have differentiated between gestured communication and true sign language, or cared much, probably, that there was a difference.

People who had learned writing before becoming deaf would have been able to use the written word to communicate. Such people would not have been common. Writing was not available to the average person in Greece,[79] and the vast population of the ancient world was not merely illiterate, but rather, non-literate.[80] In the case of deaf children, the written word as a means of communication would have been limited to the rare family that included both parents who had mastered fluency of writing and reading[81] and deaf children.[82] Written characters were not the only media by which people who could not talk could transmit information. In the folk tale of the sisters Procne and Philomela, in which Procne's husband, Tereus, cuts out Philomela's tongue in order to prevent her from telling anyone that he raped her, Philomela weaves scenes into her tapestry that depict her story.[83]

In any case, people who did not speak Greek and who, for whatever reason, had to rely on gestured communication, were not admired.[84] Furthermore, the inability to speak went beyond a simple barrier in communication. Aristotle (*History of Animals* 4.9.536 b) observed that all people born deaf (κωφοὶ) are also mute (ἔυνεοι).[85] By mute, Aristotle refers to an inability to express language, not an inability to form sounds.[86] Aristotle (*History of Animals* 4.9.536 b) observes that animals make noise; human beings speak, and though people who are born deaf have a voice, they cannot talk. For the Greeks, as for people of all pre-Enlightenment cultures, speech, language, and reason were intertwined.[87] Because the conditions (inability to hear) and symptoms (inability to speak) of deafness were indistinct, Herodotus could use "deaf" (κωφός) and "speechless" (ἄφωνος; ἔνεος) interchangeably.[88] As Herodotus' audience took for granted, deafness was synonymous with "dumbness" in its full range of meanings. Language was the hallmark of human achievement, so muteness went beyond a physical condition. An inability to speak went hand-in-hand with an inability to reason, hand-in-hand with stupidity.[89] Plato (*Theaetetus* 206 d) has Socrates say that anyone can show what he thinks about anything, unless he is speechless or deaf from birth (ἐνεὸς ἢ κωφὸς ἀπ' ἀρχῆς). The proverb recorded by Plutarch (*Moralia* 512 d) that only the oracle can understand the deaf (κωφοῦ) further highlights the difficulty faced by people unable to communicate verbally.

That muteness was seen as a grave affliction can be traced with three literary examples from the seventh century through the first century B. C. Hesiod (*Theogony* 793–98) describes the punishment for perfidious gods as a sort of temporary death, in which the god must lie for a year without breath, without voice (ἄναυδος). In the chilling final scene of the *Alcestis*, the woman whom Heracles offers to Admetus is not dead yet not quite alive, Alcestis yet not quite Alcestis.[90] The emblem of this liminal state is her muteness (ἄναυδος) (Euripides, *Alcestis* 1143). Finally, Diodorus (4.24.4–5), in his account of Heracles' travels, reports that the punishment for the young men who failed to carry out sacred rites in honor of Iolaüs was that they were struck mute (ἀφώνος), and thus, he writes, resemble dead men (τετελευτηκόσιν).

Deafness was indeed a curse, sometimes literally. The word "deaf" (κωφός) appears in the surviving Greek inscriptions almost exclusively as a curse, and a powerful one. Deprivation of hearing, because it meant a deprivation of verbal communication and perceived intelligence, meant separation from the political and intellectual arena. A curse of deafness was appropriate not only for one's political opponents, whose speech could harm, but also for anyone who had too much power.[91] Aristophanes (*Clouds* 1320) provides a comedic example of this curse when the chorus teases Strepsiades, saying that he will wish his son, soon to be diabolically forensically skilled, were mute (ἄφωνον).[92]

It is crucial to consider that concerns surrounding speech and intelligence were different for the literate elite than they were for the bulk of the population, but that it is the literate elite on whom we must rely for almost all our information about deafness. The elite valued the very skills—such as fluency in communication—that they thought deaf people lacked. On one hand, Herodotus' Greek audience knew that Croesus' son could never become king. On the other hand, the deaf child of a farmer or shepherd, even if considered utterly stupid and incapable of political activity, could certainly carry out any number of tasks. Aristotle and his circle had the luxury to despise lack of eloquence, but the average peasant would be far less concerned with his child's forensic skills.

In summary, we are confined to learning about deafness in the ancient Greek world through the filter of the literary elite. In other words, the closest we can observe everyday life for deaf people is through a partial reconstruction of attitudes toward deaf people. Deafness was perceived not as a physical handicap but as an impairment of reasoning and basic intelligence. Life in Greece for any-one who did not speak must have been frustrating, at best. While the consequences of deafness are synonymous with exile or death in the literature, it is important to remember that more people in the Greek world were interested in farming than rhetoric. While ineligibility in political and intellectual arenas may have been a hardship, the hardship is magnified out of proportion in the surviving mate-rial. Furthermore, we must be cautious about our own filter of interpretation. We should not leap to conclusions about constructions of intellectual ability and disability in the ancient world any faster than about physical ability and disability.

Notes

1. This essay is based on a chapter of my Ph. D. thesis, "Physical Disability in the Ancient Greek World." The essay also developed from my presentation of "Croesus' Other Son: Ancient Greek Attitudes to Deafness" at the meeting of the Classical Association of the Midwest and South, Omaha, 22 April 1995. Many people contributed to this essay. Alan Boegehold and Robert Garland kindly provided me with their work before publication. Roberta Cullen, Lorna Sopçak, and Ross Willits have read and commented on many drafts, as have Lois Bragg and Anthony Hogan. Three anonymous readers associated with Gary Kiger and the Society for Disability Studies offered much helpful criticism and advice. Len-nard Davis, too, has been generous and gracious. I appreciate Jenny Singleton's correspondence and suggestions. I also thank Thomas Kelly, my thesis advisor.

2. Gary Kiger et al., "Introduction," *Disability Studies: Definitions and Diversity*, ed. G. Kiger et al. (Salem, Oregon, 1994), 1.

3. Beth Haller ("Rethinking Models of Media Representation of Disability," *Disability Studies Quarterly* 15 [1995]: 29–30) includes a succinct summary of various categories by which the media have represented disability, including the medical model.

4. Kiger et al., "Introduction," *Disability Studies*, 1.

5. Pliny (*Natural History* 35.7.21) relates the story of Quintus Pedius, "born dumb" (*natura mutus esset*), who, on the advice of the orator Messala and with the approval of Augustus, had lessons in painting and was making good progress when he died. Danielle Gourevitch, "Un enfant muet de naissance s'exprime par le dessin: à propos d'un cas rapporté par Pline l'Ancien," *L'Evolution psychiatrique* 56 [1991]: 889–93 discusses this short passage fully, and compares the Latin *mutus* with the various Greek terms for muteness.

6. Herodotus' tale (1.34; 1.38; 1.85), and see Warren Dawson, "Herodotus as Medical Writer," *Bulletin of the Institute of Classical Studies* 33 (1986): 87–96.

7. Nanci Scheetz, *Orientation to Deafness* (Boston, 1993), 203. Aram Gloring and Jean Roberts ("Hearing Levels of Adults by Age and Sex," *Vital and Health Statistics* 11th ser., 11 [1965]: 16) define a person with a severe hearing impairment as anyone who has trouble understanding loud or even amplified speech.

8. Karl Kryter (*The Effects of Noise on Man* [Orlando, 1985], 220) states that people working around noise have always suf-fered deafness. Still, the noise to which he refers throughout his study is industrial noise.

9. Jiri Prazma ("Ototoxicity of Aminoglycoside Antibiotics," *Pharmacology of Hearing*, ed. R. D. Brown and E. A. Daigneault [New York, 1981], 153–95) discusses cochlear destruction caused by the AmAn drugs, the best-known of which include the streptomycin antibiotics. In antiquity, wormseed, chenopodium oil, and cinchona alkaloids could cause temporary deafness. Calvin Wells (*Bones, Bodies and Disease* [London, 1964], 111–13) discusses paleotoxicology in terms of the difficulty of identification; for example, mineral poisons remain in the tissues and are easily identified, but may have come from the soil, after death.

10. Guido Majno (*The Healing Hand: Man and Wound in the Ancient World* [Cambridge, Mass., 1975], 171–75) discusses various injuries that resulted from boxing in fourth-and third-century Greece, including the "cauliflower ear." He points out (174) that Aristophanes invented the term "ear-breaker" (κάταξις) for a boxer. A type of accident in which the ears themselves are injured is seen in an account by Plutarch (*Moralia* 470 e) of men whose noses and ears were mutilated (περικοπτομένους) as they were digging through Mt. Athos. While this tale is fantastic, designed to show an example of Xerxes' hybris in cutting through Mt. Athos, the detail of injured ears is believable.

11. Grmek (*DAGW*, 334–37) sees evidence for chickenpox, the common cold virus, and mumps. He sees evidence for the possibility of the influenza virus and poliomyelitis. He does not believe that the measles virus existed. Srboljub Živanović (*Ancient Diseases: The Elements of Paleopathology* [New York, 1982], 86, 108) finds possible skeletal evidence for polio-myelitis.

12. Grmek (*DAGW*, 122, 123, 131) discusses meningitis in ancient Greece.

13. Of course, these viruses must have taken their toll not only by causing deafness, but also by killing the victim. Mustafa Abdalla Salih ("Childhood Acute Bacterial Meningitis in the Sudan: An Epidemiological, Clinical and Laboratory Study," *Scandinavian Journal of Infectious Diseases* suppl. 66 [1990]) studied meningitis in a developing area (the Sudan), and reports (76) that both the mortality and the frequency of long-term complications, including hearing loss, was much higher than in developed countries. Among survivors in the Sudan, twenty-two percent had hearing loss (7). Antibiotics (20, 26) and vaccination (27) are the main factors responsible for diminishing the impact of the disease in developed countries.

14. Ancient writers were aware of hereditary physical disability, even if they did not recognize the underlying genetics. The Hippocratic author of *The Sacred Disease* (3) observes phlegmatic children from phlegmatic parents, bilious children from bilious parents, and so on. Aristotle (*History of Animals* 9(7).585 b) cites lame children born of lame parents; blind children produced by blind parents. Because he does not understand the genetics, he also cites (*Generation of Animals* 1.17.721 b) acquired characteristics, such as scars and brands.

15. Robert Sallares, *The Ecology of the Ancient Greek World* (Ithaca, 1991), 235. Sallares (460) mentions other ancient ecological peculiarities of Myconos. Nora Groce (*Everyone Here Spoke Sign Language: Hereditary Deafness on Martha's Vineyard* [Cambridge, Mass., 1985]) gives a modern account of island communities with a high proportions of people who are deaf—twenty-five percent of the inhabitants in the mid-nineteenth century—as a result of inbreeding. The discussion (40–43) on inbreeding is especially useful.

16. Ha-Sheng Li, "Genetic Influences on Susceptibility of the Auditory System to Aging and Environmental Factors," *Scandinavian Audiology* 21 suppl. 36 (1992): 7.

17 M. Michael Cohen and Robert J. Gorlin ("Epidemiology, Etiology, and Genetic Patterns," *Hereditary Hearing Loss and Its Syndromes*, ed. R. Gorlin et al. [New York, 1995], 9–21) discuss the varieties of genetic deafness in the modern world, listing hereditary factors, acquired factors, and unknown factors as about equal as causes of genetic hearing loss (9). These subcategories of genetic deafness in the ancient world are impossible to determine.

18. Gerhard Salomon, "Hearing Problems and the Elderly," *Danish Medical Bulletin* 33 suppl. 3 (1986): 4.

19. Grmek (*DAGW*, 103) gives 41.7 years as the average age of adults at the moment of death in Greece during Classical times. Here he follows J. Lawrence Angel, "The Length of Life in Ancient Greece," *Journal of Gerontology* 2 (1947): 20. Angel points out (23) that the data are scanty, especially for very old people. Mogens Herman Hansen (*Demography and Democracy* [Herning, Denmark, 1986], 12) calculates that in the fourth century, of all males in Attica eighteen to eighty years and older, 11.9 percent were fifty to sixty-nine years old; 8.7 percent were sixty to eighty years and older. M. I. Finley ("The Elderly in Classical Antiquity," *Greece and Rome* 28 [1981]: 157) contrasts these figures with the projection that by the end of the twentieth century, people sixty years of age and older will comprise twenty percent of the population in Great Britain.

20. The cumulative effect of noise pollution might be responsible for some hearing loss in the elderly that would not have been present in the ancient world. Ha-Sheng Li ("Genetic Influences on Susceptibility of the Auditory System to Aging and Environmental Factors," *Scandinavian Audiology* 21 suppl. 36 [1992]: 8) states that the etiology of deafness through aging is not well understood. Sava Soucek and Leslie Michaels (*Hearing loss in the Elderly: Audiometric, Electrophysiological and Histopathological Aspects* (London, 1990)) conclude (103) that hearing loss is innate to old age.

21. Even in the twentieth century this is the case. Donna Williams (*Somebody Somewhere: Breaking Free From the World of Autism* [New York, 1994], 50) explains, in her account of her own autism, that she was "meaning-deaf," but, like many autistic children, was thought to be sound-deaf.

22. An example of muteness as a result of autism can be seen in Josh Greenfeld's account of his son, *A Child Called Noah* (New York, 1972).

23. Pötscher ("Der stumme Sohn der Kroisos," *Zeitschrift für klinische Psychologie und Psychotherapie* 20 [1974]: 368) argues that Croesus' son was not deaf at all, pointing out that, in order to finally speak, he must have been able to hear all along. He suggests that Herodotus used "deaf " (κωφός) as an interchangeable word for "mute."

24. "Stone deaf" is not an exclusively modern concept, though in the ancient world it was perhaps more literal. A girl's first or second century A. D. grave stele from Smyrna (*Inschriften von Smyrna* I.549, ed. G. Petzl [Bonn, 1982]) refers to the deaf stones (Κωφαί . . . πέτραι) of the tomb.

25. It is interesting that Herodotus (1.166 and elsewhere) uses this same term for ships that are damaged so as to be utterly useless.

26. Xenophon (*Cyropaedia* 7.2.20) repeats the assessment.

27. The parallels between discounting a "defective" child and discounting a female child are provocative, and call to mind families who named only male children in census reports, as mentioned by Sarah Pomeroy ("Infanticide in Hellenistic Greece," *Images of Women in Antiquity*, ed. A. Cameron and A. Kuhrt [Detroit, 1993], 208).

28. J. A. S. Evans, *Herodotus: Explorer of the Past* (Princeton, 1991), 49.

29. Frag. 14 c *PMG*.

30. There are sixty-nine instances of the forms of κωφός in the Hippocratic Corpus.

31. Lane (*WMH*, 93) points out that about ten centuries later, deaf people appeared as a legal class for the first time, in the Code of Justinian, 3.20.7; 6.22.10.

32. The class of people who are severely deaf (δύσκωφοι) is mentioned in *Coan Foreknowledge* (193.1) in connection with symptoms they might have; specifically, if their hands tremble, their tongue is paralyzed, and they have torpor, it is a bad sign. Deaf people who are deaf from birth (οἰκωφοὶ οἱ ἐκ γενεῆς) are presented to illustrate nonfunctional vocal chords in *Fleshes* (18.8). Danielle Gourevitch ("L'a-phonie hippocratique," *Formes de pensée dans la Collection hippocratique*, ed. F. Lasserre and P. Mudry [Geneva, 1983], 302) points out that muteness (ἄφωος) appears in the Hippocratic Corpus as a symptom rather than a condition in itself, and that while the Hippocratics recognized that there were different degrees and typed of muteness, the aim of the practitioners was objective reporting, not analysis. She further points out (303–05), that the meaning of the two common terms for muteness (ἄφωνος and ἀναυοῆς) shifts from author to author and even within the Hippocratic Corpus.

33. This sort of passing deafness is seen especially frequently throughout *Epidemics*; e.g., 1.3.13(3).5, 15, 16; 1.3.13(5).26; 1.3.13(10).4, and so on. In the writings of Galen, there are twenty-five instances of the term "deaf" (κωφὸς); four in Pseudo-Galen. Of these, almost all are referrals to the temporary deafness of the Hippocratic Corpus (e.g., 17a.528.5; 17a.530.2; 17a.530.7; 17a.534.4; 17a.557.16; 17a. 560.10; 17a.585.7; 17a.587.2).

34. Deafness as a result of a misdirected lochial purge: Hippocrates, *On the Affections of Women* 41.30. Muteness as an accompanying symptom of hysteria: *On the Nature of Women* 23.1; *On the Affections of Women* 127.1; 201.13; 203.18. Danielle Gourevitch (*Le Mal d'être femme: la femme et la médecine dans la Rome antique* [Paris, 1984], 113–28) provides a good discussion of female hysteria in general. She also explains (27) that women's bodies were usually traumatically out of balance in the view of medical science, which had as its underpinnings the system of humors; that is, blood, phlegm, black bile, and yellow bile all balanced in the right proportions given the season and topography.

35. A main vein, in Hippocratic thought (*Internal Affections* 18.23–25) travels all the way from the head to the feet. If it is severed in the area of the head, deafness or blindness results. Lameness results if it is severed in the leg. Muteness, not deafness, is at least in one instance a tangible medical phenomenon: a short passage (*Fleshes* 18.8) on the physiology of speaking and muteness explains that air produces sound as it intersects the throat, moderated by the tongue.

36. Naturally, the term continues as an effective and not uncommon metaphor; for example, Plato (*Republic* 3.18.411 d) warns that the soul of a man who does not partake in the Muse will become weak, deaf (κωφόζ), and blind.

37. Huldrych Koelbing (*Arzt und Patient in der Antiken Welt* [Munich, 1977], 158) points out that although Celsus worked during the Roman, not Hellenistic, period, his work is more a compilation of Hellenistic scientific writing than a reflection of his own practice.

38. When bowels are bilious, deafness ensues, *Aphorisms* 4.28.1; deafness accompanying a bowel movement full of black matter is fatal after a hemorrhage, *Prorrhetic* 1.129; similar examples: *Prorrhetic* 1.127; *Coan Foreknowledge* 324; 623.

39. In case Celsus' treatment seems quaint, I should note Lane, *WMH*, the first part of which is written as an autobiography of Laurent Clerc, a nineteenth-century deaf man. Clerc submitted to visits to a doctor who injected mysterious liquids into his ears in an attempt to cure his deafness (5).

40. Anthony Hogan, letter to the author, 14 July 1994 points out that the treatment is still successfully used today, as a solution of turpentine is helpful in loosening an impaction of cerumen (earwax), and that the danger lies, then and now, in inserting the probe too far, and perforating the ear drum. I thank Mr. Hogan for his help, his generosity in reading several drafts of this chapter, and for his correspondence. A study undertaken by the Health Services Directorate of Canada (*Acquired Hearing Impairment in the Adult* [Ottawa, 1988], 14) confirms that partial deafness can indeed result from an impaction of earwax.

41. Robert Garland (*The Eye of the Beholder* [Ithaca, 1995], 96–97) sees Croesus' son's spontaneous recovery as a symbol that the son was, after all, worthwhile, and that Croesus' moral blindness toward his son is parallel with his senseless invasion of Persia. I thank Dr. Garland for his generosity in providing me with substantial portions of his manuscript before publication, and for his correspondence, advice, and encouragement. W. Pötscher ("Der stumme Sohn der Kroisos," *Zeitschrift für klinische Psychologie und Psychotherapie* 20 [1974], 367–68) argues that the muteness was psychogenic and not connected with deafness at all.

42. Ludwig and Emma Edelstein (*Asclepius: A Collection and Interpretation of the Testimonies*, 2 vols. [Baltimore, 1945]) have collected and translated much of *IG* IV².951, a stele from the healing site at Epidaurus, both sides of which consist of narrations of various complications and cures. For the translation of this case, see 230–31. This cure is typically miraculous, listed among other cures such as the restoration of a lost eyeball and the disappearance of scars.

43. Mabel Lang (*Cure and Cult in Ancient Corinth: A Guide to the Asklepion* [Princeton, 1977], 15) uses headache as an example of an abstract ailment. This difficulty of representation may explain the lack of reference to deafness or muteness in the surviving papyri; I have yet to see a reference to either. Physical characteristics do appear in the papyri, especially in the private documents, but usually as neutral attributes, such as scars, that identify people. A negative characteristic (e.g., not speaking) would be inefficient identification.

44. Such offerings could also represent thank offerings or pleas for cures of ear infections. Van Straten (*GG*, 105–43) catalogues votive offerings representing body parts from the Greek world. Models of ears were found on many sites.

45. Here (*History of Animals* 1.11.492 a) Aristotle associates large, projecting ears with senseless chatter.

46. Van Straten (*GG*, 110) points out that while there are no surviving examples of mouths, there is testimony for eight examples at the Athenian Asclepion. Sara Aleshire (*The Athenian Asklepion: The People, Their Dedications, and the Inventories* [Amsterdam, 1989], 41) has little to add to Van Straten's findings in her study, published eight years after Van Straten's, on the issue of votive mouths: she refers the reader to Van Straten for the discussion of mouths.

47. H. S. Versnel, "Religious Mentality in Ancient Prayer," *Faith Hope and Worship*, ed. H. S. Versnel (Leiden, 1981), 30.

48. Van Straten, GG, 83. Van Straten points out (144) that he restricted the ears, in his catalogue of body parts, to the ears which were votive offerings, not representations of gods' ears, although it is impossible to be completely sure which is which. The atmosphere and appearance of the Asclepions is just lately being reconstructed. Sara Aleshire (*Asklepios at Athens: Epigraphic and Prosopographic Essays on the Athenian Healing Cults* [Amsterdam, 1991], 46) compares the temples of Asclepius, in contrast to the stark reconstructions of bare buildings, to overcrowded antique stores or museum storerooms.

49. We see another example of comedic deafness in Herodas' mime, in which the slave Kydilla, addressing the slave Pyrrhias as "deaf " (κωφέ) tells him that his mistress is calling him, *Mime* 5.55 I. C. Cunningham (*Herodas Miamiambi* [Oxford, 1971], 155–56) argues that this term (κωφέ) is not a true vocative. There is nothing to indicate that Pyrrhias was to be taken as a literally deaf character, but the line has a slapstick tone. Cunningham (*LCL* 1993) translates the lines: "Pyrries, you deaf wretch, she is calling you" (Πυρρίης, τάλας, κωφέ, / καλεῖ σε). Similarly, a small fragment of Cratinus' comedy, "Archilochoi," frag. 6 *PCG*, provides just enough information to confirm that the gag of the deaf man and the blind man interacting existed in the fifth century. The stock gag continues; e.g., the interactions between a blind butler and deaf maid are meant to be comic in the film *Murder by Death*, dir. Robert Moore, Columbia, 1984.

50. Here, the phrase is "diminished hearing" (ἀκουεινἡττον).

51. M. I. Finley ("The Elderly in Classical Antiquity," *Greece and Rome* 28 [1981]: 156 and passim) discusses the role of the elderly in comedy.

52. Meyer Reinhold ("The Generation Gap in Antiquity," *The Conflict of Generations in Ancient Greece and Rome*, ed. M. Bertman [Amsterdam, 1976], 44) argues that the conflict of generations is particularly a fifth-century phenomenon. Gerhard Salomon ("Hearing Problems and the Elderly," *Danish Medical Bulletin* 33 suppl. 3 [1986]: 12) points out that hearing loss may magnify the traits of senility.

53. Victor Hanson, *The Western Way of War: Infantry Battle in Classical Greece* (New York, 1989), 95.

54. Victor Hanson, *The Western Way of War: Infantry Battle in Classical Greece* (New York, 1989), 95. The panic was not necessarily always noise-induced, but may have been: Hanson (147–50, 152–54) reconstructs the chaos and the noise of battle.

55. Jan Bremmer ("The Old Women of Ancient Greece," *Sexual Asymmetry*, ed. J. Blok and P. Mason [Amsterdam, 1987], 191–215) has assembled the evidence that exists. Silence in a woman was virtuous, and women's speech was, at best, considered less valuable than men's speech (e.g., Nancy Sorkin Rabinowitz, "Female Speech and Female Sexuality: Euripides' *Hippolytus* as Model," *Helios* 13 [1986]: 127–40), and it is interesting to wonder what attitudes a mute woman might have encountered, given the ideals of feminine silence. Because there is no record of such attitudes, all we can do is wonder.

56. *Greek Anthology* 11.74. "In fact," the narrator says, "she does not comprehend a word I say." This is the only significant instance of a deaf woman that I have found in the Greek material.

57. Henry Kisor (*What's That Pig Outdoors?* [New York, 1990]), throughout his autobiography, dispels the notion that a deaf person can always read lips efficiently.

58. Lane (*WMH*, 93) writes that "those who were deaf only but could speak—who had established their credentials in the eyes of hearing society and knew their oral language—have always been regarded as persons at law." That those who could speak have "always" been seen as worthwhile is probably true, but the earliest documentation, as Lane points out, is not until the Code of Justinian, sixth century A. D.

59. The question of nasal speech comes up in Pseudo-Aristotle, *Problems*, 11.2.899 a; the answer hinges on the relation between deafness and dumbness, followed by a physiological explanation about breath and tongue, mirroring the Hippocratic Corpus, *Fleshes* 8; another connection between deafness and dumbness, followed by an explanation that the nostrils of the deaf are distended because the deaf breathe more violently, 11.4.899 a; and a suggestion that deafness is a congestion in the region of the lungs, 33.14.962 b. Similarly, Galen, 8.267.14–16, describes a condition in which injured throat muscles result in a wounded voice, but specifies that a weak voice, not muteness, results (σμικρόφωνος ο ὗτε δὲ ἄφωνος).

60. Ironically, Hannah Gershon ("Who Gets to be Called Deaf? Cultural Conflicts Between Deaf Populations," Society for Disability Studies 1994 Annual Meeting, Rockville, 24 June 1994) argued that in deaf culture today, while all audiologically

deaf people are "permanent exiles" from the world of sound, late-deafened adults are "immigrants" in deaf culture, who "never lose their hearing accent," while those who grew up without hearing have a solid identity in deaf society.

61. Battus, who according to Herodotus, 4.155–58, was the seventh century B. C. founder of Cyrene, is also a good example: on one hand, his speech disorder—usually taken as a stutter—was part of his identity. On the other hand, his legend involves a full role in the political sphere. O. Masson ("Le nom de Battos, fondateur de Cyrene," *Glotta* 54 [1976]: 84–98) discusses the etymology of the name "Battus."

62. William Stokoe, "Language, Prelanguage, and Sign Language," *Seminars in Speech and Language* 11 (1990), 93.

63. Venetta Lampropoulou ("The History of Deaf Education in Greece," *The Deaf Way*, ed. C. Erting et al. [Washington, D.C., 1995], 240) suggests that deaf babies in Sparta were included among those "with disabilities" and discarded. There is no reason, though, to believe that babies born deaf were subject to infanticide, if only because the deafness would not be detected until later, as Danielle Gourevitch ("Un enfant muet de naissance s'exprime par le dessin: à propos d'un cas rapporté par Pline l'Ancien," *L'Evolution psychiatrique* 56 [1991]: 890) points out. It is possible that a child who was perceived as worthless would have received less than his or her share of necessities and thus eventually would have died, but there is no evidence for or against this.

64. Steven Pinker (*The Language Instinct* [New York, 1994], 37–38) points out that successful language acquisition must take place in childhood, and (293) that the likelihood of acquiring spoken language is steadily compromised after the age of six. Franklin Silverman, *Communication for the Speechless* (Boston, 1995), 11.

65. In extreme cases today, children without language are treated as subhuman, even "wild." "Genie" is a recent case of a "wild child" who, until thirteen years old, had been raised in near-isolation, not deaf but language-deprived. Her portrait illustrates the severe consequences of the intertwined lack of language and socialization: Genie "was unsocialized, primitive, hardly human." Susan Curtiss, *Genie: A Psycholinguistic Study of a Modern-Day "Wiled Child"* (New York, 1977), 9. Russ Rymer (Genie: An Abused Child Flight From Silence [New York, 1993]) discusses several other cases of mute children, including (205) a deaf woman misdiagnosed as mentally retarded, who grew up in the backwoods and was deprived of language until she was in her thirties. It is interesting that satyrs—subhuman inhabitants of the wilds—are vaguely associated with muteness. Silens, too, are intriguing in this context. Guy Michael Hedreen (*Silens in Attic Black-figure Vase-painting: Myth and Performance* [Ann Arbor, 1992], 1) describes silens, the mythical horse-man hybrids who are related to satyrs, but who bear more resemblance to humans than do satyrs. Plutarch (*Sulla* 27.2) relates the tale of Sulla's discovery of a Greek satyr; Sulla was unable to force it to do more than grunt. The satyr Silenus was supposed to possess unlimited wisdom but, at least according to Vergil (*Ecologues* 6.13) had to be forced to speak. One wonders about the lost Sophoclean *Deaf Satyrs*, frags. 362–63, but with only two surviving partial lines to accompany the title, one can only wonder. A. C. Pearson (ed., *The Fragments of Sophocles*, 3 vols. [Cambridge, England, 1917], 2:31) suggests that "the κωφοί" were 'blockheads,'" and discusses other scholars' theories on the content of the play.

66. Carol Padden (review of *A Man Without Words*, by Susan Schaller, *American Journal of Psychology* 105 [1992]: 652–53) writes that the "wild children" such as Victor and Genie lacked not just language, but also the ability to take part in life's social rhythm.

67. Alan L. Boegehold ("Some Modern Gestures in Ancient Greek Literature," *Transactions of the Greek Humanistic Society 1* [forthcoming]: 2–3) encourages scholars of ancient Greek to pay attention not only to the written words but also to the implied gestures. I thank Dr. Boegehold for providing me with this essay before publication. Boegehold provides a specific example in "A Signifying Gesture: Euripides, *Iphigeneia Taurica*, 965–66, *American Journal of Archaeology* 93 (1989), 81–83, in which he argues that the gesture made by Athena, suggested by the word ὠλένι, has a specific indication: an equal (thus favorable) conclusion of the sorting of votes in the trial of Orestes.

68. S. Goldin-Meadow and C. Mylander, "The Development of Morphology Without a Conventional Language Model," *From Gesture to Language in Hearing and Deaf Children*, ed. V. Volterra and C.J. Erting (New York, 1990), 165. Lane (*WMH*, 5) describes "home sign," a system of abbreviated gestures. Steven Pinker (*The Language Instinct* [New York, 1994], 36) cites a situation in Nicaragua in the 1970s in which deaf children pooled their gestures and developed what is now a codified system of gestures. Since it is not based on consistent grammar, this system is "basically pidgin."

69. Harlan Lane, *The Mask of Benevolence: Disabling the Deaf Community* (New York, 1992), 147.

70. Harlan Lane, *The Mask of Benevolence: Disabling the Deaf Community* (New York, 1992), 151. Mark Golden (*Children and Childhood in Classical Athens* [Baltimore, 1990], 35–36) discusses the agricultural labor of children—gathering stones from the field, breaking up dirt, tending animals—as a criterion that helps assess their value as an economic unit in the family.

71. William Stokoe ("Seeing Clearly Through Fuzzy Speech," *Sign Language Studies* 82 [1994], 90) argues that all language *is* gesture.

72. William Stokoe, *Semiotics and Human Sign Languages*, Approaches to Semiotics 21 (Paris, 1972), 13. Syntax is the difference between gesture and signed language.

73. Robert E. Johnson and Carol Erting ("Ethnicity and Socialization in a Classroom for Deaf Children," *The Sociolinguistics of the Deaf Community*, ed. C. Lucas [New York, 1989], 43) point out that in America, deafness goes beyond a physical disability to include a set of attitudes and behaviors. They further point out (49) that the shared experience based on a visual culture is one of the elements that creates a community among deaf people. Whether or not a deaf community existed anywhere in the ancient Greek world is impossible to determine, though one imagines that at least in the rural

areas of Greece, there were only isolated, deaf individuals. Lane (*WMH*, 112 and passim) cites "signing communities" in eighteenth-century France that, he argues, formed the basis of formal education for the deaf. In any case, it is important to distinguish between early communities of deaf people and the newer deaf community. Petra Rose and Gary Kiger ("Intergroup Relations: Political Action and Identity in the Deaf Community," Society for Disability Studies Annual Meeting, Rockville, Maryland, 23 June 1994) trace the newer, radical element of the deaf community to the Deaf Power movement in the 1970s, in which deaf people "acquired a voice" and recognized themselves as a minority with a cultural heritage.

74. M. C. Da Cunha Pereira and C. De Lemos ("Gesture in Hearing Mother-Deaf Child Interaction," *From Gesture to Language in Hearing and Deaf Children*, ed. V. Volterra and C. J. Erting [New York, 1990], 186) point out that, while deaf children in hearing families develop the skills necessary to learning sign language, a sign language does not materialize on its own, even between deaf peers. Sign language must be taught by someone proficient in it.

75. If in Athens, with the largest population of any Greek polis by far, there were 60,000 citizens ca. 500 B. C., as Chester Starr (*The Economic and Social Growth of Early Greece 800–500* B. C. [New York, 1977], 152–56) calculates, 600 citizens would have been severely deaf; sixty would have been congenitally deaf. The category of "citizens" includes male residents eligible to vote and does not include women, children, slaves, or foreign residents. If we double the population figure of 60,000 to include women, and double it again to include two children for each family, we still have only 240 congenitally deaf people up and down Attica, with no particular reason that they would be aware of each other's presence, especially given the lack of public schools. In a smaller community such as the island of Melos, with its fifth-century population of about 1,250 citizens, as Eberhard Ruschenbusch ("Tribut und Bürgerzahl im ersten athenischen Seebund," *Zeitschrift für Papyrologie und Epigraphik* 53 [1983]: 145) estimates, one or two citizens would be congenitally deaf, and about five people altogether. On one hand, these figures do not account for the possibility that, as noted earlier, the diseases that leave people deaf in the modern world may have killed people in the ancient world. On the other hand, they do not take into account genetic phenomena that might have increased the prevalence of deafness in island communities.

76. But William Stokoe ("Discovering a Neglected Language," *Sign Language Studies* 85 [1994]: 377) believes that sign language has a long history, documented or not: "In my opinion," he writes, "if the ancestor of sign language is ever found, it will turn out to be the first human, most likely a woman, who realized that gestures not only meant whatever two or more people agreed on that they meant, because they may also connect meanings—they may be words or sentences, depending on how one looks at them."

77. As William Stokoe (Language, Prelanguage, and Sign Language," *Seminars in Speech and Language* 11 [1990]: 94) points out.

78. Xenophon (*Anabasis* 4.5.33) describes soldiers with a language barrier using gestures as if mute (ἐνειοῖς). Ctesias (*FGrH* 688 F 45) refers to using signs like "the deaf and speechless" (κωφοὶ καὶ ἄλαλοι). Plato (*Cratylus* 422 d-e) too, has Socrates suggest communication by gesture, "as mute men" (ἐνεοί).

79. William Harris, *Ancient Literacy* (Cambridge, Mass., 1989), 67.

80. Rosalind Thomas (*Literacy and Orality in Ancient Greece* [Cambridge, England, 1992], 2–4) discusses the extent of non-literacy. Eric Havelock (*Origins of Western Literacy* [Toronto, 1976], 7) drives the point home by pointing out that Pindar and Plato were nearly nonliterate.

81. Eric Havelock (*Origins of Western Literacy* [Toronto, 1976], 46–47) traces the ancient development of reading fluency (Possible only when the components of the alphabet have no independent meaning at all). He argues (21) that scriptoral literacy only appeared at the beginning of the fourth century B. C.

82. Mark Golden (*Children and Childhood in Classical Athens* [Baltimore, 1990], 62–65) discusses children's education, of which reading and writing was a component (62). Golden (73–74) discusses the education of girls, which was conducted at home. While there is no evidence one way or the other, it is doubtful that a congenitally-deaf child would be thought to be capable of receiving more than rudimentary instruction, let alone formal education.

83. The tale is recorded in various sources, including the fragments of Sophocles' lost play *Tereus* (frags. 581–95, A. C. Pearson, ed., *The Fragments of Sophocles* [Cambridge, Mass., 1917]); Apollodorus, 3.14.8; Pausanias, 1.41.8–9. Only in Apollodorus' version does Philomela weave written characters (γράμματα), as opposed to images, into her robe.

84. For example, Clytemnestra, in Aeschylus, *Agamemnon* 1060–1061, commands an unresponsive Cassandra, "Speak not, but make with your barbarian hand some sign" (σὺ δ' ἀντὶ φωνῆς φράζε καρθάνω χερί). Similarly, the Phrygian messenger in Euripides, *Orestes* (1369–526), both foreign and terrified, delivers his barely coherent report by pantomime, to the impatience and disgust of his audience.

85. Pseudo-Aristotle (*Problems* 898 b) asks why those who suffer any defect from birth mostly have bad hearing, and asks in answer if it is because hearing and voice arise from the same source; he also observes (*Problems* 33.1.961 b) that men become deaf and dumb (ἔνεοι καὶ κωφοί) at the same time. This observation is echoed by Pliny (*Natural History* 10.88.192).

86. Babies who are born deaf, after all, still cry. Carol Padden and Tom Humphries (*Deaf in America* [Cambridge, Mass., 1988], 91) point out that "a widespread misconception among hearing people is that Deaf people live in a world without sound," and that the metaphor of silence "is clumsy and inadequate as a way of explaining what Deaf people know and do" (109).

87. Yves Violé O'Neill, *Speech and Speech Disorders in Western Thought Before 1600* (Westport, 1980), 3–11.

88. For example, Herodotus (1.34) uses "deaf " (κωφός) and "speechless" (ἄφωνος)(1.85) interchangeably to refer to Croesus' son. It is interesting to note that modern Greek combines the term for deaf (κωφός) and mute ($_{-1\ pt}$λαλος) into one word for "deaf-mute" (κωφάλαλος). I have not found this compound term in the ancient Greek vocabulary.

89. Harlan Lane (*The Mask of Benevolence: Disabling the Deaf Community* [New York, 1992], 147) points out that this misperception still exists today.

90. There are of course many possible interpretations. D. L. Drew ("Euripides' *Alcestis,*" *American Journal of Philology* 52 [1931]: 295–319) argues that this is the corpse of Alcestis. Whether the figure on stage was meant to be seen as alive, dead, or something in between, Drew points out (313) that even if only three speaking actors were available, her continued silence was not necessary from a technical standpoint. Charles Segal (*Art, Gender, and Communication in* Alcestis, Hippolytus, *and* Hecuba [Durham, 1993], 49) writes that Alcestis' final silence has associations with death.

91. John Gager (*Curse Tablets and Binding Spells From the Ancient World* [New York, 1992], 116–50) discusses curses and binding spells in the courtroom. While many of the curses he cites give only the bare information, such as the names of the people to be cursed, others specifically request speechlessness, such as a tablet from the Piraeus (date unknown), in which a woman's tongue is cursed to be bound, made of lead, *and* stabbed (159–60). Nonpolitical curses: *SEG* 35.214, 216, 218, 220–23. These are A. D. third-century defixiones, discussed by David Jordan ("Defixiones From a Well Near the Southwest Corner of the Athenian Agora," *Hesperia* 54 [1985]: 105–255) as curses on individual athletes. The typical curse: "may he be deaf (κωφός); speechless (-1 ptλαλος); mindless (-1 ptνους)," and so on. Although the surviving examples of curses mentioning κωφός are late, Gager (5) shows that defixiones did exist as early as the fifth century B. C. Generally, the earlier the curse tablet, the simpler the spell; the earliest often include only the name of the victim.

92. This is reminiscent of the wisdom that the priestess at the Delphic oracle gives Croesus: it is better, she says, that his son remain mute, Herodotus (1.85).

References

Primary Sources

Aeschylus. sixth/fifth centuries B. C. 1973 [1922]. Trans. H. Smyth. Loeb Classical Library. Vol. 1. Cambridge: Harvard University Press. 2 vols.

———. sixth/fifth centuries B. C. 1983 [1926]. Trans. H. Smyth. Loeb Classical Library. Vol. 2. Cambridge: Harvard University Press. 2 vols.

Apollodorus. second century B. C. 1976 [1921]. Trans. G. Frazer. Loeb Classical Library. Cambridge: Harvard University Press. 2 vols.

Aristophanes. fifth century B. C. 1982 [1924]. Trans. B. B. Rogers. Loeb Classical Library. Vol. 2. Cambridge: Harvard University Press. 3 vols.

Aristotle. fourth century B. C. 1979 [1965]. Trans. A. L. Peck. Loeb Classical Library. Cambridge: Harvard University Press. 23 vols.

———. fourth century B. C. 1991. Trans. D. M. Balme. Loeb Classical Library. Vol. 11. Cambridge: Harvard University Press. 23 vols.

———. fourth century B. C. 1979 [1942]. Trans. A. L. Peck. Loeb Classical Library. Vol. 13. Cambridge: Harvard University Press. 23 vols.

———. fourth century B. C. 1970 [1926]. Trans. W. S. Hett. Loeb Classical Library. Vol. 15. Cambridge: Harvard University Press. 23 vols.

———. fourth century B. C. 1983 [1937]. Trans. W. S. Hett. Loeb Classical Library. Vol. 15. Cambridge: Harvard University Press. 23 vols.

Athenaeus. second century A. D. 1980 [1937]. *Deipnosophistae.* Trans. C. B. Gulick. Loeb Classical Library. Vol. 6. Cambridge: Harvard University Press. 7 vols.

Celsus. first century B. C. 1971 [1935]. *De Medecina.* Trans. W. G. Spencer. Loeb Classical Library Vol. 1. Cambridge: Harvard University Press. 3 vols.

———. first century B. C. 1961 [1938]. *De Medecina.* Trans. W. G. Spencer. Loeb Classical Library. Vol. 2. Cambridge: Harvard University Press. 3 vols.

Diodorus Siculus. first century B. C. 1961 [1935]. Trans. C. H. Oldfather. Loeb Classical Library. Vol. 2. Cambridge: Harvard University Press. 12 vols.

Edelstein, Emma and Ludwig Edelstein. 1945. *Asclepius: A Collection and Interpretation of the Testimonies.* Vol. 1. Baltimore: Johns Hopkins Press. 2 vols.

Euripides. fifth century B. C. 1987. *Alcestis.* A. M. Dale, ed. Oxford: Clarendon Press.

———. fifth century B. C. 1978. *Orestes.* G. Murray, ed. 2nd ed. Vol. 2. Oxford: Clarendon Press. 3 vols.

Galen. second century A. D. 1821–33. *Medicorum Graecorum.* C. G. Kühn, ed. 20 vols. Leipzig: Knobloch.

Gager, John. 1992. *Curse Tablets and Binding Spells from the Ancient World.* New York: Oxford University Press.

The Greek Anthology. 1979. Trans. W. R. Paton. Vol. 4. Loeb Classical Library. Cambridge: Harvard University Press. 5 vols.

Herodas. third century B. C. 1971. *Herodas Miamiambi*. I. C. Cunningham, ed. Oxford: Clarendon Press.

Herodas. third century B. C. 1993. *Mimes*. In *Theophrastus*, Characters; *Herodas*, Mimes; *Cercidas and the Choliambic Poets*. Ed. and trans. I. C. Cunningham. Loeb Classical Library. Cambridge: Harvard University Press.

Herodotus. fifth century B. C. 1981–90 [1920–25]. Trans. A. D. Godley. Loeb Classical Library. Cambridge: Harvard University Press. 4 vols.

Hesiod. ca. seventh century B. C. 1990. Friedrich Solmson, ed. 3rd ed. Oxford: Clarendon Press.

Hippocrates. ca. sixth through fourth centuries B. C. 1839–1861. *Oeuvres complètes d'Hippocrate*. É. Littré, ed. Paris: Ballière. 10 vols.

Homer. ca. eighth century B. C. 1988–93 [1924–25]. *Iliad*. Trans. A. T. Murray. Loeb Classical Library. Cambridge: Harvard University Press. 2 vols.

Jacoby, Felix. 1958. *Die Fragmente der griechischen Historiker*. 3:C. Leiden: E. J. Brill.

Jordan, David. 1985. "Defixiones From a Well Near the Southwest Corner of the Athenian Agora." *Hesperia* 54: 105–255.

Kassel, R. and C. Austin. 1983. *Poetae Comici Graeci*. Vol. 4. Berlin: Walter de Gruyter. 7 vols.

Page, D. L. 1967. *Poetae Melici Graecae*. Oxford: Clarendon Press.

Pausanias. second century A. D. 1977–79 [1918–33]. Trans W. H. S. Jones. Loeb Classical Library. Cambridge: Harvard University Press. 4 Vols.

Pearson, A. C. 1917. *The Fragments of Sophocles*. Vol. 2. Cambridge: Cambridge University Press. 3 vols.

———. *The Fragments of Sophocles*. 1917. Vol. 3. Cambridge: Cambridge University Press, 1917. 3 vols.

Petzl, Georg. 1982. *Die Inschriften von Smyrna*. Inschriften Griechischer Stadte Aus Kleinasien 23. Bonn: Rudolf Habelt.

Plato. fifth/fourth centuries B. C. 1977 [1926]. Trans. H. N. Fowler. Vol. 4. Loeb Classical Library. Cambridge: Harvard University Press. 12 vols.

———. fifth/fourth centuries B. C. 1977 [1927]. Trans. H. N. Fowler. Vol. 5. Loeb Classical Library. Cambridge: Harvard University Press. 12 vols.

———. fifth/fourth centuries B. C. 1977 [1921]. Trans. H. N. Fowler. Vol. 7. Loeb Classical Library. Cambridge: Harvard University Press. 12 vols.

Pleket, H. W. and R. S. Stroud, eds. 1988. Vol. 35. *Supplementum Epigraphicum Graecum*. Amsterdam: J. C. Gieben.

Pliny. first century A. D. 1983 [1940]. *Natural History*. Trans. H. Rackham. Vol. 3. Loeb Classical Library. Cambridge: Harvard University Press. 10 vols.

———. first century A. D. 1971 [1962]. *Natural History*. Trans. D. E. Eichholz. Vol. 10. Loeb Classical Library. Cambridge: Harvard University Press. 10 vols.

Plutarch. first/second centuries A. D. 1968 [1916]. *Lives*. Trans. B. Perrin. Vol. 4. Loeb Classical Library. Cambridge: Harvard University Press. 11 vols.

———. first/second centuries A. D. 1971 [1919]. *Lives*. Trans. B. Perrin. Vol. 7. Loeb Classical Library. Cambridge: Harvard University Press. 11 vols.

———. first/second centuries A. D. 1936. *Moralia*. Trans. F. C. Babbit. Vol. 5. Loeb Classical Library. Cambridge: Harvard University Press. 15 vols.

Strabo. first century B. C./first century A. D. 1928. *Geography*. Trans. H. L. Jones. Vol. 5. Loeb Classical Library. Cambridge: Harvard University Press. 8 vols.

Vergil. first century B. C. 1978 [1916]. Trans. H. R. Fairclaugh. Loeb Classical Library. Vol. 1. Cambridge: Harvard University Press. 2 vols.

Xenophon. fifth/fourth centuries B. C. 1983 [1914]. Trans. W. Miller. Loeb Classical Library. Vol. 4. Cambridge: Harvard University Press. 7 vols.

———. fifth/fourth centuries B. C. 1979 [1923]. Trans. O. J. Todd. Loeb Classical Library. Vol. 5. Cambridge: Harvard University Press. 7 vols.

Secondary Material: Ancient Topics

Aleshire, Sara. 1991. *Asklepios at Athens: Epigraphic and Prosopographic Essays on the Athenian Healing Cults*. Amsterdam: J. C. Gieben.

———. 1989. *The Athenian Asklepion: The People, Their Dedications, and the Inventories*. Amsterdam: J. C. Gieben.

Angel, J. Lawrence. 1947. "The Length of Life in Ancient Greece." *Journal of Gerontology* 2: 18–24.

Boegehold, Alan. Forthcoming. "Some Modern Gestures in Ancient Greek Literature." *Transactions of the Greek Humanistic Society* 1.

———. 1989. "A Signifying Gesture: Euripides, *Iphageneia Taurica* 965–66." *American Journal of Archaeology* 93: 81–83.

Bremmer, Jan. 1987. "The Old Women of Ancient Greece." *Sexual Asymmetry: Studies in Ancient Society*. Ed. J. Blok and P. Mason. Amsterdam: J. C. Gieben. 191–215.

Burford, Alison. 1993. *Land and Labor in the Greek World*. Baltimore: Johns Hopkins University Press.

Dawson, Warren R. 1986. "Herodotus as a Medical Writer." *Bulletin of the Institute of Classical Studies* 33: 87–96.

Drew, D. L. 1931. "Euripides' *Alcestis*." *American Journal of Philology* 52: 295–319.

Evans, J. A. S. 1991. *Herodotus: Explorer of the Past*. Princeton: Princeton University Press.

Finley, M. I. 1981. "The Elderly in Classical Antiquity." *Greece and Rome* 28: 156–71.

Garland, Robert. 1995. *The Eye of the Beholder: Deformity and Disability in the Graeco-Roman World*. Ithaca: Cornell University Press.

Golden, Mark. 1990. *Children and Childhood in Classical Athens*. Baltimore: Johns Hopkins University Press.

Gourevitch, Danielle. 1983. "L'aphonie hippocratique." *Formes de pensée dans la Collection hippocratique*. Ed. F. Lasserre and P. Mudry. Geneva: Librairie Droz: 297–305.

———. 1991. "Un enfant muet de naissance s'exprime par le dessin: à propos d'un cas rapporté par Pline l'Ancien." *L'Evolution psychiatrique* 56: 889–93.

———. 1984. *Le Mal d'être femme: la femme et la médecine dans la Rome antique*. Paris: Société d'edition "Les Belles Lettres."

Grmek, Mirko, 1989. *Diseases in the Ancient Greek World*. Trans. M. Muellner. Baltimore: Johns Hopkins University Press.

Hansen, Mogens Herman. 1985. *Demography and Democracy: The Number of Athenian Citizens in the Fourth Century B. C.* Herning, Denmark: Systime.

Hanson, Victor Davis. 1989. *The Western Way of War: Infantry Battle in Classical Greece*. New York: Knopf.

Harris, William. 1989. *Ancient Literacy*. Cambridge: Harvard University Press.

Havelock, Eric. 1976. *Origins of Western Literacy*. Toronto: Ontario Institute for Studies in Education.

Hedreen, Guy Michael. 1992. *Silens in Attic Black-figure Vase-painting: Myth and Performance*. Ann Arbor: University of Michigan Press.

Koelbing, Huldrych. 1977. *Arzt und Patient in der Antiken Welt*. Munich: Artemis.

Lang, Mabel. 1977. *Cure and Cult in Ancient Corinth: A Guide to the Asklepion*. Princeton: American School of Classical Studies at Athens.

Majno, Guido. 1975. *The Healing Hand: Man and Wound in the Ancient World*. Cambridge: Harvard University Press.

Masson O. 1976. "Le nom de Battos, fondateur de Cyrene," *Glotta* 54: 84–98.

O'Neill, Yves Violé. 1980. *Speech and Speech Disorders in Western Thought Before 1600*. Westport: Greenwood Press.

Pötscher, W. 1974. "Der stumme Sohn der Kroisos." *Zeitschrift für klinische Psychologie und Psychotherapie* 20: 367–68.

Pomeroy, Sarah. 1993. "Infanticide in Hellenistic Greece." *Images of Women in Antiquity*. Ed. A. Cameron and A. Kuhrt. 2nd ed. Detroit: Wayne State University Press. 207–22.

Rabinowitz, Nancy Sorkin. 1986. "Female Speech and Female Sexuality: Euripides' *Hippolytus* as Model." *Helios* 13: 127–40.

Reinhold, Meyer. 1976. "The Generation Gap in Antiquity." *The Conflict of Generations in Ancient Greece and Rome*. Ed. S. Bertman. Amsterdam: Grüner. 15–54.

Ruschenbusch, Eberhard. 1983. "Tribut und Bürgerzahl im ersten athenischen Seebund." *Zeitschrift für Papyrologie und Epigraphik* 53: 125–48.

Sallares, Robert. 1991. *The Ecology of the Ancient Greek World*. Ithaca: Cornell University Press.

Segal, Charles. 1993. *Art, Gender, and Communication in* Alcestis, Hippolytus, *and* Hecuba. Durham: Duke University Press.

Starr, Chester. 1977. *The Economic and Social Growth of Early Greece 800—500 B. C.* New York: Oxford University Press.

Thomas, Rosalind. 1992. *Literacy and Orality in Ancient Greece*. Cambridge: Cambridge University Press.

Van Straten, F. T. 1981. "Gifts for the Gods." *Faith Hope and Worship*. Ed. H. S. Versnel. Leiden: E. J. Brill. 65–151.

Versnel, H. S. 1981. "Religious Mentality in Ancient Prayer." *Faith Hope and Worship*. Ed. H. S. Versnel. Leiden E. J. Brill. 1–64.

Wells, Calvin. 1964. *Bones, Bodies and Disease: Evidence of Disease and Abnormality in Early Man*. Ancient Peoples and Places 37. Bristol: Western Printing Services.

Živanović, Srboljub. 1982. *Ancient Diseases: The Elements of Paleopathology*. Trans. L. Edwards. New York: Pica Press, 1982.

Secondary Material: Modern Topics

Canadian Task Force of the Health Services Directorate. 1988. *Acquired Hearing Impairment of the Adult*. Ottawa: Minister of National Health and Welfare.

Cohen, M. Michael and Robert J. Gorlin. 1995. "Epidemiology, Etiology, and Genetic Patterns." *Hereditary Hearing Loss and Its Syndromes*. Ed. R. Gorlin, H. Toriello and M. Cohen. Oxford Monographs on Medical Genetics 28. New York: Oxford University Press. 9–21.

Curtiss, Susan. 1977. *Genie: A Psycholinguistic Study of a Modern Day "Wild Child."* New York: Academic Press.

Gershon, Hannah. 1994. "Who Gets to be Called 'Deaf'? Cultural Conflict Between Deaf Populations." Society for Disability Studies Annual Meeting. Rockville, 24 June.

Gloring, Aram and Jean Roberts. 1965. "Hearing Levels of Adults by Age and Sex." *Vital and Health Statistics Ser.* 11, 11: 1–34.

Goldin-Meadow, S. and C. Mylander. 1990. "The Development of Morphology Without a Conventional Language Model." *From Gesture to Language in Hearing and Deaf Children*. Ed. V. Volterra and C. J. Erting. New York: Springer-Verlag. 165–77.

Greenfeld, Josh. 1972. *A Child Called Noah*. New York: Washington Square Press.

Groce, Nora. 1985. *Everyone Here Spoke Sign Language: Hereditary Deafness on Martha's Vineyard*. Cambridge: Harvard University Press.

Haller, Beth. 1995. "Rethinking Models of Media Representation of Disability." *Disability Studies Quarterly* 15: 29–30.

Hogan, Anthony. 1984. Letter to the Author. 14 July.

Itard, Jean Marc Gaspard. 1962. *The Wild Boy of Aveyron (L'enfant sauvage)*. Trans. G. and M. Humphrey. New York: Meredith.

Johnson, Robert E. and Carol Erting. 1989. "Ethnicity and Socialization in a Classroom for Deaf Children." *The Sociolinguistics of the Deaf Community*. Ed. C. Lucas. New York: Academic Press. 41–83.

Kiger, Gary, Stephen Hey and J. Gary Linn. 1994. "Introduction." *Disability Studies: Definitions and Diversity*. Ed. G. Kiger, S. Hey, and J. G. Linn. Salem, Oregon: Society for Disability Studies and Willamette University. 1–4.

Kisor, Henry. 1990. *What's That Pig Outdoors? A Memoir of Deafness*. New York: Penguin Books.

Kryter, Karl. 1985. *The Effects of Noise on Man*. 2nd ed. Orlando: Academic Press.

Lampropoulou, Venetta. 1995. "The History of Deaf Education in Greece." *The Deaf Way: Perspectives from the International Conference on Deaf Culture*. Ed. C. J. Erting, R. C. Johnson, D. L. Smith, and B. D. Snider. Washington, D. C.: Gallaudet University Press. 239–49.

Lane, Harlan. *1992. The Mask of Benevolence: Disabling the Deaf Community*. New York: Knopf.

———. 1985. *When the Mind Hears: A History of the Deaf*. New York: Random House.

———. and Richard Pillard. 1978. *The Wild Boy of Burundi: A Study of an Outcast Child*. New York: Random House.

Li, Ha-Sheng. 1992. "Genetic Influence on Susceptibility of the Auditory System to Aging and Environmental Factors." *Scandinavian Audiology* 21, Supplement 36: 1–39.

Mohay, H. 1990. "The Interaction of Gesture and Speech in the Language Development of Two Profoundly Deaf Children." *From Gesture to Language in Hearing and Deaf Children*. Ed. V. Volterra and C. J. Erting. New York: Springer-Verlag. 187–204.

Murder By Death. 1984. Directed by Robert Moore. Columbia.

Padden, Carol and Tom Humphries. 1988. *Deaf in America: Voices from a Culture*. Cambridge: Harvard University Press.

Padden, Carol. 1992. Review of *A Man Without Words*, by Susan Schaller. *American Journal of Psychology* 105: 648–53.

Pereira Da Cunha, M. C. and C. De Lemos. 1990. "Gesture in Hearing Mother—Deaf Child Interaction." *From Gesture to Language in Hearing and Deaf Children*. Ed. V. Volterra and C. J. Erting. New York: Springer-Verlag. 178–86.

Pinker, Steven. 1994. *The Language Instinct: How the Mind Creates Language*. New York: William Morrow and Company.

Prazma, Jiri. 1981. "Ototoxicity of Aminoglycoside Antibiotics." *Pharmacology of Hearing: Experimental and Clinical Bases*. Ed. R. D. Brown and E. A. Daigneault. New York: John Wiley.

Rose, Petra and Gary Kiger. 1994. "Intergroup Relations: Political Action and Identity in the Deaf Community." Society for Disability Studies Annual Meeting. Rockville, 23 June.

Rymer, Russ. 1993. *Genie: An Abused Child's Flight From Silence*. New York: Harper Collins.

Salih, Mustafa Abdalla. 1990. "Childhood Acute Bacterial Meningitis in the Sudan: An Epidemiological, Clinical and Laboratory Study." *Scandinavian Journal of Infectious Diseases* Supplement 66: 1–103.

Salomon, Gerhard. 1986. "Hearing Problems and the Elderly." *Danish Medical Bulletin Special Supplement Series on Gerontology* 33, Supplement 3: 1–17.

Scheetz, Nanci. 1993. *Orientation to Deafness*. Boston: Allyn and Bacon.

Silverman, Franklin. 1995. *Communication for the Speechless: An Introduction to Nonvocal Communication Systems for the Severely Handicapped*. 3rd ed. Boston: Allyn and Bacon.

Soucek, Sava and Leslie Michaels. 1990. *Hearing Loss in the Elderly: Audiometric, Electrophysiological and Histopathological Aspects*. London: Springer-Verlag.

Stokoe, William. 1994. "Discovering a Neglected Language." *Sign Language Studies* 85: 377–82.

———. 1990. "Language, Prelanguage, and Sign Language." *Seminars in Speech and Language* 11: 92–99.

———. 1994. "Seeing Clearly Through Fuzzy Speech." *Sign Language Studies* 82: 85–91.

———. 1972. *Semiotics and Human Sign Languages*. Approaches to Semiotics 21. Paris: Mouton.

Williams, Donna. 1994. *Somebody Somewhere: Breaking Free From the World of Autism*. New York: Times Books.

Abbreviations

DAGW	M. Grmek, *Diseases in the Ancient Greek World* (Baltimore, 1989).
FGrH	F. Jacoby, Die Fragmente der griechischen Historiker (Leiden, 1923).
GG	F. Van Straten, "Gifts for the Gods," *Faith Hope and Worship* (Leiden, 1981).
LCL	Loeb Classical Library.
PCG	R. Kassel and C. Austin, *Poetae Comici Graeci* (Berlin, 1983).
PMG	D. L. Page, *Poetae Melici Graecae* (Oxford, 1967).
SEG	*Supplementum Epigraphicum Graecum*.
WMH	H. Lane, *When the Mind Hears* (New York, 1985).

3

"A Silent Exile on This Earth"

The Metaphorical Construction of Deafness in the Nineteenth Century

Douglas Baynton

Deafness is a cultural construction as well as a physical phenomenon. The difference between the hearing and the deaf is typically construed as simply a matter of audiology. For most hearing people, this is the common sense of the matter—the difference between the deaf and the hearing is that the deaf cannot hear. The result is that the relationship between the deaf and the hearing appears solely as a natural one. The meanings of "hearing" and "deaf " are not transparent, however. As with gender, age, race, and other such categories, physical difference is involved, but physical differences do not carry inherent meanings. They must be interpreted and cannot be apprehended apart from a culturally created web of meaning. The meaning of deafness is contested, although most hearing and many deaf people are not aware that it is contested, and it changes over time. It has, that is to say, a history.[1]

The meaning of deafness changed during the course of the nineteenth century for educators of the deaf, and the kind of education deaf people received changed along with it. Until the 1860s, deafness was most often described as an affliction that isolated the individual from the Christian community. Its tragedy was that deaf people lived beyond the reach of the gospel. After the 1860s, deafness was redefined as a condition that isolated people from the national community. Deaf people were cut off from the English-speaking American culture, and *that* was the tragedy. The remedies proffered for each of these kinds of isolation were dramatically different. During the early and middle decades of the nineteenth century, sign language was a widely used and respected language among educators at schools for the deaf. By the end of the century it was widely condemned and banished from many classrooms. In short, sign language was compatible with the former construction of deafness, but not with the latter.

Schools for deaf people were first established in the United States by Evangelical Protestant reformers during the Second Great Awakening. They learned sign language, much as other missionaries of the time learned Native American or African languages, and organized schools where deaf people could be brought together and given a Christian education. The first school, the American Asylum for the Deaf and Dumb at Hartford, Connecticut, was founded in 1817 by the Reverend Thomas H. Gallaudet, with a young deaf man from Paris, Laurent Clerc, as his head teacher.

With the creation of this residential school, and the others which soon followed, the deaf in the United States may be said to have become the Deaf; that is, hearing-impaired individuals became a cultural and linguistic community.[2] To be sure, wherever sufficient numbers of deaf people have congregated, a distinctive community has come into existence—we know of one such community in eighteenth-century Paris.[3] These early schools, however, gathered together larger numbers of deaf people than ever before, most of them in adolescence, placed them in a communal living situation, and taught them formally not only about the world but also about themselves. Those from small towns and the countryside—the majority—met other deaf people for the first time and learned, also for the first time, how to communicate beyond the level of pantomime and gesture. They encountered the surprising knowledge that they had a history and an identity shared by many others. Embracing a common language and common experience, they began to create an American deaf community.[4]

Beginning in the 1860s and continuing into the twentieth century, another group of reformers sought to unmake that community and culture. Central to that project was a campaign to eliminate the use of sign language in the classroom (referred to in the nineteenth century as the philosophy of "manualism") and replace it with the *exclusive* use of lip-reading and speech (known as "oralism"). Residential schools for the deaf had been manualist from their beginnings, conducting their classes in sign language, finger-spelling, and written English. Lessons in speech and lip-reading were added to curriculums in most schools for the deaf by the latter decades of the century, but this was not the crux of the issue for those who called themselves oralists. They were opposed to the use of sign language in any form, for any purpose.[5]

Afraid that deaf people were isolated from the life of the nation, and comparing the deaf community to communities of immigrants, oralists charged that the use of sign language encouraged deaf people to associate principally with each other and to avoid the hard work of learning to communicate with people who were *speaking* English. All deaf people, they thought, should be able to learn to communicate orally. They believed that a purely oral education would lead to greater assimilation, which they believed to be a goal of the highest importance.

The larger goals of the oralist movement were not achieved—the deaf community was not unmade, and sign language continued to be used within it. Most deaf people rejected the oralist philosophy, and maintained an alternative vision of what being deaf meant for them. The deaf community did not, however, control the schools, and the campaign to eliminate sign language from the classroom was largely successful. By the turn of the century, nearly 40 percent of American deaf students were taught without the use of sign language, and over half were so taught in at least some of their classes.[6] The number of children taught entirely without sign language was nearly 80 percent by the end of World War I, and oralism remained orthodox until the 1970s.[7]

Why did educators of the deaf take this road? While this widespread and rapid shift away from the use of sign language has been well documented and described, it has yet to be adequately explained. Oralists at the turn of the century, looking back upon the ascendance of their cause and the demise of manualism, explained it in terms of the march of progress.[8] Improved techniques and knowledge made the use of sign language no longer necessary, they believed. This remained the dominant view in the field until the efficacy of purely oral education began to be questioned in the 1960s and 1970s. Since most recent research and practice supports an eclectic approach that includes the use of sign language—and since, as one recent writer said with only slight exaggeration, the "Old Orthodoxy of oral-or-nothing paternalism has died a richly deserved death"—the progress model has become rather less tenable.[9]

Most deaf adults and their organizations in the nineteenth century strenuously opposed the elimination of sign language from the classroom.[10] At the Convention of American Instructors of the Deaf in 1890, an angry deaf member pointed out that "Chinese women bind their babies' feet to make them small; the Flathead Indians bind their babies' heads to make them flat." Those who prohibit sign language in the schools, he declared, "are denying the deaf their free mental growth . . . and are in the same class of criminals."[11]

Scholars today in the new and still very small field of deaf history have, in general, agreed with this assessment, and have been uniformly critical of oralism. Oralists, it has been argued, were in many cases woefully ignorant of deafness. Their faith in oralism was based more upon wishful thinking than evidence, and they were often taken in by charlatans and quacks.[12] Others, such as Alexander Graham Bell, were more knowledgeable but motivated by eugenicist fears that intermarriage among the deaf, encouraged by separate schools and the use of sign language, would lead to the "formation of a deaf variety of the human race." Bell's prestige, leadership skills, and dedication to the cause gave a tremendous boost to oralism.[13] Opponents of sign language believed that its use discouraged the learning of oral communication skills; hearing parents, eager to believe their deaf children could learn to function like hearing people, supported its proscription. State legislators were persuaded by claims that oral education would be less expensive.[14] Finally, "on the face of it, people are quite afraid of human diversity.... [This] fear of diversity leads majorities to oppress minorities"; the suppression of sign language was one more example of the suppression of a minority language by an intolerant majority.[15]

The question of why schools adopted and continued to practice manualism for over half a century has been given less attention. Manualism has seemed less in need of explanation than oralism; since it is closer to current practice, the manualist philosophy of the nineteenth century has simply come to seem more sensible. With oralism now widely rejected, the focus has been upon explaining how and why such a philosophy gained ascendance.[16] Why manualism took root so readily in the first half of the nineteenth century and why attempts to establish oral schools were unsuccessful until the decades after the Civil War are questions that have not been adequately addressed. Rather than treating manualism as merely sensible and oralism as an unfortunate aberration, seeing both as embedded in historically created constructions of deafness can illuminate them as well as the reform eras of which they were a part.

Manualism and oralism were expressions of two very different reform eras in American history. Manualism was a product of the Evangelical, romantic reform movements of the antebellum years, which emphasized moral regeneration and salvation. Reformers of this period usually traced social evils to the weaknesses of individuals and believed that the reformation of society would come about only through the moral reform of its members. The primary responsibility of the Evangelical reformer, then, was to educate and convert individuals. The Christian nation they sought, and the millennial hopes they nurtured, came with each success one step closer to fruition.

Oralism was the product of a much changed reform atmosphere after the Civil War. While Protestantism continued to be an important ingredient, the emphasis shifted from the reform of the individual to, among other things, the creation of national unity and social order through homogeneity of language and culture. Much reform of the time, oralism included, reflected widespread fears of unchecked immigration and expanding, multiethnic cities. Deaf people in both eras served as convenient, and not always willing, projection screens for the anxieties of their times. The history of deaf education is as much, or more, about concerns over national identity and selfhood as it is about pedagogical technique or theory.

Oralists and manualists have generally been portrayed as standing on opposite sides of an ideological fault line. While in many ways accurate, this formulation obscures fundamental similarities between them. Both created images of deaf people as outsiders. Implicit in these images was the message that deaf people depended upon hearing people to rescue them from their exile. And both based their methods of education upon the images they created. Where they differed was in their definition of the "outsider," and of what constituted "inside" and "outside." For the manualists, the Christian community was the measure, while for the oralists it was an American nation defined in the secular terms of language and culture. Deafness, constructed as a condition that excluded people from the community, was defined and redefined according to what their hearing educators saw as the essential community.

The manualist image of deafness can be seen in the pages of what was in 1847 a remarkable new journal. Published by the American Asylum for the Deaf and Dumb and proclaiming itself the first of its kind in the English language, the *American Annals of the Deaf and Dumb* was intended to be not only a journal of education but also a "treasury of information upon all questions and subjects related, either immediately or remotely, to the deaf and dumb." The editors noted that not only did "the deaf and dumb constitute a distinct and, in some respect, strongly marked class of human beings," they also "have a history peculiar to themselves...sustaining relations, of more or less interest, to the general history of the human race." The implication of this, and of the editors' suggestion of such topics for investigation as the "social and political condition in ancient times" of the deaf, and "a careful exposition of the philosophy of the language of signs," was that deaf people were not so much handicapped *individuals* as they were a collectivity, a people—albeit, as we shall see, an inferior one, and one in need of missionary guidance.[17]

In "The Natural Language of Signs," Gallaudet wrote that there was "scarcely a more interesting sight than a bright, cheerful deaf-mute, of one or two years of age" in the midst of its hearing family. "The strangeness of his condition, from the first moment of their discovering it, has attracted their curiosity. They wonder at it." Gallaudet and others of his generation also wondered at the deaf. The source of their wonderment, and of the "greatest delight" for the family, was the child's efforts "to convey his thoughts and emotions...by those various expressions of countenance, and descriptive signs and gestures, which his own spontaneous feelings lead him to employ." For Gallaudet, "substantial good has come out of apparent evil," for this family would now have the privilege of learning "a novel, highly poetical, and singular descriptive language, adapted as well to spiritual as to material objects."[18]

Gallaudet praised the beauty of sign language, the "picture-like delineation, pantomimic spirit, variety, and grace...the transparent beaming forth of the soul...that merely oral language does not possess." Not only should the language of signs not be denied to the deaf, but it should also be given as a gift to the hearing as well, in order to "supply the deficiencies of our oral intercourse [and] perfect the communion of one soul with another." Superior to spoken language in its beauty and emotional expressiveness, sign language brought "kindred souls into a much more close and conscious communion than...speech can possibly do."[19]

Such a language was ideal for alleviating what Gallaudet saw as the overriding problem facing deaf people: they lived beyond the reach of the gospel. They knew nothing of God and the promise of salvation, nor had they a firm basis for the development of a moral sense. An essential part of education was learning "the necessity and the mode of controlling, directing, and at times subduing" the passions. Gallaudet emphasized the need to develop the conscience, to explain vice and virtue, to employ both hope and fear and "the sanctions of religion" in order to create a moral human being.[20]

The "moral influence" with which Gallaudet was concerned, however, could not "be brought to bear...without language, and a language intelligible to such a mind." Learning to speak and read lips was a "long and laborious process, even in the comparatively few cases of complete success." Communication between student and teacher, furthermore, was not sufficient. A language was needed with which "the deaf-mute can intelligibly conduct his private devotions, and join in social religious exercises with his fellow pupils."[21]

For Gallaudet, then, to educate was to impart moral and religious knowledge. Such teaching was not primarily directed to the mind through abstractions—rather, "the heart is the principle thing which we must aim to reach"; oral language may better communicate abstraction, he believed, but "the heart claims as its peculiar and appropriate language that of the eye and countenance, of the attitudes, movements, and gestures of the body."[22] Gallaudet described the progress of the student with the use of sign language:

> Every day he is improving in this language; and this medium of moral influence is rapidly enlarging. His mind becomes more and more enlightened; his conscience more and more easily addressed; his heart more and more prepared to be accessible to the simple truths and precepts of the Word of God.[23]

The interdependence of the mind, the heart, and the conscience, of both knowledge and morality, run through these teachers' writings. Morality, and the self-discipline it required, depended upon a knowledge of God's existence as well as a heartfelt conviction that the soul was immortal and that the promise of its salvation was real. What was more, the proper development of the moral nature not only depended upon knowledge but in its turn also stimulated the higher faculties to yet greater learning.[24]

As David Walker Howe has recently pointed out, achieving inner self-discipline was important for Evangelicals not just for the sake of self-control, but for the liberation of the self as well. Liberation and control were seen by antebellum Evangelicals as "two sides of the same redemptive process." Evangelicals, according to Howe, "were typically concerned to redeem people who were not functioning as free moral agents: slaves, criminals, the insane, alcoholics, children."[25] The contributors to the *Annals* in its first year clearly placed deaf people in this same category: outsiders to the Christian community. Teachers at the Asylum at Hartford, "preeminently a Christian institution" dedicated to teaching those "truths which are received in common by all evangelical denominations," bemoaned the fact that "in this Christian land" there were still deaf people living "in utter seclusion from the direct influences of the gospel."[26] These deaf people "might almost as well have been born in benighted Asia, as in this land of light," and were "little short of a community of heathen at our very doors."[27]

Throughout this first year of the journal, images of imprisonment, darkness, blankness, and isolation were repeatedly used to describe the condition of deaf people without education. These metaphors were interconnected, as was made plain by the descriptions of the uninstructed deaf by the Reverend Collins Stone, a teacher at the Hartford school: "scarcely a ray of intellectual or moral light ever dawns upon his solitude"; "his mind is a perfect blank"; if "he dies unblessed by education, he dies in this utter moral darkness"; we must "open the doors of his prison, and let in upon him the light of truth," for the terrible fact is that "even in the midst of Christian society, he must grope his way in darkness and gloom . . . unless some kind hand penetrates his solitude."[28]

The image of the animal appeared frequently as well. Stone wrote that the uneducated deaf were reduced "to the level of mere animal life" because the "great facts and truths relating to God and a future state" are unknown to them. What "makes us differ from the animals and things around us" is the possession of a soul and an understanding of what that possession means. Without this understanding, deaf people were capable of nothing higher than "mere animal enjoyment."[29] With the use of sign language, however, as J. A. Ayres believed, "it will be seen at once that the deaf-mute is restored to his position in the human family, from which his loss had well-nigh excluded him."[30]

Writer after writer used the same or similar metaphors, with the same emphasis upon the knowledge of God and the immortality of the soul as that which distinguishes the human from the nonhuman. The Reverend Luzerne Ray, speculating upon the "Thoughts of the deaf and Dumb before Instruction," asked the reader to imagine a child born with no senses, to imagine that "the animal life of this infant is preserved, and that he grows up to be, in outward appearance at least, a man." Ray asked, "can we properly say that here would be any mind at all? . . . [C]ould there be any conscious self-existence or self-activity of a soul imprisoned within such a body?" He concluded that to answer in the affirmative would be to succumb to "the lowest form of materialism." While no such person had ever existed, uneducated deaf people living "in a state of isolation the most complete that is ever seen among men" came close.[31] Henry B. Camp, writing on the "Claims of the Deaf and Dumb upon Public Sympathy and Aid," lamented the "darkness and solitude" of the person who lives in a "condition but little superior to that of the brute creation," with "no key to unlock the prison of his own mind."[32]

For the manualists, then, the "real calamity for the deaf-mute" was "not that his ear is closed to the cheerful tones of the human voice"; and it was "not that all the treasures of literature and science, of philosophy and history . . . are to him as though they were not"; the calamity was that "the light of divine truth never shines upon his path."[33] The darkness, the emptiness, the solitude, were all of a particular kind: uneducated deaf people were cut off from the Christian community and its message.

A peculiar duality that runs throughout their writings illuminates the meaning of deafness for these teachers. Deafness was an affliction, they believed, but they called it a blessing as well. One explained that the only unusual aspect of educating deaf people on moral and religious matters was that they had "a *simplicity* of mental character and an *ignorance* of the world, highly favorable to the entrance and dominion of this highest and best motive of action" (emphasis added). The properly educated deaf person, he believed, will exhibit "a pleasing combination of strength and simplicity." The strength would come from proper education, but the simplicity was inherent in the deafness; it "flows naturally from that comparative isolation of the mind which prevents its being formed too much on the model of others."[34]

Another writer touched on the same duality when explaining the "beautiful compensation" for deafness:

Deprived of many blessings, he is also shut out from many temptations, and it is rare indeed that the claims of religion and the reasonings of morality fail to secure the ready assent both of his heart and his understanding.[35]

Deaf people were thought to have a great moral advantage in that they have been left relatively unscathed by a corrupt world. They are innocent, rather than living in darkness, and their deafness is an asylum rather than a prison. Deafness, then, confers both the benefit of innocence and the burden of ignorance: two sides of the same coin. It is a positive good if temporary and discovered by the right people but an evil if neglected and left uncultivated. The difference between virginity and barrenness (whether of women or of land) is analogous—the first is a blessed state, the second a calamity. The deaf are blessed if virginal, innocent, and fertile, but would be accursed if left forever in that state. They would then be barren. Innocence holds within it the germ of knowledge and salvation. Ignorance is only darkness.

The dark side was expressed in a poem by a former student at the Hartford school, published in the *Annals*:

> I moved—a silent exile on this earth;
> As in his dreary cell one doomed for life,
> My tongue is mute, and closed ear heedeth not;
>
> Deep silence over all, and all seems lifeless;
> The orators exciting strains the crowd
> Enraptur'd hear, while meteor-like his wit
> Illuminates the dark abyss of mind—
> Alone, left in the dark—*I hear them not.*
>
> The balmy words of God's own messenger
> Excite to love, and troubled spirits sooth—
> Religion's dew-drops bright—*I feel them not.*[36]

But some months later, a poem entitled "The Children of Silence" was published in response "to show that there are times and circumstances," in the editor's words, "when not to be able to hear must be accounted a blessing rather than a misfortune":

> Not for your ears the bitter word
> Escapes the lips once filled with love;
> The serpent speaking through the dove,
> Oh Blessed! ye have never heard.
> Your minds by mercy here are sealed
> From half the sin in man revealed.[37]

The use of "silent" and "silence" in these poems embodies the contradictions in the innocence and ignorance metaphor. It was (and is) a common description of the world of deafness, and at first glance would seem a common sense description as well. Deaf people use it as well as hearing people. In the nineteenth century, for example, journals by and for the deaf had such titles as the *Silent Worker* and *Silent World*. Today there are newspapers such as the *Silent News*, and clubs with such names as the Chicago Silent Dramatic Club.

"Silence" is not a straightforward or unproblematic description of the experience of a deaf person, however. First, few deaf people hear nothing. Most have hearing losses which are not uniform across the entire range of pitch—they will hear low sounds better than high ones, or vice versa. Sounds will often be quite distorted, but heard nevertheless. And second, for those who do not hear, what does the word silence signify? Unless they once heard and *became* deaf, the word is meaningless as a description of their experience. (Even for those who once heard, as the experience of sound recedes further into the past, so too does the significance of silence diminish.) Silence is experienced by the hearing as an absence of sound. For those who have never heard, deafness is not an absence. To be deaf is *not* to not hear for most profoundly deaf people, but a social relation—that is, a relation with other human beings, those called "hearing" and those called "deaf." What the deaf person sees in these other people is not the presence or absence of hearing, not their soundfulness or their silence, but their mode of communication—they sign, or they move their lips. That is why deaf people in the nineteenth century typically referred to themselves not as deaf people but as "mutes." That is why the sign still used today that is translated as "hearing person" is made next to the mouth, not the ear, and literally means "speaking person."

Silence is a metaphor rather than a simple description of the experience of most deaf people.[38] Deafness is a relationship, not a state, and the use of the "silence" metaphor is one indication of how the relationship is dominated by the hearing. Hearing is defined as the universal, and deafness, therefore, as an absence, as an emptiness. Silence can represent innocence and fertility, and silence can represent darkness and barrenness. In both cases it is empty. In both cases it needs to be filled. Images such as these—images of light and dark, of solitude and society, of animal and human—construct a world in which deaf people lack what hearing people alone can provide.

The absence which defined deaf people was framed as a place in which the deaf lived: a darkness within which they could not escape, a blankness and ignorance which denied them humanity. But of course the converse was also true: the problem was not only that the deaf could not see *out* but also that the hearing could not see *in*. The minds of deaf people represented impenetrable dark spaces within Christian society—or better, *without* Christian society—of which the hearing had little knowledge. Sign language was the light that could illuminate the darkness.

In 1899, the *Association Review* was established as the journal of the American Association to Promote the Teaching of Speech to the Deaf, the first president of which was Alexander Graham Bell. In the introduction to the first issue, the editor Frank Booth was able to state confidently that "the spirit prevalent in our schools is one entirely favorable to speech for the deaf, and to more and better speech teaching so soon as more favorable conditions may warrant and permit."[39] Indeed, with 55 percent of their teachers now speech teachers (as compared with 24 percent in 1886, the first year for which we have figures), the acquisition of speech was rapidly becoming the preeminent aim in the education of the deaf.[40]

The times were not only favorable to speech but quite hostile to sign language. Nearly 40 percent of American deaf students now sat in classrooms from which sign language had been banished. Within twenty years it would be 80 percent.[41] Deaf teachers were rarely hired by the schools anymore and made up less than 20 percent of the teaching corps, down from more than twice that number in the 1850s and 1860s.[42] Those who remained were increasingly confined to teaching industrial education courses, to which students who were "oral failures" were relegated. The new teacher training school established in 1891 at Gallaudet College, a liberal arts college primarily for deaf students, itself refused, as a matter of policy, to train deaf teachers.[43] Booth himself would forbid the use of sign language at the Nebraska school when he became its superintendent in 1911. "That language is not now used in the school-room," he wrote to Olaf Hanson, president of the National Association of the Deaf, "and I hope to do away with its use outside of the school-room."[44]

Booth was certainly correct that the "spirit now prevalent" was much changed. The *American Annals of the Deaf* at the turn of the century reflected the changed climate as well. Educational philosophy had shifted ground so dramatically that unabashed manualism had nearly disappeared from its pages, with the majority of opinion ranging between oralism and what was called the "combined system." The definition of the latter varied widely. In some cases it mean supplementing speech with fingerspelling but forbidding sign language; in others, speech alone was used in the classroom, with sign language permitted outside; in many cases it meant using speech with all young students and resorting later to sign language only with older "oral failures." To Edward M. Gallaudet, son of Thomas and first president of Gallaudet College, the combined system meant preserving sign language but using it in the classroom "as little as possible." He defended his tiny remnant of his father's world in an article bearing the plaintive title "Must the Sign-Language Go?"[45]

The new aversion to sign language had many causes, but a profound change in the images and meanings of deafness during the second half of the nineteenth century was fundamental. The opening article of the first issue of the *Association Review* is revealing. Reprinted from an address delivered before a meeting of the Association by John M. Tyler (president of Amherst College), "The Teacher and the State" was concerned with what teachers could do about two related national problems: the new immigration and the decline in law and order. There was a "struggle between rival civilizations" within America. "Shall her standards and aims, in one word her civilization, be those of old New England, or shall they be Canadian or Irish, or somewhat better or worse than any of these?" The burden rested upon the teachers, for "'Waterloo was won at Rugby' [and] it was the German schoolmaster who triumphed at Sedan." Furthermore, teachers could no longer focus on "purely intellectual training," for "[t]he material which we are trying to fashion has changed; the children are no longer of the former blood, stock, and training." Teachers must make up for the new immigrants' deficiencies as parents, he warned: "the emergency remains and we must meet it as best we can." If they do not, the "uncontrolled child grows into the lawless youth and the anarchistic adult."[46]

Tyler's speech was not directly about deaf people, but it must have resonated with his audience of educators of the deaf. Metaphors of deafness by the turn of the century were no longer ones of spiritual darkness but instead conjured images of foreign enclaves within American society. Articles about deaf people in the *Association Review* might just as well have been about immigrant communities, with metaphors of foreignness at work on several levels. First there was the problem of what was not commonly referred to as "the foreign language of signs."[47] Educators worried that if deaf people "are to exercise intelligently the rights of citizenship, then they must be made people of our language."[48] They insisted that "the English language must be made the vernacular of the deaf if they are not to become a class unto themselves—foreigners among their own countrymen."[49] Oralism was about much more than just speech and lip-reading. It was part of a larger argument about language and the maintenance of a national community.

The image of foreignness was not confined to the pages of the *Association Review*. A parent wrote to the superintendent of the Illinois Institution in 1898, requesting information about methods of deaf education. The answer she received was that there were two: "the English language method," and the method in which "the English language is considered a foreign language," taught through "translation from the indefinite and crude sign language."[50]

"Sign language is an evil," avowed a teacher from the Pennsylvania Institution for Deaf-Mutes, one of the first state schools to adopt the oralist philosophy, in an 1892 article in the *Silent Educator*. The mastery of English was not, by itself, the point, he argued. Sign language made deaf people "a kind of foreigners in tongue," and this was so whether or not they also mastered English. Deaf people who signed could not be full members of the English-speaking American community; they were, instead, "a sign making people who have studied English so as to carry on business relations with those who do not understand signs." Using another language was the offense, for "English is a jealous mistress. She brooks no rival. She was born to conquer and to spread all over the world. She has no equal."[51]

This was an extreme example of a usually more subtle nationalism expressed by opponents of sign language. Most oralists did not exhibit open xenophobia, insist upon Anglo-Saxon superiority, nor advocate one worldwide language. Most emphasized their belief that sign language isolated deaf people and made the deaf person an outsider who was "not an Englishman, a German, a Frenchman, or a member of any other nationality, but, intellectually, a man without a country."[52] They were convinced and deeply troubled by the conviction that signing deaf people existed apart and isolated from the life of the nation. An earlier generation of educators had believed that sign language liberated deaf people from their confinement, but for oralists it was the instrument of their imprisonment.

Even some hearing educators who had long supported sign language had begun to criticize what they termed the "clannishness" of deaf people. In 1873, Edward M. Gallaudet had condemned the conventions, associations and newspapers of deaf people, as well as their intermarriage, for discouraging the intercourse of the deaf "with their race and the world." It was injurious to the best interests of the deaf when they came to consider themselves "members of society with interests apart from the mass,... a 'community,' with its leaders and rulers, its associations and organs, and its channels of communication." Gallaudet's concerns were similar to those of the oralists, except that sign language was, he thought, still necessary—a "necessary evil." It could not be relinquished, he argued, because few people profoundly deaf from an early age could become proficient enough at oral communication for a full education or participation in religious services.[53] Oralists escalated the charge of "clannishness" to "foreignness," however, a term with more ominous connotations.

This was a metaphor of great significance for Americans of the late nineteenth century. References to deaf people as foreigners coincided with the greatest influx of immigrants in U. S. history. The new immigrants were concentrated in urban areas, and no major city was without its quilt pattern of immigrant communities. Many came from eastern and southern Europe, bringing with them cultural beliefs and habits that native-born Americans often regarded as peculiar, inferior, or even dangerous. As Frederick E. Hoxie has noted in his study of the Indian Assimilation movement (a movement contemporaneous with and sharing many characteristics with the oralist movement), in the late nineteenth century "growing social diversity and shrinking social space threatened many Americans' sense of national identity."[54] Nativism, never far from the surface of American life, resurged with calls for immigration restriction, limits on the employment of foreigners, and the proscription of languages other than English in the schools. To say that sign language made deaf people appear foreign was to make a telling point for these educators. That foreignness should be avoided at all costs was generally expressed as a self-evident truth.

"Foreignness" had two related meanings. As with the manualists' metaphor of darkness, this was a metaphor with two centers. Looking from the outside in, the metaphor suggested a space within American society that was mysterious to outsiders, into which hearing Americans could see only obscurely if at all. As such it posed vague threats of deviance from the majority culture. Looking from the inside out—that is, empathizing with what the oralists imagined to be the experience of deaf people—it seemed a place in which deaf people became trapped, from which they could not escape without assistance. "Foreignness" was both a threat and a plight. The deaf community, as one of a host of insular and alien-appearing communities, was seen as harmful to both the well-being of the nation and to its own members.

For many hearing people, what they saw looking in from the outside was troubling. Journals and magazines such as the *Silent World* and the *Deaf-Mute Journal*, written and printed by deaf people for a deaf audience, were thriving in every state. Deaf adults across the country were actively involved in local clubs, school alumnae associations, and state and national organizations. They attended churches together where sign language was used. The great majority found both their friends and their spouses within the deaf community. According to the research of Bell, the rate of intermarriage was at least 80 percent, a fact that caused him great alarm.[55]

The two chief interests of Bell's life, eugenics and deaf education, came together over this issue. In a paper published by the National Academy of Sciences in 1884, Bell warned that a "great calamity" for the nation was imminent due to the high rate of intermarriage among the deaf: the "formation of a deaf variety of the human race." The proliferation of deaf clubs, associations, and periodicals, with their tendency to "foster class-feeling among the deaf," were ominous developments. Already, he warned, "a special language adapted for the use of such a race" was in existence, "a language as different from English as French or German or Russian."[56]

While other oralists would call for legislation to "prevent the marriage of persons who are liable to transmit defects to their offspring," Bell believed such legislation would be difficult to enforce.[57] His solution was this: *(1) Determine the causes that promote intermarriages among the deaf and dumb; and*

(2) remove them" [emphasis his]. Bell identified two principal causes: "segregation for the purposes of education, and the use, as a means of communication, of a language which is different from that of the people." Indeed, he wrote, "if we desired to create a deaf variety of the race…we could not invent more complete or more efficient methods than those."[58]

Bell's fears were unfounded. His findings, published in the year of Gregor Mendel's death and before the latter's research on genetic transmission had become known, were based upon a faulty understanding of genetics. Others soon countered his empirical evidence as well; most deafness was not heritable, and marriages between deaf people produced on average no greater number of deaf offspring than mixed marriages of deaf and hearing partners.[59] But the image of an insular, inbred, and proliferating deaf community, with its own "foreign" language and culture, became a potent weapon for the oralist cause. Bell was to become one of the most prominent and effective crusaders against both residential schools and sign language.[60]

More often, oralists emphasized the empathetic side of the metaphor. They insisted that their intent was to rescue deaf people from their confinement, not to attack them. Deaf adults, however, actively defended the space from which they were urged to escape and from which deaf children were supposed to be rescued. But just as deaf people resisted the oralist conception of their needs, oralists likewise resisted the portrayal of themselves by deaf leaders as "enemies of the true welfare of the deaf."[61] As did the advocates of Indian and immigrant assimilation, they spoke of themselves as the "friends of the deaf." They tried to project themselves into that mysterious space they saw deaf people inhabiting and to empathize with the experience of deafness.

They were especially concerned that "because a child is deaf he is…considered peculiar, with all the unpleasant significance attached to the word."[62] The great failure of deaf education was that "in many cases, this opinion is justified by deaf children who are growing up without being helped…to acquire any use of language."[63] ("Language" was frequently used as a synonym for "spoken English.") Peculiarity was spoken of as part of the curse of foreignness, and "to go through life as one of a peculiar class…is the sum of human misery. No other human misfortune is comparable to this."[64] This peculiarity of deaf people was not unavoidable, but "solely the result of shutting up deaf children to be educated in sign schools, whence they emerge…aliens in their own country!"[65] Cease to educate deaf people with sign language, oralists believed, and they will "cease to be mysterious beings."[66]

Like their contemporaries in other fields of reform, oralists worried that the lives of people were diminished by being a part of such restricted communities as the deaf community; they would not, it was feared, fully share in the life of the nation. The deaf community, like ethnic communities, narrowed the minds and outlooks of its members. "The individual must be one with the race," one wrote in words that could have come from Jane Addams or John Dewey or any number of Progressive reformers, "or he is virtually annihilated"; the chief curse of deafness was "apartness from the life of the world," and it was just this that oralism was designed to remedy.[67] This was the darkness of the manualists redefined for a new world.

Oralists believed sign language was to blame for making deaf people seem foreign, peculiar, and isolated from the nation and claimed it was an inferior language that impoverished the minds of its users. This language of "beauty and grace," in the words of Thomas H. Gallaudet, now was called a wretched makeshift of the language."[68] It was "immeasurably inferior to English" and any "culture dependent upon it must be proportionately inferior."[69] The implication of foreignness, barbarism, was not left unspoken. As one opponent of sign language stated, "if speech is better for hearing people than barbaric signs, it is better for the deaf."[70] In an age when social scientists ranked cultures and languages on The evolutionary scale from savage to civilized, teachers of the deaf came to depict sign language as "characteristic of tribes low in the scale of development."[71] It was in fact identical to the gestures used by "a people of lowest type" found to exist "in the ends of the earth where no gleam of civilization had penetrated."[72] Like the races supposed to be lowest on the evolution scale, sign language was barely human.

For some it was not human at all. The metaphor of animality reappeared in different guise. Benjamin

D. Pettingill, a teacher at the Pennsylvania School for the Deaf, noted as early as 1873 that sign language was being "decried, denounced, and ridiculed...as a set of monkey-like grimaces and antics."[73] Sarah Porter, a teacher at the Kendall School, in 1894 wrote that the common charge against the use of sign language—"You look like monkeys when you make signs"—would be "hardly worth noticing except for its...incessant repetition."[74] A teacher from Scotland complained in 1899 in the pages of the *American Annals of the Deaf* that it was wrong to "impress [deaf people] with the thought that it is apish to talk on the fingers."[75]

Lewis Dudley, a trustee of the first oral school in the nation, the Clarke Institution, implied in 1880 that deaf people who used sign language themselves felt less than human. When he visited a school in which sign language was used, the children looked at him.

> with a downcast pensive look which seemed to say, "Oh, you have come to see the unfortunate; you have come to see young creatures human in shape, but only half human in attributes; you have come here much as you would go to a menagerie to see something peculiar and strange."[76]

He contrasted the demeanor of these children with that of a young girl he had met who had recently learned to speak: "the radiant face and the beaming eye showed a consciousness of elevation in the scale of being. It was a real elevation."[77] The metaphors of the subhuman and the animal had been used by the manualists to signify ignorance of the soul. To the oralists they came to signify ignorance of spoken language.

Clearly the "real calamity of the deaf-mute" had been redefined. The 1819 annual report of the American Asylum did not ask if most Americans could understand signs, but "does God understand signs?"[78] To this they answered yes and were satisfied. At mid-century the calamity still was "not that his ear is closed to the cheerful tones of the human voice," but that the deaf person might be denied "the light of divine truth."[79] When the manualist generation had spoken of deaf people being "restored to society" and to "human brotherhood," membership in the Christian community was the measure of that restoration.[80] Sign language had made it possible. The isolation of the deaf was a problem that had been solved.

By the turn of the century, however, the problem had returned. Once again educators of the deaf spoke of rescuing the deaf from their "state of almost total isolation from society," "restoring" them to "their proper and rightful place in society,"[81] and once again deaf people lived "outside." They were "outside" because "inside" had been redefined. Whereas manualists had believed that to teach their students "the gospel of Christ, and by it to save their souls, is our great duty," it was now the "grand aim of every teacher of the deaf...to put his pupils in possession of the spoken language of their country."[82] The relevant community was no longer the Christian community, but a national community defined in large part by language.

Both manualists and oralists understood deafness in the context of movements for national unity, and their metaphors came from those movements. Evangelical Protestantism brought together a nation no longer unified by the common experience of the Revolution, unsettled by rapid social and economic change, and worried about the effects of the opening of the West upon both the morality and the unity of the nation. In crafting that unity, by creating a common set of experiences for understanding of the world, Evangelicalism emphasized above any other kind of cultural or linguistic homogeneity a common spiritual understanding. When Evangelicals saw dangers in the immigration of the time, it was not foreignness *per se* that principally concerned them, but Catholicism.[83] That definition of unity was not necessarily more tolerant of difference in general, but it did mean that sign language and the deaf community were not seen as inimical to it.

The movement for national unity at the time of the rise of oralism had a different source. This time it was the multiplicity of immigrant communities crowded into burgeoning industrial cities that seemed to threaten the bonds of nationhood. Two streams converged to make sign language repugnant to many hearing Americans: at the same time that deaf people were creating a deaf community, with its own clubs, associations, and periodicals, American ethnic communities were doing the same to an extent alarming to the majority culture. At the same time that deaf children were attending separate schools in which deaf teachers taught them with both English and sign language, immigrant children were attending parochial schools in which immigrant teachers taught them in both English and their native languages.[84] The convergence was merely fortuitous, but it was not difficult to transfer anxieties from one to the other.

If the fragmentation of American society into distinct and unconnected groups was the fear that drove the oralists, the coalescence of a homogeneous society of equal individuals was the vision that drew them together. For the oralists, as for their contemporaries in other fields of reform—the assimilation of the Indian, the uplifting of the working class, the Americanization of the immigrant—equality was synonymous with sameness. The ideal was achieved when one could "walk into…our hearing schools and find the deaf boys working right along with their hearing brothers…[where] no difference is felt by the teacher."[85] Just as manualism arose within a larger Evangelical revival, so did oralism partake of the late nineteenth-century quest for national unity through the assimilation of ethnic cultures.[86]

Humans use metaphor and mental imagery to understand things of which they have no direct experience.[87] For people who are not deaf, then, the use of metaphor to understand deafness is inevitable: they can approach it no other way. The problem is that hearing people are in positions to make, on the basis of their metaphors—usually unaware that they *are* metaphors—decisions with profound and lasting effects upon the lives of deaf people. The most persistent images of deafness among hearing people have been ones of isolation and exclusion, and these are images that are consistently rejected by deaf people who see themselves as part of a deaf community and culture. Feelings of isolation may even be less common for members of this tightly knit community than among the general population.[88] The metaphors of deafness—of isolation and foreignness, of animality, of darkness and silence—are projections reflecting the needs and standards of the dominant culture, not the experiences of most deaf people.

The oralists and the manualists appeared to be opposing forces—"old fashioned" manualists fought bitterly with "progressive" oralists. The deaf community saw a clear difference, siding with the manualists and resisting with all its resources the changes in educational practice that the oralists sought. One reason was that manual schools employed deaf teachers. Oral schools generally did not—deaf people could not teach speech.[89] Furthermore, oralists simply did not believe that the deaf should exist as a social group; to hire deaf teachers would imply that deaf people had something to teach each other, that there was a significant group experience. Manualists seem to have been more egalitarian for this reason. While deaf people taught in manualist schools, however, they generally found positions of authority closed to them. Few became principals or superintendents, and probably no deaf person ever sat on a school governing board.[90] One result was that when the hearing society refashioned its images of deafness and turned toward oralism, the deaf community had limited means of resistance.

Resist it did through that combination of open and subterranean means commonly resorted to by beleaguered minorities. From the beginnings of oralism until its demise in the 1970s, deaf people organized to lobby legislatures and school boards in support of sign language in the schools.[91] Deaf parents passed sign language on to their children, and those children who were deaf and attended schools where sign language was banned surreptitiously taught others. Those unable to learn sign language as children learned it as adults when they found themselves free to associate with whomever they pleased, however they pleased; over 90 percent continued to marry other deaf people and deaf clubs and associations continued to thrive.[92] But their means of resistance within the educational establishment were scant, a legacy at least in part of the paternalism of the manualist educators.

Manualists and oralists had paternalism in common, and much else. Both groups saw deafness through their own cultural biases and sought to reshape deaf people in accordance with them. Both used similar clusters of metaphors to forge images of deaf people as fundamentally flawed, incomplete, isolated and dependent. And both used that imagery to justify not only methods of education, but also the inherent authority of the hearing over the deaf. That did not change.

Still, deaf people sided with the manualists. We do not know exactly how deaf people responded to the images created by either manualists or oralists, to what extent they internalized them, rejected them, or used them for their own purposes. The creation of alternative meanings for deafness by the deaf community has a complex history all its own, one that is still largely unwritten.[93] But while the reception of the Evangelical *message* by deaf people during the manualist years is not yet clear, the Evangelical *medium*—sign language within a sign-using community—was clearly welcomed by most. And whether or not deaf adults accepted the oralist depiction of their community as "foreign" or akin to an immigrant community, most of them clearly rejected the oralist understanding of what those images meant.

Whatever metaphors of deafness manual*ists* may have used, manual*ism* allowed the possibility of alternative constructions of deafness by deaf people themselves. So long as deaf people had their own language and community, they possessed a cultural space in which to create alternative meanings for their lives. Within that space they could resist the meanings that hearing people attached to deafness, adopt them and put them to new uses, or create their own. Oralism, whose ideal was the thoroughly assimilated deaf person, would do away with that alternative. Oralism failed, finally, and sign language survived, because deaf people chose not to relinquish the autonomous cultural space their community gave them.

Notes

1. For an example of a radically different construction of deafness than has been typical in the United States, see Nora Groce, *Everyone Here Spoke Sign Language: Hereditary Deafness on Martha's Vineyard* (Cambridge, Mass., 1985). From the sixteenth to the nineteenth century, an unusually high rate of inherited deafness on Martha's Vineyard combined with premodern village values to produce communities in which deafness was apparently not considered a significant difference at all. The hearing people in these communities were all bilingual in spoken English and a variety of British Sign Language. There were no apparent differences between the social, economic, or political lives of the hearing and the deaf, according to Groce.

2. Within forty years there would be twenty residential schools in the United States; by the turn of the century, more than fifty. See "Tabular Statement of Schools for the Deaf, 1897–98," *American Annals of the Deaf* 43 (Jan. 1898): 46–47 (hereafter cited as *Annals*).

   The use of "deaf" (with a lower case *d*) to refer primarily to an audiological condition of hearing loss, and "Deaf" (with an upper case *D*) to refer to a cultural identity (deaf people, that is, who use American Sign Language, share certain attitudes and beliefs about themselves and their relation to the hearing world, and self-consciously think of themselves as part of a separate Deaf culture) has become standard in the literature on Deaf culture. The distinction, while useful and important, is often difficult in practice to apply to individuals, especially when dealing with historical figures. I have not tried to make the distinction in this paper. See Carol Padden and Tom Humphries, *Deaf in America: Voices from a Culture* (Cambridge, Mass., 1988), 2–6.

3. Pierre Desloges, a deaf Parisian, wrote in 1779 that "matters are completely different for the deaf living in society in a great city like Paris.... In intercourse with his fellows he promptly acquires the supposedly difficult art of depicting and expressing all his thoughts.... No event—in Paris, in France, or in the four corners of the world—lies outside the scope of our discussion. We express ourselves on all subjects with as much order, precision, and rapidity as if we enjoyed the faculty of speech and hearing." Desloges's short book, *Observations d'un sourd et muet sur "Un Cours elementaire d'education des sourds et muets"* is translated in Harlan Lane, ed., *The Deaf Experience: Classics in Language and Education*, trans. Franklin Philip (Cambridge, 1984), 36.

4. The best account of the contemporary American Deaf community can be found in Padden and Humphries, *Deaf in America*. For anyone wishing to understand the world of deaf people, this small but rich and insightful book is a fine place to start. For a concise history of the formation of the deaf community in nineteenth-century United States, see John Vickrey Van Cleve and Barry Crouch, *A Place of Their Own: Creating the Deaf Community in America* (Washington, D. C., 1989); see also, Jack Gannon, *Deaf Heritage: A Narrative History of Deaf America* (Silver Spring, Md., 1981), a popular history that was written by a deaf man, published by the National Association of the Deaf, and created primarily for the deaf community.

5. I am using "sign language" here as a generic term referring to any complex means of manual communication. In the nineteenth century, as today, there were (to simplify) two forms of sign language in use: American Sign Language, a natural language that has evolved over the course of American history within the deaf community, having roots in French Sign Language, indigenous sign languages, and a variety of British Sign Language brought to Martha's Vineyard; and signed

English (called "methodical signs" in the nineteenth century), of which several varieties exists. These latter are not true languages but manual codes invented for educational use to represent English manually. Manualists in the nineteenth century at different times used both, and oralists opposed both. See Joseph D. Stedt and Donald F. Moores, "Manual Codes on English and American Sign Language: Historical perspectives and Current Realities," in Harry Borstein, ed., *Manual Communication: Implications for Education* (Washington, D.C., 1990), 1–20; James Woodward, "Historical Bases of American Sign Language," in Patricia Siple, ed., *Understanding Language Through Sign Language Research* (New York, 1978), 333–48.

6. According to Alexander Graham Bell, 23.7 percent "taught wholly by oral methods"; 14.7 percent "taught also by Manual Spelling (no Sign-language)"; 53.1 percent "with whom speech is used [in at least some classes] as a means of instruction." See "Address of the President," *Association Review* 1 (Oct. 1899), 78–79 (in 1910 renamed the *Volta Review*). Bell's figures differ somewhat from those provided by the *American Annals of the Deaf*–see, for example, Edward Allen Fay in "Progress of Speech-Teaching in the United States," *Annals* 60 (Jan. 1915): 115. Bell's method of counting, as he explains in the same issue, is more precise in that he distinguishes between those taught wholly by oral methods and those taught in part orally and in part manually.

7. "Statistics of Speech Teaching in American Schools for the Deaf," *Volta Review* 22 (June 1920): 372.

8. See, for example, J. C. Gordon, "Dr. Gordon's Report," *American Review* 1 (Dec. 1899): 213; Mary McCowen, "Educational and Social Work for the Deaf and Deafened in the Middle West," *Oralism and Auralism* 6 (Jan. 1927): 67.

9. Henry Kisor, *What's That Pig Outdoors? A Memoir of Deafness* (New York, 1990), 259; Kisor was orally educated, never learned sign language, and has been very successful communicating orally all his life. Nevertheless he condemns "the history of oralism, the unrelenting and largely unsuccessful attempt to teach *all* the deaf to speak and read lips without relying on sign language" (9).

    The reintroduction of sign language into the classroom has been even more rapid than its banishment at the turn of the century; it occurred amidst widespread dissatisfaction with oralism—after a series of studies suggested that early use of sign language had no negative effect on speech skills and positive effects on English acquisition as well as social and intellectual development. See Donald F. Moores, *Educating the Deaf: Psychology, Principals and Practices* (Boston, 1987), 10–13. Julia M. Davis and Edward J. Hardick, *Rehabilitative Audiology for Children and Adults* (New York, 1981), 319–25; Mimi WheiPing Lou, "The History of Language Use in the Education of the Deaf in the United States," in Michael Strong, ed., *Language Learning and Deafness* (Cambridge, 1988), 88–94; Leo M. Jacobs, *A Deaf Adult Speaks Out* (Washington, D. C., 1980), 26, 41–50.

10. Van Cleve and Crouch, *A Place of Their Own*, 128–41; Beryl Lieff Benderly, *Dancing Without Music: Deafness in America* (Garden City, N. Y., 1980), 127–29; Harlan Lane, *When the Mind Hears: A History of the Deaf* (New York, 1984), 371–72; Padden and Humphries, *Deaf in America*, 110–12; Oliver Sacks, *Seeing Voices: A Journey into the World of the Deaf* (Berkeley, 1989), 25–28.

11. Quoted in Lane, *When the Mind Hears.* 371

12. Lane, *When the Mind Hears*, 301–2.

13. Richard Winefield, *Never the Twain Shall Meet: Bell, Gallaudet, and the Communications Debate* (Washington, D.C., 1987), 81–96; Van Cleve and Crouch, *A Place of Their Own*, 114–27; Lane, *When the Mind Hears*, 353–61.

14. Van Cleve and Crouch, *A Place of Their Own*, 106–7, 119, 126.

15. Lane, *When the Mind Hears*, xiii, 283–85.

16. Instruction in oral communication is still given in all educational programs for deaf and hearing-impaired children. "Oralism" as a philosophy of education does not mean simply oral instruction, but is rather a philosophy that maintains that all or most deaf children can be taught this way *exclusively*. The current philosophy, known as "Total Communication," and nineteenth-century manualism have in common the use of sign language. But American Sign Language was commonly used in the nineteenth century, while today some form of signed English delivered simultaneously with speech is most common. The integration of deaf pupils into the public schools, with the use of interpreters, is now the norm. The arguments today are not for the most part between oralists and manualists but between the advocates of signed English and American Sign Language, and between mainstreaming and separate residential schooling. See Moores, *Educating the Deaf*, 1–28.

17. Luzerne Ray, "Introductory," *Annals* 1 (Oct. 1847): 4.

18. Thomas H. Gallaudet, "The Natural Language of Signs," *Annals* 1 (Oct. 1847): 55–56.

19. Ibid., 56.

20. Thomas H. Gallaudet, "The Natural Language of Signs—II" *Annals* 1 (Jan. 1848): 82, 88.

21. Ibid., 82–85.

22. Ibid., 88–89. The emphasis on the heart rather than the intellect was of course a commonplace of Second great Awakening Evangelicalism. Reason and knowledge were not, however, seen as opposed to religion, and were also highly valued; see Jean V. Matthews, *Toward a New Society: American Thought and Culture, 1800–1830* (Boston, 1991) 35.

23. Thomas H. Gallaudet, "The Natural Language of Signs—II," 86.

24. Lucius Woodruff, "The Motives to Intellectual Effort on the part of the Young Deaf-Mute," *Annals* 1 (Apr. 1848): 163–65.

25. David Walker Howe, "The Evangelical Movement and Political Culture in the North during the Second Party System," *Journal of American History* 77 (Mar. 1991): 1220.

26. Collins Stone, "The Religious State and Instruction of the Deaf and Dumb," *Annals* 1 (Apr. 1848): 144.

27. Henry B. Camp, "Claims of the Deaf and Dumb Upon Public Sympathy and Aid," *Annals* 1 (July 1848): 213–14.

28. Stone, "The Religious State," 133–34, 137.

29. Ibid., 134–35, 138.

30. J. A. Ayres, "An Inquiry into the Extent to which the Misfortune of Deafness may be Alleviated," *Annals* 1 (July 1848): 223.

31. Luzerne Ray, "Thoughts of the Deaf and Dumb before Instruction," *Annals* 1 (Apr. 1848): 150–51.

32. Camp, "Claims of the Deaf," 210–15. See also Woodruff, "The Motives to Intellectual Effort," 163–65.

33. Stone, "The Religious State," 136–37.

34. Woodruff, "The Motives to Intellectual Effort," 165–66.

35. Ayres, "An Inquiry," 224.

36. John Carlin, "The Mute's Lament," *Annals* 1 (Oct. 1847): 15. Carlin, a successful artist, was well known for his expressions of what today might be termed "self hatred." He was a contradictory individual. Although he married a deaf woman, used sign language, and was an ardent supported of the establishment of Gallaudet College, he claimed to prefer the company of hearing people and expressed contempt for deaf people and sign language. While he did not speak or lip-read, he became one of the small minority of deaf adults who supported the oralist movement. Carlin derided proposals for a separatist community of deaf people on the grounds that "it is a well known fact that the majority of them [deaf people] show little decision of purpose in any enterprise whatever." *Annals* 10 (Apr. 1858): 89. See also Lane, *When the Mind Hears*, 245–46, 275–76, 325; Van Cleve and Crouch, *A Place of Their Own*, 66, 76–78.

37. Anon., *Annals* 1 (July 1848): 209.

38. Padden and Humphries identify the use of "silence" in reference to deaf people as metaphorical. They explain that sound (to greatly simplify their argument) directly and indirectly plays an important role in the lives of deaf people and has important meanings for them, albeit quite different ones than for the hearing; *Deaf in America*, 91–109.

39. Frank Booth, "The Association Magazine," *Association Review* 1 (Oct. 1899): 4.

40. Alexander Graham Bell, "Address of the President," *Association Review* 1 (Oct. 1899): 74–75, 85.

41. Bell, "Address of the President," 78–79 (see note 6). "Statistics of Speech Teaching in American Schools for the Deaf," 372.

42. Percentages of deaf teachers by year: 1852–38 percent; 1858–41 percent; 1870–41 percent; 1880–29 percent; 1892–24 percent; 1897–18 percent; 1915–15 percent, compiled from periodic reports of schools for the deaf, published in the *American Annals of the Deaf* during the years indicated, under the heading "Tabular Statement of American Schools for the Deaf."

43. Winefield, *Never the Twain Shall Meet*, 48.

44. John Van Cleve, "Nebraska's Oral Law of 1911 and the Deaf Community," *Nebraska History* 65 (Summer 1984): 208.

45. *Annals* 44 (June 1899): 221–29.

46. John M. Tyler, "The Teacher and the State," *Association Review* 1 (Oct. 1899): 9, 12–13.

47. Katherine T. Bingham, "All Along the Line, *Association Review* 2 (Feb. 1900): 27, 29.

48. Edward C. Rider, "The Annual Report of the Northern New York Institution for the Year Ending September 30, 1898," reprinted in the *Association Review* 1 (Dec. 1899): 214–15.

49. S. G. Davidson, "The Relation of Language to Mental Development and of Speech to Language Teaching," *Association Review* 1 (Dec. 1899), 132. See also, Alexander Graham Bell, *Proceedings of the Twelfth Convention of American Instructors of the Deaf* (New York, 1890), 181.

50. Joseph C. Gordon, *The Difference Between the Two Systems of Teaching Deaf-Mute Children the English Language: Extracts from a Letter to a Parent Requesting Information Relative to the Prevailing Methods of Teaching Language to Deaf-Mutes in America* (Washington, D. C., 1898), 1.

51. J. D. Kirkhuff, "The Sign System Arraigned," *Silent Educator* 3 (Jan. 1892): 88a.

52. S. G. Davidson, "The Relation of Language Teaching to Mental Development," *National Educational Association: Journal of Proceedings and Addresses of the Thirty-Seventh Annual Meeting* (Washington, D. C., 1898), 1044.

53. Edward M. Gallaudet, "'Deaf Mute' Conventions, Associations, and Newspapers," *Annals* 18 (July 1873): 200–206.

54. Frederick E. Hoxie, *A Final Promise: The Campaign to Assimilate the Indians, 1880–1920* (Lincoln, Neb., 1984), 12.

55. Alexander Graham Bell, *Memoir Upon the Formation of a Deaf Variety of the Human Race* (Washington, D. C., 1884), 194.

56. Bell, *Memoir*, 194, 217–18, 223.

57. Mary S. Garrett, "The State of the Case," *National Educational Association: Journal of Proceedings and Addresses of the Thirty-Ninth Annual Meeting* (Washington, D. C., 1900), 663; Bell, *Memoir*, 221–22.

58. Bell, *Memoir*, 217, 221–23.

59. Edward Allen Fay, "An Inquiry Concerning the Results of Marriages of the Deaf in America," *Annals* 42 (Feb. 1897): 100–102; see also the discussion of this issue in Van Cleve and Crouch, *A Place of Their Own*, 150–52.

60. On the influence of eugenics upon Bell's work in deaf education, see Winefield, *Never the Twain Shall Meet*, 82–96; Lane, *When the Mind Hears*, 353–61; Van Cleve and Crouch, *A Place of Their Own*, 145–52; for a more sympathetic view of Bell's eugenic concerns about deafness, see Robert V. Bruce, *Bell: Alexander Graham Bell and the Conquest of Solitude*

(Ithaca, N. Y., 1973), 409–12.

61. Quoted in Padden and Humphries, *Deaf in America*, 36.

62. Helen Taylor, "The Importance of a Right Beginning," *Association Review* 1 (Dec. 1899): 159.

63. Ibid.

64. Bingham, "All Along the Line," 28–29.

65. Ibid. See also, J. C. Gordon, "Dr. Gordon's Report," *Association Review* 1 (Dec. 1899): 204.

66. Gordon, "Dr. Gordon's Report," 213.

67. Bingham, "All Along the Line," 29; see also Emma Garrett, "A Plea that the Deaf 'Mutes' of America May be Taught to Use Their Voices," *Annals* 28 (Jan. 1883): 18.

68. Thomas H. Gallaudet, "The Natural Language of Signs—II," 89; J. D. Kirkhuff, "The Sign System Arraigned," 88a.

69. Davidson, "The Relation of Language," 132.

70. Emma Garrett, "A Plea," 18.

71. Gordon, "Dr. Gordon's Report," 206.

72. Bingham, "All Along the Line," 22.

73. Benjamin D. Pettingill, "The Sign-Language," *Annals* 18 (Jan. 1873), 4.

74. Sara Harvey Porter, "The Suppression of Signs by Force," *Annals* 39 (June 1894): 171. Porter repeated this observation in 1913, when she stated that in the "old primitive fighting days the oralists cried to us, derisively: 'Your children, making signs, look like monkeys!" In the context it is not clear whether she believed those fighting days were over, or whether she was calling for their end; *Annals* 58 (May 1913): 284.

75. R. W. Dodds, "The Practical Benefits of Methods Compared," *Annals* 44 (Feb. 1899): 124.

76. Lewis J. Dudley, "Address of Mr. Dudley in 1880," *Fifteenth Annual Report of the Clarke Institution for Deaf-Mutes* (Northampton, Mass., 1882), 7.

77. Ibid.

78. From extracts reprinted in Alexander Graham Bell, "Historical Notes Concerning the Teaching of Speech to the Deaf," *Association Review* (Apr. 1902): 151.

79. Stone, "On the Religious State," 137.

80. Camp, "Claims of the Deaf," 214.

81. Bingham, "All Along the Line," 28; Taylor, "The Importance of a Right Beginning," 158.

82. J. A. Jacobs, "To Save the Souls of His Pupils, the Great Duty of a Teacher of Deaf-Mutes," *Annals* 8 (July 1856): 211; Susanna E. Hull, "The Psychological Method of Teaching Language," *Annals* 43 (Apr. 1898): 190.

83. Donald G. Matthews, "The Second Great Awakening as an Organizing Process, 1780–1830; An Hypothesis," *American Quarterly* 21 (Spring 1969): 23–43; Richard Carwardine, "The Know-Nothing Party, the Protestant Evangelical Community and American National Identity," in *Religion and National Identity,* Stuart Mews, ed. (Oxford, 1982), 449–63.

84. Rivka Shpak Lissak, *Pluralism and Progressives: Hull House and the New Immigrants, 1890–1919* (Chicago, 1989): 50–55.

85. Taylor, "The Importance of a Right beginning," 158. The equation of equality with sameness was a staple of Progressive reform thought; see Lissak, *Pluralism and Progressives*, 153.

86. Lissak, *Pluralism and Progressives*; Hoxie, *A Final Promise*; Joshua A. Fishman, *Language Loyalty in the United States: The Maintenance and Perpetuation of Non-English Mother Tongues by American Ethnic and Religious Groups* (The Hague, 1966).

87. George Lakoff, *Women, Fire, and Dangerous Things: What Categories Reveal about the Mind* (Chicago, 1987), xiv.

88. Leo M. Jacobs, *A Deaf Adult Speaks Out* (Washington, D. C., 1980), 90–100; Jerome D. Schein, *At Home Among Strangers: Exploring the Deaf Community in the United States* (Washington, D. C., 1989), 130; Paul C. Higgins, *Outsiders in a Hearing World: A Sociology of Deafness* (Beverly Hills, 1980), 69–76; James Woodward, "How You Gonna Get to Heaven if You Can't Talk with Jesus: The Educational Establishment vs. the Deaf Community," in *How You Gonna Get to Heaven if You Can't Talk with Jesus: On Depathologizing Deafness* (Silver Spring, Md., 1982), 11.

89. In the first five years of Gallaudet College (1869 to 1874), a liberal arts college exclusively for deaf students, 75 percent of its graduates became teachers at schools for the deaf. From 1894 to 1899, fewer than a third did so. See Edward P. Clarke, "An Analysis of the Schools and Instructors of the Deaf in the United States," *American Annals of the Deaf* 45 (Apr. 1900): 229.

90. Van Cleve and Crouch, *A Place of Their Own*, 128.

91. See W. Earl Hall, "To Speak or Not to Speak: That is the Question Behind the Bitter Deaf-Teaching Battle," *Iowan* 4 (Feb.–Mar. 1956) for a brief description of a battle between the Iowa Association of the Deaf and the Iowa School for the Deaf in the 1950s over this issue. See also Van Cleve, "Nebraska's Oral Law," 195–220; Van Cleve and Crouch, *A Place of Their Own*, 128–41.

92. Padden and Humphries, *Deaf in America*, 5–6; Benderly, *Dancing Without Music*, 218–39; Schein, *At Home Among Strangers*, 72–105, 106, 120.

93. Padden and Humphries, *Deaf in America*, 26–38, 110–21, explore the alternative meanings of deafness created by the deaf community; their focus is on the present, but their brief forays into the historical roots of these meanings are suggestive and insightful.

4

The Other Arms Race

David Serlin

In the November 1946 issue of *Fortune,* famous photographer Walker Evans presented some views of perfectly ordinary men walking the streets of downtown Detroit in the late afternoon.[1] Evans, a master of social realism whose photographic work for the Farm Security Administration in the mid-1930s culminated in his masterpiece with James Agee, *Let Us Now Praise Famous Men* (1939), had moved into a new phase of his career, this time focused largely on representations of postwar labor.[2] Evan's pictures of American working men in a variety of guises—in broad-brimmed caps and overalls, or in work pants and white T-shirts—were familiar to the American businessmen who made up the vast majority of *Fortune's* readers. Since the 1920s they had been accustomed to looking at images of men who marked physically the masculine exuberance and patriotic spirit embodied in icons of Americans commercial production.[3] Even into the 1950s, a disproportionate number of advertisements in *Fortune* that depicted men at work showed blue-collar workers.

For Evans, such icons of American labor were fundamental to the health of the postwar economy, since they promoted the strength and vitality of the American workingman. The text that accompanied the *Fortune* photo-essay (which may have been written by Evans himself) observed:

> The American worker...is a decidedly various fellow. His blood flows from many sources. His features tend now toward the peasant and now toward the patrician. His hat is sometimes a hat and sometimes he has moulded it into a sort of defiant signature. It is this diversity, perhaps, which makes him, in the mass, the most resourceful and versatile body of labor in the world. If the war proved anything, it demonstrated that American labor can learn new operations with extraordinary rapidity and speed-ily carry them to the highest pitch of productive efficiency. Though it may often lack the craftsmanly traditions of the older worlds, American labor's wide spectrum of temperaments rises to meet almost any challenge: in labor as in investment portfolios, diversification pays off. There is another thing to be noted about these street portraits. Here are none of those worn, lusterless, desolated faces we have seen so frequently in recent photographs of the exhausted masses of Europe. Most of these men on these pages would seem to have a solid degree of self-possession. By the grace of providence and the efforts of millions including themselves, they are citizens of a victorious and powerful nation, and they appear to have preserved a sense of themselves as individuals. When editorialists lump them as "labor," these laborers can no doubt laugh that off.[4]

From its focus on the American worker's ability to be "resourceful" and "versatile" to its insistence that what characterizes American labor is individual pride—"a solid degree of self-possession"—and not union affiliation or a European (read socialist) working-class identity, Evans's text exemplified the compulsive need among many commentators in the postwar era to correlate the male American worker with the qualities of a certain brand of normative masculinity: independence, reliability, ef-ficiency, resiliency. With the excitement of industrial production from a military economy still fresh, using one's body remained one of the primary ways that citizens (and, despite Evans's protestations, men who identified as organized members of the American working class) forged identities and af-filiations with industrial economies. In the years immediately following World War II, vast pockets of the United States were still heavily industrial. Many older cities in the Northeast and Midwest relied almost exclusively on steel, coal, iron, lumber, and oil as well as the nexus of related industries including railroads, automobile and appliance manufacturing, production of chemicals and plastics, and shipping and storage technologies. In this industrial milieu, the image of the blue-collar man still carried substantial power as a dignified symbol for corporate strength. The prominent service-oriented FIRE industries (finance, insurance, and real estate) that we now associate with large American cities for the most part represented only one segment of their diversified financial output. The image of the city as a hive of gleaming office towers housing white-collar corporate capital was still only a dream of urban planners, economic theorists, and real estate moguls that would not be realized in cities like Detroit until the 1970s.[5]

Evans's 1946 photo spread for *Fortune* was characteristic of images of the workingman's body in action, found in abundance throughout mass culture. One could trace these icons of the masculine work ethic to images by Progressive Era photographers like Lewis Hine or, somewhat later, works by muralists and photographers who created public art for the Works Progress Administration during the 1930s. Film representations of ruggedly masculine American men like James Cagney and Clark Gable were enjoyed by Depression audiences who found admiring such handsome figures a convenient escape from the economic deprivation of the era. During the work shortages of the Depression, conservative critics had sounded a note of fear over the perceived erosion of masculinity among American men. Their worst fears were realized in the early 1940s when the mobilization of hundreds of thousands of women in the labor force, combined with the prolonged absence of men from traditional positions of family and community authority, began to give a new shape to civilian domestic culture. Many were displeased by new configurations of family and marriage, not to mention the new sexual divisions of labor on the home front. In the best-selling *Generation of Vipers* (1942), for example, Philip Wylie coined the term "Momism" to describe what he perceived to be the emasculating effects of aggressive mothers and wives on the behavior of passive sons and husbands as a consequence of the reconfiguration of traditional gender roles. One could argue that after the attack on Pearl Harbor in December 1941, and the war that followed it, the bodies of American men were marked simultaneously by their solidity and their fragility, the dual norms of American heterosexual masculinity. As Walker Evans's photographs demonstrate, the two constituent aspects of the male body—its relation to productive labor and its relation to heterosexual masculinity—took on increased significance.

Professional and public discussions of workingmen, as well as representations of them working, became more complex as a result of the return of veterans—many of them wounded, disfigured, or traumatized—to positions in civilian society. One of the foremost concerns of the era was what effect trauma and disability would have on veterans' self-worth, especially in a competitive economy defined by able-bodied men. Social workers, advice columnists, physical therapists, and policymakers during and after World War II turned their attention to the perceived crisis of the American veteran, much as they had done after the Great War some thirty years earlier. As Susan Hartmann has written, "By 1944, as public attention began to focus on the postwar period, large numbers of writers and speakers…awakened readers to the social problems of demobilization, described the specific adjustments facing ex-servicemen, and prescribed appropriate behavior and attitudes for civilians." [6] Recent studies of disabled veterans of the two world wars have emphasized that such men often carried collective and national anxieties about the transition from wartime to civilian labor and its relation to the precarious status of the male body. For many workingmen these anxieties seemed hardly visible. But many male veterans of World War II with visible (and not-so-visible) disabilities came back to a country where, among other changes they encountered, gender roles were far less comprehensible or predictable than they had once seemed. How did normative models of masculinity affect disabled veterans who had to compete against the reputation and image of the able-bodied American workingman?

This chapter examines the status of disabled veterans of World War II, looking closely not only at veteran amputees but also at the design and representation of prosthetic devices developed for amputees who wanted to return to the workplace. I read the stories of veterans and their prostheses as neglected components of the historical reconstruction of gender roles and heterosexual male archetypes in early Cold War culture. Like artificial body parts created for victims of war and industrial accidents after the Civil War and World War I, prosthetics developed during the 1940s and 1950s were linked explicitly to the fragile politics of labor, employment, and self-worth for disabled veterans.[7] Discussions of prosthetics also reflected concomitant social and sexual anxieties that attended the public specter of the damaged male body. As this chapter argues, the design and construction of prostheses help to distinguish the rehabilitation of veterans after World War II from earlier periods of adjustment.

Prosthetics research and development were catalyzed, to a great extent, by the mystique attached to "medical miracles" and scientific progress in the late 1940s and early 1950s. The advent of new materials science and new bioengineering principles during the war and the application of these materials and principles to new prosthetic devices helped transform prosthetics into its own biomedical subdiscipline. The convergence of these two areas of research—making prostheses as physical objects and designing prosthetics as products of engineering science—offers important insights into the political and cultural dimensions of the early postwar period, especially in light of what we know about the social and economic restructuring of postwar society with the onset of the Cold War. By the mid-1950s the development of new materials and technologies for prostheses had become the consummate marriage of industrial engineering and domestic engineering.

This chapter uses the term "prosthetics" in two distinct though clearly overlapping ways. While the word obviously refers to artificial additions, appendages, or extensions of the human body, after World War II it referred increasingly to a biomedical and engineering subdiscipline—what mathematician Norbert Wiener, beginning in the late 1950s, would call "biocybernetics" or "cybernetic medicine." Before World War II, prostheses were made of organic, often familiar materials—such as leather, wood, glass, and metal—or were changed to accommodate the synthetic products of late nineteenth-century industrial processes such as vulcanized rubber or early plastics. By the late 1940s and early 1950s, however, prosthetic devices were constructed from a variety of new materials such as acrylic, polyurethane, and stainless steel. Furthermore, by the late 1950s and early 1960s, new biomechanical principles and cybernetic control systems had begun to be applied to the operation of artificial arms and legs. Because of these myriad changes, prosthetics themselves were entirely reimagined by the designers and engineers who made them as well as by the veteran and civilian amputees who wore them. The distinction between prosthetics as objects and prosthetics as science also enables us to reclaim both the ideological foundation and the material foundation of postwar prosthetics—to look at prostheses and the prosthetic sciences not merely as metaphorical tropes or linguistic conceits but as forms of embodied technology that predate our affinity for talking about cyborgs and cyberculture.

Many books of the past decade use the extended metaphor of the prosthesis to analyze the artificial objects that mediate human relations as well as cyberculture's mandate of virtual reality.[8] In these works, a prosthesis can refer to any machine or technology that intervenes in human subjectivity, such as a telephone, a computer, or a sexual device. As a result, the prosthesis is regularly abstracted as a postmodern tool or artifact, a symbol that reductively dematerializes the human body. As Kathleen Woodward has written, "Technology serves fundamentally as a prosthesis of the human body, one that ultimately displaces the material body."[9] Despite ubiquitous representations of prostheses or cyborgs in late twentieth and early twenty-first century culture, they hardly begin to understand the complex historical and technological origins of the body-machine interface for amputees and other prosthesis wearers. They also fail to give agency to the people who use prosthetic technology every day without glamour or fanfare.

Far from transforming them into supermen or cyborgs, prostheses provided veteran amputees with the material means through which individuals on both sides of the therapeutic divide imagined and negotiated what it meant to look and behave like a so-called normal, able-bodied workingman. For engineers and prosthetists, artificial parts were biomedical tools that could be used to rehabilitate bodies and social identities. For doctors and patients, prosthetics were powerful anthropomorphic tools that reflected contemporary fantasies about ability and employment, heterosexual masculinity, and American citizenship.

Patriotic Gore

Long before World War II ended in August 1945—the month that Japan officially surrendered to the United States after the bombing of Hiroshima and Nagasaki—images in the mass media of wounded soldiers convalescing or undergoing physical therapy occupied a regular place in news reports and popular entertainment.[10] In John Cromwell's film *The Enchanted Cottage* (1945), a young soldier played by Robert Young hides from society and his family in a remote honeymoon cottage after wartime injuries damage his handsome face.[11] *The Enchanted Cottage* updated and Americanized the substance of Sir Arthur Wing Pinero's 1925 play of the same title. Pinero's drama focused on a British veteran of World War I who symbolized the plight of facially disfigured veterans (sometimes called *les gueules cassés* by their countrymen), who were often considered social outcasts by an insensitive public.[12] In the 1945 North American production, as in the original, the cottage protects the mutilated soldier and his homely, unglamorous fiancée from parents and family members who take pity on the couple for their abnormal physical differences.

Many amputees who returned from war to their homes, hometowns, and places of work—if they could find work—suffered from a similar lack of respect, despite the best efforts of federal agencies like the Veterans Administration to meet their needs. Physicians, therapists, psychologists, and ordinary citizens alike often regarded veterans as men whose recent amputations were physical proof of emasculation or general incompetence, or else a kind of monstrous defamiliarization of the normal male body. Social policy advocates recommended that families and therapists apply positive psychological approaches to rehabilitating amputees.[13] Too often, however, such approaches were geared toward making able-bodied people more comfortable with their innate biases so they could "deal" with the disabled. This seemed to be a more familiar strategy than empowering the disabled themselves.

In William Wyler's Academy Award-winning film *The Best Years of Our Lives* (1946), real-life war veteran Harold Russell played Homer, a sensitive double amputee who tries to challenge the stereotype of the ineffectual amputee while he and his loyal girlfriend cope valiantly with his new split-hook, above-elbow prosthetic arms. Given the mixed reception of disabled veterans in the public sphere—simultaneous waves of pride and awkwardness—scriptwriters made Homer exhibit tenacious courage and resilience of spirit rather than the vulnerability or rage that visited many veteran amputees. As David Gerber has written, "The culture and politics of the 1940s placed considerable pressure on men like Russell to find individual solutions, within a constricted range of emotions, to the problem of bearing a visible disability in a world of able-bodied people."[14] Recurring images of disabled soldiers readjusting to civilian life became positive propaganda that tried to persuade able-bodied Americans that the convalescence of veterans was not a problem.

Such propaganda was to be expected in the patriotic aftermath of World War II—especially given the War Department's decision during the early 1940s to expunge all painful images of wounded or dead soldiers from the popular media.[15] The American media regularly circulated stories about amputees and their triumphant use of their prostheses. The circulation of such unduly cheery narratives of tolerance in the face of adversity implied a direct relation between physical trauma—and the ability to survive such trauma—and patriotic duty.

In the summer of 1944, for example, United States audiences were captivated by the story of Jimmy Wilson, an army private who was the only survivor of a ten-person plane crash in the Pacific Ocean. When he was found forty-four hours later amid the plane's wreckage, army doctors were forced to amputate both of his arms and legs. After Wilson returned to his hometown of Starke, Florida, surgeons outfitted him with new prosthetic arms and legs, and he became a poster boy for the plight of thousands of amputees who faced physical and psychological readjustment on their return to civilian life. In early 1945, the *Philadelphia Inquirer* initiated a national campaign to raise money for Wilson. By the end of the war in August the *Inquirer* had raised over $50,000, collected from well-known philanthropists and ordinary citizens alike, such as a group of schoolchildren who raised $26 by selling scrap iron.[16] By the winter of 1945, Wilson's trust fund had grown to over $105,000, and he pledged to use the money to get married, buy a house, and study law under the newly signed GI Bill. Wilson's celebrity status as a quadruple amputee peaked when he posed with Bess Myerson, Miss America 1945, in a brand-new Valiant, a car (whose name itself championed Wilson's patriotic reception) that General Motors designed specifically for above-ankle amputees.[17] Wilson learned how to operate the car by manipulating manual gas and brake levers on the car's steering column. Demand for the Valiant was so great that in September 1946 Congress allocated funds that provided ten thousand of these automobiles to needy amputees.[18]

If men like Jimmy Wilson were regularly celebrated as heroic and noble, it was because tales of their perseverance and resilience grew with the fervor of a Cold War mentality. Instead of allowing them to speak for themselves, the media transformed amputees into powerful visual and rhetorical symbols through which war-related disability was unequivocally identified with heroism. In the fall of 1945, for example, the Washington, DC, edition of the *Goodwill*, Goodwill Industries' newsletter devoted to raising money and collecting supplies for the war effort, published a provocative image of a handsome young veteran on crutches. Dressed stylishly in pleated pants, a twilled cotton shirt, and the greased, well-coifed hair typical of young civilian men in the early 1940s, the relaxed veteran beams beneath a visual collage including the Capitol, the Washington Monument, and the Lincoln Memorial. The text on the front of the newsletter bears a striking proclamation of patriotic support:

> We are fighting for him and others like him—Not only veterans of the war—but all who are handicapped....In the general confusion of National Reconversion—we wish to eliminate as many difficulties for them as possible—now, more than ever, we are in need of your whole-hearted support! we must not fail them![19]

Although the message is remarkable for its inclusion of all people with disabilities, the rhetorical power of words like "victory" and "support" clearly invokes the economic and social needs highlighted by veterans. The reference to "National Reconversion" addresses the expectations of a new economic organization—one that emphasizes the viability of disabled veterans as competent workers—in which public commitment to the social welfare of the disabled is one way of exercising one's patriotic duty. By making an implicit connection between the disabled veteran's individual transition to civilian society and the military's transition to a civilian economy, the newsletter amplifies the need to understand that such a transition is about both individual and collective sacrifice.

At approximately the same time, in late 1945, the Coast Guard photographic corps circulated the image of a different kind of amputee, in full military dress, that made explicit the needs of disabled veterans within the discourse of patriotism and military masculinity. In the photograph, the small body of Thomas Sortino of Chicago is shown saluting the Olympic-sized statue of Abraham Lincoln on the Mall in Washington, D.C. An accompanying caption proclaims, "A fighting coastguardsman...poses for a Memorial Day tribute to the Great Emancipator at the Lincoln shrine here." Like the *Goodwill* cartoon, the photograph uses Sortino's familiar gesture to endorse the democratic ethos of sacrifice, as if his amputation had been nothing less, or more, than what the government demanded of all its citizens during wartime—"pitching in," buying war bonds, tending victory gardens, and rationing consumer goods. Under Lincoln's attentive glare, the visual and verbal cues invoked a nostalgia for the Civil War, reinforcing the idea that those disabled during World War II fought and won the war to preserve democracy. Two newspaper articles published about the same time in the *Washington [D.C.] Evening Star* confirm this theme. One, about the Quebec-born amputee Fernand Le Clare, declares in a headline, "Canadian GI Proud to Be an American," while the other, about the Hawaiian-born disabled veteran Kenneth T. Otagaki, assures us that "This Jap Is Justly Proud That He Is an American."[20] The particular brand of normative domestic politics expressed by these images and headlines is precisely what Tom Englehardt has described as the "victory culture" of the late 1940s and early 1950s.[21]

The media's use of images of male amputees, both with and without their prostheses, was a deliberate strategy that reminded the public of the recent war, but it also served to memorialize the war-honored dead and disabled. It was, after all, yet another period all citizens would need to acclimate to, another period that mandated massive social reconstruction, policymaking, and productive transitions to civilian life for millions of people, both able-bodied and disabled, civilian and veteran. Moreover, amputee veterans were a significant part of the popular image of soldiering itself and of military culture in general. Their public presence blurred the techniques of physical rehabilitation with tacit forms of democratic participation and civic duty.[22] In 1951, for example, Senator Joseph McCarthy antagonized Secretary of State Dean Acheson (who McCarthy believed was a Communist) at a congressional hearing by invoking the name of Bob Smith, a recent veteran amputee of the Korean War, to contest some of Acheson's recent foreign policy proposals. Seamlessly combining anti-Communist hysteria with homophobic intolerance, McCarthy contrasted Smith's masculine resilience with Acheson's perceived effeminate and aristocratic stance. "I suggest that...when Bob Smith can walk," McCarthy asserted, "when he gets his artificial limbs, he first walk over to the State Department and call upon the Secretary if he is still there.... He should say to Acheson: 'You and your lace handkerchief crowd have never had to fight in the cold, so you cannot know its bitterness.... [Y]ou should not only resign from the State Department but you should remove yourself from this country and go to the nation for which you have been struggling and fighting so long.' "[23]

The ideological links forged between public exhibitions of disability, heterosexual masculinity, and patriotic commitment—usually exercised in a less spectacular fashion than McCarthy's exploitation of Smith—were not new. Since the 1860s, photographers had developed a sophisticated visual lexicon for depicting able-bodied and disabled soldiers and veterans. Alan Trachtenberg, among others, has discussed how images of wounded amputees sitting graciously for portrait photographs were rhetorical expressions of extreme patriotism (for both Northern and Southern veterans) distilled into visual form.[24] For many of these disabled veterans of the Civil War, the amputation stump, the artificial limb, and other physical markings that proved sustained injury were visual shorthand for military service. Disability, then, became their permanent uniform. Medical photographs of amputees in the nineteenth century, as Kathy Newman has argued, were sophisticated enough to capture the subjects' brutal amputations yet polished enough to preserve the genteel conventions of Victorian portrait photography.[25] This must explain why, in such photographs, the male body often appears as both disabled spectacle and eroticized object. For those reading the photographs today, these portrait sittings of handsome young men with deep wounds, radical amputations, or artificial limbs become material reflections of the photographer's desire to recuperate the soldiers' putatively lost masculinity. Perhaps medical photographers believed that by using an "objective" science of surveillance, they could displace the potentially emasculating effects of the camera's penetration into the intimate spaces of the amputee's body.

Through the public circulation of photographic images and verbal descriptions of veteran amputees, we begin to see the formation of arbitrary (though no less hierarchical) categories for thinking about disability itself. How differently, for example, does a society view disability that results from war injury or industrial accident as opposed to disability that results from congenital deformity, acquired illness, or even self-mutilation? Part of this delineation relies on the perceived difference between disability induced by modern technology or warfare and hereditary disability, attitudes toward which were influenced by antiquated notions of a "monstrous birth" even as late as the 1950s.[26] In the former, disability is material proof of one's service to the military, to the modern state, to industrial capitalism: these help to preserve patriotic values and respectable citizenship. In the latter, disability is a material stigma that marks one's rejection from competent service to society. Among men, such stigmas may confirm the male body as weak, effeminate, and inimical to normative heterosexual versions of manly competence. In the aftermath of war and the rise of the hyperpatriotic culture of the late 1940s, veteran male amputees constituted a superior category on an unspoken continuum of disabled bodies, suggesting that hierarchies of value are constructed even *within,* and sometimes *by,* groups of differently abled individuals.

Making Men Whole Again

The social and political climate of the late 1940s directly affected the ways in which images of veterans were disseminated in the public sphere. Images of amputees undergoing rehabilitation—learning to walk, eat, and perform other "normal" activities—were often used in tandem with materials to promote the agendas of postwar science and technology. This was especially true after the passage of NSC-68, the National Security Council's 1947 resolution to allocate enormous sums to the "containment" of Communism by any means necessary, which increased exponentially the military aggression and technological competition already mounting between the United States and the Soviet Union. At large, well-funded research institutions with other government contracts—such as Case Institute of Technology, Massachusetts Institute of Technology, Michigan State University, New York University, the University of California at Los Angeles, and Western Reserve University—the development of new prosthetic designs arose concomitantly with new technologies used to protect and defend national interests. Writing in 1954, Detlev Bronk, president of the National Academy of Sciences, made clear the responsibilities to nation and citizenry that were articulated through the relation between military research and rehabilitation medicine:

> Those whom this committee first sought to aid were those who suffered loss of limb in battle where they were serving their fellows. In times of war scientists have fortified the courage of our defenders by applying science to the development of better weapons. They have done significantly more; during times when it was necessary to sacrifice human lives they marshaled the resources of science for the protection of health and life. . . . [The development of prostheses] is a vivid reminder that human values are a primary concern of the scientists of freedom-loving nations.[27]

This was not the first time new materials and techniques had been applied to the design and creation of new prosthetic parts for those wounded during war. Industrial processes in the nineteenth and twentieth centuries had enabled the production of materials, such as vulcanized rubber, synthetic resins, and plastics, for use in prosthetic devices developed for veterans of the Civil War and World War I. What made new prostheses different from earlier models is that they represented the marriage of prosthetic design to military-industrial production. Both materials science and information science—hallmarks of military research and federal funding—figured prominently in experimental prosthetics developed in the late 1940s. According to Wilfred Lynch, "The development of dependable [prostheses] proceeded at a snail's pace until the emergence of 'exotic' new materials in answer to the needs of the military in World War II. The subsequent aerospace program and the high volume of burgeoning new postwar industries made the commercial production of these unique materials practical." [28] Some of these represented the conversion of military needs for civilian ones in materials such as Plexiglas, Lucite, polyester, silicone, titanium, Duralumin, stainless steel, ceramics, and high-grade plastics that flooded the industrial and consumer markets. By the fall of 1947, funding from Congress had made artificial limbs constructed from lightweight plastics available to over five thousand veterans. Newly patented technologies used in later experimental prosthetic models, such as Velcro and Siemes servomotors, grew out of wartime research in materials science and miniaturization of solid-state electronics.[29] Furthermore, scientists attempted to apply new engineering techniques derived from military-industrial research to veterans' artificial limbs. In late August 1945, just two weeks after the war ended, Paul E. Klopsteg, chairman of the National Research Council's Committee on Prosthetic Devices, announced a research program devoted to creating "power-driven" artificial limbs that resembled the "real thing" by "introducing power, either hydraulic, pneumatic, or electric" to prosthetic limbs.[30]

The association between amputees and state-of-the-art prosthetics research may have been an intentional strategy to link disabled veterans with the cutting edge of new scientific discoveries. In 1943, for example, the War Department commissioned Milton Wirtz, a civilian dentist, to develop artificial eyes using the new wonder material, acrylic.[31] Wirtz's expertise with acrylic derived from using the new material in forging dental prostheses for patients. It made him the ideal candidate to supply the armed forces with hundreds of prototype acrylic eyes, which proved to be more durable, lighter, and even more realistic than glass eyes. Wirtz's kits provided low-skilled technicians at military hospitals with easy-to-follow charts for matching the patient's eye color, and they even contained red-brown threads for simulating blood vessels. In a similar fashion, the Naval Graduate Dental Center in Annapolis, Maryland, developed a full complement of acrylic facial parts, including eye, nose, cheek, and ear prostheses. Surgeons in the field adapted these parts temporarily to the patient's face before the soldier was transferred to a military hospital for reconstructive surgery. In 1944 the Naval Graduate Dental Center also built customized cases for holding these parts that looked like velvet-lined candy box samplers. They included, among other facial features, a "Negro" ear and a "Caucasian" cheek. Interestingly, these navy prosthetists used a single mold to cast each facial part they created. This process made fabrication of parts easy; at the same time, it may have had the effect of neutralizing, or even erasing, the perceived phenotypic differences between white and black facial characteristics. One could argue that, in some small way, such a technical feat of prosthetic science anticipated by several years President Harry S. Truman's desegregation of the U.S. military in 1948.

Prosthetists and engineers working to rehabilitate disabled veterans relied on technical expertise; but they were also directly influenced by the fiercely heterosexual culture of postwar psychology, especially its orthodox zeal to preserve a soldier's masculine status. A 1957 rehabilitation manual developed by physical therapists at the University of California at Los Angeles, for example, explicitly correlated physical disability with the perceived heterosexual anxieties of the male amputee: "Will he be acceptable to wife or sweetheart? Can he live a normal sex-life? Will his children inherit anything as a result of his acquired physical defect? Can he hope to rejoin his social group? Must he give up having fun?"[32] This professional concern was associated with increasing panic about homosexuality, which predated the war but was formalized in the public imagination after the 1948 publication of Dr. Alfred Kinsey's *Sexual Behavior in the Human Male*. Among military and university researchers, this emphasis on rehabilitating the amputee's masculinity along with his body was an artifact left over from the military's deep-seated and overt homophobia.[33] As Allan Bérubé has described it, the armed forces maintained statistics throughout World War II on soldiers excused from military service for perceived homosexual behavior or for having otherwise unmasculine psychological or physiological traits.[34] At New York University, rehabilitation therapists expected that prostheses not only would permit able-bodied activity but also would confer positive self-esteem on those who participated in an experimental, technologically innovative laboratory study: "[A] good prosthesis, provided in an atmosphere of understanding and interest by people who are looking to him as a *man,* a human being, and as an important cog in an experimental program fills two interwoven needs. He can feel a lessening of the threats against which he must continually arm himself and he can utilize the potentialities of the prosthesis to a much greater extent."[35]

Attitudes like this, which equated independent activity with the perquisites of heterosexual masculinity in order to resist the potentially feminizing interventions of family members, were hardly unique in postwar rehabilitation culture. Throughout the late 1940s and 1950s, physicians, psychologists, and engineers imagined amputees as potentially troubled and socially maladjusted. Most were not even expected to fulfill their routine daily chores, let alone discharge their civic duties as sons, husbands, and citizens. For example, the physical therapists Donald Kerr and Signe Brunnstrom writing in 1956 encouraged amputees to reclaim their masculinity by rejecting dependence on others and observing strict rules of self-reliance: "From the time of surgery until he has returned to a normal life in the community, the amputee is beset by many doubts and fears.... The amputee must recognize that these attitudes are based on lack of knowledge, and he must not permit them to influence his own thinking.... [T]he family [should learn] to ignore the amputation and to expect and even require the amputee to take care of himself, to share in household duties, and to participate in social activities." [36]

In this institutional climate, prostheses were regarded not only as prescriptive tools for rehabilitating amputees but also as cultural weapons with which they might defend themselves against the onslaught of social criticism or the scrutiny of their male peers.

Apparently the social emphasis put on productive labor and its relation to masculine independence made such weapons mandatory for many veterans. Even while they were manipulated as symbols of American patriotism and stalwart defenders of national values, veterans and amputees often suffered explicit discrimination from employers in both white- and blue-collar industries. According to a 1947 interview with Fred Hetzel, director of the U.S. Employment Service for Washington, DC, "during and immediately following World War I, employers were eager to help disabled men." The difference between these two postwar periods, Hetzel argued, was that "now that the labor market has tightened up, [employers] hire the physically fit applicant almost every time. They seem to want a Superman or a Tarzan—even though wartime experience showed that disabled men often turned in better work than those not handicapped."[37]

Hetzel's comments about the privileges of the able-bodied and the biases of the "tightened" labor market echoed a storyline that was published in the comic strip *Gasoline Alley* in May and June 1946. The comic ran at approximately the same moment when double amputee Harold Russell and quadruple amputee Jimmy Wilson had ascended to popular consciousness. *Gasoline Alley* tells the story of Bix, a veteran of World War II who "lost both legs in the war and has two artificial ones" and the responses of able-bodied men who are impressed and won over by the display of Bix's normalcy. In the brief narrative, Wilmer, the shop owner, protests foreman Skeezix's decision to hire Bix as a new employee on the warehouse floor. Wilmer tells Skeezix, "It's nice to help those fellows, but we've got work to turn out—lots of it!" When Wilmer hires a former sailor for the position, he is amazed to discover that he is the same double amputee Skeezix had hired the day before. The cartoon echoes the promotion of rehabilitation medicine as one of the perquisites of the postwar economy. Skeezix declares, parroting the rhetoric of medical miracles that saturated the postwar media, "Modern medicine and surgery have been doing wonders for war casualties.... [Bix] tells me he was out dancing last night!" Apparently Bix was not alone on the dance floor. In a 1946 autobiography the writer Louise Baker observed that "[a] great wave of slick stories has pounced [on] the public recently in which disabled soldiers bounce out of their beds, strap on artificial legs, and promptly dance off with pretty nurses.... [One nurse] not only affected a miraculous cure of the poor boy's complexes, she practically put blood and bones in his [prosthetic] leg."[38] By the social standards of the mid-1940s, what evidence was more reasonable assurance of an American's normal status than Darwinian competition with other males on the dance floor?

Artifacts of popular culture like *Gasoline Alley* suggest that some sectors of the public were only too aware of the harsh standards amputees were judged by. These were standardized versions of normal, heterosexual masculinity that few men, able-bodied or otherwise, could deviate from without fear of reprisal. That Bix is able to "pass" as an able-bodied, virile veteran—and is not immediately identified as a delicate or effeminate war casualty—is the comic's principal message. While watching Bix carry an enormous carton across the shop, Wilmer declares, "You sure put one over on me. I didn't suspect [Bix] wasn't perfectly *normal*." Skeezix replies, "Practically he is.... He wants to show he's as good as anybody. That makes him better."

As the *Gasoline Alley* comic demonstrates, preconceptions about amputees as maladjusted, fragile, or even neurotic were widespread and powerful. Yet such preconceptions did not just disappear at the behest of cartoonists; they significantly influenced the way prosthetics research was conducted—and consequently represented—during the 1950s. Such representations, in other words, were hardly the purview of mass culture alone. In one photograph taken by an unknown staff photographer at Walter Reed Army Hospital in March 1952, for example, a handsome young veteran amputee was depicted in a familiar able-bodied activity: enjoying a cigarette. As usual, what was at issue was not simply his vocational or domestic rehabilitation but the crucial preservation of his masculinity. Yet the dramatic lighting and crisply graduated shapes of the amputee's body, however, seem like conventions of celebrity iconography directly descended from photographers such as Cecil Beaton or George Platt Lynes. The photograph also suggests that the prosthesis will help the veteran preserve his male competence and self-reliant citizenship. Similarly, a photograph of an older veteran reading the newspaper, taken at Walter Reed in 1949, challenges the notion that all amputees were young and virile embodiments of virtuous American character and identity. Difficult to discern in the photograph, but no less poignant, are the pinup girls painted on the amputee's legs—icons more characteristic of the noses of airplanes or the backs of bomber jackets. Customizing one's legs with images of calendar girls perpetuates the tradition of proudly decorating jeeps, tanks, airplanes, and other military transport.[40] Like other objects that celebrated the scientific and technological progress of postwar culture, such photographs taken at a military hospital known for its advanced prosthetics research were self-conscious attempts to illuminate and maintain the essential gestures of masculinity.[39] These familiar icons were disseminated throughout the world—not unlike Hollywood films, modern art, swing dancing, or phonograph records in decidedly American genres—as evidence of both domestic rehabilitation policies and the enduring legacies of American male toughness and resiliency.

Images of veterans like these served double duty. First, they served as promotional materials for large rehabilitation centers like Walter Reed, advertising their progress in prosthetics research. Such consciously crafted publicity images also assured the general public that amputees suffered no loss of ability, mobility, personality, or—most important—manhood. Smoking, reading the sports section, and in Bix's case swing dancing, were glorified matter-of-factly as normal American expressions of heterosexual male behavior. In the case of this older man, perhaps the pinup girls let him identify with blue-collar workers. Looking like rugged tattoos, they may have connoted a particular mechanical aptitude or technological competence beyond merely sitting at a desk all day. The seductive lure of blue-collar accoutrements like tattoos never disappeared but in fact expanded among white-collar workers after the United States shifted from industry to a service economy in the 1960s and 1970s. To a large degree, the singular image of the happy, efficient white-collar organization man in his corporate office may have been only a triumph of postwar marketing, the genius of Madison Avenue.[41]

Building a New Workforce

The rapid development and diffusion of new prosthetic materials and technologies in the postwar period made it possible for thousands of veterans to return to their jobs or to pursue alternative careers. Engineering departments and rehabilitation centers still needed to exercise extreme care in selecting which amputees would make good candidates for receiving experimental prostheses. Clearly the United States had a surfeit of veterans eager to participate in new research programs at military and university hospitals—most notably those sponsored by the Veterans Administration and the National Research Council's Advanced Council on Artificial Limbs. But with the fate of large federally sponsored contracts on the line, doctors and administrators made a concerted effort to choose just the right applicants as research subjects. As we have already seen, many professional discussions of veterans' social and psychological stability focused on the male amputee and his work competence, an especially potent set of concerns during a period when Freudian psychoanalysis, lobotomies, and shock therapy all held enormous medical authority as solutions to the problem of the maladjusted individual. Psychologists in both military and civilian practice in the 1940s and 1950s emphasized social adjustment—what sociologist David Riesman described in his critique of the "outer-directed personality"—in endorsing manliness and self-reliance among veterans and amputees.[42] Prosthetic laboratories, it seems, were no different.

At New York University and the University of California at Los Angeles, for example, engineers routinely gave potential prosthesis wearers a battery of psychological tests, all of which assumed that amputees suffered from war-related neuroses. In 1957 amputees at the UCLA School of Medicine were given the California Test of Personality, "designed to identify and reveal the status of certain fundamental characteristics of human nature which are highly important in determining personal, social, or vocational relationships."[43] UCLA also asked potential prosthesis wearers to describe in their own words their personal concepts of "self reliance; sense of personal worth; sense of personal freedom; feeling of belonging; freedom from withdrawing tendencies; and freedom from nervous symptoms." These questions in the testing manual all fell under the ominous category "Personal Security." In 1953, clinical researchers at NYU's College of Engineering gave prospective prosthesis wearers the Ascendance-Submission Reaction Study, a psychological test developed in the late 1930s "to discover the disposition of an individual to dominate his fellows (or be dominated by them) in various face-to-face relationships of everyday life."[44] This study examined the amputee according to his "early development—home setting; conforming or non-conforming behavior; neurotic character traits; attitude to parents; siblings; friends; cheerful or gloomy childhood; position of leadership; [and] attitude toward crippling." Through these examinations, engineers who built experimental prostheses believed they could quickly estimate the amputees' psychological profiles and citizenship values, including what the UCLA examiners called the test subjects' "social standards; social skills; freedom from anti-social tendencies; family relations; occupational relations; [and] community relations."

The relationship between psychological health and ideas about citizenship in rehabilitation programs underscored the assumptions made by engineers and therapists that much more was at stake than making the amputee a productive laborer. While the language in these manuals seems at first glance to partake of the Cold War's obsession with character and conformity, the use of the prewar Ascendance-Submission Study to measure an amputee's "conforming or nonconforming behavior" or "neurotic character traits" demonstrates that the concern with the amputee's social and political orientation in relation to his rehabilitation was not entirely new. The Cold War may have normalized the use of some of this language, but the psychological dimensions of rehabilitation medicine for amputees belonged to a much older historical discourse about the care of citizens and workers under government bureaucracies and industrial management. After World War I, for instance, European social scientists like Jules Amar applied principles from management to the rehabilitation of amputees and veterans in hospitals in Paris. Their concern was the treatment of the neurotic individual in society, but in the economic depressions that followed the Great War they were equally concerned about the impact of a generation of neurotic young veterans and amputees on the financial and political vitality of their respective nations. In the United States, where the Great War ushered in a period of unprecedented economic prosperity, psychologists also helped to develop vocational training programs for veterans to meet the needs of assembly-line production and other forms of industrial labor.[45] For rehabilitation doctors and efficiency experts between the wars, making the damaged male body productive was perhaps the greatest conceptual challenge to modern industrial capitalism.

After World War II, the new possibilities offered by prosthetics research meant that rehabilitation programs could use prostheses as technological interventions to meet the social mandates of the era, especially as they reflected a new set of economic and political attitudes about the future of work in American society. In the late 1940s Norbert Wiener, the MIT mathematician and communication theorist who coined the term "cybernetics" in 1947, was commissioned to explore the social benefits of independent function by applying advanced electronics to the problem of the inefficient prosthesis.

Wiener theorized rhapsodically about "electronic control techniques to amplify pulses provided by commands from the amputee's brain."[46] In 1949 Wiener argued that engineers had the capacity to control muscle power through electrical motors attached to self-adjusting electronic feedback chains in a classic cybernetic system: "There is very little new art in connecting an electric motor to the numerical output of the machine, using electrical amplifiers to step up the power. It is even possible to imitate the kinesthetic sense of the human body, which records the position and motion of our muscles and joints, and equip the effector organs of the machine with telltales, which report back their performance in a proper form to be used by the machine."[47] Wiener's theorizing about a cybernetic-controlled prosthesis was not unprecedented. Experiments with power-assisted prostheses had begun in earnest in Germany in the late 1940s and by the mid-1950s were taken up in Britain, the Soviet Union, and the United States. Some of these included myoelectric prostheses, which used internal batteries or external amplifiers to stimulate muscles that had survived amputation, and pneumatic limbs, which were powered by small pneumatic gas canisters attached to the body. By the end of the 1950s, cybernetic control systems were considered to be in the vanguard of artificial limb research, and prosthetists and engineers in the United States saw self-contained power sources as the future of prosthetic science. Wiener later helped to design one of the earliest myoelectric arms. Using a battery-operated amplifier, it magnified existing nerve impulses into a self-regulating feedback chain, which generated enough consistent power to lift and move the arm.[48] Variously called the "Boston arm" and the "Liberty Limb," the myoelectric arm was developed in the early 1960s by Wiener in conjunction with Harvard Medical School and sponsored by the Liberty Mutual Insurance Company of Boston.[49]

Wiener's design for a cybernetic prosthesis was humanitarian in its vision, intended to rebuild the human body rather than displace or destroy it. The "Liberty Limb" was a new biomechanical model that promised self-control and self-sufficiency for individual prosthesis wearers. Reflecting the period's emphasis on self-reliant citizenship, the myoelectric prosthesis theoretically could perform independent functions using an internal power supply. For Wiener, the internal mechanism of the cybernetic prosthesis—pulleys, cylinders, and the like—echoed the postwar society's emphatic belief that medical technology could rehumanize the physical body rather than dehumanize it. In creating a group of electronically controlled, self-sustaining artificial limbs that replaced conventional prostheses, Wiener imagined a futuristic body in which applied technical expertise and cybernetic sophistication brought mobility and independence to the nonproductive citizen, who was almost always imagined as male and predominantly working class.

In retrospect, however, Wiener's vision was diluted by the politics of international scientific competition at the height of the Cold War. At the 1958 World's Fair in Brussels the USSR's pavilion of new technological breakthroughs under Soviet science featured the world's first commercially available myoelectric artificial arm. A. Y. Kobrinski and his colleagues at the Institute of Machine Technology of the USSR's Academy of Sciences and the Central Prosthetics Research Institute perfected and built the arm in the mid-1950s.[50] Meanwhile, in the United States during the same period, Wiener's experiments with cybernetic arms had bypassed the rehabilitation center completely and ultimately found their way to a very different end-user: the industrial robot. The United States exhibited the remote-controlled robot without showing its application in a myoelectric arm, let alone any medical device utilizing cybernetic technology. The result of this discrepancy between Soviet and American approaches to prosthetic technology—the former serving rehabilitation medicine, the latter serving industry—is one of the crushing ironies of postwar labor in the United States. Wiener's good-faith efforts with the principles of cybernetics, which started with the initial intention of helping amputees achieve self-sufficiency and return to work, became principles of exploitation after they were appropriated and promoted by industry, as the United States pavilion at the Brussels World's Fair demonstrated. By the mid-1960s, when they arrived en masse, robotic arms had begun to displace manual laborers in almost every facet of large-scale manufacturing and industrial production in the United States.[51]

Anxieties over the rise of complex automated processes in the workplace were not new for American workers in the 1950s. Automation had been a point of contention between labor and management since the early part of the century, beginning with Ford's assembly lines and picking up steam with the popularity of machine-made industrial objects and technocratic management styles in the 1930s.[52] The appearance of industrial robots—which worked tirelessly and without complaint on both day and night shifts and for which coffee breaks, safe working conditions, and overtime pay were nonissues—seemed like the death knell for American laborers, who saw their bodies and their status as workers as potentially obsolete. Furthermore, this new generation of industrial robots perfectly matched the new generation of managerial theories propounded by white-collar economists and business executives in the 1950s, who spoke rapturously about the new opportunities for leisure and relaxation that would be afforded to the American worker. For older workers who had experienced these so-called leisure opportunities during the Depression, as well as for younger workers and returning veterans of the recent war, the rise of industrial robots represented yet another disruptive historical force that challenged the capacity of male workers to express their masculinity through their physical bodies.

In the scheme of postwar prostheses, Wiener's "Liberty Limb" was atypical: designed as an experimental model, it did not become available commercially in the United States until the late 1960s, and then its exorbitant cost was anathema to most patients and many insurance companies. More typical were prostheses that would help allay men's work anxieties. Updated designs meant to create work opportunities were far more common than new designs meant to produce unemployment. Designer Henry Dreyfuss, for example, whose work promoted the social benefits of ergonomics, engineered and built a prosthetic hand for the Veterans Administration in the late 1940s, and the design is still in use today. One might say that Dreyfuss's work as an industrial designer for the federal government marked the perfect cohesion of prosthetics as a tool of social engineering and of Cold War science. As he declared in his 1955 manifesto *Designing for People,* "The goal in [military projects] is a contribution to morale, the intangible force that impels soldiers to have confidence and pride in their weapons and therefore in themselves and that, in the long pull, wins battles and wars." [53] Dreyfuss had many experiences adapting his design sensibility to serve military-industrial science and technology. [54] In 1942, for example, Dreyfuss contracted with the Coordinator of Information and the Office of Strategic Services to plan strategy rooms and conference rooms for the armed forces. Dreyfuss also designed Howitzer rifles and carriages for 105-millimeter guns for the army and ship habitats for the navy. Well into the 1950s his services were retained, and he designed missile launchers as well as the ergonomic interiors of the M46 and M95 tanks. Completing the collaborative symbiosis between government and industry that so marks the Cold War period, Dreyfuss served as a consultant for Chrysler's confidential missile branch from 1954 to 1956. Following the war, however, from 1948 to 1950, Dreyfuss served as a consultant to the National Research Council's Advanced Council on Artificial Limbs.

A photograph of Dreyfuss Associates' prosthetic hand created for the Veterans Administration's Human Engineering Division was published in *Designing for People.* Appearing alongside images of familiar industrial objects, such as the round Honeywell thermostat and the black Bell telephone, the photograph would have been a noticeable departure from advertisements for artificial hands—let alone feet, legs, arms, or other parts of the body—typically produced by nineteenth- and twentieth-century prosthesis manufacturers. As Stephen Mihm has argued, late nineteenth-century catalogs by esteemed limb makers such as A. A. Marks routinely included images of workingmen using their artificial arms and legs to operate threshers and other heavy farm machines. Such images demonstrated that an artificial arm in no way compromised either the worker's masculinity or his ability to earn a living. [55] As one A. A. Marks catalog declared in 1908, "The wholesome effect an [artificial] arm has on the stump, that of keeping it in a healthy and vigorous condition, protecting it from injuries, forcing it into healthful activity, together with its ornamental aspect, are sufficient reasons for wearing one, even if utility is totally ignored." [56] By contrast, the Dreyfuss hand would have been a self-conscious alternative to these photographic images and manufacturers' endorsements. It provided a "civilized" alternative to the otherwise painful and traumatic representations of amputees and prosthesis wearers that were displayed in public, especially those doing blue-collar work, such as Bix from *Gasoline Alley. Photographic depictions of* Dreyfuss's hand for above-elbow amputees showed a shiny, rounded stainless steel hook that imitated the graceful curve of elongated fingers. With its mechanics hidden tastefully by a crisp Oxford-cloth shirtsleeve and its user signing the beginning of the name *John* in beautiful longhand, the gleaming steel hand twinkles within a well lit and expertly framed composition.

Clearly, Dreyfuss was concerned with aspects of the hand that would not have provoked much interest, or comment, among prosthesis makers or amputees fifty years earlier. As Dreyfuss commented in *Designing for People,* "If 'feel' is of importance to the housewife at her ironing board, imagine how infinitely more important it is in the artificial limbs of an amputee. We learned a great deal about this in our work for the Veterans Administration. To understand the plight of the amputee, members of our staff had artificial limbs strapped to them."[57] Dreyfuss's interest in "feel" was not a conceptual category of design that was useful or even recognizable to many early manufacturers of prostheses. Even in the 1950s, the typical goal for prosthetists was to make the worker as productive and efficient as possible, while not discounting necessary comfort and daily utility. The search for some ergonomic standard of "feel" would have stimulated the interest only of an industrial designer, especially one concerned with the appearance and feel of commercial products and home and business environments. The Dreyfuss hand may have harked back to the image of a managed worker's body from the early twentieth century, but its aesthetic details were undeniably *moderne,* a product of the design-conscious mid-1950s. The Dreyfuss hand followed the objectives of an industrial designer whose goal was to package all consumer objects according to the aesthetic criteria of beauty, harmony, and use-value. After all, Dreyfuss not only designed telephones and thermostats, but also designed window displays for Marshall Field's in Chicago and Macy's in New York as well as theatrical spaces at the 1939–40 New York World's Fair. For someone of such catholic tastes, designing and representing a prosthetic hand held similar aesthetic and ergonomic challenges. Mechanical hardware must be hidden either by the stainless steel casing or by the long-sleeved shirt in order to obey Dreyfuss's own strict design injunctions: no visible screws, a single housing, no exposed seams or joints, and no distracting colors or patterns.

Dreyfuss's prosthetic hand was clearly meant to be a model of professional solidity and masculine sophistication. To whom, then, were these new Dreyfuss hands pitched? As we have seen, representations of amputees engaged in what appear to be ordinary tasks and performing as men in familiar and recognizably masculine endeavors, both individually and collectively, were an extremely important part of rehabilitation. In the creation and representation of the Dreyfuss hand, however, we see historical evidence of industrial designers and commercial photographers grappling not with the needs of factory workers or GI amputees but with the postwar period's growing desire for a new model of American masculinity. Such a hand, ideally, would accommodate a growing army of corporate white-collar workers, not to mention those blue-collar workers encouraged—or forced—to make the professional transition to a service economy.[58] For this reason, the functionalist imperative in the Dreyfuss hand might be understood as one way of normalizing and marketing able-bodied function for amputees whose professional aspirations did not include assembly-line work. This, then, was the "other" arms race of the postwar period: not the technological cum political competition with the Soviet Union but the competition between white-collar masculinity (as symbolized by the Dreyfuss hand) and that of the blue-collar worker who formerly had proved his worthiness and aptitude through the labor he accomplished after completing rehabilitation. By the 1960s, both able-bodied and disabled men who had been trained for certain types of physical labor were seen as increasingly obsolete as more and more jobs shifted from the industrial and manufacturing sector to service contexts. The uneasy relationship between the workingman and his body remained the premier site where American masculinity continued to be refashioned throughout the postwar era. This is why Dreyfuss's hand is historically so important: it offered corporate bureaucrats a vision of a white-collar hand that was compatible with the newly emerging white-collar world that would come to dominate the workscape of American cities. Indeed, the hand forming a signature of the name "John" vindicated the consumerist ethos that dominated the 1950s by demonstrating that even amputees could sign their lives away through credit debt. The Dreyfuss hand may have promised to restore anatomical function and neutralize emasculation, but perhaps it could also confer self-esteem and cultural capital. This may be why the white-collar sophistication that Dreyfuss's design team attempted to impart through both product and marketing reflected not the contents of contemporary rehabilitation manuals but those of period magazines like *Playboy* and *Esquire,* whose advertisements regularly featured high-tech appliances or multifunctional Herman Miller furniture.[59]

The arms race in prosthetics demonstrated, in material form, the shift in ideas about labor for men as well as the status of the prosthesis as a form of social engineering. It offered a proud new consumer item that reflected a profound new sense of prosperity, as predicted by the era's foremost economic theorists and carried out by service economy workers. At the end of the war, an amputated arm or leg may have provoked associations between anatomical dysfunction and a lack of reliability, sturdiness, fortitude, or commitment. But by the mid-1950s, the utterly functionalist, aesthetically integrated, and mass-produced Dreyfuss hand offered a new kind of social prestige as well as a new model of masculine labor. Many must have believed that the Dreyfuss hand would be the wave of the future. It was a whole new hand for a whole new kind of work.

Notes

1. See Walker Evans, "Labor Anonymous," *Fortune* 34, no. 5 (November 1946): 152–153.
2. James Agee and Walker Evans, *Let Us Now Praise Famous Men* (1939; New York: Houghton Mifflin, 1988.)
3. See Terry Smith, *Making the Modern: Industry, Art, and Design in America* (Chicago: University of Chicago Press, 1994). See also *Fortune: The Art of Covering Business*, ed. Daniel Okrent (Layton, UT: Gibbs Smith, 1999).
4. Evans, "Labor Anonymous," 153. In James R. Mellow's biography *Walker Evans* (New York: Basic Books, 1999), 485–504, the author posits that Evans did indeed write the text that accompanied this Fortune photo-essay.
5. For more about the transition of large American cities from industrial to service economies, see Robert Fitch, *The Assassination of New York* (New York: Verso, 1994).
6. Susan Hartmann, "Prescriptions for Penelope: Literature on Women's Obligations to Returning World War Two Veterans," *Women's Studies* (1978): 224.
7. For historical studies of amputation and prosthetics in a nineteenth-century United States context, see Lisa Herschbach, "Prosthetic Reconstructions: Making the Industry, Re-making the Body, Modelling the Nation," *History Workshop Journal* 44 (Autumn 1997): 22–57. On prosthetics and amputation with reference to British society after World War I, see Seth Koven, "Remembering and Dismemberment: Crippled Children, Wounded Soldiers, and the Great War in Britain," *American Historical Review* 99, no.4 (October 1994): 1167–1202. For French and German responses to soldiers after World War I, see Roxanne Panchasi, "Reconstruction: Prosthetics and the Rehabilitation of the Male Body in World War I France," *differences: A Journal of Feminist Cultural Studies* 7, no.3 (1995): 109–140; Anson Rabinbach, *The Human Motor: Energy, Fatigue, and the Origins of Modernity* (Berkeley: University of California Press, 1990); and Heather Perry, "Re-Arming the Disabled Veteran: Artificially Rebuilding State and Society in World War One Germany," in *Artificial Parts, Practical Lives: Modern Histories of Prosthetics*, ed. Katherine Ort, David Serlin, and Stephen Mihm [New York: New York University Press, 2002), 60–95.
8. See Celia Lury, *Prosthetic Culture: Photography, Memory, and Identity* (New York: Routledge, 1998), and Gabriel Brahm, Jr. and Mark Driscoll, eds., *Prosthetic Territories: Politics and Hypertechnologies* (Boulder, CO: Westview Press, 1996).
9. Kathleen Woodward, "From Virtual Cyborgs to Biological Time Bombs: Technocriticsm and the Material Body," in *Culture on the Brink: Ideologies of Technology*, ed. Gretchen Bender and Timothy Druckery (Seattle: Bay Press, 1994), 50.
10. See Glenn Gritzer and Arnold Arluke, *The Making of Rehabilitation: A Political Economy of Medical Specialization, 1890–1980* (Berkeley: University of California Press, 1985), and Jafi Alyssa Lipson, "Celluloid Therapy: Rehabilitating Veteran Amputees and American Society through Film in the 1940s" (unpublished senior thesis, Harvard University, 1995), author's collection.
11. More than half a century after the film's release, *The Enchanted Cottage* is still seen as a cautionary tale about narcissism, which reduces the content of the film to its most ahistorical form. According to one online movie-review service, the film is about "two people [who] are thrown together and find love in their mutual unhappiness. Sensitive, touching romantic drama."
12. See Arthur Wing Pinero, *The Enchanted Cottage: A Fable in Three Acts* (Boston: Baker, 1925).
13. For contemporary examples of this literature, see United States Veterans Administration, *Manual of Advisement and Guidance* (Washington, DC: Government Printing Office, 1945), and James Bedford, *The Veteran and His Future Job: A Guide-Book for the Veteran* (Los Angeles: Society for Occupational Research, 1946).
14. David Gerber, "Anger and Affability: The Rise and Representation of a Repertory of Self-Presentation Skills in a World War II Disabled Veteran," *Journal of Social History* 27 (Fall 1993), 6. For more about the film, see Gerber, "Heroes and Misfits: The Troubled Social Reintegration of Disabled Veterans in The Best Years of Our Lives," *American Quarterly* 46, no.4 (December 1994): 545–74.
15. See George Roeder Jr., *The Censored War: American Visual Experience during World War Two* (New Haven: Yale UP, 1993).

16. "50,000 Mark Passed in Drive to Aid Army Multiple Amputee," *Washington Evening Star* (August 30, 1945).

17. See photograph of Wilson and Myerson published in the *Washington Times-Herald*, (January 31, 1946). See also material on Wilson in Bess Furman's *Progress in Prosthetics* (Washington, D.C.: National Science Foundation, 1962).

18. Arthur Edison, "Iwo Jima Vet First to Get Amputee Car," *New York Times-Herald*, (September 5, 1946).

19. *The Goodwill*, Washington, DC edition, 7, no.2 (Fall 1945); 1; capitals in original.

20. Newspaper clippings from the *Washington Evening Star*, probably 1945 or 1946. From the scrapbooks of the Donald Canham Collection, Otis Historical Archives, Armed Forces Institute of Pathology, Walter Reed Army Medical Center.

21. See Tom Engelhardt, *The End of Victory Culture: Cold War America and the Disillusioning of a Generation* (New York: Basic Books, 1995).

22. See Matthew Naythons, *The Face of Mercy: A Photographic History of Medicine at War* (New York: Random House, 1993)

23. Congressional Record, 1951, 5579 quoted in David M. Oshinsky, *A Conspiracy So Immense: The World of Joe McCarthy* (New York: Free Press, 1983), 196.

24. See Alan Trachtenberg, *Reading American Photographs: Images as History from Matthew Brady to Walker Evans* (New York: Noonday, 1989). See also Michael Rhode, *Index to Photographs of Surgical Cases and Specimens and Surgical Photographs*, 3rd ed. (Washington, D.C.: Otis Historical Archives, Armed Forces Institute of Pathology, Walter Reed Army Medical Center, 1996).

25. Kathy Newman, "Wounds and Wounding in the American Civil War: A Visual History," *Yale Journal of Criticism* 6, no.2 (1993): 63–86.

26. For examples of scholarship in this area, see Leslie Fielder, *Freaks: Myths and Images of the Secret Self* (New York: Simon and Schuster, 1978); Robert Bogdan, *Freak Show: Presenting Human Oddities for Amusement and Profit* (Chicago: University of Chicago Press, 1987); Rosemarie Garland Thomson, ed., *Freakery: Cultural Spectacles of the Extraordinary Body* (New York: New York University Press, 1996; and Rosamond Purcell, *Special Cases: Natural Anomalies and Historical Monsters* (San Francisco: Chronicle Books, 1997).

27. Detlev W. Bronk, foreword to *Human Limbs and Their Substitutes* (1954; New York: Hafner, 1968), iv.

28. Wilfred Lynch, *Implants: Reconstructing the Human Body* (New York: Van Nostrand Reinhold, 1982), I.

29. For more about the uses of new products developed in tandem with postwar materials science, see *Proceedings of the International Symposium on the Application of Automatic Control in Prosthetic Design* (Belgrade, Yugoslavia, 1962).

30. Cornelia Ball, "New Artificial Limbs to Be Power-Driven," *Washington Daily News*, August 27, 1945.

31. All material on Milton Wirtz and the Naval Graduate Dental Center is from the collection of the Division of Science, Medicine, and Society, National Museum of American History, Smithsonian Institution, Washington, DC.

32. Miles Anderson and Raymond Sollars, *Manual of Above-Knee Prosthesis for Physicians and Therapists* (Los Angeles: University of California School of Medicine Program, 1957), 40.

33. Army psychologists who feared that one bad apple could spoil the whole bunch taunted recruits with effeminate mannerisms and "code words" perceived to be the performative gestures and underground lingo of a vast homosexual conspiracy. The military also administered urine tests to determine whether soldiers' bodies had appropriate levels of testosterone and rejected those with too much estrogen. See "Homosexuals in Uniform," *Newsweek* (June 9, 1947), reprinted in Larry Gross and James Woods, eds., *The Lesbian and Gay Reader in Media, Society, and Politics* (New York: Columbia University Press, 1999), 78. See also Christina Jarvis, *The Male Body at War: American Masculinity During World War II* (De Kalb, IL: Northern Illinois University Press, 2004).

34. Alan Bérubé, *Coming Out Under Fire: The History of Gay Men and Women in World War Two* (New York: Free Press, 1990).

35. New York University College of Engineering Research Division, *The Function and Psychological Suitability of an Experimental Hydraulic Prosthesis for Above-the Knee Amputees*, National Research Council Report 115.15 (New York: NYU/Advisory Committee on Artificial Limbs, 1953), 48; emphasis added

36. Donald Kerr and Signe Brunnstrom, *Training of the Lower Extremity Amputee* (Springfield, IL: C.C. Thomas, 1956), vii, 3–4

37. Quoted in Steven Hall, "Amputees Find Employers Want Only Supermen," *Washington Daily News*, October 2, 1947.

38. Louise Maxwell Baker, *Out on a Limb* (New York: McGraw-Hill, 1946), 37.

39. See, for example Serge Guibault, *How New York Stole the Idea of Modern Art* (Chicago: University of Chicago Press, 1983), or Robert Haddow's discussion of the circulation of American objects during the Cold War in *Pavilions of Plenty: Exhibiting American Culture Abroad in the 1950s* (Washington, DC: Smithsonian Institution Press, 1997).

40. For an interesting discussion of pinup girls as domestic politics, see Robert B. Westbrook, "I Want a Girl, Just Like the Girl, That Married Harry James': American Women and the Problem of Political Obligation in World War Two," *American Quarterly* 42 (December 1990): 587–614.

41. See Barbara Ehrenreich, *The Hearts of Men: American Dreams and the Flight from Commitment* (Garden City, NY: Anchor Books, 1983). See also Angel Kwolek-Folland, "Gender, Self, and Work in the Life Insurance Industry, 1880-1930," in *Work Engendered: Toward a New History of American Labor*, ed. Ava Baron (Ithaca, NY: Cornell University Press, 1991). For historical background on the image of the white-collar corporate organization man, see C. Wright Mills, *White Col-*

lar (New York: Oxford University Press, 1951), and William H. Whyte, *The Organization Man* (New York: Simon and Schuster, 1954).

42. See Ellen Herman, *The Romance of American Psychology: Political Culture in the Age of Experts* (Berkeley: University of California Press, 1994), and David Riesman, Nathan Glazer and Reuel Denney, *The Lonely Crowd: A Study of the Changing American Character* (1950; Garden City, NY: Doubleday, 1953).

43. Anderson and Sollars, *Manual of Above-Knee Prosthesis for Physicians and Therapists*, 20.

44. New York University College of Engineering Research Division, *Function and Psychological Suitability of an Experimental Hydraulic Prosthesis for Above-the-Knee Amputees*, 21–22.

45. See Elspeth Brown, "The Prosthetics of Management: Motion Study, Photography, and the Industrialized Body in World War I America," in Ott et al, *Artificial Parts, Practical Lives*, 179–219. See also Rabinbach, *Human Motor*, esp. 280–88, and Michael Adas, *Machines as the Measure of Men: Science, Technology, and Ideologies of Western Dominance* (Ithaca, NY: Cornell University Press, 1989).

46. Ralph Parkman, *The Cybernetic Society* (New York: Pergamon Press, 1972), 215.

47. Norbert Wiener, "The Second Industrial Revolution and the New Concept of the Machine" (manuscript dated Sept. 13, 1949), from folder 619, Norbert Wiener Papers, Institute Archives, Massachusetts Institute of Technology.

48. For further exploration see Peter Galison's important essay "The Ontology of the Enemy: Norbert Wiener and the Cybernetic Vision," *Critical Inquiry* 21 (Autumn 1994): 228–66.

49. Sandra Tanenbaum, *Engineering Disability: Public Policy and Compensatory Technology* (Philadelphia: Temple UP, 1986), 34. For further elaboration on Weiner's impact on the development of cybernetics, see Steve Heims, *Constructing a Social Science for Postwar America: The Cybernetics Group, 1946–1953* (Cambridge: MIT Press, 1993); Evelyn Fox Keller, *Refiguring Life: Metaphors of Twentieth-Century Biology* (New York: Columbia University Press, 1995), esp. 81–118; and Lily E. Kay, "Cybernetics, Information, Life: The Emergence of Scriptural Representations of Heredity," *Configurations* 5, no.1 (Winter 1997): 23–91.

50. For further information about the history of the Soviet arm, see A.Y. Kobrinski, "Utilization of Biocurrents for Control Purposes," Report of the USSR Academy of Science, Department of Technical Sciences Energetics, and Automation 3 (1959), folder 812, Norbert Wiener Papers, Institute Archives, Massachusetts Institute of Technology.

51. Parkman, *Cybernetic Society*, 254.

52. See Amy Sue Bix, *Inventing Ourselves Out of Jobs? The Debate about Technology and Work in the Twentieth Century* (Baltimore: Johns Hopkins University Press, 2000)

53. Henry Dreyfuss, *Designing for People* (New York: Simon and Schuster, 1955), 160.

54. All information about Dreyfuss Associates is taken from chronologies in Dreyfuss's "Brown Books" microfiche, Henry Dreyfuss Papers, Henry Dreyfuss Memorial Study Center, Cooper-Hewitt National Museum of Design, New York City.

55. See Stephen Mihm, " 'A Limb Which Shall Be Presentable in Polite Society': Prosthetic Technologies in the Nineteenth Century," in Ott et al, *Artificial Parts, Practical Lives*, 220–35.

56. A.A. Marks annual merchandise catalog (New York, 1908), 226. From the collection of Katherine Ott.

57. Dreyfuss, *Designing for People*, 29.

58. For more about disruptions of gender normativity (and their consequences) in the late 1940s and early 1950s, see, for example, Richard Corber, *In the Name of National Security: Hitchcock, Homophobia, and the Political Construction of Gender in Postwar America* (Durham, NC: Duke University Press, 1993), and Alan Nadel, *Containment Culture: American Narratives, Postmodernism, and the Atomic Age* (Durham, NC: Duke University Press, 1995), esp. 117–54.

59. See "Playboy's Penthouse Apartment" (1956), reprinted in Joel Sanders, ed. *Stud: Architectures of Masculinity* (New York: Princeton Architectural Press, 1995), 54–65.

5

(Re)Writing the Genetic Body-Text
Disability, Textuality, and the Human Genome Project

James C. Wilson

If this is the Book of Life, we should not settle for a rough draft over the long term but should remain committed to producing a final, highly accurate version.
—Francis S. Collins, "Shattuck Lecture: Medical and Societal Consequences of the Human Genome Project"

So this book...maps its particular investigations along the double helix of a work's reception history and its production history. But the work of knowing demands that the map be followed into the textual field, where "the meaning of the texts" will appear as a set of concrete and always changing conditions; because the meaning is in the use, and textuality is a social condition of various times, places, and persons.
—Jerome J. McGann, *The Textual Condition*

When Francis S. Collins, the director of the National Human Genome Research Institute, delivered the 109th Shattuck Lecture at the 1999 meeting of the Massachusetts Medical Society, he likened the sequencing of the human genome to "the great expeditions—those of Lewis and Clark, Sir Edmund Hillary, and even Neil Armstrong." The search for what Collins called the "complete set of genetic instructions of the human being" was undertaken by scientists in order to "map the human genetic terrain, knowing it would lead them to previously unimaginable insights, and from there to the common good" (28). It is this concept of the genetic body-text—and the implications of the resulting construction of disability as textual error—that I wish to examine.

First, a few definitions for those readers who are not immediately familiar with genetics. A genome refers to the complete DNA code of a particular organism or species. DNA molecules are found in the nucleus of every cell, carried on chemical structures known as chromosomes. Sequencing the human genome involves identifying its roughly three billion pairs of nucleotide bases and then storing this information in computer databases. Mapping involves location analysis meant to establish linkage. In one sense linkage refers to the location of a particular gene in relation to other genes, but it can also mean correlation with a phenotype (i.e., a gene "linked" to Parkinson's). Biotechnology and pharmaceutical companies hope to make billions of dollars as the function of more and more genes is established and feasible treatment options for harmful mutations within them are developed.[1]

The expedition to sequence and map the human genome has evolved into a two-way race between the Human Genome Project and Celera Genomics, a private biotechnology company located in Rockville, Maryland. The two competitors made a joint announcement in June 2000, issuing a joint report and releasing a "working draft" of the genome. Celera intends to finish its sequence of the human genome by December 2001 (or earlier) and then to patent sequences auspicious for therapeutic development.[2] To compete with Celera, the Human Genome Project will finish computing the entire sequence by the end of 2003. The Human Genome Project is an international consortium that includes the U.S. National Institutes of Health and Department of Energy, the Wellcome Trust of London, and ten pharmaceutical companies. In contrast to Celera's for-profit approach, the Human Genome

Project has adopted a policy of releasing data every twenty-four hours to a free, publicly accessible database called GenBank.[3]

Sequencing the human genome was proclaimed to be "the single most important project in biology and the biomedical sciences—one that will permanently change biology and medicine" by members of the National Institutes of Health and Department of Energy planning groups in their "New Goals for the U.S. Human Genome Project: 1998–2003."[4] The transition to "sequence-based" biology, they announced, will aid in the development of "highly accurate DNA-based medical diagnostics and therapeutics" (Collins et al., 682). Francis S. Collins concluded his "Shattuck Lecture," subtitled "Medical and Societal Consequences of the Human Genome Project," by declaring that the project's goal was to "uncover the hereditary factors in virtually every disease" so as to make that information available for the prevention and cure of those diseases (36). Likewise, the Human Genome Project's Web page proclaims: "The ultimate goal is to use this information to develop new ways to treat, cure, or even prevent the thousands of diseases that afflict humankind." The dozens of news and research articles linked to the Human Genome Project's Web page contain repeated references to "defective genes" and "genetic mistakes."[5] Thus the stated purpose, the very promise of genome sequencing and mapping, is to "correct" errors in the genetic "instruction book" that result in disease and disability. Indeed, this promise of genetic-based medicine has enabled those involved in genetic research to successfully promote their work in the public arena and solicit enormous subsidies from the U.S. Congress (more on this later). The allied fields of genetics and molecular biology are therefore in the process of constructing a model of disability as flawed genetic text in need of rewriting.

In the remainder of this article I will argue that the concept of (re)writing the genetic body-text (in addition to being simplistic and misleading) reinforces our culture's negative constructions of disability and creates a "genetic Other." In contrast, I will suggest that a more realistic understanding of genetics as difference supports the model of disability theorized by disability studies.[6]

(Re)Writing the Genetic Body-Text

Genome sequencing—or genomics—has created the new scientific field of bioinformatics. Genomes are sequenced by high-speed robotic sequencing machines; the resulting information is transformed into an alphabetical pattern of symbols for DNA subunits called bases (C, T, A, G),[7] which are stored as digital information in computer databases. This digital information is accessible on the Internet (at sites like GenBank) to anyone who has a computer. Digitalization/alphabetization of the genetic body-text has fostered the much used analogy of DNA as a molecular language where the "letters" are bases, the "words" are genes, and the "book" is the complete genome.[8] Scientists, science writers, and science journalists frequently use this analogy to explain genomics to lay audiences. In this analogy genetics becomes textuality, and the human genome becomes the "Book of Life." Scientific journals, as well as the mass media, borrow the terminology of textual criticism, editing, and computer science as a way of making genetics comprehensible—to explain the mechanism by which DNA participates in the production of the proteins involved in all biological activities.[9]

Implicit in this textual analogy is the fiction of the standard(ized) body-text. Donna J. Haraway has referred to the sequencing of the human genome as an "act of canonization," the production of a "standard reference work...through which human diversity and its pathologies could be tamed in the exhaustive code kept by a national or international genetic bureau of standards" (215). The logic here suggests that any deviation from this authoritative genetic script results in a flawed and thus corrupted text. One recent example of this usage is "Repairing the Genome's Spelling Mistakes" by science writer Trisha Gura in *Science*. The article begins: "On the computer, correcting spelling errors takes nothing but a quick keystroke or two. Now, researchers are trying to harness the cell's own spell-check program—its DNA repair machinery—to tackle a much more difficult problem: fixing errors in the flawed genes that cause such hereditary diseases as sickle cell anemia and cystic fibrosis" (316).

Thus disease/disability is cast as textual irregularity, and those in the biomedical community become editors who attempt to amend, delete, and correct the defective texts of disabled bodies.

However, the concept of a single, authoritative text—now mostly outdated in the humanities—poses as many problems for genome sequencers as it does for textual editors. To begin with, the Human Genome Project and Celera Genomics are both constructing a hypothetical DNA sequence by assembling multiple DNA fragments into a complete genome. This "consensus" DNA sequence (even if only a statistical generalization) will be, like all composites, a fiction. Partly in response to this issue, the Human Genome Diversity Project was formed in 1993 to "explore the full range of genome diversity within the human family," according to its Web page. Stressing the importance of understanding genetic diversity, the Human Genome Diversity Project warns: "Without this Project, science will characterize 'the' human genome, with its historical and medical implications, largely in terms of what is known from a small sample of people of European origin."[10] In actuality, there is no prototypical genetic script by which to measure or evaluate all others. The notion of the "correct" genetic text resembles that of the "unitary text of modern scholarship," which hypertext theorizer George P. Landow characterizes as a "bizarrely fictional idealization" (66).

Jerome J. McGann's work in textual criticism is relevant here and can help identify the problems inherent in creating a "correct" genetic text. McGann argues that "textuality is a social condition" (1991, 16), and thus the textual condition is one of indeterminacy. "Instability is an essential feature of the text in process" (94), McGann writes, arguing that "no single 'text' of a particular work…can be imagined or hypothesized as the 'correct' one" (62). Instead, texts are produced and reproduced in a process defined by multiplicity, that is, a process that results in different texts with different intentionalities that reflect particular social and institutional conditions. All texts, McGann explains, are social products, mediated by "determinate sociohistorical conditions" (9). And perhaps most important for the purposes of this article, the "meaning" of a text is in its use.

Like McGann's literary text and Landow's hypertext, no unitary genetic script exists that can be considered definitive. "The Human Genome Project is founded upon a fallacy," writes Matt Ridley in *Genome: The Autobiography of a Species in 23 Chapters*. "There is no such thing as 'the human genome.' Neither in space nor in time can such a definitive object be defined.… Variation is an inherent and integral part of the human—or indeed any—genome" (145). No two human genomes are or can ever be alike: all exhibit mutations, deletions, and other genetic variants (beyond having different alleles for the same gene). Not only is genetic variation (in the larger sense) the norm, these variations are never fixed, but always in the process of becoming. Genomes are dynamic, constantly evolving over time, shaped by both internal and external factors (such as infectious disease, which I will discuss later). Even when mutations occur, many of them are gradually purged by genetic drift, random change (Ridley). Thus, in the final analysis, arguments that posit a correct genetic script are ultimately teleological: they imply a kind of evolutionary "final intention" that recalls the concept of authorial final intention that has so troubled modern textual scholars. As McGann, and other textual critics, has shown, the theory (McGann calls it an "ideology") of "final intentions' is "a deeply problematic concept" (1983, 68).

Though molecular genetics continues to detect genome variations, writes Lois Wingerson in *Unnatural Selection: The Promise and the Power of Human Gene Research,* "it helps to remember that in many cases it is our environment and often simply our society that defines these variations as 'disorders'" (332). I am not denying, and neither is Wingerson, that some genetic mutations (for example) can be deleterious; clearly they can. Rather, my quarrel here is with the simplistic construction of normal versus abnormal genomes and the implication of that textual fiction for people with disabilities. The Human Genome Project's Web page illustrates this construction of normality. Here we find (a typical example) that DNA testing "involves comparing the sequence of DNA bases in a patient's gene to a normal version of the gene."[11] However, since genomes are constantly changing, a normal genome is an impossibility; that would be like saying that there is a normal course of evolution.

If the Human Genome Project does indeed have the potential to "permanently change biology and medicine," as Francis S. Collins and many others in the biomedical community have argued, it also has the potential to permanently stigmatize disability as the genetic Other. To understand this danger we need to recognize that the meaning of genetic medicine is constructed by the intersection of genetic codes and social codes.

Genohype and the Myth of the All-Powerful Gene

The Human Genome Project has engendered what Neil A. Holtzman, of Genetics and Public Policy Studies at Johns Hopkins Medical Institutions, calls "genohype." The genohype can at times obscure the fact that cultural meanings are automatically coded into words like "genes" and "inherited traits." Indeed, such terms, when manipulated and proliferated by the mass media, lead to the popular assumption that genetics represents the fundamental essence, the inescapable fate of a person. This ideological baggage, Celeste Michelle Condit argues, "encourage[s] an asocial biological determinism and discriminatory attitudes with regard to both class and disability" ("Character," 178). Condit and many other critics believe that this biological/genetic determinism is inaccurate and misleading.[12]

Here it might be helpful to take a closer look at the all-powerful gene. It is important to remember that genes are conceptual as well as physical, referring to functional segments of DNA. (Up to 90 percent of human DNA is—apparently—nonfunctional and therefore categorized as "junk" DNA.)[13] The DNA segments designated as genes are functional in that they participate in the manufacture of protein by coding the order of the amino acids used to assemble the proteins. Often, scientists as well as science writers and journalists will construct a hierarchical model of this process with the gene at the top and the many other factors involved at the bottom. The active verbs most often used to describe what genes do clearly reveal this bias: genes are said to "control," to "program," to "determine," to "encode" proteins. Consider this typical example from "Gene Therapy's Focus Shifts from Rare Illnesses" by *New York Times* science journalist Andrew Pollack: "The idea is simple and eloquent. Many inherited diseases are caused by a *faulty* gene, which makes the body unable to produce some essential protein or enzyme" (my italics). Or consider this variation that relies on the familiar but awkward trope of "genes gone bad" by Emma Ross of the Associated Press: "Genes can promote or cause disease when they don't work *properly.* Some illnesses linked to genes gone bad include cancer, arthritis, diabetes, high blood pressure, Alzheimer's and multiple sclerosis" (A11, my italics). Even the Human Genome Project's Web page states: "The successes of the Human Genome Project (HGP) have even enabled researchers to pinpoint errors in genes—the smallest units of heredity—that cause or contribute to disease."[14]

How does this hierarchical model of protein production serve the biomedical community? For one thing, it makes public relations, as well as lobbying and fund-raising, easier when scientists can point to a single gene as the culprit in the production of a certain protein, linked to diabetes or breast cancer, for example. With adequate funding, so the suggestion goes, biomedical editors can rewrite this and other flawed genes that produce disease and disability so as to produce a genetically altered—and approved—text.

In actuality, other factors participate in the formation of proteins, including ribosomes, messenger RNA (mRNA), transfer RNA (tRNA), and amino acids, as well as external factors such as environmental stresses like viruses or toxins.[15] Making the situation even more complicated, some traits are polygenic (that is, they involve multiple genes). Moreover, gene expression is dynamic (meaning that in a matter of minutes genes can be switched on and off).

"We must remember that genetic functions are embedded in complex networks of biological reactions and social and economic relationships," write Ruth Hubbard and Elijah Wald in *Exploding the Gene Myth* (12). Harvard biologist Richard Lewontin calls it "bad biology" to separate genes from their environment. In his recent *The Triple Helix: Gene, Organism, and Environment*, he argues: "If we had the complete DNA sequence of an organism and unlimited computational power, we could not compute the organism, because the organism does not compute itself from its genes." He goes on to explain that "the ontogeny of an organism is the consequence of a unique interaction between the genes it carries, the temporal sequence of external environments through which it passes during its life, and random events of molecular interactions within individual cells" (17–18).

Matt Ridley examines some of the environmental factors that have shaped (and continue to shape) the human genome, including infectious disease. The great epidemic diseases of the past (such as plague, measles, smallpox, typhoid, and malaria) all left their imprint on the human genome.[16] Mutations that granted resistance to these infectious diseases thrived but in turn created a susceptibility to other disorders (such as sickle cell anemia, for example). Ridley also discusses the emerging field of "psychoneuroimmunology," which studies the link between the mind, the body, the immune system, and the genome. "The mind drives the body, which drives the genome," Ridley writes (157). All of these factors prompt Ridley to conclude: "The genome that we decipher in this generation is but a snapshot of an ever-changing document. There is no definitive edition" (146).

The point here is that genes do not act alone but participate in an integrated network of systems: biological, social, psychological, environmental, etc. Though more accurate, the integrated network model of DNA transcription poses problems to science writers and journalists eager to employ pat phrases like "genes gone bad" to relay complex information to their audiences. The integrated network model also complicates fund-raising and public relations for the scientific community. As academics know all too well, it is not so easy to get multimillion-dollar grants to investigate environmental or social systems.

Geneticizing Disability

As I begin my final section, let me just say that I am not opposed to genetic medicine. It would be absurd for those of us in the disability community to argue against genetic research or medical technology. Indeed, many people who have experienced disability are alive today because of medical technology (myself included) and are understandably grateful for any research that promises to improve the lives of the disabled. My concern here is that genomics, as the field is currently constituted and presented to the public, reinforces the social stigma attached to disability.[17] Indeed, as we have seen, the genetic model of disability as defective or corrupted text reduces people with disabilities to the level of spelling mistakes, typographical errors that need to be eliminated by genetic editors. Feminist philosopher of science Sandra Harding reminds us that science is not value-free and that its technologies participate in the "translation of social agendas into technological ones" (37). Unfortunately, many of the new technologies associated with genomics—such as genetic tests and genetic screening—raise the specter of an old social agenda that is still very much a part of medical science's professional and public discourse: eugenics.[18] In fact, philosopher Philip Kitcher has referred to genetic screening as "laissez-fair eugenics."

Underwriting the model of disability as flawed genetic text is the binary construction of normal versus abnormal. The tyranny of the norm goes back at least as far as Aristotle, whose taxonomies provide the foundation of Western intellectual tradition. Aristotle established binary opposites—normal versus abnormal—in discursive realms that encompassed poetics, rhetoric, ethics, politics, as well as the natural sciences.[19] In "Constructing Normalcy: The Bell Curve, the Novel, and the Invention of the Disabled Body in the Nineteenth Century," Lennard J. Davis traces the evolution of the norm from a concept to an ideology of human perfectibility, as measured and created by statistics, eugenics, the bell curve, and intelligence tests:

> The concept of a norm, unlike that of an ideal, implies that the majority of the population must or should somehow be part of the norm. The norm pins down that majority of the population that falls under the arch of the standard bell-shaped curve. This curve, the graph of an exponential function, that

was known variously as the astronomer's "error law," the "normal distribution," the "Gaussian density function," or simply "the bell curve," became in its own way a symbol of the tyranny of the norm. Any bell curve will always have at its extremities those characteristics that deviate from the norm. (13)

The binary construction of normal versus abnormal is equally prevalent in contemporary biomedical discourse (as we have seen previously in an example from the HGP Web page). Consider another recent example from *Science,* where Esmail D. Zanjani and W. French Anderson write in "Prospects for in Utero Human Gene Therapy": "For the neurologic genetic diseases (such as Tay-Sachs, Niemann-Pick, Lesch-Nyhan, Sandhoff, Leigh, many leukodystrophies, generalized gangliosidosis) that appear to produce irreversible damage during gestation, treatment before birth (perhaps early in pregnancy) may be required to allow the birth of a normal baby" (2084). The point here is that this binary construction masks a social hierarchy (with those who are "abnormal" at the bottom) and therefore reinforces the stigma attached to disability. Sometimes the language itself reinforces this social stigma, as in the case of science writer Trisha Gura's "Gene Defect Linked to Rett Syndrome," a report on the gene "at fault in Rett Syndrome, which afflicts at least one in 10,000 girls." "Exactly how the defect leads to the neurological decline of the afflicted girls has yet to be deciphered" (27), Gura admits, but her use of the word "afflicted," with its biblical implications of divine punishment for sin, suggests that those who have Rett syndrome are somehow deserving of their condition.[20] This newly defined category of genetically afflicted provides a clear example of the interconnection of medical and social codes, here equally complicit in stigmatizing disability.

The attempt to geneticize disability relates to what sociologist Troy Duster calls a "'drift' toward greater receptivity to genetic explanation for an increasing variety of human behaviors" (119). These behaviors include violence, homosexuality, alcoholism, criminality, polygamy, and other behaviors considered socially deviant by the dominant culture. The danger, of course, is that as more genes are mapped, sequenced, and patented, new variations in the genetic script will be identified that will stigmatize still other behaviors and conditions. As Hubbard and Wald remark, rather sarcastically, "As long as every deviation... is considered 'abnormal,' physicians, geneticists, and the biotechnology companies will not run out of customers" (71).

And, I might add, the Human Genome Project will not run out of funding. It is especially troubling to me that so much of the National Institutes of Health's research and development funding goes to genetic research and so little to directly help those who live with the diseases and impairments that the Human Genome Project claims to be attempting to remediate. For example, in 1996, the last year for which I have figures, the National Institutes of Health allocated $200 million to the Human Genome Project, while providing only $1,410,925 for AIDS research, $381,880 for breast cancer research, and $111,479 for schizophrenia research.[21] Admittedly, there are other sources of government funding for this research, such as the National Science Foundation. Nevertheless, the numbers speak for themselves about NIH priorities.

The biomedical community's success in fund-raising has come at the expense of people with disabilities in yet another way. Scientists actively participate in the creation of the "specter" of disability, which they then exploit for public relations purposes. This specter, which preys on the public's fear of disease and disability, allows scientists to justify their biomedical projects and generate research and development funding. In this bogeyman representation, disability becomes not only a personal tragedy but a public burden that costs taxpayers excessively. One sees the disability-as-burden rhetoric used repeatedly in scientific discourse and public relations materials. Consider a recent example from the *New England Journal of Medicine,* taken from a review article on "Neural-Tube Defects." The authors, all associated with the National Center for Environmental Health at the Centers for Disease Control and Prevention, review current strategies to prevent neural-tube defects such as spina bifida. In a section entitled "The Burden of Disease," the authors write:

> In addition to the emotional cost of spina bifida, the estimated monetary cost is staggering. In the
> United States alone, the total cost of spina bifida over a lifetime (the direct costs of medical, develop-

mental, and educational services and the indirect costs associated with morbidity and mortality, in 1992 dollars) for affected infants born in 1988 was almost $500 million, or $294,000 for each infant. (Botto et al., 1511)

Once again, I am not arguing against research that might someday prevent at least some spina bifidas; rather, I am pointing out that the rhetoric employed by much of this literature casts people born with these conditions as "burdens." In fact, as the authors of this article admit, neural-tube defects have been recognized since antiquity and are quite common, occurring in 1 of every 1,000 pregnancies (1509). That is, neural-tube defects are (and have always been) a regularly occurring—yes, normal—part of human variation. Perhaps the focus should be not on how to eliminate, but instead on how to accommodate, variation. Rhetoric that casts disability as burden stigmatizes people with disabilities and makes this accommodation much more difficult.

Genomics has enormous potential to advance the understanding of human diversity. We need to remember that genetics *is* variation, and that variation is not only healthy but essential for the survival of a species. Indeed, evolution could not work without genetic diversity. Stephen Jay Gould's analysis of evolution, marked by what he calls "chaos and contingency," comes to mind. Webs of life and anatomical diversity "are so intricate, so imbued with random and chaotic elements, so unrepeatable in encompassing such a multitude of unique (and uniquely interacting) objects, that standard models of simple prediction and replication do not apply" (1994, 85).[22] Any standard biology textbook will instill in its readers an appreciation of the beauty of genetic diversity: the diversity of recombination, spontaneous mutation, speciation, gene expression, and so on. As Lois Wingerson concludes, "If genetics leads us anywhere, it leads us not toward purity but toward a new understanding of variation" (338). The reality is enormous genetic heterogeneity.

If genomics, both the science and the industry, were to more effectively emphasize the normality of variation, the fact that human variation is a continuous spectrum, then surely there would be a better understanding and acceptance of disability. In turn, this acceptance could result in a commitment to accommodation rather than erasure. With its vast resources the Human Genome Project has the potential—and, I would argue, the responsibility—to further this process. And yet, to date, the opposite has happened: the Human Genome Project has pathologized disability and created the genetic Other. Here it is important to note that geneticizing disability is hardly disinterested. Constructing disability as internal genetic mistakes (rather than lack of social accommodation, as disability studies argues) allows private biotechnology companies to develop genetic tests and medicines that turn disability into opportunities for private profit while at the same time limiting public discourse of social responsibility and accommodation.

As Sandra Harding points out, "the sciences generate information that is used to produce technologies and applications that are not morally and politically neutral" (37). Thus the technologies and applications produced by sequencing the human genome raise profound moral and political issues. We should understand that genomics involves more than just compiling databases; it stands to alter the material conditions and shape the lives of the disabled in countless, concrete ways.

Notes

1. As early as 1995, over fifty biotechnology companies were developing or providing tests to diagnose genetic disorders or predict the risk of their occurrence. See Holtzman.
2. As of October 1999, Celera had filed for 6,500 provisional patents that would give it and its client drug companies—Amgen, Novartis, and Pharmacia & Upjohn—a year to decide which genes they would pursue in their search for genetic tests and genetic medicine.
3. At http://www.ncbi.nlm.nih.gov.
4. The planning groups included Francis S. Collins and Elke Jordan from the National Human Genome Research Institute and Ari Patrinos from the Office of Biological and Environmental Research at the Department of Energy.
5. At http://www.ornl.gov/TechResources/Human_Genome/resource/medicine.html.

6. The field of disability studies emerged in the early 1990s, drawing from other interdisciplinary studies (such as feminism and cultural studies) amid the interest in identity issues growing out of postmodern inquiries into subjectivity. Both a studies area and an approach, what Simi Linton calls "a location and a means to think critically about disability" (1), disability studies has developed a social theory of disability. Linton and others working in the field set aside the medical model of disability as disease or trauma and the "natural" view of it as deficit or defect. Instead, disability studies considers disability as socially constituted. How the disabled are—and historically have been—represented, situated, marginalized, educated, and employed, for example, yields a recognition that what it means to be disabled, indeed the very conditions of disability, are crucially determined by the social order in which one lives.

7. The letters represent the four bases in DNA: cytosine, thymine, adenine, and guanine.

8. An alternate but less popular analogy is the human genome as blueprint. For example, Barbara R. Jasny and Pamela J. Hines write in "Genome Prospecting" that "Much as an architect's blueprint forms the plan of a building, genomic sequence supplies the directions from which a living organism is constructed."

9. For example, consider these recent headlines from *Science*: "Faithful Translations" (September 10, 1999) and "Dirty Transcripts from Clean DNA" (April 2, 1999). Likewise, the original research articles published in *Science* make use of the same textual-editing language. For example, the authors of "A Molecular Pathway Revealing a Genetic Basis for Human Cardiac and Craniofacial Defects" claim to have discovered a gene that, when absent, triggers a common congenital heart defect associated with DiGeorge syndrome, second only to Down's syndrome in causing malformations of the heart. Ninety percent of people with DiGeorge syndrome are missing three megabases of DNA from chromosome 22, designated by the authors as a "DiGeorge deletion site" (Yamagishi et al., 1093). The first two sentences of the authors' abstract demonstrate the genetic-body-as-text model: "Microdeletions of chromosome 22q11 are the most common genetic defects associated with cardiac and craniofacial anomalies in humans. A screen for mouse genes dependent on dHAND, a transcription factor implicated in neural crest development, identified Ufd1, which maps to human 22q11 and encodes a protein involved in degradation of ubiquitinated proteins" (1158).

10. At http://www.stanford.edu/group/morrinst/hgdp/faq.html#Q1. The Human Genome Diversity Project, which is not officially connected to the Human Genome Project, has from its beginning in the early 1990s stressed the importance of understanding genetic variation and the meaning of diversity. Unfortunately, the Project has never been adequately funded and thus far has been powerless to do anything but call attention to the need to consider issues of diversity.

11. At http://www.ornl.gov/TechResources/Human_Genome/resource/medicine.html.

12. J. Weiner argues in *Time, Love, Memory: A Great Biologist and His Quest for the Origins of Behavior* that the popular construction of "a gene for _____" (fill in the blank) comes from the genetics of Thomas Hunt Morgan, an American biologist who won a 1933 Nobel prize for discoveries relating to the hereditary function of chromosomes.

13. By most estimates, there are some 30,000 to 100,000 genes in the human genome.

14. At http://www.ornl.gov/TechResources/Human_Genome/resource/medicine.html.

15. Ribosomes are tiny particles in the cell that bind to messenger RNA, which carries the genetic information needed for protein synthesis, as well as to transfer RNA, the kind of molecule that supplies the ribosome with amino acids, the building blocks of proteins. For more information, see Elizabeth Pennisi, "The Race to the Ribosome Structure."

16. According to Ridley, there are several thousand nearly complete viral genomes integrated into the human genome, most of them now inert and missing a crucial gene. For example, human endogenous retroviruses account for 1.3 percent of the human genome. Another related form, retrotransposons, account for 14.6 percent of the entire genome (125).

17. It can be argued that, curiously, genetic "causes" of disorders absolve disabled people of responsibility at the same time that they stigmatize those same people. For more on this, see Celeste M. Condit's *The Meanings of the Gene: Public Debates about Human Heredity.*

18. Coincidentally, the infamous Eugenics Record Office was located at Cold Spring Harbor, about an hour east of New York City on Long Island. Today the Cold Spring Harbor Laboratory is a major genetics research center.

19. For example, in *Generation of Animals,* his treatise on biology, Aristotle classifies both animals and humans. With humans, any physical difference that "departs from type" (the able-bodied male) becomes a "monstrosity" that, by its very essence, is less than human. The "first beginning of this deviation is when a female is formed instead of a male," Aristotle claims (IV.iii.767b). He goes on to say, "we should look upon the female state as being as it were a deformity" (IV.vi.775a). Among the most extreme cases of such "deformity" are children born with birth anomalies. "Sometimes," he writes, a child "has reached such a point that in the end it no longer has the appearance of a human being at all, but that of an animal only" (IV.iii.769b). In *Nicomachean Ethics* Aristotle takes his argument to its (il)logical conclusion, identifying the norm (or mean) with moral virtue and the abnormal with vice. Thus physical "deformity" becomes moral flaw, exposing Aristotle's binary configuration for what it really is—a social hierarchy.

20. For a discussion of how medical rhetoric constructs people with disease and/or disability as deserving of their conditions, see "Medical Discourse and Subjectivity," in G. Thomas Couser's *Recovering Bodies: Illness, Disability, and Life Writing*; and Scott L. Montgomery's "Illness and Image in Holistic Discourse: How Alternative Is 'Alternative'?" in *Cultural Critique.*

21. The numbers for HGP funding come from Ari Patrinos et al., "New Goals for the U.S. Human Genome Project: 1998–2003," *Science* 282, no. 5389 (1998): 682–89. The numbers for NIH funding of research on specific diseases come from Cary P. Gross et al., "The Relation between Funding by the National Institutes of Health and the Burden of Disease," *New England Journal of Medicine* 340, no. 24 (1999): 1881–87.

22. For a more complete discussion of evolution, see Gould's *Evolution and the History of Life.* See also *The Book of Life,* which Gould edited.

Works Cited

Aristotle. *Generation of Animals.* Trans. A. L. Peck. Cambridge: Harvard University Press, 1979.

———. *The Nicomachean Ethics.* Trans. H. Rackham. Cambridge: Harvard University Press, 1975.

Botto, Lorenzo D., Cynthia A. Moore, Muin J. Khoury, and J. David Erickson. "Neural-Tube Defects." *New England Journal of Medicine* 341, no. 20 (1999): 1509–19.

Collins, Francis S. "Shattuck Lecture: Medical and Societal Consequences of the Human Genome Project." *New England Journal of Medicine* 341, no. 1 (1999): 28–37.

Collins, Francis S., Ari Patrinos, et al. "New Goals for the U.S. Human Genome Project: 1998–2003." *Science* 282, no. 5389 (1998): 682–89.

Condit, Celeste Michelle. "The Character of 'History' in Rhetoric and Cultural Studies: Recoding Genetics." In *At the Intersection: Cultural Studies and Rhetorical Studies.* Ed. Thomas Rosteck, 168–85. New York: Guilford, 1999.

———. *The Meanings of the Gene: Public Debates about Human Heredity.* Madison: University of Wisconsin Press, 1999.

Couser, G. Thomas. *Recovering Bodies: Illness, Disability, and Life Writing.* Madison: University of Wisconsin Press, 1997.

Davis, Lennard J. "Constructing Normalcy: The Bell Curve, the Novel, and the Invention of the Disabled Body in the Nineteenth Century." In *The Disability Studies Reader.* New York: Routledge, 1997.

Duster, Troy. "The Prism of Heritability and the Sociology of Knowledge." In *Naked Science: Anthropological Inquiry into Boundaries, Power, and Knowledge.* Ed. Laura Nader. New York: Routledge, 1996. 119–30.

Gould, Stephen Jay. *Evolution and the History of Life.* New York: Basic, 2000.

———. "The Evolution of Life on the Earth." *Scientific American* (October 1994): 85–91.

———, ed. *The Book of Life.* New York: W.W. Norton, 1993.

Gura, Trisha. "Gene Defect Linked to Rett Syndrome." *Science* 286, no. 5437 (1999): 27.

———. "Repairing the Genome's Spelling Mistakes." *Science* 285, no. 5426 (1999): 316–18.

Haraway, Donna J. *Simians, Cyborgs, and Women: The Reinvention of Nature.* New York: Routledge, 1991.

Harding, Sandra. *Whose Science? Whose Knowledge?* Ithaca, N.Y.: Cornell University Press, 1991.

Holtzman, Neil A. "Are Genetic Tests Adequately Regulated?" *Science* 286, no. 5439 (1999): 409.

Hubbard, Ruth, and Elijah Wald. *Exploding the Gene Myth.* Boston: Beacon, 1997.

Jasny, Barbara R., and Pamela J. Hines. "Genome Prospecting." *Science* 286, no. 5439 (1999): 443.

Kitcher, Philip. *The Lives to Come.* New York: Simon and Schuster, 1996.

Landow, George P. *Hypertext 2.0: The Convergence of Contemporary Critical Theory and Technology.* Baltimore: Johns Hopkins University Press, 1997.

Lewontin, Richard. *The Triple Helix: Gene, Organism, and Environment.* Cambridge: Harvard University Press, 2000.

Linton, Simi. *Claiming Disability: Knowledge and Identity.* New York: New York University Press, 1998.

McGann, Jerome J. *The Textual Condition.* Princeton, N.J.: Princeton University Press, 1991.

———. *A Critique of Modern Textual Criticism.* Chicago: University of Chicago Press, 1983.

Montgomery, Scott L. "Illness and Image in Holistic Discourse: How Alternative Is 'Alternative'?" *Cultural Critique* 25 (1993): 65–89.

Pennisi, Elizabeth. "The Race to the Ribosome Structure." *Science* 285, no. 5436 (1999): 2048–51.

Pollack, Andrew. "Gene Therapy's Focus Shifts from Rare Illnesses." *New York Times on the Web,* August 4, 1998, http://www.nytimes.com.

Ridley, Matt. *Genome: The Autobiography of a Species in 23 Chapters.* New York: Harper Collins, 1999.

Ross, Emma. "Scientists Near Goal: DNA Code of Chromosome." *Cincinnati Enquirer,* October 22, 1999, A11.

Weiner, J. *Time, Love, Memory: A Great Biologist and His Quest for the Origins of Behavior.* New York: Knopf, 1999.

Wingerson, Lois. *Unnatural Selection: The Promise and the Power of Human Gene Research.* New York: Bantam, 1998.

Yamagishi, Hiroyuki, Vidu Garg, et al. "A Molecular Pathway Revealing a Genetic Basis for Human Cardiac and Craniofacial Defects." *Science* 283, no. 5405 (1999): 1158–61.

Zanjani, Esmail D., and W. French Anderson. "Prospects for in Utero Human Gene Therapy. *Science* 285, no. 5436 (1999): 2084–88.

Part II

The Politics of Disability

6

Construction of Deafness

Harlan Lane

Social Problems Are Constructed

It is obvious that our society is beset by numerous social problems. A brief historical perspective on four of them reveals something not so obvious: social problems are constructed in particular cultures, at particular times, in response to the efforts of interested parties.

The social problem of alcoholism evidently consists in this: there is a particular segment of the population that suffers from the use of alcohol; these sufferers need specially trained people to help them—for example alcoholism counselors, psychologists and psychiatrists; they need special facilities such as detoxification centers; and special organizations like AA. This understanding of alcoholism is less than fifty years old. Recall that the Temperance Movement of the last century viewed excessive drinking not as a disease but as an act of will; alcoholics victimized their families and imposed on the rest of society. The movement advocated not treatment but prohibition. Some groups favored prohibition and took the moral high ground; other groups felt justified in breaking the law. Special facilities existed then to house and treat many problem groups—mentally ill people, for example—but not people who drank too much. Only recently has a consensus developed that excessive drinking "is" a disease—a matter of individual suffering more than a political dispute. With this shift in the construction of alcoholism and alcoholics—from victimizers to victims—the evident need was for medical research to alleviate suffering; vast sums of money are now devoted to research on alcoholism, and there is now a large treatment establishment with halfway houses, hospital wards, outpatient clinics, and specialized hospitals (Gusfield, 1982).

The discovery of child abuse dates from the 1950s. Radiologists and pediatricians first decried the evidence they were seeing of parents beating their children. The Children's Bureau and the media took up the cause (it is still very present in TV and the newspapers) and made the public aware of this social problem. In the decade that followed, the states passed laws requiring reports of child abuse and providing penalties. Of course, parents did not start beating their children only in the 1950s. Rather, a social consensus emerged in that decade that a problem existed requiring laws, special welfare workers, and special budgetary provisions. In the last century, the major problems associated with children concerned poverty and child labor—a rather different and much more political construction of the problem of improper treatment of children (Gusfield, 1989).

For a very long time, the dominant construction of homosexuality, like that of alcoholism, was a moral one: men and women were making sinful choices; the problem was "owned" by the church. Later psychiatry gave it a new construction: it "is" an illness they claimed that psychiatrists could treat (Conrad & Schneider, 1980). In the third phase, Gays and Lesbians were presented as a minority group; they ask for the same protection as all other groups that are discriminated against based on the circumstances of their birth, such as blacks and women.

Disability, too, has had moral, medical and now social constructions, as numerous articles in this journal have explicated. The Disability Rights Movement has shifted the construct of disability "off the body and into the interface between people with impairments and socially disabling conditions" (Hevey, 1993, p. 426).

Alcoholism has changed from a moral failure to a disease; child abuse from an economic problem to a criminal one; homosexuality from disease to personal constitution to human rights; disability from tragic flaw to social barriers. Social problems, it seems, are partly what we make of them; they are not just out there "lying in the road to be discovered by passers-by" (Gusfield, 1984, p. 38). The particular way in which society understands alcoholism, disability and so forth determines exactly what these labels mean, how large groups of people are treated, and the problems that they face. Deafness, too, has had many constructions; they differ with time and place. Where there were many deaf people in small communities in the last century, on Martha's Vineyard, for example, as in Henniker, New Hampshire, deafness was apparently not seen as a problem requiring special intervention. Most Americans had quite a different construction of deafness at that time, however: it was an individual affliction that befell family members and had to be accommodated within the family. The great challenge facing Thomas Gallaudet and Laurent Clerc in their efforts to create the first American school for the deaf was to persuade state legislatures and wealthy Americans of quite a different construction which they had learned in Europe: Deafness was not an individual but a social problem, deaf people had to be brought together for their instruction, special "asylums" were needed. Nowadays, two constructions of deafness in particular are dominant and compete for shaping deaf peoples' destinies. The one construes deaf as a category of disability; the other construes deaf as designating a member of a linguistic minority. There is a growing practice of capitalizing Deaf when referring specifically to its second construction, which I will follow hereafter.

Disability vs. Linguistic Minority

Numerous organizations are associated with each of the prominent constructions of deafness. In the U.S., National organizations primarily associated with deafness as disability include the A. G. Bell Association (4,500 members), the American Speech-Language-Hearing Association (40,000), the American Association of Late-Deafened Adults (1,300), Self-Help for the Hard of Hearing (13,000), the American Academy of Otolaryngology, Head and Neck Surgery (5,600), and the National Hearing Aid Society (4,000). National organizations associated primarily with the construction of Deaf as a linguistic minority include the National Association of the Deaf (20,000), the Registry of Interpreters for the Deaf (2,700), and the National Fraternal Society of the Deaf (13,000) (Van Cleve, 1987; Burek, 1993).

Each construction has a core client group. No one disputes the claim of the hearing adult become deaf from illness or aging that he or she has a disability and is not a member of Deaf culture. Nor, on the other hand, has any one yet criticized Deaf parents for insisting that their Deaf child has a distinct linguistic and cultural heritage. The struggle between some of the groups adhering to the two constructions persists across the centuries (Lane, 1984) in part because there is no simple criterion for identifying most childhood candidates as clients of the one position or the other. More generally, we can observe that late deafening and moderate hearing loss tend to be associated with the disability construction of deafness while early and profound deafness involve an entire organization of the person's language, culture and thought around vision and tend to be associated with the linguistic minority construction.

In general, we identify children as members of a language minority when their native language is not the language of the majority. Ninety percent of Deaf children, however, have hearing parents who are unable to effectively model the spoken language for most of them. Advocates of the disability construction contend these are hearing-impaired children whose language and culture (though they may have acquired little of either) are in principle those of their parents; advocates of the linguistic minority construction contend that the children's native language, in the sense of primary language, must be manual language and that their life trajectory will bring them fully into the circle of Deaf culture. Two archetypes for these two constructions, disability and linguistic minority, were recently placed side by side before our eyes on the U. S. television program, "Sixty Minutes." On the one hand, seven-year-old Caitlin Parton, representing the unreconstructed disability-as-impairment: presented as a victim of a personal tragedy, utterly disabled in communication by her loss of hearing but enabled by technology, and dedicated professional efforts (yes, we meet the surgeon), to approach normal, for which she yearns, as she herself explains. On the other hand, Roslyn Rosen, then president of the National Association of the Deaf, from a large Deaf family, native speaker of ASL, proud of her status as a member of a linguistic minority, insistent that she experiences life and the world fully and has no desire to be any different (*Sixty Minutes,* 1992).

Professional Influence over Constructions

Organizations espousing each construction of deafness compete to "own" the children and define their needs. Their very economic survival depends on their success in that competition. Which construction of a social problem prevails is thus no mere academic matter. There is a body of knowledge associated with construction A and a quite different body with construction B; the theories and facts associated with construction A have been studied by the professional people who grapple with the social problem; they are the basis of their specialized training and professional credentials and therefore contribute to their self-esteem; they are used to maintain respect from clients, to obtain federal and state funding, to insure one's standing in a fraternity of like professionals; they legitimate the professional person's daily activities. Professionals examine students on this body of knowledge, give certificates, and insert themselves into the legal and social norms based on their competence in that body of knowledge. Whoever says A is a mistaken construction is of course not welcome. More than that, whoever says A is a construction is not welcome, for that implies that there could be or is another construction, B, say, which is better. What the parties to each construction want is that their construction not be seen as a construction at all; rather, they insist, they merely reflect the way things are in the world (cf. Gusfield, 1984).

These "troubled-persons industries," in the words of sociologist Joseph Gusfield, "bestow benevolence on people defined as in need" (Gusfield, 1989, p. 432). These industries have grown astronomically in recent decades (Albrecht, 1992). The professional services fueled by the disability construction of deafness are provided by some administrators of schools and training programs, experts in counseling and rehabilitation, teachers, interpreters, audiologists, speech therapists, otologists, psychologists, psychiatrists, librarians, researchers, social workers, and hearing aid specialists. All these people and the facilities they command, their clinics, operating rooms, laboratories, classrooms, offices and shops, owe their livelihood or existence to deafness problems. Gusfield cites the story about American missionaries who settled in Hawaii. They went to do good. They stayed and did well (Gusfield, 1989).

The troubled-person professions serve not only their clientele but also themselves, and are actively involved in perpetuating and expanding their activities. Teachers of the Deaf, for example, seek fewer students per teacher and earlier intervention (Johnson *et al.,* 1989). American audiologists have formally proposed testing of the hearing of all American newborns without exception. The self-aggrandizement of the troubled-persons professions when it comes to Deaf people is guided by a genuine belief in their exclusive construction of the social problem and their ability to alleviate it. Some of their promotional methods are readily seen; for example, they employ lobbyists to encourage legislation that requires and pays for their services. Other measures are more subtle; for example, the structural relation between the service provider and the client often has the effect of disempowering the client and maintaining dependency.

Lessons from Services for Blind People

The history of services to blind people illustrates some of the pitfalls of the professionalization of a social problem. Workshops for blind people have large budgets, provide good income for sighted managers, and have a national organization to lobby for their interest. Blind people, however, commonly view sheltered workshops as a dead end that involves permanent dependency. The editor of the journal *Braille Monitor* says that "professional" is a swear word among blind people, "a bitter term of mockery and disillusionment" (Vaughan, 1991). A light-house for the blind was raked over the coals in that journal for having one pay scale for blind employees and a higher one for sighted employees performing the same work; moreover, the blind employees were paid below minimum wage (Braille Monitor, 1989). The National Accreditation Council for Agencies Serving the Blind and visually Handicapped (NAC) was disowned by organizations of blind people for its efforts to keep blind people in custodial care, its refusal to hear blind witnesses, and its token representation of blind people on the board; the Council rebutted that it had to consider the needs of agencies and professionals and not just blind people. For decades blind people picketed the NAC annual meetings (Braille Monitor, 1973; Jernigan, 1973; Vaughan, 1991).

A conference convened to define the new specialization of mobility trainer for the blind concluded that it required graduate study to learn this art and that "the teaching of mobility is a task for the sighted rather than a blind individual" (quoted in Vaughan, 1991, p. 209). This approach was naturally challenged by blind consumers. At first, the American Association of Workers with the Blind required normal vision for certification; then this was seen as discriminatory, in violation of section 504 of the Rehabilitation Act of 1973. So the criteria were changed. To enter the training program, the student must be able to assess the collision path of a blind person with obstacles nearly a block away. As it turns out, the functions claimed to be essential to mobility teaching just happen to require normal vision. Needless to say, blind people have been teaching blind people how to get about for centuries (Olson, 1981).

Workers with blind people view blindness as a devastating personal tragedy although blind people themselves commonly do not. Said the president of the National Association of the Blind "We do not regard our lives…as tragic or disastrous and no amount of professional jargon or trumped up theory can made us do so" (Jernigan quoted in Olson, 1977, p. 408). As sociologist R. A. Scott explains in his classic monograph, *The Making of Blind Men,* the sighted professionals believe that the blind man's only hope for solving his problems is to submit to their long-term program of psychological services and training. To succeed, the blind man is told, he must change his beliefs about blindness, most of all, his belief that he is basically fine and only needs one or two services. The cooperative client is the one who welcomes all the services provided; the uncooperative client is the one who welcomes all the services provided; the uncooperative client is the one who fails to realize how many and great his needs are—who is in denial. The troubled-persons industries thus stand the normal relation between needs and services on its head: services do not evolve purely to meet needs; clients must recognize that they need the services provided by the professionals. Scott comments that it is easy to be deluded about the reality of these special needs. There are always a few blind clients who can be relied on to endorse these beliefs in the profound need for professional services. These blind individuals have been socialized, perhaps since childhood, to the professional construction of blindness. They confirm that blind people have the needs the agency says they have (Scott, 1981).

So it is with deafness. In much of the world, including the United States, deaf people are largely excluded from the ranks of professionals serving deaf children. In many communities it just happens that to be a teacher of deaf children you must first qualify as a teacher of hearing children, and deaf people are excluded as teachers of hearing children. In other communities, it just happens that to become a teacher of deaf children the candidate who is most capable of communicating with them is disbarred because he or she must pass an examination couched in high register English without an interpreter. And as with services for blind people, many of the professions associated with the disability construction of deafness insist that the plight of the deaf child is truly desperate—so desperate, in fact, that some professionals propose implant surgery followed by rigorous and prolonged speech and hearing therapy. The successful use of a cochlear implant in everyday communication calls on a prior knowledge of spoken language (Staller *et al.,* 1991) that only one child candidate in ten possesses (Allen *et al.,* 1994); this has not, however, deterred professionals from recruiting among the other ninety percent; it is doubtful that the cochlear-implant industry would survive, certainly not flourish, if it sold its services and equipment only to the core clientele for the disability construction.

As with service providers for blind people, the troubled-persons industry associated with deafness seeks total conformity of the client to the underlying construction of deafness as disability. In the words of an audiology textbook: "One is not simply dealing with a handicapped child, one is dealing with a family with a handicap" (Tucker & Nolan, 1984 quoted in Gregory & Hartley, 1991, p. 87). The text goes on to state: "This concept of 'total child' being child plus hearing aids is one which parents may need time to come to terms with and fully accept." The profession wants to intervene in that family's life as early as possible and seeks to provide "a saturation service" (Tucker & Nolan, 1984 quoted in Gregory & Hartley, 1991, p. 97).

The criteria for disability, presented as objective, in fact conform to the interests of the profession (Oliver, 1990). Audiologic criteria decide which children will receive special education, so the audiologist must be consulted. In most countries of the world, audiology and special education are intimately related; the role of special education is to achieve as far as possible what audiology and otology could not do—minimize the child's disability. Writes one audiologist: "Education cannot cure deafness; it can only alleviate its worst effects" (Lynas, 1986, quoted in Gregory & Hartley, 1991, p. 155). Parents generally have little say about the right educational placement for their child; neither are there any functional tests of what the child can understand in different kinds of classrooms. Instead, audiologic criteria prevail, even if they have little predictive value. For example, the academic achievement scores of children classified as severely hearing-impaired are scarcely different from those of children classified as profoundly hearing impaired (Allen, 1986). Research has shown that some children categorized as profoundly hearing impaired can understand words and sentences whereas others do not even detect sound (Osberger *et al.,* 1993). Likewise, Scott states that the official definition of blindness is "based upon a meaningless demarcation among those with severely impaired vision" (Scott, 1981, p. 42).

The Making of Deaf Men

The family that has received "saturation services" from the deafness troubled-persons industry will participate in socializing the deaf child to adapt the child's needs to those of the industry. A recent handbook for parents with implanted children states: "Parents should accept a primary role in helping their child adjust to the implant. They must assume responsibility for maintaining the implant device, for ensuring that the child is wearing it properly, and assuring that the auditory speech stimulation occurs in both the home and school" (Tye-Murray, 1992, p. xvi). "The child should wear the implant during all waking hours" (Tye-Murray, 1992, p. 18). Ultimately, the child should see the implant as part of himself, like his ears or hands. The handbook recounts enthusiastically how one implanted schoolchild, told to draw a self portrait, included the speech processor and microphone/transmitter in great detail: "This self-portrait demonstrated the child's positive image of himself and the acceptance of his cochlear implant" (Tye-Murray, 1992, p. 20).

The construction of the deaf child as disabled is legitimized early on by the medical profession and later by the special education and welfare bureaucracy. When the child is sent to a special educational program and obliged to wear cumbersome hearing aids, his or her socialization into the role of disabled person is promoted. In face-to-face encounters with therapists and teachers the child learns to cooperate in promoting a view of himself or herself as disabled. Teachers label large numbers of these deaf children emotionally disturbed or learning disabled (Lane, 1992). Once labeled as "multiply handicapped" in this way, deaf children are treated differently—for example, placed in a less demanding academic program where they learn less, so the label is self-validating. In the end, the troubled-persons industry creates the disabled deaf person.

Deaf as Linguistic Minority

From the vantage point of Deaf culture, deafness is not a disability (Jones & Pullen, 1989). British Deaf leader Paddy Ladd put it this way: "We wish for the recognition of our right to exist as a linguistic minority group...Labeling us as disabled demonstrates a failure to understand that we are not disabled in any way within our own community" (Dant & Gregory, 1991, p. 14). U. S. Deaf scholar Tom Humphries concurs: "There is no room within the culture of Deaf people for an ideology that all Deaf people are deficient. It simple does not compute. There is no "handicap" to overcome...(Humphries, 1993, p. 14). American Deaf leader MJ Bienvenu asks: "Who benefits when we attempt to work in coalition with disability groups?...How can we fight for official recognition of ASL and allow ourselves as "communication disordered" at the same time?" And she concludes: "We are proud of our language, culture and heritage. Disabled we are not!" (Bienvenu, 1989, p. 13).

Nevertheless, many in the disability rights movement, and even some Deaf leaders, have joined professionals in promoting the disability construction of all deafness. To defend this construction, one leading disability advocate, Vic Finkelstein, has advanced the following argument based on the views of the people directly concerned: Minorities that have been discriminated against, like blacks, would refuse an operation to eliminate what sets them apart, but this is not true for disabled people: "every (!) disabled person would welcome such an operation" (*Finkelstein's exclamation point*). And, from this perspective, Deaf people, he maintains, "have more in common with other disability groups than they do with groups based upon race and gender" (Finkelstein, 1991, p. 265). However, in fact, American Deaf people are more like blacks in that most would refuse an operation to eliminate what sets them apart (as Dr. Rosen did on "Sixty Minutes"). One U. S. survey of Deaf adults asked if they would like an implant operation so they could hear; more than eight out of 10 declined (Evans, 1989). When the magazine *Deaf Life* queried its subscribers, 87 percent of respondents said that they did not consider themselves handicapped.

There are other indications that American Deaf culture simply does not have the ambivalence that, according to Abberley, is called for in disability: "Impairment must be identified as a bad thing, insofar as it is an undesirable consequence of a distorted social development, at the same time as it is held to be a positive attribute of the individual who is impaired" (Abberley, 1987, p. 9). American Deaf people (like their counterparts in many other nations) think cultural Deafness is a good thing and would like to see more of it. Expectant Deaf parents, like those in any other language minority, commonly hope to have Deaf children with whom they can share their language, culture and unique experiences. One Deaf mother from Los Angeles recounted to a researcher her reaction when she noticed that her baby did not react to Fourth of July fireworks: "I thought to myself, 'She must be deaf.' I wasn't disappointed; I thought, 'It will be all right. We are both deaf, so we will know what to do' (Becker, 1980, p. 55). Likewise an expectant Deaf mother in Boston told the *Globe*, "I want my daughters to be like me, to be deaf" (Saltus, 1989, p. 27). The Deaf community, writes Paddy Ladd, "regards the birth of each and every deaf child as a precious gift" (quoted in Oliver, 1989, p. 199). Deaf and hearing scholars expressed the same view in a 1991 report to the U. S. National Institutes of Health; research in genetics to improve deaf people's quality of life is certainly important, they said, but must not become, in the hands of hearing people, research on ways of reducing the deaf minority (Padden, 1990).

Finkelstein acknowledges that many Deaf people reject the label "disabled" but he attributes it to the desire of Deaf people to distance themselves from social discrimination. What is missing from the construction of deafness is what lies at the heart of the linguistic minority construction: Deaf culture. Since people with disabilities are themselves engaged in a struggle to change the construction of disability, they surely recognize that disabilities are not "lying there in the road" but are indeed socially constructed. Why is this not applied to Deaf people? Not surprisingly, deafness is constructed differently in Deaf cultures than it is in hearing cultures.

Advocates of the disability construction for all deaf people, use the term "deaf community" to refer to all people with significant hearing impairment, on the model of "the disability community." So the term seems to legitimate the acultural perspective on Deaf people. When Ladd (*supra*) and other advocates of the linguistic minority construction speak of the Deaf community, however, the term refers to a much smaller group with a distinct manual language, culture, and social organization.[1] It is instructive, as American Deaf leader Ben Bahan has suggested, to see how ASL speakers refer to their minority; one term can be glossed as DEAF-WORLD. The claim that one is in the DEAF-WORLD, or that someone else is, is not a claim about hearing status at all; it is an expression of that self-recognition or recognition of others that is defining for all ethnic collectivities (Johnson & Erting, 1989). It is predictive about social behavior (including attitudes, beliefs and values) and language, but not about hearing status. All degrees of hearing can be found among Deaf people (it is a matter of discussion whether some hearing people with Deaf parents are Deaf), and most people who are hearing-impaired are not members of the DEAF-WORLD.

In ASL the sign whose semantic field most overlaps that of the English "disability" can be glossed in English LIMP-BLIND-ETC. I have asked numerous informants to give me examples from that category: they have responded by citing (in literal translation) people in wheelchairs, blind people, mentally retarded people, and people with cerebral palsy, but no informant has ever listed DEAF and all reject it when asked. Another term in use in the Boston area (and elsewhere), which began as a fingerspelled borrowing from English, can be glossed D–A. My informants agree that Deaf is not D–A. The sign M–H–C (roughly, "multiply-handicapped") also has some currency. When I have asked Deaf people here for examples of M–H–C, DEAF-BLIND has never been listed, and when I propose it, it is rejected.

Other important differences between culturally Deaf people and people with disabilities come to light when we consider these groups' priorities. Among the preconditions for equal participation in society by disabled persons, the U.N. *Standard Rules* (1994) list medical care, rehabilitation, and support services such as personal assistance. "Personal assistance services are the new top of the agenda issue for the disability rights movement," one chronicler reports (Shapiro, 1993, p. 251). From my observation, Deaf people do not attach particular importance to medical care, not place any special value on rehabilitation or personal assistance services,[2] not have any particular concern with autonomy and independent living. Instead, the preconditions for Deaf participation are more like those of other language minorities: culturally Deaf people campaign for acceptance of their language and its broader use in the schools, the workplace, and in public events.

Integration, in the classroom, the workforce and the community, "has become a primary goal of today's disability movement" (Shapiro, 1993, p. 144). School integration is anathema to the DEAF-WORLD. Because most Deaf children have hearing parents, they can only acquire full language and socialization in specialized schools, in particular the prized network of residential schools; Deaf children are drowning in the mainstream (Lane, 1992). While advocates for people with disabilities recoil in horror at segregated institutions, evoking images of Willowbrook and worse, the Deaf alumni of residential schools return to their alma mater repeatedly over the years, contribute to their support, send their Deaf children to them, and vigorously protest the efforts of well-meaning but grievously ill-informed members of the disability rights movement to close those schools. These advocates fail to take account of language and culture and therefore of the difference between imposed and elective segregation. Where people with disabilities cherish independence, culturally Deaf people cherish interdependence. People with disabilities may gather for political action; Deaf people traditionally gather primarily for socializing. Deaf people marry Deaf people 90 percent of the time in the U. S. (Schein, 1989).

With the shift in the construction of disability has come an emphasis on the bonds that unite people with disabilities to the rest of society with whom they generally share not only culture but also ranges of capacities and incapacities (cf. Barton, 1993). "We try to make disability fixed and dichotomous," writes Zola, "but it is fluid and continuous" (Zola, 1993, p. 24). More than 20 percent of the noninstitutionalized population of the U.S. has a disability, we are told, and over 7.7 million Americans report that hearing is their primary functional limitation (Dowler & Hirsch, 1994). This universalizing view, according to which most people have some disability at least some of the time, is strikingly at odds with the DEAF-WORLD, small, tightly knit, with its own language and culture, sharply demarcated from the rest of society: there is no slippery slope between Deaf and hearing. "Deaf people are foreigners," wrote an early president of the National Association of the Deaf, "[living] among a people whose language they can never learn" (Hanson, cited in Van Cleve & Crouch, 1989, p. ix).

It is significant that the four student leaders who led the uprising known as the Gallaudet Revolution, were Deaf children of Deaf parents, deeply imbued with a sense of DEAF-WORLD, and natively fluent in ASL. One of them explained to *USA Today* the significance of the Revolution as it relates to the construction of deafness: "Hearing people sometimes call us handicapped. But most—maybe all deaf people—feel that we're more of an ethnic group because we speak a different language...We also have our own culture...There's more of an ethnic difference than a handicap difference between us and hearing people" (Hlibok, 1988, p. 11a). The new Deaf president of Gallaudet sought to explain the difference in the underlying construction in these terms: "More people realize now that deafness is a difference, not a deficiency" (Jordan, quoted in Gannon, 1989, p. 173).

So there is no reason to think that Paddy Ladd, Tom Humphries and MJ Bienvenu are being insincere when they claim that Deaf people are not disabled. Quite the contrary: since all are leaders of Deaf communities and are steeped in deaf culture, they advance the construction of deafness that arises from their culture. Mr. Finkelstein could have been tipped off to this very different construction by observing how various groups choose to be labeled: disability groups may find labels such as "disabled" or "motorically-impaired" or "visually handicapped" distasteful and reserve for themselves the right to call someone a "crip," but Deaf culture embraces the label "Deaf" and asks that everyone use it, as in The National Association of the Deaf and The World Federation of the Deaf. It seems right to speak of "the Deaf" as we speak of "The French" or "The British." It is alien to Deaf culture on two counts to speak of its members as "people with hearing-impairment." First, it is the troubled-persons industry for deafness that invented and promoted the label in English "hearing-impaired" (Ross & Calvert, 1967; Wilson *et al.*, 1974; Castle, 1990). Second, the "people with" construction implies that the trait is incidental rather than defining, but one's culture is never an incidental trait. It seems to be an error in ordinary language to say, "I happen to be Hispanic," or "I happen to be Deaf"; who would you be, after all, if you were you and yet not Hispanic, or not Deaf? But it is acceptable to say, "I happen to have a spinal cord injury."

Deaf cultures do not exist in a vacuum. Deaf Americans embrace many cultural values, attitudes, beliefs and behaviors that are part of the larger American culture and, in some instances, that are part of ethnic minority cultures such as African-American, Hispanic-American, etc. Because hearing people have obliged Deaf people to interact with the larger hearing society in terms of a disability model, that model has left its mark on Deaf culture. In particular, Deaf people frequently have found themselves recipients of unwanted special services provided by hearing people. "In terms of its economic, political and social relations to hearing society, the Deaf minority can be viewed as a colony" (Markowicz & Woodward, 1978, p. 33). As with colonized peoples, some Deaf people have internalized the "other's" (disability) construction of them alongside their own cultural construction (Lane, 1992). For example, they may be active in their Deaf club and yet denigrate skilled use of ASL as "low sign"; "high sign" is a contact variety of ASL that is closer to English-language word order. The Deaf person who uses a variety of ASL marked as English frequently has greater access to wider resources such as education and employment. Knowing when to use which variety is an important part of being Deaf (Johnson

& Erting, 1989). Granted that culturally Deaf people must take account of the disability model of deafness, that they sometimes internalize it, and that it leaves its mark on their culture, all this does not legitimize that model—any more than granting that African-Americans had to take account of the construction of the slave as property, sometimes internalized that construction, and found their culture marked by it legitimizes that construction of their ethnic group.

Neither culturally Deaf people nor people with disabilities are a homogeneous group.[3] Many of the differences between the two that I have cited will not apply to particular subgroups or individuals; nevertheless, it should be clear that cultural Deafness involves a constellation of traits quite different from those of any disability group. Faced with these salient differences, those who would argue that Deaf people are "really" disabled, sometimes resort instead to arguing that they are "really not" like linguistic minorities (Fishman, 1982). Certainly there are differences. For example, Deaf people cannot learn English as a second language as easily as other minorities. Second and third generation Deaf children find learning English no easier than their forbears, but second and third generation immigrants to the U. S. frequently learn English before entering school. The language of the DEAF-WORLD is not usually passed on from generation to generation; instead, it is commonly transmitted by peers or associates. Normally, Deaf people are not proficient in this native language until they reach school age. Deaf people are more scattered geographically than many linguistic minorities. The availability of interpreters is even more vital for Deaf people than for many other linguistic minorities because there are so few Deaf lawyers, doctors and accountants, etc. Few Deaf people are in high-status public positions in our society (in contrast with, say, Hispanics), and this has hindered the legitimation of ASL use (Kyle, 1990, 1991; Parratt & Tipping, 1991). However, many, perhaps all, linguistic minorities have significant features that differentiate them: Members of the Chinese-American community are increasingly marrying outside their linguistic minority but this is rare for ASL speakers. Many Native American languages are dying out or have disappeared; this is not true of ASL which is unlikely ever to die out. Spanish-speaking Americans are so diverse a group that it may not be appropriate to speak of the Hispanic community in the U. S. (Wright, 1994). Neither the newer strategy of citing what is special about the ASL-speaking minority nor the older one of minimizing ASL itself hold much promise of discrediting the construction of deafness as linguistic minority.

It is undeniable that culturally Deaf people have great common cause with people with disabilities. Both pay the price of social stigma. Both struggle with the troubled-persons industries for control of their destiny. Both endeavor to promote their construction of their identity in competition with the interested (and generally better funded) efforts of professionals to promote *their* constructions. And Deaf people have special reasons for solidarity with people with hearing impairments; their combined numbers have created services, commissions and laws that the DEAF-WORLD alone probably could not have achieved. Solidarity, yes, but when culturally Deaf people allow their special identity to be subsumed under the construct of disability they set themselves up for wrong solutions and bitter disappointments.

It is because disability advocates think of Deaf children as disabled that they want to close the special schools and absurdly plunge Deaf children into hearing classrooms in a totally exclusionary program called inclusion. It is because government is allowed to proceed with a disability construction of cultural Deafness that the U. S. Office of Bilingual Education and Minority Language Affairs has refused for decades to provide special resources for schools with large numbers of ASL-using children although the law requires it to do so for children using any other non-English language. It is because of the disability construction that court rulings requiring that children who do not speak English receive instruction initially in their best language have not been applied to ASL-using children. It is because of the disability construction that the teachers most able to communicate with Britain's Deaf children are excluded from the profession on the pretext that they have a disqualifying disability. It is because lawmakers have been encouraged to believe by some disability advocates and prominent deaf figures that Deaf people are disabled that, in response to the Gallaudet Revolution, the U. S. Congress passed a law, not recognizing ASL or the DEAF-WORLD as a minority, but a law establishing another institute of *health,* The National Institute on Deafness and Other Communications Disorders [*sic*], operated by the deafness troubled persons industry, and sponsoring research to reduce hereditary deafness. It is because of the disability construction that organizations *for* the Deaf (e.g., the Royal National Institute for the Deaf) are vastly better funded by government that organizations *of* the Deaf (e.g., the British Deaf Association).

One would think that people with disabilities might be the first to grasp and sympathize with the claims of Deaf people that they are victims of a mistaken identity. People with disabilities should no more resist the self-construction of culturally Deaf people, than Deaf people should subscribe to a view of people with disabilities as tragic victims of an inherent flaw.

Changing to the Linguistic Minority Construction

Suppose our society were generally to adopt a disability construction of deafness for most late-deafened children and adults and a linguistic minority construction of Deaf people for most others, how would things change? The admirable Open University course, *Issues in Deafness* (1991) prompted these speculations.

(1) Changing the construction changes the legitimate authority concerning the social problem. In many areas, such as schooling, the authority would become Deaf adults, linguists and sociologists, among others. There would be many more service providers from the minority: Deaf teachers, foster and adoptive parents, information officers, social workers, advocates. Non-Deaf service providers would be expected to know the language, history, and culture of the Deaf linguistic minority.

(2) Changing the construction changes how behavior is construed. Deaf people would be expected to use ASL (in the U. S.) and to have interpreters available; poor speech would be seen as inappropriate.

(3) Changing the construction may change the legal status of the social problem group. Most Deaf people would no longer claim disability benefits or services under the present legislation for disabled people. The services to which the Deaf linguistic minority has a right in order to obtain equal treatment under the law would be provided by other legislation and bureaucracies. Deaf people would receive greater protection against employment discrimination under civil rights laws and rulings. Where there are special provisions to assist the education of linguistic minority children, Deaf children would be eligible.

(4) Changing the construction changes the arena where identification and labeling take place. In the disability construction, deafness is medicalized and labeled in the audiologist's clinic. In the construction as linguistic minority, deafness is viewed as a social variety and would be labeled in the peer group.

(5) Changing the construction changes the kinds of intervention. The Deaf child would not be operated on for deafness but brought together with other Deaf children and adults. The disability construction orients hearing parents to the question, what can be done to mitigate my child's impairment? The linguistic minority construction presents them with the challenge of insuring that their child has language and role models from the minority (Hawcroft, 1991).

Obstacles to Change

The obstacles to replacing a disability construction of deafness for much of the concerned population with a linguistic minority construction are daunting. In the first place, people who have little familiarity with deafness find the disability construction self-evident and the minority construction elusive. As I argue in *The Mask of Benevolence* (Lane, 1992), hearing people led to reflect on deafness generally begin by imagining themselves without hearing—which is, of course, to have a disability but not to be Deaf. Legislators can easily grasp the disability construction, not so the linguistic minority construction. The same tendency to uncritically accept the disability model led *Sixty Minutes* to feature a child from among the nine percent of childhood implant candidates who were deafened after learning English rather than from the 91 percent who do not identify with the English-speaking majority (Allen *et al.*, 1994). Not only did the interviewer find the disability construction of deafness easier to grasp but no doubt the producers thought heir millions of viewers would do likewise. Social problems are a favorite theme of the media but they are almost always presented as private troubles—deafness is no exception—because it makes for more entertaining viewing.

The troubled-persons industry associated with deafness—the "audist establishment" (Lane, 1992)—vigorously resists efforts to replace their construction of deafness. Audist policy is that ASL is a kind of primitive prosthesis, a way around the communication impasse caused by deaf peoples' disability. The audists control teacher training programs, university research facilities, the process of peer review for federal grant monies, the presentations made at professional meetings, and publications in professional journals; they control promotion and through promotion, salary. They have privileged access to the media and to law-making bodies when deafness is at issue. Although they lack the credibility of Deaf people themselves, they have expert credentials and they are fluent in speaking and writing English so law and policy makers and the media find it easier to consult them.

When a troubled-persons industry recasts social problems as private troubles it can treat, it is protecting its construction by removing the appearance of a social issue on which there might be political disagreement. The World Health Organization, for example, has medicalized and individualized what is social; services are based on an individualized view of disability and are designed by professionals in the disability industry (Oliver, 1991). The U. S. National Institute on Deafness and Other Communications Disorders proclaims in its very title the disability construction of deafness that it seeks to promote. The American Speech-Language Hearing Association, for example, has the power of accrediting graduate programs for training professionals who work with Deaf people; a program that deviated too far from the disability construction could lose its accreditation; without accreditation its students would not be certified; without the promise of certification, no one would enter the training program.

Some of the gravest obstacles to broader acceptance of the linguistic minority model come from members of the minority itself. Many members of the minority were socialized in part by professionals (and parents) to adopt a disabled role. Some Deaf people openly embrace the disability construction and thus undercut the efforts of other Deaf people to discredit it. Worse yet, many opportunities are provided to Deaf people (e.g., access to interpreters) on the condition that they adopt the alien disability construction. This double blind—accept our construction of your life or give up your access to equal citizenship—is a powerful form of oppression. Thus, many members of the DEAF-WORLD endorsed the Americans with Disabilities Act with its provisions for deaf people, all the while believing they are not disabled but lending credence to the claim that they are. In a related double blind, Deaf adults who want to become part of the professions serving Deaf people, find that they must subscribe to audist views of rehabilitation, special education, etc.

Exponents of the linguistic minority construction are at a further disadvantage because there is little built-in cultural transmission of their beliefs. The most persuasive advocates for Deaf children, their parents, must be taught generation after generation the counter-intuitive linguistic minority construction because most are neither Deaf themselves nor did they have Deaf parents.

A further obstacle arising within the DEAF-WORLD to promoting the linguistic minority construction concerns, ironically, the form that much Deaf political activism takes. Ever since the first congresses of Deaf people organized in response to the Congress of Milan in 1880, Deaf leaders have appeared before friendly Deaf audiences to express their outrage—to preach to the converted. Written documents—position papers, articles and proceedings—have similarly been addressed to and read by primarily the DEAF-WORLD. It is entirely natural to prefer audiences with whom one shares language and culture, the more so as Deaf people have rarely been permitted to address audiences comprised of hearing professionals. Admittedly, preaching to the converted has value—it may evoke fresh ideas and it builds solidarity and commitment. Advocates of the disability construction do the same; childhood implant conferences, for example, rigorously exclude the voices of the cautious or frankly opposed.

I hope it may be allowed, however, to someone who has been invited to address numerous Deaf audiences and is exasperated by the slow pace of reform to point out that too much of this is an obstacle to true reform because it requires effort, permits the illusion that significant action has been taken, and yet changes little since Deaf people themselves are not responsible for the spread of the disability construction and have little direct power to change its range of application. What part of the battle is won when a Deaf leader receives a standing ovation from a Deaf audience? In the tradition of Deaf activism during the International Congress on the Education of the Deaf in Manchester in 1985, and during the Gallaudet Revolution, the past year have seen a striking increase in Europe of Deaf groups turning outward and presenting their views to hearing people and the media uninvited, particularly in opposition to cochlear implant surgery on Deaf children (Lane, 1994).

Production Change

Despite all the obstacles, there are powerful social forces to assist the efforts of the DEAF-WORLD to promote the linguistic minority construction. The body of knowledge developed in linguistics, history, sociology, and anthropology (to mention just four disciplines) concerning Deaf communities has influenced Deaf leadership, bureaucratic decision-making, and legislation. The civil rights movement has given great impetus to the belief that minorities should define themselves and that minority leaders should have a significant say in the conduct of minority affairs. Moreover, the failure of the present predominant disability construction to deliver more able deaf children is a source of professional and public embarrassment and promotes change. Then, too, Deaf children of Deaf parents are frequently insulated against the disability construction to a degree by their early language and cultural acquisition within the DEAF-WORLD. These native ASL-users have important allies in the DEAF-WORLD, among hearing children of Deaf parents, and among disaffected hearing professionals. The Gallaudet Revolution did not change the disability construction on a large scale but it led to inroads against it. Growing numbers of schools, for example, are turning to the linguistic minority construction to guide their planning, curricula, teacher selection and training.

Numerous organizations have committed extensive effort and money to promoting the disability construction. What can the national associations of the Deaf do to promote the linguistic minority construction? Publications like the British Deaf Association *News* or the National Association of the Deaf *Deaf American* are an important step because they provide a forum for national political discussion. However, the discussion has lacked focus. In addition to a forum, such associations need an explicit political agenda and a plan for implementing it. Such an agenda might include, illustratively, building a greater awareness of the difference between hearing-impairment and cultural Deafness; greater acceptance of the national sign language; removal or reduction of language barriers; improving culturally sensitive health care. Nowhere I know of are such agendas made explicit—given priorities, implementation, a time plan. If these were published they could provide the needed focus for the debate. Commentary on the agenda and plan would be invited as well as rebuttals to the commentaries in subsequent issues. Such agendas, plans and debates are buttressed by scholarship. An important resource to develop is a graduate program in public administration or political science focused on the DEAF-WORLD and the promotion of the linguistic minority construction.

Notes

I acknowledge gratefully helpful discussions with Ben Bahan, and Robert Hoffmeister, Boston University; Alma Bournazian, Northeastern University; Robert E. Johnson, Gallaudet University; Osamu Nagase, United Nations Program on Disability; MJ Bienvenu, the Bicultural Center; and helpful criticism from two unidentified journal reviewers.

1. Padden (1980) makes a distinction between a deaf community, a group of Deaf and hearing individuals who work to achieve certain goals, and a Deaf culture, to which Deaf members of that community belong.
2. In an effort to retain the disability construction of deafness, it has been suggested that sign language interpreters should be viewed as personal assistants. However, the services of these highly trained professionals are frequently not personal but provided to large audiences and they "assist" hearing people as well as, and at the same time as, Deaf people. Nor is interpreting between any other two languages (for example, at the United Nations) considered personal assistance.
3. I am not contending that there is a unitary homogenous DEAF-WORLD. My claims about Deaf culture are best taken as hypotheses for further verification, all the more as I am not a member of the DEAF-WORLD. My means of arriving at cultural principles are the usual ones for an outsider: encounters, ASL language and literature (including stories, legends, anecdotes, poetry, plays, humor, rituals, sign play), magazines and newspaper stories, films, histories, informants, scholarly studies, and the search for principles of coherence. See Stokoe (1994) and Kyle (1990).

References

Albrecht, G. L. (1992) *The Disability Business: Rehabilitation in America* (Newbury Park CA, Sage).

Aberley, P. (1987) The concept of oppression and the development of a social theory of disability, *Disability, Handicap and Society,* 2, pp. 5–19.

Allen, T. E. (1986) Patterns of academic achievement among hearing-impaired students: 1974 and 1983, in: A. N. Schildroth & M. A. Karchmer (Eds.) *Deaf Children in America* (San Diego, College-Hill).

Allen, T. E., Rawlings, B. W. & Remington, E. (1994) Demographic and audiologic profiles of deaf children in Texas with cochlear implants, *American Annals of the Deaf,* 138, pp. 260–266.

Barton, L. (1993) The struggle for citizenship: the case of disabled people, *Disability, Handicap and Society,* 8, pp. 235–248.

Becker, G. (1980) *Growing Old in Silence* (Berkeley, University of California Press).

Bienvenu, M. J. (1989) Disability, *The Bicultural Center News,* 13 (April), p. 1.

Braille Monitor (1973) NAC—unfair to the blind, *Braille Monitor,* 2, pp. 127–128.

Braille Monitor (1989) Blind workers claim wages exploitative, *Braille Monitor,* 6, p. 322.

Burek, D. M. (Ed.) (1993) *Encyclopedia of Associations* (Detroit, Gale Research).

Castle, D. (1990) Employment bridges cultures, *Deaf American,* 40, pp. 19–21.

Conrad, P. & Schneider, J. (1980) *Deviance and Medicalization: from Badness to Sickness* (Columbia, OH, Merrill).

Cant, T. & Gregory, S. (1991) Unit 8. The social construction of deafness, in: Open University (Eds.) *Issues in Deafness* (Milton Keynes, Open University).

Dowler, D. L. & Hirsh, A. (1994) Accommodations in the workplace for people who are deaf or hard of hearing, *Technology and Disability,* 3, pp. 15–25.

Evans, J. W. (1989) Thoughts on the psychosocial implications of cochlear implantation in children, in: E. Owens & D. Kessler (Eds.) *Cochlear Implants in Young Deaf Children* (Boston, Little, Brown).

Finkelstein, V. (1991) 'We' are not disabled, 'you' are, in: S. Gregory & G. M. Hartley (Eds.) *Constructing Deafness* (London, Pinter).

Fishman, J. (1982) A critique of six papers on the socialization of the deaf child, in: J. B. Christiansen (Ed.) *Conference highlights: National Research Conference on the Social Aspects of Deafness,* pp. 6–20 (Washington, DC, Gallaudet College).

Gannon, J. (1989) *The Week the World Heard Gallaudet* (Washington, DC, Gallaudet University Press).

Gregory, S. & Hartley, G. M. (Eds.) (1991) *Constructing Deafness* (London, Pinter).

Gusfield, J. (1982) Deviance in the welfare state: the alcoholism profession and the entitlements of stigma, in: M. Lewis (Ed.) *Research in Social Problems and Public Policy,* Vol. 2 (Greenwich, CT, JAI press).

Gusfield, J. (1984) On the side: practical action and social constructivism in social problems theory, in: J. Schneider & J. Kitsuse (Eds.) *Studies in the Sociology of Social Problems* (Rutgers, NJ, Ablex).

Gusfield, J. (1989) Constructing the ownership of social problems: fun and profit in the welfare state, *Social Problems,* 36, pp. 431–441.

Hawcroft, L. (1991) Block 2, unit 7. Whose welfare?, in: Open University (Eds.) *Issues in Deafness* (Milton Keynes, Open University).

Hevey, D. (1993) From self-love to the picket line: strategies for change in disability representation, *Disability, Handicap and Society,* 8, pp. 423–430.

Hlibok, G. (1988) Quoted in *USA Today,* 15 March, p. 11a.

Humphries, T. (1993) Deaf culture and cultures, in: K. M. Christensen & G. L. Delgado (Eds.) *Multicultural Issues in Deafness* (White Plains, NY, Longman).

Jernigan, K. (1973) Partial victory in the NAC battle—and the beat goes on, *Braille Monitor,* January, pp. 1–3.

Johnson, R. E. & Erting, C. (1989) Ethnicity and socialization in a classroom for deaf children, in: C. Lucas (Ed.) *The sociolinguistics of the Deaf Community,* pp. 41–84 (New York, Academic Press).

Johnson, R. E. Liddell, S. K. & Erting, CJ. (1989) Unlocking the curriculum: principles for achieving access in deaf education, *Gallaudet Research Institute Working Papers,* 89–3.

Jones, L. & Pullen, G. (1989) 'Inside we are all equal': a European social policy survey of people who are deaf, in: L. Barton (Ed.) *Disability and Dependency* (Bristol, PA, Taylor & Francis/Falmer Press).

Kyle, J. (1990) The Deaf community: culture, custom and tradition, in: S. Prillwitz & T. Vollhaber (Eds.) *Sign Language Research and Application* (Hamburg, Signum).

Kyle, J. (1991) Deaf people and minority groups in the UK, in: S. Gregory & G. M. Hartley (Eds.) *Constructing Deafness* (London, Pinter).

Lane, H. (1984) *When the Mind Hears: a history of the deaf* (New York, Random House).

Lane, H. (1992) *The Mask of Benevolence: disabling the deaf community* (New York, Alfred Knopf).

Lane, H. (1994) The cochlear implant controversy, *World Federation of the Deaf News,* 2–3, pp. 22–28.

Lynas, W. (1986) *Integrating the Handicapped into Ordinary Schools: a study of hearing-impaired pupils* (London, Croom Helm).

Markowicz, H. & Woodward, J. (1978) Language and the maintenance of ethnic boundaries in the deaf community, *Communication and Cognition,* 11, pp. 29–38.

Oliver, M. (1989) Disability and dependency: a creation of industrial societies, in: L. Barton (Ed.) *Disability and Dependency,* pp. 6–22 (Bristol, PA, Taylor & Francis/Falmer Press).

Oliver, M. (1990) *The Politics of Disablement* (New York, St. Martin's Press).

Oliver, M. (1991) Multispecialist and multidisciplinary—a recipe for confusion? 'Too many cooks spoil the broth', *Disability, Handicap & Society,* 6, pp. 65–68.

Olson, C. (1977) Blindness can be reduced to an inconvenience, *Journal of Visual Impairment and Blindness,* 11, pp. 408–409.

Olson, C. (1981) Paper barriers, *Journal of Visual Impairment and Blindness,* 15, pp. 337–339.

Open University (1991) *Issues in Deafness* (Milton Keynes, Open University).

Osberger, M. J., Maso, M. & Sam, L. K. (1993) Speech intelligibility of children with cochlear implants, tactile aids, or hearing aids, *Journal of Speech and Hearing Research,* 36, pp. 186–203.

Padden, C. (1980) The deaf community and the culture of deaf people, in: C. Baker & R. Battison (Eds.) *Sign Language and the Deaf Community: essays in honor of William C. Stokoe,* pp. 89–103 (Silver Spring, MD, National Association of the Deaf).

Padden, C. (Ed.) (1990) *Report of the Working Group on Deaf Community Concerns* (Bethesda, MD, National Institute on Deafness and Other Communication Disorders).

Parratt, D. & Tipping, B. (1991) The state, social work and deafness, in: S. Gregory & G. M. Hartley (Eds.) *Constructing Deafness* (London, Pinter).

Ross, M. & Calvert, D. R. (1967) Semantics of deafness, *Volta Review,* 69, pp. 644–649.

Saltus, R. (1989) Returning to the world of sound, *Boston Globe,* 10 July, pp. 27, 29.

Schein, J. D. (1989) *At Home Among Strangers* (Washington, DC, Gallaudet University Press).

Schneider, J. & Kitsuse, J. (Eds.) (1989) *Studies in the Sociology of Social Problems* (Rutgers, NJ, Ablex).

Scott, R. A. (1981) *The Making of Blind Men* (New Brunswick, NJ, Transaction).

Shapiro, J. P. (1993) *No Pity: people with disabilities forging a new Civil Rights Movement* (New York: Times Books).

Sixty Minutes (1992) Caitlin's story, 8 November.

Staller, S. S., Better, A. L., Brimacombe, J. A., Mecklenburg, D. J. & Arndt, P. (1991) Pediatric performance with the Nucleus 22-channel cochlear implant system, *American Journal of Otology,* 12 (Suppl.), pp. 126–136.

Stokos, W. (1994) An SLS print symposium [on culture]: an introduction, *Sign Language Studies,* 83, pp. 97–102.

Tucker, I. & Nolan, M. (1984) *Educational Audiology* (London, Croom Helm).

Tye-Murray, N. (1992) *Cochlear Implants and Children: a handbook for parents, teachers and speech professionals* (Washington, DC, A. G. Bell Association).

United Nations (1994) *The Standard Rules on the Equalization of Opportunities for Persons with Disabilities* (New York, United Nations).

Van Cleve, J. (Ed.) (1987) *The Gallaudet Encyclopedia of Deaf People and Deafness* (New York, McGraw-Hill).

Vaughan, C. E. (1991) The social basis of conflict between blind people and agents of rehabilitation, *Disability, Handicap & Society,* 6, pp. 203–217.

Wilson, G. B., Ross, M. & Calvert, D. R. (1974) An experimental study of the semantics of deafness, *Volta Review,* 76, pp. 408–414.

Wright, L. (1994) Annals of politics: one drop of blood, *The New Yorker,* 25 July, pp. 46–55.

Zola, I. K. (1993) Disability statistics, what we count and what it tells us, *Journal of Disability Policy Studies,* 4, pp. 9–39.

7

Abortion and Disability
Who Should and Who Should Not Inhabit the World?

Ruth Hubbard

Political agitation and education during the past few decades have made most people aware of what constitutes discrimination against blacks and other racial and ethnic minorities and against women. And legal and social measures have been enacted to begin to counter such discrimination. Where people with disabilities are concerned, our level of awareness is low, and the measures that exist are enforced haphazardly. Yet people with disabilities and disability-rights advocates have stressed again and again that it is often far easier to cope with the physical aspects of a disability than with the discrimination and oppression they encounter because of it (Asch, 1988; Asch and Fine, 1988). People shun persons who have disabilities and isolate them so they will not have to see them. They fear them as though the disability were contagious. And it is, in the sense that it forces us to face our own vulnerability.

Most of us would be horrified if a scientist offered to develop a test to diagnose skin color prenatally so as to enable racially mixed people (which means essentially everyone who is considered black and many of those considered white in the Americas) to have light-skinned children. And if the scientist explained that because it is difficult to grow up black in America, he or she wanted to spare people suffering because of the color of their skin, we would counter that it is irresponsible to use scientific means to reinforce racial prejudices. Yet we see nothing wrong, and indeed hail as progress, tests that enable us to try to avoid having children who have disabilities or are said to have a tendency to acquire a specific disease or disability later in life.

The scientists and physicians who develop and implement these tests believe they are reducing human suffering. This justification seems more appropriate for speed limits, seat-belt laws, and laws to further occupational safety and health than for tests to avoid the existence of certain kinds of people. When it comes to women or to racial or ethnic groups, we insist that it is discriminatory to judge individuals on the basis of their group affiliation. But we lump people with disabilities as though all disabilities were the same and always devastating and as though all people who have one were alike.

Health and physical prowess are poor criteria of human worth. Many of us know people with a disease or disability whom we value highly and so-called healthy people whom we could readily do without. It is fortunate for human variety and variability that most of us are not called on to make such judgments, much less to implement them.

It is not new for people to view disability as a form of pollution, evidence of sin. Disability has been considered divine punishment or, alternatively, the result of witches' spells. In our scientific and medical era we look to heredity for explanations unless there is an obvious external cause, such as an accident or infectious disease. Nowadays, even if an infection can explain the disability, scientists have begun to suggest that our genes might have made us unusually susceptible to it.

In a sense, hereditary disabilities are contagious because they can be passed from one generation to the next. For this reason, well before there was a science of genetics, scientists proposed eugenic measures to stem the perpetuation of "defects."

The Rise of Eugenics in Britain and the United States

Eugenics met its apotheosis under the Nazis, which is why many Germans oppose genetic testing and gene therapy and their use is being hotly debated in the parliament. Germans tend to understand better than people in other countries what can happen when the concern that people with disabilities will become social and economic burdens or that they will lead to a deterioration of the race begins to dictate so-called preventive health policies. They are aware that scientists and physicians were the ones who developed the Nazi policies of "selection and eradication" (*Auslese und Ausmerze*) and who oversaw their execution. What happened under the Nazis has been largely misrepresented and misinterpreted in this country, as well as among Nazi apologists in Germany. To make what happened clearer, I shall briefly review the scientific underpinnings of the Nazi extermination program, which are obscured when these practices are treated as though they were incomprehensible aberrations without historical roots or meaning—a holocaust.

German eugenics, the attempt to improve the German race, or *Volk*, by ridding it of inferior and foreign elements, was based on arguments and policies developed largely in Great Britain and the United States during the latter part of the nineteenth and the beginning of the twentieth centuries. (In what follows I shall not translate the german word *Volk* because it has no English equivalent. The closest is "people," singular, used as a collective noun, as in "the German people *is* patriotic." But "people," singular, does not convey the collectivity of *Volk* because to us "people" means individuals. Therefore, we would ordinarily phrase my example, "the German people *are* patriotic.")

The term *eugenics* is derived from the Greek word for "well born." It was coined in 1883 by Francis Galton, cousin of Charles Darwin, as "a brief word to express the science of improving the stock, which is by no means confined to questions of judicious mating, but which, especially in the case of man [*sic*], takes cognizance of all the influences that tend in however remote a degree to give the more suitable races or strains of blood a better chance of prevailing speedily over the less suitable than they otherwise would have had" (pp. 24–25). Galton later helped found the English Eugenics Education Society and eventually became its honorary president.

British eugenics counted among its supporters many distinguished biologists and social scientists. Even as late as 1941, while the Nazis were implementing their eugenic extermination program, the distinguished biologist Julian Huxley (1941)—brother of Aldous—opened a semipopular article entitled "The Vital Importance of Eugenics" with the words: "Eugenics is running the usual course of many new ideas. It has ceased to be regarded as a fad, is now receiving serious study, and in the near future, will be regarded as an urgent practical problem." In the article, he argues that it is crucial for society "to ensure that mental defectives [*sic*] shall not have children" and defines as mentally defective "someone with such a feeble mind that he cannot support himself or look after himself unaided." (Notice the mix of eugenics and economics.) He says that he refuses to enter into the argument over whether such "racial degeneration" should be forestalled by "prohibition of marriage" or "segregation in institutions" combined with "sterilization for those who are at large." He states as fact that most "mental defects" are hereditary and suggests that it would therefore be better if one could "discover how to diagnose the carriers of the defect" who are "apparently normal." "If these could but be detected, and then discouraged *or prevented* from reproducing, mental defects could very speedily be reduced to negligible proportions among our population" (my emphasis). It is shocking that at a time when the Nazi program of eugenic sterilization and euthanasia was in full force across the Channel, Huxley expressed regret that it was "at the moment very difficult to envisage methods for putting even a limited constructive program [of eugenics] into effect" and complained that "that is due as much to difficulties in our present socioeconomic organization as to our ignorance of human heredity, and most of all to the absence of a eugenic sense in the public at large."

The American eugenics movement built on Galton and attained its greatest influence between 1905 and 1935. An underlying concern of the eugenicists is expressed in a statement by Lewis Terman (1924), one of the chief engineers of I.Q. testing: "The fecundity of the family stocks from which our most gifted children come appears to be definitely on the wane.... It has been figured that if the present differential birth rate continues 1,000 Harvard graduates will, at the end of 200 years, have but 56 descendants, while in the same period, 1,000 S. Italians will have multiplied to 100,000." To cope with this dire eventuality, eugenics programs had two prongs: "positive eugenics"—encouraging the "fit" (read "well-to-do") to have lots of children—and "negative eugenics"—preventing the "unfit" (defined to include people suffering from so-called insanity, epilepsy, alcoholism, pauperism, criminality, sexual perversion, drug abuse, and especially feeble-mindedness) from having any.

Many distinguished American geneticists supported eugenics, but none was more active in promoting it than Charles Davenport, who, after holding faculty appointments at Harvard and the University of Chicago, in 1904 became director of the "station for the experimental study of evolution," which he persuaded the Carnegie Institution of Washington to set up in Cold Spring Harbor on Long Island. His goal was to collect large amounts of data on human inheritance and store them in a central office. In 1910, he managed to persuade the heiress to the Harriman railroad fortune to fund the Eugenics Record Office at Cold Spring Harbor, for which he got additional money from John D. Rockefeller, Jr. He appointed Harry W. Laughlin, a Princeton Ph. D., as superintendent and recruited a staff of young graduates from Radcliffe, Vassar, Cornell, Harvard, and other elite institutions as fieldworkers to accumulate interview data about a large number of so-called mental and social defectives. The office and its staff became major resources for promoting the two legislative programs that formed the backbone of U. S. eugenics: involuntary-sterilization laws and the Immigration Restriction Act of 1924.

The first sterilization law was enacted in Indiana in 1907, and by 1931 some thirty states had compulsory-sterilization laws on their books. Aimed in general at the insane and "feeble-minded" (broadly interpreted to include many recent immigrants and other people who did badly on I.Q. tests because they were functionally illiterate or barely spoke English), these laws often extended to so-called sexual perverts, drug fiends, drunkards, epileptics, and "other diseased and degenerate persons" (Ludmerer, 1972). Although most of these laws were not enforced, by January 1935 some twenty thousand people in the United States had been forcibly sterilized, nearly half of them in California. Indeed, the California law was not repealed until 1980 and eugenic-sterilization laws are still on the books in about twenty states.

The eugenic intent of the Immigration Restriction Act of 1924 was equally explicit. It was designed to decrease the proportion of poor immigrants from southern and eastern Europe so as to give predominance to Americans of British and north European descent. This goal was accomplished by restricting the number of immigrants allowed into the United States from any one country in each calendar year to at most 2 percent of U.S. residents who had been born in that country as listed in the Census of 1890 (so, thirty-four years earlier). The date 1890 was chosen because it established as a baseline the ethnic composition of the U.S. population prior to the major immigrations from eastern and southern Europe, which began in the 1890s. Laughlin of the Eugenics Record Office was one of the most important lobbyists and witnesses at the Congressional hearings that preceded passage of the Immigration Restriction Act and was appointed "expert eugenical agent" of the House Committee on Immigration and Naturalization (Kevles, 1985).

Racial Hygiene in Germany

What was called eugenics in the United States and Britain came to be known as racial hygiene in Germany. It was the response to several related and widely held beliefs: (1) that humane care for people with disabilities would enfeeble the "race" because they would survive to pass their disabilities on to their children; (2) that not just mental and physical diseases and so-called defects, but also poverty, criminality, alcoholism, prostitution, and other social problems were based in biology and inherited; and (3) that genetically inferior people were reproducing faster than superior people and would eventually displace them. Although these beliefs were not based in fact, they fueled racist thinking and social programs in Britain and the United States as well as in Germany.

German racial hygiene was founded in 1895, some dozen years after Galton's eugenics, by a physician, Alfred Plötz, and was based on much the same analysis of social problems as the British and American eugenics movements were. In 1924, Plötz started the *Archive of Race- and Socio-biology (Archiv für Rassen- und Gesellschaftsbiologie)* and the next year helped found the Society for Racial Hygiene (Gesellschaft für Rassenhygiene). German racial hygiene initially did not concern itself with preventing the admixture of "inferior" races, such as Jews or gypsies, in contrast to the British and American movements where miscegenation with blacks, Asians, Native Americans, and immigrants of almost any sort was one of the major concerns. The recommended means for preventing racial degeneration in Germany, as elsewhere, was sterilization. Around 1930 even some German socialists and communists supported the eugenic sterilization of inmates of psychiatric institutions, although the main impetus came from the Nazis. The active melding of anti-Semitism and racial hygiene in Germany began during World War I and accelerated during the 1920s, partly in response to economic pressures and a scarcity of available positions, which resulted in severe competition for jobs and incomes among scientists and physicians, many of whom were Jews.

Racial hygiene was established as an academic discipline in 1923, when Fritz Lenz, a physician and geneticist, was appointed to the newly created Chair of Racial Hygiene at the University of Munich, a position he kept until 1933, when he moved to the Chair of Racial Hygiene at the University of Berlin. Lenz, Eugen Fischer, and Erwin Baer coauthored the most important textbook on genetics and racial hygiene in German. Published in 1921, it was hailed in a review in the *American Journal of Heredity* in 1928 as "the standard textbook of human genetics" in the world (quoted in Proctor, 1988, p. 58). In 1931, it was translated into English, and the translation was favorably reviewed in Britain and the United States despite its blatant racism, or perhaps because of it. By 1933, eugenics and racial hygiene were being taught in most medical schools in Germany.

Therefore the academic infrastructure was in place when the Nazis came to power and began to build a society that gave biologists, anthropologists, and physicians the opportunity to put their racist and eugenic theories into practice. Looking back on this period, Eugen Fischer, who directed the Kaiser Wilhelm Institute for Anthropology, Human Genetics, and Eugenics in Berlin from 1927 to 1942, wrote in a newspaper article in 1943: "It is special and rare good luck when research of an intrinsically theoretical nature falls into a time when the general world view appreciates and welcomes it and, what is more, when its practical results are immediately accepted as the basis for governmental procedures" (quoted in Müller-Hill, 1984, p. 64; my translation). It is not true, as has sometimes been claimed, that German scientists were perverted by Nazi racism. Robert Proctor (1988) points out that "it was largely medical scientists who *invented* racial hygiene in the first place" (p. 38; original emphasis).

A eugenic-sterilization law, drafted along the lines of a "Model Sterilization Law" published by Laughlin (the superintendent of Davenport's Eugenics Record Office at Cold Spring Harbor), was being considered in 1932 by the Weimar government. On July 14, 1933, barely six months after Hitler took over, the Nazi government passed its eugenic-sterilization law. This law established genetic health courts (*Erbgesundheitsgerichte*), presided over by a lawyer and two physicians, one of whom was to be an expert on "hereditary pathology" (*Erbpathologie*), whose rulings could be appealed to similarly constituted supreme genetic health courts. However, during the entire Nazi period only about 3 percent of lower-court decisions were reversed. The genetic health courts could order the sterilization of people on grounds that they had a "genetically determined" disease, such as "inborn feeble-mindedness, schizophrenia, manic-depressive insanity, hereditary epilepsy, Huntington's disease, hereditary blindness, hereditary deafness, severe physical malformations, and severe alcoholism" (Müller-Hill, 1984, p. 32; my translation). The law was probably written by Dr. Ernst Rüdin, professor of psychiatry and director of the Kaiser Wilhelm Institute for Genealogy and Demography of the German Research Institute for Psychiatry in Munich. The official commentary and interpretation of the law was published under his name and those of an official of the Ministry of the Interior, also a medical doctor, and of a representative of the Health Ministry in the Department of the Interior who was a doctor of laws. All practicing physicians were sent copies of the law and commentaries describing the acceptable procedures for sterilization and castration.

The intent of the law was eugenic, not punitive. Physicians were expected to report patients and their close relatives to the nearest local health court and were fined if they failed to report someone with a so-called hereditary disease. Although some physicians raised the objection that this requirement invaded the doctor-patient relationship, the health authorities argued that this obligation to notify then was no different from requirements that physicians report the incidence of specific infectious diseases or births and deaths. The eugenic measures were to be regarded as health measures pure and simple. And this is the crucial point: the people who designed these policies and the later policies of euthanasia and mass extermination as well as those who oversaw their execution looked on them as sanitary measures, required in this case to cure not individual patients but the collective—the *Volk*—of threats to its health (Lifton, 1987; Proctor, 1988).

As early as 1934, Professor Otmar von Verschuer, then dean of the University of Frankfurt and director of its Institute for Genetics and Racial Hygiene and later the successor of Fischer as director of the Kaiser Wilhelm Institute for Anthropology, Human Genetics, and Eugenics in Berlin, urged that patients should not be looked on, and treated, as individuals. Rather the patient is but "one part of a much larger whole or unity: of his family, his race, his *Volk*" (quoted in Proctor, 1988, p. 105). Minister of the Interior Wilhelm Frisch estimated that at least half a million Germans had genetic diseases, but some experts thought that the true figure was more like one in five, which would be equivalent to thirteen million. In any event, by 1939 some three to four hundred thousand people had been sterilized, with a mortality of about 0.5 percent (Proctor, 1988, pp. 108–109). After that there were few individual sterilizations. Later, large numbers of people were sterilized in the concentration camps, but that was done without benefit of health courts, as part of the program of human experimentation.

The eugenic-sterilization law of 1933 did not provide for sterilization on racial grounds. Nonetheless, in 1937 about five hundred racially mixed children were sterilized; the children had been fathered by black French colonial troops brought to Europe from Africa after World War I to occupy the Rhineland (the so-called Rheinlandbastarde).

The first racist eugenic measures were passed in 1935. They were the Nürnberg antimiscegenation, or blood-protection laws, which forbade intermarriage or sexual relations between Jews and non-Jews and forbade Jews from employing non-Jews in their homes. The Nürnberg laws also included a "Law for the Protection of the Genetic Health of the German People," which required premarital medical examinations to detect "racial damage" and required people who were judged "damaged" to marry only others like themselves, provided they first submitted to sterilization. The Nürnberg laws were considered health laws, and physicians were enlisted to enforce them. So-called positive eugenics was practiced by encouraging "genetically healthy" German women to have as many children as possible. They were persuaded to do so by means of propaganda, economic incentives, breeding camps, and strict enforcement of the law forbidding abortion except for eugenic reasons (Koonz, 1987).

The next stage in the campaign of "selection and eradication" was opened at the Nazi party congress in 1935, where plans were made for the "destruction of lives not worth living." The phrase was borrowed from the title of a book published much earlier, in 1920, by Alfred Hoche, professor of psychiatry and director of the Psychiatric Clinic at Freiburg, and Rudolf Binding, professor of jurisprudence at the University of Leipzig. In their book, entitled *The Release for Destruction of Lives Not Worth Living (Die Freigabe zur Vernichtung lebensunwerten Lebens)*, these professors argued for killing "worthless" people, whom they defined as those who are "mentally completely dead" and those who constitute "a foreign body in human society" (quoted in Chorover, 1979, p. 97). At the time the program was initiated, the arguments focused on the money wasted in keeping institutionalized (hence "worthless") people alive, for in the early stages the rationale of the euthanasia campaign was economic as much as eugenic. Therefore the extermination campaign was directed primarily at inmates of state psychiatric hospitals and children living in state institutions for the mentally and physically disabled. Jews were specifically excluded because they were not considered worthy of euthanasia. (Here, too, the Nazis were not alone. In 1942, as the last inmates of German mental hospitals were being finished off, Dr. Foster Kennedy, an American psychiatrist writing in the official publication of the American

Psychiatric Association, advocated killing mentally retarded children of five and older (Proctor, 1988). The arguments were phrased in humane terms like these: "Parents who have seen the difficult life of a crippled or feebleminded child must be convinced that though they have the moral obligation to care for the unfortunate creatures, the wider public should not be obliged … to assume the enormous costs that long-term institutionalization might entail" (quoted in Proctor, 1988, p. 183). This argument calls to mind the statement by Bentley Glass (1971) about parents not having "a right to burden society with a malformed or a mentally incompetent child."

In Germany, the propaganda was subtle and widespread. For example, Proctor (1988, p. 184) cites practice problems in a high school mathematics text published for the school year 1935–36, in which students were asked to calculate the costs to the Reich of maintaining mentally ill people in various kinds of institutions for different lengths of time and to compare the costs of constructing insane asylums and housing units. How is that for relevance?

Although the euthanasia program was planned in the mid-1930s, it was not implemented until 1939, when wartime dislocation and secrecy made it relatively easy to institute such extreme measures. Two weeks before the invasion of Poland an advisory committee commissioned by Hitler issued a secret report recommending that children born with Down syndrome, microcephaly, and various deformities be registered with the Ministry of the Interior. Euthanasia, like sterilization, was to proceed with the trappings of selection. Therefore physicians were asked to fill out questionnaires about all children in their care up to age three who had any of these kinds of disabilities. The completed questionnaires were sent to three-man committees of medical experts charged with marking each form "plus" or "minus." Although none of these "experts" ever saw the children, those whose forms were marked "plus" were transferred to one of a number of institutions where they were killed. Some of the oldest and most respected hospitals in Germany served as such extermination centers. By 1941 the program was expanded to include older children with disabilities and by 1943, to include healthy Jewish children. Also in 1939, evaluation forms were sent to psychiatric institutions for adults for selection and so-called euthanasia.

By September 1941 over seventy thousand inmates had been killed at some of the most distinguished psychiatric hospitals in Germany, which had been equipped for this purpose with gas chambers, disguised as showers, and with crematoria (Lifton, 1986; Proctor, 1988). (When the mass extermination of Jews and other "undesirables" began shortly thereafter, these gas chambers were shipped east and installed at Auschwitz and other extermination camps.) Most patients were gassed or killed by injection with legal drugs, but a few physicians were reluctant to intervene so actively and let children die of slow starvation and the infectious diseases to which they became susceptible, referring to this as death from "natural" causes. Relatives were notified that their family member had died suddenly of one of a number of infectious diseases and that the body had been cremated for reasons of public health. Nevertheless, rumors began to circulate, and by 1941 hospital killings virtually ceased because of protests, especially from the Church.

There is a direct link between this campaign of "selection and eradication" and the subsequent genocide of Jews, gypsies, communists, homosexuals, and other "undesirables." Early on these people were described as "diseased" and their presence, as an infection or a cancer in the body of the *Volk*. Proctor (1988, p. 194) calls this rationalization "the medicalization of antisemitism." The point is that the Nazi leaders shouted anti-Semitic and racist propaganda from their platforms, but when it came to devising the measures for ridding the Thousand Year Reich of Jews, gypsies, and the other undesirables, the task was shouldered by the scientists and physicians who had earlier devised the sterilization and euthanasia programs for the mentally or physically disabled. Therefore, nothing came easier than a medical metaphor: Jews as cancer, Jews as disease. And so the Nazi extermination program was viewed by its perpetrators as a gigantic program in sanitation and public health. It started with quarantining the offending organisms in ghettoes and concentration camps and ended with the extermination of those who did not succumb to the "natural" consequences of the quarantine, such as the various epidemics and hunger.

Yet a measure of selection was practiced throughout the eradication process: It was still *Auslese* as well as *Ausmerze*. At every step choices were made of who could still be used and who had become "worthless." We have read the books and seen the films that show selections being made as the cattle cars emptied the victims into the concentration camps: to work or to die? That is where Joseph Mengele, an M. D./Ph. D., selected the twins and other unfortunates to use as subjects for his scientific experiments at Auschwitz, performed in collaboration with Professor von Verschuer, at that time director of the Kaiser Wilhelm Institute for Anthropology, Human Genetics, and Eugenics in Berlin. And von Verschuer was not the only distinguished scientist who gratefully accepted the human tissues and body fluids provided by Mengele. After the war it became fashionable to characterize the experiments as "bad science," but as Beno Müller-Hill (1984) emphasizes, nothing about them would be considered "bad" were they done with mice. What was "bad" was not their scientific content but the fact that they were being done with "disenfranchised human beings" (p. 97).

Prenatal Testing: Who Should Inhabit the World?

I want to come back to the present, but I needed to go over this history in order to put my misgivings and those of some of the Germans who are opposing genetic testing into the proper perspective. I can phrase the problem best by rephrasing a question Hannah Arendt asks in the epilogue of her commentary on the trial of Adolf Eichmann. Who has the "right to determine who should and who should not inhabit the world?" (1977). That's what it comes down to.

So let me be clear: I am not suggesting that prenatal diagnosis followed by abortion is similar to euthanasia. Fetuses are not people. And a woman must have the right to terminate her pregnancy, whatever her reasons. I am also not drawing an analogy between what the Nazis did and what we and others in many of the industrialized countries are doing now. Because the circumstances are different, different things are being done and for different reasons. But a similar eugenic ideology underlies what happened then and the techniques now being developed. So it is important that we understand how what happened then came about—and not in some faraway culture that is altogether different from ours but in the heart of Europe, in a country that has produced artists, writers, composers, philosophers, jurists, scientists, and physicians the equal of any in the Western world. Given that record, we cannot afford to be complacent.

Scientists and physicians in this and other countries are once more engaged in developing the means to decide what lives are worth living and who should and should not inhabit the world. Except that now they provide only the tools, while pregnant women themselves have to make the decisions, euphemistically called choices. No one is forced to do anything. A pregnant woman must merely "choose" whether to terminate a wanted pregnancy because she has been informed that her future child will have a disability (although, as I have said before, usually no one can tell her how severe the disability will be). If she "chooses" not to take the tests or not to terminate a pregnancy despite a positive result, she accepts responsibility for whatever the disability will mean to that child and to her and the rest of her family. In that case, her child, her family, and the rest of society can reproach her for having so-to-speak "caused" that human being's physical pain as well as the social pain he or she experiences because our society does not look kindly on people with disabilities.

There is something terribly wrong with this situation, and although it differs in many ways from what went wrong in Germany, at base are similar principles of selection and eradication. Lest this analogy seem too abstract, let me give a few examples of how the principle of selection and eradication now works in practice.

Think of people who have Huntington's disease; as you may remember they were on the list of people to be sterilized in Germany. Huntington's disease is a degenerative disease of the nervous system and is unusual among hereditary diseases in that it is inherited as what geneticists call a dominant trait. In other words, even people in whom only one of the pair of genes that is involved with regulating the relevant metabolic processes is affected manifest the disease. Most other gene-mediated diseases, such as Tay-Sachs disease or sickle-cell anemia, are so-called recessives: Only people in whom both members of the relevant pair of genes are affected manifest the disease. In the case of recessive diseases, people with only one affected gene are called carriers: They do not have the disease and usually do not even know that they carry a gene for it. To inherit a recessive disease such as sickle-cell anemia, a child must get an affected gene from each of its parents; to inherit a dominant disease, such as Huntington's disease, it is enough is she or he gets an affected gene from either parent.

The symptoms of Huntington's disease usually do not appear until people are in their thirties, forties, or fifties—in other words, after most people who want to have children have already had one or more. Woody Guthrie had Huntington's disease, but he did not become ill until after he had lived a varied and productive life, produced a large legacy of songs, and fathered his children. At present, there is no cure for Huntington's disease, although scientists have been working to find one. However, a test has been developed that makes it possible to establish with fair reliability whether a person or fetus carries the gene for Huntington's disease, provided a sufficient number of people in that family is willing to be tested.

The existence of this test puts people with a family history of Huntington's disease in an outrageous position: Although they themselves are healthy and do not know whether they will get the disease, they must decide whether to be tested, whether to persuade as many of their relatives as possible to do the same, and whether to test their future child prenatally so they can terminate the pregnancy if the test reveals that the fetus has the gene for Huntington's disease. If it does and they decide on abortion, they are as much as saying that a life lived in the knowledge that one will eventually die of Huntington's disease is not worth living. What does that say about their own life and the lives of their family members who now know that they have the gene for Huntington's disease? If the fetus has the gene and they do not abort, they are knowingly wishing a cruel, degenerative disease on their future child. And if they refuse the test, they can be accused of sticking their heads in the sand. This is an obscene "choice" for anyone to have to make!

Some other inherited diseases also do not become evident until later in life, such as retinitis pigmentosa, a degenerative eye disease. People with this disease are born with normal vision, but their eyesight deteriorates, although usually not until midlife, and they may eventually lose their sight. (People with this disease presumably also were slated for sterilization by the Nazis because it is a form of "hereditary blindness.") There are different patterns of inheritance of retinitis pigmentosa, and prenatal diagnosis is becoming available for one of these patterns and being sought for others. What are prospective parents to do when confronted with the "choice" of aborting a pregnancy because their future child may become blind at some time during its life?

Another, rather different, problem arises with regard to the so-called neural-tube defects (NTDs), a group of developmental disorders which, in fact, are not inherited. They include anencephaly (failure to develop a brain) and spina bifida (failure of the spinal column, and sometimes also the overlying tissues, to close properly) Babies with anencephaly die before birth or shortly thereafter. The severity of the health problems of children who have spina bifida depends on where along the spinal column the defect is located and can vary from life-threatening to relatively mild. The incidence of NTDs varies geographically and tends to be higher in industrialized than in nonindustrialized areas. Women who carry a fetus with a neural-tube defect have a grater than usual concentration of a specific substance, called alpha-feto-protein, in their blood. A blood test has been developed to detect NTDs prenatally, and California now requires that all pregnant women in the state be offered this test. The women are first counseled about NTDs and about the test and then have to sign a consent or refusal form. If they refuse, that is the end of it. If they consent, they can later refuse to abort the fetus even if the test is positive. This procedure sounds relatively unproblematical, although the requirement to sign a refusal form is coercive. (You cannot walk away; you must say no.) The trouble is that although the test detects virtually all fetuses who have NTDs, it yields a large number of false positive results that suggest that the fetus has a NTD although it does not.

Let us look at some numbers. In California there are about two hundred thousand births a year and the incidence of NTDs is about one per thousand. So, about 200 pregnant women a year carry fetuses with NTDs and 199,800 do not. However, about 5 percent of women test positive on a first test. In other words, if all pregnant women agreed to be tested, 10,000 women would have a positive test, 9,800 of which would be false positives. Those 10,000 women would then have to undergo the stress of worrying as well as further tests in order to determine who among them is in fact carrying a fetus with a NTD. And no test will tell the 200 women whose fetus, in fact, has a NTD how severe their child's health problem will be. All this testing with uncertain results must be offered at this time, when health dollars in California, as elsewhere, have been cut to the bone, and increasing numbers of pregnant women are coming to term with little or no prenatal services of any sort.

The reason I have spelled this problem out in such detail is to make it clear that in many of these situations parents have only the most tenuous basis for making their decisions. Because of the fear of raising a child with a serious disability, many women "choose" to abort a wanted pregnancy if they are told that there is any likelihood whatever that their future child may have a health problem. At times like that we seem to forget that we live in a society in which every day people of all ages are disabled by accidents—at work, on the street, or at home—many of which could be prevented if the necessary money were spent, the necessary precautions taken. What is more, because of the deteriorating economic conditions of poor people and especially women, increasing numbers of babies are born with disabilities that could easily be prevented and are prevented in most other industrialized nations. I question our excessive preoccupation with inherited diseases while callousness and economic mismanagement disable and kill increasing numbers of children and adults.

To say again, I am not arguing against a woman's right to abortion. Women must have that right because it involves a decision about our bodies and about the way we will spend the rest of our lives. But for scientists to argue that they are developing these tests out of concern for the "quality of life" of future children is like the arguments about "lives not worth living." No one can make that kind of decision about someone else. No one these days openly suggests that certain kinds of people be killed; they just should not be born. Yet that involves a process of selection and a decision about what kinds of people should and should not inhabit the world.

German women, who know the history of Nazi eugenics and how genetic counseling centers functioned during the Nazi period, have organized against the new genetic and reproductive technologies (Duelli Klein, Corea, and Hubbard, 1985). They are suspicious of prenatal testing and counseling centers because some of the scientists and physicians working in them are the same people who designed and implemented the eugenics program during the Nazi period. Others are former co-workers or students of these Nazi professors.

Our history is different, but not different enough. Eugenic thinking is part of our heritage and so are eugenic sterilizations. Here they were not carried over to mass exterminations because we live in a democracy with constitutional safeguards. But, as I mentioned before, even in recent times black, Hispanic, and Native-American women have been sterilized against their wills (Rodriguez-Trias, 1982). We do not exalt the body of the people, as a collective, over that of individuals, but we come dangerously close to doing so when we question the "right" of parents to bear a child who has a disability or when we draw unfavorable comparisons between the costs of care for children with disabilities and the costs of prenatal diagnosis and abortion. We come mighty close when we once again let scientists and physicians make judgments about who should and who should not inhabit the world and applaud them when they develop the technologies that let us implement such judgments. Is it in our interest to have to decide not just whether we want to bear a child but what kind of children to bear? If we try to do that we become entirely dependent on the decisions scientists and physicians make about what technologies to develop and what disabilities to "target." Those decisions are usually made on grounds of professional interest, technical feasibility, and economic and eugenic considerations, not out of a regard for the needs of women and children.

Problems with Selective Abortion

I want to be explicit about how I think a woman's right to abortion fits into this analysis and about some of the connections I see between what the Nazis did and what is happening now. I repeat: A woman must have the right to abort a fetus, whatever her reasons, precisely because it is a decision about her body and about how she will live her life. But decisions about what kind of baby to bear inevitably are bedeviled by overt and unspoken judgments about which lives are "worth living."

Nazi eugenic practices were fairly coercive. The state decided who should not inhabit the world, and lawyers, physicians, and scientists provided the justifications and means to implement these decisions. In today's liberal democracies the situation is different. Eugenic principles are part of our largely unexamined and unspoken preconceptions about who should and who should not inhabit the world, and scientists and physicians provide the ways to put them into practice. Women are expected to implement the society's eugenic prejudices by "choosing" to have the appropriate tests and "electing" not to initiate or to terminate pregnancies if it looks as though the outcome will offend. And to a considerable extent not initiating or terminating these pregnancies may indeed be what women want to do. But one reason we want to is that society promises much grief to parents of children it deems unfit to inhabit the world. People with disabilities, like the rest of us, need opportunities to act in the world, and sometimes that means that they need special provisions and consideration.

So once more, yes, a woman must have the right to terminate a pregnancy, whatever her reasons, but she must also feel empowered not to terminate it, confident that the society will do what it can to enable here and her child to live fulfilling lives. To the extent that prenatal interventions implement social prejudices against people with disabilities they do not expand our reproductive rights. They constrict them.

Focusing the discussion on individualistic questions, such as every woman's right to bear healthy children (which in some people's minds quickly translates into her duty not to "burden society" with unhealthy ones) or the responsibility of scientists and physicians to develop techniques to make that possible, obscures crucial questions such as: How many women have economic access to these kinds of choices? How many have the educational and cultural background to evaluate the information they can get from physicians critically enough to make an informed choice? It also obscures questions about a humane society's responsibilities to satisfy the requirements of people with special needs and to offer them the opportunity to participate as full-fledged members in the culture.

Our present situation connects with the Nazi past in that once again scientists and physicians are making the decisions about what lives to "target" as not worth living by deciding which tests to develop. Yet if people are to have real choices, the decisions that determine the context within which we must choose must not be made in our absence—by professionals, research review panels, or funding organizations. And the situation is not improved by inserting a new group of professionals—bioethicists—between the technical professionals and the public. This public—the women and men who must live in the world that the scientific/medical/industrial complex constructs—must be able to take part in the process by which such decisions are made. Until mechanisms exist that give people a decisive voice in setting the relevant scientific and technical agendas and until scientists and physicians are made accountable to the people whose lives they change, technical innovations do not constitute new choices. They merely replace previous social constraints with new ones.

Works Cited

Arendt, Hannah. 1977. *Eichmann in Jerusalem: A Report on the Banality of Evil.* New York: Penguin.
Asch, Adrienne. 1988. "Reproductive Technology and Disability." In Sherrill Cohen and Nadine Taub, eds., *Reproductive Laws for the 1990s.* Clifton, N. J.: Humana Press.

Asch, Adrienne, and Michelle Fine. 1988. "Introduction: Beyond Pedestals." In Michelle Fine and Adrienne Asch, eds., *Women with Disabilities*. Philadelphia: Temple University Press.

Chrorover, Stephan L. 1979. *From Genesis to Genocide*. Cambridge, Mass.: MIT Press.

Duelli Klein, Renate, Gena Corea, and Ruth Hubbard. 1985. "German Women say No to Gene and Reproductive Technology: Reflections on a Conference in Bonn, West Germany, April 19–21, 1985." *Feminist Forum: Women's Studies International Forum* 9(3):I–IV.

Galton, Francis. 1883. *Inquiries into Human Faculty*. London: Macmillan.

Glass, Bentley. 1971. "Science: Endless Horizons or Golden Age?" *Science* 171: 23–29.

Kevles, Daniel J. 1985. *In the Name of Eugenics: Genetics and the Uses of Human Heredity*. New York: Knopf.

Koonz, Claudia. 1987. *Mothers in the Fatherland: Women, the Family and Nazi Politics*. New York: St. Martin's Press.

Lifton, Robert J. 1986. *The Nazi Doctors*. New York: Basic Books.

Ludmerer, Kenneth M. 1972. *Genetics and American Society*. Baltimore: Johns Hopkins University Press.

Müller-Hill, Benno. 1984. *Tödliche Wissenshaft*. Reinbek, West Germany: Rowohlt. (Translation 1988. *Murderous Science*. Oxford: Oxford University Press.)

Proctor, Robert N. 1988. *Racial Hygiene: Medicine and the Nazis*. Cambridge: Harvard University Press.

Rodriguez-Trias, Helen. 1982. *In Labor: Women and Power in the Birthplace*. New York: Norton.

Terman, Lewis M. 1924. "The Conservation of Talent." *School and Society* 19(483): 359–364.

8

Disability Rights and Selective Abortion

Marsha Saxton

Disability rights activists are now articulating a critical view of the widespread practice of prenatal diagnosis with the intent to abort if the pregnancy might result in a child with a disability. Underlying this critique are historical factors behind a growing activism in the United States, Germany, Great Britain, and many other countries, an activism that confronts the social stigmatization of people with disabilities.

For disabled persons, women's consciousness-raising groups in the 1960s and 1970s offered a model for connecting with others in an "invisible" oppressed social group and confirming the experience of pervasive social oppression. ("That happened to you, too?") Participants in such groups began to challenge a basic tenet of disability oppression: that disability *causes* the low socioeconomic status of disabled persons. Collective consciousness-raising has made it clear that stigma is the cause.

Effective medical and rehabilitation resources since the 1950s have also contributed to activism. Antibiotics and improved surgical techniques have helped to alleviate previously fatal conditions. Consequently, disabled people are living longer and healthier lives, and the population of people with severely disabling conditions has increased. Motorized wheelchairs, lift-equipped wheelchair vans, mobile respirators, and computer and communication technologies have increased the mobility and access to education and employment for people previously ostracized because of their disabilities.

Effective community organizing by blind, deaf, and mobility-impaired citizen groups and disabled student groups flourished in the late 1960s and resulted in new legislation. In 1973 the Rehabilitation Act Amendments (Section 504) prohibited discrimination in federally funded programs. The Americans with Disabilities Act of 1990 (ADA) provides substantial civil rights protection and has helped bring about a profound change in the collective self-image of an estimated 45 million Americans. Today, many disabled people view themselves as part of a distinct minority and reject the pervasive stereotypes of disabled people as defective, burdensome, and unattractive.

It is ironic that just when disabled citizens have achieved so much, the new reproductive and genetic technologies are promising to eliminate births of disabled children—children with Down's syndrome, spina bifida, muscular dystrophy, sickle cell anemia, and hundreds of other conditions. The American public has apparently accepted these screening technologies based on the "commonsense" assumptions that prenatal screening and selective abortion can potentially reduce the incidence of disease and disability and thus improve the quality of life. A deeper look into the medical system's views of disability and the broader social factors contributing to disability discrimination challenges these assumptions.

Reproductive Rights in a Disability Context

There is a key difference between the goals of the reproductive rights movement and the disability rights movement regarding reproductive freedom: the reproductive rights movement emphasizes the right to have an abortion; the disability rights movement, the right *not to have to have* an abortion.

105

Disability rights advocates believe that disabled women have the right to bear children and be mothers, and that all women have the right to resist pressure to abort when the fetus is identified as potentially having a disability.

Women with disabilities raised these issues at a conference on new reproductive technologies (NRTs) in Vancouver in 1994.[1] For many of the conference participants, we were an unsettling group: women in wheelchairs; blind women with guide dogs; deaf women who required a sign-language interpreter; women with scarring from burns or facial anomalies; women with missing limbs, crutches, or canes. I noticed there what we often experience from people who first encounter us: averted eyes or stolen glances, pinched smiles, awkward or overeager helpfulness—in other words, discomfort accompanied by the struggle to pretend there was none.

It was clear to me that this situation was constraining communication, and I decided to do something about it. I approached several of the nondisabled women, asking them how they felt about meeting such a diverse group of disabled women. Many of the women were honest when invited to be: "I'm nervous. Am I going to say something offensive?" "I feel pretty awkward. Some of these women's bodies are so different!" One woman, herself disabled, said that she'd had a nightmare image of a disabled woman's very different body. One woman confessed: "I feel terrible for some of these unfortunate disabled women, but I know I'm not supposed to feel pity. That's awful of me, right?"

This awkwardness reveals how isolated the broader society and even progressive feminists are from people with disabilities. The dangerous void of information about disability is the *context* in which the public's attitudes about prenatal diagnosis and selective abortion are formed. In the United States this information void has yielded a number of unexamined assumptions, including the belief that the quality and enjoyment of life for disabled people is necessarily inferior, that raising a child with a disability is a wholly undesirable experience, that selective abortion will save mothers from the burdens of raising disabled children, and that ultimately we as a society have the means and the right to decide who is better off not being born.

What the women with disabilities were trying to do at the Vancouver conference, and what I wish to do in this essay, is explain how selective abortion or *eugenic abortion,* as some disability activists have called it, not only oppresses people with disabilities but also hurts all women.

Eugenics and the Birth Control Movement

The eugenic interest that stimulates reliance on prenatal screening and selective abortion today has had a central place in reproductive politics for more than half a century. In the nineteenth century, eugenicists believed that most traits, including such human "failings" as pauperism, alcoholism, and thievery, as well as such desired traits as intelligence, musical ability, and "good character," were hereditary. They sought to perfect the human race through controlled procreation, encouraging those from "healthy stock" to mate and discouraging reproduction of those eugenicists defined as socially "unfit," that is, with undesirable traits. Through a series of laws and court decisions American eugenicists mandated a program of social engineering. The most famous of these was the 1927 U.S. Supreme Court ruling in *Buck v. Bell.*[2]

Leaders in the early birth control movement in the United States, including Margaret Sanger, generally embraced a eugenic view, encouraging white Anglo-Saxon women to reproduce while discouraging reproduction among nonwhite, immigrant, and disabled people. Proponents of eugenics portrayed disabled women in particular as unfit for procreation and as incompetent mothers. In the 1920s Margaret Sanger's group, the American Birth Control League, allied itself with the director of the American Eugenics Society, Guy Irving Burch. The resulting coalition supported the forced sterilization of people with epilepsy, as well as those diagnosed as mentally retarded and mentally ill. By 1937, in the midst of the Great Depression, twenty-eight states had adopted eugenics sterilization laws aimed primarily at women for whom "procreation was deemed inadvisable." These laws sanctioned the sterilizations of over 200,000 women between the 1930s and the 1970s.[3]

While today's feminists are not responsible for the eugenic biases of their foremothers, some of these prejudices have persisted or gone unchallenged in the reproductive rights movement today.[4] Consequently, many women with disabilities feel alienated from this movement. On the other hand, some pro-choice feminists have felt so deeply alienated from the disability community that they have been willing to claim, "The right wing wants to force us to have defective babies."[5] Clearly, there is work to be done.

Disability-Positive Identity versus Selective Abortion

It is clear that some medical professionals and public health officials are promoting prenatal diagnosis and abortion with the intention of eliminating categories of disabled people, people with Down's syndrome and my own disability, spina bifida, for example. For this reason and others, many disability activists and feminists regard selective abortion as "the new eugenics." These people resist the use of prenatal diagnosis and selective abortion.

The resistance to selective abortion in the disability activist community is ultimately related to how we define ourselves. As feminists have transformed women's sense of self, the disability community has reframed the experience of having a disability. In part, through developing a sense of community, we've come to realize that the stereotyped notions of the "tragedy" and "suffering" of "the disabled" result from the *isolation* of disabled people in society. Disabled people with no connections to others with disabilities in their communities are, indeed, afflicted with the social role assignment of a tragic, burdensome existence. It is true, most disabled people I know have told me with certainty, that the disability, the pain, the need for compensatory devices and assistance can produce considerable inconvenience. But the inconvenience becomes minimal once the disabled person makes the transition to a typical everyday life. It is discriminatory attitudes and thoughtless behaviors, and the ensuing ostracism and lack of accommodation, that make life difficult. That oppression is what's most disabling about disability.

Many disabled people have a growing but still precarious sense of pride in an identity as "people with disabilities." With decades of hard work, disability activists have fought institutionalization and challenged discrimination in employment, education, transportation, and housing. We have fought for rehabilitation and Independent Living programs, and we have proved that disabled people can participate in and contribute to society.

As a political movement, the disability rights community has conducted protests and effective civil disobedience to publicize our demand for full citizenship. Many of our tactics were inspired by the women's movement and the black civil rights movement in the 1960s. In the United States we fought for and won one of the most far-reaching pieces of civil rights legislation ever, the Americans with Disabilities Act. This piece of legislation is the envy of the international community of disability activists, most of whom live in countries where disabled people are viewed with pity and charity, and accorded low social and legal status. Disability activists have fought for mentor programs led by adults with disabilities. We see disabled children as "the youth" of the movement, the ones who offer hope that life will continue to improve for people with disabilities for generations to come.

In part because of our hopes for disabled children, the "Baby Doe" cases of the 1980s caught the attention of the growing disability rights movement. These cases revealed that "selective nontreatment" of disabled infants (leaving disabled infants to starve because the parents or doctors choose not to intervene with even routine treatments such as antibiotics) was not a thing of the past. In this same period, we also took note of the growing number of "wrongful birth" suits—medical malpractice suits brought against physicians, purportedly on behalf of disabled children, by parents who feel that the child's condition should have been identified prenatally.[6] These lawsuits claim that disabled babies, once born, are too great a burden, and that the doctors who failed to eliminate the "damaged" fetuses should be financially punished.

But many parents of disabled children have spoken up to validate the joys and satisfactions of raising a disabled child. The many books and articles by these parents confirm the view that discriminatory attitudes make raising a disabled child much more difficult than the actual logistics of care.[7] Having developed a disability-centered perspective on these cases, disabled adults have joined with many parents of disabled children in challenging the notion that raising a child with a disability is necessarily undesirable.

The attitudes that disabled people are frightening or inhuman result from lack of meaningful interaction with disabled people. Segregation in this case, as in all cases, allows stereotypes to abound. But beyond advocating contact with disabled people, disability rights proponents claim that it is crucial to challenge limiting definitions of "acceptably human." Many parents of children with Down's syndrome say that their children bring them joy. But among people with little exposure to disabled people, it is common to think that this is a romanticization or rationalization of someone stuck with the burden of a damaged child.

Many who resist selective abortion insist that there is something deeply valuable and profoundly human (though difficult to articulate in the sound bites of contemporary thought) in meeting and loving a child or adult with a severe disability. Thus, contributions of human beings cannot be judged by how we fit into the mold of normalcy, productivity, or cost-benefit. People who are different from us (whether in color, ability, age, or ethnic origin) have much to share about what it means to be human. We must not deny ourselves the opportunity for connection to basic humanness by dismissing the existence of people labeled "severely disabled."

Mixed Feelings: Disabled People Respond to Selective Abortion

The disability *activist* community has begun to challenge selective abortion. But among disabled people as a whole, there is no agreement about these issues. After all, the "disability community" is as diverse as any other broad constituency, like "the working class" or "women." Aspects of this issue can be perplexing to people with disabilities because of the nature of the prejudice we experience. For example, the culture typically invalidates our bodies, denying our sexuality and our potential as parents. These cultural impulses are complexly intertwined with the issue of prenatal testing. Since the early 1990s, disability rights activists have been exploring and debating our views on selective abortion in the disability community's literature.[8] In addition, just like the general population's attitudes about *abortion,* views held by people with disabilities about *selective abortion* relate to personal experience (in this case, personal history with disability) and to class, ethnic, and religious backgrounds.

People with different kinds of disabilities may have complex feelings about prenatal screening tests. While some disabled people regard the tests as a kind of genocide, others choose to use screening tests during their own pregnancies to avoid the birth of a disabled child. But disabled people may also use the tests differently from women who share the larger culture's anti-disability bias.

Many people with dwarfism, for example, are incensed by the idea that a woman or couple would choose to abort simply because the fetus would become a dwarf. When someone who carries the dwarfism trait mates with another with the same trait, there is a likelihood of each partner contributing one dominant dwarfism gene to the fetus. This results in a condition called "double dominance" for the offspring, which, in this "extra dose of the gene" form, is invariably accompanied by severe medical complications and early death. So prospective parents who are carriers of the dwarfism gene, or are themselves dwarfs, who would readily welcome a dwarf child, might still elect to use the screening test to avoid the birth of a fetus identified with "double dominance."

Deafness provides an entirely different example. There is as yet no prenatal test for deafness, but if, goes the ethical conundrum, a hearing couple could eliminate the fetus that would become a deaf child, why shouldn't deaf people, proud of their own distinct sign-language culture, elect for a deaf child and abort a fetus (that would become a hearing person) on a similar basis?

Those who challenge selective or eugenic abortion claim that people with disabilities are the ones who have the information about what having a disability is like. The medical system, unable to cure or fix us, exaggerates the suffering and burden of disability. The media, especially the movies, distort our lives by using disability as a metaphor for evil, impotence, eternal dependence, or tragedy—or coversely as a metaphor for courage, inspiration, or sainthood. Disabled people alone can speak to the women facing these tests. Only we can speak about our real lives, our ordinary lives, and the lives of disabled children.

"Did You Get Your Amnio Yet?": The Pressure to Test and Abort

How do women decide about tests, and how do attitudes about disability affect women's choices? The reproductive technology market has, since the mid-1970s, gradually changed the experience of pregnancy. Some prenatal care facilities now present patients with their ultrasound photo in a pink or blue frame. Women are increasingly pressured to use prenatal testing under a cultural imperative claiming that this is the "responsible thing to do." Strangers in the supermarket, even characters in TV sit-coms, readily ask a woman with a pregnant belly, "Did you get your amnio yet?" While the ostensible justification is "reassurance that the baby is fine," the underlying communication is clear: screening out disabled fetuses is the right thing, "the healthy thing," to do. As feminist biologist Ruth Hubbard put it, "Women are expected to implement the society's eugenic prejudices by 'choosing' to have the appropriate tests and 'electing' not to initiate or to terminate pregnancies if it looks as though the outcome will offend."[9]

Often prospective parents have never considered the issue of disability until it is raised in relation to prenatal testing. What comes to the minds of parents at the mention of the term *birth defects*? Usually prospective parents summon up the most stereotyped visions of disabled people derived from telethons and checkout-counter charity displays. This is not to say that all women who elect selective abortion do so based on simple, mindless stereotypes. I have met women who have aborted on the basis of test results. Their stories and their difficult decisions were very moving. They made the decisions they felt were the only ones possible for them, given information they had been provided by doctors, counselors, and society.

Indeed, some doctors and counselors do make a good-faith effort to explore with prospective parents the point at which selective abortion may seem clearly "justifiable," with respect to the severity of the condition or the emotional or financial costs involved. These efforts are fraught with enormous social and ethical difficulty. Often, however, unacknowledged stereotypes prevail, as does a commitment to a libertarian view ("Let people do whatever they want!"). Together, these strains frequently push prospective parents to succumb to the medical control of birth, while passively colluding with pervasive disability discrimination.

Among the most common justifications of selective abortion is that it "ends suffering." Women as cultural nurturers and medical providers as official guardians of well-being are both vulnerable to this message. Health care providers are trying, despite the profit-based health care system, to improve life for people they serve. But the medical system takes a very narrow view of disease and "the alleviation of suffering." What is too often missed in medical training and treatment are the *social factors* that contribute to suffering. Physicians, by the very nature of their work, often have a distorted picture of the lives of disabled people. They encounter disabled persons having health problems, complicated by the stresses of a marginalized life, perhaps exacerbated by poverty and race or gender discrimination, but because of their training, the doctors tend to project the individual's overall struggle onto the disability as the "cause" of distress. Most doctors have few opportunities to see ordinary disabled individuals living in their communities among friends and family.

Conditions receiving priority attention for prenatal screening include Down's syndrome, spina bifida, cystic fibrosis, and fragile X, all of which are associated with mildly to moderately disabling clinical outcomes. Individuals with these conditions can live good lives. There are severe cases, but the medical system tends to underestimate the functional abilities and overestimate the "burden" and suffering of people with these conditions. Moreover, among the priority conditions for prenatal screening are diseases that occur very infrequently. Tay-Sachs disease, for example, a debilitating, fatal disease that affects primarily Jews of eastern European descent, is often cited as a condition that justifies prenatal screening. But as a rare disease, it's a poor basis for a treatment mandate.

Those who advocate selective abortion to alleviate the suffering of children may often raise that cornerstone of contemporary political rhetoric, *cost-benefit*. Of course, cost-benefit analysis is not woman-centered, yet women can be directly pressured or subtly intimidated by both arguments. It may be difficult for some to resist the argument that it is their duty to "save scarce health care dollars," by eliminating the expense of disabled children. But those who resist these arguments believe the value of a child's life cannot be measured in dollars. It is notable that families with disabled children who are familiar with the actual impact of the disabilities tend not to seek the tests for subsequent children.[10] The bottom line is that the cost-benefit argument disintegrates when the outlay of funds required to provide services for disabled persons is measured against the enormous resources expended to test for a few rare genetic disorders. In addition, it is important to recognize that promotion and funding of prenatal tests distract attention and resources from addressing possible environmental causes of disability and disease.

Disabled People and the Fetus

I mentioned to a friend, an experienced disability activist, that I planned to call a conference for disabled people and genetics professionals to discuss these controversial issues. She said, "I think the conference is important, but I have to tell you, I have trouble being in the same room with professionals who are trying to eliminate my people." I was struck by her identification with fetuses as "our people."

Are those in the disability rights movement who question or resist selective abortion trying to save the "endangered species" of disabled fetuses? When this metaphor first surfaced, I was shocked to think of disabled people as the target of intentional elimination, shocked to realize that I identified with the fetus as one of my "species" that I must try to protect.

When we refer to the fetus as a *disabled* (rather than defective) fetus, we *personify* the fetus via a term of pride in the disability community. The fetus is named as a member of our community. The connection disabled people feel with the "disabled fetus" may seem to be in conflict with the pro-choice stance that the fetus is only a part of the woman's body, with no independent human status.[11]

Many of us with disabilities might have been prenatally screened and aborted if tests had been available to our mothers. I've actually heard people say, "Too bad that baby with [x disease] didn't 'get caught' in prenatal screening." (This is the sentiment of "wrongful birth" suits.) It is important to make the distinction between a pregnant woman who chooses to terminate the pregnancy because she *doesn't want to be pregnant* as opposed to a pregnant woman who *wanted to be pregnant* but rejects a particular fetus, a particular potential child. Fetuses that are wanted are called "babies." Prenatal screening results can turn a "wanted baby" into an "unwanted fetus."

It is difficult to contemplate one's own hypothetical nonexistence. But I know several disabled teenagers, born in an era when they could have been "screened out," for whom this is not at all an abstraction. In biology class their teachers, believing themselves to be liberal, raised abortion issues. These teachers, however, were less than sensitive to the disabled students when they talked about "eliminating the burden of the disabled" through technological innovation.

In the context of screening tests, those of us with screenable conditions represent living adult fetuses that didn't get aborted. We are the constituency of the potentially aborted. Our resistance to the systematic abortion of "our young" is a challenge to the "nonhumanness," the nonstatus of the fetus. This issue of the humanness of the fetus is a tricky one for those of us who identify both as pro-choice feminists and as disability rights activists. Our dual perspective offers important insights for those who are debating the ethics of the new reproductive technologies.

Disentangling Patriarchal Control and Eugenics from Reproductive Freedom

The issue of selective abortion is not just about the rights or considerations of disabled people. Women's rights and the rights of all human beings are implicated here.

When disability rights activists challenge the practice of selective abortion, as we did in Vancouver, many feminists react with alarm. They feel "uncomfortable" with language that accords human status to the fetus. One woman said: "You can't talk about the fetus as an entity being supported by advocates. It's too 'right to life.'" Disabled women activists do not want to be associated with the violent anti-choice movement. In the disability community we make a clear distinction between our views and those of anti-abortion groups. There may have been efforts to court disabled people to support anti-abortion ideology, but anti-abortion groups have never taken up the issues of expanding resources for disabled people or parents of disabled children, never lobbied for disability legislation. They have shown no interest in disabled people after they are born.[12]

But a crucial issue compels some of us to risk making people uncomfortable by discussing the fetus: we must clarify the connection between control of "defective fetuses" and the control of women as vessels or producers of quality-controllable products. This continuum between control of women's bodies and control of the *products of women's bodies* must be examined and discussed if we are going to make headway in challenging the ways that new reproductive technologies can increasingly take control of reproduction away from women and place it within the commercial medical system.

A consideration of selective abortion as a control mechanism must include a view of the procedure as a wedge into the "quality control" of all humans. If a condition (like Down's syndrome) is unacceptable, how long will it be before experts use selective abortion to manipulate—eliminate or enhance—other (presumed genetic) socially charged characteristics: sexual orientation, race, attractiveness, height, intelligence? Pre-implantation diagnosis, now used with in vitro fertilization, offers the prospect of "admission standards" for all fetuses.

Some of the pro-screening arguments masquerade today as "feminist" when they are not. Selective abortion is promoted in many doctors' offices as a "reproductive option" and "personal choice." But as anthropologist Rayna Rapp notes, "Private choices always have public consequences."[13] When a woman's individual decision is the result of social pressure, it can have repercussions for all others in the society.

How is it possible to defend selective abortion on the basis of "a woman's right to choose" when this "choice" is so constrained by oppressive values and attitudes? Consider the use of selective abortion for sex selection. The feminist community generally regards the abortion of fetuses on the basis of gender—widely practiced in some countries to eliminate female fetuses—as furthering the devaluation of women. Yet women have been pressed to "choose" to perpetuate their own devaluation.[14] For those with "disability-positive" attitudes, the analogy with sex selection is obvious. Oppressive assumptions, not inherent characteristics, have devalued who this fetus will grow into.

Fetal anomaly has sometimes been used as a *justification* for legal abortion. This justification reinforces the idea that women are horribly oppressed by disabled children. When disability is sanctioned as a justification for legal abortion, then abortion for sex selection may be more easily sanctioned as well. If "choice" is made to mean choosing the "perfect child," or the child of the "right gender," then pregnancy is turned into a process and children are turned into products that are perfectible through technology. Those of us who believe that pregnancy and children must not be commodified believe that real "choice" must include the birth of a child with a disability.

To blame a woman's oppression on the characteristics of the fetus is to obscure and distract us from the core of the "choice" position: women's control over our own bodies and reproductive capacities. It also obscures the different access to "choice" of different groups of women. At conferences I've been asked, "Would I want to force a poor black woman to bear a disabled child?" That question reinforces what feminists of color have been saying, that the framework of "choice" trivializes the issues for nonprivileged women. It reveals distortions in the public's perception of users of prenatal screening; in fact, it is the middle and upper class who most often can purchase these "reproductive choices." It's not poor women, or families with problematic genetic traits, who are creating the market for tests. Women with aspirations for the "perfect baby" are establishing new "standards of care." Responding to the lure of consumerism, they are helping create a lucrative market that exploits the culture's fear of disability and makes huge profits for the biotech industry.

Some proponents argue that prenatal tests are feminist tools because they save women from the excessive burdens associated with raising disabled children.[15] This is like calling the washer-dryer a feminist tool; technological innovation may "save time," even allow women to work outside the home, but it has not changed who does the housework. Women still do the vast majority of child care, and child care is not valued as real work. Rather, raising children is regarded as women's "duty" and is not valued as "worth" paying mothers for (or worth paying teachers or day-care workers well). Selective abortion will not challenge the sexism of the family structure in which women provide most of the care for children, for elderly parents, and for those disabled in accidents or from nongenetic diseases. We are being sold an illusion that the "burden" and problems of motherhood are being alleviated by medical science. But using selective abortion to eliminate the "burden" of disabled children is like taking aspirin for an ulcer. It provides temporary relief that both masks and exacerbates the underlying problems.

The job of helping disabled people must not be confused with the traditional devaluing of women in the caregiver role. Indeed, women can be overwhelmed and oppressed by their work of caring for disabled family members. But this is *not caused by the disabilities per se.* It is caused by lack of community services and inaccessibility, and greatly exacerbated by the sexism that isolates and overworks women caregivers. Almost any kind of work with people, if sufficiently shared and validated, can be meaningful, important, joyful, and productive.

I believe that at this point in history the decision to abort a fetus with a disability even because it "just seems too difficult" must be respected. A woman who makes this decision is best suited to assess her own resources. But it is important for her to realize this "choice" is actually made under duress. Our society profoundly limits the "choice" to love and care for a baby with a disability. This failure of society should not be projected onto the disabled fetus or child. No child is "defective." A child's disability doesn't ruin a woman's dream of motherhood. Our society's inability to appreciate and support people is what threatens our dreams.

In our struggle to lead our individual lives, we all fall short of adhering to our own highest values. We forget to recycle. We ride in cars that pollute the planet. We buy sneakers from "developing countries" that exploit workers and perpetuate the distortions in world economic power. Every day we have to make judgment calls as we assess our ability to live well and right, and it is always difficult, especially in relation to raising our own children—perhaps in this era more so than ever—to include a vision of social change in our personal decisions.

Women sometimes conclude, "I'm not saintly or brave enough to raise a disabled child." This objectifies and distorts the experience of mothers of disabled children. They're not saints; they're ordinary women, as are the women who care for spouses or their own parents who become disabled. It doesn't take a "special woman" to mother a disabled child. It takes a caring parent to raise any child. If her child became disabled, any mother would do the best job she could caring for that child. It is everyday life that trains people to do the right thing, sometimes to be leaders.

Disabled Women Have a Legitimate Voice in the Abortion Debate!

Unfortunately, I've heard some ethicists and pro-choice advocates say that disabled people should not be allowed a voice in the selective abortion debate because "they make women feel guilty." The problem with this perspective is evident when one considers that there is no meaningful distinction between "disabled people" and "women." Fifty percent of adults with disabilities are women, and up to 20 percent of the female population have disabilities. The many prospective mothers who have disabilities or who are carriers of genetic traits for disabling conditions may have particular interests either in challenging or in utilizing reproductive technologies, *and* these women have key perspectives to contribute.

Why should hearing the perspectives of disabled people "make women feel guilty"? The unhappy truth is that so many decisions that women make about procreation are fraught with guilt and anxiety because sexism makes women feel guilty about their decisions. One might ask whether white people feel guilty when people of color challenge them about racism. And if so, doesn't that ultimately benefit everyone?

Do I think a woman who has utilized selective abortion intended to oppress *me* or wishes I were not born? Of course not. No more than any woman who has had an abortion means to eliminate the human race. Surely one must never condemn a woman for making the best choice she can with the information and resources available to her in the crisis of decision. In resisting prenatal testing, we do not aim to blame any individual woman or compromise her individual control over her own life or body. We *do* mean to offer information to empower her and to raise her awareness of the stakes involved for her as a woman and member of the community of all women.

A Proposal for the Reproductive Rights Movement

The feminist community is making some headway in demanding that women's perspectives be included in formulating policies and practices for new reproductive technologies, but the disability-centered aspects of prenatal diagnosis remain marginalized. Because the technologies have emerged in a society with entrenched attitudes about disability and illness, the tests have become embedded in medical "standards of care." They have also become an integral part of the biotech industry, a new "bright hope" of capitalist health care and the national economy. The challenge is great, the odds discouraging.

Our tasks are to gain clarity about prenatal diagnosis, challenge eugenic uses of reproductive technologies, and support the rights of all women to maintain control over reproduction. Here are some suggestions for action:

- We must actively pursue close connections between reproductive rights groups and disabled women's groups with the long-range goal of uniting our communities, as we intend to do with all other marginalized groups.
- We must make the issue of selective abortion a high priority in our movements' agendas, pushing women's groups and disability and parent groups to take a stand in the debate on selective abortion, instead of evading the issue.
- We must recognize disability as a feminist issue. All females (including teenagers and girls) will benefit from information and discussion about disability *before* they consider pregnancy, so they can avoid poorly informed decisions.
- Inclusion of people with disabilities must be part of the planning and outreach of reproductive rights organizations. Inclusion involves not only use of appropriate language and terminology for disability issues but also *involvement of disabled people* as resources. Women's organizations

must learn about and comply with the Americans with Disabilities Act (or related laws in other countries). If we are going to promote far-reaching radical feminist programs for justice and equality, we must surely comply with minimal standards set by the U.S. Congress.

- We must support family initiatives—such as parental leave for mothers and fathers, flex- and part-time work, child care resources, programs for low-income families, and comprehensive health care programs—that help *all* parents and thus make parenting children with disabilities more feasible.

- We must convince legislatures, the courts, and our communities that fetal anomaly must never be used again as a justification or a defense for safe and legal abortion. This is a disservice to the disability community and an insupportable argument for abortion rights.

- We must make the case that "wrongful life" suits should be eliminated. "Wrongful birth" suits (that seek damages for the cost of caring for a disabled child) should be carefully controlled only to protect against medical malpractice, not to punish medical practitioners for not complying with eugenic policy.

- We must break the *taboo* in the feminist movement against discussing the fetus. Getting "uncomfortable" will move us toward clarity, deepening the discussion about women's control of our bodies and reproduction.

- In response to the imperative from medical providers to utilize reproductive technologies, we can create programs to train "NRT peer counselors" to help women to learn more about new reproductive technologies, become truly informed consumers, and avoid being pressured to undergo unwanted tests. *People with disabilities must be included as NRT peer counselors.*

- We can help ourselves and each other gain clarity regarding the decision to abort a fetus with a disability. To begin with, we can encourage women to examine their motivations for having children, ideally before becoming pregnant. We can ask ourselves and each other: What needs are we trying to satisfy in becoming a mother? How will the characteristics of the potential child figure into these motivations? What opportunities might there be for welcoming a child who does not meet our ideals of motherhood? What are the benefits of taking on the expectations and prejudices of family and friends? Have we met and interacted meaningfully with children and adults with disabilities? Do we have sufficient knowledge about disability, and sufficient awareness of our own feelings about disabled people, for our choices to be based on real information, not stereotypes?

Taking these steps and responding to these questions will be a start toward increasing our clarity about selective abortion.

Caring about Ourselves and Each Other

Here are some things I have learned while working to educate others on this issue. I try to be patient with potential allies, to take time to explain my feelings. I try to take nothing for granted, try not to get defensive when people show their confusion or disagreement. I must remember that these issues are hard to understand; they run contrary to common and pervasive assumptions about people and life. I have to remember that it took me a long time to begin to understand disability stereotyping myself. At the same time, I have very high expectations for people. I believe it is possible to be pushy but patient and loving at the same time.

To feminist organizations attempting to include disabled women in discussions of abortion and other feminist issues: forgive us for our occasional impatience. To disabled people: forgive potential allies for their ignorance and awkwardness. At meetings we disabled people hope to be heard, but we also perceive the "discomfort" that nondisabled people reveal, based on lack of real information about who we are. *There is no way around this awkward phase.* Better to reveal ignorance than to pretend and thereby preclude getting to know each other as people. Ask questions; make mistakes!

I sometimes remember that not only have I taken on this cutting-edge work for future generations, but I'm doing this *for myself now.* The message at the heart of widespread selective abortion on the basis of prenatal diagnosis is the greatest insult: some of us are "too flawed" in our very DNA to exist; we are unworthy of being born. This message is painful to confront. It seems tempting to take on easier battles, or even just to give in. But fighting for this issue, our right and worthiness to be born, is the fundamental challenge to disability oppression; it underpins our most basic claim to justice and equality—we are indeed worthy of being born, worth the help and expense, and we know it! The great opportunity with this issue is to think and act and take leadership in the place where feminism, disability rights, and human liberation meet.

Notes

1. *New reproductive technologies* is the term often used to describe procreative medical technologies, including such prenatal diagnostic tests as ultrasound, alpha fetal protein (AFP) blood screening, amniocentesis, chorionic villi screening (CVS, a sampling of a segment of the amniotic sac), and the whole host of other screening tests for fetal anomalies. NRTs also include in vitro fertilization and related fertility-enhancing technologies. The conference, "New Reproductive Technologies: The Contradictions of Choice; the Common Ground between Disability Rights and Feminist Analysis," held in Vancouver, November 1994, was sponsored by the DisAbled Women's Network (DAWN), and the National Action Council on the Status of Women (NAC).
2. David J. Kevles, *In the Name of Eugenics* (New York: Knopf, 1985).
3. Not long after eugenics became a respectable science in the United States, Nazi leaders modeled state policies on their brutal reading of U.S. laws and practices. After their rise to power in 1933 the Nazis began their "therapeutic elimination" of people with mental disabilities, and they killed 120,000 people with disabilities during the Holocaust. See Robert J. Lifton, *The Nazi Doctors: Medical Killing and the Psychology of Genocide* (New York: Basic Books, 1986).
4. Marlene Fried, ed., *From Abortion to Reproductive Freedom: Transforming a Movement* (Boston: South End Press, 1990), 159.
5. Michelle Fine and Adrienne Asch, "The Question of Disability: No Easy Answers for the Women's Movement," *Reproductive Rights Newsletter* 4, no. 3 (Fall 1982). See also Rita Arditti, Renate Duelli Klein, and Shelley Minden, *Test-Tube Women: What Future for Motherhood?* (London: Routledge and Kegan Paul, 1984); Adrienne Asch, "The Human Genome and Disability Rights," *Disability Rag and Resource,* February 1994, 12–13; Adrienne Asch and Michelle Fine, "Shared Dreams: A Left Perspective on Disability Rights and Reproductive Rights," in *From Abortion to Reproductive Freedom,* ed. Fried; Lisa Blumberg, "The Politics of Prenatal Testing and Selective Abortion," in *Women with Disabilities: Reproduction and Motherhood,* special issue of *Sexuality and Disability Journal* 12, no. 2 (Summer 1994); Michelle Fine and Adrienne Asch, *Women with Disabilities: Essays in Psychology, Culture, and Politics* (Philadelphia: Temple University Press, 1988); Laura Hershey, "Choosing Disability," *Ms.,* July/August 1994; Ruth Hubbard and Elijah Wald, *Exploding the Gene Myth: How Genetic Information Is Produced and Manipulated by Scientists, Physicians, Employers, Insurance Companies, Educators and Law Enforcers* (Boston: Beacon Press, 1993); Marsha Saxton, "The Politics of Genetics," *Women's Review of Books* 9, no. 10–11 (July 1994); Marsha Saxton, "Prenatal Screening and Discriminatory Attitudes about Disability, in *Embryos, Ethics and Women's Rights: Exploring the New Reproductive Technologies,* ed. Elaine Hoffman Baruch, Amadeo F. D'Adamo, and Joni Seager (New York: Haworth Press, 1988); Marsha Saxton and Florence Howe, eds., *With Wings: An Anthology by and about Women with Disabilities* (New York: Feminist Press, 1987).
6. Adrienne Asch, "Reproductive Technology and Disability," in *Reproductive Laws for the 1990s: A Briefing Handbook,* ed. Nadine Taub and Sherrill Cohen (New Brunswick, N.J.: Rutgers University Press, 1989).
7. Helen Featherstone, *A Difference in the Family: Life with a Disabled Child* (New York: Basic Books, 1980).
8. To my knowledge, Anne Finger was the first disability activist to raise this issue in the U.S. women's literature. In her book *Past Due: Disability, Pregnancy, and Birth* (Seattle: Seal Press, 1990), which includes references to her earlier writings, Finger describes a small conference where feminists and disability activists discussed this topic. German and British disability activists and feminists pioneered this issue.
9. Ruth Hubbard, *The Politics of Women's Biology* (New Brunswick, N.J.: Rutgers University Press, 1990), 197.
10. Dorothy Wertz, "Attitudes toward Abortion among Parents of Children with Cystic Fibrosis," *American Journal of Public Health* 81, no. 8 (1991).
11. This view must be reevaluated in the era of in vitro fertilization (IVF), where the embryo or a genetically prescreened embryo (following "pre-implantation diagnosis") can be fertilized outside the woman's body and frozen or can be implanted

in another woman. Such a fetus has come to have legal status apart from the mother's body: for example, in divorce cases where the fate of these fetuses is decided by the courts.

12. Many "pro-life" groups support abortion for "defective fetuses." Most state laws, even conservative ones, allow later-stage abortions when the fetus is "defective."

13. Rayna Rapp, "Accounting for Amniocentesis," in *Knowledge, Power, and Practice: The Anthropology of Medicine in Everyday Life,* ed. Shirley Lindenbaum and Margaret Lock (Berkeley: University of California Press, 1993).

14. Suneri Thobani, "From Reproduction to Mal[e] Production: Women and Sex Selection Technology," in *Misconceptions: The Social Construction of Choice and the New Reproductive Technologies,* vol. I, ed. Gwynne Basen, Margaret Eichler, and Abby Lippman (Quebec: Voyager Publishing, 1994).

15. Dorothy C. Wertz and John C. Fletcher, "A Critique of Some Feminist Challenges to Prenatal Diagnosis," *Journal of Women's Health 2* (1993).

9

Universal Design
The Work of Disability in an Age of Globalization

Michael Davidson

"Today, something we do will touch your life." (Union Carbide advertisement)

Global Bodies

My title refers to the architectural design that provides access to the built environment for all people, disabled or not. The phrase takes on more insidious implications in a globalized environment where structural adjustment politics (SAPs) instituted during the worldwide debt crises of the 1970s and 1980s protected global finance from default by allowing debtor nations to continue making interest payments on foreign loans at the expense of social programs, education, and healthcare in countries that had incurred such debts. In this sense, universal design refers to the global aspirations of wealthy countries in configuring development around growth rather than social improvement. For persons with disabilities, universal design poses the conundrum that increased access promised by the internationalization of social services, healthcare, and technology is thwarted by limiting the meaning of access to new markets and economic opportunities.

A global perspective on disability must begin with some incontrovertible facts. There are more than a half billion disabled people in the world today. One in ten persons lives with a cognitive or physical disability, and according to UN estimates, 80 percent live in developing countries.[1] More than 50 percent of the people in the world's forty-six poorest countries are without access to modern healthcare. Approximately three billion people in developing countries do not have access to sanitation facilities, and one billion in those countries lack safe drinking water. The developing world carries 90 percent of the disease burden, yet these countries have access to 10 percent of world health resources.[2] As Paul Farmer Points out, "HIV has become the world's leading infectious cause of adult deaths... [but most] of the 42 million people now infected, most live in the developing world and cannot afford the drugs that might extend their lives."[3] In Africa, governments transfer to northern creditors four times more in debt payments than they spend on the health and education of their citizens. In Nicaragua, where three fourths of the population live below the poverty line, debt repayments exceed the total social-sector budget. In Bolivia, where 80 percent of the highland population lives in poverty, debt repayments for 1997 accounted for three times the spending allocated for rural poverty reduction.[4] Although the United States has pledged two-hundred million dollars to the UN Global Aids fund, it receives two-hundred million dollars *weekly* from debt repayments.[5] There are more than one-hundred-ten million land mines in sixty-four countries. There are one and a half mines per person in Angola, where one-hundred-twenty people per month become amputees. There are twelve million land mines in Afghanistan, one for every two people. It seems hardly necessary to add that land mines are created not to kill but to disable, thereby maximizing the impact of bodily damage on the extended family and community.[6]

How might the incorporation of such facts into disability studies modify or even challenge some of its primary concerns? What might a critical disability studies perspective bring to the globalization debate? To some extent, the two terms—disability and globalization—are linked in much earlier forms of internationalization and consolidation. U.S. Immigration laws in the nineteenth century, for example, were often written around bodies deemed "unhealthy" or "diseased" and therefore unfit for national citizenship. New racial panics about immigrants and miscegenation were often framed by narratives of bodily deformity and weakness. Nayan Shah has shown how Chinese migrant laborers in the latter nineteenth-century were marginalized during the immigration process, their bodies examined and regulated according to perceived epidemiological hazards that they posed to white America.[7] The same could be said for international labor history which is a story of workplace impairments, chronic lung disease, repetitive stress disorders and psychological damage caused by "fordist" modes of production and "taylorized" efficiency. And as industrial societies created new forms of disability, so they developed a health and rehabilitation service industry which they exported to developing countries."[8] Such examples suggest that many aspects of what we call international modernity are founded upon the unequal valuation of some bodies over others.

At another level, linking disability and globalization serves to direct the focus of economic stabilization onto the physical bodies in whose name those strategies are often legitimated. We understand the ways that political violence and civil conflict create disability through warfare, landmines, and displacement, but we need to remember the structural violence that maintains disability through seemingly innocuous economic systems and political consensus.[9] Union Carbide's buoyant motto that I use for my epigraph, "Today, something we do will touch your life," means something very different for the three-hundred-thousand residents of Bhopal, India "touched" by that company in 1984.[10] The ways that global capital "touches" the body allow us to rethink the separation of bodies and public spaces, of bodies without organs and organizations without bodies. Just as national borders are being redrawn around new corporate trading zones and partnerships, so the borders of the body are being rethought in an age of neo-natal screening, genetic engineering, and body modification. Disability studies has monitored such remappings as they impact social attitudes about nontraditional bodies, but it has not paid adequate attention to the political economy of the global body. As a result, disability studies risks remaining a vestige of an earlier identity politics rather than a critical intervention into social justice at large.

A common refrain in disability studies is that disability is the one identity category that, if we live long enough, everyone will inhabit. White people will not become black, and men will not become women, but most people will become disabled. This has led some disability scholars to posit disability as a kind of ur-identity that, by virtue of its ubiquitousness and fluidity, its crossing of racial, sexual, gendered categories, challenges the integrity of identity politics altogether.[11] While it is true that many of us will become disabled, it is just as certain that those who become disabled earlier in life, who have the least access to medical insurance and healthcare, who suffer longer and die younger, who have the least legal redress are poor and live in an underdeveloped country. Malnutrition may not be on the minority world agenda of disability issues, but in the majority world defined by the World Health Organization, it is on the front line. Hence the first challenge that globalization poses for disability studies is a consideration of class and the unequal distribution of wealth.

When we consider disability as a global phenomenon we are forced to reevaluate some of the keywords of disability studies—stigma, normalcy, ableism, bodily difference—from a comparative cultural perspective.[12] We must ask to what extent the discourse of "disability" is underwritten by a Western, state-centered model that assumes values of individual rights and equality guaranteed by legal contract. The Americans with Disabilities Act (ADA) recognizes both the material and social meanings of disability, but its ability to mitigate issues of access and employment discrimination presumes a level of economic prosperity and political stability that does not easily translate. What is considered a disability in the first world may be a physical advantage or blessing in another: "[the] disfiguring scar in Dallas becomes an honorific mark in Dahomey."[13] And when U.S. policy makers attempt to intervene in global health crises in developing countries, they often bring Western assumptions about social normalization that undermine the goodwill gesture. The 1984 Reagan administration's executive order banning U.S. government financial support for U.S. and foreign family planning agencies that provided information about abortion—the so-called "Mexico City Policy"—is typical of this gesture. Thus the attempt to study disability through the social model as a set of discourses about a hypothetical, normal body, must be situated within individual cultural landscapes.

And it is landscape that motivates the theoretical armature of my paper. Arjun Appadurai describes the cultural logic of globalization as a series of "imaginary landscapes"—ethnoscapes, mediascapes, technoscapes, financescapes, and ideoscapes—that define "historically situated imaginations of person and groups spread around the globe."[14] Appadurai's theory of "scapes" is particularly useful for explaining the multiple, overlapping sites in which disability is produced and perpetuated. If we imagine that disability is something that bodies "have" or display, then we restrict the meaning of the term to a medical definition of that impairment. But if we imagine that disability as defined within regimes of pharmaceutical exchange, labor migration, ethnic displacement, epidemiology, genomic research, and trade wars, then the question must be asked differently: does disability exist in a cell, a body, a building, a race, a DNA molecule, a set of residential schools, a special education curriculum, a sweatshop, a rural clinic? The implications of seeing disability spatially force us to re-think the embodied character of impairment and disease.[15]

When we consider the *place* of disability, we begin to see the extent to which physical and cognitive impairment is directly related to material conditions and structures of power. The increased presence of depression among female *maquiladora* workers along the Mexico/U.S. border or cancers among agricultural workers in the California Central Valley must be linked to labor and migration in export processing zones following the passage of NAFTA.[16] Harlan Lane's description of Deaf persons as a colonial regime invokes the rhetoric of postcoloniality and imperialism to describe a physical condition (deafness) as well as a set of cultural practices relating to the use of manual signing that have little to do with an ability to hear and everything to do with community and culture. Keith Wailoo's work on sickle cell anemia in Memphis shows how a disease found predominantly among persons of African descent and characterized by acute physical pain became visible as a disease when changes in civil rights laws began to recognize the historic pain of black people.[17] The global market in body parts is inextricable from what Appadurai calls the "ethnoscape"—contexts of labor migration, sexual tourism, and ethnic conflicts through which this market does its business. In such cases, does disability rest with the person with kidney disease or with the so-called "donor" who sells the kidney, with the wealthy recipient whose life is sustained by an operation or the immigrant whose health is drastically compromised as a result of it? Obviously phrased in this way, disability is as much about national and cultural power differentials as it is a matter of medicine and bodies.

Disability Studies in a Global Perspective

The salient feature of U.S., Canadian, and British work in disability studies in the past ten years is a shift from a medical to a social model of impairment. The medical definition of disability locates impairment in the individual as someone who lacks the full complement of physical and cognitive elements of true personhood and who must be cured or rehabilitated. The social model locates disability not in the individual's impairment but in the environment—in social attitudes, institutional structures, and physical or communicational barriers that prevent full participation as citizen subject. Much of this work is reinforced by language in the Americans with Disabilities Act (1990) that recognizes that a person in a wheelchair becomes disabled when he or she encounters a building without elevators or when a sight impaired person tries to use an ATM machine without Braille signage. It also recognizes that one may be equally disabled by social stigma. Phrases like "wheelchair bound," "retarded," or "deaf and dumb" are no less oppressive than lack of physical access since they mark how certain bodies are interpreted and read.

In the humanities, this social model has been accompanied by a disability hermeneutics that looks critically at the ways disabled characters in literature have been seen as sites of moral failing, pity, or sexual panic. David Mitchell and Sharon Snyder have seen this analogical treatment of disability as a "narrative prosthesis" by which a disabled character serves as a crutch to shore up normalcy somewhere else.[18] The disabled character is prosthetic in the sense that he or she provides an illusion of bodily wholeness upon which the novel erects its formal claims to totality, in which ethical or moral failings in one sphere are signified through physical limitations in another. In Richard Wright's *Native Son*, Mrs. Dalton's blindness could be read as a sign of the moral limits of white liberal attitudes that mask racism. Wright is less interested in blindness itself than the way it enables a story about racial violence and liberal guilt. In *A Christmas Carol* Charles Dickens does not use Tiny Tim to condemn the treatment of crippled children in Victorian society but to finesse Scrooge's awakening to charity and human kindness towards others. By regarding disability as a "narrative prosthesis," Mitchell and Snyder underscore the ways that the material bodies of blind or crippled persons are deflected onto an able bodied normalcy that the story must reinforce. Indeed, narrative's claim to formal coherence is underwritten by that which it cannot contain, as evidenced by the carnival grotesques, madwomen in attics, blind prophets, and mute soothsayers that underwrite much narrative theory.

Despite Mitchell and Snyder's important warnings about the dangers of analogical treatments of disability, there are cases in which a prosthesis is *still* a prosthesis. The first world texts that have been the site of most work in disability studies may very well have narrative closure as their telos, but regarded in a more globalized environment, the social meaning of both disability and narrative may have to be expanded. In Mohsen Makhmalbaf's 2001 film, *Kandahar,* the main character, a female journalist, Nafas (Niloufar Pazira) is traveling from the Iranian border to Kandahar in Afghanistan to save her sister from what appears to be an immanent suicide attempt. The film is set during the Taliban regime, and Nafas wears a *burqa* while traveling, her clothing serving as a metaphor for the limits to female agency but also providing a degree of protection from threatening forces she encounters along the way. In one scene, Nafas observes a group of amputated Afghani men on crutches lurching across the desert to retrieve prosthetic legs that have been parachuted out of a Red Cross airplane. The image of prosthetic legs falling gracefully to earth is a powerful, if bizarre, image of post-colonial disruptions.

It would be tempting to regard the prostheses as representing the unreality of everyday life under the Taliban or as surrogates for the *burqa*, metaphors for gendered and sexual limits within religious fundamentalism. But at another level, the prosthetic appendages testify to the pervasiveness of historical impairments caused by thousands of land mines left by both Soviets and mujahadin after the war. Here disability is not a metaphor but a lived reality for tens of thousands of people who have endured the ravages of post-colonial wars and factionalist struggles. In Ato Quayson's terms, "to have full disclosure about the social and political grounds of an impairment is perforce to go beyond the impairment and to engage the social, political, and cultural forces that produce disability."[19] "Full disclosure" in the case of *Kandahar* is located not merely in the explosion that led to amputation but in the long history of colonization, political occupation, and nationalisms that mark both landscape and landmine.

Just as "prosthesis" within a global disability perspective must be looked at historically, so must the term "narrative." It is impossible to consider cultural forms in Africa without mentioning the role of AIDS activism and especially the Treatment Action Campaign (TAC) that has legislated for increased access to antiretroviral drugs. Here, representations of disability and social action converge in performances designed to educate and entertain. Moreover, due to the informational nature of this performance—what some call "edutainment"—issues of readability mean something very different from what they do in Western narrative theory. Within Theatre for Development performances around HIV/AIDS, the stage may be an open clearing or flatbed truck, a movable stage or community center where performances occur. The audience is encouraged to participate in the performance, often taking on roles themselves or shouting encouragement to the actors. Traditional oral and folkloric materials may be fused with references to proper nutrition and safe sex; street protests merge with street theater; popular culture (comics, hip hop) combines with classic theater. The work of art in an age of globalization may be a tape cassette about the need to wear a condom.

If disability studies has been reticent on the subject of globalization, recent literature on globalization has been silent about disability. Such work often mentions the ill effects of multinational corporations and structural adjustment policies on healthcare systems, but they devote scant attention to disability as a cultural problem.[20] Where disability studies has focused much of its attention on the role of stigma and social marginalization, anti-globalist theory tends to treat disabled persons as victims of economic processes rather than subjects. Often themes of powerlessness and dependency are filtered through the rhetoric of disability, as in Gillian Hart's important book on South Africa, *Disabling Globalization* which, despite its title, never mentions AIDS or the country's active disability rights movement.[21] Richard Wolff's essay, "World Bank/Class Blindness" excoriates development theorists who ignore class issues in formulating economic policy, using the word "blindness" throughout the essay to describe ignorance and obtuseness.[22] I do not mean to dismiss globalization theory by focusing on ableist rhetoric, but such usage underscores how easily a critique of class blindness may dismiss blindness itself.

What if we submitted Wolff's appeal for a reading of class as a contributor to the production of surplus to specific disabled] people's lives? Two examples come to mind. In 1983, the Centers for Disease Control (CDC) observed that pooled blood products (rather than the life-styles of gay men) were responsible for AIDS among hemophilia patients. In 1984, the Bayer unit of Cutter Biological sold millions of dollars worth of its blood-clotting factor for hemophiliacs to Asia and Latin America when it discovered that the company had large stores of product that were now unsaleable in the United States and Europe. Instead of destroying the tainted product and alerting distributors abroad, Bayer continued to sell factor in Malaysia, Singapore, Indonesia, Japan, and Argentina where thousands of hemophiliacs and other patients needing transfusions became infected with HIV. These events were occurring despite the fact that the company had developed a safer, heat-treated product that it was selling in the United States and Europe. In a statement to the *New York Times*, Bayer officials claimed that they had "behaved responsibly, ethically and humanely" in continuing to sell the old product in these parts of the world.[23] Not only did Bayer continue to sell infected product, it continued to *make* the old type of factor in order to fill orders from several large fixed-price contracts. The result was a worldwide HIV infection rate of 90% among severe hemophiliacs and a four million dollar profit for Bayer. Although similar scandals erupted within the United States Canada, Japan, and France, the practice of transnational corporations selling unwanted products to developing countries in order to maintain the bottom line at home is the specter haunting a globalized economy.[24] Supporters of a global marketplace will argue that despite local inequities, a free market will ultimately benefit those most in need, but this assumption obviously depends on what one means by "free." When HIV infected recipients of blood transfusions become "collateral damage" in a worldwide trade war, one wonders who is being served by open markets.

My second example concerns the definitions that the World Bank uses for persons with disabilities in order to calculate cost effective interventions in health policy. In its 1993 World Development Report, "Investing in Health," the World Bank applied the concept of the Disability Adjusted Life Years (DALY) as an indicator of the "time lived with a disability and the time lost due to premature mortality."[25] The language of the report is full of references to "global burdens" and the "cost effectiveness of different interventions at reducing the disease burdens due to a particular condition."[26] Obviously the World Bank is trying to do the right thing by assessing priorities for intervention in health matters, but by defining individuals by lost productivity instead of medical need, the bank imposes an actuarial value on its largesse. Those deemed least useful in certain cultures—women, children, aged, and disabled persons will, as Nirmala Erevelles says, "have little or no entitlement to health services at public expense."[27]

In both of these examples, the lack of monitoring or quality control on pharmaceutical products, the application of cost-benefit analysis to matters of health and mortality, and the ability of transnational corporations like Bayer to control worldwide distribution and prevent competition are only the most obvious ways that internationalization of healthcare creates—rather than eliminates—disability and calls into question the degree to which markets can ever achieve the kind of equality that free market economists advocate.

Development, Devaluation, and Disability

I want now to provide several cultural examples that read the scapes of globalization through a disability optic. My ocular metaphor calls attention to the importance of performance in all of my examples, but it also reinforces the ways that disability focalizes the inherently unrepresentable quality of global economic processes. As critics have pointed out, the homogenization of commodities, signage, and technology that we associate with globalization creates a placelessness for which mimetic criteria seem inadequate. In Raymond Williams's terms, globalization could be seen as a "structure of feeling" that cannot be contained in a single image or narrative.[28] We could imagine this structure of feeling around globalization as a kind of phantom limb phenomenon that registers a phantasmatic "whole body" that can no longer be constituted by an appeal to national origins or cultural integrity.

The films of Jibril Diop Mambety, Senegal's best known film maker, are often based on traditional folk tales, yet their retellings of the trickster, Yadikoon, or the animal fables of rabbit and hyena, are placed in contemporary settings. As the title to his incomplete final trilogy indicates, he tells the story of "les petites gens," the "little people," marginalized by devaluations, both human and economic. In addition to being poor, Mambety's characters are often disabled, played by nonprofessional, disabled actors who, far from serving as metaphors for an Africa "crippled" by debt are often the moral centers of each tale. Disability in these films is used to frame the burdens produced in the social and political infrastructure of Senegal following the 1994 devaluation of the West African Franc (CFA) by European and American financial institutions.[29] Almost overnight, the value of domestic products was cut in half, the price of a sack of rice doubled, export prices plummeted. In Mambety's films, the financescape of devaluation is manifest in the various ways that the market is depicted—from the lottery ticket seller of *Le franc*, who embodies the economic world of poor Africans after devaluation to the dusty, bustling marketplace of Dakar in *La petite vendeuse de* Soleil to the hardscrabble country store that is the centerpiece of *Hyenas*. Framing these local economic sites stand the anonymous corporate buildings of Dakar, looming over the "little" dramas of Mambety's characters. This financescape is combined with both mediascape and ethnoscape through which global information (newspapers, radio) is passed and communal identities (religious institutions, family units) interrupted. In *Le Franc*, the Muslim call to prayer comes via the same public address system that broadcasts the winning lottery ticket numbers. Religious and economic rituals vie for a common electronic voice in the marketplace. By situating each of his disabled characters in relation to a massive economic shift in west African finance, Mambety studies the impact of devaluation and development on those most affected.

Mambety's last film, *La petite vendeuse de* soleil (*The Little Girl Who Sold* The Sun), tells of a twelve year old paraplegic girl, Sili Laam, who begs for money in the crowded market of Dakar with her blind grandmother. Seeing that boys make more money by selling the local paper, *Soleil*, she tries her entrepreneurial hand as a news vendor. Her resilience and toughness carry her through the crowded, competitive world of the market where street vendors vie for the smallest share and where corrupt police lurk at the edges. Sili's paraplegia, possibly due to polio, suggests the condition of all bodies kept in poverty by structural adjustment, but she is not reduced to being a "cripple." We see her moving forcefully through the crowd, getting a ride to Dakar in a horse cart, dancing in a yellow dress with other girls, defending herself against threatening police and predatory gangs, giving her earnings to beggars in the market. The theme of structural adjustment is manifest through references to the devaluation of the CFA in the headlines that Lili shouts. Lili's market is dominated by a combination of individual initiative and corruption, not the blessings of free trade. However flawed, it is also a market in which mixtures of people and products converge—a place where disabled citizens mutually support each other and where exchange of products coincides with sharing of opinions and ideas.[30]

Throughout the film, Lili establishes a friendship with a young boy, Babou Seck, who protects her from a gang of threatening news vendors. In this last scene of the film, Lili and Babou are selling papers whose headlines read "Afrique quitte le franc zone" (Africa has left the franc zone), announcing a future, as yet unrealized francophone Africa that has severed its dependence on the French franc and must adapt to a world economy. Lili is set upon by a gang of boys who knock her down and steal her crutch. Babou tries unsuccessfully to retrieve it. "What do we do now?" Babou asks to which Lili responds, "We continue." He hoists her onto his back and carries her through a crowded arcade of the market. The other vendors fade back into the stalls, leaving only the sound of Babou's footsteps echoing through the hall. The moral of the story—perhaps too bluntly stated—is that in a society damaged by fluctuating, international markets and plagued by local corruption, the salvific value is mutual aid and support, not dependence or victimization. In short, Mambety allows us to witness an alternative form of development, one based on self-reliance rather than ruthless competition.

Mambety is constantly aware of the relationship between disability and market driven poverty, a connection made concrete in a scene that takes place at a ferry dock called "Goree," a reference to the infamous Goree Island slave port in West Africa from which slaves were sent to the new world. Lili is often viewed by a young man in a wheelchair who cradles a large boombox in his arms and who, for a few coins, plays music. He functions as a kind of silent chorus, his music providing entertainment and perhaps a site of resistance (he plays songs celebrating African freedom fighters), his disabled perspective becomes the viewer's vantage from which we too see Lili. Finally, Lili must negotiate a literally rocky terrain—streets with potholes and puddles of water, garbage strewn about, making the term "access" seem laughable. Clearly, a country that must divert all of its resources to settling its international debts cannot be bothered with providing better infrastructure and curb cuts. At the end of the film, Mambety provides a voice over moral in a male voice: "This tale is thrown to the sea," suggesting that it is up to the audience to uncork the bottle and read its meanings into the future. But Lili delivers the last words by saying, "The first to breathe it will go to heaven," providing a redemptive parable of emancipation through mutual (not foreign) aid.

My second example concerns a number of recent films, plays, and novels that deal with the international organ trade in which the body quite literally becomes a commodity, its components exchanged in a worldwide market that mirrors the structural inequality between wealth and poverty. Nancy Scheper-Hughes points out that organ transplantation "now takes place in a trans-national space with both donors and recipients following the paths of capital and technology in the global economy."[31] Nor is "space" a metaphor. Lawrence Cohen describes what he calls the "kidneyvakkam" of India where many poor residents have undergone kidney operations and where the day's buying and selling prices of organs are publicly posted.[32] Transplantation narratives reinforce the links between the space of the body and the global space of capital, between a body regarded as a totality of parts and a communicational and media space in which those parts are sold, packaged in ice chests, and shipped around the world. And organ trafficking is a discursive matter. Rumors of children stolen, soldiers's bodies "looted," and hospital patients misdiagnosed for their organs add a Gothic element to the organ sale narrative, a literary-subgenre that Scheper-Hughes calls "neo-cannibalism."[33]

We could divide transplantation narratives into two forms. The first, typified by films like *Dirty Pretty Things* and *Central Station*, might be called "organ diaspora stories." These situate the context of body part trafficking within an ethnoscape of transnational labor flows, black market crime, and moral panic. In Walter Salles' 1998 movie, *Central Station*, a young orphaned boy is rescued by a woman who writes letters for poor, illiterate city dwellers in her Rio de Janeiro stall. Her decision to save the boy is motivated by fears that he will become a victim of unscrupulous body part salesmen in a country where everyone at birth is declared a universal organ donor. In Stephen Frears' *Dirty Pretty Things*, organ sales occur within a the migrant worker population in London—from the sleazy black market broker, Senor Juan, to the Somalian man who has had his kidney removed to Okwe, who, as both illegal immigrant and doctor, is constantly tempted to use his medical skills illegally to alleviate economic problems. The second form of transplantation narrative is a more futuristic one that imagines a world in which the ideal of replacing an aging or disabled body with new parts retrofits a nineteenth-century eugenics story in a globalized environment. In Manjula Padmanabhan's *Harvest* the play's characters are divided up into "Donors," poor, Bombay city dwellers, and "Receivers" wealthy, first world customers for body parts.[34] In Andrew Niccol's *Gattaca*, a man with congenital heart disease purchases "pure" DNA stock from a paraplegic but otherwise eugenically perfect male in order to participate in a space program. Such science fiction fantasies are, of course, present day potentialities, and one of the cultural functions that such representations serves is to bring into visibility the links between medical technology, racialist science, infomatics, and global economy.

Dirty Pretty Things (2003) depicts a modern London in which the entire population comes from elsewhere, employed as service workers, hotel clerks, prostitutes, cab drivers, and hospital orderlies. The film concerns a Nigerian immigrant, Okwe (Chiwte Ejiofor) who had been a doctor in his native country but who now works illegally in London as a desk clerk at a hotel. What little sleep he gets he obtains on the couch of a fellow immigrant, Senay (Audrey Tautou), a young Turkish Muslim woman who works clandestinely as a maid in the same hotel. While checking on a room whose toilet is overflowing, Okwe discovers a human heart stuck in the plumbing, and after checking with his friend at the hospital, realizes that the manager of the hotel, Senor Juan, has been conducting a black market business in organ sales. Because Okwe is illegally in the country and needs his job, he cannot go to the police, and the hotel manager threatens to turn him in to immigration authorities if he pursues the matter. Just as the clandestine organ trade is part of an invisible global economy, so its actors must remain invisible to the "normal" functioning of touristic London.

The dirty and pretty things that maintain the hotel's functioning also support the marginal existence of the vast immigrant labor force. The oxymoronic blazon of the film—a heart in a toilet bowl—defines the existence of individuals whose lifeblood is wasted in repetitive, unremunerative labor under constant surveillance, whose bodies are literally waste products. Whatever romance Okwe and Senay might share is thwarted by the constant presence of immigration police and the possibility of deportation. Forced to flee her hotel job and a second job in a sweatshop, Senay turns to the only option available to her—to offer her own kidney to Senor Juan—for a passport and passage out of the country. Okwe realizes what she is about to do and offers the manager to do the operation himself so that it will be hygienic. He prepares the hotel room with proper surgical equipment but ends up drugging Senor Juan instead and substituting him as the kidney patient. Okwe completes the operation, with the help of Senay and other friends, and delivers the organ to the broker. When the broker sees Okwe and his subaltern assistants, he says "I've never seen you before," and Okwe responds, "Oh yes you have. We're the ones who drive your cars, clean your rooms and suck your cocks."[35] This is a particularly vivid representation of the status of immigrant labor in a globalized economy. This necessary but invisible laboring body is metonymized in a kidney exchanged with a wealthy client whose life is prolonged while that of the immigrant donor is compromised.

At one point in *Dirty Pretty Things* Senay asks Okwe why he came to London. He replies, "It's an African story." He is speaking about the post-colonial diaspora of Africans throughout the Western world, but he could equally be speaking about the diaspora of HIV/AIDS within Africa. There is a relationship between the two African stories insofar as poverty and transnational labor movements drive both. What form does this "African Story" take? Can Western theories of textuality and aesthetic coherence account for the story of post-Apartheid Africa, especially when it concerns disability and development? Most importantly, how does the context of AIDS challenge the division between art and politics, cultural forms and social movements? These questions emerge forcefully in Theater for Development projects in which performance has become central to pedagogical efforts to explain government policies or health issues.[36] Although activists are sometimes skeptical about Theater for Development as a tool of state interests, there is a growing acceptance of its importance in addressing HIV/AIDS. Theater for Development is reminiscent of other forms of activist theater—Luis Valdez's "Actos" or the militant theater of the U.S. Black Nationalism—that combine pedagogy and audience participation. As "edutainment," these new cultural forms challenge formalist aesthetics, their sometimes didactic message and instrumental character elaborated through popular genres involving puppetry, dance, hiphop music, comics, posters, and mime.

In speaking of *Kandahar* I referred to Nafas' use of a tape cassette to record her difficult desert journey; I now want to conclude with reference to another tape cassette, forged in the Theater for Development arena, whose function, far from representing an outlawed interiority, establishes an imagined community among travelers. "Yiriba" is a thirty-minute tape cassette developed by several local NGO's and CIDA (the Canadian Agency for International Development) designed to be distributed among long-distance truck drivers who cover routes in West Africa's "AIDS" corridor.[37] This hugely popular tape features the voices of two well known Malian griots, Djeli Daouda Dembele and his wife Hawa Dembele, who warn truck drivers of the dangers of sexually transmitted diseases, using traditional oral tales and musical accompaniment. Daouda tells the story of a truck driver, Yiriba, who is approached by a good looking woman, Korotouma, at a truck stop, who asks for a lift to the next town. They end up at a hotel and begin to engage in sexual activity. When Yiriba produces a condom, Korotouma chastizes him for thinking she might be a prostitute. Yiriba delivers a speech about the need for prudence—"Both of us travel a lot, and we meet many people every day. This condom will protect you and me. I must say we hardly know one another." Korotouma, insulted, leaves and takes up with another driver, Seydou. The same scenario occurs, but Seydou does not use a condom and, as a result, becomes infected with HIV. When Yiriba visits his now ailing friend, he learns that Seydou has infected other women as well as his wife, causing her to become infertile. Finally, because of his illness, Seydou has entrusted his truck to his apprentice who promptly steals it, leaving him without a means of livelihood. Throughout the tale, Hawa Dembele sings a refrain: "I have traveled to the East, to the West, to the North, and to the South. I have never encountered a similar fever, Father of the griots."

There are several stylistic features of the tape that link the tape to traditional story telling traditions and that make this more than a simple cautionary tale. The griot poses as the "great bard of truck drivers" and urges solidarity with each other during the long night drives. The Dembeles act both as story tellers and actors who take on various roles. Daoda also praises the AIDS doctors of West Africa and mentions truck stops, cities and health centers that drivers are likely to encounter. Most significantly, he praises rig owners "who help their drivers when these latter fall ill."[38]

"Yiriba" raises provocative questions about the work of art in an age of globalization. The cassette exists in a liminal space between several cultural forms, some archaic (the griot tale) and some modern (truck routes, tape recorders). It is, in James Clifford's terms, a form of "traveling culture," crossing national, ethnic, and linguistic boundaries, linking truck drivers from different areas who share the same routes and the same potential for HIV infection.[39] Daouda and Hawa can count on their fame as storytellers among their listeners to validate their message—and along the way, to legitimate the NGO's that sponsor the tape. Thus the cautionary story of "Yiriba," simple though it may seem on the surface, brings the AIDS story and the African story together.

The Work of the ADA in an Age of Globalization

Thus far I have stressed the ways in which disability—like the aesthetic—challenges ideas of bodily and cognitive normalcy. Cultural forms such as the ones I have briefly mentioned permit us to examine globalization through what I have been calling a disability optic, one that like the camera obscura permits us to see the familiar upside down. In the United States we benefit from legal statutes like the ADA—as well as section 504 of the 1973 Rehabilitation Act and the 1975 Individuals with Disabilities Education Act—that provide a safety net for those who otherwise would fall through the cracks. This safety net is a privilege that a wealthy country can—and should—afford, but as a result, "universal design" remains largely a first world concept rather than a global reality. And like all legal protections, the ADA is vulnerable to change. In recent years, there have been several major challenges to the ADA, and in the current business-friendly administration more are likely to appear. The Rehnquist Court overturned cases on appeal that would expand the class of persons protected, especially plaintiffs with correctable disabilities (high blood pressure, nearsightedness) or cases that would contradict existing state statutes. A more ominous fact is that of the numerous claims made under ADA protection, 95 percent are decided in favor of employers, leading many in the disability rights movement to conclude that legal arguments for limiting the class and kinds of cases applicable under federal protection are often based on cost-accounting rather than the welfare of the plaintiffs. In an era of increasingly privatized healthcare, restrictions on Medicare, and the possible evacuation of Social Security, the ADA may become more of a symbolic document than a map for redress.[40]

In my introduction I described disability as a series of sites that include the spaces of the body but that extend into a more public arena of communities and institutions. If we think of disability as located in societal barriers, not in individuals, then disability must be seen as a matter of social justice. The remedy for social justice as Nancy Fraser points out, involves synthesizing a politics of recognition and a politics of redistribution, a theory of justice based on cultural identities and one based on the reorganization of material resources around those identities.[41] Disability would seem to be the test cast for such a synthesis since any recognition of, say, children with developmental disabilities, will require, as Michael Berubé says, access to "a free and appropriate public education in the least restrictive environment."[42] Recognition of disability as a civil right entails making sure that a person with a disability has access to the buildings, classrooms, and courts where those rights are learned and adjudicated. As Berubé says, if the ADA "were understood as broad civil rights law … [pertaining] to the entire population of the country, then maybe disability law would be understood not as fringe addition to civil rights law but as its very fulfillment."[43]

Adapting these remarks, I would suggest that if disability were considered as a matter of global human rights rather than as a "healthcare problem," perhaps the ADA could serve as a roadmap for universal design in its best estate. Rather than seeing globalization narrowly as providing greater access to computer chips, phone lines, raw materials, and cheap labor, it could be seen as something relating to all of us who have bodies, the spirit of inclusion promised by the ADA might extend beyond its current national jurisdiction. This would entail a recognition on the part of wealthier nations that access to public spaces, healthcare, social justice cannot be made contingent on private sector interests or moral/ideological restrictions. Such recognition is not likely to come soon, and so we must look to the fruitful alliances among local community organizations, church groups, NGO's, health centers, and political action campaigns that have formed a vital global disability rights movement. Under the motto, "Nothing About Us Without Us," this network of nonaligned organizations is providing both access and knowledge across—and in some cases against—the economic landscape that often confuses "development" with "growth."

Notes

1. James I. Charlton, *Nothing About Us Without Us: Disability, Oppression and Empowerment*. (Berkeley: U of California Press, 2000), p. 8. See also Lennard Davis, *Enforcing Normalcy: Disability, Deafness, and the Body* (London: Verso, 1995), p. 7.

2. World Health figures quoted in *Dying for Growth: Global Inequality and the Health of the Poor*, ed. Jim Young Kim et al, (Monroe, Maine: Common Courage Press, 2000), p 4.

3. Paul Farmer, "Introduction." *Global AIDS: Myths and Facts.*(Cambridge: South End Press, 2003), p. xvii.

4. *Dying for Growth*, p. 25.

5. Louise Bourgault, *Playing for Life: Performance in Africa in the Age of AIDS.* (Durham: Carolina Academic Press, 2003), p. 261.

6. James Charlton, "The Disability Rights Movement as a Counter-Hegemonic Popular Social Movement." Unpublished MS, p. 5. See also David Levi Strauss, "Broken Wings," in *Between the Eyes: Essays on Photography and Politics* (New York: Aperture, 2003), pp. 56–64.

7. Nayan Shah, *Contagious Divides: Epidemics and Race in San Francisco's Chinatown* (Berkeley: U of California Press, 2001).

8. Chris Holden and Peter Beresford, "Globalization and Disability," *Disability Studies Today*, ed. Colin Barnes, Mike Oliver, and Len Barton (London: Polity Press, 2002), p. 194.

9. On "structural violence," see Johan Galtung, "Violence, Peace and Peace Research." *Journal of Peace Research* 3 (1969), p. 171. See also *Dying for Growth* (pp. 102-4) and Paul Farmer, *Pathologies of Power: Health, Human Rights, and the New War on the Poor* (Berkeley: U of California Press, 2003), pp. 29–50.

10. This ad appeared in *Scientific American* 231:1 (July 1974), p. 9.

11. See, for example, Lennard Davis, *Bending Over Backwards: Disability, Dismodernism and Other Difficult Positions* (New York: New York U Press, 2002), p. 25.

12. For discussions of global disability from a social science perspective see the following: Brigitte Holzer, Arthur Vreede, Gabriele Weight, ed. *Disability in Different Cultures: Reflections on Local Concepts* (New Brunswick: Transaction Publishers, 1999); Benedicte Ingstad and Susan Reynolds Whyte, ed. *Disability and Culture* (Berkeley: U of California Press, 1995); Mark Priestley, ed. *Disability and the Life Course: Global Perspectives* (Cambridge: Cambridge U Press, 2001).

13. J. Hanks quoted in Colin Barnes and Geof Mercer, *Disability* (London: Polity Press, 2003), p. 135.

14. Arjun Appadurai, *Modernity at Large: Cultural Dimensions of Globalization* (Minneapolis: U of Minnesota Press 1996), p. 33.

15. Keith Wailoo, *Dying in the City of the Blues: Sickle Cell Anemia and the Politics of Race and Health* (Chapel Hill: U of North Carolina Press, 2001), p. 6. On the "space" of disease, see Keith Wailoo, "Inventing the Heterozygote: Molecular Biology, Racial Identity, and the Narratives of Sickle Cell Disease, Tay-Sachs, and Cystic Fibrosis." *Race, Nature, and the Politics of Difference*, ed. Donald S. Moore, Jake Kosek, and Anand Pandian (Durham: Duke U Press, 2004), pp. 236-53. Charles Rosenberg and Janet Golden, eds. *Framing Disease: Studies in Cultural History* (New Brunswick: Rutgers U Press, 1992).

16. Howard Frumkin, Mauricio Hernandez-Avila, Felipe Espinsoa Torres, "Maquiladoras: A Case Study of Free Trade Zones." *Occupational and Environmental Health* 1.2 (April/June, 1995): 96-109. See also Joel Brenner, Jennifer Ross, Janie Simmons, and Sarah Zaidi, "Neoliberal Trade and Investment and the Health of *Maquiladora* Workers on the U.S.-Mexico Border." *Dying for Growth*, pp. 261–90.

17. Keith Wailoo, *Dying in the City of the Blues*, 10–11.

18. David T. Mitchell and Sharon L. Snyder, *Narrative Prosthesis: Disability and the Dependencies of Discourse* (Ann Arbor: U of Michigan Press, 2001).

19. Ato Quayson, *Calibrations*, p. 117.

20. See, for example, David Held and Anthony McGrew, ed. *The Global Transformations Reader: An Introduction to the Globalization Debate* (Cambridge: Polity, 2000); Jim Young Kim, et al, *Dying for Growth*; Rob Wilson and Wimal Dissanayake, ed. *Global/Local: Cultural Production and the Transnational Imaginary* (Durham: Duke U Press, 1996; Amitava Kumar, ed. *World Bank Literature* (Minneapolis: U of Minnesota Press, 2003); Fredric Jameson and Masao Miyoshi, ed. *The Cultures of Globalization* (Durham: Duke U Press, 1999; Joseph E. Stiglitz, *Globalization and its Discontents* (New York: Norton, 2003).

21. Gillian Hart, *Disabling Globalization: Places of Power in Post-Apartheid South Africa* (Berkeley: U of California Press, 2002).

22. Richard Wolff, "World Bank / Class Blindness," *World Bank Literature*, ed. Amitava Kumar (Minneapolis: U of Minnesota Press, 2003), pp. 174–83.

23. Walt Bogdanich and Eric Koli, "2 Paths of Bayer Drug in 80's: Riskier Type Went Overseas." *New York Times* (May 22, 2003), C5.

24. In contrast, Cuba initiated an HIV screening program early, once it was suspected that HIV was blood borne. According to Paul Farmer, in 1983 Cuba "banned the importation of factor VIII and other hemo-derivatives, and the Ministry of Public Health ordered the destruction of twenty thousand units of blood product." These actions have resulted in Cuba's having one of the lowest incidence of HIV infection in the western hemisphere. Farmer, *Pathologies of Power*, 70.

25. Nuria Homedes, "The Disability-Adjusted Life Year (DALY) Definition, Measurement and Potential Use." Human Capital Development and Operations Policy Working Papers available at http://www.worldbank.org/html/extdr/hnp/hddflash/workp/wp_00068.html, 3. See also David Wasserman et al. eds. *Quality of Life and Human Difference* (Cambridge: Cambridge U Press, 2005).

26. Homedes, 8.

27. Nirmala Erevelles, "Disability in the New World Order: The Political Economy of World Bank Intervention in (Post/Neo)colonial Context." (Unpublished manuscript, p. 5)

28. This aspect of globalization is developed in Lisa Lowe, "The Metaphoricity of Globalization." Unpublished MS, p. 3. I am grateful to Professor Lowe for allowing me to see this unpublished manuscript.

29. On the 1994 devaluation, see Manthia Diawara, "Toward a Regional Imaginary in Africa." *World Bank Literature,* p. 65.

30. On the cultural function of West African markets, see Diawara, pp. 73–80.

31. Nancy Sheper-Hughes, "The End of the Body: The Global Traffic in Organs for Transplant Surgery," available at http://www.sunsite.berkeley.edu/biotech/organsswatch/pages/cadraft.html

32. Lawrence Cohen, "Where it Hurts: Indian Material for an Ethics of Organ Transplantation." *Daedalus* 128:4 (Fall, 1999), pp. 4–5.

33. On rumor and organ trafficking see Scheper-Hughes, "Theft of Life: The Globalization of Organ Stealing Rumours." *Anthropology Today,* vol. 12, no. 3 (June, 1996), pp. 3–11; Claudia Castaneda, *Figurations: Child, Bodies, Worlds* (Durham: Duke U Press, 2002)..

34. Manjula Padmanabhan, *Harvest. Postcolonial Plays: An Anthology,* Ed. Helen Gilbert (London: Routledge, 2001), pp. 214–49.

35. Stephen Frears, *Dirty Pretty Things* (Miramax and BBC Films, 2003).

36. On Theatre for Development, see *African Theatre in Development,* ed. Martin Banham, James Gibbs, Femi Osofisan, ed.(Bloomington, U of Indiana Press, 1999); *Politics and Performance: Theatre, Poetry and Song in Southern Africa,* ed. Liz Gunner (Johannesburg: Witwatersrand U Press, 2001); Louise M. Bourgault, *Playing for Life: Performance in Africa in the Age of AIDS* (Durham: Caroline Academic Press, 2003).

37. "Yiriba" is discussed in Louise Bourgault, *Playing for Life: Performance in Africa in the Age of AIDS,* pp. 132–38. A CD-ROM accompanies the book that includes clips of plays, dances, songs, and "edutainment" performances.

38. Bourgault, p. 137.

39. James Clifford, *Routes: Travel and Translation in the Late Twentieth-Century* (Cambridge: Harvard U Press, 1997).

40. Documentation of judicial responses to the ADA can be seen in *Backlash Against the ADA: Reinterpreting Disability Rights,* Linda Hamilton Kriger, ed. (Ann Arbor: U of Michigan Press, 2003).

41. Nancy Fraser, *Justice Interruptus: Critical Reflections on the 'Postsocialist' Condition* (New York: Routledge, 1997), p. 12.

42. Michael Berube, "Citizenship and Disability." *Dissent* (Spring, 2003), p. 3.

43. Berube, p. 3.

Part III

Stigma and Illness

10

Selections from *Stigma*

Erving Goffman

Stigma and Social Identity

The Greeks, who were apparently strong on visual aids, originated the term *stigma* to refer to bodily signs designed to expose something unusual and bad about the moral status of the signifier. The signs were cut or burnt into the body and advertised that the bearer was a slave, a criminal, or a traitor—a blemished person, ritually polluted, to be avoided, especially in public places. Later, in Christian times, two layers of metaphor were added to the term: the first referred to bodily signs of holy grace that took the form of eruptive blossoms on the skin; the second, a medical allusion to this religious allusion, referred to bodily signs of physical disorder. Today the term is widely used in something like the original literal sense, but is applied more to the disgrace itself than to the bodily evidence of it. Furthermore, shifts have occurred in the kinds of disgrace that arouse concern. Students, however, have made little effort to describe the structural preconditions of stigma, or even to provide a definition of the concept itself. It seems necessary, therefore, to try at the beginning to sketch in some very general assumptions and definitions.

Preliminary Conceptions

Society establishes the means of categorizing persons and the complement of attributes felt to be ordinary and natural for members of each of these categories. Social settings establish the categories of persons likely to be encountered there. The routines of social intercourse in established settings allow us to deal with anticipated others without special attention or thought. When a stranger comes into our presence, then, first appearances are likely to enable us to anticipate hxs category and attributes, his "social identity"—to use a term that is better than "social status" because personal attributes such as "honesty" are involved, as well as structural ones, like "occupation." We lean on these anticipations that we have, transforming them into normative expectations, into righteously presented demands. Typically, we do not become aware that we have made these demands or aware of what they are until an active question arises as to whether or not they will be fulfilled. It is then that we are likely to realize that all along we had been making certain assumptions as to what the individual before us ought to be. Thus, the demands we make might better be called demands made "in effect" and the character we impute to the individual might better be seen as an imputation made in potential retrospect—a characterization "in effect," a *virtual social* identity. The category and attributes he could in fact be proved to possess will be called his *actual social identity*.

While the stranger is present before us, evidence can arise of his possessing an attribute that makes him different from others in the category of persons available for him to be, and of a less desirable kind—in the extreme, a person who is quite thoroughly bad, or dangerous, or weak. He is thus reduced in our minds from a whole and usual person to a tainted, discounted one. Such an attribute is a stigma, especially when its discrediting effect is very extensive; sometimes it is also called a failing, a shortcoming, a handicap. It constitutes a special discrepancy between virtual and actual social identity. Note that there are other types of discrepancy between virtual and actual social identity, for example the kind that causes us to reclassify an individual from one socially anticipated category to a different but equally well-anticipated one, and the kind that causes us to alter our estimation of the individual upward. Note, too, that not all undesirable attributes are at issue, but only those which are incongruous with our stereotype of what a given type of individual should be.

The term stigma, then, will be used to refer to an attribute that is deeply discrediting, but it should be seen that a language of relationships, not attributes, is really needed. An attribute that stigmatizes one type of possessor can confirm the usualness of another, and therefore is neither creditable nor discreditable as a thing in itself. For example, some jobs in America cause holders without the expected college education to conceal this fact; other jobs, however, can lead the few of their holders who have a higher education to keep this a secret, lest they be marked as failures and outsiders. Similarly, a middle class boy may feel no compunction in being seen going to the library; a professional criminal, however, writes:

> I can remember before now on more than one occasion, for instance, going into a public library near where I was living, and looking over my shoulder a couple of times before I actually went in just to make sure no one who knew me was standing about and seeing me do it.[1]

So, too, an individual who desires to fight for his country may conceal a physical defect, lest his claimed physical status be discredited; later, the same individual, embittered and trying to get out of the army, may succeed in gaining admission to the army hospital, where he would be discredited if discovered in not really having an acute sickness.[2] A stigma, then, is really a special kind of relationship between attribute and stereotype, although I don't propose to continue to say so, in part because there are important attributes that almost everywhere in our society are discrediting.

The term stigma and its synonyms conceal a double perspective: does the stigmatized individual assume his differentness is known about already or is evident on the spot, or does he assume it is neither known about by those present nor immediately perceivable by them? In the first case one deals with the plight of the *discredited*, in the second with that of the *discreditable*. This is an important difference, even though a particular stigmatized individual is likely to have experience with both situations. I will begin with the situation of the discredited and move on to the discreditable but not always separate the two.

Three grossly different types of stigma may be mentioned. First there are abominations of the body—the various physical deformities. Next there are blemishes of individual character perceived as weak will, domineering or unnatural passions, treacherous and rigid beliefs, and dishonesty, these being inferred from a known record of, for example, mental disorder, imprisonment, addiction, alcoholism, homosexuality, unemployment, suicidal attempts, and radical political behavior. Finally there are the tribal stigma of race, nation, and religion, these being stigma that can be transmitted through lineages and equally contaminate all members of a family.[3] In all of these various instances of stigma, however, including those the Greeks had in mind, the same sociological features are found: an individual who might have been received easily in ordinary social intercourse possesses a trait that can obtrude itself upon attention and turn those of us whom he meets away from him, breaking the claim that his other attributes have on us. He possesses a stigma, an undesired differentness from what we had anticipated. We and those who do not depart negatively from the particular expectations at issue I shall call the *normals*.

The attitudes we normals have toward a person with a stigma and the actions we take in regard to him, are well known, since these responses are what benevolent social action is designed to soften and ameliorate. By definition, of course, we believe the person with a stigma is not quite human. On this assumption we exercise varieties of discrimination, through which we effectively, if often unthinkingly, reduce his life chances. We construct a stigma-theory, an ideology to explain his inferiority and account for the danger he represents, sometimes rationalizing an animosity based on other differences, such as those of social class.[4] We use specific stigma terms such as cripple, bastard, moron in our daily discourse as a source of metaphor and imagery, typically without giving thought to the original meaning.[5] We tend to impute a wide range of imperfections on the basis of the original one,[6] and at the same time to impute some desirable but undesired attributes, often of a supernatural cast, such as "sixth sense," or "understanding":[7]

> For some, there may be a hesitancy about touching or steering the blind, while for others, the perceived failure to see may be generalized into a gestalt of disability, so that the individual shouts at the blind as if they were deaf or attempts to lift them as if they were crippled. Those confronting the blind may have a whole range of belief that is anchored in the stereotype. For instance, they think they are subject to unique judgment, assuming the blinded individual draws on special channels of information unavailable to others.[8]

Further, we may perceive his defensive response to his situation as a direct expression of his defect, and then see both defect and response as just retribution for something he or his parents or his tribe did, and hence a justification of the way we treat him.[9]

Now turn from the normal to the person he is normal against. It seems generally true that members of a social category may strongly support a standard of judgment that they and others agree does not directly apply to them. Thus it is that a businessman may demand womanly behavior from females or ascetic behavior from monks, and not construe himself as someone who ought to realize either of these styles of conduct. The distinction is between realizing a norm and merely supporting it. The issue of stigma does not arise here, but only where there is some expectation on all sides that those in a given category should not only support a particular norm but also realize it.

Also, it seems possible for an individual to fail to live up to what we effectively demand of him, and yet be relatively untouched by this failure; insulated by his alienation, protected by identity beliefs of his own, he feels that he is a full-fledged normal human being, and that we are the ones who are not quite human. He bears a stigma but does not seem to be impressed or repentant about doing so. This possibility is celebrated in exemplary tales about Mennonites, Gypsies, shameless scoundrels, and very orthodox Jews.

In America at present, however, separate systems of honor seem to be on the decline. The stigmatized individual tends to hold the same beliefs about identity that we do; this is a pivotal fact. His deepest feelings about what he is may be his sense of being a "normal person," a human being like anyone else, a person, therefore, who deserves a fair chance and a fair break.[10] (Actually, however phrased, he bases his claims not on what he thinks is due *everyone*, but only everyone of a selected social category into which he unquestionably fits, for example, anyone of his age, sex, profession, and so forth.) Yet he may perceive, usually quite correctly, that whatever others profess, they do not really "accept" him and are not ready to make contact with him on "equal grounds."[11] Further, the standards he has incorporated from the wider society equip him to be intimately alive to what others see as his failing, inevitably causing him, if only for moments, to agree that he does indeed fall short of what he really ought to be. Shame becomes a central possibility, arising from the individual's perception of one of his own attributes as being a defiling thing to possess, and one he can readily see himself as not possessing.

The immediate presence of normals is likely to reinforce this split between self-demands and self, but in fact self-hate and self-derogation can also occur when only he and a mirror are about:

> When I got up at last...and had learned to walk again, one day I took a hand glass and went to a long mirror to look at myself, and I went alone. I didn't want anyone...to know how I felt when I saw myself for the first time. But here was no noise, no outcry; I didn't scream with rage when I saw myself. I just felt numb. That person in the mirror *couldn't* be me. I felt inside like a healthy, ordinary, lucky person—oh, not like the one in the mirror! Yet when I turned my face to the mirror there were my own eyes looking back, hot with shame...when I did not cry or make any sound, it became impossible that I should speak of it to anyone, and the confusion and the panic of my discovery were locked inside me then and there, to be faced alone, for a very long time to come.[12]

Over and over I forgot what I had seen in the mirror. It could not penetrate into the interior of my mind and become an integral part of me. I felt as if it had nothing to do with me; it was only a disguise. But is was not the kind of disguise which is put on voluntarily by the person who wears it, and which is intended to confuse other people as to one's identity. My disguise had been put on me without my consent or knowledge like the ones in fairy tales, and it was I myself who was confused by it, as to my own identity. I looked in the mirror, and was horror-struck because I did not recognize myself. In the place where I was standing, with that persistent romantic elation in me, as if I were a favored fortunate person to whom everything was possible, I saw a stranger, a little, pitiable, hideous figure, and a face that became, as I stared at it, painful and blushing with shame. It was only a disguise, but it was on me, for life. It was there, it was there, it was real. Everyone of those encounters was like a blow on the head. They left me dazed and dumb and senseless every time, until slowly and stubbornly my robust persistent illusion of well-being and of personal beauty spread all through me again, and I forgot the irrelevant reality and was all unprepared and vulnerable again.[13]

The central feature of the stigmatized individual's situation in life can now be stated. It is a question of what is often, if vaguely, called "acceptance." Those who have dealings with him fail to accord him the respect and regard which the uncontaminated aspects of his social identity have led them to anticipate extending, and have led him to anticipate receiving; he echoes this denial by finding that some of his own attributes warrant it.

How does the stigmatized person respond to his situation? In some cases it will be possible for him to make a direct attempt to correct what he sees as the objective basis of his failing, as when a physically deformed person undergoes plastic surgery, a blind person eye treatment, an illiterate remedial education, a homosexual psychotherapy. (Where such repair is possible, what often results is not the acquisition of fully normal status, but a transformation of self from someone with a particular blemish into someone with a record of having corrected a particular blemish.) Here proneness to "victimization" is to be cited, a result of the stigmatized person's exposure to fraudulent servers selling speech correction, skin lighteners, body stretchers, youth restorers (as in rejuvenation through fertilized egg yolk treatment), cures through faith, and poise in conversation. Whether a practical technique or fraud is involved, the quest, often secret, that results provides a special indication of the extremes to which the stigmatized can be will to go, and hence the painfulness of the situation that leads them to these extremes. One illustration may be cited:

Miss Peck [a pioneer New York social worker for the hard of hearing] said that in the early days the quacks and get-rich-quick medicine men who abounded saw the League [for the hard of hearing] as their happy hunting ground, ideal for the promotion of magnetic head caps, miraculous vibrating machines, artificial eardrums, blowers, inhalers, massagers, magic oils, balsams, and other guaranteed, sure-fire, positive, and permanent cure-alls for incurable deafness. Advertisements for such hokum (until the 1920s when the American Medical Association moved in with an investigation campaign) beset the hard of hearing in the pages of the daily press, even in reputable magazines.[14]

The stigmatized individual can also attempt to correct his condition indirectly by devoting much private effort to the mastery of areas of activity ordinarily felt to be closed on incidental and physical grounds to one with his shortcoming. This is illustrated by the lame person who learns or re-learns to swim, ride, play tennis, or fly an airplane, or the blind person who becomes expert at skiing and mountain climbing.[15] Tortured learning may be associated, of course, with the tortured performance of what is learned, as when an individual, confined to a wheelchair, manages to take to the dance floor with a girl in some kind of mimicry of dancing.[16] Finally, the person with a shameful differentness can break with what is called reality, and obstinately attempt to employ an unconventional interpretation of the character of his social identity.

The stigmatized individual is likely to use his stigma for "secondary gains," as an excuse for ill success that has come his way for other reasons:

For years the scar, harelip or misshapen nose has been looked on as a handicap, and its importance in the social and emotional adjustment is unconsciously all embracing. It is the "hook" on which the patient has hung all inadequacies, all dissatisfactions, all procrastinations and all unpleasant duties of social life, and he has come to depend on it not only as a reasonable escape from competition but as a protection from social responsibility.

   When one removes this factor by surgical repair, the patient is cast adrift from the more or less acceptable emotional protection it has offered and soon he finds, to his surprise and discomfort, that life is not all smooth sailing even for those with unblemished, "ordinary" faces. He is unprepared to cope with this situation without the support of a "handicap," and he may turn to the less simple, but similar, protection of the behavior patterns of neurasthenia, hysterical conversion, hypochondriasis or the acute anxiety states.[17]

He may also see the trials he has suffered as a blessing in disguise, especially because of what it is felt that suffering can teach one about life and people:

> But now, far away from the hospital experience, I can evaluate what I have learned. [A mother permanently disabled by polio writes.] For it wasn't only suffering: it was also learning through suffering. I know my awareness of people has deepened and increased, that those who are close to me can count on me to turn all my mind and heart and attention to their problems. I could not have learned *that* dashing all over a tennis court.[18]

Correspondingly, he can come to re-assess the limitations of normals, as a multiple sclerotic suggests:

> Both healthy minds and healthy bodies may be crippled. The fact that "normal" people can get around, can see, can hear, doesn't mean that they are seeing or hearing. They can be very blind to the things that spoil their happiness, very deaf to the pleas of others for kindness; when I think of them I do not feel any more crippled or disabled than they. Perhaps in some way I can be the means of opening their eyes to the beauties around us: things like a warm handclasp, a voice that is anxious to cheer, a spring breeze, music to listen to, a friendly nod. These are important to me, and I like to feel that I can help them.[19]

And a blind writer.

> That would lead immediately to the thought that there are many occurrences which can diminish satisfaction in living far more effectively than blindness, and that lead would be an entirely healthy one to take. In this light, we can perceive, for instance, that some inadequacy like the inability to accept human love, which can effectively diminish satisfaction of living almost to the vanishing point, is far more a tragedy than blindness. But it is unusual for the man who suffers from such a malady even to know he has it and self pity is, therefore, impossible for him.[20]

And a cripple:

> As life went on, I learned of many, many different kinds of handicap, not only the physical ones, and I began to realize that the words of the crippled girl in the extract above [words of bitterness] could just as well have been spoken by young women who had never needed crutches, women who felt inferior and different because of ugliness, or inability to bear children, or helplessness in contacting people, or many other reasons.[21]

   The responses of the normal and of the stigmatized that have been considered so far are ones which can occur over protracted periods of time and in isolation from current contacts between normals and stigmatized.[22] This book, however, is specifically concerned with the issue of "mixed contacts"—the moments when stigmatized and normal are in the same "social situation," that is, in one another's immediate physical presence, whether in a conversation-like encounter or in the mere co-presence of an unfocused gathering.

   The very anticipation of such contacts can of course lead normals and the stigmatized to arrange life so as to avoid them. Presumably this will have larger consequences for the stigmatized, since more arranging will usually be necessary on their part:

Before her disfigurement [amputation of the distal half of her nose] Mrs. Dover, who lived with one of her two married daughters, had been an independent, warm and friendly woman who enjoyed traveling, shopping, and visiting her many relatives. The disfigurement of her face, however, resulted in a definite alteration in her way of living. The first two or three years she seldom left her daughter's home, preferring to remain in her room or to sit in the backyard. "I was heartsick," she said; "the door had been shut on my life."[22]

Lacking the salutary feed-back of daily social intercourse with others, the self-isolate can become suspicious, depressed, hostile, anxious, and bewildered. Sullivan's version may be cited:

The awareness of inferiority means that one is unable to keep out of consciousness the formulation of some chronic feeling of the worst sort of insecurity, and this means that one suffers anxiety and perhaps even something worse, if jealousy is really worse than anxiety. The fear that others can disrespect a person because of something he shows means that he is always insecure in his contact with other people; and this insecurity arises, not from mysterious and somewhat disguised, sources, as a great deal of our anxiety does, but from something which he knows he cannot fix. Now that represents an almost fatal deficiency of the self-system, since the self is unable to disguise or exclude a definite formulation that reads, "I am inferior. Therefore people will dislike me and I cannot be secure with them."[24]

When normals and stigmatized do in fact enter one another's immediate presence, especially when they there attempt to sustain a joint conversational encounter, there occurs one of the primal scenes of sociology; for, in many cases, these moments will be the ones when the causes and effects of stigma must be directly confronted on both sides.

These stigmatized individual may find that he feels unsure of how we normals will identify him and receive him.[25] An illustration may be cited from a student of physical disability:

Uncertainty of status for the disabled person obtains over a wide range of social interactions in addition to that of employment. The blind, the ill, the deaf, the crippled can never be sure what the attitude of a new acquaintance will be, whether it will be rejective or accepting, until the contact has been made. This is exactly the position of the adolescent, the light-skinned Negro, the second generation immigrant, the socially mobile person and the woman who has entered a predominantly masculine occupation.[26]

This uncertainty arises not merely from the stigmatized individual's not knowing which of several categories he will be placed in, but also, where the placement is favorable, from his knowing that in their hearts the others may be defining him in terms of his stigma:

And I always feel this with straight people—that whenever they're being nice to me, pleasant to me, all the time really, underneath they're only assessing me as a criminal and nothing else. It's too late for me to be any different now to what I am, but I still feel this keenly, that that's their only approach, and they're quite incapable of accepting me as anything else.[27]

Thus in the stigmatized arises the sense of not knowing what the others present are "really" thinking about him.

Further, during mixed contacts, the stigmatized individual is likely to feel that he is "on,"[28] having to be self-conscious and calculating about the impression he is making, to a degree and in areas of conduct which he assumes others are not.

Also, he is likely to feel that the usual scheme of interpretation for everyday events has been undermined. His minor accomplishments, he feels, may be assessed as signs of remarkable and noteworthy capacities in the circumstances. A professional criminal provides an illustration:

"You know, it's really amazing you should read books like this, I'm staggered I am. I should've thought you'd read paper-backed thrillers, things with lurid covers, books liked that. And here you are with Claud Cockburn, Hugh Klare, Simone de Beauvoir, and Lawrence Durrell!"

You know, he didn't see this as an insulting remark at all: in fact, I think he thought he was being honest in telling me how mistaken he was. And that's exactly the sort of patronizing you get from straight people if you're a criminal. "Fancy that!" they say. "In some ways you're just like a human being!" I'm not kidding, it makes me want to choke the bleeding life out of them.[29]

A blind person provides another illustration:

His once most ordinary deeds—walking nonchalantly up the street, locating the peas on his plate, lighting a cigarette—are no longer ordinary. He becomes an unusual person. If he performs them with finesse and assurance they excite the same kind of wonderment inspired by a magician who pulls rabbits out of hats.[30]

At the same time, minor failings or incidental impropriety may, he feels, be interpreted as a direct expression of his stigmatized differentness. Ex-mental patients, for example, are sometimes afraid to engage in sharp interchanges with spouse or employer because of what a show of emotion might be taken as a sign of. Mental defectives face a similar contingency:

It also happens that if a person of low intellectual ability gets into some sort of trouble the difficult is more or less automatically attributed to "mental defect" whereas if a person of "normal intelligence" gets into a similar difficulty, it is not regarded as symptomatic of anything in particular.[31]

A one-legged girl, recalling her experience with sports, provides other illustrations:

Whenever I fell, out swarmed the women in droves, clucking and fretting like a bunch of bereft mother hens. It was kind of them, and in retrospect I appreciate their solicitude, but at the time I resented and was greatly embarrassed by their interference. For they assumed that no routine hazard to skating—no stick or stone—upset my flying wheels. It was a foregone conclusion that *I* fell because I was a poor, helpless cripple.[32]

Not one of them shouted with outrage, "That dangerous wild bronco threw her!"—which, God forgive, he did technically. It was like a horrible ghostly visitation of my old roller-skating days. All the good people lamented in chorus, "That poor, poor girl fell off!"[33]

When the stigmatized person's failing can be perceived by our merely directing attention (typically, visual) to him—when, in short, he is a discredited, not discreditable, person—he is likely to feel that to be present among normals nakedly exposes him to invasions of privacy,[34] experienced most pointedly perhaps when children simply stare at him.[35] This displeasure in being exposed can be increased by the conversations strangers may feel free to strike up with him, conversations in which they express what he takes to be morbid curiosity about his condition, or in which they proffer help that he does not need or want.[36] One might add that there are certain classic formulae for these kinds of conversations: "My dear girl, how did you get your quiggle"; "My great uncle had a quiggle, so I feel I know all about your problem"; "You know I've always said that Quiggles are good family men and look after their own poor"; "Tell me, how do you manage to bathe with a quiggle?" The implication of these overtures is that the stigmatized individual is a person who can be approached by strangers at will, providing only that they are sympathetic to the plight of persons of his kind.

Given what the stigmatized individual may well face upon entering a mixed social situation, he may anticipatorily respond by defensive cowering. This may be illustrated from an early study of some German unemployed during the Depression, the words being those of a 43-year-old mason:

How hard and humiliating it is to bear the name of an unemployed man. When I go out, I cast down my eyes because I feel myself wholly inferior. When I go along the street, it seems to me that I can't be compared with an average citizen, that everybody is pointing at me with his finger. I instinctively avoid meeting anyone. Former acquaintances and friends of better times are no longer so cordial. They greet me indifferently when we meet. They no longer offer me a cigarette and their eyes seem to say, "You are not worth it, you don't work."[37]

A crippled girl provides an illustrative analysis:

> When...I began to walk out alone in the streets of our town...I found then that wherever I had to pass three or four children together on the sidewalk, if I happened to be alone, they would shout at me,...Sometimes they even ran after me, shouting and jeering. This was something I didn't know how to face, and it seemed as if I couldn't bear it....
>
> For awhile those encounters in the street filled me with a cold dread of all unknown children ...
>
> One day I suddenly realized that I had become so self-conscious and afraid of all strange children that, like animals, they knew I was afraid, so that even the mildest and most amiable of them were automatically prompted to derision by my own shrinking and dread.[38]

Instead of cowering, the stigmatized individual may attempt to approach mixed contacts with hostile bravado, but this can induce from others its own set of troublesome reciprocation. It may be added that the stigmatized person sometimes vacillates between cowering and bravado, racing from one to the other, thus demonstrating one central way in which ordinary face-to-face interaction can run wild.

I am suggesting, then, that the stigmatized individual—at least "visibly" stigmatized one—will have special reasons for feeling that mixed social situations make for anxious unanchored interaction. But if this is so, then it is to be suspected that we normals will find these situations shaky too. We will feel that the stigmatized individual is either too aggressive or too shamefaced, and in either case too ready to read unintended meanings into our actions. We ourselves may feel that if we show direct sympathetic concern for his condition, we may be overstepping ourselves; and yet if we actually forget that he has a failing we are likely to make impossible demands of him or unthinkingly slight his fellow-sufferers. Each potential source of discomfort for him when we are with him can become something we sense he is aware of, aware that we are aware of, and even aware of our state of awareness about his awareness; the stage is then set for the infinite regress of mutual consideration that Meadian social psychology tells us how to begin but not how to terminate.

Given what both the stigmatized and we normals introduce into mixed social situations, it is understandable that all will not go smoothly. We are likely to attempt to carry on as though in fact he wholly fitted one of the types of person naturally available to us in the situation, whether this means treating him as someone better than we feel he might be or someone worse than we feel he probably is. If neither of these tacks is possible, then we may try to act as if he were a "non-person," and not present at all as someone of whom ritual notice is to be taken. He, in turn, is likely to go along with these strategies, at least initially.

In consequence, attention is furtively withdrawn from its obligatory targets, and self-consciousness and "other-consciousness" occurs, expressed in the pathology of interaction—uneasiness.[39] As described in the case of the physically handicapped:

> Whether the handicap is overtly and tactlessly responded to as such or, as is more commonly the case, no explicit reference is made to it, the underlying condition of heightened, narrowed, awareness causes the interaction to be articulated too exclusively in terms of it. This, as my informants described it, is usually accompanied by one or more of the familiar signs of discomfort and stickiness: the guarded references, the common everyday words suddenly made taboo, the fixed stare elsewhere, the artificial levity, the compulsive loquaciousness, the awkward solemnity.[40]

In social situations with an individual known or perceived to have a stigma, we are likely, then, to employ categorizations that do not fit, and we and he are likely to experience uneasiness. Of course, there is often significant movement from this starting point. And since the stigmatized person is likely to be more often faced with these situations than are we, he is likely to become the more adept at managing them.

Notes

1. T. Parker and R. Allerton, *The Courage of His Convictions* (London: Hutchinson & Co., 1962), p. 109.

2. In this connection see the review by M. Meltzer, "Countermanipulation through Malingering," in A. Biderman and H. Zimmer, eds., *The Manipulation of Human Behavior* (New York: John Wiley & Sons, 1961), pp. 277–304.

3. In recent history, especially in Britain, low class status functioned as an important tribal stigma, the sins of the parents, or at least their millieu, being visited on the child, should the child rise improperly far above his initial station. The management of class stigma is of course a central theme in the English novel.

4. D. Riesman, "Some Observations Concerning Marginality," *Phylon,* Second Quarter, 1951, 122.

5. The case regarding mental patients is represented by T. J. Scheff in a forthcoming paper.

6. In regard to the blind, see E. Henrich and L. Kriegel, eds., *Experiments in Survival* (New York: Associatino for the Aid of Crippled Children, 1961), pp. 152 and 186; and H. Chevigny, *My Eyes Have a Cold Nose* (New Haven, Conn.: Yale University Press, paperbound, 1962), p. 201.

7. In the words of one blind woman, "I was asked to endorse a perfume, presumably because being sightless my sense of smell was super-discriminating." See T. Keitlen (with N. Lobsenz), *Farewell to Fear* (New York: Avon, 1962), p. 10.

8. A. G. Gowman, *The War Blind in American Social Structure* (New York: American Foundation for the Blind, 1957), p. 198.

9. For examples, see Macgregor *et al., op. cit.,* throughout.

10. The notion of "normal human being" may have its source in the medical approach to humanity or in the tendency of large-scale bureaucratic organizations, such as the nation state, to treat all members in some respects as equal. Whatever its origins, it seems to provide the basic imagery through which laymen currently conceive of themselves. Interestingly, a convention seems to have emerged in popular life-story writing where a questionable person proves his claim to normalcy by citing his acquisition of a spouse and children, and, oddly, by attesting to his spending Christmas and Thanksgiving with them.

11. A criminal's view of this nonacceptance is presented in Parker and Allerton, *op. cit.,* pp. 110–111.

12. K. B. Hathaway, *The Little Locksmith* (New York: Coward-McCann, 1943), p. 41, in Wright, *op. cit.,* p. 157.

13. *Ibid.,* pp. 46–47. For general treatments of the self-disliking sentiments, see K. Lewin, *Resolving Social Conflicts,* Part III (New York: Harper & Row, 1948); A. Kardiner and L. Ovesey, *The Mark of Oppression: A Psychological Study of the American Negro* (New York: W. W. Norton & Company, 1951); and E. H. Erikson, *Childhood and Society* (New York: W. W. Norton & Company, 1950).

14. F. Warfield, *Keep Listening* (New York: The Viking Press, 1957), p. 76. See also H. von Hentig, *The Criminal and His Victim* (New Haven, Conn.: Yale University Press, 1948), p. 101.

15. Keitlen, *op. cit.,* Chap. 12, pp. 117–129 and Chap. 14, pp. 137–149. See also Chevigny, *op. cit.,* pp. 85–86.

16. Henrich and Kriegel, *op. cit.,* p. 49.

17. W. Y. Baker and L. H. Smith, "Facial Disfigurement and Personality," *Journal of the American Medical Association,* CXII (1939), 303. Macgregor *et al., op. cit.,* p. 57ff., provide an illustration of a man who used his big red nose for a crutch.

18. Henrich and Kriegel, *op. cit.,* p. 19.

19. *Ibid.,* p. 35.

20. Chevigny, *op. cit.,* p. 154.

21. F. Carlin, *And Yet We Are Human* (London: Chatto & Windus, 1962), pp. 23–24.

22. For one review, see G. W. Allport, *The Nature of Prejudice* (New York: Anchor Books, 1958).

23. Macgregor *et al., op. cit.,* pp. 91–92.

24. From *Clinical Studies in Psychiatry,* H. S. Perry, M. L. Gawel, and M. Gibbon, eds. (New York: W. W. Norton & Company, 1956), p. 145.

25. R. Barker, "The Social Psychology of Physical Disability," *Journal of Social Issues,* IV (1948), 34, suggests that stigmatized persons "live on a social-psychological frontier," constantly facing new situations. See also Macgregor *et al., op. cit.,* p. 87, where the suggestion is made that the grossly deformed need suffer less doubt about their reception in interaction than the less visibly deformed.

26. Barker, *op. cit.,* p. 33.

27. Parker and Allerton, *op. cit.,* p. III.

28. This special kind of self-consciousness is analyzed in S. Messinger, *et al.,* "Life as Theater: Some Notes on the Dramaturgic Approach to Social Reality," *Sociometry,* XXV (1962), 98–110.

29. Parker and Allerton, *op. cit.,* p. III.

30. Chevigny, *op. cit.,* p. 140.

31. L. A. Dexter, "A Social Theory of Mental Deficiency," *American Journal of Mental Deficiency,* LXII (1958), 923. For another study of the mental defective as a stigmatized person, see S. E. Perry, "Some Theoretical Problems of Mental Deficiency and Their Action Implications," *Psychiatry,* XVII (1954), 45–73.

32. Baker, *Out on a Limb* (New York: McGraw-Hill Book Company, n.d.), p. 22.

33. *Ibid.,* p. 73.

34. This theme is well treated in R. K. White, B. A. Wright, and T. Dembo, "Studies in Adjustment to Visible Injuries: Evaluation of Curiosity by the Injured," *Journal of Abnormal and Social Psychology*, XLIII (1948), 13–28.

35. For example, Henrich and Kriegel, *op. cit.,* p. 184.

36. See Wright, *op. cit.,* "The Problem of Sympathy," pp. 233–237.

37. S. Zawadski and P. Lazarsfeld, "The Psychological Consequences of Unemployment," *Journal of Social Psychology,* VI (1935), 239.

38. Hathaway, *op. cit.,* pp. 155–157, in S. Richardson, "The Social Psychological Consequences of Handicapping," unpublished paper presented at the 1962 American Sociological Association Convention, Washington, D. C., 7–8.

39. For a general treatment, see E. Goffman, "Alienation from Interaction," *Human Relations,* X (1957), 47–60.

40. F. Davis, "Deviance Disavowal: The Management of Strained Interaction by the Visibly Handicapped," *Social Problems,* IX (1961), 123. See also White, Wright, and Dembo, *op. cit.,* pp. 26–27.

11

Stigma
An Enigma Demystified

Lerita M. Coleman

Nature caused us all to be born equal; if fate is pleased to disturb this plan of the general law, it is our responsibility to correct its caprice, and to repair by our attention the usurpations of the stronger.

—Maurice Blanchot

What is stigma and why does stigma remain? Because stigmas mirror culture and society, they are in constant flux, and therefore the answers to these two questions continue to elude social scientists. Viewing stigma from multiple perspectives exposes its intricate nature and helps us to disentangle its web of complexities and paradoxes. Stigma represents a view of life; a set of personal and social constructs; a set of social relations and social relationships; a form of social reality. Stigma has been a difficult concept to conceptualize because it reflects a property, a process, a form of social categorization, and an affective state.

> Two primary questions, then, that we as social scientists have addressed are how and why during certain historical periods. In specific cultures or within particular social groups, some human differences are valued and desired, and other human differences are devalued, feared, or stigmatized. In attempting to answer these questions, I propose another view of stigma, one that takes into account its behavioral, cognitive, and affective components and reveals that stigma is a response to the dilemma of difference.

The Dilemma

No two human beings are exactly alike: there are countless ways to differ. Shape, size, skin color, gender, age, cultural background, personality, and years of formal education are just a few of the infinite number of ways in which people can vary. Perceptually, and in actuality, there is greater variation on some of these dimensions than on others. Age and gender, for example, are dimensions with limited and quantifiable ranges; yet they interact exponentially with other physical or social characteristics that have larger continua (e.g., body shape, income, cultural background) to create a vast number of human differences. Goffman states, though, that "stigma is equivalent to an undesired differentness" (see Stafford & Scott). The infinite variety of human attributes suggests that what is undesired or stigmatized is heavily dependent on the social context and to some extent arbitrarily defined. The large number of stigmatizable attributes and several taxonomies of stigmas in the literature offer further evidence of how arbitrary the selection of undesired differences may be (see Ainlay & Crosby; Becker & Arnold; Solomon; Stafford & Scott).

What is most poignant about Goffman's description of stigma is that it suggests that all human differences are potentially stigmatizable. As we move out of one social context where a difference is desired into another context where the difference is undesired, we begin to feel the effects of stigma.

This conceptualization of stigma also indicates that those possessing power, the dominant group, can determine which human differences are desired and undesired. In part, stigmas reflect the value judgments of a dominant group.

Many people, however, especially those who have some role in determining the desired and undesired differences of the zeitgeist, often think of stigma only as a property of individuals. They operate under the illusion that stigma exists only for certain segments of the population. But the truth is that any "nonstigmatized" person can easily become "stigmatized." "Nearly everyone at some point in life will experience stigma either temporarily or permanently.... Why do we persist in this denial?" (Zola, 1979, p. 454). Given that human differences serve as the basis for stigmas, being or feeling stigmatized is virtually an inescapable fate. Because stigmas differ depending upon the culture and the historical period. It becomes evident that it is mere chance whether a person is born into a nonstigmatized or severely stigmatized group.

Because stigmatization often occurs within the confines of a psychologically constructed or actual social relationship, the experience itself reflects relative comparisons, the contrasting of desired and undesired differences. Assuming that flawless people do not exist, relative comparisons give rise to a feeling of superiority in some contexts (where one possesses a desired trait that another person is lacking) but perhaps a feeling of inferiority in other contexts (where one lacks a desired trait that another person possesses). It is also important to note that it is only when we make comparisons that we can feel different. Stigmatization or feeling stigmatized is a consequence of social comparison. For this reason, stigma represents a continuum of undesired differences that depend upon many factors (e.g., geographical location, culture, life cycle stage) (see Becker & Arnold).

Although some stigmatized conditions appear escapable or may be temporary, some undesired traits have graver social consequences than others. Being a medical resident, being a new professor, being 7 feet tall, having cancer, being black, or being physically disfigured or mentally retarded can all lead to feelings of stigmatization (feeling discredited or devalued in a particular role), but obviously these are not equally stigmatizing conditions. The degree of stigmatization might depend on how undesired the difference is in a particular social group.

Physical abnormalities, for example, may be the most severely stigmatized differences because they are physically salient, represent some deficiency or distortion in the bodily form, and in most cases are unalterable. Other physically salient differences, such as skin color or nationality, are considered very stigmatizing because they also are permanent conditions and cannot be changed. Yet the stigmatization that one feels as a result of being black or Jewish or Japanese depends on the social context, specifically social contexts in which one's skin color or nationality is not a desired one. A white American could feel temporarily stigmatized when visiting Japan due to a difference in height. A black student could feel stigmatized in a predominantly white university because the majority of the students are white and white skin is a desired trait. But a black student in a predominantly black university is not likely to feel the effects of stigma. Thus, the sense of being stigmatized or having a stigma is inextricably tied to social context. Of equal importance are the norms in that context that determine which are desirable and undesirable attributes. Moving from one social or cultural context to another can change both the definitions and the consequences of stigma.

Stigma often results in a special kind of downward mobility. Part of the power of stigmatization lies in the realization that people who are stigmatized or acquire a stigma lose their place in the social hierarchy. Consequently, most people want to ensure that they are counted in the nonstigmatized "majority." This, of course, leads to more stigmatization.

Stigma, then, is also a term that connotes a relationship. It seems that this relationship is vital to understanding the stigmatizing process. Stigma allows some individuals to feel superior to others. Superiority and inferiority, however, are two sides of the same coin. In order for one person to feel superior, there must be another person who is perceived to be or who actually feels inferior. Stigmatized people are needed in order for the many nonstigmatized people to feel good about themselves.

On the other hand, there are many stigmatized people who feel inferior and concede that other persons are superior because they possess certain attributes. In order for the process to occur (for one person to stigmatize another and have the stigmatized person feel the effects of stigma), there must be some agreement that the differentness is inherently undesirable. Moreover, even among stigmatized people, relative comparisons are made, and people are reassured by the fact that there is someone else who is worse off. The dilemma of difference, therefore, affects both stigmatized and nonstigmatized people.

Some might contend that this is the very old scapegoat argument, and there is some truth to that contention. But the issues here are more finely intertwined. If stigma is a social construct, constructed by cultures, by social groups, and by individuals to designate some human differences as discrediting, then the stigmatization process is indeed a powerful and pernicious social tool. The inferiority/superiority issue is a most interesting way of understanding how and why people continue to stigmatize.

Some stigmas are more physically salient than others, and some people are more capable of concealing their stigmas or escaping from the negative social consequences of being stigmatized. The ideal prototype (e.g., young, white, tall, married, male, with a recent record in sports) that Stafford cites may actually possess traits that would be the source of much scorn and derision in another social context. Yet, by insulating himself in his own community, a man like the one described in the example can ensure that his "differentness" will receive approbation rather than rejection, and he will not be subject to constant and severe stigmatization. This is a common response to stigma among people with some social influence (e.g., artists, academics, millionaires). Often, attributes or behaviors that might otherwise be considered "abnormal" or stigmatized are labeled as "eccentric" among persons of power or influence. The fact that what is perceived as the "ideal" person varies from one social context to another, however, is tied to Martin's notion that people learn ways to stigmatize in each new situation.

In contrast, some categories of stigmatized people (e.g., the physically disabled, members of ethnic groups, poor people) cannot alter their stigmas nor easily disguise them. People, then, feel permanently stigmatized in contexts where their differentness is undesired and in social environments that they cannot easily escape. Hence, power, social influence, and social control play a major role in the stigmatization process.

In summary, stigma stems from differences. By focusing on differences we actively create stigmas because any attribute or difference is potentially stigmatizable. Often we attend to a single different attribute rather than to the large number of similar attributes that any two individuals share. Why people focus on differences and denigrate people on the basis of them is important to understanding how some stigmas originate and persist. By reexamining the historical origins of stigma and the way children develop the propensity to stigmatize, we can see how some differences evolve into stigmas and how the process is linked to the behavioral (social control), affective (fear, dislike), and cognitive (perception of differences, social categorization) components of stigma.

The Origins of *Stigma*

The phrase *to stigmatize* originally referred to the branding or marking of certain people (e.g., criminals, prostitutes) in order to make them appear different and separate from others (Goffman, 1963). The act of marking people in this way resulted in exile or avoidance. In most cultures, physical marking or branding has declined, but a more cognitive manifestation of stigmatization—social marking—has increased and has become the basis for most stigmas (Jones *et al.*, 1984). Goffman points out, though, that stigma has retained much of its original connotation. People use differences to exile or avoid others. In addition, what is most intriguing about the ontogenesis of the stigma concept is the broadening of its predominant affective responses such as dislike and disgust to include the emotional reaction of fear. Presently, *fear* may be instrumental in the perpetuation of stigma and in maintaining its original social functions. Yet as the developmental literature reveals, fear is not a natural but an acquired response to differences of stigmas.

Sigelman and Singleton offer a number of insightful observations about how children learn to stigmatize. Children develop a natural wariness of strangers as their ability to differentiate familiar from novel objects increases (Sroufe, 1977). Developmental psychologists note that stranger anxiety is a universal phenomenon in infants and appears around the age of seven months. This reaction to differences (e.g., women versus men, children versus adults, blacks versus whites) is an interesting one and, as Sigelman and Singleton point out, may serve as a prototype for stigmatizing. Many children respond in a positive (friendly) or negative (fearful, apprehensive) manner to strangers. Strangers often arouse the interest (Brooks & Lewis, 1976) of children but elicit negative reactions if they intrude on their personal space (Sroufe, 1977). Stranger anxiety tends to fade with age, but when coupled with self-referencing it may create the conditions for a child to learn how to respond to human differences or how to stigmatize.

Self-referencing, or the use of another's interpretation of a situation to form one's own understanding of it, commonly occurs in young children. Infants often look toward caregivers when encountering something different, such as a novel object, person, or event (Feinman, 1982). The response to novel stimuli in an ambiguous situation may depend on the emotional displays of the caregiver; young children have been known to respond positively to situations if their mothers respond reassuringly (Feinman, 1982). Self-referencing is instrumental to understanding the development of stigmatization because it may be through this process that caregivers shape young children's responses to people, especially those who possess physically salient differences (Klinnert, Campos, Sorce, Emde, & Svejda, 1983). We may continue to learn about how to stigmatize from other important figures (e.g., mentors, role models) as we progress through the life cycle. Powerful authority figures may serve as the source of self-referencing behavior in new social contexts (Martin).

Sigelman and Singleton also point out that preschoolers notice differences and tend to establish preferences but do not necessarily stigmatize. Even on meeting other children with physical disabilities, children do not automatically eschew them but may respond to actual physical and behavioral similarities and differences. There is evidence, moreover, indicating that young children are curious about human differences and often stare at novel stimuli (Brooks & Lewis, 1976). Children frequently inquire of their parents or of stigmatized persons about their distinctive physical attributes. In many cases, the affective response of young children is interest rather than fear.

Barbarin offers a poignant example of the difference between interest and fear in his vignette about Myra, a child with cancer. She talks about young children who are honest and direct about her illness, an attitude that does not cause her consternation. What does disturb her, though, are parents who will not permit her to baby-sit with their children for *fear* that she might give them cancer. Thus, interest and curiosity about stigma or human differences may be natural for children, but they must *learn* fear and avoidance as well as which categories or attributes to dislike, *fear*, or stigmatize. Children may learn to stigmatize without ever grasping "why" they do so (Martin), just as adults have beliefs about members of stigmatized groups without ever having met any individuals from the group (Crocker & Lutsky). The predisposition to stigmatize is passed from one generation to the next through social learning (Martin) or socialization (Crocker & Lutsky; Stafford & Scott).

Sigelman and Singleton agree with Martin that social norms subtly impinge upon the information-processing capacities of young children so that negative responses to stigma later become automatic. At some point, the development of social cognition must intersect with the affective responses that parents or adults display toward stigmatized people. Certain negative emotions become attached to social categories (e.g., *all* ex-mental patients are dangerous, *all* blacks are angry or harmful). Although the attitudes (cognitions) about stigma assessed in paper-and-pencil tasks may change in the direction of what is socially acceptable, the affect and behavior of elementary- and secondary-school children as well as adults reflect the early negative affective associations with stigma. The norms about stigma, though, are ambiguous and confusing. They teach young children to avoid or dislike stigmatized people, even though similar behavior in adults is considered socially unacceptable.

Stigma as a Form of Cognitive Processing

The perceptual processing of human differences appears to be universal. Ainlay and Crosby suggest that differences arouse us; they can please or distress us. From a phenomenological perspective, we carry around "recipes" and "typifications" as structures for categorizing and ordering stimuli. Similarly, social psychologists speak of our need to categorize social stimuli in such terms as *schemas* and *stereotypes* (Crocker & Lutsky). These approaches to the perception of human differences indirectly posit that stigmatizing is a natural response, a way to maintain order in a potentially chaotic world of social stimuli. People want to believe that the world is ordered.

Although various approaches to social categorization may explain how people stereotype on the basis of a specific attribute (e.g., skin color, religious beliefs, deafness), they do not explain the next step—the negative imputations. Traditional approaches to sociocognitive processing also do not offer ideas about how people can perceptually move beyond the stereotype, the typification, or stigma to perceive an individual. Studies of stereotyping and stigma regularly reveal that beliefs about the inferiority of a person predominate in the thoughts of the perceiver (Crocker & Lutsky).

Stigma appears to be a special and insidious kind of social categorization or, as Martin explains, a process of generalizing from a single experience. People are treated categorically rather than individually, and in the process are devalued (Ainlay & Crosby; Barbarin; Crocker & Lutsky; Stafford & Scott). In addition, as Crocker and Lutsky point out, coding people in terms of categories (e.g., "X is a redhead") instead of specific attributes ("X has red hair") allows people to feel that stigmatized persons are fundamentally different and establishes greater psychological and social distance.

A discussion of the perceptual basis of stigma inevitably leads back to the notion of master status (Goffman, 1963). Perceptually, stigma becomes the master status, the attribute that colors the perception of the entire person. All other aspects of the person are ignored except those that fit the stereotype associated with the stigma (Kanter, 1979). Stigma as a form of negative stereotyping has a way of neutralizing positive qualities and undermining the identity of stigmatized individuals (Barbarin). This kind of social categorization has also been described by one sociologist as a "discordance with personal attributes" (Davis, 1964). Thus, many stigmatized people are not expected to be intelligent, attractive, or upper class.

Another important issue in the perception of human differences or social cognition is the relative comparisons that are made between and within stigmatized and nonstigmatized groups. Several authors discuss the need for people to accentuate between-group differences and minimize within-group differences as a requisite for group identity (Ainlay & Crosby; Crocker & Lutsky; Sigelman & Singleton). Yet these authors do not explore in depth the reasons for denigrating the attributes of the out-group members and elevating the attributes of one's own group, unless there is some feeling that the out-group could threaten the balance of power. Crocker and Lutsky note, however, that stereotyping is frequently tied to the need for self-enhancement. People with low self-esteem are more likely to identify and maintain negative stereotypes about members of stigmatized groups; such people are more negative in general. This line of reasoning takes us back to viewing stigma as a means of maintaining the status quo through social control. Could it be that stigma as a perceptual tool helps to reinforce the differentiation of the population that in earlier times was deliberately designated by marking? One explanation offered by many theorists is that stereotypes about stigmatized groups help to maintain the exploitation of such groups and preserve the existing societal structure.

Are there special arrangements or special circumstance, Ainlay and Crosby ask, that allow people to notice differences but not denigrate those who have them? On occasion, nonstigmatized people are able to "break through" and to see a stigmatized person as a real, whole person with a variety of attributes, some similar traits and some different from their own (Davis, 1964). Just how frequently and in what ways does this happen?

Ainlay and Crosby suggest that we begin to note differences within a type when we *need* to do so. The example they give about telephones is a good one. We learn differences among types of telephones, appliances, schools, or even groups of people when we need to. Hence stereotyping or stigmatizing is not necessarily automatic; when we want to perceive differences we perceive them, just as we perceive similarities when we *want* to. In some historical instances, society appears to have recognized full human potential when it was required, while ignoring certain devalued traits. When women were needed to occupy traditionally male occupations in the United States during World War II, gender differences were ignored as they have been ignored in other societies when women were needed for combat. Similarly, the U. S. armed forces became racially integrated when there was a need for more soldiers to fight in World War II (Terry, 1984).

Thus, schemas or stereotypes about stigmatized individuals can be modified but only under specific conditions. When stigmatized people have essential information or possess needed expertise, we discover that some of their attributes are not so different, or that they are more similar to us than different. "Cooperative interdependence" stemming from shared goals may change the nature of perceptions and the nature of relationships (Crocker & Lutsky). Future research on stigma and on social perception might continue to investigate the conditions under which people are less likely to stereotype and more likely to respond to individuals rather than categories (cf., Locksley, Borgida, Brekke, & Hepburn, 1980; Locksley, Hepburn & Ortiz, 1982).

The Meaning of Stigma for Social Relations

I have intimated that "stigmatized" and "nonstigmatized" people are tied together in a perpetual inferior/superior relationship. This relationship is key to understanding the meaning of stigma. To conceptualize stigma as a social relationship raises some vital questions about stigma. These questions include (a) when and under what conditions does an attribute become a stigmatized one? (b) can a person experience stigmatization without knowing that a trait is devalued in a specific social context? (c) does a person feel stigmatized even though in a particular social context the attribute is not stigmatized or the stigma is not physically or behaviorally apparent? (d) can a person refuse to be stigmatized or destigmatize an attribute by ignoring the prevailing norms that define it as a stigma?

These questions lead to another one: Would stigma persist if stigmatized people did not feel stigmatized or inferior? Certainly, a national pride did not lessen the persecution of the Jews, nor does it provide freedom for blacks in South Africa. These two examples illustrate how pervasive and powerful the social control aspects of stigma are, empowering the stigmatizer and stripping the stigmatized of power. Yet a personal awakening, a discover that the responsibility for being stigmatized does not lie with oneself, is important. Understanding that the rationale for discrimination and segregation based on stigma lies in the mind of the stigmatizer has led people like Mahatma Gandhi and civil rights activist Rosa Parks to rise above the feeling of stigmatization, to ignore the norms, and to disobey the exiting laws based on stigma. There have been women, elderly adults, gays, disabled people, and many others who at some point realized that their fundamental similarities outweighed and outnumbered their differences. It becomes clear that, in most oppressive situations the primary problem lies with the stigmatizer and not with the stigmatized (Sartre, 1948; Schur, 1980, 1983). Many stigmatized people also begin to understand that the stigmatizer, having established a position of false superiority and consequently the need to maintain it, is enslaved to the concept that stigmatized people are fundamentally inferior. In fact, some stigmatized individuals question the norms about stigma and attempt to change the social environments for their peers.

In contrast, there are some stigmatized persons who accept their devalued status as legitimate. Attempting to "pass" and derogating others like themselves are two ways in which stigmatized people effectively accept the society's negative perceptions of their stigma (Goffman, cited in Gibbons). It is clear, especially from accounts of those who move from a nonstigmatized to a stigmatized role, that stigmatization is difficult to resist if everyone begins to reinforce the inferior status with their behavior. Two of the most common ways in which nonstigmatized people convey a sense of fundamental inferiority to stigmatized people are social rejection or social isolation and lowered expectations.

There are many ways in which people communicate social rejection such as speech, eye contact, and interpersonal distance. The stigmatized role, as conceptualized by the symbolic interactionism approach, is similar to any other role (e.g., professor, doctor) in which we behave according to the role expectations of others and change our identity to be congruent with them. Thus, in the case of stigma, role expectations are often the same as the stereotypes. Some stigmatized people become dependent, passive, helpless, and childlike because that is what is expected of them.

Social rejection or avoidance affects not only the stigmatized individual but everyone who is socially involved, such as family, friends, and relatives (Barbarin). This permanent form of social quarantine forces people to limit their relationships to other stigmatized people and to those for whom the social bond outweighs the stigma, such as family members. In this way, avoidance or social rejection also acts as a form of social control or containment (Edgerton, 1967; Goffman, 1963; Schur, 1983; Scott, 1969). Social rejection is perhaps most difficult for younger children who are banned from most social activities of their peers.

Social exile conveys another message about expectations. Many stigmatized people are not encouraged to develop or grow, to have aspirations or to be successful. Barbarin reports that children with cancer lose friendships and receive special, lenient treatment from teachers. They are not expected to achieve in the same manner as other children. Parents, too, sometimes allow stigmatized children to behave in ways that "normal" children in the same family are not permitted to do. Social exclusion as well as overprotection can lead to decreased performance. Lowered expectations also lead to decreased self-esteem.

The negative identity that ensues becomes a pervasive personality trait and inhibits the stigmatized person from developing other parts of the self. Another detrimental aspect of stigmatization is the practice of treating people, such as the ex-con and ex-mental patient who are attempting to reintegrate themselves into society, as if they still had the stigma. Even the terms we use to describer such persons suggest that role expectations remain the same despite the stigmatized person's efforts to relinquish them. It seems that the paradoxical societal norms that establish a subordinate and dependent position for stigmatized people while ostracizing them for it may stem from the need of nonstigmatized people to maintain a sense of superiority. Their position is supported and reinforced by their perceptions that stigmatized people are fundamentally inferior, passive, helpless, and childlike.

The most pernicious consequence of bearing a stigma is that stigmatized people may develop the same perceptual problems that nonstigmatized people have. They begin to see themselves and their lives through the stigma, or as Sartre (1948) writes about the Jews, they "allow themselves to be poisoned by the stereotype and live in fear that they will correspond to it" (p. 95). As Gibbons observes, stigmatized individuals sometimes blame their difficulties on the stigmatized trait, rather than confronting the root of their personal difficulties. Thus, normal issues that one encounters in life often act as a barrier to growth for stigmatized people because of the attributional process involved.

The need to maintain one's identity manifests itself in a number of ways, such as the mischievous behavior of the adolescent boy with cancer cited in Barbarin's chapter. "Attaining normalcy within the limits of stigma" (Tracy & Gussow, 1978) seems to be another way of describing the need to establish or recapture one's identity (Weiner, 1975).

Stigma uniquely alters perceptions in other ways, especially with respect to the notion of "normality", and raises other questions about the dilemma of difference. Most people do not want to be perceived as different or "abnormal." Becker and Arnold and Gibbons discuss normalization as attempts to be "not different" and to appear "normal." Such strategies include "passing" or disguising the stigma and acting "normal" by "covering up"—keeping up with the pace of nonstigmatized individuals (Davis,

1964; Gibbons; Goffman, 1963; Weiner, 1975). For stigmatized people, the idea of normality takes on an exaggerated importance. Normality becomes the supreme goal for many stigmatized individuals until they realize that there is no precise definition of normality except what they would be without their stigma. Given the dilemma of difference that stigma reflects, it is not clear whether anyone can ever feel "normal."

Out of this state of social isolation and lowered expectations, though, can arise some positive consequences. Although the process can be fraught with pain and difficulty, stigmatized people who manage to reject the perceptions of themselves as inferior often come away with greater inner strength (Jones et al., 1984). They learn to depend on their own resources and, like the earlier examples of Mahatma Gandhi and Rosa Parks, they begin to question the bases for defining normality. Many stigmatized people regain their identity through redefining normality and realizing that it is acceptable to be who they are (Ablon, 1981; Barbarin; Becker, 1980; Becker & Arnold).

Fear and Stigma

Fear is important to a discussion of how and why stigma persists. In many cultures that do not use the term *stigma*, there is some emotional reaction beyond interest or curiosity to differences such as children who are born with birthmarks, epilepsy, or a caul. Certain physical characteristics or illnesses elicit fear because the etiology of the attribute or disease is unknown, unpredictable, and unexpected (Sontag, 1979). People even have fears about the sexuality of certain stigmatized groups such as persons who are mentally retarded, feeling that if they are allowed to reproduce they will have retarded offspring (Gibbons). It seems that what gives stigma its intensity and reality is fear.

The nature of the fear appears to vary with the type of stigma. For most stigmas stemming from physical or mental problems, including cancer, people experience fear of contagion even though they know that the stigma cannot be developed through contact (see Barbarin). This fear usually stems from not knowing about the etiology of a condition, its predictability, and its course.

The stigmatization of certain racial, ethnic, and gender categories may also be based on fear. This fear, though, cannot stem from contagion because attributes (of skin color, ethnic background, and gender) cannot possibly be transmitted to nonstigmatized people. One explanation for the fear is that people want to avoid "courtesy stigmas" or stigmatization by association (Goffman, 1963). Another explanation underlying this type of fear may be the notion of scarce resources. This is the perception that if certain groups of people are allowed to have a share in all resources, there will not be enough: not enough jobs, not enough land, not enough water, or not enough food. Similar explanations from the deviance literature suggest that people who stigmatize feel threatened and collectively feel that their position of social, economic, and political dominance will be dismantled by members of stigmatized groups (Schur, 1980, 1983). A related explanation is provided by Hughes, who states, "that it may be that those whose positions are insecure and whose hopes for the higher goals are already fading express more violent hostility to new people" (1945, p. 356). This attitude may account for the increased aggression toward members of stigmatized groups during dire economic periods.

Fear affects not only nonstigmatized but stigmatized individuals as well. Many stigmatized people (e.g., ex-cons, mentally retarded adults) who are attempting to "pass" live in fear that their stigmatized attribute will be discovered (Gibbons). These fears are grounded in a realistic assessment of the negative social consequences of stigmatization and reflect the long-term social and psychological damage to individuals resulting from stigma.

At some level, therefore, most people are concerned with stigma because they are fearful of its unpredictable and uncontrollable nature. Stigmatization appears uncontrollable because human differences serve as the basis for stigmas. Therefore, *any* attribute can become a stigma. No one really ever knows when or if he or she will acquire a stigma or when societal norms might change to stigmatize a trait he or she already possesses. To deny this truth by attempting to isolate stigmatized people or escape from stigma is a manifestation of the underlying fear.

The unpredictability of stigma is similar to the unpredictability of death. Both Gibbons and Barbarin note that the development of a stigmatized condition in a loved one or in oneself represents a major breach of trust—a destruction of the belief that life is predictable. In a sense, stigma represents a kind of death—a social death. Nonstigmatized people, through avoidance and social rejection, often treat stigmatized people as if they were invisible, nonexistent, or dead. Many stigmas, in particular childhood cancer, remove the usual disguises of mortality. Such stigmas can act as a symbolic reminder of everyone's inevitable death (see Barbarin's discussion of Ernest Becker's (1973) *The Denial of Death*). These same fears can be applied to the acquisition of other stigmas (e.g., mental illness, physical disabilities) and help to intensify and perpetuate the negative responses to most stigmatized categories. Thus, irrational fears may help stigmatization to be self-perpetuating with little encouragement needed in the form of forced segregation from the political and social structure.

The ultimate answers about why stigma persists may lie in an examination of why people fear differences, fear the future, fear the unknown, and therefore stigmatize that which is different and unknown. An equally important issue to investigate is how stigmatization may be linked to the fear of being different.

Conclusion

Stigma is clearly a very complex multidisciplinary issue, with each additional perspective containing another piece of this enigma. A multidisciplinary approach allowed us as social scientists to perceive stigma as a whole; to see from within it rather than to look down upon it. Our joint perspectives have also demonstrated that there are many shared ideas across disciplines, and in many cases only the terminology is different.

Three important aspects of stigma emerge from this multidisciplinary examination and may forecast its future. They are fear, stigma's primary affective component; stereotyping, its primary cognitive component; and social control, its primary behavioral component. The study of the relationship of stigma to fear, stereotyping, and social control may elucidate our understanding of the paradoxes that a multidisciplinary perspective reveals. It may also bring us closer to understanding what stigma really is—not primarily a property of individuals as many have conceptualized it to be but a humanly constructed perception, constantly in flux and legitimizing our negative responses to human differences (Ainlay & Crosby). To further clarify the definition of stigma, one must differentiate between an "undesired differentness" that is likely to lead to feelings of stigmatization and actual forms of stigmatization. *It appears that stigmatization occurs only when the social control component is imposed, or when the undesired differentness leads to some restriction in physical and social mobility and access to opportunities that allow an individual to develop his or her potential. This definition combines the original meaning of stigma with more contemporary connotations and uses.*

In another vein, stigma is a statement about personal and social responsibility. People irrationally feel that, by separating themselves from stigmatized individuals, they may reduce their own risk of acquiring the stigma (Barbarin). By isolating individuals, people feel they can also isolate the problem. If stigma is ignored, the responsibility for its existence and perpetuation can be shifted elsewhere. Making stigmatized people feel responsible for their own stigma allows nonstigmatized people to relinquish the onus for creating or perpetuating the conditions that surround it.

Changing political and economic climates are also important to the stigmatization and destigmatization process. What is economically feasible or politically enhancing for a group in power will partially determine what attributes are stigmatized, or at least how they are stigmatized. As many sociologists have suggested, some people are stigmatized for violating norms, whereas others are stigmatized for being of little economic or political value (Birenbaum & Sagarin, 1976, cited in Stafford & Scott). We should admit that stigma persists as a social problem because it continues to have some of its original social utility as a means of controlling certain segments of the population and ensuring that power is not easily exchanged. Stigma helps to maintain the existing social hierarchy.

One might then ask if there will ever be societies or historical periods without stigma. Some authors hold a positive vision of the future. Gibbons, for example, suggests that as traditionally stigmatized groups become more integrated into the general population, stigmatizing attributes will lose some of their onus. But historical analysis would suggest that new stigmas will replace old ones. Educational programs are probably of only limited help, as learning to stigmatize is a part of early social learning experiences (Martin; Sigelman & Singleton). The social learning of stigma is indeed very different from learning about the concept abstractly in a classroom. School experiences sometimes merely reinforce what children learn about stigmatization from parents and significant others.

From a sociological perspective, the economic, psychological and social benefits of stigma sustain it. Stigmas will disappear when we no longer need to legitimize social exclusion and segregation (Zola, 1979). From the perspective of cognitive psychology, when people find it necessary or beneficial to perceive the fundamental similarities they share with stigmatized people rather than the differences, we will see the beginnings of a real elimination of stigma. This process may have already occurred during some particular historical period or within particular societies. It is certainly an important area for historians, anthropologists, and psychologists to explore.

Although it would seem that the core of the problem lies with the nonstigmatized individuals, stigmatized people also play an important role in the destigmatization process. Stigma contests, or the struggles to determine which attributes are devalued and to what extent they are devalued, involve stigmatized and nonstigmatized individuals alike (Schur, 1980). Stigmatized people, too, have choices as to whether to accept their stigmatized condition and the negative social consequences or continue to fight for more integration into nonstigmatized communities. Their cognitive and affective attitudes toward themselves as individuals and as a group are no small element in shaping societal responses to them. As long as they continue to focus on the negative, affective components of stigma, such as low self-esteem, it is not likely that their devalued status will change. Self-help groups may play an important role in countering this tendency.

There is volition or personal choice. Each stigmatized or nonstigmatized individual can choose to feel superior or inferior, and each individual can make choices about social control and about fear. Sartre (1948) views this as the choice between authenticity or authentic freedom, and inauthenticity or fear of being oneself. Each individual can choose to ignore social norms regarding stigma. Personal beliefs about a situation or circumstance often differ from norms, but people usually follow the social norms anyway, fearing to step beyond conformity to exercise their own personal beliefs about stigma (see Ainlay & Crosby and Stafford & Scott, discussions of personal versus socially shared forms of stigma). Changing human behavior is not as simple as encouraging people to exercise their personal beliefs. As social scientists, we know a number of issues may be involved in the way personal volition interacts with social norms and personal values.

The multidisciplinary approach could be used in a variety of creative ways to study stigma and other social problems. Different models of how stigma has evolved and is perpetuated could be subject to test by a number of social scientists. They could combine their efforts to examine whether stigma evolves in a similar manner in different cultures, or among children of different cultural and social backgrounds, or during different historical periods. The study of stigma encompasses as many factors and dimensions as are represented in a multidisciplinary approach. All of the elements are interactive and in constant flux. The effective, cognitive, and behavioral dimensions are subject to the current cultural, historical, political, and economic climates, which are in turn linked to the norms and laws. We know that the responses of stigmatized and nonstigmatized individuals may at times appear to be separate, but that they are also interconnected and may produce other responses when considered together. This graphic portrayal of the issues vital to the study of stigma is neither exhaustive nor definitive. It does suggest, however, that a multidimensional model of stigma is needed to understand how these factors, dimensions, and responses co-vary.

We need more cross-disciplinary research from researchers who do not commonly study stigma. For example, a joint project among historians, psychologists, economists, and political scientists might examine the relationship between economic climate, perceptions of scarcity, and stigmatization. Other joint ventures by anthropologists and economists could design research on how much income is lost over a lifetime by members of a stigmatized category (e.g., blind, deaf, overweight), and how this loss adversely affects the GNP and the overall economy. Another example would be work by political scientists and historians or anthropologists to understand the links between the stigmatization of specific attributes and the maintenance of social control and power by certain political groups. Psychologists might team up with novelists or anthropologists to use case studies to understand individual differences or to examine how some stigmatized persons overcome their discredited status. Other studies of the positive consequences of stigma might include a joint investigation by anthropologists and psychologists of cultures that successfully integrate stigmatized individuals into nonstigmatized communities and utilize whatever resources or talents a stigmatized person has to offer (as the shaman is used in many societies) (Halifax, 1979, 1982).

The study of stigma by developmental and social psychologists, sociologists, anthropologists, economists, and historians may also offer new insights into the evolution of sex roles and sex role identity across the life cycle and during changing economic climates. Indeed, linguists, psychologists, and sociologists may be able to chronicle the changes in identity and self-concept of stigmatized and nonstigmatized alike, by studying the way people describe themselves and the language they use in their interactions with stigmatized and nonstigmatized others (Coleman, 1985; Edelsky & Rosengrant, 1981).

The real challenge for social scientists will be to better understand the need to stigmatize; the need for people to reject rather than accept others; the need for people to denigrate rather than uplift others. We need to know more about the relationship between stigma and perceived threat, and how stigma may represent "the kinds of deviance that it seeks out" (Schur, 1980, p. 22). Finally, social scientists need to concentrate on designing an optimal system in which every member of society is permitted to develop one's talents and experience one's full potential regardless of any particular attribute. If such a society were to come about, then perhaps some positive consequences would arise from the dilemma of difference.

References

Ablon, J. 1981. "Stigmatized Health Conditions." *Social Science and Medicine*, 15: 5–9.

Ainlay, S. and F. Cosby. 1986. "Stigma, Justice and the Dilemma of Difference." In S. Ainlay, G. Becker, and L. M. Coleman, *The Dilemma of Difference: A Multicultural View of Stigma*, 17–38. New York: Plenum.

Barbarin, O. 1986. "Family Experience of Stigma in Childhood Cancer." In S. Ainlay, G. Becker, and L. M. Coleman, *The Dilemma of Difference: A Multicultural View of Stigma*. New York: Plenum, 163–184.

Becker, G. 1980. *Growing Old in Silence*. Berkeley: University of California Press.

Becker, G. and R. Arnold. 1986. "Stigma as Social and Cultural Construct." In S. Ainlay, G. Becker, and L. M. Coleman, *The Dilemma of Difference: A Multicultural View of Stigma*. New York. Plenum, 39–58.

Brooks, J. and Lewis, M. 1976. "Infants' responses to strangers: Midget, adult, and child." *Child Development* 47: 323–332.

Coleman, L. 1985. "Language and the evolution of identity and self-concept." In F. Kessel, ed., *The development of language and language researchers: Essays in honor of Roger Brown*. Hillsdale, N. J.: Erlbaum.

Crocker, J. and N. Lutsky. 1986. "Stigma and the Dynamics of Social Cognition." In S. Ainlay, G. Becker, and L. M. Coleman, *The Dilemma of Difference: A Multicultural View of Stigma* New York. Plenum, 95–122.

Davis, F. 1964. "Deviance disavowal: The management of strained interaction by the visibly handicapped." In H. Becker, ed., *The Other Side*. New York: Free Press, 119–138.

Edelsky, C. and Rosengrant, T. 1981. "Interactions with handicapped children: Who's handicapped?" *Sociolinguistic Working Paper 92.* Austin, TX: Southwest Educational Development Laboratory.

Edgerton, R. G. 1967. *The Cloak of Competence: Stigma in the Lives of the Mentally Retarded.* Berkeley: University of California Press.

Feinman, S. 1982. "Social referencing in infancy." Merrill-*Palmer Quarterly* 28: 445–70. Gibbons, F. X. 1986. "Stigma and Interpersonal Relations." In S. Ainlay, G. Becker, and L. M. Coleman, *The Dilemma of Difference: A Multicultural View of* Stigma. New York. Plenum. 123–144.

Goffman. E. 1963. *Stigma: Notes on the Management of Spoiled Identity.* Englewood Cliffs, N.J.: Prentice Hall.

Hallifax, J. 1979. *Shamanic Voices: A Survey of Visionary Narratives.* New York: Dutton.

———. 1982. *Shaman: The Wounded Healer.* London: Thames and Hudson.

Jones. E. E., A. Farina, A. H. Hastof, H. Markus, D. T. Miller, and R. A. Scott, 1984. *Social Stigma: The Psychology of Marked Relationships.* New York: Freeman.

Kanter, R. M. 1979. *Men and Women of the Corporation.* New York: Basic Books.

Klinnert, M. D., J. J. Campos, J. F. Sorce, R. Emde and M. Svejda. 1983. "Emotions as behavior regulators: Social referencing in infancy." In R. Plutchik & H. Kellerman, eds. *Emotion Theory, Research, and Experience. Vol. II. Emotions in Early Development.* New York: Academic Press, 57–88.

Locksley, A., E. Borgida, N. Brekke, and C. Hepburn. 1980. "Sexual stereotypes and social judgment." *Journal of Personality and Social Psychology*, 39: 821–31.

Locksley, A., C. Hepburn, and V. Ortiz. 1982. "Social stereotypes and judgments of individuals: An instance of the base-rate fallacy." *Journal of Experimental Social Psychology.* 18: 23–42.

Martin, L. G. 1986. "Stigma: A Social Learning Perspective." In S. Ainlay, G. Becker, and L. M. Coleman, *The Dilemma of Difference: A Multicultural View of Stigma.* New York. Plenum, 1–16.

Sartre, J. 1948. *Anti-Semite and Jew.* New York: Schocken Books.

Schur, E. 1980. *The Politics Of Deviance: A Sociological Introduction.* Englewood Cliffs, N. J.: Prentice Hall.

———. 1983. *Labeling Women Deviant: Gender, Stigma, and Social Control.* Philadelphia: Temple University Press.

Scott, R., 1969. *The Making of Blind Men.* New York: Russel Sage Foundation.

Sigelman, C. and L. C. Singleton. 1986. "Stigmatization in Childhood: A Survey of Developmental Trends and Issues." In S. Ainlay, G. Becker, and L. M. Coleman, *The Dilemma of Difference: A Multicultural View of Stigma.* New York. Plenum. 185–210.

Solomon, Howard M. 1986. "Stigma and Western Culture: A Historical Approach" In S. Ainlay, G. Becker, and L. M. Coleman, *The Dilemma of Difference: A Multicultural View of Stigma.* New York: Plenum, 59–76.

Sontag, S. 1979. *Illness as metaphor.* New York: Random House.

Sroufe, L. A. 1977. "Wariness of strangers and the study of infant development." *Child Development*, 48: 731–46.

Stafford, M and R. Scott. 1986. "Stigma, Deviance and Social Control: Some Conceptual Issues." In S. Ainlay, G. Becker, and L. M. Coleman, *The Dilemma of Difference: A Multicultural View of Stigma.* New York. Plenum, 77–94.

Terry, W. 1984. *Bloods: An Oral History of the Vietnam War by Black Veterans.* New York: Random House.

Tracy, G. S., and Gussow, Z. 1978. "Self-help health groups: A grass-roots response to a need for services." *Journal of Applied Behavioral Science*: 81–396.

Weiner, C. L., 1975. "The burden of rheumatoid arthritis: Tolerating the uncertainty." *Social Science and Medicine*: 99, 97–104.

Zola, I. Z. 1979. "Helping one another: A speculative history of the self-help movement. *Archive of Physical Medicine and Rehabilitation*: 60, 452.

12

AIDS and Its Metaphors

Susan Sontag

Because of countless metaphoric flourishes that have made cancer synonymous with evil, having cancer has been experienced by many as shameful, therefore something to conceal, and also unjust, a betrayal by one's body. Why me? the cancer patient exclaims bitterly. With AIDS, the shame is linked to an imputation of guilt; and the scandal is not at all obscure. Few wonder, Why me? Most people outside of Sub-Saharan Africa who have AIDS know (or think they know) how they got it. It is not a mysterious affliction that seems to strike at random. Indeed, to get AIDS is precisely to be revealed, in the majority of cases so far, as a member of a certain "risk group," a community of pariahs. The illness flushes out an identity that might have remained hidden from neighbors, job-mates, family, friends. It also confirms an identity and, among the risk group in the United States most affected in the beginning, homosexual men, has been a creator of community as well as an experience that isolates the ill and exposes them to harassment and persecution.

Getting cancer, too, is sometimes understood as the fault of someone who has indulged in "unsafe" behavior—the alcoholic with cancer of the esophagus, the smoker with lung cancer: punishment for living unhealthy lives. (In contrast to those obliged to perform unsafe occupations, like the worker in a petrochemical factory who gets bladder cancer.) More and more linkages are sought between primary organs or systems and specific practices that people are invited to repudiate, as in recent speculation associating colon cancer and breast cancer with diets rich in animal fats. But the unsafe habits associated with cancer, among other illnesses—even heart disease, hitherto little culpabilized, is now largely viewed as the price one pays for excesses of diet and "life-style"—are the result of a weakness of the will or a lack of prudence, or of addiction to legal (albeit very dangerous) chemicals. The unsafe behavior that produces AIDS is judged to be more than just weakness. It is indulgence, delinquency—addictions to chemicals that are illegal and to sex regarded as deviant.

The sexual transmission of this illness, considered by most people as a calamity one brings on oneself, is judged more harshly than other means—especially since AIDS is understood as a disease not only of sexual excess but of perversity. (I am thinking, of course, of the United States, where people are currently being told that heterosexual transmission is extremely rare, and unlikely—as if Africa did not exist.) An infectious disease whose principal means of transmission is sexual neces-sarily puts at greater risk those who are sexually more active—and is easy to view as a punishment for that activity. True of syphilis, this is even truer of AIDS, since not just promiscuity but a specific sexual "practice" regarded as unnatural is named as more endangering. Getting the disease through a sexual practice is thought to be more willful, therefore deserves more blame. Addicts who get the illness by sharing contaminated needles are seen as committing (or completing) a kind of inadvertent suicide. Promiscuous homosexual men practicing their vehement sexual customs under the illusory conviction, fostered by medical ideology with its cure-all antibiotics, of the relative innocuousness of all sexually transmitted diseases, could be viewed as dedicated hedonists—though it's now clear that their behavior was no less suicidal. Those like hemophiliacs and blood-transfusion recipients, who cannot by any stretch of the blaming faculty be considered responsible for their illness, may be as ruth-lessly ostracized by frightened people, and potentially represent a greater threat because, unlike the already stigmatized, they are not as easy to identify.

Infectious disease to which sexual fault is attached always inspire fears of easy contagion and bizarre fantasies of transmission by nonvenereal means in public places. The removal of doorknobs and the installation of swinging doors on U.S. Navy ships and the disappearance of the metal drinking cups affixed to public water fountains in the United States in the first decades of the century were early consequences of the "discovery" of syphilis's "innocently transmitted infection"; and the warning to generations of middle-class children always to interpose paper between bare bottom and the public toilet seat is another trace of the horror stories about the germs of syphilis being passed to the innocent by the dirty that were rife once and are still widely believed. Every feared epidemic disease, but especially those associated with sexual license, generates a preoccupying distinction between the disease's putative carriers (which usually means just the poor and, in this part of the world, people with darker skins) and those defined—health professionals and other bureaucrats do the defining—as "the general population." AIDS has revived similar phobias and fears of contamination among *this* disease's version of "the general population": white heterosexuals who do not inject themselves with drugs or have sexual relations with those who do. Like syphilis a disease of, or contracted from, dangerous others, AIDS is perceived as afflicting, in greater proportions than syphilis ever did, the already stigmatized. But syphilis was not identified with certain death, death that follows a protracted agony, as cancer was once imagined and AIDS is now held to be.

That AIDS is not a single illness but a syndrome, consisting of a seemingly open-ended list of contributing or "presenting" illnesses which constitute (that is, qualify the patient as having) the disease, makes it more a product of definition or construction than even a very complex, multiform illness like cancer. Indeed, the contention that AIDS is invariably fatal depends partly on what doctors decided to define as AIDS—and keep in reserve as distinct earlier stages of the disease. And this decision rests on a notion no less primitively metaphorical than that of a "full-blown" (or "full-fledged") disease.[1] "Full-blown is the form in which the disease is inevitably fatal. As what is immature is destined to become mature, what buds to become full-blown (fledglings to become full-fledged)—the doctors' botanical or zoological metaphor makes development or evolution into AIDS the norm, the rule. I am not saying that the metaphor creates the clinical conception, but I am arguing that it does much more than just ratify it. It lends support to an interpretation of the clinical evidence which is far from proved or, yet, provable. It is simply too early to conclude, of a disease identified only seven years ago, that infection will always produce something to die from, or even that everybody who has what is defined as AIDS will die of it. (As some medical writers have speculated, the appalling mortality rates could be registering the early, mostly rapid deaths of those most vulnerable to the virus—because of diminished immune competence, because of genetic predisposition, among other possible co-factors—not the ravages of a uniformly fatal infection.) Construing the disease as divided into distinct stages was the necessary way of implementing the metaphor of "full-blown disease." But it also slightly weakened the notion of inevitability suggested by the metaphor. Those sensibly interested in hedging their bets about how uniformly lethal infection would prove could use the standard three-tier classification—HIV infection, AIDS-related complex (ARC), and AIDS—to entertain either of two possibilities or both: the less catastrophic one, that *not* everybody infected would "advance" or "graduate" from HIV infection, and the more catastrophic one, that everybody would.

It is more catastrophic reading of the evidence that for some time has dominated debate about the disease, which means that a change in nomenclature is under way. Influential administrators of the way the disease is understood have decided that there should be no more of the false reassurance that might be had from the use of different acronyms for different stages of the disease. (It could never have been more than minimally reassuring.) Recent proposals for redoing terminology—for instance, to phase out the category of ARC—do not challenge the construction of the disease in stages, but do place additional stress on the *continuity* of the disease process. "Full-blown disease" is viewed as more inevitable now, and that strengthens the fatalism already in place.[2]

From the beginning the construction of the illness had depended on notions that separated one group of people from another—the sick from the well, people with ARC from people with AIDS, them and us—while implying the imminent dissolution of these distinctions. However hedged, the predictions always sounded fatalistic. Thus, the frequent pronouncements by AIDS specialists and public health officials on the chances of those infected with the virus coming down with "full-blown" disease have seemed mostly an exercise in the management of public opinion, dosing out the harrowing news in several steps. Estimates of the percentage expected to show symptoms classifying them as having AIDS within five years, which may be too low—at the time of this writing, the figure is 30 to 35 percent—are invariably followed by the assertion that "most," after which comes "probably all," those infected will eventually become ill. The critical number, then, is not the percentage of people likely to develop AIDS within a relatively short time but the *maximum* interval that could elapse between infection with HIV (described as lifelong and irreversible) and appearance of the first symptoms. As the years add up in which the illness has been tracked, so does the possible number of years between infection and becoming ill, now estimated, seven years into the epidemic, at between ten and fifteen years. This figure, which will presumably continue to be revised upward, does much to maintain the definition of AIDS as an inexorable, invariably fatal disease.

The obvious consequence of believing that all those who "harbor" the virus will eventually come down with the illness is that those who test positive for it are regarded as people-with-AIDS, who just don't have it...yet. It is only a matter of time, like any death sentence. Less obviously, such people are often regarded as if they *do* have it. Testing positive for HIV (which usually means having been tested for the presence not of the virus but of antibodies to the virus) is increasingly equated with being ill. Infected *means* ill, from that point forward. "Infected but not ill," that invaluable notion of clinical medicine (the body "harbors" many infections), is being superseded by biomedical concepts which, whatever their scientific justification, amount to reviving the antiscientific logic of defilement, and make infected-but-healthy a contradiction in terms. Being ill in this new sense can have many practical consequences. People are losing their jobs when it is learned that they are HIV-positive (though it is not legal in the United States to fire someone for that reason) and the temptation to conceal a positive finding must be immense. The consequences of testing HIV-positive are even more punitive for those selected populations—there will be more—upon which the government has already made testing mandatory. The U.S. Department of Defense has announced that military personnel discovered to be HIV-positive are being removed "from sensitive, stressful jobs," because of evidence indicating that mere infection with the virus, in the absence of any other symptoms, produces subtle changes in mental abilities in a significant minority of virus carriers. (The evidence cited: lower scores on certain neurological tests given to some who had tested positive, which could reflect mental impairment caused by exposure to the virus, though most doctors think this extremely improbably, or could be caused—as officially acknowledged under questioning—by "the anger, depression, fear, and panic" of people who have just learned that they are HIV-positive.) And, of course, testing positive now makes one ineligible to immigrate everywhere.

In every previous epidemic of an infectious nature, the epidemic is equivalent to the number of tabulated cases. This epidemic is regarded as consisting *now of* that figure plus a calculation about a much larger number of people apparently in good health (seemingly healthy, but doomed) who are infected. The calculations are being made and remade all the time, and pressure is building to identify these people, and to tag them. With the most up-to-date biomedical testing, it is possible to create a new class of lifetime pariahs, the future ill. But the result of this radical expansion of the notion of illness created by the triumph of modern medical scrutiny also seems a throwback to the past, before the era of medical triumphalism, when illnesses were innumerable, mysterious, and the progression from being seriously ill to dying was something normal (not, as now, medicine's lapse or failure, destined to be corrected). AIDS, in which people are understood as ill before they are ill; which produces a seemingly innumerable array of symptom-illnesses; for which there are only palliatives; and which brings to many a social death the precedes the physical one—AIDS reinstates something like a premodern experience of illness, as described in Donne's *Devotions*, in which "every thing that disorders a faculty and the function of that is a sicknesse," which starts when we

> are preafflicted, super-afflicted with these jealousies and suspitions, and apprehensions of Sicknes, before we can call it a sicknes; we are not sure we are ill; one hand askes the other by the pulse, and our eye asks our own urine, how we do.... we are tormented with sicknes, and cannot stay till the torment come. . . .

whose agonizing outreach to every part of the body makes a real cure chimerical, since what "is but an accident, but a symptom of the main disease, is so violent, that the Physician must attend the cure of that" rather than "the cure of the disease it self," and whose consequence is abandonment:

> As Sicknesse is the greatest misery, so the greatest misery of sicknes is solitude; when the infectiousness of the disease deterrs them who should assist, from coming; even the Physician dares scarce come.... it is an Outlawry, an Excommunication upon the patient. . . .

In premodern medicine, illness is described as it is experienced intuitively, as a relation of outside and inside: an interior sensation or something to be discerned on the body's surface, by sight (or just below, by listening, palpating), which is confirmed when the interior is opened to viewing (in surgery, in autopsy). Modern—that is, effective—medicine is characterized by far more complex notions of what is to be observed inside the body: not just the disease's results (damaged organs) but its cause (microorganisms), and by a far more intricate typology of illness.

In the older era of artisanal diagnoses, being examined produced an immediate verdict, immediate as the physician's willingness to speak. Now an examination means tests. And being tested introduces a time lapse that, given the unavoidably industrial character of competent medical testing, can stretch out for weeks: an agonizing delay for those who think they are awaiting a death sentence or an acquittal. Many are reluctant to be tested out of dread of the verdict, out of fear of being put on a list that could bring future discrimination or worse, and out of fatalism (what good would it do?). The usefulness of self-examination for the early detection of certain common cancers, much less likely to be fatal if treated before they are very advanced, is now widely understood. Early detection of an illness thought to be inexorable and incurable cannot seem to bring any advantage.

Like other diseases that arouse feelings of shame, AIDS is often a secret, but not from the patient. A cancer diagnosis was frequently concealed from patients by their families; an AIDS diagnosis is at least as often concealed from their families by patients. And as with other grave illnesses regarded as more than just illnesses, many people with AIDS are drawn to whole-body rather than illness-specific treatments, which are thought to be either ineffectual or dangerous. (The disparagement of effective, scientific medicine for offering treatments that are *merely* illness-specific, and likely to be toxic, is a recurrent misconjecture of opinion that regards itself as enlightened.) This disastrous choice is still being made by some people with cancer, an illness that surgery and drugs can often cure. And a predictable mix of superstition and resignation is leading some people with AIDS to refuse antiviral chemotherapy, which, even in the absence of a cure, has proved of some effectiveness (in slowing down the syndrome's progress and in staving off some common presenting illnesses), and instead to seek to heal themselves, often under the auspices of some "alternative medicine" guru. But subjecting an emaciated body to the purification of a macrobiotic diet is about as helpful in treating AIDS as having oneself bled, the "holistic" medical treatment of choice in the era of Donne.

Notes

1. The standard definition distinguishes between people with the disease or syndrome "fulfilling the criteria for the sur-veillance definition of AIDS" from a larger number infected with HIV and symptomatic "who do not fulfill the empiric criteria for the full-blown disease. This constellation of signs and symptoms in the context of HIV infection has been

termed the AIDS-related complex (ARC)." Then follows the obligatory percentage. "It is estimated that approximately 25 percent of patients with ARC will develop full-blown disease within 3 years." Harrison's *Principles of Internal Medicine,* 11th edition (1987), p. 1394.

The first major illness known by an acronym, the condition called AIDS does not have, as it were, natural borders. It is an illness whose identity is designed for purposes of investigation and with tabulation and surveillance by medical and other bureaucracies in view. Hence, the unselfconscious equating in the medical textbook of what is empirical with what pertains to surveillance, two notions deriving from quite different models of understanding. (AIDS is what fulfills that which is referred to as either the "criteria for the surveillance definition" or the "empiric criteria": HIV infection plus the presence of one or more diseases included on the roster drown up by the disease's principal administrator of definition in the United States, the federal Centers for Disease Control in Atlanta.) This completely stipulative definition with its metaphor of maturing disease decisively influences how the illness is understood.

2. The 1988 Presidential Commission on the epidemic recommended "de-emphasizing" the use of the term ARC because it "tends to obscure the life-threatening aspects of this stage of illness." There is some pressure to drop the term AIDS, too. The report by the President Commission pointedly used the acronym HIV for the epidemic itself, as part of a recommended shift from "monitoring disease" to "monitoring infection." Again, one of the reasons given is that the present terminology masks the true gravity of the menace. ("This longstanding concentration on the clinical manifestations of AIDS rather than on all stages of HIV infection [i.e., from initial infection to seroconversion, to an antibody-positive asymptomatic stage, to full-blown AIDS] has had the unintended effect of misleading the public as to the extent of infection in the population. . . .") It does seem likely that the disease will, eventually, be renamed. *This* change in nomenclature would justify officially the policy of including the infected but asymptomatic among the ill.

Part IV

Theorizing Disability

13

Reassigning Meaning

Simi Linton

The present examination of disability has no need for the medical language of symptoms and diagnostic categories. Disability studies looks to different kinds of signifiers and the identification of different kinds of syndromes for its material. The elements of interest here are the linguistic conventions that structure the meanings assigned to disability and the patterns of response to disability that emanate from, or are attendant upon, those meanings.

The medical meaning-making was negotiated among interested parties who packaged their version of disability in ways that increased the ideas' potency and marketability. The disability community has attempted to wrest control of the language from the previous owners, and reassign meaning to the terminology used to describe disability and disabled people. This new language conveys different meanings, and, significantly, the shifts serve as metacommunications about the social, political, intellectual, and ideological transformations that have taken place over the past two decades.

Naming Oppression

It has been particularly important to bring to light language that reinforces the dominant culture's views of disability. A useful step in that process has been the construction of the terms *ableist* and *ableism,* which can be used to organize ideas about the centering and domination of the nondisabled experience and point of view. *Ableism* has recently landed in the *Reader's Digest Oxford Wordfinder* (Tulloch 1993), where it is defined as "discrimination in favor of the able-bodied." I would add, extrapolating from the definitions of *racism* and *sexism,* that *ableism* also includes the idea that a person's abilities or characteristics are determined by disability or that people with disabilities as a group are inferior to nondisabled people. Although there is probably greater consensus among the general public on what could be labeled racist or sexist language than there is on what might be considered ableist, that may be because the nature of the oppression of disabled people is not yet as widely understood.

Naming the Group

Across the world and throughout history various terminologies and meanings are ascribed to the types of human variations known in contemporary Westernized countries as disabilities. Over the past century the term *disabled* and others, such as *handicapped* and the less inclusive term *crippled,* have emerged as collective nouns that convey the idea that there is something that links this disparate group of people. The terms have been used to arrange people in ways that are socially and economically convenient to the society.

There are various consequences of the chosen terminology and variation in the degree of control that the named group has over the labeling process. The terms *disability* and *disabled people* are the most commonly used by disability rights activists, and recently policy makers and health care professionals have begun to use these terms more consistently. Although there is some agreement on terminology, there are disagreements about what it is that unites disabled people and whether disabled people should have control over the naming of their experience.

The term *disability,* as it has been used in general parlance, appears to signify something material and concrete, a physical or psychological condition considered to have predominantly medical significance. Yet it is an arbitrary designation, used erratically both by professionals who lay claim to naming such phenomena and by confused citizens. A project of disability studies scholars and the disability rights movement has been to bring into sharp relief the processes by which *disability* has been imbued with the meaning(s) it has and to reassign a meaning that is consistent with a sociopolitical analysis of disability. Divesting it of its current meaning is no small feat. As typically used, the term *disability* is a linchpin in a complex web of social ideals, institutional structures, and government policies. As a result, many people have a vested interest in keeping a tenacious hold on the current meaning because it is consistent with the practices and policies that are central to their livelihood or their ideologies. People may not be driven as much by economic imperatives as by a personal investment in their own beliefs and practices, in metaphors they hold dear, or in their own professional roles. Further, underlying this tangled web of needs and beliefs, and central to the arguments presented in this book is an epistemological structure that both generates and reflects current interpretations.[1]

A glance through a few dictionaries will reveal definitions of disability that include incapacity, a disadvantage, deficiency, especially a physical or mental impairment that restricts normal achievement; something that hinders or incapacitates, something that incapacitates or disqualifies. Legal definitions include legal incapacity or disqualification. *Stedman's Medical Dictionary* (1976) identifies *disability* as a "medicolegal term signifying loss of function and earning power," whereas *disablement* is a "medicolegal term signifying loss of function without loss of earning power" (400). These definitions are understood by the general public and by many in the academic community to be useful ones. *Disability* so defined is a medically derived term that assigns predominantly medical significance and meaning to certain types of human variation.

The decision to assign medical meanings to *disability* has had many and varied consequences for disabled people. One clear benefit has been the medical treatments that have increased the well-being and vitality of many disabled people, indeed have saved people's lives. Ongoing attention by the medical profession to the health and well-being of people with disabilities and to prevention of disease and impairments is critical. Yet, along with these benefits, there are enormous negative consequences that will take a large part of this book to list and explain. Briefly, the medicalization of disability casts human variation as deviance from the norm, as pathological condition, as deficit, and, significantly, as an individual burden and personal tragedy. Society, in agreeing to assign medical meaning to *disability,* colludes to keep the issue within the purview of the medical establishment, to keep it a personal matter and "treat" the condition and the person with the condition rather than "treating" the social processes and policies that constrict disabled people's lives. The disability studies' and disability rights movement's position is critical of the domination of the medical definition and views it as a major stumbling block to the reinterpretation of *disability* as a political category and to the social changes that could follow such a shift.

While retaining the term *disability,* despite its medical origins, a premise of most of the literature in disability studies is that *disability* is best understood as a marker of identity. As such, it has been used to build a coalition of people with significant impairments, people with behavioral or anatomical characteristics marked as deviant, and people who have or are suspected of having conditions, such as AIDS or emotional illness, that make them targets of discrimination.[2] As rendered in disability studies scholarship, disability has become a more capacious category, incorporating people with a range of physical, emotional, sensory, and cognitive conditions. Although the category is broad, the term is used to designate a specific minority group. When medical definitions of *disability* are dominant, it is logical to separate people according to biomedical condition through the use of diagnostic categories and to forefront medical perspectives on human variation. When disability is redefined as a social/political category, people with a variety of conditions are identified as *people with disabilities* or *disabled people*, a group bound by common social and political experience. These designations, as reclaimed by the community, are used to identify us as a constituency, to serve our needs for unity and identity, and to function as a basis for political activism.

The question of who "qualifies" as disabled is as answerable or as confounding as questions about any identity status. One simple response might be that you are disabled if you say you are. Although that declaration won't satisfy a worker's compensation board, it has a certain credibility with the disabled community. The degree and significance of an individual's impairment is often less of an issue than the degree to which someone identifies as disabled. Another way to answer the question is to say that disability "is mostly a social distinction . . . a marginalized status" and the status is assigned by "the majority culture tribunal" (Gill 1994, 44). But the problem gets stickier when the distinction between disabled and nondisabled is challenged by people who say, "Actually, we're all disabled in some way, aren't we?" (46). Gill says the answer is no to those whose difference "does *not* significantly affect daily life and the person does not [with some consistency] present himself/herself to the world at large as a disabled person" (46). I concur with Gill; I am not willing or interested in erasing the line between disabled and nondisabled people, as long as disabled people are devalued and discriminated against, and as long as naming the category serves to call attention to that treatment.

Over the past twenty years, disabled people have gained greater control over these definitional issues. *The disabled or the handicapped* was replaced in the mid-70s by *people with disabilities* to maintain disability as a characteristic of the individual, as opposed to the defining variable. At the time, some people would purposefully say *women and men with disabilities* to provide an extra dimension to the people being described and to deneuter the way *the disabled* were traditionally described. Beginning in the early 90s *disabled people* has been increasingly used in disability studies and disability rights circles when referring to the constituency group. Rather than maintaining disability as a secondary characteristic, *disabled* has become a marker of the identity that the individual and group wish to highlight and call attention to.

In this book, the terms *disabled and nondisabled* are used frequently to designate membership within or outside the community. Disabled is centered, and nondisabled is placed in the peripheral position in order to look at the world from the inside out, to expose the perspective and expertise that is silenced. Occasionally, *people with disabilities* is used as a variant of *disabled people*. The use of *nondisabled* is strategic: to center disability. Its inclusion in this chapter is also to set the stage for postulating about the nondisabled position in society and in scholarship in later chapters. This action is similar to the strategy of marking and articulating "whiteness." The assumed position in scholarship has always been the male, white, nondisabled scholar; it is the default category. As recent scholarship has shown, these positions are not only presumptively hegemonic because they are the assumed universal stance, as well as the presumed neutral or objective stance, but also undertheorized. The nondisabled stance, like the white stance, is veiled. "*White* cannot be said quite out loud, or it loses its crucial position as a precondition of vision and becomes the object of scrutiny" (Hara-way 1989, 152). Therefore, centering the disabled position and labeling its opposite nondisabled focuses attention on both the structure of knowledge and the structure of society.

Nice Words

Terms such as *physically challenged,* the *able disabled, handicapable,* and *special people/children* surface at different times and places. They are rarely used by disabled activists and scholars (except with palpable irony). Although they may be considered well-meaning attempts to inflate the value of people with disabilities, they convey the boosterism and do-gooder mentality endemic to the paternalistic agencies that control many disabled people's lives.

Physically challenged is the only term that seems to have caught on. Nondisabled people use it in conversation around disabled people with no hint of anxiety, suggesting that they believe it is a positive term. This phrase does not make much sense to me. To say that I am physically challenged is to state that the obstacles to my participation are physical, not social, and that the barrier is my own disability. Further, it separates those of us with mobility impairments from other disabled people, not a valid or useful partition for those interested in coalition building and social change. Various derivatives of the term *challenged* have been adopted as a description used in jokes. For instance, "vertically challenged" is considered a humorous way to say short, and "calorically challenged" to say fat. A review of the Broadway musical *Big* in the *New Yorker* said that the score is "melodically challenged."

I observed a unique use of *challenged* in the local Barnes and Nobles superstore. The children's department has a section for books on "Children with Special Needs." There are shelves labeled "Epilepsy" and "Down Syndrome." A separate shelf at the bottom is labeled "Misc. Challenges," indicating that it is now used as an organizing category.

The term *able disabled* and *handicapable* have had a fairly short shelf life. They are used, it seems, to refute common stereotypes of incompetence. They are, though, defensive and reactive terms rather than terms that advance a new agenda.

A number of professions are built around the word *special*. A huge infrastructure rests on the idea that *special children* and *special education* are valid and useful structuring ideas. Although dictionaries insist that *special* be reserved for things that surpass what is common, are distinct among others of their kind, are peculiar to a specific person, have a limited or specific function, are arranged for a particular purpose, or are arranged for a particular occasion, experience teaches us that *special* when applied to education or to children means something different.

The naming of disabled children and the education that "is designed for students whose learning needs cannot be met by a standard school curriculum" (*American Heritage Dictionary* 1992) as *special* can be understood only as a euphemistic formulation, obscuring the reality that neither the children nor the education are considered desirable and that they are not thought to "surpass what is common."

Labeling the education and its recipients special may have been a deliberate attempt to confer legitimacy on the educational practice and to prop up a discarded group. It is also important to consider the unconscious feelings such a strategy may mask. It is my feeling that the nation in general responds to disabled people with great ambivalence. Whatever antipathy and disdain is felt is in competition with feelings of empathy, guilt, and identification. The term *special* may be evidence not of a deliberate maneuver but of a collective "reaction formation," Freud's term for the unconscious defense mechanism in which an individual adopts attitudes and behaviors that are opposite to his or her own true feelings, in order to protect the ego from the anxiety felt from experiencing the real feelings.

The ironic character of the word *special* has been captured in the routine on *Saturday Night Live*, where the character called the "Church Lady" declares when she encounters something distasteful or morally repugnant, "Isn't that special!"

Nasty Words

Some of the less subtle or more idiomatic terms for disabled people such as: *cripple, vegetable, dumb, deformed, retard,* and *gimp* have generally been expunged from public conversation but emerge in various types of discourse. Although they are understood to be offensive or hurtful, they are still used in jokes and in informal conversation.

Cripple as a descriptor of disabled people is considered impolite, but the word has retained its metaphoric vitality, as in "the exposé in the newspaper crippled the politician's campaign." The term is also used occasionally for its evocative power. A recent example appeared in *Lingua Franca* in a report on research on the behaviors of German academics. The article states that a professor had "documented the postwar careers of psychiatrists and geneticists involved in gassing thousands of cripples and schizophrenics" (Allen 1996, 37). *Cripple* is used rather loosely here to describe people with a broad range of disabilities. The victims of Nazi slaughter were people with mental illness, epilepsy, chronic illness, and mental retardation, as well as people with physical disabilities. Yet *cripple* is defined as "one that is partially disabled or unable to use a limb or limbs" (*American Heritage Dictionary* 1992) and is usually used only to refer to people with mobility impairments. Because *cripple* inadequately and inaccurately describes the group, the author of the report is likely to have chosen this term for its effect.

Cripple has also been revived by some in the disability community who refer to each other as "crips" or "cripples." A performance group with disabled actors call themselves the "Wry Crips." "In reclaiming 'cripple,' disabled people are taking the thing in their identity that scares the outside world the most and making it a cause to revel in with militant self-pride" (Shapiro 1993, 34).

A recent personal ad in the *Village Voice* shows how "out" the term is:

> **TWISTED CRIP:** Very sexy, full-figured disabled BiWF artist sks fearless, fun, oral BiWF for hot, no-strings nights. Wheelchair, tattoo, dom. Shaved a + N/S No men/sleep-overs.

Cripple, gimp and freak as used by the disability community have transgressive potential. They are personally and politically useful as a means to comment on oppression because they assert our right to name experience.

Speaking about Overcoming and Passing

The popular phrase *overcoming a disability* is used most often to describe someone with a disability who seems competent and successful in some way, in a sentence something like "She has overcome her disability and is a great success." One interpretation of the phrase might be that the individual's disability no longer limits her or him, that sheer strength or willpower has brought the person to the point where the disability is no longer a hindrance. Another implication of the phrase may be that the person has risen above society's expectation for someone with those characteristics. Because it is physically impossible to *overcome* a disability, it seems that what is *overcome* is the social stigma of having a disability. This idea is reinforced by the equally confounding statement "I never think of you as disabled." An implication of these statements is that the other members of the group from which the individual has supposedly moved beyond are not as brave, strong, or extraordinary as the person who has *overcome* that designation.

The expression is similar in tone to the phrase that was once more commonly used to describe an African American who was considered exceptional in some way: "He/she is a credit to his/her race." The implication of this phrase is that the "race" is somehow discredited and needs people with extraordinary talent to give the group the credibility that it otherwise lacks. In either case, talking about the person who is African American or talking about the person with a disability, these phrases are often said with the intention of complimenting someone. The compliment has a double edge. To accept it, one must accept the implication that the group is inferior and that the individual is unlike others in that group.

The ideas imbedded in the *overcoming* rhetoric are of personal triumph over a personal condition. The idea that someone can *overcome* a disability has not been generated within the community; it is a wish fulfillment generated from the outside. It is a demand that you be plucky and resolute, and not let the obstacles get in your way. If there are no curb cuts at the corner of the street so that people who use wheelchairs can get across, then you should learn to do wheelies and jump the curbs. If there are no sign language interpreters for deaf students at the high school, then you should study harder, read lips, and stay up late copying notes from a classmate. When disabled people internalize the demand to "overcome" rather than demand social change, they shoulder same kind of exhausting and self-defeating "Super Mom" burden that feminists have analyzed.

The phrase *overcome a disability* may also be a shorthand version of saying "someone with a disability overcame many obstacles." Tremblay (1996) uses that phrase when describing behaviors of disabled World War II veterans upon returning to the community: "[T]heir main strategies were to develop individualized strategies to overcome the obstacles they found in the community" (165). She introduces this idea as a means to describe how the vets relied on their own ingenuity to manage an inaccessible environment rather than demand that the community change to include them.

In both uses of *overcome*, the individual's responsibility for her or his own success is paramount. If we, as a society, place the onus on individuals with disabilities to work harder to "compensate" for their disabilities or to "overcome" their condition or the barriers in the environment, we have no need for civil rights legislation or affirmative action.

Lest I be misunderstood, I don't see working hard, doing well, or striving for health, fitness, and well-being as contradictory to the aims of the disability rights movement. Indeed, the movement's goal is to provide greater opportunity to pursue these activities. However, we shouldn't be impelled to do these because we have a disability, to prove to some social overseer that we can perform, but we should pursue them because they deliver their own rewards and satisfactions.

A related concept, familiar in African American culture as well as in lesbian and gay culture, is that of *passing*. African Americans who pass for white and lesbians and gays who pass for straight do so for a variety of personal, social, and often economic reasons. Disabled people, if they are able to conceal their impairment or confine their activities to those that do not reveal their disability, have been known to pass. For a member of any of these groups, passing may be a deliberate effort to avoid discrimination or ostracism, or it may be an almost unconscious, Herculean effort to deny to oneself the reality of one's racial history, sexual feelings, or bodily state. The attempt may be a deliberate act to protect oneself from the loathing of society or may be an unchecked impulse spurred by an internalized self-loathing. It is likely that often the reasons entail an admixture of any of these various parts.

Henry Louis Gates, Jr. (1996) spoke of the various reasons for passing in an essay on the literary critic Anatole Broyard. Broyard was born in New Orleans to a family that identified as "Negro." His skin was so light that for his entire career as "one of literary America's foremost gatekeepers" (66) the majority of people who knew him did not know this. His children, by then adults, learned of his racial history shortly before he died. Sandy Broyard, Anatole's wife, remarked that she thought that "his own personal history continued to be painful to him. . . . In passing, you cause your family great anguish, but I also think conversely, do we look at the anguish it causes the person who is passing? Or the anguish that it was born out of?" (75).

When disabled people are able to pass for nondisabled, and do, the emotional toll it takes is enormous. I have heard people talk about hiding a hearing impairment to classmates or colleagues for years, or others who manage to conceal parts of their body, or to hide a prosthesis. These actions, though, may not result in a family's anguish; they may, in fact, be behaviors that the family insists upon, reinforces, or otherwise shames the individual into. Some disabled people describe how they were subjected to numerous painful surgeries and medical procedures when they were young not so much, they believe, to increase their comfort and ease of mobility as to fulfill their families' wish to make them appear "more normal."

Even when a disability is obvious and impossible to hide on an ongoing basis, families sometimes create minifictions that disabled people are forced to play along with. Many people have told me that when family pictures were taken as they were growing up, they were removed from their wheelchairs, or they were shown only from the waist up, or they were excluded from pictures altogether. The messages are that this part of you, your disability or the symbol of disability, your wheelchair, is unacceptable, or, in the last case, you are not an acceptable member of the family.

I was recently in an elementary school when class pictures were taken, and I learned that it is the custom for all the children who use wheelchairs to be removed from their chairs and carried up a few steps to the auditorium stage and placed on folding chairs. I spoke with people at the school who said they have thought about raising money to build a ramp to the stage, but in the meantime this was the solution. I wondered, of course, why they have to take pictures on the stage when it is inaccessible. The families of these children or the school personnel might even persist with this plan, believing that these actions have a positive effect on children, that they demonstrate that the disabled child is "just like everybody else." But these fictions are based more clearly on the projections of the adults than on the unadulterated feelings of the child. The message that I read in this action: You are like everyone else, but only as long as you hide or minimize your disability.

Both passing and overcoming take their toll. The loss of community, the anxiety, and the self-doubt that inevitably accompany this ambiguous social position and the ambivalent personal state are the enormous cost of declaring disability unacceptable. It is not surprising that disabled people also speak of "coming out" in the same way that members of the lesbian and gay community do. A woman I met at a disability studies conference not long ago said to me in the course of a conversation about personal experience: "I'm five years old." She went on to say that despite being significantly disabled for many years, she had really only recently discovered the disabled community and allied with it. For her, "coming out" was a process that began when she recognized how her effort to "be like everyone else" was not satisfying her own needs and wishes. She discovered other disabled people and began to identify clearly as disabled, and then purchased a motorized scooter, which meant she didn't have to expend enormous energy walking. She told this tale with gusto, obviously pleased with the psychic and physical energy she had gained. Stories such as hers provide evidence of the personal burdens many disabled people live with. Shame and fear are personal burdens, but if these tales are told, we can demonstrate how the personal is indeed the political. And further, that the unexamined connections between the personal and political are the curricular.

Normal/Abnormal

Normal and *abnormal* are convenient but problematic terms used to describe a person or group of people. These terms are often used to distinguish between people with and without disabilities. In various academic disciplines and in common usage, *normal* and *abnormal* assume different meanings. In psychometrics, *norm* or *normal* are terms describing individuals or characteristics that fall within the center of the normal distribution on whatever variable is being measured. However, as the notion of *normal* is applied in social science contexts and certainly in general parlance, it implies its obverse—*abnormal*—and they both become value laden. Often, those who are not deemed normal are devalued and considered a burden or problem, or are highly valued and regarded as a potential resource. Two examples are the variables of height and intelligence. Short stature and low measured intelligence are devalued and labeled abnormal, and people with those characteristics are considered disabled. Tall people (particularly males) and high scores on IQ tests are valued, and, although not normal in the statistical sense, are not labeled abnormal or considered disabled.[3]

Davis (1995) describes the historical specificity of the use of *normal* and thereby calls attention to the social structures that are dependent on its use. "[T]he very term that permeates our contemporary life—the normal—is a configuration that arises in a particular historical moment. It is part of a notion of progress, of industrialization, and of ideological consolidation of the power of the bourgeoisie. The implications of the hegemony of normalcy are profound and extend into the very heart of cultural production" (49).

The use of the terms *abnormal* and *normal* also moves discourse to a high level of abstraction, thereby avoiding concrete discussion of specific characteristics and increasing ambiguity in communication. In interactions, there is an assumed agreement between speaker and audience of what is normal that sets up an aura of empathy and "us-ness." This process "enhances social unity among those who feel they are normal" (Freilich, Raybeck, and Savishinsky 1991, 22), necessarily excluding the other or abnormal group.

These dynamics often emerge in discussions about disabled people when comparisons are made, for instance, between "the normal" and "the hearing impaired," or "the normal children" and "the handicapped children." The first example contrasts two groups of people; one defined by an abstract and evaluative term (the normal), the other by a more specific, concrete, and nonevaluative term (the hearing impaired). In the second comparison, the "handicapped children" are labeled abnormal by default. Setting up these dichotomies avoids concrete discussion of the ways the two groups of children actually differ, devalues the children with disabilities, and forces an "us and them" division of the population.

The absolute categories *normal* and *abnormal* depend on each other for their existence and depend on the maintenance of the opposition for their meaning. Sedgwick (1990), in *Epistemology of the Closet*, comments on a similar pattern in the forced choice categories homosexual and heterosexual:

> [C]ategories presented in a culture as symmetrical binary oppositions—heterosexual/homosexual, in this case—actually subsist in a more unsettled and dynamic tacit relation according to which, first, term B is not symmetrical with but subordinated to term A; but, second, the ontologically valorized term A actually depends for its meaning on the simultaneous subsumption and exclusion of term B; hence, third, the question of priority between the supposed central and the supposed marginal category of each dyad is irresolvably unstable, an instability caused by the fact that term B is constituted as at once internal and external to term A. (9–10)

Despite the instability and the relational nature of the designations *normal* and *abnormal*, they are used as absolute categories. They have achieved their certainty by association with empiricism, and they suffer from empiricism's reductive and simplifying tendencies. Their power and reach are enormous. They affect individuals' most private deliberations about their worth and acceptability, and they determine social position and societal response to behavior. The relationship between abnormality and disability accords to the nondisabled the legitimacy and potency denied to disabled people. And, central to our concerns here, the reification of *normal* and *abnormal* structures curriculum. Courses with titles such as "Abnormal Psychology," "Sociology of Deviance," "Special Education," and "Psychopathology" assume the internal consistency of a curriculum focused on "the abnormal" and depend on the curriculum of the "normal" being taught elsewhere. In fact, this organization of knowledge implicitly suggests that the rest of the curriculum is "normal."

Rosemarie Garland Thomson (1997) has coined the term *the normate*, which, like *nondisabled*, is useful for marking the unexamined center. "This neologism names the veiled subject position of cultural self, the figure outlined by the array of deviant others whose marked bodies shore up the normate's boundaries. The term *normate* usefully designates the social figure through which people can represent themselves as definitive human beings" (8). By meeting *normal* on some of its own terms, *normate* inflects its root, and challenges the validity, indeed the possibility, of normal. At the same time, its ironic twist gives a more flavorful reading of the idea of normal.

Passivity versus Control

Language that conveys passivity and victimization reinforces certain stereotypes when applied to disabled people. Some of the stereotypes that are particularly entrenched are that people with disabilities are more dependent, childlike, passive, sensitive, and miserable and are less competent than people who do not have disabilities. Much of the language used to depict disabled people relates the lack of control to the perceived incapacities, and implies that sadness and misery are the product of the disabling condition.

These deterministic and essentialist perspectives flourish in the absence of contradictory information. Historically, disabled people have had few opportunities to be active in society, and various social and political forces often undermine the capacity for self-determination. In addition, disabled people are rarely depicted on television, in films, or in fiction as being in control of their own lives—in charge or actively seeking out and obtaining what they want and need. More often, disabled people are depicted as pained by their fate or, if happy, it is through personal triumph over their adversity. The adversity is not depicted as lack of opportunity, discrimination, institutionalization, and ostracism; it is the personal burden of their own body or means of functioning.

Phrases such as *the woman is a victim of cerebral palsy* implies an active agent (cerebral palsy) perpetrating an aggressive act on a vulnerable, helpless "victim." The use of the term *victim*, a word typically used in the context of criminal acts, evokes the relationship between perpetrator and victim. Using this language attributes life, power, and intention to the condition and disempowers the person with the disability, rendering him or her helpless and passive. Instead, if there is a particular need to note what an individual's disability is, saying *the woman has cerebral palsy* describes solely the characteristic of importance to the situation, without imposing extraneous meaning.

Grover (1987) analyzes the word *victim* as used to describe people with AIDS. She notes that the term implies fatalism, and therefore "enable[s] the passive spectator or the AIDS 'spectacle' to remain passive." Use of the term may also express the unconscious wish that the people with AIDS may have been "complicit with, to have courted, their fate" (29), in which case the individual would be seen as a *victim* of her or his own drives. This is particularly apparent when the phrase *innocent victim* is used to distinguish those who acquire HIV from blood transfusions or other medical procedures from those who contract HIV from sexual contact or shared needles. This analysis is also pertinent to people with other disabilities because a number of belief systems consider disability, or some disabilities, as punishment for sin in this or a former life.

Disabled people are frequently described as *suffering from* or *afflicted with* certain conditions. Saying that someone is *suffering from* a condition implies that there is a perpetual state of suffering, uninterrupted by pleasurable moments or satisfactions. *Afflicted* carries similar assumptions. The verb *afflict* shares with *agonize, excruciate, rack, torment,* and *torture* the central meaning "to bring great harm or suffering to someone" (*American Heritage Dictionary* 1992, 30). Although some people may experience their disability this way, these terms are not used as descriptors of a verified experience but are projected onto disability. Rather than assume suffering in the description of the situation, it is more accurate and less histrionic to say simply that a person *has a disability*. Then, wherever it is relevant, describe the nature and extent of the difficulty experienced. My argument here isn't to eliminate descriptions of suffering but to be accurate in their appointment. It is interesting that AIDS activists intentionally use the phrase *living with AIDS* rather than *dying from AIDS*, not to deny the reality of AIDS but to emphasize that people are often actively engaged in living even in the face of a serious illness.

The ascription of passivity can be seen in language used to describe the relationship between disabled people and their wheelchairs. The phrases *wheelchair bound* or *confined to a wheelchair* are frequently seen in newspapers and magazines, and heard in conversation. A more puzzling variant was spotted in *Lingua Franca*, which described the former governor of Alabama, George Wallace, as the "slumped, wheelchair-ridden 'Guv'nah'" (Zalewski 1995, 19). The choice here was to paint the wheelchair user as *ridden*, meaning "dominated, harassed, or obsessed by" (*American Heritage Dictionary* 1992), rather than the rider in the wheelchair. The various terms imply that a wheelchair restricts the individual, holds a person prisoner. Disabled people are more likely to say that someone *uses a wheelchair*. The latter phrase not only indicates the active nature of the user and the positive way that wheelchairs increase mobility and activity but recognizes that people get in and out of wheelchairs for different activities: driving a car, going swimming, sitting on the couch, or, occasionally, for making love.

A recent oral history conducted with disabled Canadian World War II veterans and other disabled people who are contemporaries of the vets recounts their memories of the transition from hospital-style wicker wheelchairs used to transport patients to self-propelled, lighter-weight, folding chairs that were provided to disabled people, mostly to veterans, in the years following the war. Prior to the new chairs, one man recalls that "one was often confined to bed for long periods of time. . . . There were a few cerebral palsy chaps there. . . . If they transgressed any rule . . . they'd take their wheelchairs away from them and leave them in bed for two weeks" (Tremblay 1996, 153). In this and other interviews the value of wheelchairs is revealed. A vet described how the medical staff's efforts were geared toward getting veterans to walk with crutches, but when the vets discovered the self-propelled chairs they realized "it didn't make much sense spending all that energy covering a short distance [on crutches] . . . when you could do it quickly and easily with a wheelchair. . . . It didn't take long for people to get over the idea that walking was that essential" (158–59). Another veteran recalled how the staff's emphasis on getting the men to walk "delayed our rehabilitation for months and months" (159). The staff obviously understood the value of the wheelchair to disabled people; otherwise they would not have used it as a means of control, yet they resisted purchasing the new self-push chairs for some time after they were made available. It is that type of manipulation and control, along with architectural and attitudinal barriers, that confine people. It is not wheelchairs.

Multiple Meanings

Are *invalid,* with the emphasis on the first syllable, and *invalid,* with the emphasis on the second, synonyms or homonyms? Does the identical housing of *patient,* the adjective, and *patient,* the noun, conflate the two meanings? Did their conceptual relationship initially determine their uniform casing?

For instance, *invalid* is a designation used to identify some disabled people. The term is seen most prominently on the sides of vans used to transport people with mobility impairments. Disabled people, desperate for accessible transportation, must use vans with the dubious appellation *"Invalid Coach"* printed in bold letters on the side. Aside from this being a fertile source of jokes about the aptness of these notoriously bad transportation services being identified as "not factually or legally valid; falsely based or reasoned; faulty" (*American Heritage Dictionary* 1992), those on the inside of the bus suffer the humiliation of being written off so summarily. Both *invalids* share the Latin root *invalidus,* which means weak. It could be argued that some disabilities do result in weakening of the body, or, more likely, parts of the body, but the totalizing noun, *invalid,* does not confine the weakness to the specific bodily functions; it is more encompassing.

The homonymic *patient/patient,* is, I think, not coincidental or irrelevant. The noun *patient* is a role designation that is always relational. A patient is understood to belong to a doctor or other health care professional, or more generally to an institution. As a noun, *patient* is a neutral description of the role of "one who receives medical attention, care, or treatment" (*American Heritage Dictionary* 1992). The adjective *patient* moves beyond the noun's neutral designation to describe a person who is capable of "bearing or enduring pain, difficulty, provocation, or annoyance with calmness" as well as "tolerant . . . persevering . . . constant . . . not hasty" (*American Heritage Dictionary* 1992). The "good" patient is one who does not challenge the authority of the practitioner or institution and who complies with the regimen set out by the expert, in other words a patient. Disabled people, who have often spent a great deal of time as patients, discuss the ways that we have been socialized in the medical culture to be compliant, and that has often undermined our ability to challenge authority or to function autonomously. Further, the description of disabled people as patients in situations where we are not, reinforces these ideas.[4]

Reflections on the *Dis* in Disability

Before discussing the prefix *dis,* let's examine a similar bound morpheme that conveys meaning and significantly modifies the words it is attached to. The suffix *ette,* when appended to nouns, forms words meaning small or diminutive, as in *kitchenette;* female, as in *usherette;* or imitation or inferior kind, as in *leatherette* (*American Heritage Dictionary* 1992). These various meanings of *ette* slip around in our minds to influence how we interpret other words with the same suffix. So, for instance, although the word *leatherette* is used to tell us it is not the real thing and an inferior version of leather, *usherette* becomes, by association, not only the female version of usher but denotes a poor imitation. *Usherette* becomes, like *kitchenette,* the diminutive version. These various meanings tumble into one another, propagating new meanings, unintended and imprecise. I recently met a woman who told me that she had been a Rockette at Radio City Music Hall in Rockefeller Center for twenty years. I realized that this string of high-kicking, synchronized dancing women are perpetually cast as the smaller, imitation, inferior and female counterparts of the great male barons, the Rockefellers.

The prefix *dis,* like the suffix *ette,* has similarly unchecked impulses. Although *ette* qualifies its base and reduces it to the more diminutive and less valid version, a relationship is maintained between the base and its amended version. However, the prefix *dis* connotes separation, taking apart, sundering in two. The prefix has various meanings such as not, as in *dissimilar;* absence of, as in *disinterest;* opposite of, as in *disfavor;* undo, do the opposite of, as in *disarrange;* and deprive of, as in *disfranchise.* The Latin root *dis* means apart, asunder. Therefore, to use the verb *disable,* means, in part, to deprive of capability or effectiveness. The prefix creates a barrier, cleaving in two ability and its absence, its opposite. Disability is the "not" condition, the repudiation of ability.

Canguilhem (1991), in his explorations of the normal and the pathological, recognizes the way that prefixes signal their relationship to the words they modify. He asserts that

> the pathological phenomena found in living organisms are nothing more than quantitative variations, greater or lesser according to corresponding physiological phenomena. Semantically, the pathological is designated as departing from the normal not so much by *a-* or *dys-* as by *hyper-* or *hypo-*. . . . [T]his approach is far from considering health and sickness as qualitatively opposed, or as forces joined in battle." (42)

Ette, hyper and *hypo,* and *dis* have semantic consequences, but, moreover, each recapitulates a particular social arrangement. The suffix *ette* not only qualifies the meaning of the root word it is attached to but speaks of the unequal yet dynamic relationship between women and men, in which "woman was, as we see in the profoundly influential works of Aristotle, not the equal opposite of man but a failed version of the supposedly defining type" (Minnich 1990, 54). The medical prefixes *hyper* and *hypo* are typically attached to medical conditions that are temporary or circumscribed. People with those conditions are not socially marked and separated as are those with the more pronounced, and long standing conditions known as disabilities. With *hyper* and *hypo* conditions, there is less semantic and social disjuncture. However, the construction of *dis/ability* does not imply the continuum approach Canguilhem finds in diagnostic categories. *Dis* is the semantic reincarnation of the split between disabled and nondisabled people in society.

Yet *women and men with disabilities, disabled people,* and the *disability community* are terms of choice for the group. We have decided to reassign meaning rather than choose a new name. In retaining *disability* we run the risk of preserving the medicalized ideas attendant upon it in most people's idea of disability. What I think will help us out of the dilemma is the naming of the political category in which *disability* belongs. Women is a category of *gender,* and black or Latino/a are categories of *race/ethnicity,* and it is the recognition of those categories that has fostered understanding of the political meaning of *women* and *black.* Although *race* and *gender* are not perfect terms because they retain biological meanings in many quarters, the categories are increasingly understood as axes of oppression; axes along which power and resources are distributed. Although those of us within the disability community recognize that power is distributed along disability lines, the naming and recognition of the axis will be a significant step in gaining broader recognition of the issues. Further, it will enrich the discussion of the intersections of the axes of class, race, gender and sexual orientation, and disability.

Constructing the axis on which disabled and nondisabled fall will be a critical step in marking all points along it. Currently, there is increased attention to the privileged points on the continua of race, gender, and sexual orientation. There is growing recognition that the white, the male, and the heterosexual positions need to be noted and theorized. Similarly, it is important to examine the nondisabled position and its privilege and power. It is not the neutral, universal position from which disabled people deviate, rather, it is a category of people whose power and cultural capital keep them at the center.

In this book, though, disabled people's perspectives are kept central and are made explicit, partly to comment on how marginal and obscure they typically are, and partly to suggest the disciplinary and intellectual transformation consequent on putting disability studies at the center.

Notes

1. Various authors have discussed issues related to definitions of *disability*. See Wendell (1996), Longmore (1985b, 1987), and Hahn (1987), and also the June Isaacson Kailes (1995) monograph *Language Is More Than a Trivial Concern!* which is available from the Institute on Disability Culture, 2260 Sunrise Point Road, Las Cruces, New Mexico 88011.

2. The definition of *disability* under the Americans with Disabilities Act is consistent with the sociopolitical model employed in disability studies. A person is considered to have a disability if he or she:
   - has a physical or mental impairment that substantially limits one or more of his or her major life activities;
   - has a record of such an impairment; or
   - is regarded as having such an impairment.

   The last two parts of this definition acknowledge that even in the absence of a substantially limiting impairment, people can be discriminated against. For instance, this may occur because someone has a facial disfigurement or has, or is suspected of having, HIV or mental illness. The ADA recognizes that social forces, such as myths and fears regarding disability, function to substantially limit opportunity.

3. I am indebted to my colleague John O'Neill for his input on these ideas about the use of the term *normal*.

4. See June Isaacson Kailes's (1995), *Language Is More Than a Trivial Concern!* for a discussion on language use.

Works Cited

Allen, A. 1996. Open secret: A German academic hides his past—in plain sight. *Lingua Franca* 6 (3): 28–41.

American Heritage Dictionary. 1992. 3rd ed. Boston: Houghton Mifflin.

Cangiulhem, G. 1991. *The normal and the pathological.* New York: Zone Books.

Davis, L. J. 1995. *Enforcing normalcy: Disability, deafness, and the body.* London: Verso.

Freilich, M., Raybeck, D., and Savishinsky, J. 1991. *Deviance: Anthropological perspectives.* New York: Bergin and Garvey.

Gates, H. L., Jr. 1996. White like me. *New Yorker* 72 (16): 66–81.

Gill, C. J. 1994. Questioning continuum. In B. Shaw, ed., *The ragged edge: The disability experience from the pages of the first fifteen years of "The Disability Rag,"* 42–49. Louisville, Ky.: Advocado Press.

Grover, J.Z. 1987. AIDS: Keywords. In Douglas Crimp, ed., *AIDS: Cultural analysis,* 17–30. Cambridge: MIT Press.

Hahn, H. 1987. Disability and capitalism: Advertising the acceptably employable image. *Policy Studies Journal* 15 (3): 551–70.

Haraway, D. 1989. *Primate visions: Gender, race, and nature in the world of modern science.* New York: Routledge.

Kailes, J. I. 1995. *Language is more than a trivial concern!* (Available from June Isaacson Kailes, Disability Policy Consultant, 6201 Ocean Front Walk, Suite 2, Plaza del Rey, California 90293-7556).

Longmore, P. K. 1985. The life of Randolph Bourne and the need for a history of disabled people. *Reviews in American History* 586 (December) 581–587.

———. 1987. Uncovering the hidden history of people with disabilities. *Reviews in American History* 15 (3) (September): 355–364.

Minnick, E. K. 1990. *Transforming knowledge.* Philadelphia: Temple UP.

Sedgwick, E. K. 1990. *Epistemology of the closet.* Berkeley: U of California P.

Shapiro, J. P. 1993. *No pity: People with disabilities forging a new civil rights movement.* New York: Times Books.

Steadman's Medical Dictionary. 1976. 23d ed. Baltimore: Williams and Wilkins.

Tremblay, M. 1996. Going back to civvy street: A historical account of the Everest and Jennings wheelchair for Canadian World War II veterans with spinal cord injury. *Disability and Society* 11(2): 146–169.

Tulloch, S., ed. 1993. *The Reader's Digest Oxford wordfinder.* Oxford, Eng.: Clarendon Press.

Wendell, S. 1996. *The rejected body: Feminist philosophical reflections on disability.* New York: Routledge.

14

Disability in Theory
From Social Constructionism
to the New Realism of the Body

Tobin Siebers

In the hall of mirrors that is world mythology, there are none more ghastly, more disturbing to the eye, than the three Graiae, sisters of Medusa—whose own ghastliness turns onlookers to stone. Possessed of a single eye and six empty eye sockets, the three hags pass their eyeball from greedy hand to greedy hand in order to catch a glimpse of the world around them. Is the lone eyeball of the Graiae blind while in transit from eye socket to eye socket? Or does it stare at the world as it moves from hand to hand? If so, the eye is more than a metaphor for the experience of the disabled body. It is its reality, and therefore should tell us something about the construction of reality. The hand is the socket of seeing for the Graiae, just as it is for every other blind person. The blind alone do not live this way. All disabled bodies create this confusion of tongues—and eyes and hands and other body parts. For the deaf, the hand is the mouth of speech, the eye, its ear. Deaf hands speak. Deaf eyes listen.

Disability offers a challenge to the representation of the body—this is often said. Usually, it means that the disabled body provides insight into the fact that all bodies are socially constructed—that social attitudes and institutions determine far greater than biological fact the representation of the body's reality. The idea that representation governs the body, of course, has had enormous influence on cultural and critical theory, especially in gender studies. The women's movement radicalized interpretation theory to the point where repressive constructions of the female form are more universally recognized, and recent work by gay and lesbian activists has identified the ways that heterosexual models map the physique of the erotic body to the exclusion of nonnormative sexualities. Disability studies has embraced many of these theories because they provide a powerful alternative to the medical model of disability.[2] The medical model situates disability exclusively in individual bodies and strives to cure them by particular treatment, isolating the patient as diseased or defective. Social constructionism makes it possible to see disability as the effect of an environment hostile to some bodies and not to others, requiring advances in social justice rather than medicine. Thanks to the insight that the body is socially constructed, it is now more difficult to justify prejudices based on physical appearance and ability, permitting a more flexible definition of human beings in general.

But what I have in mind—perhaps I should say *in hand*—is another kind of insight: the disabled body changes the process of representation itself. Blind hands envision the faces of old acquaintances. Deaf eyes listen to public television. Tongues touch-type letters home to Mom and Dad. Feet wash the breakfast dishes. Mouths sign autographs.[3] Different bodies require and create new modes of representation. What would it mean for disability studies to take this insight seriously? Could it change body theory as usual if it did?

1. Social Constructionism

Let us step back from our places, as if we have put our hands on something prickly, and rearrange the objects of discourse on the usual table of thought. We have a theory of the body called *social constructionism*. It exists in weak and strong senses, but its correctness and theoretical power are very nearly unchallenged on the current academic scene. In its weak sense, it posits that the dominant ideas, attitudes, and customs of a society influence the perception of bodies. In a racist society, for example, black people may feel uncomfortable seeing themselves in the mirror, while in an ableist society passing civil rights legislation to permit greater access for people with disabilities is thought unnecessary because the reigning myth explains that they neither understand nor desire to enter "normal" society. Social constructionism in the weak sense tries to advance a commonsense approach to thinking about how people victimize individuals unlike them. This is not to say that this commonsense approach is so very common, as any person with a disability will explain at great length: people easily perceive when someone is different from them but rarely acknowledge the violence of their perceptions.

Unlike weak constructionism, the strong version does not rely on human ignorance or misunderstanding to account for prejudices of sex, gender, race, and ability but on a linguistic model that describes representation itself as a primary ideological force. Strong constructionism posits that the body does not determine its own representation in any way because the sign precedes the body in the hierarchy of signification. In fact, political ideologies and cultural mores exert the greatest power, social constructionists claim, when they anchor their authority in natural objects such as the body. Michel Foucault defined *biopower* as the force that constitutes the materiality of any human subject; it forms, secures, and normalizes human subjects through a process of "subjection" (*History of Sexuality* 140–41, 143–44). The techniques of biopower—statistics, demographics, eugenics, medicalization, sterilization—are all familiar to scholars of disability studies. They create the political alliance between knowledge and power in the modern state, but biopower is not merely a political force, controlled by one or two institutions. Biopower determines for Foucault the way that human subjects experience the materiality of their bodies. The human subject has no body, nor does the subject exist, prior to its subjection as representation. Bodies are linguistic effects driven, first, by the order of representation itself and, second, by the entire array of social ideologies dependent on this order.

If it is true that bodies matter to people with disabilities, it may be worth thinking at greater length about the limits of social construction. Judith Butler, for example, has recently made the case that constructionism is inadequate to the task of understanding material bodies (xi). Butler herself tends to isolate bodies in pain and abject bodies as resources for rethinking the representation of physicality. The "exclusionary matrix by which subjects are formed," she explains, "requires the simultaneous production of a domain of abject beings, those who are not yet 'subjects,' but who form the constitutive outside to the domain of the subject" (3). Abject beings have bodies and desires that cannot be incorporated into social norms, Butler argues, and so they inhabit the border between the acceptable and unacceptable, marking it out for the benefit of mainstream society. In short, people with disabilities are not yet "subjects" in Foucault's disciplinary sense: their bodies appear as a speck of reality uncontrolled by the ideological forces of society. It is as if Butler has caught a glimpse of a badly turned ankle under the petticoats of the "normal" world, and this vision of disability somehow provides a means to resist subjection. Disabled bodies come to represent what Rosemarie Garland Thomson calls the "freak show." "Disability is the unorthodox made flesh," she writes, "refusing to be normalized, neutralized, or homogenized" (23).

Disability exposes with great force the constraints imposed on bodies by social codes and norms. In a society of wheelchair users, stairs would be nonexistent, and the fact that they are everywhere in our society seems an indication only that most of our architects are able-bodied people who think unseriously about access. Obviously, in this sense, disability looks socially constructed. It is tempting, in fact, to see disability exclusively as the product of a bad match between social design and some human bodies, since this is so often the case. But disability may also trouble the theory of social construction. Disability scholars have begun to insist that strong constructionism either fails to account for the difficult physical realities faced by people with disabilities or presents their body in ways that are conventional, conformist, and unrecognizable to them. These include the habits of privileging performativity over corporeality, favoring pleasure to pain, and describing social success in terms of intellectual achievement, bodily adaptability, and active political participation. The disabled body seems difficult for the theory of social construction to absorb: disability is at once its best example and a significant counterexample.

According to Foucault, madness, criminality, and sexuality are modern inventions, and his major writings are dedicated to tracking their involvement with social repression and exclusion.[4] Not surprisingly, these topics involve him with the representation of disability, but his treatment of it reveals tangles in the social construction argument not always visible elsewhere in his work. The chapter on "docile bodies" in *Discipline and Punish: The Birth of the Prison* (1975) begins by describing the ideal figure of the soldier before the modern age took control of it: "[T]he soldier was someone who could be recognized from afar; he bore certain signs: the natural signs of his strength and his courage, the marks, too, of his pride; his body was the blazon of his strength and valour . . ." (135). Foucault also emphasizes a long description of the soldier's body in which health dominates: "[A]n erect head, a taut stomach, broad shoulders, long arms, strong fingers, a small belly, thick thighs, slender legs and dry feet" (135). His point is to contrast this soldier with the soldier of the modern age: "By the late eighteenth century," he writes, "the soldier has become something that can be made; out of a formless clay, an inapt body, the machine required can be constructed; posture is gradually corrected; a calculated constraint runs slowly through each part of the body, mastering it, making it pliable . . ." (135). The contrast between the two ideas of the body could not be more strident. Foucault uses natural metaphors to describe the health and vigor of the pre-modern soldier, while deliberately representing the modern one as malleable, weak, and machinelike. Docility begins to resemble disability, and it is not meant as a term of celebration. The docile body is a bad invention—a body "that may be subjected, used, transformed and improved" (136).

Hidden underneath the docile body—the body invented by the modern age and now recognized as the only body—is the able body. Foucault's account is a not-so-subtle retelling of the Fall in which well-being and ability are sacrificed to enter the modern age. The new docile body replaces the able body. Health and naturalness disappear. Human beings seem more machinelike. The docile body requires supports and constraints, its every movement based on a calculation. This narrative, incidentally, is not limited to Foucault's account of the docile or disabled body. It dominates his observations on madness, sexuality, and criminality as well. Underneath each lies a freer and less compromised version—madness more mad than unreasonable, sex more polymorphously perverse than any plurality of modern sexualities, criminality more outrageous and unsociable than the criminal code imagines. The point is often made that Foucault reveals with great force the structure of exclusion at the core of modern history; it has never been remarked that he describes what has been excluded as purer and fitter conceptions of the body and mind.

This picture is wrong, of course, and many disability scholars know it. They understand that recent body theory, whatever its claims, has never confronted the disabled body. Most obviously, it represents the docile body as an evil to be eradicated. If the docile body is disabled, however, it means that recent body theory has reproduced the most abhorrent prejudices of ableist society. Lennard Davis has argued that disability is as much a nightmare for the discourse of theory as for ableist society, and he provides a succinct description of the ways in which current theory avoids the harsh realities of the body: "[T]he body is seen as a site of *jouissance*, a native ground of pleasure, the scene of an excess that defies reason, that takes dominant culture and its rigid, powerladen vision of the body to task. . . . The nightmare of that body is the one that is deformed, maimed, mutilated, broken, diseased. . . . Rather than face this ragged image, the critic turns to the fluids of sexuality, the gloss of lubrication, the glossary of the body as text, the heteroglossia of the intertext, the glossolalia of the schizophrenic. But almost never the body of the differently abled" (5).[5] Many social constructionists assume that it is extremely difficult to see through the repressive apparatus of modern society to any given body, but when they do manage to spot one, it is rarely disabled. It is usually a body that feels good and looks good—a body on the brink of discovering new kinds of pleasure, new uses for itself, and more and more power.

The central issue for the politics of representation is not whether bodies are infinitely interpretable but whether certain bodies should be marked as defective and how the people who have these bodies may properly represent their interests in the public sphere. More and more people now believe that disabled bodies should not be labeled as defective, although we have a long way to go, but we have not even begun to think about how these bodies might represent their interests in the public sphere for the simple reason that our theories of representation do not take account of them. Only by beginning to conceive of the ways that disabled bodies change the process of representation, both politically and otherwise, might we begin to tackle the difficult issues of how access bears on voting rights, how current theories of political subjectivity limit citizenship for the mentally disabled, and why economic theories cast people with disabilities exclusively as burdens.

2. Pain and More Pain

Only 15% of people with disabilities are born with their impairments. Most people become disabled over the course of their life. This truth has been accepted only with difficulty by mainstream society; it prefers to think of people with disabilities as a small population, a stable population, that neverthe-less makes enormous claims on the resources of everyone else. Most people do not want to consider that life's passage will lead them from ability to disability. The prospect is too frightening, the disabled body, too disturbing. In fact, even this picture is overly optimistic. The cycle of life runs in actual-ity from disability to temporary ability back to disability, and that only if you are among the most fortunate, among those who do not fall ill or suffer a severe accident. The human ego does not easily accept the disabled body. It prefers pleasure. Perhaps this is because, as Freud explained, the ego ex-ists on the surface of the body like skin. It thrives on surface phenomena and superficial glimmers of enjoyment. No doubt, this explains why the body posited by social constructionism is a body built for pleasure, a body infinitely teachable and adaptable. It has often been claimed that the disabled body represents the image of the Other. In fact, the able body is the true image of the Other. It is a prop for the ego, a myth we all accept for the sake of enjoyment, for we all learn early on, as Jacques Lacan has explained, to see the clumsiness and ineptitude of the body in the mirror as a picture of health—at least for a little while.

Pain is a subjective phenomenon, perhaps the most subjective of phenomena. It is therefore tempt-ing to see it as a site for describing individuality. This temptation is troublesome for two reasons. First, individuality, whatever its meaning, is a social object, which means that it must be communicable as a concept. Individuality derived from the incommunicability of pain easily enforces a myth of hyper individuality, a sense that each individual is locked in solitary confinement where suffering is the only object of contemplation. People with disabilities are already too politically isolated for this myth to be attractive. Second, both medical science and rehabilitation represent the pain of the disabled body as individual, which has also had dire consequences for the political struggles of people with disabilities. The first response to disability is to treat it, and this almost always involves cataloguing what is most distinctive about it. Treatment programs regard each disability as completely individual, with the end result that people with disabilities are robbed of a sense of political community by those whom they need to address their pain. No two blind people appear to have the same medical problem or political interests. The paraplegic and the elderly have even less basis in the current climate to gather together for political purposes. The struggle for civil rights is completely different from the usual process for people with disabilities because they must fight against their individuality rather than to establish it—unlike political action groups based on race and gender.

Consequently, the greatest stake in disability studies at the present moment is to find ways to represent pain and to resist current models that blunt the political effectiveness of these representations. I stress the importance of pain not because pain and disability are synonymous but to offer a challenge to current body theory and to expose to what extent its dependence on social constructionism collaborates with the misrepresentation of the disabled body in the political sphere.[6] There are only a few images of pain acceptable on the current scene, and none of them is realistic from the standpoint of people who suffer pain daily. The dominant model defines pain as either regulatory or resistant. In the first case, pain is the tool used by society to enforce its norms. The second case usually spins off from the first, describing pain as a repressive effect that nevertheless produces an unmanageable supplement of suffering that marks out the individual as a site of resistance to social regulation. Despite the dominant principle that individuality is only an ideological construction, many theorists turn to pain to represent a form of individuality that escapes the forces of social domination. Indeed, pain often comes to represent individuality as such, whether individuality is a part of the theory or not.

Judith Butler's argument in *Bodies That Matter: On the Discursive Limits of "Sex"* (1993) provides a clear example of the dominant model of pain. She claims that society uses the pain of guilt to produce conformity with what she calls the "morphology" of the heterosexual body. This morphology relies on ideas of a proper body strictly enforced by social taboo: "To the extent that such supporting *ideas* are regulated by prohibition and pain, they can be understood as the forcible and materialized effects of regulatory power. But precisely because prohibitions do not always work, that is, do not always produce the docile body that fully conforms to the social ideal, they may delineate body surfaces that do not signify conventional heterosexual polarities" (64).

For Butler, pain has a delineating effect on our awareness of our bodies; it "may be one way," she explains, "in which we come to have an idea of our body at all" (65). But the painful prohibitions against homosexuality also mold human desire and the body in an artificial way, constructing heterosexuality at a grave cost—a fusion of fantasy and fetishism that allies love with illness. In effect, pain forces the body to conform, but the construction of this conformity is too burdensome to support, and it produces as a byproduct another kind of pain from which a less repressive individuality may spring, in Butler's specific case, the individuality of the lesbian body.

Notice that pain in current body theory is rarely physical. It is more likely to be based on the pain of guilt or social repression. Society creates pain, but this creation backfires, producing a resource to struggle against society—this is the dominant theoretical conception of pain. I do not want to underestimate the amount of psychic pain produced by society; nor do I want to deny that psychic pain translates into physical pain. Clearly, the pain of disability is less bearable because people with disabilities suffer intolerance and loneliness every day. They hurt because the able-bodied often refuse to accept them as members of the human community. And yet most people with a disability understand that physical pain is an enemy. It hovers over innumerable daily actions, whether the disability is painful in itself or only the occasion for pain because of the difficulty of navigating one's environment. The great challenge every day is to manage the body's pain, to get out of bed in the morning, to overcome the well of pain that rises in the evening, to meet the hundred daily obstacles that are not merely inconveniences but occasions for physical suffering.

When body theorists do represent pain as physical—infrequent as this is—the conventional model still dominates their descriptions. They present suffering and disability either as a way of reconfiguring the physical resources of the body or of opening up new possibilities of pleasure.[7] Pain is most often soothed by the joy of conceiving the body differently from the norm. Frequently, the objects that people with disabilities are forced to live with—prostheses, wheelchairs, braces, and other devices—are viewed not as potential sources of pain but as marvelous examples of the plasticity of the human form or as devices of empowerment. Some theorists have gone so far as to argue that pain remaps the body's erotic sites, redistributing the erogenous zones, breaking up the monopoly of the genitals, and smashing the repressive and aggressive edifice of the ego. Rare is the theoretical account where physical suffering remains harmful for very long.[8]

Consider Donna Haraway's justly famous theory of the cyborg, "a hybrid of machine and organism" (149).[9] Haraway embraces hybridization to defeat social conformity and to awaken new possibilities for women's empowerment. She represents the cyborg as a world-changing fiction for women and a resource for escaping the myths of progress and organic history. Haraway's cyborgs are spunky, irreverent, and sexy; they accept with glee the ability to transgress old boundaries between machine and animal, male and female, and mind and body. They supposedly make up a future, fortunate race, but in fact they exist everywhere today. Our cyborgs are people with disabilities, and Haraway does not shy away from the comparison. Severe disability is her strongest example of complex hybridization: "Perhaps paraplegics and other severely-handicapped people can (and sometimes do) have the most intense experiences of complex hybridization with other communication devices" (178). Moreover, she views the prosthetic device as a fundamental category for preparing the self and body to meet the demands of the information age. "Prosthesis is semiosis," she explains, "the making of meanings and bodies, not for transcendence but for power-charged communication" (244). Haraway is so preoccupied with power and ability that she forgets what disability is. Prostheses always increase the cyborg's abilities; they are a source only of new powers, never of problems.[10] The cyborg is always more than human—and never risks to be seen as subhuman. To put it simply, the cyborg is not disabled.

It is easy to mythologize disability as an advantage. Disabled bodies are so unusual and bend the rules of representation to such extremes that they must mean something extraordinary. They quickly become sources of fear and fascination for able-bodied people, who cannot bear to look at the unruly sight before them but also cannot bear not to look. Every person with a disability can recount the stories. Here is one of mine. I wore a steel leg brace throughout my childhood, and one early summer evening, an angry neighborhood boy challenged me to a fistfight, but he had one proviso: he wanted me to remove my steel brace because he thought it would give me unfair advantage. He was afraid I would kick him. I refused to remove my brace, but not because I wanted an additional weapon. I had hardly the strength to lift my leg into a kick, let alone the ability to do him harm. I refused to remove the brace because I knew that at some point in the fight this angry boy or someone else would steal my brace from the ground and run away with it, and I would be left both helpless and an object of ridicule for the surrounding mob of children. I know the truth about the myth of the cyborg, about how able-bodied people try to represent disability as a marvelous advantage, because I am a cyborg myself.

Physical pain is highly individualistic, unpredictable, and raw as reality. It pits the mind against the body in ways that make the opposition between thought and ideology in most current body theory seem trivial. It offers few resources for resisting ideological constructions of masculinity and femininity, the erotic monopoly of the genitals, the violence of ego, or the power of capital. Pain is not a friend to humanity. It is not a secret resource for political change. It is not a well of delight for the individual. Theories that encourage these interpretations are not only unrealistic about pain; they contribute to an ideology of ability that marginalizes people with disabilities and makes their stories of suffering and victimization both politically impotent and difficult to believe.

3. These Blunt, Crude Realities

I have been using, deliberately, the words *reality* and *real* to describe the disabled body, but we all know that the real has fallen on hard times. The German idealists disabled the concept once and for all in the eighteenth century. More recently, the theory of social construction has made it impossible to refer to "reality" without the scare quotes we all use so often. Advocates of reality risk appearing philosophically naive or politically reactionary. This is as true for disability studies as for other areas of cultural and critical theory.

And yet the word is creeping back into usage in disability studies, even among the most careful thinkers. Disability activists are prone to refer to the difficult physical realities faced by people with disabilities. Art works concerning disability or created by artists with disabilities do not hesitate to represent the ragged edges and blunt angles of the disabled body in a matter of fact way (see, for example, Jim Ferris and David Hevey). Their methods are deliberate and detailed, as if they are trying to get people to see something that is right before their eyes and yet invisible to most. The testimony of sufferers of disability includes gritty accounts of their pain and daily humiliations—a sure sign of the rhetoric of realism. Cheryl Marie Wade provides a powerful but not untypical example of the new realism of the body:

> To put it bluntly—because this need is blunt as it gets—we must have our asses cleaned after we shit and pee. Or we have others' fingers inserted into our rectums to assist shitting. Or we have tubes of plastic inserted inside us to assist peeing or we have re-routed anuses and pissers so we do it all into bags attached to our bodies. These blunt, crude realities. Our daily lives.... The difference between those of us who need attendants and those who don't is the difference between those who know privacy and those who don't. We rarely talk about these things, and when we do the realities are usually disguised in generic language or gimp humor. Because, let's face it: we have great shame about this need. This need that only babies and the "broken" have.... And yes, this makes us different from you who have privacy of the body.... If we are ever to be really at home in the world and in ourselves, then we must say these things out loud. And we must say them with real language. (88–89)

Wade experiences a corporeality rarely imagined by the able-bodied. Her account ruptures the dominant model of pain found in body theory today, projects a highly individual dimension of feeling, and yet speaks in the political first person plural. She describes the reality, both physical and political, of those people with disabilities who need care, and risk paying for it with their independence and personal self-esteem as they struggle to maintain some portion of equality with their caregivers. The inequality threatening people with these kinds of disabilities at every instant derives from a body politic—the real physical expectation that all people beyond a certain age will perform their own bodily hygiene. What sea change in social attitudes about the body could bring an end to this expectation? Crudely put, unless all adults have their ass wiped by someone else, unless the caregiver cannot wipe his or her own ass, the people who alone require this service will be represented as weak or inferior.

A renewed acceptance of bodily reality has specific benefits for disability studies, and few of the risks associated with realism, as far as I can tell. It is difficult to think of disability activists as being philosophically naive or politically conservative, given the radical demands they have been making on society and its institutions. First, people with disabilities build communities through a more transparently political process than other groups; since they cannot rely on seemingly more natural associations, such as family history, race, age, gender, or geographical point of origin, they tend to organize themselves according to health-care needs, information sharing, and political advocacy. Second, their commitment to political struggle is so obvious and urgent that their ideas are difficult to dismiss on philosophical grounds, especially given that ours is an age of political interpretation. Third, the views associated with disability studies turn many of the burning moral and political issues of our times on their head. Consider some disability perspectives on assisted suicide, abortion, and genetic research. Assisted suicide takes on an entirely different meaning for the disabled, and often in contradictory ways. On the one hand, whether you consider suicide a personal right or not, it is still the case that the majority of people may choose to end their own life, but some people with disabilities are deprived of this choice because they do not have the physical means to act by themselves. On the other hand, many disability activists view assisted suicide as a device to guilt-trip people with disabilities into ending their life for the "good" of society. The abortion of fetuses who will have physical or mental impairments does not mean the same thing to people with disabilities as it does to the able-bodied who view health as an essential human trait. Some disability activists have asked whether the wish to have a healthy baby is not as prejudicial as the wish to have a light-skinned baby. The vast sums of money being spent today on genetic research strike many in the disability community as a drain on resources that could be spent to support the needs of people who require immediate assistance with their impairments. It looks as if the government would rather eradicate people with disabilities than assist them. None of these arguments is easily described as conservative or politically reactionary. Finally, disability activists have no reverence for conventional economic policy, which represents people with disabilities as a small but needy group that requires more resources than it deserves, and they have a radical view of political autonomy and freedom because their notion of independence allows for a great deal of support to encourage people with disabilities to practice their civil rights. An acceptance of the physical realities of the disabled body simply makes it impossible to view our society in the same light.

Restoring a sense of the reality of the disabled body, however, does have some risks. One worth stressing is the temptation to view disability and pain as more real than their opposites. The perception already exists that broken bodies and things are more real than anything else. The discourse of literary realism began in the nineteenth century to privilege representations of trash, fragments, and imperfect bodies, while modern art turned to the representation of human difference and defect, changing the sense of aesthetic beauty to a rawer conception. These discourses soon penetrated society at large. Somehow, today, a photograph of a daisy in a garden seems less real than a photograph of garbage blowing down a dirty alley. Incidentally, literary and cultural theorists often obey the same rules. A closer look at many of the major concepts of current theory—hybridity, heterogeneity, difference, performativity—would reveal that each works as a substitute for the real, countering the illusion that "reality" is sound, smooth, and simple with the claim that it is in fact sick, ragged, and complex.

The disabled body is no more real than the able body—and no less real. In fact, serious consideration of the disabled body exposes that our current theories of reality are not as sophisticated as we would like to think. They prefer complexity to simplicity, but they lop off a great deal of reality in the process, most notably, the hard simple reality of the body. More often than not, these theories are driven by ethical concerns rather than the desire to represent what happens to bodies in the world. They are part of a rhetoric that exists less to explain how the body works than to make claims about how it "ought" to work in the society we all apparently desire.

Notice I am not claiming either that the body exists apart from social forces or that it represents something more *real*, *natural*, or *authentic* than things of culture. I am claiming that the body has its own forces and that we need to recognize them if we are to get a less one-sided picture of how bodies and their representations affect each other for good and for bad. The body is, first and foremost, a biological agent teeming with vital and often chaotic forces. It is not inert matter subject to easy manipulation by social representations. The body is alive, which means that it is as capable of influencing and transforming social languages as they are capable of influencing and transforming it.[11]

The most urgent issue for disability studies is the political struggle of people with disabilities, and this struggle requires a realistic conception of the disabled body. In practice, this means resisting the temptation to describe the disabled body as either power laden or as a weapon of resistance useful only to pierce the false armor of reality erected by modern ideologies. It means overturning the dominant image of people with disabilities as isolated victims of disease or misfortune who have nothing in common with each other or the able-bodied. Finally, it means opposing the belief that people with disabilities are needy, selfish, and resentful—and will consequently take more than their fair share of resources from society as a whole.

People with disabilities usually realize that they must learn to live with their disability, if they are to live life as a human being. The challenge is not to adapt their disability into an extraordinary power or an alternative image of ability. The challenge is to function. I use this word advisedly and am prepared to find another if it offends. People with disabilities want to be able to function: to live with their disability, to come to know their body, to accept what it can do, and to keep doing what they can for as long as they can. They do not want to feel dominated by the people on whom they depend for help, and they want to be able to imagine themselves in the world without feeling ashamed.

Sooner or later, whatever we think an object is, we come to esteem it not for what we think it is but for what it really is—if we are lucky. We still lack the means to represent what disabled bodies are because there are false notions everywhere and these bodies change what representation is. But people with disabilities are working on it, and they hope to be lucky. What would it mean to esteem the disabled body for what it really is?

4. Epilogue

In April 1999, the Supreme Court began grappling with the purposely vague wording of the Americans with Disabilities Act of 1990, raising the question whether a person who can restore normal functioning by wearing glasses or taking a pill for hypertension can be considered disabled. One high profile example for the Court concerned a lawsuit brought against United Airlines by two nearsighted women who were not accepted for jobs as pilots. At one point in the hearing Justice Antonin Scalia removed his glasses and waved them in the air, proclaiming "I couldn't do my current job without them."[12] Shortly afterward, the Court handed down a decision much in the style of Justice Scalia's gesture, gutting the ADA and ruling to restrict the definition of disability to the *truly disabled*.

Although justice is blind, Judge Scalia put his glasses back on after making his dramatic gesture. But I imagine a different scenario, one that touches upon the reality of those disabled people for whom remedies are not so easily available and resources are scarce. When Justice Scalia waved his glasses in the air, the greedy hands of Justice David Souter stole them and moved them to his eyes—"Now I can do my job!" he exclaimed—after which the greedy hands of Justice Sandra Day O'Connor filched the glasses from him—"Now I can do my job!" she exclaimed—and on and on.

Notes

1. Disability studies may also be in the position to offer significant adjustments to current theories of the gendered and sexed body. Some of this work has already begun. See, for example, Tom Shakespeare, Kath Gillespie-Sells, and Dominic Davies.

2. This little list runs the gamut of mythologies and realities connected with the representation of the disabled body, from freak show to mundane to metaphorical, and might serve as a warm-up for thinking about how different bodies transform language. A specific and provocative example of how bodies affect the process of representation can be found in the recent work of transgender and intersex activists (*intersex* being the accepted term among these theorists for *hermaphrodites*). Intersex bodies, David Valentine and Riki Anne Wilchins argue, defy the basis of existing categories, requiring new languages that seem confusing but more accurately represent their biology. For example, *his* or *her* is replaced with *hir*. Other examples of new linguistic usage appear in the e-mail signatures of two transgender activists: "[J]ust your average, straight white guy with a cunt who really digs lezzie chicks like me" and "just your average butch lesbian intersexed white guy with a clitoral recession and a vaginoplasty who wants her dick back" (218).

3. Disability scholars are currently debating whether people with disabilities were better off before the inception of modernity, and this debate usually relies on the social construction argument. One example among many is found in Davis's path-breaking study of deafness, *Enforcing Normalcy: Disability, Deafness, and the Body* (1995): "This study aims to show that disability, as we know the concept, is really a socially driven relation to the body that became relatively organized in the eighteenth and nineteenth centuries. This relation is propelled by economic and social factors and can be seen as part of a more general project to control and regulate the body that we have come to call crime, sexuality, gender, disease, subalternity, and so on. Preindustrial societies tended to treat people with impairments as part of the social fabric, although admittedly not kindly, while postindustrial societies, instituting 'kindness,' ended up segregating and ostracizing such individuals through the discursivity of disability" (3). See also Simi Linton, et al., esp. 6; Martha Edwards; Michael Oliver's *The Politics of Disablement: A Sociological Approach* (1990); and James Trent's *Inventing the Feeble Mind: A History of Mental Retardation in the United States* (1984).

4. Susan Bordo also critiques the postmodern pleasure body, which she calls the "plastic body," arguing that we cannot always choose our own bodies. The emphasis on *heterogeneity* and *indeterminacy* in recent body theory, she explains, reflects a disembodied ideal of freedom. This theoretical trend is not only incompatible with the experiences of people with disabilities; it mimics the fantasy, often found in medical models, that the body is immaterial as long as the imagination is free. See Bordo 38–39, 227–28, 247, and 275.

5. Pain is a notoriously complex issue in disability studies. On the one hand, a focus on pain risks describing disability as if it were related exclusively to the physical body and not to social barriers, suggesting that disability is only and always about physical limitation. On the second hand, people with disabilities often complain that the social construction argument denies the pain of impairment and suggests that it can be overcome simply by changing cultural attitudes. On the

third hand, some people with disabilities are not in physical pain and dispute the association between pain and disability. A politically effective theory of pain needs to mediate between these three alternatives. For more on the role of pain in disability studies, see Oliver, esp. ch. 3.

6. A major exception is Elaine Scarry, who makes it clear that pain is physical, but her own commitments make her work less useful than it could be for disability studies because she is more interested in describing how physical pain disturbs the social realm than the individual body. Her major examples of pain are torture and warfare, and these have a powerful impact on her theory. According to Scarry, pain is a "pure physical experience of negation, an immediate sensory rendering of 'against,' of something being against one, and of something one must be against. Even though it occurs within oneself, it is at once identified as "not oneself," 'not me,' as something so alien that it must right now be gotten rid of" (52). The subjective effects of pain, then, are objectified in the other, and consequently the gap between self and other widens to the point where it causes an enormous tear in the social fabric. Pain unmakes the world precisely because it usually lodges the source of suffering in the social realm. This idea of pain works extremely well for torture and warfare, where the presence of the torturer or enemy easily embodies otherness, but less so for disability where suffering has to do not specifically with the destruction of the social realm but with the impairment of the body. Rather than objectifying their body as the other, people with disabilities often work to identify with it, for only a knowledge of their body will decrease pain and permit them to function in society. Unfortunately, this notion of the body as self has been held against people with disabilities. It is represented in the psychological literature as a form of pathological narcissism, with the result that they are represented as mentally unfit in addition to being physically unfit. On this last point, see Siebers on narcissism and disability.

7. A notable exception, important for disability studies, is the feminist discourse on rape; it rejects the idea that pain translates into pleasure, insisting that physical pain and feelings of being dominated are intolerable.

8. For other critiques of Haraway, see Susan Wendell 44–45 and David Mitchell and Sharon Snyder 28–29.

9. When prostheses fit well, they still fit badly. They require the surface of the body to adjust—that is rarely easy—and impart their own special wounds. My mother wore a false eye; it fit at first, but as the surrounding tissue began to shrink, it soon twisted and turned in its orbit, inflaming her eye socket and becoming easily infected. I wear a plastic brace. It quiets the pain in my lower back, but I have developed a painful bunion, and the brace rubs my calf raw, especially in the heat of summer. Every user of a prosthesis has similar stories.

10. Haraway, although eschewing the language of realism, makes a case for the active biological agency of bodies, calling them "material-semiotic generative nodes" (200). By this last phrase, she means to describe the body as both constructed and generative of constructions and to dispute the idea that it is merely a ghostly fantasy produced by the power of language.

11. In 1990, when the ADA was passed, the number of Americans with disabilities was estimated at 43 million. That number falls well short if one includes the one in three Americans who wear glasses or the 50 million who take medicine for hypertension. See Linda Greenhouse, "Justices Wrestle With the Definition of "Disability" (1999), and also Leslie Kaufman, who concludes her report on the legal issues posed to the Supreme Court as follows: "If the court decides that poor eyesight or hypertension are equally limiting, millions more Americans might wake up this spring to find themselves on the rolls of the disabled." Predictably, the Court found that 43 million disabled Americans were enough and ruled to restrict the definition of disability established by the ADA. See Greenhouse, "High Court Limits Who Is Protected by Disability Law" (1999).

Works Cited

Bordo, Susan. *Unbearable Weight: Feminism, Western Culture, and the Body*. Berkeley: U of California P, 1993.

Butler, Judith. *Bodies That Matter: On the Discursive Limits of "Sex."* New York: Routledge, 1993.

Couser, Thomas, ed. "The Empire of the 'Normal': A Forum on Disability and Self-Representation." *American Quarterly* 52 (2000): 305–43.

Davis, Lennard J. *Enforcing Normalcy: Disability, Deafness, and the Body*. London: Verso, 1995.

Edwards, Martha. "The Cultural Context of Deformity in the Ancient Greek World." *Ancient History Bulletin* 10.3–4 (1996): 79–92.

Ferris, Jim. "Uncovery to Recovery: Reclaiming One Man's Body on a Nude Photo Shoot." *Michigan Quarterly Review* 37 (1998): 503–18.

Foucault, Michel. *Discipline and Punish: The Birth of the Prison*. Trans. Alan Sheridan. New York: Vintage, 1995.

———. *The History of Sexuality*. Vol. 1: *An Introduction*. Trans. Robert Hurley. New York: Vintage, 1980.

Greenhouse, Linda. "High Court Limits Who Is Protected by Disability Law." *New York Times* 23 June 1999: A1+.

———. "Justices Wrestle With the Definition of Disability: Is It Glasses? False Teeth?" *New York Times* 28 Apr. 1999: A26.

Haraway, Donna J. *Simians, Cyborgs, and Women: The Reinvention of Nature*. New York: Routledge, 1991.

Hevey, David. *The Creatures Time Forgot: Photography and Disability Imagery*. New York: Routledge, 1992.

Kaufman, Leslie. "From Eyeglasses to Wheelchairs: Adjusting the Legal Bar for Disability." *New York Times* 18 Apr. 1999: A1.

Linton, Simi, Susan Mello, and John O'Neill. "Disability Studies: Expanding the Parameters of Diversity." *Radical Teacher* 47 (1995): 4–10.

Mitchell, David T., and Sharon L. Snyder. "Introduction: Disability Studies and the Double Bind of Representation." *The Body and Physical Difference: Discourses of Disability*. Ed. David T. Mitchell and Sharon L. Snyder. Ann Arbor: U of Michigan P, 1997. 1–31.

Oliver, Michael. *Understanding Disability: From Theory to Practice*. New York: St. Martin's, 1996.

Scarry, Elaine. *The Body in Pain: The Making and Unmaking of the World*. New York: Oxford UP, 1985.

Shakespeare, Tom, Kath Gillespie-Sells, and Dominic Davies. *The Sexual Politics of Disability: Untold Desires*. London: Cassell, 1996.

Siebers, Tobin. "Tender Organs, Narcissism, and Identity Politics." *Disability Studies: Enabling the Humanities*. Ed. Brenda Jo Brueggemann, Sharon L. Snyder, and Rosemarie Garland Thomson. New York: PMLA, 2001.

Thomson, Rosemarie Garland. *Extra-ordinary Bodies: Figuring Physical Disability in American Culture and Literature*. New York: Columbia UP, 1997.

Valentine, David, and Riki Anne Wilchins. "One Percent on the Burn Chart: Gender, Genitals, and Hermaphrodites with Attitude." *Social Text* 15 (1997): 215–22.

Wade, Cheryl Marie. "It Ain't Exactly Sexy." *The Ragged Edge: The Disability Experience from the Pages of the First Fifteen Years of* The Disability Rag. Ed. Barrett Shaw. Louisville, KY: Advocado Press, 1994.

Wendell, Susan. *The Rejected Body: Feminist Philosophical Reflections on Disability*. New York: Routledge, 1996.

15

On the Government of Disability
Foucault, Power, and the Subject of Impairment

Shelley Tremain

We believe that feelings are immutable, but every sentiment, particularly the noblest and most disinterested, has a history. We believe in the dull constancy of instinctual life and imagine that it continues to exert its force indiscriminately in the present as it did in the past ... We believe, in any event, that the body obeys the exclusive laws of physiology and that it escapes the influence of history, but this too is false.

—Foucault, "Nietzsche, Genealogy, History"[1]

Introduction: Bio-power and Its Objects

In the field of Disability Studies, the term "impairment" is generally taken to refer to an objective, transhistorical and transcultural entity of which modern bio-medicine has acquired knowledge and understanding and which it can accurately represent. Those in Disability Studies who assume this realist ontology are concerned to explain why social responses to "impairment" vary between historical periods and cultural contexts—that is, why people "with impairments" are included in social life in some places and periods and are excluded from social life in some places and periods.[2] Against these theorists, I will argue that this allegedly timeless entity (impairment) is an historically specific effect of knowledge/power. In order to advance this claim, I assume nominalism.[3]

Nominalists hold the view that there are no phenomena or states of affairs whose identities are independent of the concepts we use to understand them and the language with which we represent them. Some philosophers think this is a misguided stance. For these thinkers, objects such as photons, stars, and horses with which the natural sciences concern themselves *existed as* photons, stars, and horses long before any human being encountered them and presumed to categorize or classify them. Compelling arguments have been made, nevertheless, according to which not even the objects of the natural sciences (say, photons, stars, and Shetland ponies) have identities until someone names them.[4]

I want to set aside questions regarding the metaphysical status of these objects. In this paper, the only ontological commitments that interest me are those that pertain to elements of human history and culture. My aim is to show that impairment is an historical artifact of the regime of "bio-power"; therefore, I will restrict myself to claims that apply to objects of the human sciences.

Foucault's term "bio-power" (or "bio-politics") refers to the endeavor to rationalize the problems that the phenomena characteristic of a group of living human beings, when constituted as a population, pose to governmental practice: problems of health, sanitation, birthrate, longevity, and race. Since the late eighteenth century, these problems have occupied an expanding place in the government of individuals and populations. Bio-power is then the strategic movement of relatively recent forms of power/knowledge to work toward an increasingly comprehensive management of these problems in the life of individuals and the life of populations. These problems (and their management), Foucault thinks, are inextricable from the framework of political rationality within which they emerged and developed their urgency; namely, liberalism.[5]

The objectification of the body in eighteenth-century clinical discourse was one pole around which bio-power coalesced. As feminist historian Barbara Duden notes, in that historical context the modern body was created as the effect and object of medical examination, which could be used, abused, transformed, and subjugated. The doctor's patient had come to be treated in a way that had at one time been conceivable only with cadavers. This new clinical discourse about "the body" created and caused to emerge new objects of knowledge and information and introduced new, inescapable rituals into daily life, all of which became indispensable to the self-understandings, perceptions, and epistemologies of the participants in the new discourse. For the belief took hold that the descriptions that were elaborated in the course of these examinations truly grasped and reflected "reality."[6]

The dividing practices that were instituted in the spatial, temporal, and social compartmentalization of the nineteenth-century clinic worked in concert with the treatment of the body as a thing. Foucault introduced the term "dividing practices" to refer to modes of manipulation that combine a scientific discourse with practices of segregation and social exclusion in order to categorize, classify, distribute and manipulate subjects who are initially drawn from a rather undifferentiated mass of people. Through these practices, subjects become *objectivized* as (for instance) mad or sane, sick or healthy, criminal or good. Through these practices of division, classification, and ordering, furthermore, subjects become tied to an identity and come to understand themselves scientifically.[7] In short, this "subject" must not be confused with modern philosophy's *cogito*, autonomous self, or rational moral agent.

Technologies of normalization facilitate the systematic creation, identification, classification, and control of social anomalies by which some subjects can be divided from others. Foucault explains the rationale behind normalizing technologies in this way:

> [A] power whose task is to take charge of life needs continuous regulatory and corrective mechanisms…Such a power has to qualify, measure, appraise, and hierarchize, rather than display itself in its murderous splendor; it does not have to draw the line that separates the enemies of the sovereign from his obedient subjects; …it effects distributions around the norm … [T]he law operates more and more as a norm, and …the juridical institution is increasingly incorporated into a continuum of apparatuses (medical, administrative, and so on) whose functions are for the most part regulatory.[8]

The power of the modern state to produce an ever-expanding and increasingly totalizing web of social control is inextricably intertwined with and dependent upon its capacity to generate an increasing specification of individuality in this way. As John Rajchman puts it, the "great complex idea of normality" has become the means through which to identify subjects and make them identify themselves in ways that make them governable.[9]

The approach to the "objects" of bio-medicine that I have outlined relies upon an anti-realism that conflicts with the ontological assumptions that condition dominant discourses of disability theory. In addition, this approach assumes a conception of power that runs counter to the conception of power those discourses on disability take for granted.

Generally speaking, disability theorists and researchers (and activists) continue to construe the phenomena of disablement within what Foucault calls a "juridico-discursive" notion of power. In the terms of juridical conceptions, power is a fundamentally repressive thing possessed, and exercised over others, by an external authority such as a particular social group, a class, an institution, or the state. The "social model of disability," in whose framework a growing number of theorists and researchers conduct their work, is an example of the juridical conception of power that predominates in Disability Studies. Developed to oppose "individual" or "medical" models of disability, which represent that state of affairs as the detrimental consequences of an intrinsic deficit or personal flaw, the "social model" has two terms of reference, which are taken to be mutually exclusive. They are: *impairment* and *disability*.[10] As the formalized articulation of a set of principles generated by the Union for the Physically Impaired Against Segregation (UPIAS), the social model defines *impairment* as "the lack of a limb or part thereof or a defect of a limb, organ or mechanism of the body." By contrast, *disability* is defined as "a form of disadvantage which is imposed on top of one's impairment, that is, the disadvantage or restriction of activity caused by a contemporary social organization that takes little or no account of people with physical impairments."[11] Thus, Michael Oliver (one of the first proponents of the model) stresses that although "disablement *is* nothing to do with the body," impairment is "*nothing less than a description of the physical body.*"[12]

Several interlocutors within Disability Studies have variously objected that insofar as proponents of the social model have forced a strict separation between the categories of impairment and disability, the former category has remained untheorized.[13] Bill Hughes and Kevin Paterson have remarked, for example, that although the impairment-disability distinction de-medicalizes disability, it renders the impaired body the exclusive jurisdiction of medical interpretation.[14] I contend that this amounts to a failure to analyze how the sort of bio-medical practices in whose analysis Foucault specialized have been complicit in the historical emergence of the category of impairment and contribute to its persistence.

Hughes and Paterson allow that the approach to disability that I recommend would be a worthwhile way to map the constitution of impairment and examine how regimes of truth about disabled bodies have been central to governance of them.[15] These authors claim nevertheless that the approach ultimately entails the "theoretical elimination of the material, sensate, palpable body."[16] This argument begs the question, however; for the materiality of the "(impaired) body" is precisely that which ought to be contested. In the words of Judith Butler, "there is no reference to a pure body which is not at the same time a further formation of that body."[17] Moreover, the historical approach to disability that I recommend does not deny the materiality of the body; rather, the approach assumes that the materiality of "the body" cannot be dissociated from the historically contingent practices that bring it into being, that is, bring it into being as that sort of thing. Indeed, it seems politically naive to suggest that the term "impairment" is value-neutral, that is, "merely descriptive," as if there could ever be a description that was not also a *prescription* for the formulation of the object (person, practice, or thing) to which it is claimed to innocently refer.[18] Truth-discourses that purport to describe phenomena contribute to the construction of their objects.

It is by now a truism that intentional action always takes place under a description. The possible courses of action from which people may choose, as well as their behavior, self-perceptions, habits, and so on are not independent of the descriptions available to them under which they may act; nor do the available descriptions occupy some vacuous discursive space. Rather, descriptions, ideas, and classifications work in a cultural matrix of institutions, practices, power relations, and material interactions between people and things. Consider, for example, the classification of "woman refugee." The classification of "woman refugee" not only signifies a person; it is in addition a legal entity, and a paralegal one to which immigration boards, schools, social workers, activists, and others classified in that way may refer. One's classification (or not) as a "woman refugee," moreover, may mean the difference between escaping from a war-torn country, obtaining safe shelter, and receiving social assistance and medical attention, or not having access to any of these.[19] In short, the ways in which concepts, classifications, and descriptions are imbricated in institutional practices, social policy, intersubjective relations, and medical discourses structure the field of possible action for humans.

This, then, is the place in which to make explicit the notion of power upon which my argument relies. Following Foucault, I assume that power is more a question of *government* than one of confrontation between adversaries. Foucault uses the term "government" in its broad, sixteenth-century sense, which encompasses any mode of action, more or less considered and calculated, that is bound to structure the field of possible action of others.[20] Discipline is the name that Foucault gives to forms of government that are designed to produce a "docile" body, that is, one that can be subjected, used, transformed, and improved.[21] Disciplinary practices enable subjects to act in order to constrain them.[22] For juridical power *is* power (as opposed to mere physical force or violence) only when it addresses individuals who are free to act in one way or another. Despite the fact that power appears to be repressive, the exercise of power consists in guiding the possibilities of conduct and putting in order the possible outcomes. The production of these practices, these *limits* of possible conduct, furthermore, is a concealing. Concealment of these practices allows the naturalization and legitimation of the discursive formation in which they circulate.[23] To put the point another way, the production of seeming acts of choice (*limits* of possible conduct) on the everyday level of the subject makes possible hegemonic power structures.

In what follows, I will show that the allegedly real entity called "impairment" is an effect of the forms of power that Foucault identifies. I take what might seem a circuitous route to arrive at this thesis. For in order to indicate how bio-power naturalizes and materializes its objects, I trace a genealogy of practices in various disciplinary domains (clinical psychology, medico-surgical, and feminist) that produce two "natural" sexes. In turn, I draw upon these analyses in order to advance my argument that "impairment" (the foundational premise of the social model) is an historical artifact of this regime of knowledge/power.

Both "natural sex" and "natural impairment" have circulated in discursive and concrete practices as nonhistorical (biological) matter of the body, which is molded by time and class, is culturally shaped, or *on which* culture is imprinted. The matter of sex and of impairment itself has remained a prediscursive, that is, politically neutral, given. When we acknowledge that matter is an *effect* of certain historical conditions and contingent relations of social power, however, we can begin to identify and resist the ways in which these factors have material-*ized* it.

Governing Sex and Gender

In the first edition (1933) of the Oxford English Dictionary, there is no entry for "gender" that describes it as a counterpart to "sex" in the modern sense; instead, in the first edition of the OED, "gender" is described as a direct substitute for sex. In the second edition (1962) of the OED, a section appended to the main entry for "gender" reads: "In mod[ern]. (esp. feminist) use, a euphemism for the sex of a human being, often intended to emphasize the social and cultural, as opposed to biological, distinctions between the sexes." Examples cited to demonstrate this usage include ones taken from feminist scholarship in addition to ones drawn from earlier clinical literature on gender role and identity that developed out of research on intersexuality ("hermaphroditism") in the 1950s.[24]

In fact, it was in the context of research on intersex that Johns Hopkins psychologist John Money and his colleagues, the psychiatrists John and Joan Hampson, introduced the term "gender" to refer to the psycho-social aspects of sex identity. For Money and his colleagues, who at the time aimed to develop protocols for the treatment of intersexuality, required a theory of identity that would enable them to determine which of two "sexes" to assign to their clinical subjects. They deemed the concept of *gender* (construed as the psycho-social dimensions of "sex") as one that would enable them to make these designations.[25]

In 1972, Money and Anke Ehrhardt popularized this idea that sex and gender comprise two separate categories. The term "sex," they instructed, refers to physical attributes that are anatomically and physiologically determined; by contrast, the term "gender," they said, refers to the internal conviction that one is either male or female (gender identity) and the behavioral expressions of that conviction.[26] They claimed that their theory of gender identity enabled medical authorities to understand the experience of a given subject who was manifestly one "sex," but who wished to be its ostensible other. Nevertheless, in the terms of their sex-gender paradigm, "normal development" was defined as congruence between one's "gender identity" and one's "sexual anatomy."[27] Indeed, although Money and his colleagues concluded from their studies with intersexed people that neither sexual behavior nor orientation as "male" or "female" have an innate, or instinctive, basis, they did not recant the foundational assumption of their theory, namely, there are only two sexes. To the contrary, they continued to maintain that intersexuality resulted from fundamentally *abnormal* processes; thus, they insisted that their patients required immediate treatment because they *ought* to have become either a male or a female.[28]

Despite the prescriptive residue of the sex-gender formation, it appealed to early "second-wave" feminists because of its motivational assumption that everyone has a "gender identity" that is detachable from each one's so-called "sex." Without questioning the realm of anatomical or biological sex, feminists took up the sex-gender paradigm in order to account for culturally specific forms of an allegedly universal oppression of women.

The distinction between sex and gender that Gayle Rubin articulated in 1975 through an appropriation of structuralist anthropology and Lacanian psychoanalysis has arguably been the most influential one in feminist discourse. By drawing on Claude Levi-Strauss's nature-culture distinction, Rubin cast *sex* as a natural (i.e., prediscursive) property (attribute) of bodies and *gender* as its culturally specific configuration. As Rubin explained it, "Every society has a sex-gender system—a set of arrangements by which the biological raw material of human sex and procreation is shaped by human, social intervention and satisfied in a conventional manner."[29] For Rubin, in other words, sex is a product of nature as gender is a product of culture.

The structuralist nature-culture distinction on which Rubin's sex-gender distinction relies was putatively invented to facilitate cross-cultural anthropological analyses; however, the universalizing framework of structuralism obscures the multiplicity of cultural configurations of "nature." Because structuralist analysis presupposes that nature is prediscursive (that is, prior to culture) and singular, it cannot interrogate what counts as "nature" within a given cultural and historical context, in accordance with what interests, whose interests, and for what purposes.[30] In fact, the theoretical device known as the nature-culture distinction is already circumscribed within a culturally-specific epistemological frame. As Sandra Harding remarks, the way in which contemporary western society distinguishes between nature and culture is both modern and culture-bound. In addition, the culture-nature distinction is interdependent on a field of other binary oppositions that have structured western modes of thought. Some of these others are: reason-emotion, mind-body, objectivity-subjectivity, and male-female. In the terms of this dichotomous thinking, the former term of each respective pair is privileged and assumed to provide the *form* for the latter term of the pair, whose very recognition is held to depend upon (that is, *require)* the transparent and stable existence of that former term.[31] In the terms of this dichotomous thinking, furthermore, any thing (person, object, or state of affairs) that threatens to undermine the stable existence of the former term, or to reveal its artifactual character (and hence the artifactual character of the opposition itself) must be obscured, excluded, or nullified.

To be sure, some feminists early criticized the nature-culture distinction and identified binary discourse as a dimension of the domination of those who inhabit "natural" categories (women, people of color, animals, and the non-human environment).[32] These early feminist critiques of the nature-culture distinction did not, however, extend to one of its derivatives: the sex-gender distinction. Donna Haraway asserts that feminists did not question the sex-gender distinction because it was too useful a tool with which to counter arguments for biological determinism in "sex difference" political struggles.[33]

The political and explanatory power of the category of gender depend precisely upon relativizing and historicizing the category of sex, as well as the categories of biology, race, body, and nature. Each of these categories has, in its own way, been regarded as foundational to gender; yet, none of them is an objective entity with a transhistorical and transcultural identity. In this regard, Nigerian anthropologist Oyeronke Oyewumi, for one, has criticized European and Euro-American feminists for their proposition according to which all cultures "organize their social world through a perception of human bodies as male or female." Oyewumi's criticism puts into relief how the imposition of a system of gender can alter how racial and ethnic differences are understood. In a detailed analysis, Oyewumi shows that in Yoruba culture, relative age is a far more significant social organizer than sex. Yoruba pronouns, for example, indicate who is older or younger than the speaker; they do not make reference to "sex."[34] In short, the category of sex (as well as the categories of biology, race, body, and nature) must be considered in the specific historical and cultural contexts in which it has emerged as salient.

Foucault makes remarks in another context that cast further suspicion on how the construct of an allegedly prediscursive "nature" operates within the terms of the sex-gender distinction. While the category of "sex" is generally taken to be a self-evident fact of nature and biology, Foucault contends that "sex is the most speculative, most ideal, and most internal element in a deployment of sexuality organized by power in its grip on bodies and their materiality, their forces, energies, sensations, and pleasures."[35] For Foucault, the materialization and naturalization of "sex" are integral to the operations of bio-power. In the final chapter of volume one of *The History of Sexuality*, Foucault explains that "the notion of 'sex' made it possible to group together, in an artificial unity, anatomical elements, biological functions, conducts, sensations, and pleasures, and it enabled one to make use of this fictitious unity as a causal principle, an omnipresent meaning."[36] In other words, the category of "sex" is actually a phantasmatic *effect* of hegemonic power which comes to pass as the *cause* of a naturalized heterosexual human desire.

Now, it might seem counterintuitive to claim (as Foucault does) that there is no such thing as "sex" prior to its circulation in discourse, for "sex" is generally taken to be the most fundamental, most value-neutral aspect of an individual. Thus, one might wish to object that even a die-hard anti-realist must admit that there are certain sexually differentiated parts, functions, capacities, and hormonal and chromosomal differences that exist for human bodies. I should emphasize, therefore, that my argument does not entail the denial of material differences between bodies. Rather, my argument is that these differences are always already signified and formed by discursive and institutional practices. In short, what counts as "sex" is actually formed through a series of contestations over the criteria used to distinguish between two natural sexes, which are alleged to be mutually exclusive.[37] Because "sex" inhabits haunted terrain in this way, an array of scientific, medical, and social discourses must be continuously generated to refresh its purportedly definitive criteria. Of course, dominant beliefs about gender infect these discourses, conditioning what kinds of knowledge scientists endeavor to produce about sex in the first place. As the work on intersexuality of Fausto-Sterling and others shows, however, the regulatory force of knowledge/power about the category of sex is nevertheless jeopardized by the birth of infants whose bodies do not conform to normative ideals of sexual dimorphism, that is, infants who are both "male" and "female," or neither.

Recall that Money and his colleagues appraised intersexed bodies to be "abnormal" and in need of immediate medical treatment, despite concluding that sexed identity had no instinctual or innate basis. The clinical literature produced by those upon whom authority is conferred to make such pronouncements is in fact replete with references to the birth, or expected birth, of an intersexed infant as (for instance) "a medical emergency," "a neonatal surgical emergency," and "a devastating problem."[38] Since this is the almost universal reaction of medical practitioners to the birth (or expected birth) of an intersexual baby, substantial resources are mobilized to "correct" these so-called *unfortunate errors of nature*, including genetic "therapies" known to carry risks to the unborn, multiple surgeries that often result in genital insensitivity from repeated scarring, and life-long regimens of hormone treatments.[39] That these culturally condoned practices of genetic manipulation, surgical mutilation, and chemical control (these *technologies of normalization*) circulate as remedial measures performed on the basis of spurious projections about the future best interests of a given infant de-politicizes their disciplinary character; in addition, the role they play in naturalizing binary sex-gender and upholding heterosexual normativity remains disguised.

The argument according to which "sex" is an effect of contingent discursive practices is likely to encounter significant resistance from the domains of evolutionary and molecular biology (among others). I should underscore, therefore, that these disciplines do not stand apart from other discourses of knowledge/power about sex. On the contrary, social and political discourses on sex-gender have contributed to the production of evolutionary arguments and descriptions used in the physiology of reproduction, as well as to the identification of the objects of endocrinology (hormone science). From genitalia, to the anatomy of the gonads, and then to human chemistry, the signs of gender have been thoroughly integrated into human bodies. Fausto-Sterling points out, for example, that by defining as "sex hormones" groups of cells that are, in effect, multi-site chemical growth regulators, researchers *gendered* the chemistry of the body and rendered nearly invisible the far-reaching, non-sexual roles these regulators play in "male" and "female" development. As Fausto-Sterling explains it, with each choice these scientists and researchers made about how to measure and name the molecules they studied, they naturalized prevailing cultural ideas about gender.[40] In short, the emergence of scientific accounts about sex in particular and human beings in general can be understood only if scientific discourses and social discourses are seen as inextricable elements of a cultural matrix of ideas and practices.

Consider that if the category of sex is itself a *gendered* category (that is, politically invested and naturalized, but not natural), then there really is no *ontological* distinction between sex and gender. As Butler explains it, the category of "sex" cannot be thought as prior to gender as the sex-gender distinction assumes, since gender is required in order to think "sex" at all.[41] In other words, gender is not the product of culture and sex is not the product of nature, as Rubin's distinction implies. Instead, gender is the means through which "sexed nature" is produced and established as *natural*, as *prior to* culture, and as a politically neutral surface *on which* culture acts.[42] Rather than the manifestation of some residing essence or substrate, moreover, "gender identity" is the stylized *performance* of gender, that is, the sum total of acts believed to be produced as its "expression."

The claim that relations of power animate the production of sex as the naturalized foundation of gender draws upon Foucault's argument that juridical systems of power generate the subjects they subsequently come to represent. Recall that although juridical power appears to regulate political life in purely negative (repressive) terms by prohibiting and controlling subjects, it actually governs subjects by guiding, influencing, and limiting their actions in ways that seem to accord with the exercise of their freedom; that is, juridical power enables subjects to act in order to constrain them. By virtue of their subjection to such structures, subjects are in effect formed, defined, and reproduced in accordance with the requirements of them. That the practices of gender performance (construed as the cultural expression of a "natural sex") seem to be dictated by individual choice, therefore, conceals the fact that complicated networks of power have already limited the possible interpretations of that performance.[43] For only those genders that conform to highly regulated norms of cultural intelligibility may be lived without risk of reprisal.

The Subject of Impairment

Tom Shakespeare has claimed that the "achievement" of the U.K. disability movement (informed by the social model) has been to "break the causal link" between "our bodies" (impairment) and "our social situation" (disability).[44] Recall that the social model was intended to counter "individual" (or "medical") models of disability that conceptualized that state of affairs as the unfortunate consequences of a personal attribute or characteristic. In the terms of the social model, impairment neither equals, nor causes, disability; rather, disability is a form of social disadvantage that is imposed on top of one's impairment. In addition, impairment is represented as a real entity, with unique and characteristic properties, whose identity is distinguishable from, though may intersect with, the identities of an assortment of other bodily "attributes."

Proponents of the social model explicitly argue: (1) disablement is not a necessary consequence of impairment, and (2) impairment is not a sufficient condition for disability. Nevertheless, an unstated premise of the model is: (3) impairment is a necessary condition for disability. For proponents of the model do not argue that people who are excluded, or discriminated against, on the basis of (say) skin color are by virtue of that fact disabled, nor do they argue that racism is a form of disability. Equally, intersexed people who are socially stigmatized, and who may have been surgically "corrected" in infancy or childhood, do not seem to qualify as "disabled."[45] On the contrary, only people who *have* or are presumed to *have* an "impairment" get to count as "disabled." Thus, the strict division between the categories of impairment and disability that the social model is claimed to institute is in fact a chimera.

Notice that if we combine the foundational (i.e., necessary) premise of the social model (impairment) with Foucault's argument that modern relations of power produce the subjects they subsequently come to represent (that is, *form* and *define* them by putting in place the limits of their possible conduct), then, it seems that subjects are produced who "have" impairments because this identity meets certain requirements of contemporary political arrangements. My discussion below of the U.K. government's Disability Living Allowance policy shows, for example, that in order to make individuals productive and governable within the juridical constraints of that regime, the policy actually contributes to the production of the "subject of impairment" that it is claimed to merely recognize and represent. Indeed, it would seem that the identity of the subject of the social model ("people with impairments") is actually formed in large measure by the political arrangements that the model was designed to contest. Consider that if the identity of the subject of the social model is actually produced in accordance with those political arrangements, then a social movement that grounds its claims to entitlement in that identity will inadvertently *extend* those arrangements.

If the "impairments" alleged to underlie disability are actually constituted in order to sustain, and even augment, current social arrangements, they must no longer be theorized as essential, biological characteristics (attributes) of a "real" body upon which recognizably disabling conditions are imposed. Instead, those allegedly "real" impairments must now be identified as constructs of disciplinary knowledge/power that are incorporated into the self-understandings of some subjects. As *effects* of an historically specific political discourse (namely, bio-power), impairments are materialized as universal attributes (properties) of subjects through the iteration and reiteration of rather culturally specific regulatory norms and ideals about (for example) human function and structure, competency, intelligence, and ability. As universalized attributes of subjects, furthermore, impairments are naturalized as an interior identity or essence *on which* culture acts in order to camouflage the historically contingent power relations that materialized them *as* natural.[46]

In short, impairment has been disability all along. Disciplinary practices into which the subject is inducted and divided from others produce the illusion that they have a prediscursive, or natural, antecedent (impairment), one that in turn provides the justification for the multiplication and expansion of the regulatory effects of these practices. The testimonials, acts, and enactments of the disabled subject are *performative* insofar as the allegedly "natural" impairment that they are purported to disclose, or manifest, has no existence prior to or apart from those very constitutive performances. That the discursive object called *impairment* is claimed to be the embodiment of natural deficit or lack, furthermore, obscures the fact that the constitutive power relations that define and circumscribe "impairment" have already put in place broad outlines of the forms in which that discursive object will be materialized.

Thus, it would seem that insofar as proponents of the social model claim that disablement is not an inevitable consequence of impairment, they misunderstand the productive constraints of modern power. For it would seem that the category of impairment emerged and in part persists in order to legitimize the disciplinary practices that generated it in the first place.

The public and private administration and management (government) of impairment contribute to its objectivization. In one of the only detailed applications of Foucauldian analyses to disability, Margrit Shildrick and Janet Price demonstrate how impairment is naturalized and materialized in the context of a particular piece of welfare policy—the U.K.'s Disability Living Allowance (DLA)—that is designed to distribute resources to those who need assistance with "personal care" and "getting around." Shildrick and Price argue that although the official rationale for the policy is to ensure that the particularity of certain individuals does not cause them to experience undue hardship that the welfare state could ameliorate, the questionnaire that prospective recipients must administer to themselves abstracts from the heterogeneity of *their own* bodies to produce a regulatory category—impairment—that operates as a homogeneous entity in the *social* body.[47]

The definitional parameters of the questionnaire, and indeed the motivation behind the policy itself, posit an allegedly pre-existing and stable entity (impairment) on the basis of regulatory norms and ideals about (for example) function, utility, and independence. By virtue of responses to the questions posed on the form, moreover, a potential recipient/subject is enlisted to elaborate individuated specifications of this impairment. In order to do this (and to produce the full and transparent report that the government bureaucrats demand), the given potential recipient must document the most minute experiences of pain, disruptions of a menstrual cycle, lapses of fatigue, and difficulty in operating household appliances and associate these phenomena in some way with this abstraction. Thus, through a performance of textual confession ("the more you can tell us, the easier it is for us to get a clear picture of what you need"), the potential recipient is made a subject of impairment (in addition to being made a subject of the state), and is rendered "docile," that is, one to be used, enabled, subjugated, and improved.[48]

Despite the fact that the questions on the DLA form seem intended to extract very idiosyncratic detail from subject/recipients, the differences that they produce are actually highly coordinated and managed ones. Indeed, the innumerable questions and subdivisions of questions posed on the form establish a system of differentiation and individuation whose totalizing effect is to grossly restrict individuality.[49] For the more individualizing the nature of the state's identification of us, the farther the reach of its normalizing disciplinary apparatus in the administration of our lives. This, Foucault believes, is a characteristic and troubling property of the development of the practice of government in western societies: the tendency toward a form of political sovereignty that is a government "of all and of each," one whose concerns are to totalize and to individualize.[50]

Because Foucault maintains that there is no outside of power, that power is everywhere, that it comes from everywhere,[51] some writers in Disability Studies have suggested that his approach is nihilistic, offering little incentive to the disabled people's movement.[52] Clearly, this conclusion ignores Foucault's dictum that "there is no power without potential refusal or revolt."[53] In fact, Foucault's governmentality approach holds that the disciplinary apparatus of the modern state that puts in place the limits of possible conduct by materializing discursive objects through the repetition of regulatory norms also, by virtue of that repetitive process, brings into discourse the very conditions for subverting that apparatus itself. The regime of bio-politics in particular has generated a new kind of counter-politics (one that Foucault calls "strategic reversibility"). For individuals and *juridically constituted* groups of individuals have responded to governmental practices directed in increasingly intimate and immediate ways to "life," by formulating needs and imperatives of that same "life" as the basis for political counter-demands.[54]

The disabled people's movement is a prime example of this sort of counter-discourse; that is, the disciplinary relations of power that produce subjects have also spawned a defiant movement whose organizing tool (the social model of disability) has motivated its subject to advance demands under the auspices of that subjectivity. The current state of disability politics could moreover be regarded as an historical effect of what Foucault describes as the "polymorphism" of liberal govern(-)mentality, which is its capacity to continually refashion itself in a practice of auto-critique.[55] Yet, insofar as the identity of that subject (people with impairments) is a naturalized construct of the relations of power that the model was designed to rebut, the subversive potential of claims that are grounded in it will actually be limited. As Wendy Brown argues, disciplinary power manages liberalism's production of politicized subjectivity by neutralizing (that is, re-*de*-politicizing) identity through normalizing practices. For politicized identity both produces and potentially accelerates that aspect of disciplinary society that incessantly characterizes, classifies, and specializes through on-going surveillance, unremitting registration, and perpetual assessment.[56] Identities of the subject of the social model can therefore be expected to proliferate, splinter, and collide with increasing frequency as individualizing and totalizing diagnostic and juridical categories offer ever more finely tuned distinctions between and varieties of (for instance) congenital and acquired impairments, physical, sensory, cognitive, language, and speech impairments, mental illnesses, chronic illnesses, and environmental illnesses, aphasia, dysphasia, dysplasia, and dysarthria, immune deficiency syndromes, attention deficit disorders, attention deficit hyperactivity disorders, and autism.

This, then, is the paradox of contemporary identity politics, a paradox with which Disability Studies and the disabled people's movement must soon come to terms. Many feminists have long since realized that a political movement whose organizing tools are identity-based shall inevitably be contested as exclusionary and internally hierarchical. As I suggest elsewhere, a disabled people's movement that grounds its claims to entitlement in the identity of its subject ("people with impairments") can expect to face similar criticisms from an ever-increasing number of constituencies that feel excluded from and refuse to identify with those demands for rights and recognition; in addition, minorities internal to the movement will predictably pose challenges to it, the upshot of which are that those hegemonic descriptions eclipse their respective particularities.[57]

In short, my argument is that the disabled people's movement should develop strategies for advancing claims that make no appeal to the very identity upon which that subjection relies. Brown suggests, for example, that counter-insurgencies ought to supplant the language of "I am" ("with its defensive closure on identity, its insistence on the fixity of position, and its equation of social with moral positioning") with the language of "I want this for us."[58] We should, in other words, formulate demands in terms of "what we want," not "who we are." In a rare prescriptive moment, Foucault too suggests that the target for insurgent movements in the present is to refuse subjecting individuality, not embrace it. As Foucault puts it, the political, ethical, social, philosophical problem of our day is not to liberate ourselves from the state and the state's institutions, but to liberate ourselves both from the state and the type of individualization that is linked to the state.[59]

The agenda for a critical Disability Studies movement, furthermore, should be to articulate the disciplinary character of that identity, that is, articulate the ways that disability has been naturalized *as* impairment by identifying the constitutive mechanisms of truth and knowledge within scientific and social discourses, policy, and medico-legal practice that have produced that contingent discursive object and continue to amplify its regulatory effects. Disability theorists and researchers ought to conceive of this form of inquiry as a "critical ontology of ourselves." A critical ontology of ourselves, Foucault writes, must not be considered as a theory, doctrine, or permanent body of knowledge; rather, this form of criticism must be conceived as a "limit-attitude," that is, an ethos, a philosophical life in which the critique of what we are is at the same time the historical analysis of the limits imposed on us.[60] In particular, the critical question that disability theorists engaged in an historical ontology would ask is this: Of what is given to us as universal, necessary, and obligatory, how much is occupied by the singular, the contingent, the product of arbitrary constraints? Lastly, a critical ontology of our current situation would be genealogical:

> [I]t will not deduce from the form of what we are what it is impossible for us to do and to know; but it will separate out, from the contingency that has made us what we are, the possibility of no longer being, doing, or thinking what we are, do or think. It is not seeking to make possible a metaphysics that has finally become a science; it is seeking to give new impetus, as far and wide as possible, to the undefined work of freedom.[61]

Notes

1. Michel Foucault, "Nietzsche, Genealogy, History," in Donald F. Bouchard (ed.), *Language, Counter-Memory, Practice: Selected Essays and Interviews by Michel Foucault*, trans. Donald F. Bouchard and Sherry Simon (Ithaca, N.Y.: Cornell University Press, 1977), p. 153.

2. See, for instance, Colin Barnes, "Theories of Disability and the Origins of the Oppression of Disabled People in Western Society," in Len Barton (ed.), *Disability and Society: Emerging Issues and Insights* (Harlow: Longman, 1996), pp. 43–60; Mark Priestley, "Constructions and Creations: Idealism, Materialism, and Disability Theory," *Disability & Society* 13 (1998): 75–94.

3. With an array of other diverse and even competing discourses, the nominalist approach to disability that I take in this paper has been identified as "idealist" and claimed to "lack...explanatory power." See Priestley, "Constructions and

Creations"; see also Carol Thomas, *Female Forms: Experiencing and Understanding Disability* (Buckingham: Open University Press, 1999). I contend, however, that these criticisms rely upon a misconstrual of those discourses in general and a misunderstanding of nominalism in particular.

4. See Ian Hacking, *The Social Construction of What?* (Cambridge, Mass.: Harvard University Press, 1999). See also Barry Allen, *Truth in Philosophy* (Cambridge, Mass.: Harvard University Press, 1993).

5. See Michel Foucault, "The Birth of Biopolitics," in *Ethics: Subjectivity and Truth*, ed. Paul Rabinow (New York: New Press, 1997), p. 73. See also Barry Allen, "Foucault and Modern Political Philosophy," in Jeremy Moss (ed.), *The Later Foucault* (London: Sage Publications, 1998), pp. 293–352; and "Disabling Knowledge," in G. Madison and M. Fairbairn (eds.), *The Ethics of Postmodernity* (Evanston: Northwestern University Press, 1999), 89–103.

6. Barbara Duden, *The Woman Beneath the Skin: A Doctor's Patients in Eighteenth-Century Germany*, trans. Thomas Dunlap (Cambridge, Mass.: Harvard University Press, 1991), pp. 1–4.

7. Michel Foucault, "The Subject and Power," appended to Hubert Dreyfus and Paul Rabinow, *Michel Foucault: Beyond Structuralism and Hermeneutics* (Chicago: University of Chicago Press, 1983), pp. 208, 212.

8. Michel Foucault, *The History of Sexuality, Vol. 1: An Introduction*, trans. Robert Hurley (New York: Random House, 1978), p. 144.

9. See John Rajchman, *Truth and Eros: Foucault, Lacan, and the Question of Ethics* (New York: Routledge, 1991), p. 104.

10. Michael Oliver, *The Politics of Disablement* (London: Macmillan Education, 1990), pp. 4–11.

11. UPIAS, *The Fundamental Principles of Disability* (London: Union of the Physically Impaired Against Segregation, 1976). See Michael Oliver, *Understanding Disability: From Theory to Practice* (London: Macmillan, 1996), p. 22.

12. Oliver, *Understanding Disability*. p. 35; emphasis added.

13. See, for instance, Tom Shakespeare and Nicholas Watson, "Habeamus Corpus? Sociology of the Body and the Issue of Impairment," paper presented at Quincentennial Conference on the History of Medicine, Aberdeen, 1995; Bill Hughes and Kevin Paterson, "The Social Model of Disability and the Disappearing Body: Towards a Sociology of Impairment," *Disability & Society* 12 (1997): 325–40; Mairian Corker, "Differences, Conflations and Foundations: The Limits to the 'Accurate' Theoretical Representation of Disabled People's Experience," *Disability & Society* 14 (1999): 627–42.

14. Hughes and Paterson, "Social Model," p. 330.

15. Ibid., p. 332.

16. Ibid., pp. 333–34. See also Shakespeare and Watson, "Habeamus Corpus?"

17. Judith Butler, *Bodies that Matter: On the Discursive Limits of 'Sex'* (New York: Routledge, 1993), p. 10.

18. Cf. Corker, "Differences, Conflations and Foundations."

19. Hacking, *The Social Construction of What?* pp. 31, 103–4.

20. Foucault, "The Subject and Power," p. 221.

21. Michel Foucault, *Discipline and Punish: The Birth of the Prison*, trans. Alan Sheridan (New York: Pantheon Books, 1977), p. 136.

22. Cf. Hughes and Paterson, "Social Model," p. 334.

23. Judith Butler, *Gender Trouble: Feminism and the Subversion of Identity*, 10th anniversary ed. (New York: Routledge, 1999), p. 2.

24. Bernice L. Hausman, *Changing Sex: Transsexualism, Technology, and the Idea of Gender* (Durham: Duke University Press, 1995), p. 7.

25. Ibid., passim.

26. John Money and Anke Ehrhardt, *Man and Woman, Boy and Girl* (Baltimore: Johns Hopkins University Press, 1972), p. 257; quoted in Anne Fausto-Sterling, *Sexing the Body: Gender Politics and the Construction of Sexuality* (New York: Basic Books, 2000), p. 4.

27. Fausto-Sterling, *Sexing the Body*, p. 7.

28. Ibid., p. 46.

29. Gayle Rubin, "The Traffic in Women: Notes on the 'Political Economy' of Sex," in Rayna R. Reiter (ed.), *Toward an Anthropology of Women* (New York: Basic Books, 1975), p. 165.

30. See Butler, *Gender Trouble*, p. 48.

31. Sandra Harding, "The Instability of the Analytical Categories of Feminist Theory," in Micheline R. Malson, Jean F. O'Barr, Sarah Westphal-Wihl, and Mary Wyer (eds.), *Feminist Theory in Practice and Process* (Chicago: University of Chicago Press, 1989), p. 31.

32. See, for example, Sandra Harding, *The Science Question in Feminism* (Ithaca: Cornell University Press, 1986), pp. 163–96.

33. Donna Haraway, "'Gender' for a Marxist Dictionary: The Sexual Politics of a Word," in *Simians, Cyborgs, and Women: The Reinvention of Nature* (New York: Routledge, 1991), p. 134.

34. Oyeronke Oyewumi, "De-confounding Gender: Feminist Theorizing and Western Culture, a Comment on Hawkesworth's 'Confounding Gender,'" *Signs* 23 (1998): 1049–62, p. 1053; quoted in Fausto-Sterling, *Sexing the Body*, pp. 19–20.

35. Foucault, *The History of Sexuality, Vol. 1*, p. 155.

36. Ibid.

37. See Butler, *Bodies that Matter*.

38. Fausto-Sterling, *Sexing the Body*, pp. 275–76 n. 1.

39. Fausto-Sterling, *Sexing the Body*. See also Cheryl Chase, "Affronting Reason," in Dawn Atkins (ed.), *Looking Queer: Body Image and Identity in Lesbian, Bisexual, Gay, and Transgender Communities* (New York: The Harrington Park Press, 1998); A.D. Dreger, *Hermaphrodites and the Medical Invention of Sex* (Cambridge, Mass.: Harvard University Press, 1998); Shelley Tremain, Review of Atkins (ed.), *Looking Queer: Body Image and Identity in Lesbian, Bisexual, Gay and Transgender Communities*, in *Disability Studies Quarterly* 18 (1998): 198–99; and Shelley Tremain, "Queering Disabled Sexuality Studies," *Journal of Sexuality and Disability* 18 (2000): 291–99.

40. Fausto-Sterling, *Sexing the Body*, pp. 147–59.

41. Butler, *Gender Trouble*, p. 143.

42. Ibid., pp. 10–11.

43. See Butler, *Gender Trouble*.

44. Tom Shakespeare, "A Response to Liz Crow," *Coalition* (September 1992), p. 40; quoted in Oliver, *Understanding Disability*, p. 39.

45. The analogical arguments that disability researchers and theorists make from "sex" not only reinstitute and contribute to the naturalization and materialization of binary sex—in addition, these arguments facilitate and contribute to the naturalization and materialization of impairment. To take one example, in order to argue that degrading cultural norms and values, exclusionary discursive and social practices, and biased representations produce disability, disability theorists have come to depend upon analogical arguments that illustrate how these phenomena operate in the service of sexism (e.g., Oliver, *The Politics of Disablement*). To take another example, the analogy from sexism is used to identify inconsistencies and double standards between the treatment of sexual discrimination in public policy and law and the treatment in the same domains of disability discrimination (e.g., Anita Silvers, David Wasserman, and Mary B. Mahowald, *Disability, Difference, Discrimination: Perspectives on Justice in Bioethics and Public Policy* [Lanham: Rowman & Littlefield, 1998]). The analogical structure of these arguments requires that one appeal to clear distinctions between males and females, and men and women, as well as assume a stable and distinct notion of impairment. In the terms of these analogical arguments, furthermore, "sex" and "impairment" are represented as separate and real entities, each with unique properties, and each of whose identity can be distinguished from that of the other. The heterosexual assumptions that condition this manner of argumentation in Disability Studies preclude consideration of the implications for work in the discipline of the questions that intersexuality raises (see Tremain, "Queering Disabled Sexuality Studies"; and Shelley Tremain, Review of Thomas, *Female Forms: Experiencing and Understanding Disability*, in *Disability & Society* 15 (2000): 825–29.

46. Cf. Paul Abberley, "The Concept of Oppression and the Development of a Social Theory of Disability," *Disability, Handicap & Society* 2 (1987): 5–19; and Carol Thomas, *Female Forms*.

47. Margrit Shildrick and Janet Price, "Breaking the Boundaries of the Broken Body," *Body & Society* 2 (1996): 93–113, p. 101.

48. Ibid., p. 102.

49. Ibid., pp. 101–2.

50. Foucault, "The Subject and Power"; Colin Gordon, "Governmental Rationality: An Introduction," in Graham Burchell, Colin Gordon, and Peter Miller (eds.), *The Foucault Effect: Studies in Governmentality* (Chicago: University of Chicago Press, 1991), p. 3.

51. Foucault, *The History of Sexuality, Vol. 1*, p. 93.

52. See, for example, Thomas, *Female Forms*, p. 137.

53. Michel Foucault, "Power and Sex," in *Politics, Philosophy, Culture: Interviews and Other Writings (1977–1984)*, ed. Lawrence D. Kritzman (London: Routledge, 1988), p. 84.

54. Gordon, "Governmental Rationality," p. 5.

55. Foucault, "The Birth of Biopolitics," pp. 74–77.

56. Wendy Brown, *States of Injury: Power and Freedom in Late Modernity* (Princeton: Princeton University Press, 1995), pp. 59, 65.

57. See Tremain, Review of Thomas, *Female Forms*.

58. Brown, *States of Injury*, p. 75.

59. Foucault, "The Subject and Power," p. 216.

60. Michel Foucault, "What is Enlightenment?" in *Ethics, Subjectivity and Truth*, p. 319.

61. Ibid., p. 315.

16

The Social Model of Disability

Tom Shakespeare

Introduction

In many countries of the world, disabled people and their allies have organised over the last three decades to challenge the historical oppression and exclusion of disabled people (Driedger, 1989; Campbell and Oliver, 1996; Charlton, 1998). Key to these struggles has been the challenge to over-medicalized and individualist accounts of disability. While the problems of disabled people have been explained historically in terms of divine punishment, karma or moral failing, and post-Enlightenment in terms of biological deficit, the disability movement has focused attention onto social oppression, cultural discourse, and environmental barriers.

The global politics of disability rights and deinstitutionalisation has launched a family of social explanations of disability. In North America, these have usually been framed using the terminology of minority groups and civil rights (Hahn, 1988). In the Nordic countries, the dominant conceptualisation has been the relational model (Gustavsson et al., 2005). In many countries, the idea of normalisation and social role valorisation has been inspirational, particularly amongst those working with people with learning difficulties (Wolfensburger, 1972). In Britain, it has been the social model of disability which has provided the structural analysis of disabled people's social exclusion (Hasler, 1993).

The social model emerged from the intellectual and political arguments of the *Union of Physically Impaired Against Segregation* (UPIAS). This network had been formed after Paul Hunt, a former resident of the Lee Court Cheshire Home, wrote to *The Guardian* newspaper in 1971, proposing the creation of a consumer group of disabled residents of institutions. In forming the organization and developing its ideology, Hunt worked closely with Vic Finkelstein, a South African psychologist, who had come to Britain in 1968 after being expelled for his anti-apartheid activities. UPIAS was a small, hardcore group of disabled people, inspired by Marxism, who rejected the liberal and reformist campaigns of more mainstream disability organisations such as the Disablement Income Group and the Disability Alliance. According to their policy statement (adopted December 1974), the aim of UPIAS was to replace segregated facilities with opportunities for people with impairments to participate fully in society, to live independently, to undertake productive work and to have full control over their own lives. The policy statement defined disabled people as an oppressed group and highlighted barriers:

> We find ourselves isolated and excluded by such things as flights of steps, inadequate public and personal transport, unsuitable housing, rigid work routines in factories and offices, and a lack of up-to-date aids and equipment. (UPIAS Aims paragraph 1)

Even in Britain, the social model of disability was not the only political ideology on offer to the first generation of activists (Campbell and Oliver, 1996). Other disabled-led activist groups had emerged, including the Liberation Network of People with Disabilities. Their draft Liberation Policy, published in 1981, argued that while the basis of social divisions in society was economic, these divisions were sustained by psychological beliefs in inherent superiority or inferiority. Crucially, the Liberation Network argued that people with disabilities, unlike other groups, suffered inherent problems because of their disabilities. Their strategy for liberation included: developing connections with other disabled people and creating an inclusive disability community for mutual support; exploring social conditioning and positive self-awareness; the abolition of all segregation; seeking control over media representation; working out a just economic policy; encouraging the formation of groups of people with disabilities.

However, the organization which dominated and set the tone for the subsequent development of the British disability movement, and of disability studies in Britain, was UPIAS. Where the Liberation Network was dialogic, inclusive and feminist, UPIAS was hard-line, male-dominated, and determined. The British Council of Organisations of Disabled People, set up as a coalition of disabled-led groups in 1981, adopted the UPIAS approach to disability. Vic Finkelstein and the other BCODP delegates to the first Disabled People's International World Congress in Singapore later that year, worked hard to have their definitions of disability adopted on the global stage (Driedger, 1989). At the same time, Vic Finkelstein, John Swain and others were working with the Open University to create an academic course which would promote and develop disability politics (Finkelstein, 1998). Joining the team was Mike Oliver, who quickly adopted the structural approach to understanding disability, and was to coin the term "social model of disability" in 1983.

What Is the Social Model of disability?

While the first UPIAS Statement of Aims had talked of social problems as an added burden faced by people with impairment, the Fundamental Principles of Disability discussion document, recording their disagreements with the reformist Disability Alliance, went further:

> In our view, it is society which disables physically impaired people. Disability is something imposed on top of our impairments, by the way we are unnecessarily isolated and excluded from full participation in society. Disabled people are therefore an oppressed group in society. (UPIAS, 1975)

Here and in the later development of UPIAS thinking are the key elements of the social model: the distinction between disability (social exclusion) and impairment (physical limitation) and the claim that disabled people are an oppressed group. Disability is now defined, not in functional terms, but as

> the disadvantage or restriction of activity caused by a contemporary social organisation which takes little or no account of people who have physical impairments and thus excludes them from participation in the mainstream of social activities. (UPIAS, 1975)

This redefinition of disability itself is what sets the British social model apart from all other socio-political approaches to disability, and what paradoxically gives the social model both its strengths and its weaknesses.

Key to social model thinking is a series of dichotomies:

1. Impairment is distinguished from disability. The former is individual and private, the latter is structural and public. While doctors and professions allied to medicine seek to remedy impairment, the real priority is to accept impairment and to remove disability. Here there is an analogy with feminism, and the distinction between biological sex (male and female) and social gender (masculine and feminine) (Oakley, 1972). Like gender, disability is a culturally and historically specific phenomenon, not a universal and unchanging essence.

2. The social model is distinguished from the medical or individual model. Whereas the former defines disability as a social creation—a relationship between people with impairment and a disabling society—the latter defines disability in terms of individual deficit. Mike Oliver writes:

> Models are ways of translating ideas into practice and the idea underpinning the individual model was that of personal tragedy, while the idea underpinning the social model was that of externally imposed restriction. (Oliver, 2004, 19)

Medical model thinking is enshrined in the liberal term "people with disabilities," and in approaches that seek to count the numbers of people with impairment, or to reduce the complex problems of disabled people to issues of medical prevention, cure or rehabilitation. Social model thinking mandates barrier removal, anti-discrimination legislation, independent living and other responses to social oppression. From a disability rights perspective, social model approaches are progressive, medical model approaches are reactionary.

3. Disabled people are distinguished from non-disabled people. Disabled people are an oppressed group, and often non-disabled people and organisations—such as professionals and charities—are the causes or contributors to that oppression. Civil rights, rather than charity or pity, are the way to solve the disability problem. Organisations and services controlled and run by disabled people provide the most appropriate solutions. Research accountable to, and preferably done by, disabled people offers the best insights.

For more than ten years, a debate has raged in Britain about the value and applicability of the social model (Morris, 1991; Crow, 1992; French, 1993; Williams, 1999; Shakespeare and Watson 2002). In response to critiques, academics and activists maintain that the social model has been misunderstood, misapplied, or even wrongly viewed as a social theory. Many leading advocates of the social model approach maintain that the essential insights developed by UPIAS in the 1970s still remain accurate and valid three decades later.

Strengths of the Social Model

As demonstrated internationally, disability activism and civil rights are possible without adopting social model ideology. Yet the British social model is arguably the most powerful form which social approaches to disability have taken. The social model is simple, memorable, and effective, each of which is a key requirement of a political slogan or ideology. The benefits of the social model have been shown in three main areas.

First, the social model, called "the big idea" of the British disability movement (Hasler, 1993), has been effective *politically* in building the social movement of disabled people. It is easily explained and understood, and it generates a clear agenda for social change. The social model offers a straightforward way of distinguishing allies from enemies. At its most basic, this reduces to the terminology people use: "disabled people" signals a social model approach, whereas "people with disabilities" signals a mainstream approach.

Second, by identifying social barriers to be removed, the social model has been effective *instrumentally* in the liberation of disabled people. Michael Oliver argues that the social model is a "practical tool, not a theory, an idea or a concept" (2004, 30). The social model demonstrates that the problems disabled people face are the result of social oppression and exclusion, not their individual deficits. This places the moral responsibility on society to remove the burdens which have been imposed, and to enable disabled people to participate. In Britain, campaigners used the social model philosophy to name the various forms of discrimination which disabled people (Barnes, 1991), and used this evidence as the argument by which to achieve the 1995 Disability Discrimination Act. In the subsequent decade, services, buildings and public transport have been required to be accessible to disabled people, and most statutory and voluntary organizations have adopted the social model approach.

Third, the social model has been effective *psychologically* in improving the self-esteem of disabled people and building a positive sense of collective identity. In traditional accounts of disability, people with impairments feel that they are at fault. Language such as "invalid" reinforce a sense of personal deficit and failure. The focus is on the individual, and on her limitations of body and brain. Lack of self-esteem and self-confidence is a major obstacle to disabled people participating in society. The social model has the power to change the perception of disabled people. The problem of disability is relocated from the individual, to the barriers and attitudes which disable her. It is not the disabled person who is to blame, but society. She does not have to change, society does. Rather than feeling self-pity, she can feel anger and pride.

Weaknesses of the Social Model

The simplicity which is the hallmark of the social model is also its fatal flaw. The social model's benefits as a slogan and political ideology are its drawbacks as an academic account of disability. Another problem is its authorship by a small group of activists, the majority of whom had spinal injury or other physical impairments and were white heterosexual men. Arguably, had UPIAS included people with learning difficulties, mental health problems, or with more complex physical impairments, or more representative of different experiences, it could not have produced such a narrow understanding of disability.

Among the weaknesses of the social model are:

1. The neglect of impairment as an important aspect of many disabled people's lives. Feminists Jenny Morris (1991), Sally French (1993), and Liz Crow (1992) were pioneers in this criticism of the social model neglect of individual experience of impairment:

> As individuals, most of us simply cannot pretend with any conviction that our impairments are irrelevant because they influence every aspect of our lives. We must find a way to integrate them into our whole experience and identity for the sake of our physical and emotional well-being, and, subsequently, for our capacity to work against Disability. [Crow, 1992, 7]

The social model so strongly disowns individual and medical approaches, that it risks implying that impairment is not a problem. Whereas other socio-political accounts of disability have developed the important insight that people with impaired are disabled by society as well as by their bodies, the social model suggests that people are disabled by society not by their bodies. Rather than simply opposing medicalization, it can be interpreted as rejecting medical prevention, rehabilitation or cure of impairment, even if this is not what either UPIAS, Finkelstein, Oliver, or Barnes intended. For individuals with static impairments, which do not degenerate or cause medical complications, it may be possible to regard disability as entirely socially created. For those who have degenerative conditions which may cause premature death, or which any condition which involves pain and discomfort, it is harder to ignore the negative aspects of impairment. As Simon Williams has argued,

> . . . endorsement of disability solely as social oppression is really only an option, and an erroneous one at that, for those spared the ravages of chronic illness. (Williams, 1999, 812)

Carol Thomas (1999) has tried to develop the social model to include what she calls "impairment effects," in order to account for the limitations and difficulties of medical conditions. Subsequently, she subsequently suggested that a relational interpretation of the social model enables disabling aspects to be attributed to impairment, as well as social oppression:

> once the term "disability" is ring-fenced to mean forms of oppressive social reactions visited upon people with impairments, there is no need to deny that impairment and illness cause some restrictions of activity, or that in many situations both disability and impairment effects interact to place limits on activity. (2004, 29)

One curious consequence of the ingenious reformulation is that only people with impairment who face oppression can be called disabled people. This relates to another problem:

2. The social model assumes what it needs to prove: that disabled people are oppressed. The sex/gender distinction defines gender as a social dimension, not as oppression. Feminists claimed that gender relations *involved* oppression, but did not define gender relations *as* oppression. However, the social model defines disability as oppression. In other words, the question is not whether disabled people are oppressed in a particular situation, but only the extent to which they are oppressed. A circularity enters into disability research: it is logically impossible for a qualitative researcher to find disabled people who are not oppressed.

3. The analogy with feminist debates about sex and gender highlights another problem: the crude distinction between impairment (medical) and disability (social). Any researcher who does qualitative research with disabled people immediately discovers that in everyday life it is very hard to distinguish clearly between the impact of impairment, and the impact of social barriers (see Watson, 2002; Sherry, 2002). In practice, it is the interaction of individual bodies and social environments which produces disability. For example, steps only become an obstacle if someone has a mobility impairment: each element is necessary but not sufficient for the individual to be disabled. If a person with multiple sclerosis is depressed, how easy is it to make a causal separation between the effect of the impairment itself; her reaction to having an impairment; her reaction to being oppressed and excluded on the basis of having an impairment; other, unrelated reasons for her to be depressed? In practice, social and individual aspects are almost inextricable in the complexity of the lived experience of disability.

Moreover, feminists have now abandoned the sex/gender distinction, because it implies that sex is not a social concept. Judith Butler (1990) and others show that what we think of as sexual difference is always viewed through the lens of gender. Shelley Tremain (2002) has claimed similarly that the social model treats impairment as an unsocialized and universal concept, whereas, like sex, impairment is always already social.

4. The concept of the barrier-free utopia. The idea of the enabling environment, in which all socially imposed barriers are removed, is usually implicit rather than explicit in social model thinking, although it does form the title of a major academic collection (Swain et al., 1993). Vic Finkelstein (1981) also wrote a simple parable of a village designed for wheelchair users to illustrate the way that social model thinking turned the problem of disability on its head. Yet despite the value of approaches such as Universal Design, the concept of a world in which people with impairments were free of environmental barriers is hard to operationalize.

For example, numerous parts of the natural world will remain inaccessible to many disabled people: mountains, bogs, beaches are almost impossible for wheelchair users to traverse, while sunsets, birdsong, and other aspects of nature are difficult for those lacking sight or hearing to experience. In urban settings, many barriers can be mitigated, although historic buildings often cannot easily be adapted. However, accommodations are sometimes incompatible because people with different impairments may require different solutions: blind people prefer steps and defined curbs and indented paving, while wheelchair users need ramps, dropped curbs, and smooth surfaces. Sometimes, people with the same impairment require different solutions: some visually impaired people access text in Braille, others in large print, audio tape or electronic files. Practicality and resource constraints make it unfeasible to overcome every barrier: for example, the New York subway and London Underground systems would require huge investments to make every line and station accessible to wheelchair users. A copyright library of five million books could never afford to provide all these texts in all the different formats that visually impaired users might potentially require. In these situations, it seems more practical to make other arrangements to overcome the problems: for example, Transport for London have an almost totally accessible fleet of buses, to compensate those who cannot use the tube, while libraries increasingly have arrangements to make particular books accessible on demand, given notice.

Moreover, physical and sensory impairments are in many senses the easiest to accommodate. What would it mean to create a barrier free utopia for people with learning difficulties? Reading and writing and other cognitive abilities are required for full participation in many areas of contemporary life in developed nations. What about people on the autistic spectrum, who may find social contact difficult to cope with: a barrier free utopia might be a place where they did not have to meet, communicate with, or have to interpret other people. With many solutions to the disability problem, the concept of addressing special needs seems more coherent than the concept of the barrier free utopia. Barrier free enclaves are possible, but not a barrier free world.

While environments and services can and should be adapted wherever possible, there remains disadvantage associated with having many impairments which no amount of environmental change could entirely eliminate. People who rely on wheelchairs, or personal assistance, or other provision are more vulnerable and have fewer choices than the majority of able-bodied people. When Michael Oliver claims that

> An aeroplane is a mobility aid for non-flyers in exactly the same way as a wheelchair is a mobility aid for non-walkers. (Oliver, 1996, 108)

his suggestion is amusing and thought provoking, but cannot be taken seriously. As Michael Bury has argued,

> It is difficult to imagine any modern industrial society (however organised) in which, for example, a severe loss of mobility or dexterity, or sensory impairments, would not be 'disabling' in the sense of restricting activity to some degree. The reduction of barriers to participation does not amount to abolishing disability as a whole. (Bury, 1997, 137)

Drawing together these weaknesses, a final and important distinction needs to be made. The disability movement has often drawn analogies with other forms of identity politics, as I have done in this chapter. The disability rights struggle has even been called the "Last Liberation Movement" (Driedger, 1989). Yet while disabled people do face discrimination and prejudice, like women, gay and lesbian people, and minority ethnic communities, and while the disability rights movement does resemble in its forms and activities many of these other movements, there is a central and important difference. There is nothing intrinsically problematic about being female or having a different sexual orientation, or a different skin pigmentation or body shape. These other experiences are about wrongful limitation of negative freedom. Remove the social discrimination, and women and people of color and gay and lesbian people will be able to flourish and participate. But disabled people face both discrimination and intrinsic limitations. This claim has three implications. First, even if social barriers are removed as far as practically possible, it will remain disadvantageous to have many forms of impairment. Second, it is harder to celebrate disability than it is to celebrate Blackness, or Gay Pride, or being a woman. "Disability pride" is problematic, because disability is difficult to recuperate as a concept, as it refers either to limitation and incapacity, or else to oppression and exclusion, or else to both dimensions. Third, if disabled people are to be emancipated, then society will have to provide extra resources to meet the needs and overcome the disadvantage which arises from impairment, not just work to minimize discrimination (Bickenbach et al., 1999).

Beyond the Social Model?

In this chapter, I have tried to offer a balanced assessment of the strengths and weaknesses of the British social model of disability. While acknowledging the benefits of the social model in launching the disability movement, promoting a positive disability identity, and mandating civil rights legislation and barrier removal, it is my belief that the social model has now become a barrier to further progress.

As a researcher, I find the social model unhelpful in understanding the complex interplay of individual and environmental factors in the lives of disabled people. In policy terms, it seems to me that the social model is a blunt instrument for explaining and combating the social exclusion that disabled people face, and the complexity of our needs. Politically, the social model has generated a form of identity politics which has become inward looking and separatist.

A social approach to disability is indispensable. The medicalization of disability is inappropriate and an obstacle to effective analysis and policy. But the social model is only one of the available options for theorizing disability. More sophisticated and complex approaches are needed, perhaps building on the WHO initiative to create the International Classification of Functioning, Disability and Health. One strength of this approach is the recognition that disability is a complex phenomenon, requiring different levels of analysis and intervention, ranging from the medical to the socio-political. Another is the insight that disability is not a minority issue, affecting only those people defined as disabled people. As Irving Zola (1989) maintained, disability is a universal experience of humanity.

Bibliography

Barnes, C. (1991). *Disabled People in Britain and Discrimination*. London: Hurst and Co.

Bickenbach, J. E., Chatterji, S., Badley, E. M., and Ustun, T. B. (1999). "Models of Disablement, Universalism and the International Classification of Impairments, Disabilities and Handicaps." *Social Science and Medicine*, 48: 1173–1187

Butler, J (1990). *Gender Trouble: Feminism and the Subversion of Identity*. New York: Routledge.

Bury, M. (1997). *Health and Illness in a Changing Society*. London: Routledge.

Campbell, J. and Oliver, M. (1996). *Disability Politics: Understanding Our Past, Changing Our Future*. London: Routledge.

Charlton J (1998). *Nothing About Us Without Us: Disability, Oppression and Empowerment*. Berkeley: University of California Press.

Crow, L. (1992). "Renewing the Social Model of Disability." *Coalition*, July: 5–9

Dreidger, D. (1989). *The Last Civil Rights Movement*. London: Hurst.

Finkelstein, V. (1981). "To Deny or Not to Deny Disability." In *Handicap in a Social World*, edited by A Brehin et al. Sevenoaks: OUP/Hodder and Stoughton.

Finkelstein, V. (1998). "Emancipating disability studies." In *The Disability Reader: Social Science Perspectives,* edited by T. Shakespeare. London: Cassell.

French, S. (1993). "Disability, Impairment or Something in Between." In *Disabling Barriers, Enabling Environments*, edited by John Swain, Sally French, Colin Barnes, Carol Thomas London: Sage, 17–25.

Gustavsson, A., Sandvin, J., Traustadóttir, R., and Tossebrø, J (2005). *Resistance, Reflection and Change: Nordic disability research*. Lund, Sweden: Studentlitteratur..

Hahn, H. (1988). "The Politics of Physical Differences: Disability and Discrimination." *Journal of Social Issues*, 44 (1) 39–47

Hasler, F. (1993). "Developments in the Disabled People's Movement." In *Disabling Barriers, Enabling Environments*, edited by J. Swain , Sally French, Colin Barnes, Carol Thomas et al. London: Sage.

Oakley, A. (1972). *Sex, Gender and Society*. London: Maurice Temple Smith.

Oliver, M. (1996). *Understanding Disability: From Theory to Practice*. Basingstoke: Macmillan.

Oliver, M. (2004). "The Social Model in Action: If I Had a Hammer." In *Implementing the Social Model of Disability: Theory and Research*, edited by C. Barnes and G. Mercer.: Leeds: The Disability Press.

Morris, J. (1991). *Pride Against Prejudice*. London: Women's Press.

Shakespeare, T. and Watson, N. (2001). "The Social Model of Disability: An Outdated ideology?" In *Exploring Theories and Expanding Methodologies: Where Are We and Where Do We Need to Go? Research in Social Science and Disability volume 2*, edited by S. Barnarrt and B. M. Altman. Amsterdam: JAI.

Sherry, M. (2002). "If Only I Had a Brain." Unpublished PhD dissertation, University of Queensland.

Swain, J., Finkelstein, V., French, S., and Oliver, M.. eds. (1993). *Disabling Barriers, Enabling Environments*. London: OUP/ Sage.

Thomas, C. (1999). *Female Forms*. Buckingham: Open University Press.

Thomas, C. (2004). "Developing the Social Relational in the Social Model of Disability: A Theoretical Agenda." In *Implementing the Social Model of Disability: Theory and Rresearch*, edited by C. Barnes and G. Mercer. Leeds: The Disability Press.

Tremain, S. (2002). "On the Subject of Impairment." In *Disability/Postmodernity: Embodying Disability Theory*, edited by M. Corker and T. Shakespeare, pp. 32–47. London: Continuum.

Union of the Physically Impaired Against Segregation (1974/5). Policy Statement, available at http://www.leeds.ac.uk/disability-studies/archiveuk/archframe.htm; accessed August 10, 2005.

Union of the Physically Impaired Against Segregation (1975). Fundamental Principles, available at http://www.leeds.ac.uk/disability-studies/archiveuk/archframe.htm; accessed August 10, 2005.

Watson, N. (2002). "Well, I Know This Is Going to Sound Very Strange to You, But I Don't See Myself as a Disabled Person: Identity and Disability." *Disability and Society*, 17, 5, pp 509–528.

Williams, S. J. (1999). "Is Anybody There? Critical Realism, Chronic Illness, and the Disability Debate." *Sociology of Health and Illness*, 21, 6, pp 797–819

Wolfensberger, W. (1972). *The Principle of Normalization in Human Services*. Toronto: National Institute on Mental Retardation.

Zola, I. K. (1989). "Towards the Necessary Universalizing of a Disability Policy." *The Milbank Quarterly*, vol. 67, suppl.2, Pt. 2., 401–428.

17

Narrative Prosthesis and the Materiality of Metaphor

David Mitchell and Sharon Snyder

Literature and the Undisciplined Body of Disability

This chapter prefaces the close readings to come by deepening our theory of narrative prosthesis as shared characteristics in the literary representation of disability. We demonstrate one of a variety of approaches in disability studies to the "problem" that disability and disabled populations pose to all cultures. Nearly every culture views disability as a problem in need of a solution, and this belief establishes one of the major modes of historical address directed toward people with disabilities. The necessity for developing various kinds of cultural accommodations to handle the "problem" of corporeal difference (through charitable organizations, modifications of physical architecture, welfare doles, quarantine, genocide, euthanasia programs, etc.) situates people with disabilities in a profoundly ambivalent relationship to the cultures and stories they inhabit. The perception of a "crisis" or a "special situation" has made disabled people the subject of not only governmental policies and social programs but also a primary object of literary representation.

Our thesis centers not simply upon the fact that people with disabilities have been the object of representational treatments, but rather that their function in literary discourse is primarily twofold: disability pervades literary narrative, first, as a stock feature of characterization and, second, as an opportunistic metaphorical device. We term this perpetual discursive dependency upon disability *narrative prosthesis*. Disability lends a distinctive idiosyncrasy to any character that differentiates the character from the anonymous background of the "norm." To exemplify this phenomenon, the opening half of this chapter analyzes the Victorian children's story *The Steadfast Tin Soldier* in order to demonstrate that disability serves as a primary impetus of the storyteller's efforts. In the second instance, disability also serves as a metaphorical signifier of social and individual collapse. Physical and cognitive anomalies promise to lend a "tangible" body to textual abstractions; we term this metaphorical use of disability the *materiality of metaphor* and analyze its workings as narrative prosthesis in our concluding discussion of Sophocles' drama *Oedipus the King*. We contend that disability's centrality to these two principle representational strategies establishes a conundrum: while stories rely upon the potency of disability as a symbolic figure, they rarely take up disability as an experience of social or political dimensions.

While each of the chapters that follow set out some of the key cultural components and specific historical contexts that inform this history of disabled representations, our main objective addresses the development of a representational or "literary" history. By "literary" we mean to suggest a form of writing that explicitly values the production of what narrative theorists such as Barthes, Blanchot, and Chambers have referred to as "open-ended" narrative.[1] The identification of the open-ended narrative differentiates a distinctively "literary" component of particular kinds of storytelling: those texts that not only deploy but explicitly foreground the "play" of multiple meanings as a facet of their discursive production. While this definition does not overlook the fact that all texts are inherently "open" to a multiplicity of interpretations, our notion of literary narrative identifies works that *stage* the arbitrariness of linguistic sign systems as a characterizing feature of their plots and commentaries. Not only do the artistic and philosophical works under discussion here present themselves as available to a multiplicity of readings, they openly perform their textual *inexhaustibility*. Each shares a literary objective of destabilizing sedimented cultural meanings that accrue around ideas of bodily "deviance." Thus, we approach the writings of Montaigne, Nietzsche, Shakespeare, Melville, Anderson, Dunn, and an array of post-1945 American authors as writers who interrogate the objectives of narrative in general and the corporeal body in particular as discursive products. Their narratives all share a self-reflexive mode of address about their own textual production of disabled bodies.

This textual performance of ever-shifting and unstable meanings is critical in our interpretive approach to the representation of disability. The close readings that follow hinge upon the identification of disability as an ambivalent and mutable category of cultural and literary investment. Within literary narratives, disability serves as an interruptive force that confronts cultural truisms. The inherent vulnerability and variability of bodies serves literary narratives as a metonym for that which refuses to conform to the mind's desire for order and rationality. Within this schema, disability acts as a metaphor and fleshly example of the body's unruly resistance to the cultural desire to "enforce normalcy."[2] The literary narratives we discuss all deploy the mutable or "deviant" body as an "unbearable weight" (to use Susan Bordo's phrase) in order to counterbalance the "meaning-laden" and ethereal projections of the mind. The body's weighty materiality functions as a textual and cultural other—an object with its own undisciplined language that exceeds the text's ability to control it.

As many theorists have pointed out, this representational split between body and mind/text has been inherited from Descartes (although we demonstrate that disability has been entrenched in these assumptions throughout history). Keeping in mind that the perception of disability shifts from one epoch to another, and sometimes within decades and years, we want to argue that the disabled body has consistently held down a "privileged" position with respect to thematic variations on the mind/body split. Whether a culture approaches the body's materiality as a denigrated symbol of earthly contamination (such as in early Christian cultures), or as a perfectible *technē* of the self (as in ancient Athenian culture), or as an object of medical interpretation (as in Victorian culture), or as specular commodity in the age of electronic media (as is the case in postmodernism), disability perpetually serves as the symbolical symptom to be interpreted by discourses on the body. Whereas the "able" body has no definitional core (it poses as transparently "average" or "normal"), the disabled body surfaces as any body capable of being narrated as "outside the norm." Within such a representational schema, literary narratives revisit disabled bodies as a reminder of the "real" physical limits that "weigh down" transcendent ideals of the mind and knowledge-producing disciplines. In this sense, disability serves as the *hard kernel* or recalcitrant corporeal matter that cannot be deconstructed away by the textual operations of even the most canny narratives or philosophical idealisms.[3]

For our purposes in this book, the representation of disability has both allowed an interrogation of static beliefs about the body and also erupted as the unseemly *matter* of narrative that cannot be textually undone. We therefore forward readings of disability as a narrative device upon which the literary writer of "open-ended" narratives depends for his or her disruptive punch. Our phrase *narrative prosthesis* is meant to indicate that disability has been used throughout history as a crutch upon which literary narratives lean for their representational power, disruptive potentiality, and analytical insight. Bodies show up in stories as dynamic entities that resist or refuse the cultural scripts assigned to them. While we do not simply extol these literary approaches to the representation of the body (particularly in relation to recurring tropes of disability), we want to demonstrate that the disabled body represents a potent symbolic site of literary investment.

The reasons for this dependency upon disability as a device of characterization and interrogation are many, and our concept of narrative prosthesis establishes a variety of motivations that ground the narrative deployment of the "deviant" body. However, what surfaces as a theme throughout these chapters is the paradoxical impetus that makes disability into both a destabilizing sign of cultural prescriptions about the body *and* a deterministic vehicle of characterization for characters constructed as disabled. Thus, in works as artistically varied and culturally distinct as Shakespeare's *Richard III*, Montaigne's "Of Cripples," Melville's *Moby-Dick*, Nietzsche's *Thus Spoke Zarathustra*, Anderson's *Winesburg, Ohio*, Faulkner's *The Sound and the Fury*, Salinger's *The Catcher in the Rye*, Lee's *To Kill a Mockingbird*, Kesey's *One Flew Over the Cuckoo's Nest*, Dunn's *Geek Love*, Powers's *Operation Wandering Soul*, and Egoyan's *The Sweet Hereafter*, the meaning of the relationship between having a physical disability and the nature of a character's identity come under scrutiny. Disability recurs in these works as a potent force that challenges cultural ideals of the "normal" or "whole" body. *At the same time, disability also operates as the textual obstacle that causes the literary operation of open-endedness to close down or stumble.*

This "closing down" of an otherwise permeable and dynamic narrative form demonstrates the historical conundrum of disability. Characters such as Montaigne's "les boiteux," Shakespeare's "hunchback'd king," Melville's "crippled" captain, Nietzsche's interlocutory "throng of cripples," Anderson's storied "grotesques," Faulkner's "tale told by an idiot," Salinger's fantasized commune of deaf-mutes, Lee's racial and cognitive outsiders, Kesey's ward of acutes and chronics, Dunn's chemically altered freaks, and Power's postapocalyptic wandering children provide powerful counterpoints to their respective cultures' normalizing Truths about the construction of deviance in particular, and the fixity of knowledge systems in general. Yet each of these characterizations also evidences that the artifice of disability binds disabled characters to a programmatic (even deterministic) identity. Disability may provide an explanation for the origins of a character's identity, but its deployment usually proves either too programmatic or unerringly "deep" and mysterious. In each work analyzed in this book, disability is used to underscore, in the words of Richard Powers, adapting the theories of Lacan, that the body functions "like a language" as a dynamic network of misfirings and arbitrary adaptations (*Goldbug* 545). Yet, this defining corporeal unruliness consistently produces characters who are indentured to their biological programming in the most essentializing manner. Their disabilities surface to explain everything or nothing with respect to their portraits as embodied beings.

All of the above examples help to demonstrate one of the central assumptions undergirding this book: *disability is foundational to both cultural definition and to the literary narratives that challenge normalizing prescriptive ideals.* By contrasting and comparing the depiction of disability across cultures and histories, one realizes that disability provides an important barometer by which to assess shifting values and norms imposed upon the body. Our approach in the chapters that follow is to treat disability as a narrative device—an artistic prosthesis—that reveals the pervasive dependency of artistic, cultural, and philosophical discourses upon the powerful alterity assigned to people with disabilities. In short, disability characterization can be understood as a prosthetic contrivance upon which so many of our cultural and literary narratives rely.

The (In)visibility of Prosthesis

The hypothesis of this *discursive dependency* upon disability strikes most scholars and readers at first glance as relatively insubstantial. During a recent conference of the Herman Melville Society in Völös, Greece, we met a scholar from Japan interested in representations of disability in American literature. When asked if Japanese literature made use of disabled characters to the same extent as American and European literatures, he honestly replied that he had never encountered any. Upon further reflection, he listed several examples and laughingly added that of course the Nobel Prize winner Kenzaburo Oë wrote almost exclusively about the subject. This "surprise" about the pervasive nature of disabled images in national literatures catches even the most knowledgeable scholars unaware. Without developed models for analyzing the purpose and function of representational strategies of disability, readers tend to filter a multitude of disability figures absently through their imaginations.

For film scholarship, Paul Longmore has perceptively formulated this paradox, asking why we screen so many images of disability and simultaneously screen them out of our minds. In television and film portraits of disability, Longmore argues, this screening out occurs because we are trained to compartmentalize impairment as an isolated and individual condition of existence. Consequently, we rarely connect together stories of people with disabilities as evidence of a wider systemic predicament. This same phenomenon can be applied to other representational discourses.

As we discussed in our introduction to *The Body and Physical Difference*, our current models of minority representations tend to formulate this problem of literary/critical neglect in the obverse manner (5). One might expect to find the argument in the pages to come that disability is an ignored, overlooked, or marginal experience in literary narrative, that its absence marks an ominous silence in the literary repertoire of human experiences. In pursuing such an argument one could rightly redress, castigate, or bemoan the neglect of this essential life experience within discourses that might have seen fit to take up the important task of exploring disability in serious terms. Within such an approach, disability would prove to be an unarticulated subject whose real-life counterparts could then charge that their own social marginality was the result of an attendant representational erasure outside of medical discourses. Such a methodology would theorize that disability's absence proves evidence of a profound cultural repression to escape the reality of biological and cognitive differences.

However, what we hope to demonstrate in this book is that disability has an unusual literary history. Between the social marginality of people with disabilities and their corresponding representational milieus, disability undergoes a different representational fate. While racial, sexual, and ethnic criticisms have often founded their critiques upon a pervasive absence of their images in the dominant culture's literature, this book argues that images of disabled people abound in history.[4] Even if we disregard the fact that entire fields of study have been devoted to the assessment, cataloging, taxonomization, pathologization, objectification, and rehabilitation of disabled people, one is struck by disability's prevalence in discourses outside of medicine and the hard sciences. Once a reader begins to seek out representations of disability in our literatures, it is difficult to avoid their proliferation in texts with which one believed oneself to be utterly familiar. Consequently, as in the discussion of images of disability in Japanese literature mentioned above, the representational prevalence of people with disabilities is far from absent or tangential. As we discussed in the previous chapter, scholarship in the humanities study of disability has sought to pursue previously unexplored questions of the utility of disability to numerous discursive modes, including literature. Our hypothesis in *Narrative Prosthesis* is a paradoxical one: disabled peoples' social invisibility has occurred in the wake of their perpetual circulation throughout print history. This question is not simply a matter of stereotypes or "bad objects," to borrow Naomi Schor's phrase.[5] Rather, the interpretation of representations of disability strikes at the very core of cultural definitions and values. What is the significance of the fact that the earliest known cuneiform tablets catalog 120 omens interpreted from the "deformities" of Sumerian fetuses and irregularly shaped sheep's and calf's livers? How does one explain the disabled gods, such as the blind Hod, the one-eyed Odin, the one-armed Tyr, who are central to Norse myths, or Hephaestus, the "crook-footed god," in Greek literature? What do these modes of representation reveal about cultures as they forward or suppress physical differences? Why does the "visual" spectacle of so many disabilities become a predominating trope in the nonvisual textual mediums of literary narratives?

Supplementing the Void

What calls stories into being, and what does disability have to do with this most basic preoccupation of narrative? Narrative prosthesis (or the dependency of literary narratives upon disability) forwards the notion that all narratives operate out of a desire to compensate for a limitation or to reign in excess. This narrative approach to difference identifies the literary object par excellence as that which has become extraordinary—a deviation from a widely accepted norm. Literary narratives begin a process of explanatory compensation wherein perceived "aberrancies" can be rescued from ignorance, neglect, or misunderstanding for their readerships. As Michel de Certeau explains in his well-known essay "The Savage 'I,' " the new world travel narrative in the fifteenth and sixteenth centuries provides a model for thinking about the movement of all narrative. A narrative is inaugurated "by the search for the strange, which is presumed different from the place assigned it in the beginning by the discourse of the culture" from which it originates (69). The very need for a story is called into being when something has gone amiss with the known world, and, thus, the language of a tale seeks to comprehend that which has stepped out of line. In this sense, stories compensate for an unknown or unnatural deviance that begs an explanation.

Our notion of narrative prosthesis evolves out of this specific recognition: a narrative issued to resolve or correct—to "prostheticize" in David Wills's sense of the term—a deviance marked as improper to a social context. A simple schematic of narrative structure might run thus: first, a deviance or marked difference is exposed to a reader; second, a narrative consolidates the need for its own existence by calling for an explanation of the deviation's origins and formative consequences; third, the deviance is brought from the periphery of concerns to the center of the story to come; and fourth, the remainder of the story rehabilitates or fixes the deviance in some manner. This fourth step of the repair of deviance may involve an obliteration of the difference through a "cure," the rescue of the despised object from social censure, the extermination of the deviant as a purification of the social body, or the revaluation of an alternative mode of being. Since what we now call disability has been historically narrated as that which characterizes a body as deviant from shared norms of bodily appearance and ability, disability has functioned throughout history as one of the most marked and remarked upon differences that originates the act of storytelling. Narratives turn signs of cultural deviance into textually marked bodies.

In one of our six-year-old son's books entitled *The Steadfast Tin Soldier,* this prosthetic relation of narrative to physical difference is exemplified. The story opens with a child receiving a box of tin soldiers as a birthday gift. The twenty-five soldiers stand erect and uniform in every way, for they "had all been made from the same tin spoon" (Campbell 1). Each of the soldiers comes equipped with a rifle and bayonet, a blue and red outfit signifying membership in the same regiment, black boots, and a stern military visage. The limited omniscient narrator inaugurates the conflict that will propel the story by pointing out a lack in one soldier that mars the uniformity of the gift: "All of the soldiers were exactly alike, with the exception of one, who differed from the rest in having only one leg" (2). This unfortunate blemish, which mars the otherwise flawless ideal of the soldiers standing in unison, becomes the springboard for the story that ensues. The incomplete leg becomes a locus for attention, and from this imperfection a story issues forth. The twenty-four perfect soldiers are quickly left behind in the box for the reason of their very perfection and uniformity—the "ideal" or "intended" soldier's form promises no story. As Barbara Maria Stafford points out, "there [is] only a single way of being healthy and lovely, but an infinity of ways of being sick and wretched" (284). This infinity of ways helps to explain the pervasive dependency of literary narratives upon the trope of disability. Narrative interest solidifies only in the identification and pursuit of an anomaly that inaugurates the exceptional tale or the tale of exception.

The story of *The Steadfast Tin Soldier* stands in a prosthetic relation to the missing leg of the titular protagonist. The narrative in question (and narrative in a general sense) rehabilitates or compensates for its "lesser" subject by demonstrating that the outward flaw "attracts" the storyteller's—and by extension the reader's—interest. The act of characterization is such that narrative must establish the exceptionality of its subject matter to justify the telling of a story. A subject demands a story only in relation to the degree that it can establish its own extra-ordinary circumstances.[6] The normal, routine, average, and familiar (by definition) fail to mobilize the storytelling effort because they fall short of the litmus test of exceptionality. The anonymity of normalcy is no story at all. Deviance serves as the basis and common denominator of all narrative. In this sense, the missing leg presents the aberrant soldier as the story's focus, for his physical difference exiles him from the rank and file of the uniform and physically undifferentiated troop. Whereas a sociality might reject, isolate, institutionalize, reprimand, or obliterate this liability of a single leg, narrative embraces the opportunity that such a "lack" provides—in fact, wills it into existence—as the impetus that calls a story into being. Such a paradox underscores the ironic promise of disability to all narrative.

As we point out in chapter 4, on the performance history of disabled avengers descended from Shakespeare's *Richard III*: Difference demands display. Display demands difference. The arrival of a narrative must be attended by the "unsightly" eruption of the anomalous (often physical in nature) within the social field of vision. The (re)mark upon disability begins with a stare, a gesture of disgust, a slander or derisive comment upon bodily ignominy, a note of gossip about a rare or unsightly presence, a comment upon the unsuitability of deformity for the appetites of polite society, or a sentiment about the unfortunate circumstances that bring disabilities into being. This ruling out-of-bounds of the socially anomalous subject engenders an act of violence that stories seek to "rescue" or "reclaim" as worthy of narrative attention. Stories always perform a compensatory function in their efforts to renew interest in a previously denigrated object. While there exist myriad inroads to the identification of the anomalous—femininity, race, class, sexuality—disability services this narrative appetite for difference as often as any other constructed category of deviance.

The politics of this recourse to disability as a device of narrative characterization demonstrates the importance of disability to storytelling itself. Literary narratives support our appetites for the exotic by posing disability as an "alien" terrain that promises the revelation of a previously uncomprehended experience. Literature borrows the potency of the lure of difference that a socially stigmatized condition provides. Yet the reliance upon disability in narrative rarely develops into a means of identifying people with disabilities as a disenfranchised cultural constituency. The ascription of absolute singularity to disability performs a contradictory operation: a character "stands out" as a result of an attributed blemish, but this exceptionality divorces him or her from a shared social identity. As in the story of *The Steadfast Tin Soldier,* a narrative disability establishes the uniqueness of an individual character and is quickly left behind as a purely biological fact. Disability marks a character as "unlike" the rest of a fiction's cast, and once singled out, the character becomes a case of special interest who retains originality to the detriment of all other characteristics. Disability cannot be accommodated within the ranks of the norm(als), and, thus, the options for dealing with the difference that drives the story's plot is twofold: a disability is either left behind or punished for its lack of conformity.

In the story of *The Steadfast Tin Soldier* we witness the exercise of both operations on the visible difference that the protagonist's disability poses. Once the soldier's incomplete leg is identified, its difference is quickly nullified. Nowhere in the story does the narrator call attention to a difficult negotiation that must be attempted as a result of the missing appendage. In fact, like the adventurer of de Certeau's paradigmatic travel narrative, the tin figure undergoes a series of epic encounters without further reference to his limitation: after he falls out of a window, his bayonet gets stuck in a crack; a storm rages over him later that night; two boys find the figure, place him into a newspaper boat, and sail him down the gutter into a street drain; he is accosted by a street rat who poses as gatekeeper to the underworld; the newspaper boat sinks in a canal where the soldier is swallowed by a large fish; and finally he is returned to his home of origin when the family purchases the fish for dinner and discovers the one-legged figure in the belly. The series of dangerous encounters recalls the epic adventure of the physically able Odysseus on his way home from Troy; likewise, the tin soldier endures the physically taxing experience without further remark upon the incomplete leg in the course of the tale. The journey and ultimate return home embody the cyclical nature of all narrative (and the story of disability in particular)—the deficiency inaugurates the need for a story but is quickly forgotten once the difference is established.

However, a marred appearance cannot ultimately be allowed to return home unscathed. Near the end of the story the significance of the missing leg returns when the tin soldier is reintroduced to his love—the paper maiden who pirouettes upon one leg. Because the soldier mistakes the dancer as possessing only one leg like himself, the story's conclusion hinges upon the irony of an argument about human attraction based upon shared likeness. If the maiden shares the fate of one-leggedness, then, the soldier reasons, she must be meant for him. However, in a narrative twist of deus ex machina the blemished soldier is inexplicably thrown into the fire by a boy right at the moment of his imagined reconciliation with the "one-legged" maiden. One can read this ending as a punishment for his willingness to desire someone physically perfect and therefore unlike himself. Shelley's story of Frankenstein ends in the monster's anticipated obliteration on his own funeral pyre in the wake of his misinterpretation as monstrous, and the tin soldier's fable reaches its conclusion in a similar manner. Disability inaugurates narrative, but narrative inevitably punishes its own prurient interests by overseeing the extermination of the object of its fascination.

In the remainder of this chapter we discuss the ramifications of this narrative recourse to disability as a device of characterization and narrative "rehabilitation." Specifically, we analyze the centrality of the disability's "deviant" physiognomy to literary strategies of representation, and discuss disability as that which provides writers with a means of moving between the micro and macro levels of textual meaning that we phrase the materiality of metaphor.

The Physiognomy of Disability

What is the significance of disability as a pervasive category of narrative interest? Why do the convolutions, distortions, and ruptures that mark the disabled body's surface prove seductive to literary representation? What is the relationship of the external evidence of disability's perceived deviances and the core of the disabled subject's being? The disabled body occupies a crossroads in the age-old literary debate about the relationship of form to content. Whereas the "unmarred" surface enjoys its cultural anonymity and promises little more than a confirmation of the adage of a "healthy" mind in a "healthy" body, disability signifies a more variegated and sordid series of assumptions and experiences. Its unruliness must be tamed by multiple mappings of the surface. If form leads to content or "embodies" meaning, then disability's disruption of acculturated bodily norms also suggests a corresponding misalignment of subjectivity itself.

In *Volatile Bodies* Elizabeth Grosz argues that philosophy has often reduced the body to a "fundamental continuity with brute, inorganic matter" (8). Instead of this reductive tendency, Grosz calls for a more complex engagement with our theorizations of the body: "the body provides a point of mediation between what is perceived as purely internal and accessible only to the subject and what is external and publicly observable, a point from which to rethink the opposition between the inside and the outside" (20). Approaching the body as a mediating force between the outside world and internal subjectivity would allow a more thoroughgoing theory of subjectivity's relationship to materiality. In this way, Grosz argues that the body should not be understood as a receptacle or package for the contents of subjectivity, but rather plays an important role in the formation of psychic identity itself.

Disability will play a crucial role in the reformulation of the opposition between interior and exterior because physical differences have so often served as an example of bodily form following function or vice versa. The mutability of bodies causes them to change over time (both individually and historically), and yet the disabled body is sedimented within an ongoing narrative of breakdown and abnormality. However, while we situate our argument in opposition to reading physical disability as a one-to-one correspondence with subjecthood, we do not deny its role as a foundational aspect of identity. The disabled subject's navigation of social attitudes toward people with disabilities, medical pathologies, the management of embodiment itself, and daily encounters with "perfected" physicalities in the media demonstrates that the disabled body has a substantial impact upon subjectivity as a whole. The study of disability must understand the impact of the experience of disability upon subjectivity *without simultaneously situating the internal and external body within a strict mirroring relationship to one another.*

In literature this mediating role of the external body with respect to internal subjectivity is often represented as a relation of strict correspondence. Either the "deviant" body deforms subjectivity, or "deviant" subjectivity violently erupts upon the surface of its bodily container. In either instance the corporeal body of disability is represented as manifesting its own internal symptoms. Such an approach places the body in an automatic physiognomic relation to the subjectivity it harbors. As Barbara Maria Stafford has demonstrated, practices of interpreting the significance of bodily appearances since the eighteenth century have depended upon variations of the physiognomic method.

> Physiognomics was body criticism. As corporeal connoisseurship, it diagnosed unseen spiritual qualities by scrutinizing visible traits. Since its adherents claimed privileged powers of detection, it was a somewhat sinister capability.... The master eighteenth-century physiognomist, Lavater, noted that men formed conjectures "by reasoning from the exterior to the interior." He continued: "What is universal nature but physiognomy. Is not everything surface and contents? Body and soul? External effect and internal faculty? Invisible principle and visible end?" (84)

For cultures that operated upon models of bodily interpretation prior to the development of internal imaging techniques, the corporeal surface was freighted with significance. Physiognomy became a paradigm of access to the ephemeral and intangible workings of the interior body. Speculative qualities such as moral integrity, honesty, trustworthiness, criminality, fortitude, cynicism, sanity, and so forth, suddenly became available for scrutiny by virtue of the "irregularities" of the body that enveloped them. For the physiognomist, the body allowed meaning to be inferred from the outside in; such a speculative practice resulted in the ability to anticipate intangible qualities of one's personhood without having to await the "proof" of actions or the intimacy of a relationship developed over time. By "reasoning from the exterior to the interior," the trained physiognomist extracted the meaning of the soul without the permission or participation of the interpreted.

If the "external effect" led directly to a knowledge of the "internal faculty," then those who inhabited bodies deemed "outside the norm" proved most ripe for a scrutiny of their moral or intellectual content. Since disabled people by definition embodied a form that was identified as "outside" the normal or permissible, their visages and bodily outlines became the physiognomist's (and later the pathologist's) object par excellence. Yet, the "sinister capability" of physiognomy proves more complex than just the exclusivity of interpretive authority that Stafford suggests. If the body would offer a surface manifestation of internal symptomatology, then disability and deformity automatically preface an equally irregular subjectivity. Physiognomy proves a deadly practice to a population already existing on the fringes of social interaction and "humanity." While the "authorized" physiognomist was officially sanctioned to interpret the symbology of the bodily surface, the disabled person became every person's Rorschach test. While physiognomists discerned the nuances of facial countenances and phrenologists surveyed protuberances of the skull, the extreme examples offered by those with physical disabilities and deformities invited the armchair psychology of the literary practitioner to participate in the symbolic manipulation of bodily exteriors.

Novelists, dramatists, philosophers, poets, essayists, painters, and moralists all flocked to the site of a physiognomic circus from the eighteenth century on. "Irregular" bodies became a fertile field for symbolists of all stripes. Disability and deformity retained their fascination for would-be interpreters because their "despoiled" visages commanded a rationale that narrative (textual or visual) promised to decipher. Because disability represents that which goes awry in the normalizing bodily schema, narratives sought to unravel the riddle of anomaly's origins. Such a riddle was inherently social in its making. The physiognomic corollary seemed to provide a way in to the secrets of identity itself. The chapters that follow demonstrate that the problem of the representation of disability is not the search for a more "positive" story of disability, as it has often been formulated in disability studies, *but rather a thoroughgoing challenge to the undergirding authorization to interpret that disability invites.* There is a politics at stake in the fact that disability inaugurates an explanatory need that the unmarked body eludes by virtue of its physical anonymity. To participate in an ideological system of bodily norms that promotes some kinds of bodies while devaluing others is to ignore the malleability of bodies and their definitively mutant natures.

Stafford's argument notwithstanding, the body's manipulation by physiognomic practices did not develop as an exclusively eighteenth-century phenomenon. Our own research demonstrates that while physiognomics came to be consolidated as a scientific ideology in the eighteenth and nineteenth centuries, people with disabilities and deformities have always been subject to varieties of this interpretive practice. Elizabeth Cornelia Evans argues that physiognomic beliefs can be traced back as far as ancient Greece. She cites Aristotle as promoting physiognomic reasoning when he proclaims, "It is possible to infer character from physique, if it is granted that body and soul change together in all natural affections…For if a peculiar affection applies to any individual class, e.g., courage to lions, there must be some corresponding sign for it; for it has been assumed that body and soul are affected together" (7). In fact, one might argue that physiognomics came to be consolidated out of a general historical practice applied to the bodies of disabled peoples. If the extreme evidence of marked physical differences provided a catalog of reliable signs, then perhaps more minute bodily differentiations could also be cataloged and interpreted. In this sense, people with disabilities ironically served as the historical locus for the invention of physiognomy.

As we pointed out earlier, the oldest surviving tablets found along the Tigris River in Mesopotamia and dated from 3000 to 2000 B.C. deployed a physiognomic method to prognosticate from deformed fetuses and irregular animal livers. The evidence of bodily anomalies allowed royalty and high priests to forecast harvest cycles, geographic conditions, the outcomes of impending wars, and the future of city-states. The symbolic prediction of larger cultural conditions from physical differences suggests one of the primary differences between the ancient and modern periods: physical anomalies metamorphosed from a symbolic interpretation of worldly meanings to a primarily individualized locus of information. The movement of disability from a macro to a micro level of prediction underscores our point that disability has served as a foundational category of cultural interpretation. The longstanding practice of physiognomic readings demonstrates that disability and deformity serve as the impetus to analyze an otherwise obscured meaning or pattern at the individual level. In either case the overdetermined symbolism ascribed to disabled bodies obscured the more complex and banal reality of those who inhabited them.

The readings to come demonstrate that while on a historical level the meaning of disability shifted from a supernatural and cultural to an individual and medical symbology, literary narratives persisted in integrating both interpretive possibilities into their story lines. The final section of this chapter analyzes this dual appeal of disability to literary metaphorics. Here we want to end by pointing out that the knee-jerk impulse to interpretation that disability has historically instigated hyperbolically determines its symbolic utility. This subsequent overdetermination of disability's meanings turns disabled populations into the vehicle of an insatiable cultural fascination. Literature has dipped into the well of disability's meaning-laden depths throughout the development of the print record. In doing so, literary narratives bolstered the cultural desire to pursue disability's bottomless interpretive possibilities. The inexhaustibility of this pursuit has led to the reification of disabled people as fathomless mysteries who simultaneously provoke and elude cultural capture.

The Materiality of Metaphor

Like Oedipus (another renowned disabled fictional creation), cultures thrive upon solving the riddle of disability's rhyme and reason. When the limping Greek protagonist overcomes the Sphinx by answering "man who walks with a cane" as the concluding answer to her three-part query, we must assume that his own disability served as an experiential source for this insight. The master riddle solver in effect trumps the Sphinx's feminine otherness with knowledge gleaned from his own experience of inhabiting an alien body. In doing so, Oedipus taps into the cultural reservoir of disability's myriad symbolic associations as an interpretive source for his own riddle-solving methodology. Whereas disability usually provides the riddle in need of a narrative solution, in this instance the experience of disability momentarily serves as the source of Oedipus's interpretive mastery. Yet, Sophocles' willingness to represent disability as a mode of experience-based knowledge proves a rare literary occasion and a fleeting moment in the play's dramatic structure.

While Oedipus solves the Sphinx's riddle in the wake of his own physical experience as a lame interpreter and an interpreter of lameness, his disability remains inconsequential to the myth's plot. Oedipus's disability—the result of Laius's pinning of his infant son's ankles as he sends him off to die of exposure—"marks" his character as distinctive and worthy of the exceptional tale. Beyond this physical fact, Sophocles neglects to explore the relationship of the body's mediating function with respect to Oedipus's kingly subjectivity. Either his "crippling" results in an insignificant physical difference, or the detailing of his difference can be understood to embody a vaguely remembered history of childhood violence enacted against him by his father. The disability remains a physical fact of his character that the text literally overlooks once this difference is established as a remnant of his repressed childhood. Perhaps those who share the stage with Oedipus either have learned to look away from his disability or have imbibed the injunction of polite society to refuse commentary upon the existence of the protagonist's physical difference.

However, without the pinning of Oedipus's ankles and his resulting lameness two important aspects of the plot would be compromised. First, Oedipus might have faltered at the riddle of the Sphinx like others before him and fallen prey to the voracious appetite of the she-beast; second, Sophocles' protagonist would lose the physical sign that literally connects him to an otherwise inscrutable past. In this sense, Oedipus's physical difference secures key components of the plot that allow the riddle of his identity to be unraveled. At the same time, his disability serves as the source of little substantive commentary in the course of the drama itself. Oedipus as a "lame interpreter" establishes the literal source of his ability to solve the baffling riddle and allows the dramatist to metaphorize humanity's incapacity to fathom the dictums of the gods. This movement exemplifies the literary oscillation between micro and macro levels of metaphorical meaning supplied by disability. Sophocles later moves to Oedipus's self-blinding as a further example of how the physical body provides a corporeal correlative to the ability of dramatic myth to bridge personal and public symbology.

What is of interest for us in this ancient text is the way in which one can read its representational strategy as a paradigm for literary approaches to disability. The ability of disabled characters to allow authors the metaphorical "play" between macro and micro registers of meaning-making establishes the role of the body in literature as a liminal point in the representational process. In his study of editorial cartoonings and caricatures of the body leading up to the French Revolution, Antoine de Baecque argues that the corporeal metaphor provided a means of giving the abstractions of political ideals an "embodied" power. To "know oneself " and provide a visual correlative to a political commentary, French cartoonists and essayists deployed the body as a metaphor because the body "succeeds in *connecting* narrative and knowledge, meaning and knowing" most viscerally (5). This form of textual embodiment concretizes an otherwise ephemeral concept within a corporeal essence. To give an abstraction a body allows the idea to simulate a foothold in the material would that it would otherwise fail to procure.

Whereas an ideal such as democracy imparts a weak and abstracted notion of governmental and economic reform, for example, the embodied caricature of a hunchbacked monarch overshadowed by a physically superior democratic citizen proved more powerful than any ideological argument. Instead of political harangue, the body offers an illusion of fixity to a textual effect:

> [Body] metaphors were able simultaneously to describe the event and to make the description attain the level of the imaginary. The deployment of these bodily *topoi*—the degeneracy of the nobility, the impotence of the king, the herculean strength of the citizenry, the goddesses of politics appearing naked like Truth, the congenital deformity of the aristocrats, the bleeding wound of the martyrs—allowed political society to represent itself at a pivotal moment of its history....One must pass through the [bodily] forms of a narrative in order to reach knowledge. (4–5)

Such a process of giving body to belief exemplifies the corporeal seduction of the body to textual mediums. The desire to access the seeming solidity of the body's materiality offers representational literatures a way of grasping that which is most unavailable to them. For de Baecque, representing a body in its specificity as the bearer of an otherwise intangible concept grounds the reality of an ideological meaning. The passage through a bodily form helps secure a knowledge that would otherwise drift away of its own insubstantiality. The corporeal metaphor offers narrative the one thing it cannot possess—an anchor in materiality. Such a process embodies the materiality of metaphor; and literature is the writing that aims to concretize theory through its ability to provide an embodied account of physical, sensory life.

While de Baecque's theory of the material metaphor argues that the attempt to harness the body to a specific ideological program provides the text with an illusory opportunity to embody Truth, he overlooks the fact that the same process embeds the body within a limiting array of symbolic meanings: crippling conditions equate with monarchical immobility, corpulence evidences tyrannical greed, deformity represents malevolent motivation, and so on. Delineating his corporeal catalog, the historian bestows upon the body an elusive, general character while depending for his readings almost exclusively upon the potent symbolism of disabled bodies in particular. Visible degeneracy, impotency, congenital deformity, festering ulcerations, and bleeding wounds in the passage previously quoted provide the contrastive bodily coordinates to the muscular, aesthetic, and symmetrical bodies of the healthy citizenry. One cannot narrate the story of a healthy body or national reform movement without the contrastive device of disability to bear out the symbolic potency of the message. The materiality of metaphor via disabled bodies gives all bodies a tangible essence in that the "healthy" corporeal surface fails to achieve its symbolic effect without its disabled counterpart.

As George Canguilhem has pointed out, the body only calls attention to itself in the midst of its breakdown or disrepair (209). The representation of the process of breakdown or incapacity is fraught with political and ideological significance. To make the body speak essential truths, one must give a language to it. Elaine Scarry argues that "there is ordinarily no language for [the body in] pain" (13). However, we would argue that the body itself has no language, since language is something foreign to its nonlinguistic materiality. It must be spoken for if its meanings are to prove narratable. The narration of the disabled body allows a textual body to *mean* through its long-standing historical representation as an overdetermined symbolic surface; the disabled body also offers narrative the illusion of grounding abstract knowledge within a bodily materiality. *If the body is the Other of text, then textual representation seeks access to that which it is least able to grasp.* If the nondysfunctional body proves too uninteresting to narrate, the disabled body becomes a paramount device of characterization. Narrative prosthesis, or the dependency upon the disabled body, proves essential to (even the essence of) the stories analyzed in the chapters to come.

Notes

1. Many critics have designated a distinctive space for "the literary" by identifying those works whose meaning is inherently elastic and multiple. Maurice Blanchot identifies literary narrative as that which refuses closure and readerly mastery—"to write [literature] is to surrender to the interminable" (27). In his study of Balzac's *Sarrasine*, Roland Barthes characterizes the "plural text" as that which is allied with a literary value whose "networks are many and interact, without any one of them being able to surpass the rest; the text is a galaxy of signifiers, not a structure of signifieds; it has no beginning; it is reversible; we gain access to it by several entrances, none of which can be authoritatively declared to be the main one" (5). Ross Chambers's analysis of oppositionality argues that literature strategically deploys the "play" or "leeway" in discursive systems as a means of disturbing the restrictive prescriptions of authoritative regimes (iv). As our study develops, we demonstrate that the strategic "open-endedness" of literary narrative is paralleled by the multiplicity of meanings bequeathed to people with disabilities in history. In doing so, we argue not only that the open-endedness of literature challenges sedimented historical truths, but that disability has been one of the primary weapons in literature's disruptive agenda.

2. In his important study *Enforcing Normalcy*, Lennard Davis theorizes the "normal" body as an ideological construct that tyrannizes over those bodies that fail to conform. Accordingly, while all bodies feel insubstantial when compared to our

abstract ideals of the body, disabled people experience a form of subjugation or oppression as a result of this phenomenon. Within such a system, we will argue in tandem with Davis that disability provides the contrastive term against which the concepts health, beauty, and ability are determined: "Just as the conceptualization of race, class, and gender shapes the lives of those who are not black, poor, or female, so the concept of disability regulates the bodies of those who are 'normal.' In fact, the very concept of normalcy by which most people (by definition) shape their existence is in fact tied inexorably to the concept of disability, or rather, the concept of disability is a function of a concept of normalcy. Normalcy and disability are part of the same system" (2).

3. Following the theories of Lacan, Slavoj Zizek in *The Sublime Object of Ideology* extracts the notion of the "hard kernel" of ideology. For Zizek, it represents the underlying core of belief that refuses to be deconstructed away by even the most radical operations of political critique. More than merely a rational component of ideological identification, the "hard kernel" represents the irrationality behind belief that secures the interpellated subject's "illogical" participation in a linguistically permeable system.

4. There is an equivalent problem to the representation of disability in literary narratives within our own critical rubrics of the body. The disabled body continues to fall outside of critical categories that identify bodies as the product of cultural constructions. While challenging a generic notion of white, male body as ideological proves desirable in our own moment within the realms of race, gender, sexuality, and class, there has been a more pernicious history of literary and critical approaches to the disabled body. In our introduction to *The Body and Physical Difference*, we argue that minority discourses in the humanities tend to deploy the evidence of "corporeal aberrancy" as a means of identifying the invention of an ideologically encoded body: "While physical aberrancy is often recognized as constructed and historically variable it is rarely remarked upon as its own legitimized or politically fraught identity" (5).

5. For Naomi Schor the phrase "bad objects" implies a discursive object that has been ruled out of bounds by the prevailing academic politics of the day, or one that represents a "critical perversion" (xv). Our use of the phrase implies both of these definitions in relation to disability. The literary object of disability has been almost entirely neglected by literary criticism in general until the past few years, when disability studies in the humanities have developed; and "disability" as a topic of investigation still strikes many as a "perverse" interest for academic contemplation. To these two definitions we would also add that the labeling of disability as a "bad object" nonetheless overlooks the fact that disabilities fill the pages of literary interest. The reasons for overabundance of images of disability in literature is the subject of this book.

6. The title of Thomson's *Extraordinary Bodies: Figuring Disabiltiy in American Culture and Literature* forwards the term extraordinary in order to play off of its multiple nuances. It can suggest the powerful sentimentality of overcoming narratives so often attached to stories about disabled people. It can also suggest those whose bodies are the products of overdetermined social meaning that exaggerate physical differences or perform them as a way of enhancing their exoticness. In addition, we share with Thomson the belief that disabled bodies prove extraordinary in the ways in which they expose the variety and mutable nature of physicality itself.

Works Cited

Blanchot, Maurice. *The Space of Literature*. 1955. Trans. Ann Smock. Lincoln: U of Nebraska P, 1982.

Chambers, Ross. *Room For Maneuver: Reading the Oppositional in Narrative*. Chicago: U of Chicago P, 1991.

Davis, Lennard. *Enforcing Normalcy: Disability, Deafness, and the Body*. New York: Verso, 1995.

Mitchell, David and Snyder, Sharon (eds.) *The Body and Physical Difference: Discourses of Disability*. Ann Arbor: U of Michigan P, 1997.

Schor, Naomi. *Bad Objects: Essays Popular and Unpopular*. Durham, NC: Duke UP, 1995.

Thomson, Rosemarie Garland. *Extraordinary Bodies: Figuring Disability in American Culture and Literature*. New York: Columbia UP, 1997.

Zizek, Slavoj. *The Sublime Object of Ideology*. New York: Verso, 1999.

18

The Dimensions of Disability Oppression
An Overview

James I. Charlton

The vast majority of people with disabilities have always been poor, powerless, and degraded. Disability oppression is a product of both the past and the present. Some aspects of disability oppression are remnants of ancien régimes of politics and economics, customs and beliefs, and others can be traced to more recent developments. To understand the consequences and implications for people with disabilities an analysis is called for which considers how the overarching structures of society influence this trend. This is especially relevant in light of the United Nations' contention that their condition is worsening: "Handicapped people remain *outcasts* around the world, living in shame and squalor among populations lacking not only in resources to help them but also in understanding. And with their numbers growing rapidly, their plight is getting worse.... The normal perception is that nothing can be done for disabled children. This has to do with prejudice and old-fashioned thinking that this punishment comes from God, some evil spirits or magic.... We have a catastrophic human rights situation.... They [disabled persons] are a group without power."[1]

There is a great deal to say about disability oppression, not only because it is complex and multi-faceted but also because we have so little experience conceptualizing its phenomenology and logic. Until very recently most analyses of why people with disabilities have been and continue to be poor, powerless, and degraded have been mired in an anachronistic academic tradition that understands the "status" of people with disabilities in terms of deviance and stigma. This has been compounded by the lack of participation by people with disabilities in these analyses. Fortunately, this has begun to change. Disability rights activists have recently undertaken important and fruitful efforts to frame disability oppression. These projects, however insightful, have been limited by their scope and inability to account for the systemic nature of disability oppression. For example, in the article "Malcolm Teaches Us, Too," in the *Disability Rag,* Marta Russell writes,

> Malcolm's most important message was to love blackness, to love black culture. Malcolm insisted that loving blackness itself was an act of resistance in a white dominated society. By exposing the internalized racial self-hatred that deeply penetrated the psyches of U.S. colonized black people, Malcolm taught that blacks could decolonize their minds by coming to blackness to be spiritually renewed, transformed. He believed that, only then, could blacks unite to gain the equality they rightfully deserved.... It is equally important for disabled persons to recognize what it means to live as a disabled person in a physicalist society—that is, one which places its value on physical agility, we're disvalued. Our oppression by able-bodied persons is rife with the message: There is something wrong, something "defective" with us—because we have a disability.... We must identify with ourselves and others like us. Like Malcolm sought for his race, disabled persons must build a culture which will unify us and enable us to gain our human rights. (1994:11–12)

There is much of value for the DRM in what Russell says. She is patently correct, for instance, to point people with disabilities toward Malcolm X in terms of recognition and identity, self-hatred and self-respect. But she, like Malcolm X, is wrong on the question of where the basis of oppression lies. Both identify oppression with the Other, a view that is quite prevalent among disability rights activists. For Russell, the Other is able-bodied people; for Malcolm, it was white people (although he began to change this view shortly before his assassination). Both situate oppression in the realm of the ideas of others and not in systems or structures that marginalize people for political-economic and sociocultural reasons. As the great Mexican novelist Julio Cortazar writes in *Hopscotch*, "Nothing can be denounced if the denouncing is done within the system that belongs to the thing denounced" ([1966]1987: chap. 99). My project then is as much a polemic directed at the disability rights movement as at a more general public. My point to other activists is that the logic of disability oppression closely parallels the oppression of other groups. It is a logic bound up with political-economic needs and belief systems of domination. From these priorities and values has evolved a world system dominated by the laws of capital and profit and the ethos of individualism and image worship. This point is just as important as my call to the general public, especially the international community, to recognize and respond to an extraordinary human rights tragedy, what former UN Secretary General Javier Perez de Cuellar once called "the silent emergency."

Political Economy and the World System

Political economy is crucial in constructing a theory of disability oppression because poverty and powerlessness are cornerstones of the dependency people with disabilities experience. As the social science of how politics and economics influence and limit everyday life, political economy is primarily concerned with issues of class because class positions groups of people in relation to economic production and exchange, political power and privilege. Today, class not only structures the political and economic relationships between the worker, peasant, farmer, intellectual, small-scale entrepreneur, government bureaucrat, army general, banker, and industrialist, it mediates family and community life insofar as relationships exist in these which affect people's economic viability.[2] In political-economic terms, everyday life is informed by where and how individuals, families, and communities are incorporated into a world system dominated by the few who control the means of production and force. This has been the case for a long time. The logic of this system regulates and explains who survives and prospers, who controls and who is controlled, and, not simply metaphorically, who is on the inside and who is on the outside (of power).

Perhaps the most fitting characterization of the socioeconomic condition of people with disabilities is that they are outcasts. This is how they are portrayed in the UN report cited at the beginning of this chapter. It was also repeated by many of the disability rights activists I interviewed. It seems reasonable to ask, why is this depiction so common? The answer is two-sided, sociocultural and political-economic. On one side are the panoply of reactionary and iconoclastic attitudes about disability. These are addressed briefly in the next section and in depth in chapter 4. On the other side stands a political-economic formation that does not need and in fact cannot accommodate a vast group of people in its production, exchange, and reproduction. Put differently, people with disabilities, like many others, are preponderantly part of a worldwide phenomenon that James O'Connor called "surplus population" (1973:161)[3] and Istvan Meszaros called "superfluous people" (1995:702).

The extent and implications of this phenomenon are experienced differently. For example, it is readily apparent that people, even those with disabilities, living in the more economically developed regions of the world have higher "standards of living" than their counterparts in the Third World. The United States and Europe have safety nets that catch "outcasts" before their very livelihoods are called into question. This is not necessarily the case in the Third World.

The 300 million to 400 million people with disabilities who live in the periphery, like the vast majority of people in those regions, exist in abject poverty, but I would go further and argue that, for social and cultural reasons, their lives are even more difficult. These are the poorest and most powerless people on earth.

As the global economy developed, it created more than just the wandering gypsies of southern Europe and the *posseiros* (squatters) of South America. It created an enormous number of outcasts who must be set apart from what Karl Marx called the "reserve army of labor"—a resource to be tapped in times of economic expansion (although Marx uses them interchangeably in *Grundrisse* [1973:491]). For hundreds of millions of outcasts—beggars and others who depend on charity for survival; prostitutes, drug dealers, and others who survive through criminal activities; the homeless, refugees, and others forced to live somewhere besides their home or homeland;[4] and many others—will seldom, if ever, under ordinary circumstances be used in the production, exchange, and distribution of political and economic goods and services. They are essentially declassed. So many people fall into this category that U.S. economists have created the category "underclass" to refer to them. The UN has even created the preposterous category "admissible levels of poverty" to describe the condition of the best-off among these people.

People with disabilities, at least as a group, may have been the first to join the ranks of the underclass. Since feudalism and even earlier, they have lived outside the economy and political process.[5] It should be noted, of course, that few people with physical disabilities survived for very long in precapitalist economies.

The emergence and development of capitalism had an extraordinarily profound and positive impact on people with disabilities. For the first time, probably in the mid-1700s in parts of Europe, people living outside the spheres of production and exchange, the "surplus people," could rely on others to survive. Family members and friends who could accumulate more than the barest minimum necessary for survival had the "luxury" of being able to care for others. A century later the political-economic conditions were such that charities, which supported a large number of people, were established. Those who were cared for by these charities most often were the mentally ill, the blind, the alcoholic, the chronically ill. My analysis throughout this book centers on the political-economic and sociocultural relationships born out of these times and how they have developed differently in different economic zones and in different cultures. Essentially, I will argue, as Audre Lorde does in *Sister Outsider,* that these formations now not only stand as barriers to progress but also are the basis for peoples' oppression: "Institutionalized rejection of *difference* is an absolute necessity in a profit economy which needs outsiders as surplus people. As members of such an economy, we have *all* been programmed to respond to the human differences between us with fear and loathing and to handle that difference in one of three ways: ignore it, and if that is not possible, copy it if we think it is dominant, or destroy it if we think it is subordinate. But we have no patterns for relating across our human differences as equals. As a result, those differences have been misnamed and misused in the service of separation and confusion" (1984:77).

Culture(s) and Belief Systems

The modern world is composed of thousands of cultures, each with its own ways of thinking about other people, nature, family and community, social phenomena, and so on. Culture is sustained through customs, rituals, mythology, signs and symbols, and institutions such as religion and the mass media. Each of these informs the beliefs and attitudes that contribute to disability oppression. These attitudes are almost universally pejorative. They hold that people with disabilities are pitiful and that disability itself is abnormal. This is one of the social norms used to separate people with disabilities through classification systems that encompass education, housing, transportation, health care, and family life.

For early anthropologists, "culture" meant how values were attached to belief systems (Kroeber and Kluckhorn 1952:180–182). Since then the meaning of the term "culture" has become so contested that some have argued for its abandonment. Others consider it simply a "lived experience" or "lived antagonistic experiences." For Clifford Geertz, one of anthropology's preeminent theorists, the "culture concept...denotes a historically transmitted pattern of meanings embodied in symbols, a system of inherited conceptions expressed in symbolic forms by means of which men communicate, perpetuate, and develop their knowledge and attitudes toward life" (1973:89). Geertz's theory has many adherents, but it has also garnered its share of criticism, most commonly that it neglects the influence of politics and power. In *Ideology and Modern Culture,* John Thompson postulates a more reasonable position. Thompson's formulation is that the study of symbols as a way to interpret cultures must be done contextually, by recognizing that power relations order the experiences of everyday life in which these signs and symbols are produced, transmitted, and received:

> The symbolic conception is a suitable starting point for the development of a constructive approach to the study of cultural phenomena. But the weakness of this conception—in the form it appears, for instance, in the writings of Geertz—is that it gives insufficient attention to the structured social relations within which symbols and symbolic actions are always embedded. Hence, I formulate what I call the structural conception of culture. Cultural phenomena, according to this conception, may be understood as symbolic forms in structured contexts, and cultural analysis may be construed as the study of the meaningful constitution and social contextualization of symbolic forms. (1990:123)

My notion of culture(s) is similar to Thompson's. Contrary to many traditions in anthropology, cultures are not independent or static formations. They interface and interact in the everyday world with history, politics and power, economic conditions and institutions, and nature. To neglect these important influences seems to miss important interstices where culture happens, is expressed, and, most important, is experienced. The point is not that one culture makes people do or think this and another that but that ideas and beliefs are informed by and in cultures and that cultures are partial expressions of a world in which the dualities of domination/subordination, superiority/inferiority, normality/abnormality are relentlessly reinforced and legitimized. Anthropologists may be able to find obscure cultures in which these dualities are not determinant, but this does not minimize their overarching influence.

The essential problem of recent anthropological work on culture and disability is that it perpetuates outmoded beliefs and continues to distance research from lived oppression. Contributors to Benedicte Ingstad and Susan Reynolds Whyte's *Disability and Culture* seem to be oblivious to the extraordinary poverty and degradation of people with disabilities. The book does add to our understanding of how the conceptualization and symbolization of disability takes place, but its language and perspective are still lodged in the past. In the first forty pages alone we find the words *suffering, lameness, interest group, incapacitated, handicapped, deformities.* Notions of oppression, dominant culture, justice, human rights, political movement, and self-determination are conspicuously absent. We can read hundreds of pages without even contemplating degradation. Unlike these anthropologists and of course many others, my thesis is that backward attitudes about disability are not the basis for disability oppression, disability oppression is the basis for backward attitudes.

(False) Consciousness and Alienation

The third component of disability oppression is its psychological internalization. This creates a (false) consciousness and alienation that divides people and isolates individuals. Most people with disabilities actually come to believe they are less normal, less capable than others. Self-pity, self-hate, shame, and other manifestations of this process are devastating for they prevent people with disabilities from knowing their real selves, their real needs, and their real capabilities and from recognizing the options they in fact have. False consciousness and alienation also obscure the source of their oppression. They cannot recognize that their self-perceived pitiful lives are simply a perverse mirroring of a pitiful world order. In this regard people with disabilities have much in common with others who also have internalized their own oppression. Marx called this "the self-annihilation of the worker" and Frantz Fanon "the psychic alienation of the colonized." In *Femininity and Domination*, Sandra Lee Bartky exposes the roles of alienation, narcissism, and shame in the oppression of women. Each of these examples highlights the centrality of consciousness to any discussion of oppression. Consciousness, like culture, means different things to different people. Carl Jung said it is "everything that is not unconscious." Sartre said "consciousness is being" or "being-in-itself." For the Egyptian novelist Naguib Moufouz, it is "an awareness of the concealed side." Recently there have been attempts to develop a neurobiological theory of consciousness, the best known of which is Gerald Edelman's *The Remembered Present* (1989).

Whole philosophical systems and schools of psychology are built on the concept of consciousness. Appropriately, most postulate stages or types, even archetypes of consciousness. For Jung, everything important was interior, was "thought." The highest consciousness was individuation, or self-realization (the "summit"). This required gaining command of all four thought functions: sensation, feeling, thinking, and intuition. When one arrives at the intersection of these functions, "one opens one's eyes" (Campbell 1988:xxvi–xxx).

Marxism typically understood consciousness as metaphorical spirals of practice (experience) and theory (thought) intertwined. These spirals move incrementally, quantitatively. Consciousness, however, is not a linear progression. At points this quantitative buildup congeals into a "rupture," or a qualitative or transformational leap to another stage of consciousness where another spiral-like phenomenon begins. Consciousness can leap from being-in-itself (existence as is) to being-for-itself (consciously desiring change), Marx's equivalent of a leap in self-realization. While Jung's and, before him, Freud's great contribution to modern psychology was the discovery of the importance of the unconscious, their systems excluded political and social conditions. They were asocial and apolitical. This is where idealism (e.g., Jung, Hegel) and materialism (e.g., Marx, Sartre) split most dramatically. Sartre's withering critique of psychology began with this difference. According to Sartre, "the Ego is not in consciousness, which is utterly translucent, but in the world" (Sartre [1943] 1957:xii). For Sartre, consciousness has three stages, being-in-itself, being-for-itself, and being-for-others, which reflects a growing awareness. He argues that consciousness is intentional, it has a direction. In his attack on traditional psychology, Sartre is saying one must step back and ponder reality (there is a "power of withdrawal") because reality has a thoroughgoing impact on consciousness.

Consciousness is an awareness of oneself and the world. Furthermore, consciousness has depth, and as one moves through this space one's perception of oneself and the world changes. This does not automatically entail greater self-clarity. Movement through this "space-depth" is contingent on factors such as intelligence, curiosity, character, personality, experience, and chance; political-economic and cultural structures (class, race, gender, disability, age, sexual preference); and social institutions.

Evolution of consciousness depends on how one perceives and what questions one asks. What one concludes from the thousands of impulses and impressions one receives throughout life depends on, following Albert Einstein, where the observer is and how he or she observes. Take sunsets as an example. We "see" sunsets. But how we see a sunset depends on the weather (e.g., clouds), who we are with and our state of mind at the time, the vantage point (boat, beach, high-rise building), and so on. How we see a sunset is dependent on what we think a sunset is. For many, it is the descent of the sun below the perceived horizon. I can confirm this personally, having watched tourists jump into their tour bus immediately after the sun disappears. For others, the sunset continues until the sun's rays shine back against the darkening sky and produce a sublime radiance.

The point is that consciousness cannot be separated from the real world, from politics and culture. There is an important relationship between being and consciousness.[6] Social being informs consciousness, and consciousness informs being. There is a mutual interplay. Consciousness is not a container that ideas and experiences are poured into. Consciousness is a process of awareness that is influenced by social conditions, chance, and innate cognition.

People are sometimes described as not having consciousness. This is not so. Everyone has consciousness; it is just that for some, probably most, that consciousness is partially false. From childhood, people are constantly bombarded with the values of the dominant culture. These values reflect the "naturalness" of superiority and inferiority, dominance and subordination.

Power and Ideology

The greatest challenge in conceptualizing oppression of any kind is understanding how it is organized and how it is reproduced. It is relatively easy to outline general characteristics such as poverty, degradation, exclusion, and so on. But to answer these questions, we must examine the diffuse circuitry of power and ideology. This exercise is particularly difficult because power and ideology not only organize the way in which individuals experience politics, economics, and culture, they contradictorily obscure or illuminate why and how the dimensions of (disability) oppression are reproduced.

Oppression is a phenomenon of power in which relations between people and between groups are experienced in terms of domination and subordination, superiority and inferiority. At the center of this phenomenon is control. Those with power control; those without power lack control. Power presupposes political, economic, and social hierarchies, structured relations of groups of people, and a system or regime of power. This system, the existing power structure, encompasses the thousands of ways some groups and individuals impose control over others.

Power is diffuse, ambiguous, and complicated: "Power is more general and operates in a wider space than force; it includes much more, but is less dynamic. It is more ceremonious and even has a certain measure of patience.... [S]pace, hope, watchfulness and destructive intent, can be called the actual body of power, or, more simply, power itself " (Canetti [1962] 1984:281). It is not simply a system of oppressors and oppressed. There are many kinds and experiences of power: employer/employee, men/women, dominant race/subordinated race, parent/child, principal/teacher, teacher/student, doctor/patient, to name some. Power more accurately should be considered power(s). These power relations are irreducible products of history. These histories of power(s) collectively make up the regime of power informing the manner and method of governing.

Power should not be confused with rule, however. A ruling class, historically forged by political and economic factors, governs. But other privileged groups and individuals have and exercise power. In the obscure vernacular of French philosophy, the relationship of power between those who are privileged and those who are not is *overdetermined* by class rule.[7]

There are many ways for significantly empowered classes and groups to exercise and maintain power. All regimes, regardless of political philosophy, have ruled through a combination of force and coercion, legitimation and consent. In the Western democracies and parts of the Third World, consent is prevalent and force seldom used. In many parts of the Third World, though, state-sponsored repression is common. The repressive practices of Third World dictatorships are well known and documented. In these countries there exists a pathology between military control and consent. People fear the government and the military because these institutions promote fear through constant harassment and repression.

The primary method through which power relations are reproduced is not physical—military force and state coercion—but metaphysical—people's consent to the existing power structure. This is certainly the case for the hundreds of millions of people with disabilities throughout the world. In chapter 5, I analyze the passive acquiescence of people with disabilities, individually and collectively, in the face of extraordinary lived oppression.

The passive acquiescence to oppression is partially based in what the British cultural historian Raymond Williams has called the "spiritual character" of power: "In particular, ideology needs to be studied to find out how it justifies and boosts the economic activities of particular classes; that is, the study of ideology enables us to study the intention of the articulate classes and the spiritual character of a particular class's rule" (1973:6). Williams is suggesting that the dominant classes and culture constantly and everywhere impress on people the naturalness or normality of their power and privilege. Williams, following Antonio Gramsci, called this process *hegemony*.[8] Hegemony is projected multidimensionally and multidirectionally. It is not projected like a motion picture projects images. The impulses and impressions, beliefs and values, standards and manners are projected more like sunlight. Hegemony is diffuse and appears everywhere as natural. It (re)enforces domination not only through the (armed) state but also throughout society: in families, churches, schools, the workplace, legal institutions, bureaucracy, and culture.

Schooling is a particularly notable example of this process because it cuts across so many boundaries and affects so many, including people with disabilities. If, as we are led to believe, the mission of schooling is teaching and learning, then the logical questions are, who gets to teach? what is taught? how do students learn? and, most important, why? First, let me suggest that schooling has two principal "political" functions. Its narrow purpose is to teach acquiescence to power structures operating in the educational arena. Its broad purpose is to teach acquiescence to the larger status quo, especially the discipline of its workforce.

How does this work? First teachers are trained. Then their training (knowledge) is certified and licensed. Education is "professionalized." Teachers become educational experts. Students sit in rows, all pointing toward this repository of knowledge. The teacher pours his or her knowledge into the students' "empty" heads didactically. There is little sharing of knowledge between the teacher and the student,[9] for the teacher has learned that the process is unidirectional. The curriculum itself is standardized and licensed by state education officials, often the same body that licenses teachers. Moreover, administrators are far removed from the classroom, their only regular contact with students being discipline. They allow little innovation and flexibility. Many administrators continue the same rules and programs for decades. Power comes from above. Everyone and everything in the schooling process is authorized. Students are, in Jürgen Habermas's term, *steered*. Numerous studies have shown that girls are treated differently from boys regardless of the teacher's gender. Students from some families are encouraged and others discouraged. Some, for example, students with disabilities, are segregated in different schools or classrooms.[10]

The latter point is particularly important for understanding the fundamental connections between ideology and power as they relate to disability. Students with disabilities, as soon as their disability is recognized by school officials, are placed on a separate track. They are immediately labeled by authorized (credentialed) professionals (who never themselves have experienced these labels) as LD, ED EMH, and so on. The meaning and definition of the labels differ, but they all signify inferiority on their face. Furthermore, these students are constantly told what they can (potentially/expect to) do and what they cannot do from the very date of their labeling. This happens as a natural matter of course in the classroom.

All activists I interviewed who had a disability in grade school or high school told similar kinds of horror stories—detention and retention, threats and insults, physical and emotional abuse. In Chicago, I have colleagues and friends who were told they could not become teachers because they used wheelchairs; colleagues and friends who are deaf and went through twelve years of school without a single teacher who was proficient in sign language (they were told it was good for them because they should learn to read lips). I have visited segregated schools that required its personnel to wear white lab coats (to impress on the disabled students that they were first and foremost sickly). I know of a student art exhibition that was canceled because some drawings portrayed the students growing up to be doctors and other "unrealistic vocations."

It is possible to identify numerous ways that students with disabilities are controlled and taught their place: (1) labeling; (2) symbols (e.g., white lab coats, "Handicapped Room" signs); (3) structure (pull-out programs, segregated classrooms, "special" schools, inaccessible areas); (4) curricula especially designed for students with disabilities (behavior modification for emotionally disturbed kids, training skills without knowledge instruction for significantly mentally retarded students and students with autistic behavior) or having significant implications for these students; (5) testing and evaluation biased toward the functional needs of the dominant culture (Stanford-Binet and Wexler tests); (6) body language and disposition of school culture (teachers almost never look into the eyes of students with disabilities and practice even greater patterns of superiority and paternalism than they do with other students); and (7) discipline (physical restraints, isolation/time-out rooms with locked doors, use of Haldol and other sedatives).[11]

Special Education, like so many other reforms won by the popular struggle, has been transformed from a way to increase the probability that students with disabilities will get some kind of an education into a badge of inferiority and a rule-bound, bureaucratic process of separating and then warehousing millions of young people that the dominant culture has no need for. While this process is uneven, with a minority benefiting from true inclusionary practices, the overarching influences of race and class preclude any significant and meaningful equalization of educational opportunities.[12]

The sociopolitical implications of this process are clear to many disability rights activists.

> *Danilo Delfin:* "Disability rights advocacy in Southeast Asia is very hard. Children are taught never to argue with their teacher. It is a long socialization process."

The Chicago educators and disability rights activists Carol Gill and Larry Voss interviewed twenty-one people who went through Special Education. Their survey respondents indicated that they believed that Special Education made them more passive and convinced them of their lot in life.[13]

We can begin to see the similarities between power and hegemony. Power, as Elias Canetti reminds us, is "more general and operates in a wider space than force," and hegemony, according to Raymond Williams, is "a whole body of practices and expectations, over the whole of living: our senses and assignments of energy, our shaping perceptions of ourselves and our world. It is a lived system of meaning and values...but a culture which has also to be seen as the lived dominance and subordination of particular classes" (Eagleton 1989:110). The meanings and values of society are defined by the powerful. Hegemony is omnipresent. It is embedded in the social fabric of life.

One of the ironies of hegemony is that the dominant culture's success in inculcating its contrived value system is contingent on the extent to which that worldview makes sense. On one level, and I will consider this in greater detail later, the legitimation of the dominant culture, marked by acquiescence and consent, is founded on real-world experiences. This is what Ellen Meiksins Wood means when she writes in *The Retreat from Class,*

> What gives this political form its peculiar hegemonic power...is that the consent it commands from the dominated classes does not simply rest on their submission to an acknowledged ruling class or their acceptance of its right to rule. The parliamentary democratic state is a unique form of class rule because it casts doubt on the very existence of a ruling class. It does not achieve this by pure mystification. As always hegemony has two sides. It is not possible unless it is plausible. (1986:149)

We can recognize this clearly when it comes to disability. People with disabilities are usually seen as sick and pitiful, and in fact many became disabled through disease and most live in pitiful conditions. Furthermore, most people with disabilities are only noticed when they are being lifted up steps, or walk into an obstacle, or are being assisted across a street. Historically, most people with disabilities live apart from the rest of society. Most people do not regularly interact with people with disabilities in the classroom, at work, at the movies, and so on. Instead of curing the social conditions that cause disease and desperation, or removing the steps that necessitate assistance, the dominant culture explains the pitiful conditions people are forced to live in by creating a stratum or group of "naturally" pitiful individuals to conceal its pitiful status quo. The dominant culture turns reality on its head.

Today the mass media play the greatest role in what Noam Chomsky and Edward Herman (1988) called "manufacturing consent" through the use of filters that select and shape information. Indeed, its role in creating and promoting images has grown exponentially in recent times as its capacity to project images has grown. The philosopher Roger Gottlieb links the mass media's role in maintaining order to creating an "authorized reality." He echoes Wood's earlier point that this created truth must actually reflect certain aspects of reality:

In this complex sense, the media, like the state and the doctor, serve as authority figures. Their authority is derived from the compelling power of the images they produce—just as the authority of the medieval church derived from the size of its cathedrals.... And it is not foolishness or stupidity that leads us to take these images so seriously. It is the fact that real needs are manipulated into false hopes. Our needs for sexuality, love, community, an interesting life, family respect, and self-respect are transformed by the ubiquitous images of an unattainable reality into the sense that our sexuality, family, and personal lives are unreal. And it is this mechanism that sustains social authorities no longer believed to be legitimate. (1987:156, 159)

What images of disability are most prevalent in the mass media? Television shows depicting the helpless and angry cripple as a counterpoint to a poignant story about love or redemption. Tragic news stories about how drugs or violence have "ruined" someone's life by causing him or her to become disabled, or even worse, stories of the heroic person with a disability who has "miraculously," against all odds, become a successful person (whatever that means) and actually inched very close to being "normal" or at least to living a "normal" life. Most despicable are the telethons "for" *crippled* people, especially, poor, pathetic, crippled children. These telethons parade young children in front of the camera while celebrities like Jerry Lewis pander to people's goodwill and pity to get their money. In the United States surveys have shown that more people form attitudes about disabilities from telethons than from any other source.[14]

These images merge nicely with the language used to describe people with disabilities.[15] Consider, for example, "cripple," "invalid," "retard." In Zimbabwe, the term is *chirema*, which literally translates as "useless." In Brazil, the term is *pena*, which is slang for an affliction that comes as punishment. These terms are evidence of how people with disabilities are dehumanized. The process of assigning "meaning" through language, signs, and symbols is relentless and takes place most significantly in families, religious institutions, communities, and schools.

The dehumanization of people with disabilities through language (as just one obvious example) has a profound influence on consciousness. They, like other oppressed peoples, are constantly told by the dominant culture what they cannot do and what their place is in society. The fact that most oppressed people accept their place (read: oppression) is not hard to comprehend when we consider all the ideological powers at work. Their false consciousness has little to do with intelligence. It does have to do with two interactive and mutually dependent sources. The first is the capacity of ruling regimes to instill its values in the mass of people through double-speak, misdirection (blame the victim), naturalized inferiority, and legitimated authority. This is *hegemony*. The second is the psychological devastation people experience which creates self-pity and self-annihilation and makes self-awareness, awareness of peers, and awareness of their own humanity extremely difficult. This is *alienation*. Hegemony and alienation are two sides of the same phenomenon—ideological domination.[16]

In the case of disability, domination is organized and reproduced principally by a circuitry of power and ideology that constantly amplifies the normality of domination and compresses difference into classification norms (through symbols and categories) of superiority and normality against inferiority and abnormality.

Notes

1. Einar Helander, at a press conference on the release of the United Nations Report *Human Rights and Disabled Persons* (*Chicago Tribune*, December 5, 1993). Herlander has written a number of reports for the UN, including Prejudice and Dignity and, with Padmani Mendis, Gunnel Nelson, and Ann Goerdt, Training in the Disabled Community.
2. For example, unpaid domestic labor contributes to the socially necessary sustenance and nurturance of paid nondomestic labor, and the people, prominently women, involved in this work should be considered part of the laboring class. See Ferguson 1989.
3. O'Connor does not mean to imply that people defined as surplus are unnecessary. He means they are irrelevant to the present political-economic system. The notion of surplus people was explicitly developed to account for the treatment of people with mental retardation in Farber 1968.

4. To a great extent, exiles have avoided this "declassing." They have, at least in many cases, become incorporated into new economic milieus subsequent to their forced expulsion from their homeland.

5. Much has been written about precapitalist economic formations. There have been a number of efforts to refine the classification of their primitive, feudal, or semifeudal characteristics: "archaic" (Polanyi 1944); "tributary" (Amin 1990); "precapitalist" (Dobb 1946). Many have simply used the term "traditional."

6. This is in sharp distinction not only to psychology, as discussed earlier, but also to the German idealist philosophy of Kant, Hegel, and Schopenhauer. For these people separated society and being from consciousness and thought. For example, in *The Phenomenology of Mind* Hegel extinguishes any social relationship to truth or any civil or state (government) relationship to justice. Later, in *The Science of Logic*, he merged the two. Thought *is* being, and there is a distinction between reality and actuality.

7. Overdetermination is a theory associated primarily with Louis Althusser. Trying to avoid orthodox Marxism's theory that economic relations determine all social relations, he conceived the notion that the "superstructures" (language, law, custom, religion, etc.) have their own "specific effectivity." But Althusser argues that these distinct realities are subject to the "determination in the last instance by the [economic] mode of production," although there is "the relative autonomy of the superstructures and their specific effectivity" (1964: 111). This is overdetermination. While I do not subscribe to Althusser's idea that superstructures (his structuralism), I do believe that overdetermination is an insightful way of thinking about relationships. In this case, while powers have their own specific effectivity, they are ordered by class rule. Once the ensemble of power relationships is configured or ordered, these relationships evolve primarily from their internal dynamics.

8. The theory of hegemony is one of the great contributions of the Italian communist Antonio Gramsci, who insisted that the principal way power was projected by the capitalist ruling class (Italy in the 1920s) was through hegemony or ideological domination. In his *The Two Revolutions* Carl Boggs argues that Gramsci's theory of hegemony penetrated the realm of power where ideology (most notably culture) and political economy met: "For Gramsci ideas, beliefs, cultural preferences, and even myths and superstitions possessed a certain material reality of their own since in their power to inspire people towards action, they interact with economic conditions, which other wise would be nothing more than empty abstractions" (1984: 158).

9. See Paulo Friere's "banking theory" in *The Pedagogy of the Oppressed* (1973)

10. Freire is probably the best-known theorist of hegemonic practices of schooling. He has been influential in developing counterhegemonic education. He is associated with literacy campaigns in Cuba, Guinea-Bissau, Nicaragua, and Brazil. In *Ideology, Culture, and the Process of Schooling*, the critical theorist and educator Henry Giroux writes, "According to Freire, it is the cultural institutions of the dominant elite that play a major role in inculcating the oppressed with myths and beliefs that later become anchored in their psyches and character structure. To the degree that repressive institutions are successful in universalizing the belief system of the oppressor class, people will consent to their own exploitation and powerlessness" (1988: 134).

  Samuel Bowles and Herbert Gintis (1976), Michael Apple (1979), Henry Giroux (1988), Paulo Freire (1968, 1973, 1987), and Michel Focault (1980) successfully demonstrate the role of schooling in the production of a monoculture and the reproduction of existing power relations. It is ironic that while the literature theorizing the hegemonic practices of schooling has burgeoned in recent years, the voices of radical educators, especially those critical theorists who have promoted such views, have been silent on disability, inclusion, and special education, where the oppression and control of students has been the greatest. While this omission of radical pedagogy does not compare to the common outrageous treatment of students with disabilities, it is just as telling of the status of students with disabilities.

11. Joseph Tropea's article, "Bureaucratic Order and Special Children," is useful because3 of its focus on the historical socioeconomic necessities that framed early attempts to warehouse "incorrigible, backward and otherwise defective pupils" (1987:32)

12. The same regulations that are being used to provide students with access are also being implemented in such a way that many students are being inappropriately removed from regular education, resulting in questionable educational benefit and possible harm (Gartner and Lipsky 1987). This is particularly true in the area of high-incidence mild disabilities, the so-called educable mentally handicapped, learning disabled, and behaviorally/emotionally disordered. Special education is increasingly used to segregate students labeled "mildly handicapped"—students whom schools have difficulty serving or whom they choose not to serve. These programs often have a disproportionate enrollment of racial minority students. For instance, though African-American students make up 16 percent of the public school population, they represent 35 percent of those labeled educable mentally handicapped.

13. An unpublished paper that Gill and Voss developed at the Chicago Institute of Disability Research: "Inclusion Beyond the Classroom: Asking Persons with Disabilities About Education."

14. In 1993 the magazine Vanity Fair ran a series on telethons. Most of the commentary centered on the "worth" of a life with disability. This brought Paul Longmore's work to the fore. Longmore, a leading disability rights academic then at Stanford University, had decisively shown elsewhere that telethons promoting charities are the principal ideological mediums transmitting and inculcating attitudes about disability in the United States. Longmore writes that the four major telethons—Easter Seals, Arthritis Foundation, United Cerebral Palsy, and Muscular Dystrophy Association—reach a combined audience of 250 million people and their message "is hegemonic in creating attitudes and ideas about disability" (Longmore, quoted in Bennets 1993:2

15. For the purposes of this book, I use the term "language" as it is commonly understood. I recognize that Ferdinand de Saussure in his Course in General Linguistics distinguished "language" from "speech" to argue that language is unable to be transformed, that it is an unconscious code. Emile Durkheim argued that this "split" was the basis of society. In this sense I am most often exploring speech, although I make the point numerous times that language, as it is used, is interiorized and its meaning inculcated.

16. Some people argue that ideology is partisan in that it is inherently at the service of the dominant culture; others argue that it is neutral and a contested terrain of ideas. Just before he died, Sartre defined ideology in the former terms: ""Ideology…is an ensemble of ideas which underlies alienated acts and reflects them….Ideologies represent powers and are active. Philosophies are formed in opposition to ideologies, although they reflect them to a certain extent while at the same time criticizing them and going beyond them" (Schilpp 1991:20). Sartre sees ideology as always partisan. Slavoj Zizek, editor of Mapping Ideology, thinks ideology is more limited and more neutral: "Ideology either exerts an influence that is crucial but constrained to some narrow social stratum, or its role in social reproduction is marginal" (1994: 14). For the purposes of this book it is most useful to think of ideology as a system of ideas and beliefs that are projected.

Works Cited

Louis Althusser. 1964. *For Marx.* London: Verso.

Amin, Samir. 1990. *Maldevelopment: Anatomy of Global Failure.* London: Zed Press.

———, Arrighi, Giovanni; Gunder, Frank, Andre; and Wallerstein, Immanuel. 1990. *Transforming the Revolution: Social Movements in the World System.* New York: Monthly Review Press.

Apple, Michael. 1979. *Ideology and Curriculum.* London: Routledge and Kegan Paul.

Bennets, L. 1993. "Letter from Las Vegas." *Vanity Fair* (September). 82–96

Boggs, Carl. 1984. *The Two Revolutions: Gramsci and the Dilemmas of Western Marxism.* Boston: South End Press.

Bowles, Samuel and Gintis, Herbert. 1976. *Schooling in Capitalist America.* New York: Basic Books.

Maurice, Dobb. 1946. *Studies in the Development of Capitalism.* London: Oxford Press.

Farber. 1968. *Mental Retardation: Its Social Context and Social Consequences.* Boston: Houghton Mifflin.

Ferguson, Ann. 1989. *Blood at the Root.* London: Pandora.

Freire, P. 1987. *Education for Critical Consciousness.* New York: Continuum.

———. 1973. *The Pedagogy of the Oppressed.* New York: Seabury Press.

———. 1968. *Cultural Action for Freedom.* Cambridge, Mass: Center for the Study of Change.

Gartner, Alan, and Kerzner Lipsky, Dorothy. 1987. "Beyond Special Education:Toward a Quality System for All Students" In *Harvard Educational Review* 57 (4): 367–396.

Giroux, Henry A. 1988. *Ideology, Culture, and the Process of Schooling.* Philadelphia: Temple University Press.

Polanyi, Karl. 1944. *The Great Transformation.* New York: Rinehart.

Schlipp, Paul Arthur, ed. 1991. *The Philosophy of Jean-Paul Sartre.* Lasalle, Ill: Open Court.

Tropea, Joseph. 1987. "Bureaucratic Order and Special Children: Urban Schools 1890s–1940s." *History of Education Quarterly* 27 (1): 29–52.

Zizek, Slavoj, ed. 1994. *Mapping Ideology.* London: Verso.

Part V

The Question of Identity

19

The End of Identity Politics and the Beginning of Dismodernism
On Disability as an Unstable Category

Lennard J. Davis

There are times when the black man is locked into his body. Now, "for a being who has acquired conscious-ness of himself and of his body, who has attained the dialectic of subject and object, the body is no longer a cause of the structure of consciousness, it has become an object of consciousness."

—Frantz Fanon, citing Merleau-Ponty, *Black Skin, White Masks*

At times we might look back nostalgically to the moment when identity was relatively simple, when it was possible to say that one *was* black or white, male or female, "Indian" or not. It might once have been possible to answer the question that James Weldon Johnson's narrator in *The Autobiography of an Ex-Colored Man* asks his mother "Are you white?" with her clear reply, "No, I am not white..." (8). But the issue of identity by race, gender, or sexual orientation, particularly in America, has become more clouded, fuzzier, grainier than it used to be. And so, the issue of a disability identity has begun to enter murkier grounds.

When I discussed the idea of clouding the issue of disability identity, a prominent disability scholar advised me not to pursue this line of thinking. "We're not ready to dissolve disability identity. We're just beginning to form it." While I agree that there is a strategic kind of identity politics one might want to pursue, especially early on in an academic or political movement, I also think that ignoring the current seismic shifts in identity politics would be equally disastrous and could lead to major instability in the near future. If disability studies were to ignore the current intellectual moment and plow ahead using increasingly antiquated models, the very basis for the study of the subject could be harmed by making its premises seem irrelevant, shoddily thought through, and so on.

In effect, we do have to acknowledge that, unlike race, class, gender, sexual preference, and the like, disability is a relatively new category. Although the category has existed for a long time, its present form as a political and cultural formation has only been around since the 1970s, and has come into some kind of greater visibility since the late 1980s. The political and academic movement around disability is at best a first- or second-wave enterprise. The first wave of any struggle involves the establishment of the identity against the societal definitions that were formed largely by oppression. In this first phase, the identity—be it blackness, or gayness, or Deafness—is hypostasized, normalized, turned positive against the negative descriptions used by the oppressive regime. Thus "Black is Beautiful," "Gay Pride," and "Deaf Power" might be seen as mere reappropriations of a formerly derogatory discourse. The first phase also implies a pulling together of forces, an agreement to agree for political ends and group solidarity, along with the tacit approval of an agenda for the establishment of basic rights and prohibitions against various kinds of discrimination and ostracism.

In a second wave, a newer generation of people within the identity group, ones who have grown up with the libratory models well in place, begin to redefine the struggle and the subject of study.

They no longer seek group solidarity since they have a firm sense of identity. In a second wave, the principals are comfortable about self-examining, finding diversity within the group, and struggling to redefine the identity in somewhat more nuanced and complex ways. Often this phase will produce conflict within a group rather than unity. We've seen this most dramatically in the feminist movement when second-wave thinkers like Judith Butler have critiqued earlier essentialist notions that pulled the movement together initially. The conflict can come from differences that have been suppressed for the sake of maintaining a unified front so that the group could emerge in the first place and resist the formerly oppressive categorization and treatment.

Disability studies is, as I have said, a relatively new field of study. Its earliest proponents were writing in the 1970s and 1980s. The second wave of disability writing can be seen as emerging in the 1990s. Both the first and second waves have had a strong interest in preserving the notion of a distinct and clear entity known variously as "people with disabilities" (PWDs) or "Deaf people." In the case of PWDs, the interest has been in creating a collectivity where before there had been disunity. In the past, people with disabilities did not identify as such. Medical definitions of impairments were developed with no need to create unity among diverse patient groups. Wheelchair users saw no commonality with people with chronic fatigue syndrome or Deaf people. Given the American ethic of individuality and personal achievement, there would have been little incentive for PWDs to identify with the "handicaps" of other people. Rather, the emphasis would have been on personal growth, or overcoming the disability, and normalization through cure, prosthesis, or medical interventions. With the return of veterans from the Vietnam war, a movement grew up around civil rights for people with disabilities, which culminated in the Americans with Disabilities Act of 1990. By the beginning of the millennium disability activism, consciousness, and disability studies is well established, although many areas of the ADA are being rolled back in the courts and in the legislature.[1]

To begin with, one might want to point out the obvious point that history repeats itself. As Marx wrote about the failed revolution in France, people tend to model political movements on those of the past. For people with disabilities the civil rights model was seen as more progressive and better than the earlier charity and medical models. In the earlier versions, people with disabilities were seen variously as poor, destitute creatures in need of the help of the church or as helpless victims of disease in need of the correction offered by modern medical procedures. The civil rights model, based on the struggles of African Americans in the United States, seemed to offer a better paradigm. Not plagued by God nor beset by disease, people with disabilities were seen as minority citizens deprived of their rights by a dominant ableist majority.

Along with this model went the social model, which saw disability as a constructed category, not one bred into the bone. This social model is in dialogue with what is often referred to as the British model, which sees a distinction between impairment and disability. Impairment is the physical fact of lacking an arm or a leg. Disability is the social process that turns an impairment into a negative by creating barriers to access. The clearest example of this distinction is seen in the case of wheelchair users. They have impairments that limit mobility, but are not disabled unless they are in environments without ramps, lifts, and automatic doors. So, as long as the minority and/or social model held fast, this model seems to have worked pretty well, or at least as well as the civil rights model itself worked.

Enter postmodernity. The postmodern critique is one that destabilizes grand, unifying theories, that renders problematic desires to unify, to create wholes, to establish foundations. One could fill archives with what has been said or written about the culture wars, the science wars, and whatever other wars. In terms of identity, there has been an interesting and puzzling result. The one area that remained relatively unchallenged despite the postmodern deconstructionist assault was the notion of group identity. Indeed, the postmodern period is the one that saw the proliferation of multiculturality. One could attack the shibboleths of almost any ground of knowledge, but one could never attack the notion of being, for example, African American, a woman, or gay. To do so would be tantamount to being part of the oppressive system that created categories of oppressed others. One could interrogate the unity of the novel, science, even physics, but one could not interrogate one's right to be female, of color, or queer. Given this resistant notion of identity, the disability movement quite rightly desired to include disability as part of the multicultural quilt. If all the identities were under the same tent, then disability wanted to be part of the academic and cultural solidarity that being of a particular, oppressed minority represented.

Yet, within that strong notion of identity and identity politics, a deconstructive worm of thought began its own parasitic life. That worm targeted "essentialism." Just as no one wants to be a vulgar Marxist, no one wanted to be an essentialist. Essentialists—and there were fewer and fewer of them very soon after we began to hear the word—were putatively accused of claiming in a rather simple-minded way that being a woman or an ethnic minority was somehow rooted in the body. That identity was tied to the body, written on the body. Rather, the way out of this reductionist mode was to say that the body and identities around the body were socially constructed and performative. So while postmodernism eschewed the whole, it could accept that the sum of the parts made up the whole in the form of the multicultural, rainbow quilt of identities.[2] Social constructionism and performativity seemed to offer the way out of the problem caused by the worm of essentialism, but it also created severe problems in shaping notions of identity.[3] If all identities are socially constructed or performative, is there a core identity there? Is there a there?

Disability offers us a way to rethink some of these dilemmas, but in order to do so, I think we need to reexamine the identity of disability, and to do so without flinching, without hesitating because we may be undoing a way of knowing. As with race, gender, and sexual orientation, we are in the midst of a grand reexamination. Disability, as the most recent identity group on the block, offers us the one that is perhaps least resistant to change or changing thoughts about identity. And, most importantly, as I will argue, disability may turn out to be the identity that links other identities, replacing the notion of postmodernism with something I want to call "dismodernism."

I am arguing that disability can be seen as the postmodern subject position for several reasons. But the one I want to focus on now is that these other discourses of race, gender, and sexuality began in the mid-nineteenth century, and they did so because that is when the scientific study of humans began. The key connecting point for all these studies was the development of eugenics.[4] Eugenics saw the possible improvement of the race as being accomplished by diminishing problematic peoples and their problematic behaviors—these peoples were clearly delineated under the rubric of feeble-mindedness and degeneration as women, people of color, homosexuals, the working classes, and so on. All these were considered to be categories of disability, although we do not think of them as connected in this way today. Indeed, one could argue that categories of oppression were given scientific license through these medicalized, scientificized discourses, and that, in many cases, the specific categories were established through these studies.

Postmodernity along with science now offers us the solvent to dissolve many of these categories. In the area of race, we now know, for example, that there is no genetic basis to the idea that race, in its eugenic sense, exists. Thus far, no one has been able to identify a person as belonging to a specific "race" through DNA analysis. In fact, DNA analysis lets us understand that the category of race does not exist in physiological terms. Further, DNA analysis tells us that there is more genetic variation within a group we have called a race than within the entire human gene pool. Indeed, no one is even able to tell us how many races there are, and fine distinctions between phenotypes tend to dissolve the notion of categorical racial identities even further. The Human Genome Project offered up the possibility of mapping with certainty the complete sequence of approximately 3.2 billion pairs of nucleotides that make us human. But the project has left us with more questions than it has answered. For example, scientists are puzzling over the relatively low count of genes in the human genome. It had been estimated that humans would have approximately 100,000 genes, but the study yielded a mere 30,000, putting Homo sapiens on par with the mustard cress plant (25,000 genes) in terms of genetic complexity.[5] More annoying and less known is the fact that the two groups who analyzed the genome, the privately owned Celera group and the government-financed consortium of academic centers, have come up with only 15,000 that they jointly agree on. Fifteen thousand more genes do not overlap in either analysis.[6] Considerable doubt exists as to whether these genes are "real."

More to the point, there is considerable confusion over race in relation to genetics. On the one hand, we are told that the mapped human genome, taken from the DNA of one or two individuals, is the same for all humans. We are further informed that there is relatively little diversity in our genetic makeup. But we are also told that various "races" and ethnic groups have differing genetic markers for disability, defect, and disease. The contradiction is one that has been little explored, and those who have pursued the point have come under criticism for racializing genetics.[7] Central to the confusion is the category of race itself. If we say, on the one hand, that there is no genetic way to ascertain race, and we also say that we have examined certain racial groups and discovered a greater chance of finding a particular gene, then we have indeed mixed our scientific categories.[8]

If we step back from the genetic level, we might want to investigate identity questions at the cellular level. Here, tellingly, we could investigate the HeLa cells widely used in laboratories and schools in what is called an "immortal cell line," much like the lines developed currently for stem-cell research. These cells all derive from an African American woman named Henrietta Lacks who died in 1951 of cervical cancer. The cells were taken without the permission of Ms. Lacks, and became so widespread as to be ubiquitous. For the point of view of this discussion, the cells were presumed to be universal until 1967, when a geneticist named Stanley Gartler announced that at least eighteen other cell lines had been contaminated by the HeLa cells. He determined this by insisting that the presence of G6PD (glucose-6-phosphate dehydrogenase), an enzyme which is a factor in red blood cell production, had been a marker in all these lines and that this type of enzyme "has been found only in Negroes" (61).[9] Thus, during the early period of genetic research previously universal cells were racialized at the cellular level. But the appearance of race at the cellular level is no longer possible or relevant. The markers thought to be of a specific racial group have no validity for that identificatory purpose.

The issue of race is also complicated by the use of in vitro fertilization in a recent case of "scrambled eggs," in which a fertility doctor implanted in a woman's womb not only her own fertilized embryo but that of another couple as well. The resulting birth was of fraternal twins, one white and the other black.[10] Such complications of reproductive technologies will certainly lead to other kinds of choices being made by parents and physicians, intentional as well as unintentional, with the effect of rendering even more complex racial or even gender identity.[11] Finally, the patrolled area of "mixed race" is being interrogated. The fact that multiracial identifications have been prohibited on national censuses is now being challenged. The reasons for keeping single-race checkoff boxes is itself a highly politicized and tactical arena in which, understandably, oppressed groups have gained redress and power by creating a unified subject. Where censuses allow a mixed-race checkoff, the statistical stronghold of race may well become weakened with questionable results.

In the area of gender, we are also seeing confusions in otherwise fixed categories. A culture of transgendered peoples is now being more widely permitted and the right to be transgendered is being actively fought for. The neat binaries of male and female are being complicated by volition, surgery, and the use of pharmaceuticals. Intersexuals, formerly known as hermaphrodites, were routinely operated upon at birth to assign them a specific gender. That move is now being contested by groups of adult intersexuals. Some feel they were assigned the wrong gender, and others feel that they would have liked to remain indeterminate. Transsexuals now routinely occupy various locations along a gender continuum, demarcating their place by clothing and other style-related choices, surgical corrections, and hormonal therapy. Even on the genetic level, females who are genetically male and males who are genetically female are a naturally occurring phenomenon. The gender determination is suppressed or enhanced in these cases of "Turner Syndrome" or "Klinefelter Syndrome," so that the genetic markers do not express the expected sexual phenotypes.[12]

Likewise, ethnicity is increasingly seen as problematic. Indeed, writers like Benedict Anderson have shown us that the idea of the nation is formed out of the suppression of ethnicities, although those ethnicities can end up forming new national consciousnesses. Steven Steinberg asserts that ethnicity is only one generation deep, and that all citizens become Americans after that generation, with only a thin veneer of food choices or other accoutrements of their ethnic origin to hold onto.[13]

Sexual orientation, which in the heyday of identity politics had a fairly definitive hold on defining a self, is now being questioned by many under the rubric of "queer studies." Whereas once the choice of sexual partner indicated who one was—gay, lesbian, heterosexual, or bisexual—now, in an era of dissolving boundaries, sexual orientation has become strangely unhinged, especially with the advent of transgender politics. When a male-to-female transsexual marries a person who defines herself as a woman, should that relationship be called lesbian? If an intersexual person chooses a person of either gender, or another intersexual, how do we define the relationship? In such cases, sexual orientation becomes the only option that does not define the person in all ways as fitting into a discrete category. The change from the expression "sexual preference" to "sexual orientation" serves to indicate something hardwired into a person's identity.

There has been some suggestion that there exists a "gay" gene, which, if it could be found definitively, would somehow settle the issue of gayness. But what we are seeing in the development of the Human Genome Project is that genetics is not the court of last resort in the story of life. No one gene determines the course of a human life. At this moment, while much good science has gone into the project of genetics, there is still no gene therapy that works. In addition, the low number of genes in the recent mapping indicates that genes alone will not tell the story. Further, even where genes are shown to contribute to disease, as in for example the case of Jewish women of Eastern European origin who carry a marker for a type of breast cancer, there is no good explanation for why only one-third of all such women will eventually develop breast cancer. If genes were the uncomplicated set of instructions that we are told they are, in a process of scientific grandiosity sometimes referred to as "geno-hype," there would be a one-for-one correspondence between the incidence of markers and the occurrence of disease.

Ultimately, if the grounds for an essentialist view of the human body are being challenged, so are the notions that identity is socially constructed. Most coherent of these critiques is Ian Hacking's *The Social Construction of What?* Hacking shows, to my satisfaction at least, that the idea of social constructionism, while very useful in many regards, is itself tremendously underdeveloped theoretically and methodologically. And it has reached the end of its shelf life. Once shocking and daring, now it has simply become a way of saying that objects in the world have a history of shifting feelings, concepts, and durations. In addition, Walter Benn Michaels has recently said at a public presentation at the University of Illinois at Chicago in March 2001, that if we agree that there is no biological basis for race, then how does it make sense to say there is a social construction of it? Michaels gives the example that if we agree there is no scientific basis for the existence of unicorns, does it make sense to say let's talk about the social construction of the unicorn?

So, if we follow this line of thinking, joining forces with the major critique of identity, we find ourselves in a morass in terms of identity politics and studies. There are various tactics one can take in the face of this conceptual dead end. One can object vehemently that X does indeed exist, that people have suffered for being X, and still do. Therefore, while there may be no basis in theory for being X, large numbers of people are nevertheless X and suffer even now for being so. Or one can claim that although no one has been able to prove the biological existence of X, they will be able to do so someday. In the gap between then and now, we should hold onto the idea of being X. Or one could say that despite the fact that there is no proof of the existence of X, one wants to hold to that identity because it is, after all, one's identity. Finally, we can say that we know X isn't really a biologically valid identity, but we should act strategically to keep the category so that we can pass laws to benefit groups who have been discriminated against because of the pseudo-existence of this category.

All these positions have merit, but are probably indefensible rationally. The idea of maintaining a category of being just because oppressive people in the past created it so they could exploit a segment of the population, does not make sense. To say that one wants to memorialize that category based on the suffering of people who occupy it makes some sense, but does the memorialization have to take the form of continuing the identity?[14] Even attempts to remake the identity will inevitably end up relying on the categories first used to create the oppression. Finally, strategic essentialism, as it is called, is based on several flawed premises, most notably the idea that we can keep secret our doubts so that legislators and the general public won't catch on. This Emperor's New Clothes approach is condescending to all parties, including the proponents of it.

Let us pause for a moment here to take into consideration the concept of disability as a state of injury, to use Wendy Brown's term. One of the central motivations for the Human Genome Project is the elimination of "genetic defects." The argument is based on a vision of the "correct" or "real" genome being one without errors or mistakes. Somewhere, in some empyrean there exists the platonic human genome. This genome is a book or text made up of letters sequenced in the right order without "mistakes." As such, it is in fact a sacred text and our correct reading of it is not unlike the vision that the fundamentalist has that his or her sacred text is infallible. However, the problem is that, as it stands now, the human genome is in need of fixing to make it perfect. Errors of transcription have ruined the primal perfection of the text. The problem is related to exegesis and amanuensis. Thus, people with genetic diseases have "birth defects" and are "defective."

This explanation, like most, is partial and error-laden. It is based on a pre-postmodern definition of human subjects as whole, complete, perfect, self-sustaining. This is the neoclassical model of Pico della Mirandola, Descartes, Locke, Hume, Kant, and so on. But if we think of cystic fibrosis or sickle cell anemia as "defects" in an otherwise perfect and whole human subject, are we making a grand mistake? Clearly, the people who have such genetic conditions are in grave peril. Few, if any, will live to a ripe old age. Each will have health issues. It would be in the interest of both those people and their physicians to heal their illnesses. Since there is no cure for these diseases at the present time, it seems reasonable to think that we can eliminate the defect by means of genetic medicine. So the idea that one would want to fix these genetic defects seems more than logical.

Yet the model involved in the idea of birth "defect" comes to us direct and unaltered from a eugenic model of the human body. Words like "fit," "normal," "degenerate," "feeble," "defect," and "defective" are all interlaced. Their roots lie directly in the "scientific" study of humans that reached its liminal threshold in the middle of the nineteenth century. We now openly repudiate eugenics, mainly because of the Nazis' use of "negative eugenics," that is, the direct elimination of "defectives" from the human race. This seems so horrendous to us that the term is no longer used. But organizations in the United States and England have simply morphed their names into ones that use the term "genetics," preserving the Latin linguistic root in both eugenic and genetic. Now eugenics (or genetics) is carried out through two avenues—prenatal screening, which works some of the time, and genetic engineering, which has not worked on humans so far. In both cases, the aim is to improve the human stock and to remove genetic defects. With the advent of the Human Genome and genetic sequencing projects, the illusion is that single genes will be discovered that can be "fixed" with an improved consequence. There is, of course, the problem of the "single gene" hypothesis, now being hotly debated in the context of the latest claim that there is a single gene for speech.[15]

Many would claim that for behaviors like speech, sexual orientation, or intelligence, there can be no single gene or genetic causality. So the premise that we can fix a single gene is itself a problem. Further, the idea of a "mistake" is also problematic. Take the examples I have given of sickle-cell anemia and cystic fibrosis. The genetic markers for both these are recessive, which means that a great number of the population will have genetic information (or misinformation) for these diseases. It turns out that people who carry the trait are resistant to malaria (in the case of sickle-cell anemia) and cholera (in the case of cystic fibrosis). If we posit that other "defects" are also protective against pandemic diseases, we can see that the simple elimination of such defects might be a complicated process with a possibly dubious result. What we are discussing is an algorithm of collective protectivity through genetic diversity versus harm to select individuals. I'm not arguing for a trade-off, but I think evolution has made that trade-off and our genes contain the history of humans and pandemics.

The use of genetic testing to avoid giving birth to children with genetic defects is itself problematic. On a simple statistical level, it can probably only be done in relatively wealthy countries and among middle- and upper-class people. Paradoxically, the effect of doing so may actually serve to increase the incidence of the condition because each time a person is born with the disease, two of the inherited traits end with the person upon his or her death. By bypassing this draconian form of genetic regulation, we may actually be contributing to the increased distribution of the trait in the gene pool, particularly in developing countries. The effect shows us that the simple answer of fixing the defect itself is not simple. Further, we may be tampering with the ability of humans to survive pandemics that we know about and others that we don't know about. How many people, for example, are now protected against developing active AIDS because they carry a trait for a "defect"?

Another aspect of this "defect" scenario is that a new issue is beginning to arise in the courts—the right not to be born. French courts upheld this idea in regard to women who did not receive genetic testing and who gave birth to children who were, for example, born without an arm. The courts endorsed compensatory payments to such children who had the right to not be born and whose parents were not able to exercise that right because of lack of information. The legislature in a subsequent act voided the court's ruling. Nevertheless, here indeed is a slippery slope, which many people with disabilities have regarded with suspicion. They rightly claim that their parents might have aborted them had they known of their upcoming impairment as children. On the other side of the disability divide, Deaf parents and parents of small stature have the ability to screen for the birth of a hearing child or a normal-sized child and to abort. And, of course, in countries like India and China, genetic testing is used to abort female fetuses. In the United States, the American Society for Reproductive Medicine, which sets the standards for most fertility clinics, officially stated that it is sometimes acceptable for couples to choose the sex of their children by selecting either male or female embryos and discarding the rest.[16] These cases begin to blur the notion of what a "defect" is and is not. Designer babies, as foreseen in the film *Gattaca,* can begin to be seen as those who will not contain, for example, genes for breast cancer or high blood pressure. The possibilities are limitless.

Some of the issues I've outlined here are the result of a destabilization of the categories we have known concerning the body. The body is never a single physical thing so much as a series of attitudes toward it. The grand categories of the body were established during the Renaissance and the Enlightenment, and then refined through the use of science and eugenics. Postmodernism along with science has assaulted many of these categories of self and identity. What we need now is a new ethics of the body that acknowledges the advances of science but also acknowledges that we can't simply go back to a relatively simple notion of identity. Genetics offers the way back, without, thus far, being able to deliver on that promise.

What I would like to propose is that this new ethics of the body begin with disability rather than end with it. To do so, I want to make clear that disability is itself an unstable category. I think it would be a major error for disability scholars and advocates to define the category in the by-now very problematic and depleted guise of one among many identities. In fact I argue that disability can capitalize on its rather different set of definitions from other current and known identities. To do this, it must not ignore the instability of its self-definitions but acknowledge that their instability allows disability to transcend the problems of identity politics. In setting up this model we must also acknowledge that not only is disability an unstable category but so is its doppelgänger—impairment.

In the social model, disability is presented as a social and political problem that turns an impairment into an oppression either by erecting barriers or by refusing to create barrier-free environments (where barrier is used in a very general and metaphoric sense). But impairment is not a neutral and easily understood term. It relies heavily on a medical model for the diagnosis of the impairment. For example, is Asperger's Syndrome or hysteria an impairment or the creation of the *folie à deux* of the observing physician and the cooperating patient?[17] Is anorexia or ADD an impairment or a disability? Particularly with illnesses that did not exist in the past, the plethora of syndromes and conditions that have sprouted in the hearts and minds of physicians and patients—conditions like attention deficit disorder, fugue states, pseudoneurotic schizophrenia, or borderline psychosis—we have to question the clear line drawn between the socially constructed "disability" and the preexistent and somatic "impairment." Ian Hacking, in *Mad Travelers: Reflections on the Reality of Transient Mental Illnesses,* points out that fidgety children were not considered to have impairments until ADD began. Is the impairment bred into the bone, or can it be a creation of a medical—technological—pharmaceutical complex?

Further, it is hard if not impossible to make the case that the actual category of disability really has internal coherence. It includes, according to the Americans with Disabilities Act of 1990, conditions like obesity, attention deficit disorder, diabetes, back pain, carpal tunnel syndrome, severe facial scarring, chronic fatigue syndrome, skin conditions, and hundreds of other conditions. Further, the law specifies that if one is "regarded" as having these impairments, one is part of the protected class.

The perceived legal problem is that the protected class is too large, and that is one of the reasons there is a perceived backlash in the United States against the ADA. In response to initial concerns that too many people with minor conditions were qualifying as disabled, the federal courts have issued very narrow interpretations of disability.[18] While we must deplore the fact that approximately 95 percent of cases brought before the courts are currently decided in favor of employers, we may also understand that some of this backlash is generated by a fear of creating a protected class that is too large. As with affirmative action, there is also general resentment among the populace that certain minority groups have special rights and privileges with regard to college admissions, job hiring, and so on. I want to be clear that I am not arguing against the protection of historically oppressed groups, as I will explain further. But I am calling attention to the increasingly ineffective means of achieving a goal of equality and equity in housing, jobs, and public accommodations.

Indeed, the protected class will only become larger as the general population ages. With the graying of the baby boomers, we will see a major increase in the sheer numbers of people with disabilities. As noted in the Introduction, the World Health Organization (WHO) predicts that by the year 2020, there will be more than 690 million people over the age of sixty-five, in contrast with today's 380 million. Two-thirds of the elderly will be in developing and under-developed nations. The increase in the elderly population will cause a major change in the disease patterns of these countries. There will be increasing rates of cancer, kidney failure, eye disease, diabetes, mental illness, and other chronic, degenerative illnesses such as cardiovascular disease. Although we may want to call all these senior citizens people with disabilities, what will that mean? Will we have to start making decisions about who is disabled and who is not? What Occam's razor will we use to hone the definition then? And how will this majority of older people redefine disability, since they did not grow up with a disability or acquire one early in life? Who will get to claim the definition of disability or the lack of one?

Complicating the issue of disability identity is the notion of cure. Just as people can slip into disability in the blink of an eye or the swerve of a wheel, so too can people be cured. Indeed, although we don't expect this in the near future, it is possible to imagine a world in which disability decreases from 15 to 20 percent of the population to just 2 or 3 percent. Just as we saw a major reduction in infectious diseases in the West over the previous century, so too may we see a decrease in disabilities. Gene therapy, colossally unsuccessful up until this point, could have a major although unlikely breakthrough and become the treatment of choice for many illnesses. Stem cell research could lead to the regeneration of many tissues that are the cause of degenerative and traumatic diseases and conditions. And technological fixes may become much more sophisticated, so that, for example, cochlear implants, now very problematic even if you believe in the concept, could become foolproof. Indeed, this specter is rather terrifying and offensive to many Deaf people, and with good reason. Advances in biotechnology could create natural and effective gaits for paraplegics or useful prostheses that might be virtually indistinguishable from human limbs. Indeed, political issues aside, the possibility does exist of cures for many impairments that now define a group we call "people with disabilities." We must recall though, that cures will of course only be available to people with means in wealthy countries.

What we are discussing is the instability of the category of disability as a subset of the instability of identity in a postmodern era. It would be understandable if one responded to what I've suggested by saying that, notwithstanding this instability, the category must be left alone. It must be maintained for all the reasons I had suggested earlier. Or, as one of my students responded, "What will happen to the handicapped parking space, if what you advocated happens?" True, but I want to propose that the very rationale for disability activism and study is good enough, indeed better than good enough, rationale for many people—people other than those we now call People with Disabilities. Rather than ignore the unstable nature of disability, rather than try to fix it, we should amplify that quality to distinguish it from other identity groups that have, as I have indicated, reached the limits of their own projects. Indeed, instability spells the end of many identity groups; in fact it can create a dismodernist approach to disability as a neoidentity.

What characterizes the limitations of the identity group model is its exclusivity (which contains the seeds of its own dissolution through the paradox of the proliferation of identity groups). Indeed, you have to be pretty *unidentified* in this day and age to be without an identity. So the very criticism of the category of disability as being too large, as containing too big a protected class, is actually a *fait accompli* with the notion of identity in general. We should not go on record as saying that disability is a fixed identity, when the power behind the concept is that disability presents us with a malleable view of the human body and identity.

Enlightenment thought would have it that the human is a measurable quantity, that all men are created equal, and that each individual is paradoxically both the same and different. Or perhaps, as Kierkegaard put it, "the single individual is the particular that has its *telos* in the universal."[19] In the past much of the paradoxical attitude toward citizens with disabilities arose from the conflict between notions of the equality of universal rights and the inequality of particular bodies.[20]

For all the hype of postmodern and deconstructive theory, these intellectual attempts made little or no impression on identity politics. Rather, those who pushed identity had very strong Enlightenment notions of the universal and the individual. The universal subject of postmodernism may be pierced and narrative-resistant but that subject was still whole, independent, unified, self-making, and capable. The dismodern era ushers in the concept that difference is what all of us have in common. That identity is not fixed but malleable. That technology is not separate but part of the body. That dependence, not individual independence, is the rule. There is no single clockmaker who made the uniform clock of the human body. The watchword of dismodernism could be: Form follows dysfunction.

What dismodernism signals is a new kind of universalism and cosmopolitanism that is reacting to the localization of identity. It reflects a global view of the world. To accomplish a dismodernist view of the body, we need to consider a new ethics of the body. We may take Kierkegaard's by-now naïve belief in the universal and transform it, knowing that this new universalism cannot be a return to Enlightenment values. Rather it must be a corrective to the myths not only of the Enlightenment but of postmodernism as well.

A new ethics of the dismodernist body consists of three areas: The first concerns the official stance—care *of* the body is now a requirement for existence in a consumer society. We are encouraged and beseeched to engage in this care; indeed, it is seen as a requirement of citizenship. This care of the body involves the purchase of a vast number of products for personal care and grooming, products necessary to having a body in our society. Although we are seen as self-completing, the contemporary body can only be completed by means of consumption. This is the official stance: that the contemporary human body is incomplete without deodorant, hair gel, sanitary products, lotions, perfumes, shaving creams, toothpastes, and so on.[21] In addition, the body is increasingly becoming a module onto which various technological additions can be attached. The by-now routine glasses, contact lenses, and hearing aids are supplemented by birth-control implants, breast implants, penile implants, pacemakers, insulin regulators, monitors, and the like. Further work will also intimately link us to more sophisticated cybertechnology. All this contributes to what Zygmund Bauman calls "the privatization of the body," which he sees as the "primal scene of postmodern ambivalence." The aim and goal, above all, is to make this industrial-modeled, consumer-designed body appear "normal." And even people with disabilities have to subscribe to this model and join the ranks of consumers.[22]

Another official area pertains to care *for* the body, an area that also links the economy with the body. Here we must confront an entire industry devoted to caring for the human body. We are discussing the healthcare industry and the dependent care industry. Included here are physicians' private practices, clinics, medical insurance companies, medical laboratories, hospitals, extended-care facilities, hospitals, hospices, nursing homes, in-home caregivers, pharmacies, manufacturers of assistive devices, and organizations that promote the research, development, and care of certain kinds of illnesses and conditions. In most countries, this industry makes up the largest sector of the economy. There are obviously huge economic advantages to the creation and maintenance of the disability industry. It is important to recall that since huge financial commitments are being made to the abnormal body, the ethics involved in the distribution of resources and the shaping of this industry is a major part of our approach to an ethical society. By and large, this industry is controlled and dominated by people who are not people with disabilities.

Finally, to secure a dismodernist ethics, in opposition or in some cases in alliance with the official stance, we need to discuss caring *about* the body. This is the area I would most like to emphasize. If we care about the body, that is to say care about the issues I have raised, we finally begin to open up and develop a dismodernist discourse of the body and the uses of bodies. This area begins with attention paid to human rights and civil rights that have to be achieved to bring people with disabilities to the awareness of other identity groups. Here we must discuss the oppression of so-called abnormal bodies, and the treatment of the poor with disabilities. Class again becomes an issue in identity. We must focus on the poor, since by all estimates the majority of people with disability are poor, unemployed, and undereducated. In the United States, only one-third of people with disabilities are employed, versus upward of 70 percent of "normal" workers. Indeed, many people with disabilities end up in prisons—particularly those with cognitive and affective disabilities. A *New York Times* article (August 7, 2000) pointed out that one in ten death row inmates are mentally retarded. Since the majority of people in the United States become quadriplegic or paraplegic from gunshot wounds, a disproportionate number of African American males are so impaired. And therefore a large number of these males with disabilities are also in prisons, often without adequate accommodations.

On an international level, land mines create impairments on a daily basis, and this fact combined with other technologies of war and extremely poor working conditions in sweatshop environments creates a level of disability in so-called developing countries that requires attention and thought. The treatment of women and female babies—including the abortion of female fetuses, the use of clitorectomies, the oppression of gay, lesbian, bisexual, and transgendered people—often intersects in familiar and unfamiliar ways with the mechanisms of disablement. It can be said that the most oppressed person in the world is a disabled female, Third World, homosexual, woman of color. In addition, the absence of adequate wheelchairs in poor countries, along with inadequate street and public accommodation facilities create a virtually inaccessible world for people with mobility impairments.

My point is that with a dismodernist ethic, you realize that caring *about* the body subsumes and analyzes care *of* and care *for* the body. The latter two produce oppressive subjection, while the former gives us an ethic of liberation. And the former always involves the use of culture and symbolic production in either furthering the liberation or the oppression of people with disabilities.

An ethics of the body provides us with a special insight into the complex and by now dead end of identity politics. The problem presented to us by identity politics is the emphasis on an exclusivity surrounding a specific so-called identity. Writers like Kenneth Warren, K. Anthony Appiah, Paul Gilroy, Wendy Brown, Walter Benn Michaels, Thomas Holt, and others are now critiquing the notion of a politics based on specific identities and on victim status. Disability studies can provide a critique of and a politics to discuss how all groups, based on physical traits or markings, are selected for disablement by a larger system of regulation and signification. So it is paradoxically the most marginalized group—people with disabilities—who can provide the broadest way of understanding contemporary systems of oppression.

This new way of thinking, which I am calling dismodernism, rests on the operative notion that postmodernism is still based on a humanistic model. Politics have been directed toward making all identities equal under a model of the rights of the dominant, often white, male, "normal" subject. In a dismodernist mode, the ideal is not a hypostatization of the normal (that is, dominant) subject, but aims to create a new category based on the partial, incomplete subject whose realization is not autonomy and independence but dependency and interdependence. This is a very different notion from subjectivity organized around wounded identities; rather, *all* humans are seen as wounded. Wounds are not the result of oppression, but rather the other way around. Protections are not inherent, endowed by the creator, but created by society at large and administered to all. The idea of a protected class in law now becomes less necessary since the protections offered to that class are offered to all. Thus, to belatedly answer my student, normal parking becomes a subset of handicapped parking.

The dismodernist subject is in fact disabled, only completed by technology and by interventions. Rather than the idea of the complete, independent subject, endowed with rights (which are in actuality conferred by privilege), the dismodernist subject sees that metanarratives are only "socially created" and accepts them as that, gaining help and relying on legislation, law, and technology. It acknowledges the social and technological to arrive at functionality. As the quadriplegic is incomplete without the motorized wheelchair and the controls manipulated by the mouth or tongue, so the citizen is incomplete without information technology, protective legislation, and globalized forms of securing order and peace. The fracturing of identities based on somatic markers will eventually be seen as a device to distract us from the unity of new ways of regarding humans and their bodies to further social justice and freedom.

We can thus better understand how the by now outdated postmodern subject is a ruse to disguise the hegemony of normalcy. Foucault is our best example. His work is, as Edward Said has noted, in *Power, Politics and Culture: Interview with Edward W. Said,* a homage to power, not an undermining of it. Said calls Foucault a "scribe" of power because of his fascination with the subject. For Foucault the state is power and citizens are docile bodies. This overtly sadomasochistic model is one that is part of a will-to-power, a fantasy of utter power and utter subjection. That model appeared to be postmodern, but was in fact the nineteenth century of Freud, Sacher-Masoch, and imperialism writ large. Instead, dismodernism doesn't require the abjection of wounds or docility to describe the populace, or the identity groups within. Rather it replaces the binary of docility and power with another—impairment and normalcy. Impairment is the rule, and normalcy is the fantasy. Dependence is the reality, and independence grandiose thinking. Barrier-free access is the goal, and the right to pursue happiness the false consciousness that obscures it. Universal design becomes the template for social and political designs.

The rhizomatic vision of Deleuze's solution to the postmodernist quandary presented by power, with its decentered, deracinated notion of action, along with the neorationalist denial of universals, leaves us with a temporary, contingent way of thinking about agency and change. The dismodernist vision allows for a clearer, more concrete mode of action—a clear notion of expanding the protected class to the entire population; a commitment to removing barriers and creating access for all. This includes removing the veil of ideology from the concept of the normal, and denying the locality of identity. This new ethic permits, indeed encourages, cosmopolitanism, a new kind of empire, to rephrase Hardt and Negri, that relies on the electronic senses as well as the neoclassical five. It moves beyond the fixity of the body to a literally constructed body, which can then be reconstructed with all the above goals in mind.

Clearly, what I am describing is the beginning of a long process. It began with the efforts of various identities to escape oppression based on their category of oppression. That struggle is not over and must continue. While there is no race, there is still racism. But dismodernism argues for a commonality of bodies within the notion of difference. It is too easy to say, "We're all disabled." But it is possible to say that we are all disabled by injustice and oppression of various kinds. We are all nonstandard, and it is under that standard that we should be able to found the dismodernist ethic.

What is universal in life, if there are universals, is the experience of the limitations of the body. Yet the fantasy of culture, democracy, capitalism, sexism, and racism, to name only a few ideologies, is the perfection of the body and its activities. As Paul Gilroy writes, "The reoccurrence of pain, disease, humiliation, grief, and care for those one loves can all contribute to an abstract sense of human similarity powerful enough to make solidarities based on cultural particularity appear suddenly trivial."[23] It is this aspect of experience, a dismodern view, that seems suddenly to be, at the beginning of the twenty-first century, about the only one we can justify.

Notes

1. For more on this, see a special issue of the *Berkeley Journal of Employment and Labor Law* 22:1 (2000), and also Leslie Francis and Anita Silvers, eds., *Americans with Disabilities: Exploring Implications of the Law for Individuals and Institutions* (New York: Routledge, 2000)

2. I have written more about this aspect of identity and disability in chapter 5 of *Bending Over Backwards: Disability, Dismodernism and Other Difficult Positions* (New York: New York University Press, 2002)..

3. See Ian Hacking, *The Social Construction of What?* (Cambridge: Harvard U P, 1999; rpt. 2001).

4. I have made this point elsewhere. See Lennard J. Davis, *Enforcing Normalcy: Disability, Deafness, and the Body* (London: Verso, 1995) for greater exposition.

5. Let us not even consider the further problem that in order to locate a gene, we have to cordon off "good DNA" from "junk" DNA may have a role to play in "influencing" the good DNA. Thus the exact science of genetics begins to resemble other explanatory systems requiring influence based on humors, astrological causes, and so on. Indeed, many human traits are polygenic, involving several different genes working in coordination with each other and with other processes.

6. Raymond Bonniet and Sarah Rimer, *New York Times* (August 24, 2001), A13

7. See Steve Olsen, "The Genetic Archeology of Race," *Atlantic Monthly* (April 2001).

8. See works like Tukufu Zuberi, *Thicker than Blood: An Essay on How Racial Statistics Lie* (Minneapolis: University of Minnesota Press, 2001).

9. For the most complete discussion of HeLa cells in regard to racial politics, see Hannah Landecker, "Immortality, In Vitro: A History of the HeLa Cell Line," in *Biotechnology and Culture: Bodies, Anxieties, Ethics,* ed. Paul E. Brodwin (Bloomington: Indiana UP, 2000), 53-72.

10. Dwight Garner, *New York Times Sunday Magazine* (March 25, 2001).

11. Although, as Dorothy Roberts has pointed out, prenatal technology is still very much a site of racial discrimination. See her "Race and the New Reproduction," *Hastings Law Journal* 47: 4 (1996).

12. For more on this subject, see Leslie Feinberg, *Transgender Warriors: Making History from Joan of Arc to Dennis Rodman* (Boston: Beacon Press, 1996). Also see Bob Beale, "New Insights into the X and Y Chromosomes," *The Scientist* (July 23, 2001) 15 (15): 18.

13. Steven Steinberg, *The Ethnic Myth* (Boston: Beacon Press, 2001).

14. See Wendy Brown, *States of Injury: Power and Freedom in Late Modernity* (Princeton: Princeton UP, 1995).

15. Nicholas Wade, *New York Times* (October 4, 2001

16. Gina Kolata, *New York Times* (September 28, 2001), A14.

17. See Ian Hacking's discussion of transient mental illnesses in *Mad Travelers: Reflections on the Reality of Transient Mental Illnesses* (Charlottesville: University of Virginia, 1998).

18. For an extensive discussion of the legal issues around disability, see a special issue of the *Berkeley Journal of Employment and Labor Law* 21: 1 (2000). For background on many of these issues, see Ruth O'Brien, *Crippled Justice: The History of Modern Disabiltiy Policy in the Workplace* (Chicago: U of Chicago P, 2001).

19. Soren Kierkegaard, *Fear and Trembling*, trans. Alastair Hanney (London: Penguin, 1985), 83

20. See my chapter, "Constructing Normalcy: The Bell Curve, the Novel, and the Invention of the Disabled Body in the Nineteenth Century," in this volume.

21. As an assignment, I ask my students to tally up the cost of all the products they buy for their bodies. The annual cost is astounding.

22. Magazines like *We* and *Poz* generate income by selling trendy and sexy wheelchairs and other equipment for people with disabilities. Of course, the routine body care products are called for here as well.

23. Paul Gilroy, *Against Race: Imagining Political Culture beyond the Color Line* (Cambridge: Harvard UP, 2000), 17.

20

Toward a Feminist Theory of Disability

Susan Wendell

In 1985, I fell ill overnight with what turned out to be a disabling chronic disease. In the long struggle to come to terms with it, I had to learn to live with a body that felt entirely different to me—weak, tired, painful, nauseated, dizzy, unpredictable. I learned at first by listening to other people with chronic illness or disabilities; suddenly able-bodied people seem to me profoundly ignorant of everything I most needed to know. Although doctors told me there was a good chance I would eventually recover completely, I realized after a year that waiting to get well, hoping to recovery my healthy body, was a dangerous strategy. I began slowly to identify with my new, disabled body and to learn to work with it. As I moved back into the world, I also began to experience the world as structure for people who have no weaknesses.[1] The process of encountering the able-bodied world led me gradually to identify myself as a disabled person, and to reflect on the nature of disability.

Some time ago, I decided to delve into what I assumed would be a substantial philosophical literature in medical ethics on the nature and experience of disability. I consulted *The Philosopher's Index*, looking under "Disability," "Handicap," "Illness," and "Disease." This was a depressing experience. At least 90 percent of philosophical articles on these topics are concerned with two questions: Under what conditions is it morally permissible/right to kill/let die a disabled person and how potentially disabled does a fetus have to be before it is permissible/right to prevent its being born? Thus, what I have to say here about disability is not a response to philosophical literature on the subject. Instead, it reflects what I have learned from the writings of other disabled people (especially disabled women), from talking with disabled people who have shared their insights and experiences with me, and from my own experience of disability. It also reflects my commitment to feminist theory, which offers perspectives and categories of analysis that help to illuminate the personal and social realities of disability, and which would, in turn, be enriched by a greater understanding of disability.

We need a theory of disability. It should be a social and political theory, because disability is largely socially constructed, but it has to be more than that; any deep understanding of disability must include thinking about the ethical, psychological and epistemic issues of living with disability. This theory should be feminist, because more than half of disabled people are women and approximately 16 percent of women are disabled (Fine and Asch 1988), and because feminist thinkers have raised the most radical issues bout cultural attitudes to the body. Some of the same attitudes about the body which contribute to women's oppression generally also contribute to the social and psychological disablement of people who have physical disabilities. In addition, feminists are grappling with issues that disabled people also face in a different context: Whether to stress sameness or difference in relation to the dominant group and in relation to each other; whether to place great value on independence from the help of other people, as the dominant culture does, or to question a value-system which distrusts and devalues dependence on other people and vulnerability in general; whether to take full integration into male dominated/able-bodied society as the goal, seeking equal power with men/able-bodied people in that society, or whether to preserve some degree of separate culture, in which the abilities, knowledge and values of women/the disabled are specifically honoured and developed.[2]

Disabled women struggle with both the oppressions of being women in male-dominated societies and the oppressions of being disabled in societies dominated by the able-bodied. They are bringing the knowledge and concerns of women with disabilities into feminism and feminist perspectives into the disability rights movement. To build a feminist theory of disability that takes adequate account of our differences, we will need to know how experiences of disability and the social oppression of the disabled interact with sexism, racism and class oppression. Michelle Fine and Adrienne Asch and the contributors to their 1988 volume, *Women and Disabilities*, have made a major contribution to our understanding of the complex interactions of gender and disability. Barbara Hillyer Davis has written in depth about the issue of dependency/independence as it relates to disability and feminism (Davis 1984). Other important contributions to theory are scattered throughout the extensive, primarily experiential, writing by disabled women;[3] this work offers vital insights into the nature of embodiment and the experience of oppression.

Unfortunately, feminist perspectives on disability are not yet widely discussed in feminist theory, nor have the insights offered by women writing about disability been integrated into feminist theorizing about the body. My purpose in writing this essay is to persuade feminist theorists, especially feminist philosophers, to turn more attention to constructing a theory of disability and to integrating the experiences and knowledge of disabled people into feminist theory as a whole. Toward this end I will discuss physical disability[4] from a theoretical perspective, including: some problems of defining it (here I will criticize the most widely used definitions—those of the United Nations); the social construction of disability from biological reality on analogy with the social construction of gender; cultural attitudes toward the body which oppress disabled people while also alienating the able-bodied from their own experiences of embodiment; the "otherness" of disabled people; the knowledge that disabled people could contribute to culture from our diverse experiences and some of the ways this knowledge is silenced and invalidated. Along the way, I will describe briefly three issues discussed in disability theory that have been taken up in different contexts by feminist theory: sameness vs. difference, independence vs. dependency and integration vs. separatism.

I do not presume to speak for disabled women. Like everyone who is disabled, I have a particular standpoint determined in part by both my physical condition and my social situation. My own disability may be temporary; it could get better or worse. My disability is usually invisible (except when I use a walking stick). I am a white university professor who has adequate medical and long-term disability insurance; that makes me very privileged among the disabled. I write what I can see from my standpoint. Because I do not want simply to describe my own experience but to understand it in a much larger context, I must venture beyond what I know first-hand. I rely on others to correct my mistakes and fill in those parts of the picture I cannot see.

Who Is Physically Disabled?

The United Nations offers the following definitions of and distinctions among impairment, disability and handicap:

> "*Impairment*: Any loss or abnormality of psychological, physiological, or anatomical structure or function. *Disability*: Any restriction or lack (resulting from an impairment) of ability to perform an activity in the manner or within the range considered normal for a human being. *Handicap*: A disadvantage for a given individual, resulting from an impairment or disability, that limits or prevents the fulfillment of a role that is normal, depending on age, sex, social and cultural factors, for that individual."
>
> Handicap is therefore a function of the relationship between disabled persons and their environment. It occurs when they encounter cultural, physical or social barriers which prevent their access to the various systems of society that are available to other citizens. Thus, handicap is the loss or limitation of opportunities to take part in the life of the community on an equal level with others. (U.N. 1983: 1.c. 6–7)

These definitions may be good enough for the political purposes of the U.N. They have two advantages: First, they clearly include many conditions that are not always recognized by the general public as disabling, for example, debilitating chronic illnesses that limit people's facilities but do not necessarily cause any visible disability, such as Crohn's Disease. Second, the definition of "handicap" explicitly recognizes the possibility that the primary cause of a disabled person's inability to do certain things may be social—denial of opportunities, lack of accessibility, lack of services, poverty, discrimination—which it often is.

However, by trying to define "impairment" and "disability" in physical terms and "handicap" in cultural, physical and social terms, the U.N. document appears to be making a shaky distinction between the physical and the social aspects of disability. Not only the "normal" roles for one's age, sex, society, and culture, but also "normal" structure and function, and "normal" ability to perform an activity, depend on the society in which the standards of normality are generated. Paradigms of health and ideas about appropriate kinds and levels of performance are culturally dependent. In addition, within each society there is much variation from the norm of any ability; at what point does this variation become disability? The answer depends on such factors as what activities a society values and how it distributes labour and resources. The idea that there is some universal, perhaps biologically or medically describable paradigm of human physical ability is an illusion. Therefore, I prefer to use a single term, "disability," and to emphasize that disability is socially constructed from biological reality.

Another objection I have to the U.N. definitions is that they imply that women can be disabled, but not handicapped, by being unable to do things which are not considered part of the normal role for their sex. For example, if a society does not consider it essential to a woman's normal role that she be able to read, then a blind woman who is not provided with education in Braille is not handicapped, according to these definitions.

In addition, these definitions suggest that we can be disabled, but not handicapped, by the normal process of aging, since although we may lose some ability, we are not handicapped unless we cannot fulfill roles that are normal *for our age*. Yet a society which provides few resources to allow disabled people to participate in it will be likely to marginalize *all* the disabled, including the old, and to define the appropriate roles of old people as very limited, thus handicapping them. Aging is disabling. Recognizing this helps us to see that disabled people are not "other," that they are really "us." Unless we die suddenly, we are all disabled eventually. Most of us will live part of our lives with bodies that hurt, that move with difficulty or not at all, that deprive us of activities we once took for granted or that others take for granted, bodies that make daily life a physical struggle. We need an understanding of disability that does not support a paradigm of humanity as young and healthy. Encouraging everyone to acknowledge, accommodate and identify with a wide range of physical conditions is ultimately the road to self-acceptance as well as the road to liberating those who are disabled now.

Ultimately, we might eliminate the category of "the disabled" altogether, and simply talk about individuals' physical abilities in their social context. For the present, although "the disabled" is a category of "the other" to the able-bodied, and for that very reason it is also a politically useful and socially meaningful category to those who are in it. Disabled people share forms of social oppression, and the most important measures to relieve that oppression have been initiated by disabled people themselves. Social oppression may be the only thing the disabled have in common;[5] our struggles with our bodies are extremely diverse.

Finally, in thinking about disability we have to keep in mind that a society's labels do not always fit the people to whom they are applied. Thus, some people are perceived as disabled who do not experience themselves as disabled. Although they have physical conditions that disable other people, because of their opportunities and the context of their lives, they do not feel significantly limited in their activities (see Sacks 1988); these people may be surprised or resentful that they are considered disabled. On the other hand, many people whose bodies cause them great physical, psychological and economic struggles are not considered disabled because the public and/or the medical profession do not recognize their disabling conditions. These people often long to be perceived as disabled, because society stubbornly continues to expect them to perform as healthy people when they cannot and refuses to acknowledge and support their struggles.[6] Of course, no one wants the social stigma associated with disability, but social recognition of disability determines the practical help a person receives from doctors, government agencies, insurance companies, charity organizations, and often from family and friends. Thus, how a society defines disability and whom it recognizes as disabled are of enormous psychological, economic and social importance, both to people who are experiencing themselves as disabled and to those who are not but are nevertheless given the label.

There is no definitive answer to the question: Who is physically disabled? Disability has social, experiential and biological components, present and recognized in different measures for different people. Whether a particular physical condition is disabling changes with time and place, depending on such factors as social expectations, the state of technology and its availability to people in that condition, the educational system, architecture, attitudes towards physical appearance, and the pace of life. (If, for example, the pace of life increases without changes in other factors, more people become disabled simply because fewer people can keep up the "normal" pace.)

The Social Construction of Disability

If we ask the questions: Why are so many disabled people unemployed or under-employed, impoverished, lonely, isolated; why do so many find it difficult or impossible to get an education (Davis and Marshall 1987; Fine and Asch 1988, 10–11); why are they victims of violence and coercion; why do able-bodied people ridicule, avoid, pity, stereotype and patronize them?, we may be tempted to see the disabled as victims of nature or accident. Feminists should be, and many are, profoundly suspicious of this answer. We are used to countering claims that insofar as women are oppressed they are oppressed by nature, which puts them at a disadvantage in the competition for power and resources. We know that if being biologically female is a disadvantage, it is because a social context makes it a disadvantage. From the standpoint of a disabled person, one can see how society could minimize the disadvantages of most disabilities, and, in some instances, turn them into advantages.

Consider an extreme case: the situation of physicist Stephen Hawking, who has had Amyotrophic Lateral Sclerosis (Lou Gehrig's Disease) for more than 26 years. Professor Hawking can no longer speak and is capable of only the smallest muscle movements. Yet, in his context of social and technological support, he is able to function as a professor of physics at Cambridge University; indeed he says his disability has given him the *advantage* of having more time to think, and he is one of the foremost theoretical physicists of our time. He is a courageous and talented man, but he is able to live the creative life he has only because of the help of his family, three nurses, a graduate student who travels with him to maintain his computer-communications systems, and the fact that his talent had been developed and recognized before he fell seriously ill (*Newsweek* 1988).

Many people consider providing resources for disabled people a form of charity, superogatory in part because the disabled are perceived as unproductive members of society. Yet most disabled people are placed in a double-bind: they have access to inadequate resources because they are unemployed or underemployed, and they are unemployed or underemployed because they lack the resources that would enable them to make their full contribution to society (Matthews 1983; Hannaford 1985). Often governments and charity organizations will spend far more money to keep disabled people in institutions where they have no chance to be productive than they will spend to enable the same people to live independently and productively. In addition, many of the "special" resources the disabled need merely compensate for bad social planning that is based on the illusion that everyone is young, strong, healthy (and, often, male).

Disability is also frequently regarded as a personal or family problem rather than a matter for social responsibility. Disabled people are often expected to overcome obstacles to participation by their own extraordinary efforts, or their families are expected to provide what they need (sometimes at great personal sacrifice). Helping in personal or family matters is seen as superogatory for people who are not members of the family.

Many factors contribute to determining whether providing a particular resource is regarded as a social or a personal (or family) responsibility.[7] One such factor is whether the majority can identify with people who need the resource. Most North Americans feel that society should be organized to provide short-term medical care made necessary by illness or accident, I think because they can imagine themselves needing it. Relatively few people can identify with those who cannot be "repaired" by medical intervention. Sue Halpern makes the following observation:

> Physical health is contingent and often short-lived. But this truth eludes us as long as we are able to walk by simply putting one foot in front of the other. As a consequence, empathy for the disabled is unavailable to most able-bodied persons. Sympathy, yes, empathy, no, for every attempt to project oneself into that condition, to feel what it is like not to be ambulatory, for instance, is mediated by an ability to walk (Halpern 1988, 3).

If the able-bodied saw the disabled as potentially themselves or as their future selves, they would be more inclined to feel that society should be organized to provide the resources that would make disabled people fully integrated and contributing members. They would feel that "charity" is as inappropriate a way of thinking about resources for disabled people as it is about emergency medical care of education.

Careful study of the lives of disabled people will reveal how artificial the line is that we draw between the biological and the social. Feminists have already challenged this line in part by showing how processes such as childbirth, menstruation and menopause, which may be presented, treated, and therefore experienced as illnesses or disabilities, are socially constructed from biological reality (Rich 1976; Ehrenreich and English 1979). Disabled people's relations to our bodies involve elements of struggle which perhaps cannot be eliminated, perhaps not even mitigated, by social arrangements. *But much of what is disabling about our physical conditions is also a consequence of social arrangements* (Finger 1983; Fine and Asch 1988) which could, but do not, either compensate for our physical conditions, or accommodate them so that we can participate fully, or support our struggles and integrate us into the community *and our struggles into the cultural concept of life as it is ordinarily lived.*

Feminists have shown that the world has been designed for men. In North America at least, life and work have been structured as though no one of any importance in the public world, and certainly no one who works outside the home for wages, has to breast-feed a baby or look after a sick child. Common colds can be acknowledged publicly, and allowances made for them, but menstruation cannot. Much of the world is also structured as though everyone is physically strong, as though all bodies are "ideally shaped," as though everyone can walk, hear and see well, as though everyone can work and play at a pace that is not compatible with any kind of illness or pain, as though no one is ever dizzy or incontinent or simply needs to sit or lie down. (For instance, where could you sit down in a supermarket if you needed to?) Not only the architecture, but the entire physical and social organization of life, assumes that we are either strong and healthy and able to do what the average able-bodied person can do, or that we are completely disabled, unable to participate in life.

In the split between the public and the private worlds, women (and children) have been relegated to the private, and so have the disabled, the sick and the old (and mostly women take care of them). The public world is the world of strength, the positive (valued) body, performance and production, the able-bodied and youth. Weakness, illness, rest and recovery, pain, death and the negative (de-valued) body are private, generally hidden, and often neglected. Coming into the public world with illness, pain or a de-valued body, we encounter resistance to mixing the two worlds; the split is vividly revealed. Much of our experience goes underground, because there is no socially acceptable way of expressing it and having our physical and psychological experience acknowledged and shared. A few close friends may share it, but there is a strong impulse to protect them from it too, because it seems so private, so unacceptable. I found that, after a couple of years of illness, even answering the question,

"How are you?" became a difficult, conflict-ridden business. I don't want to alienate my friends from my experience, but I don't want to risk their discomfort and rejection by telling them what they don't want to know.[8]

Disabled people learn that many, perhaps most, able-bodied people do not want to know about suffering caused by the body. Visibly disabled women report that curiosity about medical diagnoses, physical appearance and the sexual and other intimate aspects of disability is more common than willingness to listen and try to understand the experience of disability (Matthews 1983). It is not unusual for people with invisible disabilities to keep them entirely secret from everyone but their closest friends.

Contrary to what Sue Halpern says, it is not simply because they are in able bodies that the able-bodied fail to identify with the disabled. Able-bodied people can often make the imaginative leap into the skins of people physically unlike themselves; women can identify with a male protagonist in a story, for example, and adults can identify with children or with people much older than themselves. Something more powerful than being in a different body is at work. Suffering caused by the body, and the inability to control the body, are despised, pitied, and above all, feared. This fear, experienced individually, is also deeply embedded in our culture.

The Oppression of Disabled People Is the Oppression of Everyone's Real Body

Our real human bodies are exceedingly diverse—in size, shape, colour, texture, structure, function, range and habits of movements, and development—and they are constantly changing. Yet we do not absorb or reflect this simple fact in our culture. Instead, we idealize the human body. Our physical ideals change from time to time, but we always have ideals. These ideals are not just about appearance; they are also ideals of strength and energy and proper control of the body. We are perpetually bombarded with images of these ideals, demands for them, and offers of consumer products and services to help us achieve them.[9] Idealizing the body prevents everyone, able-bodied and disabled, from identifying with and loving her/his real body. Some people can have the illusion of acceptance that comes from believing that their bodies are "close enough" to the ideal, but this illusion only draws them deeper into identifying with the ideal and into the endless task of reconciling the reality with it. Sooner or later they must fail.

Before I became disabled, I was one of those people who felt "close enough" to cultural ideals to be reasonably accepting of my body. Like most feminists I know, I was aware of some alienation from it, and I worked at liking my body better. Nevertheless, I knew in my heart that too much of my liking still depended on being "close enough." When I was disabled by illness, I experienced a much more profound alienation from my body. After a year spent mostly in bed, I could barely identify my body as my own. I felt that "it" was torturing "me," trapping me in exhaustion, pain and inability to do many of the simplest things I did when I was healthy. The shock of this experience and the effort to identify with a new, disabled body, made me realize I had been living a luxury of the able-bodied. The able-bodied can postpone the luxury of identifying with their *real* bodies. The disabled don't have the luxury of demanding that their bodies fit the physical ideals of their culture. As Barbara Hillyer Davis says: "For all of us the difficult work of finding (one's) self includes the body, but people who live with disability in a society that glorifies fitness and physical conformity are forced to understand more fully what bodily integrity means" (Davis 1984, 3).

In a society which idealizes the body, the physically disabled are marginalized. People learn to identify with their own strengths (by cultural standards) and to hate, fear and neglect their own weaknesses. The disabled are not only de-valued for their de-valued bodies (Hannaford 1985), they are constant reminders to the able-bodied of the negative body—of what the able-bodied are trying to avoid, forget and ignore (Lessing 1981). For example, if someone tells me she is in pain, she reminds me of the existence of pain, the imperfection and fragility of the body, the possibility of my own pain, the *inevitability* of it. The less willing I am to accept all these, the less I want to know about her pain; if I cannot avoid it in her presence, I will avoid her. I may even blame her for it. I may tell myself that she *could have* avoided it, in order to go on believing that I *can* avoid it. I want to believe I am not like her; I cling to the differences. Gradually, I make her "other" because I don't want to confront my real body, which I fear and cannot accept.[10]

Disabled people can participate in marginalizing ourselves. We can wish for bodies we do not have, with frustration, shame, self-hatred. We can feel trapped in the negative body; it is our internalized oppression to feel this. Every (visibly or invisibly) disabled person I have talked to or read has felt this; some never stop feeling it. In addition, disabled women suffer more than disabled men from the demand that people have "ideal" bodies, because in patriarchal culture people judge women more by their bodies than they do men. Disabled women often do not feel seen (because they are often not seen) by others as whole people, especially not as sexual people (Campling 1981; Matthews 1983; Hannaford 1985; Fine and Asch 1988). Thus, part of their struggle against oppression is a much harder version of the struggle able-bodied women have for a realistic *and positive* self-image (Bogle and Shaul 1981). On the other hand, disabled people who cannot hope to meet the physical ideals of a culture can help reveal that those ideals are not "natural" or "normal" but artificial social creations that oppress everyone.

Feminist theorists have probed the causes of our patriarchal culture's desire for control of the body—fear of death, fear of the strong impulses and feelings the body give us, fear of nature, fear and resentment of the mother's power over the infant (de Beauvoir 1949; Dinnerstein 1976; Griffin 1981). Idealizing the body and wanting to control it go hand-in-hand; it is impossible to say whether one causes the other. A physical ideal gives us the goal of our efforts to control the body, and the myth that total control is possible deceives us into striving for the ideal. The consequences for women have been widely discussed in the literature of feminism. The consequences for disabled people are less often recognized. In a culture which loves the idea that the body can be controlled, those who cannot control their bodies are seen (and may see themselves) as failures.

When you listen to this culture in a disabled body, you hear how often health and physical vigour are talked about as if they were moral virtues. People constantly praise others for their "energy," their stamina, their ability to work long hours. Of course, acting on behalf of one's health can be a virtue, and undermining one's health can be a vice, but "success" at being healthy, like beauty, is always partly a matter of luck and therefore beyond our control. When health is spoken of as a virtue, people who lack it are made to feel inadequate. I am not suggesting that it is always wrong to praise people's physical strength or accomplishments, any more than it is always wrong to praise their physical beauty. But just as treating cultural standards of beauty as essential virtues for women harms most women, treating health and vigour as moral virtues for everyone harms people with disabilities and illnesses.

The myth that the body can be controlled is not easily dispelled, because it is not very vulnerable to evidence against it. When I became ill, several people wanted to discuss with me what I thought I had done to "make myself " ill or "allow myself " to become sick. At first I fell in with this, generating theories about what I had done wrong; even though I had always taken good care of my health, I was able to find some (rather far-fetched) accounts of my responsibility for my illness. When a few close friends offered hypotheses as to how *they* might be responsible for my being ill, I began to suspect that something was wrong. Gradually, I realized that we were all trying to believe that nothing this important is beyond our control.

Of course, there are sometimes controllable social and psychological forces at work in creating ill health and disability (Kleinman 1988). Nevertheless our cultural insistence on controlling the body blames the victims of disability for failing and burdens them with self-doubt and self-blame. The search for psychological, moral and spiritual causes of illness, accident and disability is often a harmful expression of this insistence on control (see Sontag 1977).

Modern Western medicine plays into and conforms to our cultural myth that the body can be controlled. Collectively, doctors and medical researchers exhibit very little modesty about their knowledge. They focus their (and our) attention on cures and imminent cures, on successful medical interventions. Research, funding and medical care are more directed toward life-threatening conditions than toward chronic illnesses and disabilities. Even pain was relatively neglected as a medical problem until the second half of this century. Surgery and saving lives bolster the illusion of control much better than does the long, patient process of rehabilitation or the management of long-term illness. These latter, less visible functions of medicine tend to be performed by nurses, physiotherapists and other low-prestige members of the profession. Doctors are trained to do something to control the body, to "make it better" (Kleinman 1988); they are the heroes of medicine. They may like being in the role of hero, but we also like them in that role and try to keep them there, because *we* want to believe that someone can always "make it better."[11] As long as we cling to this belief, the patients who cannot be "repaired"—the chronically ill, the disabled and the dying—will symbolize the failure of medicine and more, the failure of the Western scientific project to control nature. They will carry this stigma in medicine and in the culture as a whole.

When philosophers of medical ethics confine themselves to discussing life-and-death issues of medicine, they help perpetuate the idea that the main purpose of medicine is to control the body. Life-and-death interventions are the ultimate exercise of control. If medical ethicists looked more closely at who needs and who receives medical help, they would discover a host of issues concerning how medicine and society understand, mediate, assist with and integrate experiences of illness, injury and disability.

Because of the heroic approach to medicine, and because disabled people's experience is not integrated into the culture, most people know little or nothing about how to live with long-term or life-threatening illness, how to communicate with doctors and nurses and medical bureaucrats about these matters, how to live with limitation, uncertainty, pain, nausea, and other symptoms when doctors cannot make them go away. Recently, patients' support groups have arisen to fill this gap for people with nearly every type of illness and disability. They are vitally important sources of knowledge and encouragement for many of us, but they do not fill the cultural gulf between the able-bodied and the disabled. The problems of living with a disability are not private problems, separable from the rest of life and the rest of society. They are problems which can and should be shared throughout the culture as much as we share the problems of love, work and family life.

Consider the example of pain. It is difficult for most people who have not lived with prolonged or recurring pain to understand the benefits of accepting it. Yet some people who live with chronic pain speak of "making friends" with it as the road to feeling better and enjoying life. How do they picture their pain and think about it; what kind of attention do they give it and when; how do they live around and through it, and what do they learn from it? We all need to know this as part of our education. Some of the fear of experiencing pain is a consequence of ignorance and lack of guidance. The effort to avoid pain contributes to such widespread problems as drug and alcohol addiction, eating disorders, and sedentary lives. People with painful disabilities can teach us about pain, because they *can't* avoid it and have had to learn how to face it and live with it. The pernicious myth that it is possible to avoid almost all pain by controlling the body gives the fear of pain greater power than it should have and blames the victims of unavoidable pain. The fear of pain is also expressed or displaced as a fear of people in pain, which often isolates those with painful disabilities. All this is unnecessary. People *in* pain and knowledge *of* pain could be fully integrated into our culture, to everyone's benefit.

If we knew more about pain, about physical limitation, about loss of abilities, about what it is like to be "too far" from the cultural ideal of the body, perhaps we would have less fear of the negative body, less fear of our own weaknesses and "imperfections," of our inevitable deterioration and death. Perhaps we could give up our idealizations and relax our desire for control of the body; until we do, we maintain them at the expense of disabled people and at the expense of our ability to accept and love our own real bodies.

Disabled People as "Other"

When we make people "other," we group them together as the objects of *our* experience instead of regarding them as fellow *subjects* of experience with whom we might identify. If you are "other" to me, I see you primarily as symbolic of something else—usually, but not always, something I reject and fear and that I project onto you. We can all do this to each other, but very often the process is not symmetrical, because one group of people may have more power to call itself the paradigm of humanity and to make the world suit its own needs and validate its own experiences.[12] Disabled people are "other" to able-bodied people, and (as I have tried to show) the consequences are socially, economically and psychologically oppressive to the disabled and psychologically oppressive to the able-bodied. Able-bodied people may be "other" to disabled people, but the consequences of this for the able-bodied are minor (most able-bodied people can afford not to notice it). There are, however, several political and philosophical issues that being "other" to a more powerful group raises for disabled people.

I have said that for the able-bodied, the disabled often symbolize failure to control the body and the failure of science and medicine to protect us all. However, some disabled people also become symbols of heroic control against all odds; these are the "disabled heroes," who are comforting to the able-bodied because they reaffirm the possibility of overcoming the body. Disabled heroes are people with visible disabilities who receive public attention because they accomplish things that are unusual even for the able-bodied. It is revealing that, with few exceptions (Helen Keller and, very recently, Stephen Hawking are among them), disabled heroes are recognized for performing feats of physical strength and endurance. While disabled heroes can be inspiring and heartening to the disabled, they may give the able-bodied the false impression that anyone can "overcome" a disability. Disabled heroes usually have extraordinary social, economic and physical resources that are not available to most people with those disabilities. In addition, many disabled people are not capable of performing physical heroics, because many (perhaps most) disabilities reduce or consume the energy and stamina of people who have them and do not just limit them in some particular kind of physical activity. Amputee and wheelchair athletes are exceptional, not because of their ambition, discipline and hard work, but because they are in better health than most disabled people can be. Arthritis, Parkinsonism and stroke cause severe disability in far more people than do spinal cord injuries and amputations (Bury 1979). The image of the disabled hero may reduce the "otherness" of a few disabled people, but because it creates an ideal which most disabled people cannot meet, it *increases* the "otherness" of the majority of disabled people.

One recent attempt to reduce the "otherness" of disabled people is the introduction of the term, "differently-abled." I assume the point of using this term is to suggest that there is nothing *wrong* with being the way we are, just different. Yet to call someone "differently-abled" is much like calling her "differently-coloured" or "differently-gendered." It says: "This person is not the norm or paradigm of humanity." If anything, it increases the "otherness" of disabled people, because it reinforces the paradigm of humanity as young, strong and healthy, with all body parts working "perfectly," from which this person is "different." Using the term "differently-abled" also suggests a (polite? patronizing? protective? self-protective?) disregard of the special difficulties, struggles and suffering disabled people face. We are *dis-abled*. We live with particular social and physical struggles that are partly consequences of the conditions of our bodies and partly consequences of the structures and expectations of our societies, but they are struggles which only people with bodies like ours experience.

The positive side of the term "differently-abled" is that it might remind the able bodied that to be disabled in some respects is not to be disabled in all respects. It also suggests that a disabled person may have abilities that the able-bodied lack in virtue of being able-bodied. Nevertheless, on the whole, the term "differently-abled" should be abandoned, because it reinforces the able-bodied paradigm of humanity and fails to acknowledge the struggles disabled people face.

The problems of being "the other" to a dominant group are always politically complex. Our solution is to emphasize similarities to the dominant group in the hope that they will identify with the oppressed, recognize their rights, gradually give them equal opportunities, and eventually assimilate them. Many disabled people are tired of being symbols to the able-bodied, visible only or primarily for their disabilities, and they want nothing more than to be seen as individuals rather than as members of the group, "the disabled." Emphasizing similarities to the able-bodied, making their disabilities unnoticeable in comparison to their other human qualities may bring about assimilation one-by-one. It does not directly challenge the able-bodied paradigm of humanity, just as women moving into traditionally male arenas of both may produce a gradual change in the paradigms. In addition, assimilation may be very difficult for the disabled to achieve. Although the able-bodied like disabled tokens who do not seem very different from themselves, they may *need* someone to carry the burden of the negative body as long as they continue to idealize and try to control the body. They may therefore resist the assimilation of most disabled people.

The reasons in favour of the alternative solution to "otherness"—*emphasizing differences* from the able-bodied—are also reasons for emphasizing similarities among the disabled, especially social and political similarities. Disabled people share positions of social oppression that separate us from the able-bodied, and we share physical, psychological and social experiences of disability. Emphasizing differences from the able-bodied demands that those differences be acknowledged and respected and fosters solidarity among the disabled. It challenges the able-bodied paradigm of humanity and creates the possibility of a deeper challenge to the idealization of the body and the demand for its control. Invisibly disabled people tend to be drawn to solutions that emphasize difference, because our need to have our struggles acknowledged is great, and we have far less experience than those who are visibly disabled of being symbolic to the able-bodied.

Whether one wants to emphasize sameness or difference in dealing with the problem of being "the other" depends in part on how radically one wants to challenge the value-structure of the dominant group. A very important issue in this category for both women and disabled people is the value of independence from the help of others, so highly esteemed in our patriarchal culture and now being questioned in feminist ethics (see, for example, Sherwin 1984, 1987; Kittay and Meyers 1987) and discussed in the writings of disabled women (see, for example, Fisher and Galler 1981; Davis 1984; Frank 1988). Many disabled people who can see the possibility of living as independently as any able-bodied person, or who have achieved this goal after long struggle, value their independence above everything. Dependence on the help of others is humiliating in a society which prizes independence. In addition, this issue holds special complications for disabled women; reading the stories of women who became disabled as adults, I was struck by their struggle with shame and loss of self-esteem at being transformed from people who took physical care of others (husbands and children) to people who were physically dependent. All this suggests that disabled people need every bit of independence we can get. Yet there are disabled people who will always need a lot of help from other individuals just to survive (those who have very little control of movement, for example), and to the extent that everyone considers independence necessary to respect and self-esteem, those people will be condemned to be de-valued. In addition, some disabled people spend tremendous energy being independent in ways that might be considered trivial in a culture less insistent on self-reliance; if our culture valued *interdependence* more highly, they could use that energy for more satisfying activities.

In her excellent discussion of the issue of dependency and independence, Barbara Hillyer Davis argues that women with disabilities and those who care for them can work out a model of *reciprocity* for all of us, if we are willing to learn from them. "Reciprocity involves the difficulty of recognizing each other's needs, relying on the other, asking and receiving help, delegating responsibility, giving and receiving empathy, respecting boundaries" (Davis 1984, 4). I hope that disabled and able-bodied feminists will join in questioning our cultural obsession with independence and ultimately replacing it with such a model of reciprocity. If *all* the disabled are to be fully integrated into society without symbolizing failure, then we have to change social values to recognize the value of depending on other and being depended upon. This would also reduce the fear and shame associated with dependency in old age—a condition most of us will reach.

Whether one wants to emphasize sameness or difference in dealing with the problems of being "other" is also related to whether one sees anything valuable to be preserved by maintaining, either temporarily or in the long-run, some separateness of the oppressed group. Is there a special culture of the oppressed group or the seeds of a special culture which could be developed in a supportive context of solidarity? Do members of the oppressed group have accumulated knowledge or ways of knowing which might be lost if assimilation takes place without the dominant culture being transformed?

It would be hard to claim that disabled people as a whole have an alternative culture or even the seeds of one. One sub-group, the deaf, has a separate culture from the hearing, and they are fighting for its recognition and preservation, as well as for their right to continue making their own culture (Sacks 1988). Disabled people do have both knowledge and ways of knowing that are not available to the able-bodied. Although ultimately I hope that disabled people's knowledge will be integrated into the culture as a whole, I suspect that a culture which fears and denigrates the real body would rather silence this knowledge than make the changes necessary to absorb it. It may have to be nurtured and cultivated separately while the able-bodied culture is transformed enough to receive and integrate it.

The Knowledge of Disabled People and How It Is Silenced

In my second year of illness, I was reading an article about the psychological and philosophical relationship of mind to body. When the author painted a rosy picture of the experience of being embodied, I was outraged at the presumption of the writer to speak for everyone from a healthy body. I decided I didn't want to hear *anything* about the body from anyone who was not physically disabled. Before that moment, it had not occurred to me that there was a world of experience from which I was shut out while I was able-bodied.

Not only do physically disabled people have experiences which are not available to the able-bodied, they are in a better position to transcend cultural mythologies about the body, because they *cannot* do things that the able-bodied fell they *must* do in order to be happy, "normal" and sane. For example, paraplegics and quadriplegics have revolutionary things to teach about the possibilities of sexuality which contradict patriarchal culture's obsession with the genitals (Bullard and Knight 1981). Some people can have orgasms in any part of their bodies where they feel touch. One man said he never knew how good sex could be until he lost the feeling in his genitals. Few able-bodied people know these things, and, to my knowledge, no one has explored their implications for the able-bodied.

If disabled people were truly heard, an explosion of knowledge of the human body and psyche would take place. We have access to realms of experience that our culture has not tapped (even for medical science, which takes relatively little interest in people's *experience* of their bodies). Like women's particular knowledge, which comes from access to experiences most men do not have, disabled people's knowledge is dismissed as trivial, complaining, mundane (or bizarre), *less than* that of the dominant group.

The cognitive authority (Addelson 1983) of medicine plays an important role in distorting and silencing the knowledge of the disabled. Medical professionals have been given the power to describe and validate everyone's experience of the body. If you go to doctors with symptoms they cannot observe directly or verify independently of what you tell them, such as pain or weakness or numbness or dizziness or difficulty concentrating, and if they cannot find an objectively observable cause of those symptoms, you are likely to be told that there is "nothing wrong with you," no matter how you feel. Unless you are very lucky in your doctors, no matter how trustworthy and responsible you were considered to be *before* you started saying you were ill, your experience will be invalidated.[13] *Other* people are the authorities on the reality of the experiences of your body.

When you are very ill, you desperately need medical validation of your experience, not only for economic reasons (insurance claims, pensions, welfare and disability benefits all depend upon official diagnosis), but also for social and psychological reasons. People with unrecognized illnesses are often abandoned by their friends and families.[14] Because almost everyone accepts the cognitive authority of medicine, the person whose bodily experience is radically different from medical descriptions of her/his condition is invalidated as a knower. Either you decide to hide your experience, or you are socially isolated with it by being labelled mentally ill[15] or dishonest. In both cases you are silenced.

Even when your experience is recognized by medicine, it is often re-described in ways that are inaccurate from your standpoint. The objectively observable condition of your body may be used to determine the severity of your pain, for instance, regardless of your own reports of it. For example, until recently, relatively few doctors were willing to acknowledge that severe phantom limb pain can persist for months or even years after an amputation. The accumulated experience of doctors who were themselves amputees has begun to legitimize the other patients' reports (Madruga 1979).

When you are forced to realize that other people have more social authority than you do to describe your experience of your own body, your confidence in yourself and your relationship to reality is radically undermined. What can you know if you cannot know that you are experiencing suffering or joy; what can you communicate to people who don't believe you know even this?[16] Most people will censor what they tell or say nothing rather than expose themselves repeatedly to such deeply felt invalidation. They are silenced by fear and confusion. The process is familiar from our understanding of how women are silenced in and by patriarchal culture.

One final caution: As with women's "special knowledge," there is a danger of sentimentalizing disabled people's knowledge and abilities and keeping us "other" by doing so. We need to bring this knowledge into the culture and to transform the culture and society so that everyone can receive and make use of it, so that it can be fully integrated, along with disabled people, into a shared social life.

Conclusion

I have tried to introduce the reader to the rich variety of intellectual and political issues that are raised by experiences of physical disability. Confronting these issues has increased my appreciation of the insights that feminist theory already offers into cultural attitudes about the body and the many form of social oppression. Feminists have been challenging medicine's authority for many years now, but not, I think, as radically as we would if we knew what disabled people have to tell. I look forward to the development of a full feminist theory of disability.[17] We need a theory of disability for the liberation of both disabled and able-bodied people, since the theory of disability is also the theory of the oppression of the body by a society and its culture.

Notes

Many thanks to Kathy Gose, Joyce Frazee, Mary Barnes, Barbara Beach, Elliot Gose and Gordon Renwick for helping me to think about these questions, and to Maureen Ashfield for helping me to research them. Thanks also to the editors of the issue of *Hypatia* in which this article was originally published, Virginia Warren, and two anonymous reviewers for their work on editing an earlier version of the paper.

1. Itzhak Perlman, when asked in a recent CBC interview about the problems of the disabled, said disabled people have two problems: the fact that the world is not made for people with any weaknesses but for supermen and the attitudes of able-bodied people.
2. An excellent description of this last issue as it confronts the deaf is found in Sacks 1988.
3. See Matthews 1983; Hannaford 1985; Rooney and Israel (eds.) 1985, esp. the articles by Jill Weiss, Charlynn Toews, Myra Rosenfield, and Susan Russell; and, for a doctor's theories, Kleinman 1988.
4. We also need a feminist theory of mental disability, but I will not be discussing mental disability in this essay.
5. In a recent article in *Signs*, Linda Alcoff argues that we should define "woman" thus: "woman is a position from which a feminist politics can emerge rather than a set of attributes that are 'objectively identifiable.'" (Alcoff 1988, 435). I think a similar approach may be the best one for defining "disability."

6. For example, Pelvic Inflammatory Disease causes severe prolonged disability in some women. These women often have to endure medical diagnoses of psychological illness and the skepticism of family and friends, in addition to having to live with chronic severe pain. See Moore 1985.

7. Feminism has challenged the distribution of responsibility for providing such resources as childcare and protection from family violence. Increasingly many people who once thought of these as family or personal concerns now think of them as social responsibilities.

8. Some people save me that trouble by *telling me* I am fine and walking away. Of course, people also encounter difficulties with answering "How are you?" during and after crises, such as separation from a partner, death of a loved one, or a nervous breakdown. There is a temporary alienation from what is considered ordinary shared experience. In disability, the alienation lasts longer, often for a lifetime, and, in my experience, is more profound.

9. The idealization of the body is clearly related in complex ways to the economic processes of a consumer society. Since it pre-dated capitalism, we know that capitalism did not cause it, but it is undeniable that idealization now generates tremendous profits and that the quest for profit demands the reinforcement of idealization and the constant development of new ideals.

10. Susan Griffin, in a characteristically honest and insightful passage, describes an encounter with the fear that makes it hard to identify with disabled people. See Griffin 1982, 648–649.

11. Thanks to Joyce Frazee for pointing this out to me.

12. When Simone de Beauvoir uses this term to elucidate men's view of women (and women's view of ourselves), she emphasizes that Man is considered essential, Woman inessential; Man is the Subject, Woman the Other (de Beauvoir 1952, xvi). Susan Griffin expands upon this idea by showing how we project rejected aspects of ourselves onto groups of people who are designated the Other (Griffin 1981).

13. Many women with M.S. have lived through this nightmare in the early stages of their illness. Although this happens to men too, women's experience of the body, like women's experience generally, is more likely to be invalidated (Hannaford 1985).

14. Accounts of the experience of relatively unknown, newly discovered, or hard-to-diagnose diseases and conditions confirm this. See, for example, Jeffreys 1982, for the story of an experience of Chronic Fatigue Syndrome, which is more common in women than in men.

15. Frequently people with undiagnosed illnesses are sent by their doctors to psychiatrists, who cannot help and may send them back to their doctors saying they must be physically ill. This can leave patients in a dangerous medical and social limbo. Sometimes they commit suicide because of it (Ramsay 1986). Psychiatrists who know enough about living with physical illness or disability to help someone cope with it are rare.

16. For more discussion of his subject, see Zaner 1983 and Rawlinson 1983.

17. At this stage of the disability rights movement, it is impossible to anticipate everything that a full feminist theory will include, just as it would have been impossible to predict in 1970 the present state of feminist theory of mothering. Nevertheless, we can see that besides dealing more fully with the issues I have raised here, an adequate feminist theory of disability will examine all the ways in which disability is socially constructed; it will explain the interaction of disability with gender, race and class position; it will examine every aspect of the cognitive authority of medicine and science over our experiences of our bodies; it will discuss the relationship of technology to disability; it will question the belief that disabled lives are not worth living or preserving when it is implied in our theorizing about abortion and euthanasia; it will give us a detailed vision of the full integration of disabled people in society, and it will propose practical political strategies for the liberation of disabled people and the liberation of the able-bodied from the social oppression of their bodies.

References

Addelson, Kathryn P. 1983. The man of professional wisdom. In *Discovering reality*. Sandra Harding and Merrill B. Hintikka, eds. Boston: D. Reidel.

Alcoff, Linda. 1988. Cultural feminism versus poststructuralism: The identity crisis in feminist theory. *Signs: Journal of Women in Culture and Society* 13(3): 405–436.

Bullard, David G. and Susan E. Knight, eds. 1981. *Sexuality and physical disability*. St. Louis: C. V. Mosby.

Bury, M. R. 1979. Disablement in society: Towards an integrated perspective. *International Journal of Rehabilitation Research* 2(1): 33–40.

Beauvoir, Simone de. 1952. *The second sex*. New York: Alfred A. Knopf.

Campling, Jo, ed. 1981. *Images of ourselves—women with disabilities talking*. London: Routledge and Kegan Paul.

Davis, Barbara Hillyer. 1984. Women, disability and feminism: Notes toward a new theory. *Frontiers: A Journal of Women Studies* VIII(1): 1–5.

Davis, Melanie and Catherine Marshall. 1987. Female and disabled: Challenged women in education. *National Women's Studies Association Perspectives* 5: 39–41.

Dinnerstein, Dorothy. 1976. *The mermaid and the minotaur: Sexual arrangements and human malaise*. New York: Harper and Row.

Ehrenreich, Barbara and Dierdre English. 1979. *For her own good: 150 years of the experts' advice to women*. New York: Anchor.

Fine, Michelle and Adrienne Asch, eds. 1988. *Women with disabilities: Essays in psychology, culture and politics*. Philadelphia: Temple University Press.

Finger, Anne. 1983. Disability and reproductive rights. *off our backs* 13(9): 18–19.

Fisher, Bernice and Robert Galler. 1981. Conversation between two friends about feminism and disability. *off our backs* 11(5): 14–15.

Frank, Gelya. 1988. On embodiment: A case study of congenital limb deficiency in American culture. In *Women with disabilities*. Michelle Fine and Adrienne Asch, eds. Philadelphia: Temple University Press.

Griffin, Susan. 1981. *Pornography and silence: Culture's revenge against nature*. New York: Harper and Row.

Halpern, Sue M. 1988. Portrait of the artist. Review of *Under the eye of the clock* by Christopher Nolan. *The New York Times Review of Books*, June 30: 3–4.

Hannaford, Susan. 1985. *Living outside inside. A disabled woman's experience. Towards a social and political perspective*. Berkeley: Canterbury Press.

Jeffreys, Toni. 1982. *The mile-high staircase*. Sydney: Hodder and Stoughton Ltd.

Kittay, Eva Feder and Diana T. Meyers, eds. 1987. *Women and moral theory*. Totowa, NJ: Rowman and Littlefield.

Kleinman, Arthur. 1988. *The illness narratives: Suffering, healing, and the human condition*. New York: Basic Books.

Lessing, Jill. 1981. Denial and disability. *off our backs* 11(5): 21.

Madruga, Lenor. 1979. One *step at a time*. Toronto: McGraw-Hill.

Matthews, Gwyneth Ferguson. 1983. *Voices from the shadows: Women with disabilities speak out*. Toronto: Women's Educational Press.

Moore, Maureen. 1985. Coping with pelvic inflammatory disease. In *Women and Disability*. Frances Rooney and Pat Israel, eds. *Resources for Feminist Research* 14(1).

Newsweek. 1988. Reading God's mind. June 13. 56–59.

Ramsay, A. Melvin. 1986. *Postviral fatigue syndrome, the saga of Royal Free disease*. London: Gower Medical Publishing.

Rawlinson, Mary. 1983. The facticity of illness and the appropriation of health. In *Phenomenology in a pluralistic context*. William L. McBride and Calvin O. Schrag, eds. Albany: SUNY Press.

Rich, Adrienne. 1976. *Of woman born: Motherhood as experience and institution*. New York: W. W. Norton.

Rooney, Frances and Pat Israel, eds. 1985. *Women and disability. Resources for Feminist Research* 14(1).

Sacks, Oliver. 1988. The revolution of the deaf. *The New York Review of Books*, June 2, 23–28.

Shaul, Susan L. and Jane Elder Bogle. 1981. Body image and the woman with a disability. In *Sexuality and physical disability*. David G. Bullard and Susan E. Knight, eds. St. Louis: C. V. Mosby.

Sherwin. Susan. 1984–85. A feminist approach to ethics. *Dalhousie Review* 64(4): 704–713.

Sherwin, Susan. 1987. Feminist ethics and in vitro fertilization. In *Science, morality and feminist theory*. Marsha Hanen and Kai Nielsen, eds. Calgary: The University of Calgary Press.

Sontag, Susan. 1977. *Illness as metaphor*. New York: Random House.

U.N. Decade of Disabled Persons 1983–1992. 1983. *World programme of action concerning disabled persons*. New York: United Nations.

Whitbeck, Caroline. Afterword to the maternal instinct. In *Mothering: Essays in feminist theory*. Joyce Trebilcot, ed. Totowa: Rowman and Allanheld.

Zaner, Richard M. 1983. Flirtations or engagement? Prolegomenon to a philosophy of medicine. In *Phenomenology in a pluralistic context*. Wilharn L. McBride and Calvin O. Schrag, eds. Albany: SUNY Press.

21

Integrating Disability, Transforming Feminist Theory

Rosemarie Garland-Thomson

Disability Studies and Feminist Studies

Over the last several years, disability studies has moved out of the applied fields of medicine, social work, and rehabilitation to become a vibrant new field of inquiry within the critical genre of identity studies that has developed so productively in the humanities over the last twenty or so years. Charged with the residual fervor of the civil rights movement, women's studies and race studies established a model in the academy for identity-based critical enterprises that followed, such as gender studies, queer studies, disability studies, and a proliferation of ethnic studies, all of which have enriched and complicated our understandings of social justice, subject formation, subjugated knowledges, and collective action.

Even though disability studies is now flourishing in disciplines such as history, literature, religion, theater, and philosophy in precisely the same way feminist studies did twenty-five years ago, many of its practitioners do not recognize that disability studies is part of this larger undertaking that can be called identity studies. Indeed, I must wearily conclude that much of current disability studies does a great deal of wheel reinventing. This is largely due to the fact that many disability studies scholars simply don't know either feminist theory or the institutional history of women's studies. All too often the pronouncements in disability studies of what we need to start addressing are precisely issues that feminist theory has been grappling with for years. This is not to say that feminist theory can be transferred wholly and in tact over to the study of disability studies, but it is to suggest that feminist theory can offer profound insights, methods, and perspectives that would deepen disability studies.

Conversely, feminist theories all too often do not recognize disability in their litanies of identities that inflect the category of woman. Repeatedly, feminist issues that are intricately entangled with disability—such as reproductive technology, the place of bodily differences, the particularities of oppression, the ethics of care, the construction of the subject—are discussed without any reference to disability. Like disability studies practitioners unaware of feminism, feminist scholars are often simply unacquainted with disability studies perspectives. The most sophisticated and nuanced analyses of disability, in my view, come from scholars conversant with feminist theory. And the most compelling and complex analyses of gender intersectionality take into consideration what I call the ability/disability system—along with race, ethnicity, sexuality, and class.

I want to give the omissions I am describing here the most generous interpretation I can. The archive, Foucault has shown us, determines what we can know. There has been no archive, no template for understanding disability as a category of analysis and knowledge, as a cultural trope and an historical community. So just as the now widely recognized centrality of gender and race analyses to all knowledge was unthinkable thirty years ago, disability is still not an icon on many critical desktops now. I think, however, that feminist theory's omission of disability differs from disability studies' ignorance of feminist theory. I find feminist theory and those familiar with it quick to grasp the broad outlines of disability theory and eager to consider its implications. This, of course, is because feminist theory itself has undertaken internal critiques and proved to be porous and flexible. Disability studies is news, but feminist theory is not. Nevertheless, feminist theory is still resisted for exactly the same reasons that scholars might resist disability studies: the assumption that it is narrow, particular, and has little to do with the mainstream of academic practice and knowledge (or with themselves). This reductive notion that identity studies are intellectual ghettos limited to a narrow constituency demanding special pleading is the persistent obstacle that both feminist theory and disability studies must surmount.

Disability studies can benefit from feminist theory and feminist theory can benefit from disability studies. Both feminism and disability studies are comparative and concurrent academic enterprises. Just as feminism has expanded the lexicon of what we imagine as womanly, has sought to understand and destigmatize what we call the subject position of woman, so has disability studies examined the identity disability in the service of integrating disabled people more fully into our society. As such, both are insurgencies that are becoming institutionalized underpinning inquiries outside and inside the academy. A feminist disability theory builds on the strengths of both.

Feminist Disability Theory

My title here, "Integrating Disability, Transforming Feminist Theory," invokes and links two notions, integration and transformation, both of which are fundamental to the feminist project and to the larger civil rights movement that informed it. Integration suggests achieving parity by fully including that which has been excluded and subordinated. Transformation suggests reimagining established knowledge and the order of things. By alluding to integration and transformation, I set my own modest project of integrating disability into feminist theory in the politicized context of the civil rights movement in order to gesture toward the explicit relation that feminism supposes between intellectual work and a commitment to creating a more just, equitable, and integrated society.

This essay aims to amplify feminist theory by articulating and fostering feminist disability theory. In naming feminist disability studies here as an academic field of inquiry, I am sometimes describing work that is already underway, some of which explicitly addresses disability and some which gestures implicitly to the topic. At other times, I am calling for study that needs to be done to better illuminate feminist thought. In other words, this essay in part sets an agenda for future work in feminist disability theory. Most fundamentally, though, the goal of feminist disability theory, as I lay it out in this essay, is to augment the terms and confront the limits of the ways we understand human diversity, the materiality of the body, multiculturalism, and the social formations that interpret bodily differences. The fundamental point I will make here is that integrating disability as a category of analysis and a system of representation deepens, expands, and challenges feminist theory.

Academic feminism is a complex and contradictory matrix of theories, strategies, pedagogies and practices. One way to think about feminist theory is to say that it investigates how culture saturates the particularities of bodies with meanings and probes the consequences of those meanings. Feminist theory is a collaborative, interdisciplinary inquiry and a self-conscious cultural critique that interrogates how subjects are multiply interpellated: in other words, how the representational systems of gender, race, ethnicity, ability, sexuality, and class mutually produce, inflect, and contradict one another. These systems intersect to produce and sustain ascribed, achieved, and acquired identities, both those that claim us and those that we claim for ourselves. A feminist disability theory introduces the ability/disability system as a category of analysis into this diverse and diffuse enterprise. It aims to extend current notions of cultural diversity and to more fully integrate the academy and the larger world it helps shape.

A feminist disability approach fosters more complex understandings of the cultural history of the body. By considering the ability/disability system, feminist disability theory goes beyond explicit disability topics such as illness, health, beauty, genetics, eugenics, aging, reproductive technologies, prosthetics, and access issues. Feminist disability theory addresses such broad feminist concerns as the unity of the category "woman," the status of the lived body, the politics of appearance, the medicalization of the body, the privilege of normalcy, multiculturalism, sexuality, the social construction of identity, and the commitment to integration. To borrow Toni Morrison's notion that blackness is an idea that permeates American culture, disability too is a pervasive, often unarticulated, ideology informing our cultural notions of self and other (Playing in the Dark 19). Disability—like gender—is a concept that pervades all aspects of culture: its structuring institutions, social identities, cultural practices, political positions, historical communities, and the shared human experience of embodiment.

Integrating disability into feminist theory is generative, broadening our collective inquires, questioning our assumptions, and contributing to feminism's multiculturalism. Introducing a disability analysis does not narrow the inquiry, limit the focus to only women with disabilities, or preclude engaging other manifestations of feminisms. Indeed, the multiplicity of foci we now call feminisms is not a group of fragmented, competing subfields, but rather a vibrant, complex conversation. In talking about "feminist disability theory," I am not proposing yet another discrete "feminism," but suggesting instead some ways that thinking about disability transforms feminist theory. Integrating disability does not obscure our critical focus on the registers of race, sexuality, ethnicity, or gender, nor is it additive (to use Gerda Lerner's famous idea). Rather, considering disability shifts the conceptual framework to strengthen our understanding of how these multiple systems intertwine, redefine, and mutually constitute one another. Integrating disability clarifies how this aggregate of systems operate together, yet distinctly, to support an imaginary norm and structure the relations that grant power, privilege, and status to that norm. Indeed, the cultural function of the disabled figure is to act as a synecdoche for all forms that culture deems non-normative.

We need to study disability in a feminist context to direct our highly honed critical skills toward the dual scholarly tasks of unmasking and reimagining disability, not only for people with disabilities but for everyone. As Simi Linton puts it, studying disability is "a prism through which one can gain a broader understanding of society and human experience" (1998, 118). It deepens the understanding of gender and sexuality, individualism and equality, minority group definitions, autonomy, wholeness, independence, dependence, health, physical appearance, aesthetics, the integrity of the body, community, and ideas of progress and perfection in every aspect of culture. A feminist disability theory introduces what Eve Sedgwick has called a "universalizing view" of disability that will replace an often persisting "minoritizing view." Such a view will cast disability as "an issue of continuing, determinative importance in the lives of people across the spectrum" (1990, 1). In other words, understanding how disability operates as an identity category and cultural concept will enhance how we understand what it is to be human, our relationships with one another, and the experience of embodiment. The constituency for a feminist disability theory is all of us, not only women with disabilities: disability is the most human of experiences, touching every family and—if we live long enough—touching us all.

The Ability/Disability System

Feminist disability theory's radical critique hinges on a broad understanding of disability as a pervasive cultural system that stigmatizes certain kinds of bodily variations. At the same time, this system has the potential to incite a critical politics. The informing premise of feminist disability theory is that disability, like femaleness, is not a natural state of corporeal inferiority, inadequacy, excess, or a stroke of misfortune. Rather, disability is a culturally fabricated narrative of the body, similar to what we understand as the fictions of race and gender. The disability/ability system produces subjects by differentiating and marking bodies. Although this comparison of bodies is ideological rather than biological, it nevertheless penetrates into the formation of culture, legitimating an unequal distribution of resources, status, and power within a biased social and architectural environment. As such, disability has four aspects: first, it is a system for interpreting and disciplining bodily variations; second, it is a relationship between bodies and their environments; third, it is a set of practices that produce both the able-bodied and the disabled; fourth, it is a way of describing the inherent instability of the embodied self. The disability system excludes the kinds of bodily forms, functions, impairments, changes, or ambiguities that call into question our cultural fantasy of the body as a neutral, compliant instrument of some transcendent will. Moreover, disability is a broad term within which cluster ideological categories as varied as sick, deformed, abnormal, crazy, ugly, old, feebleminded, maimed, afflicted, mad, or debilitated—all of which disadvantage people by devaluing bodies that do not conform to cultural standards. Thus the disability system functions to preserve and validate such privileged designations as beautiful, healthy, normal, fit, competent, intelligent—all of which provide cultural capital to those who can claim such status, who can reside within these subject positions. It is, then, the various interactions between bodies and world that materialize disability from the stuff of human variation and precariousness.

A feminist disability theory denaturalizes disability by unseating the dominant assumption that disability is something that is wrong with someone. By this I mean, of course, that it mobilizes feminism's highly developed and complex critique of gender, class, race, ethnicity, and sexuality as exclusionary and oppressive systems rather than as the natural and appropriate order of things. To do this, feminist disability theory engages several of the fundamental premises of critical theory: 1) that representation structures reality; 2) that the margins define the center; 3) that gender (or disability) is a way of signifying relationships of power; 4) that human identity is multiple and unstable; 5) that all analysis and evaluation have political implications.

In order to elaborate on these premises, I discuss here four fundamental and interpenetrating domains of feminist theory and suggest some of the kinds of critical inquiries that considering disability can generate within these theoretical arenas. These domains are: 1) representation; 2) the body; 3) identity; 4) activism. While I have disentangled these domains here for the purposes of setting up a schematic organization for my analysis, these domains are, of course, not discrete in either concept or practice, but rather tend to be synchronous.

Representation

The first domain of feminist theory that can be deepened by a disability analysis is representation. Western thought has long conflated femaleness and disability, understanding both as defective departures from a valued standard. Aristotle, for example, defined women as "mutilated males." Women, for Aristotle, have "improper form;" we are "monstrosit[ies]" (1944, 27–8; 8–9). As what Nancy Tuana calls "misbegotten men," women thus become the primal freaks in western history, envisioned as what we might now call congenitally deformed as a result of their what we might now term a genetic disability (1993, 18). More recently, feminist theorists have argued that female embodiment is a disabling condition in sexist culture. Iris Marion Young, for instance, examines how enforced feminine comportment delimits women's sense of embodied agency, restricting them to "throwing like a girl" (1990b,141). Young asserts that, "Women in a sexist society are physically handicapped" (1990b, 153). Even the general American public associates femininity and disability. A recent study on stereotyping showed that housewives, disabled people, blind people, so-called retarded people, and the elderly were judged as being similarly incompetent. Such a study suggests that intensely normatively feminine positions—such as a housewife—are aligned with negative attitudes about people with disabilities (Fiske 2001).[11]

Recognizing how the concept of disability has been used to cast the form and functioning of female bodies as non-normative can extend feminist critiques. Take, for example, the exploitation of Saartje Bartmann, the African woman exhibited as a freak in nineteenth-century Europe (Fausto Sterling 1995, Gilman 1985). Known as the Hottentot Venus, Bartmann's treatment has come to represent the most egregious form of racial and gendered degradation. What goes unremarked in studies of Bartmann's display, however, is the ways that the language and assumptions of the ability/disability system were implemented to pathologize and exoticize Bartmann. Her display invoked disability by presenting as deformities or abnormalities the characteristics that marked her as raced and gendered. I am not suggesting that Bartmann was disabled, but rather that the concepts of disability discourse framed her presentation to the western eye. Using disability as a category of analysis allows us to see that what was normative embodiment in her native context became abnormal to the western mind. More important, rather than simply supposing that being labeled as a freak is a slander, a disability analysis presses our critique further by challenging the premise that unusual embodiment is inherently inferior. The feminist interrogation of gender since Simone de Beauvoir has revealed how women are assigned a cluster of ascriptions, like Aristotle's, that mark us as Other. What is less widely recognized, however, is that this collection of interrelated characterizations is precisely the same set of supposed attributes affixed to people with disabilities.

The gender, race, and ability systems intertwine further in representing subjugated people as being pure body, unredeemed by mind or spirit. This sentence of embodiment is conceived of as either a lack or an excess. Women, for example, are considered castrated,—or to use Marge Piercy's wonderful term—"penis-poor" (1969). They are thought to be hysterical, or to have overactive hormones. Women have been cast as alternately having insatiable appetite in some eras and as pathologically self-denying in other times. Similarly, disabled people supposedly have extra chromosomes or limb deficiencies. The differences of disability are cast as atrophy, meaning degeneration, a hypertrophy, meaning enlargement. People with disabilities are described as having aplasia, meaning absence or failure of formation, or hypoplasia, meaning underdevelopment. All these terms police variation and reference a hidden norm from which the bodies of people with disabilities and women are imagined to depart.

Female, disabled, and dark bodies are supposed to be dependent, incomplete, vulnerable, and incompetent bodies. Femininity and race are the performance of disability. Women and the disabled are portrayed as helpless, dependent, weak, vulnerable, and incapable bodies. Women, the disabled, and people of color are always ready occasions for the aggrandizement of benevolent rescuers, whether strong males, distinguished doctors, abolitionists, or Jerry Lewis hosting his Telethons. For example, an 1885 medical illustration of a pathologically "love deficient" woman who fits the cultural stereotype of the ugly woman or perhaps the lesbian suggests how sexuality and appearance slide into the terms of disability. This illustration shows that the language of deficiency and abnormality used to simultaneously devalue women who depart from the mandates of femininity by equating them with disabled bodies. Such an interpretive move economically invokes the subjugating effect of one oppressive system to deprecate people marked by another system of representation.

Subjugated bodies are pictured as either deficient or as profligate. For instance, what Susan Bordo describes as the too-muchness of women also haunts disability and racial discourses, marking subjugated bodies as ungovernable, intemperate, or threatening (1993). The historical figure of the monster, as well, invokes disability, often to serve racism and sexism. Although the term has expanded to encompass all forms of social and corporeal aberration, *monster* originally described people with congenital impairments. As departures from the normatively human, monsters were seen as category violations or grotesque hybrids. The semantics of monstrosity are recruited to explain gender violations such as Julia Pastrana, for example, the Mexican Indian "bearded woman," whose body was displayed in nineteenth-century freak shows both during her lifetime and after her death. Pastrana's live and later embalmed body spectacularly confused and transgressed established cultural categories. Race, gender, disability, and sexuality augmented one another in Pastrana's display to produce a spectacle of embodied otherness that is simultaneously sensational, sentimental, and pathological (Thomson 1999). Furthermore much current feminist work theorizes figures of hybridity and excess such as monsters, grotesques, and cyborgs to suggest their transgressive potential for a feminist politics (Haraway 1991, Braidotti 1994, Russo 1994). However, this metaphorical invocation seldom acknowledges that these figures often refer to the actual bodies of people with disabilities. Erasing real disabled bodies from the history of these terms compromises the very critique they intend to launch and misses an opportunity to use disability as a feminist critical category.

Such representations ultimately portray subjugated bodies not only as inadequate or unrestrained but at the same time as redundant and expendable. Bodies marked and selected by such systems are targeted for elimination by varying historical and cross-cultural practices. Women, people with disabilities or appearance impairments, ethnic others, gays and lesbians, and people of color are variously the objects of infanticide, selective abortion, eugenic programs, hate crimes, mercy killing, assisted suicide, lynching, bride burning, honor killings, forced conversion, coercive rehabilitation, domestic violence, genocide, normalizing surgical procedures, racial profiling, and neglect. All these discriminatory practices are legitimated by systems of representation, by collective cultural stories that shape the material world, underwrite exclusionary attitudes, inform human relations, and mold our senses of who we are. Understanding how disability functions along with other systems of representation clarifies how all the systems intersect and mutually constitute one another.

The Body

The second domain of feminist theory that a disability analysis can illuminate is the investigation of the body: its materiality, its politics, its lived experience, and its relation to subjectivity and identity. Confronting issues of representation is certainly crucial to the cultural critique of feminist disability theory. But we should not focus exclusively on the discursive realm. What distinguishes a feminist disability theory from other critical paradigms is that it scrutinizes a wide range of material practices involving the lived body. Perhaps because women and the disabled are cultural signifiers for the body, their actual bodies have been subjected relentlessly to what Michel Foucault calls "discipline" (1979). Together, the gender, race, ethnicity, sexuality, class, and ability systems exert tremendous social pressures to shape, regulate, and normalize subjugated bodies. Such disciplining is enacted primarily through the two interrelated cultural discourses of medicine and appearance.

Feminist disability theory offers a particularly trenchant analysis of the ways that the female body has been medicalized in modernity. As I have already suggested, both women and the disabled have been imagined as medically abnormal—as the quintessential "sick" ones. Sickness is gendered feminine. This gendering of illness has entailed distinct consequences in everything from epidemiology and diagnosis to prophylaxis and therapeutics.

Perhaps feminist disability theory's most incisive critique is revealing the intersections between the politics of appearance and the medicalization of subjugated bodies. Appearance norms have a long history in western culture, as is witnessed by the anthropometric composite figures of ideal male and female bodies made by Dudley Sargent in 1893. The classical ideal was to be worshiped rather than imitated, but increasingly in modernity the ideal has migrated to become the paradigm which is to be attained. As many feminist critics have pointed out, the standardization of the female body that the beauty system mandates has become a goal to be achieved through self-regulation and consumerism (Wolf 1991, Haiken 1997). Feminist disability theory suggests that appearance and health norms often have similar disciplinary goals. For example, the body braces developed in the 1930s to "correct" scoliosis, discipline the body to conform to the dictates of both the gender and the ability systems by enforcing standardized female form similarly to the nineteenth-century corset, which, ironically, often disabled female bodies. Although both devices normalize bodies, the brace is part of medical discourse while the corset is cast as a fashion practice.

Similarly, a feminist disability theory calls into question the separation of reconstructive and cosmetic surgery, recognizing their essentially normalizing function as what Sander L. Gilman calls "aesthetic surgery" (1998). Cosmetic surgery, driven by gender ideology and market forces, now enforces feminine body standards and standardizes female bodies toward what I have called the "normate"—the corporeal incarnation of culture's collective, unmarked, normative characteristics (1997, 8). Cosmetic surgery's twin, reconstructive surgery, eliminates disability and enforces the ideals of what might be thought of as the normalcy system. Both cosmetic and reconstructive procedures commodify the body and parade mutilations as enhancements that correct flaws so as to improve the psychological well being of the patient. The conception of the body as what Susan Bordo terms "cultural plastic" increasingly through surgical and medical interventions pressures people with disabilities or appearance impairments to become what Michel Foucault calls "docile bodies." (1993, 246; 1979, 135). The twin ideologies of normalcy and beauty posit female and disabled bodies, particularly, as not only spectacles to be looked at, but as pliable bodies to be shaped infinitely so as to conform to a set of standards called "normal" and "beautiful."

Normal has inflected beautiful in modernity. What is imagined as excess body fat, the effects of aging, marks of ethnicity such as "jewish" noses, bodily particularities thought of as blemishes or deformities, and marks of history such as scarring and impairments are now expected to be surgically erased to produce an unmarked body. This visually unobtrusive body may then pass unnoticed within the milieu of anonymity that is the hallmark of social relations beyond the personal in modernity. The point of aesthetic surgery, as well as the costuming of power, is not to appear unique—or to "be yourself," as the ads endlessly promise—but rather not to be conspicuous, not to look different. This flight from the nonconforming body translates into individual efforts to look normal, neutral, unmarked, to *not* look disabled, queer, ugly, fat, ethnic, or raced. For example, beauty is set out comparatively and supposedly self-evidently in an 1889 treatise called *The New Physiogomy* which juxtaposed a white, upper-class English face called "Princess Alexandra" with a stereotypical face of an Irish immigrant, called "Sally Muggins" in a class and ethnic-based binary of apparently self-evident beauty and ugliness. Beauty, then, dictates corporeal standards that create not distinction but utter conformity to a bland look that is at the same time unachievable so as to leash us to consumer practices that promise to deliver such sameness. In the language of contemporary cosmetic surgery, the unreconstructed female body is persistently cast as having abnormalities that can be corrected by surgical procedures which supposedly improve one's appearance by producing ostensibly natural looking noses, thighs, breasts, chins, and so on. Thus, our unmodified bodies are presented as unnatural and abnormal while the surgically altered bodies are portrayed as normal and natural. The beautiful woman of the twenty-first century is sculpted surgically from top to bottom, generically neutral, all irregularities regularized, all particularities expunged. She is thus non-disabled, deracialized, and de-ethnicized.

In addition, the politics of prosthetics enters the purview of feminism when we consider the contested use of breast implants and prostheses for breast cancer survivors. The famous 1993 *New York Times* cover photo of the fashion model, Matushka, baring her mastectomy scar or Audre Lorde's account of breast cancer in *The Cancer Journals* challenge the sexist assumption that the amputated breast must always pass for the normative, sexualized one either through concealment or prosthetics (1980). A vibrant feminist conversation has emerged about the politics of the surgically altered, the disabled, breast. Diane Price Herndl challenges Audre Lorde's refusal of a breast prosthesis after mastectomy and Iris Marion Young's classic essay "Breasted Experience" queries the cultural meanings of breasts under the knife (2002; 1990a).

Another entanglement of appearance and medicine involves the spectacle of the female breast, both normative and disabled. In January 2000, the San Francisco-based Breast Cancer Fund mounted "Obsessed with Breasts," a public awareness poster campaign showing women boldly displaying mastectomy scars. The posters parodied familiar commercial media sites—a Calvin Klein perfume ad, a Cosmopolitan magazine cover, and a Victoria Secret catalog cover—that routinely parade women's breasts as upscale soft porn. The posters replace the now unremarkable eroticized breast with the forbidden image of the amputated breast. In doing so, they disrupt the visual convention of the female breast as sexualized object for male appropriation and pleasure. The posters thus produce a powerful visual violation by exchanging the spectacle of the eroticized breast, which has been desensationalized by its endless circulation, with the medicalized image of the scarred breast, which has been concealed from public view. The Breast Cancer Fund used these remarkable images to challenge both sexism in medical research and treatment for breast cancer as well as the oppressive representational practices that make everyday erotic spectacles of women's breasts while erasing the fact of the amputated breast.

Feminist disability theory can press far its critique of the pervasive will-to-normalize the non-standard body. Take two related examples: first, the surgical separation of conjoined twins and, second, the surgical assignment of gender for the intersexed, people with ambiguous genitalia and gender characteristics. Both these forms of embodiment are regularly—if infrequently—occurring, congenital bodily variations that spectacularly violate sacred ideologies of western culture. Conjoined twins contradict our notion of the individual as discrete and autonomous—actually, quite similarly to the way pregnancy does. Intersexed infants challenge our insistence that biological gender is unequivocally binary. So threatening to the order of things is the natural embodiment of conjoined twins and intersexed people that they are almost always surgically normalized through amputation and mutilation immediately after birth (Clark and Myser 1996, Dreger 1998a, Kessler 1990, Fausto-Sterling 2000). Not infrequently, one conjoined twin is sacrificed to save the other from the supposed abnormality of their embodiment. Such mutilations are justified as preventing suffering and creating well adjusted individuals. So intolerable is their insult to dominant ideologies about who patriarchal culture insists that we are that the testimonies of adults with these forms of embodiment who say that they do not want to be separated is routinely ignored in establishing the rationale for "medical treatment." (Dreger 1998b). In truth, these procedures benefit not the affected individuals, but rather they expunge the kinds of corporeal human variations that contradict the ideologies the dominant order depends upon to anchor truths it insists are unequivocally encoded in bodies.

I do not want to oversimplify here by suggesting that women and disabled people should not use modern medicine to improve their lives or help their bodies function more fully. But the critical issues are complex and provocative. A feminist disability theory should illuminate and explain, not become ideological policing or set orthodoxy. The kinds of critical analyses I'm discussing here offer a counter logic to the overdetermined cultural mandates to comply with normal and beautiful at any cost. The medical commitment to healing, when coupled with modernity's faith in technology and interventions that control outcomes, has increasingly shifted toward an aggressive intent to fix, regulate, or eradicate ostensibly deviant bodies. Such a program of elimination has often been at the expense of creating a more accessible environment or providing better support services for people with disabilities. The privileging of medical technology over less ambitious programs such as rehabilitation has encouraged the cultural conviction that disability can be extirpated, inviting the belief that life with a disability is intolerable. As charity campaigns and telethons repeatedly affirm, cure rather than adjustment or accommodation is the overdetermined cultural response to disability (Longmore 1997). For instance, a 1949 March of Dimes poster shows an appealing little girl stepping out of her wheelchair into the supposed redemption of walking: "Look, I Can Walk Again!" the text proclaims while at once charging the viewers with the responsibility of assuring her future ambulation. Nowhere do we find posters suggesting that life as a wheelchair user might be full and satisfying, as many people who actually use them find their lives to be. This ideology of cure is not isolated in medical texts or charity campaigns, but in fact permeates the entire cultural conversation about disability and illness. Take, for example, the discourse of cure in get well cards. A 1950 card, for instance, urges its recipient to "snap out of it." Fusing racist, sexist, and ablist discourses, the card recruits the Mammy figure to insist on cure. The stereotypical racist figure asks, " Is you sick, Honey?" and then exhorts the recipient of her care to "jes hoodoo all dat illness out o you."

The ideology of cure directed at disabled people focuses on changing bodies imagined as abnormal and dysfunctional rather than on exclusionary attitudinal, environmental and economic barriers. The emphasis on cure reduces the cultural tolerance for human variation and vulnerability by locating disability in bodies imagined as flawed rather than social systems in need of fixing. A feminist disability studies would draw an important distinction between prevention and elimination. Preventing illness, suffering, and injury is a humane social objective. Eliminating the range of unacceptable and devalued bodily forms and functions the dominant order calls disability is, on the other hand, a eugenic undertaking. The ostensibly progressive socio-medical project of eradicating disability all too often is enacted as a program to eliminate people with disabilities through such practices as forced sterilization, so-called physician-assisted suicide and mercy killing, selective abortion, institutionization, and segregation policies.

A feminist disability theory extends its critique of the normalization of bodies and the medicalization of appearance to challenge some widely held assumptions about reproductive issues as well. The cultural mandate to eliminate the variations in form and function that we think of as disabilities has undergirded the reproductive practices of genetic testing and selective abortion (Saxton 1998, Parens and Asch 2000, Rapp 1999). Some disability activists argue that the "choice" to abort fetuses with disabilities is a coercive form of genocide against the disabled (Hubbard 1990). A more nuanced argument against selective abortion comes from Adrienne Asch and Gail Geller, who wish to preserve a woman's right choose whether to bear a child, but who at the same time objects to the ethics of selectively aborting a wanted fetus because it will become a person with a disability (1996). Asch and Geller counter the quality-of-life and prevention-of-suffering arguments so readily invoked to justify selective abortion, as well as physician-assisted suicide, by pointing out that we cannot predict or—more precisely—control in advance such equivocal human states as happiness, suffering, or success. Neither is any amount of prenatal engineering going to produce the life that any of us desire and value. Indeed, both hubris and a lack of imagination characterize the prejudicial and reductive assumption that having a disability ruins lives. A vague notion of suffering and its potential deterrence drives much of the logic of elimination that rationalizes selective abortion (Kittay 2000). Life chances and quality are simply far too contingent to justify prenatal prediction.

Similarly, genetic testing and applications of the Human Genome Project as the key to expunging disability are often critiqued as enactments of eugenic ideology, what the feminist biologist Evelyn Fox Keller calls a "eugenics of normalcy" (1992). The popular utopian notion that all forms of disability can be eliminated through prophylactic manipulation of genetics will only serve to intensify the prejudice against those who inevitably will acquire disabilities through aging and encounters with the environment. In the popular celebrations of the Human Genome Project as the quixotic pinnacle of technological progress, seldom do we hear a cautionary logic about the eugenic implications of this drive toward what Priscilla Wald calls "Future Perfect" (2000, 1). Disability scholars have entered the debate over so-called physician-assisted suicide, as well, by arguing that oppressive attitudes toward disability distort the possibility of unbiased free choice (Battin, et. al.1998). The practices of genetic and prenatal testing as well as physician-administered euthanasia, then, become potentially eugenic practices within the context of a culture deeply intolerant of disability. Both the rhetoric and the enactment of this kind of disability discrimination create a hostile and exclusionary environment for people with disabilities that perhaps exceeds the less virulent architectural barriers that keep them out of the workforce and the public sphere.

Integrating disability into feminism's conversation about the place of the body in the equality and difference debates produces fresh insights as well. Whereas liberal feminism emphasizes sameness, choice, and autonomy, cultural feminism critiques the premises of liberalism. Out of cultural feminism's insistence on difference and its positive interpretation of feminine culture comes the affirmation of a feminist ethic of care. This ethic of care contends that care giving is a moral benefit for its practitioners and for humankind. A feminist disability studies complicates both the feminist ethic of care and liberal feminism in regard to the politics of care and dependency.

A disability perspective nuances feminist theory's consideration of the ethics of care by examining the power relations between the givers and receivers of care. Anita Silvers has argued strongly that being the object of care precludes the equality that a liberal democracy depends upon and undermines the claim to justice as equality that undergirds a civil rights approach used to counter discrimination (1995). Eva Kittay, on the other hand, formulates a "dependency critique of equality" (1999, 4), which asserts that the ideal of equality under liberalism repudiates the fact of human dependency, the need for mutual care, and the asymmetries of care relations. Similarly, Barbara Hillyer has called attention to dependency in order to critique a liberal tendency in the rhetoric of disability rights (1993). Disability itself demands that human interdependence and the universal need for assistance be figured into our dialogues about rights and subjectivity.

Identity

The third domain of feminist theory that a disability analysis complicates is identity. Feminist theory has productively and rigorously critiqued the identity category of woman, on which the entire feminist enterprise seemed to rest. Feminism increasingly recognizes that no woman is ever *only* a woman, that she occupies multiple subject positions and is claimed by several cultural identity categories (Spelman 1988). This complication of *woman* compelled feminist theory to turn from an exclusively male/female focus to look more fully at the exclusionary, essentialist, oppressive, and binary aspects of the category woman itself. Disability is one such identity vector that disrupts the unity of the classification woman and challenges the primacy of gender as a monolithic category.

Disabled women are, of course, a marked and excluded—albeit quite varied—group within the larger social class of women. The relative privileges of normative femininity are often denied to disabled women (Fine and Asch 1988). Cultural stereotypes imagine disabled women as asexual, unfit to reproduce, overly dependent, unattractive—as generally removed from the sphere of true womanhood and feminine beauty. Woman with disabilities often must often struggle to have their sexuality and rights to bear children recognized (Finger 1990). Disability thus both intensifies and attenuates the cultural scripts of femininity. Aging is a form of disablement that disqualifies older women from the limited power allotted females who are young and meet the criteria for attracting men. Depression, anorexia, and agoraphobia are female-dominant, psycho-physical disabilities that exaggerate normative gendered roles. Feminine cultural practices such as foot binding, clitorectomies, and corsetting, as well as their less hyperbolic costuming rituals such as stiletto high heels, girdles, and chastity belts—impair women's bodies and restrict their physical agency, imposing disability on them.

Banishment from femininity can be both a liability and a benefit. Let me offer—with some irony-an instructive example from popular culture. Barbie, that cultural icon of femininity, offers a disability analysis that clarifies both how multiple identity and diversity is commodified and how the commercial realm might offers politically useful feminist counterimages. Perhaps the measure of a group's arrival into the mainstream of multiculturalism is to be represented in the Barbie pantheon. While Barbie herself still identifies as able-bodied—despite her severely deformed body—we now have several incarnations of Barbie's "friend," Share-A-Smile Becky. One Becky uses a cool hot pink wheelchair; another is Paralympic Champion Becky, brought out for the 2000 Sydney Olympics in a chic red-white-and-blue warm-up suit with matching chair. Most interesting however is Becky, the school photographer, clad in a preppy outfit, complete with camera and red high-top sneakers. As she perkily gazes at an alluring Barbie in her camera's viewfinder, this Becky may be the incarnation of what one scholar has called "Barbie's queer assessories" (Rand 1995).

A disabled, queer Becky is certainly a provocative and subversive fusion of stigmatized identities, but more important is that Becky challenges notions of normalcy in feminist ways. The disabled Becky, for example, wears comfortable clothes: pants with elastic-waists no doubt, sensible shoes, and roomy shirts. Becky is also one of the few dolls who has flat feet and legs that bend at the knee. The disabled Becky is dressed and poised for agency, action, and creative engagement with the world. In contrast, the prototypical Barbie performs excessive femininity in her restrictive sequined gowns, crowns, and push-up bras. So while Becky implies on the one hand that disabled girls are purged from the feminine economy, on the other hand Becky also suggests that disabled girls might be liberated from those oppressive and debilitating scripts. The last word on Barbies comes from a disability activist who quipped that he'd like to outfit a disabled doll with a power wheelchair chair and a briefcase to make her a civil rights lawyer who enforces the Americans with Disabilities Act. He wants to call her "Sue-Your-Ass-Becky."[22] I think she'd make a very good role model.

The paradox of Barbie and Becky, of course, is that the ultra-feminized Barbie is a target for sexual appropriation both by men and beauty practices while the disabled Becky escapes such sexual objectification at the potential cost of losing her sense of identity as a feminine sexual being. Some disabled women negotiate this possible identity crisis by developing alternate sexualities, such as lesbianism

(Brownsworth and Raffo 1999). However, what Harlan Hahn calls the "asexual objectification" of people with disabilities complicates the feminist critique of normative sexual objectification (1988). Consider the 1987 *Playboy* magazine photos of the paraplegic actress Ellen Stohl. After becoming disabled, Stohl wrote to editor Hugh Hefner that she wanted to pose nude for *Playboy* because "sexuality is the hardest thing for disabled persons to hold onto." ("Meet Ellen Stohl," 68.) For Stohl, it would seem that the performance of excessive feminine sexuality was necessary to counter the social interpretation that disability cancels out sexuality. This confirmation of normative heterosexuality was then for Stohl no Butlerian parody, but rather was the affirmation she needed as a disabled woman to be sexual at all.

Ellen Stohl's presentation by way of the sexist conventions of the porn magazine illuminates the relation between identity and the body, an aspect of subject formation that disability analysis can offer. Although binary identities are conferred from outside through social relations, these identities are nevertheless inscribed on the body as either manifest or incipient visual traces. Identity's social meaning turns on this play of visibility. The photos of Stohl in *Playboy* both refuse and insist on marking her impairment. The centerfold spread—so to speak—of Stohl nude and masturbating erases her impairment to conform to the sexualized conventions of the centerfold. This photo expunges her wheelchair and any other visual clues to her impairment. In other words, to avoid the cultural contradiction of a sexual disabled woman, the pornographic photos must offer up Stohl as visually nondisabled. But to appeal to the cultural narrative of overcoming disability that sells so well, seems novel, and capitalizes on sentimental interest, Stohl must be visually dramatized as disabled at the same time. So *Playboy* includes several shots of Stohl that mark her as disabled by picturing her in her wheelchair, entirely without the typical porn conventions. In fact, the photos of her using her wheelchair invoke the asexual poster child. Thus, the affirmation of Stohl's sexuality she sought by posing nude in the porn magazine came at the expense of denying through the powerful visual register her identity as a woman with a disability, even while she attempted to claim that identity textually.

Another aspect of subject formation that disability confirms is that identity is always in transition. Disability reminds us that the body is, as Denise Riley asserts, "an unsteady mark, scarred in its long decay" (Riley 1999, 224). As Caroline Walker Bynum's intriguing work on werewolf narratives suggests, the body is in a perpetual state of transformation (1999). Caring for her father for over twenty years of Alzheimer's disease prompted Bynum to investigate how we can understand individual identity as continuous even though both body and mind can and do change dramatically, certainly over a lifetime and sometimes quite suddenly. Disability invites us to query what the continuity of the self might depend upon if the body perpetually metamorphoses. We envision our racial, gender, or ethnic identities as tethered to bodily traits that are relatively secure. Disability and sexual identity, however, seem more fluid, although sexual mutability is imagined as elective where disability is seldom conceived of as a choice. Disability is an identity category that anyone can enter at any time, and we will all join it if we live long enough. As such, disability reveals the essential dynamism of identity. Thus, disability attenuates the cherished cultural belief that the body is the unchanging anchor of identity. Moreover, it undermines our fantasies of stable, enduring identities in ways that may illuminate the fluidity of all identity.

Disability's clarification of the body's corporeal truths suggests as well that the body/self materializes—in Judith Butler's sense—not so much through discourse, but through history (1993). The self materializes in response to an embodied engagement with its environment, both social and concrete. The disabled body is a body whose variations or transformations have rendered it out of sync with its environment, both the physical and the attitudinal environments. In other words, the body becomes disabled when it is incongruent both in space and the milieu of expectations. Furthermore, a feminist disability theory presses us to ask what kinds of knowledge might be produced through having a body radically marked by its own particularity, a body that materializes at the ends of the curve of human variation. For example, an alternative epistemology that emerges from the lived experience of disability is nicely summed up in Nancy Mairs' book title, *Waist High in the World*, which she irreverently considered calling "cock high in the world." What perspectives or politics arise from encountering the world from such an atypical position? Perhaps Mairs' epistemology can offer us a critical positionality called sitpoint theory, a neologism I can offer that interrogates the ableist assumptions underlying the notion of standpoint theory (Harstock 1983).

Our collective cultural consciousness emphatically denies the knowledge of bodily vulnerability, contingency, and mortality. Disability insists otherwise, contradicting such phallic ideology. I would argue that disability is perhaps the essential characteristic of being human. The body is dynamic, constantly interactive with history and environment. We evolve into disability. Our bodies need care; we all need assistance to live. An equality model of feminist theory sometimes prizes individualistic autonomy as the key to women's liberation. A feminist disability theory, however, suggests that we are better off learning to individually and collectively accommodate the body's limits and evolutions than trying to eliminate or deny them.

Identity formation is at the center of feminist theory. Disability can complicate feminist theory often quite succinctly by invoking established theoretical paradigms. This kind of theoretical intertextuality inflects familiar feminist concepts with new resonance. Let me offer several examples: the idea of "compulsory ablebodiedness," which Robert McRuer has coined, extends Adrienne Rich's famous analysis of "compulsory heterosexuality" (2001, 1986). Joan Wallach Scott's germinal work on gender is recruited when we discuss disability as "a useful category of analysis" (1988, 1). The feminist elaboration of the gender system informs my use of the disability system. Lennard Davis suggests that the term *normalcy studies* supplant the name *disability studies*, in the way that *gender studies* sometimes succeeds *feminism* (1995). The oft invoked distinction between sex and gender clarifies a differentiation between impairment and disability, even though both binaries are fraught. The concept of performing disability, cites (as it were) Judith Butler's vigorous critique of essentialism (1990). Reading disabled bodies as exemplary instances of "docile bodies" invokes Foucault (1979). To suggest that identity is lodged in the body, I propose that the body haunts the subject, alluding to Susan Bordo's notion regarding masculinity that "the penis haunts the phallus" (1994, 1). My own work has complicated the familiar discourse of the gaze to theorize what I call the stare, which I argue produces disability identity. Such theoretical shorthand impels us to reconsider the ways that identity categories cut across and redefine one another, pressuring both the terms *woman* and *disabled*.

A feminist disability theory can also highlight intersections and convergences with other identity-based critical perspectives such as queer and ethnic studies. Disability coming-out stories, for example, borrow from gay and lesbian identity narratives to expose what previously was hidden, privatized, medicalized in order to enter into a political community. The politicized sphere into which many scholars come out is feminist disability studies, which enables critique, claims disability identity, and creates affirming counter narratives. Disability coming-out narratives raise questions about the body's role in identity by asking how markers so conspicuous as crutches, wheelchairs, hearing aides, guide dogs, white canes, or empty sleeves could ever have been closeted.

Passing as nondisabled complicates ethnic and queer studies' analyses of how this seductive but psychically estranging access to privilege operates. Some of my friends, for example, have measured their regard for me by saying, "But I don't think of you as disabled." What they point to in such a compliment is the contradiction they find between their perception of me as a valuable, capable, lovable person and the cultural figure of the disabled person whom they take to be precisely my opposite: worthless, incapable, and unlovable. People with disabilities themselves routinely announce that they don't consider themselves as disabled. Although they are often repudiating the literal meaning of the word *disabled*, their words nevertheless serve to disassociate them from the identity group of the disabled. Our culture offers profound disincentives and few rewards to identifying as disabled. The trouble, of course, with such statements is that they leave intact without challenge the oppressive stereotypes that permit, among other things, the unexamined use of disability terms such as *crippled, lame, dumb, idiot, moron* as verbal gestures of derision. The refusal to claim disability identity is in part due to a lack of ways to understand or talk about disability that are not oppressive. People with disabilities and those who care about them flee from the language of *crippled* or *deformed* and have no other alternatives. Yet, the civil rights movement and the accompanying Black-is-beautiful identity politics have generally shown white culture what is problematic with saying to Black friends, "I don't think of you as Black." Nonetheless, by disavowing disability identity, many of us learned to save ourselves from devaluation by a complicity that perpetuates oppressive notions about ostensibly "real" disabled people. Thus, together we help make the alternately menacing and pathetic cultural figures who rattle tin cups or rave on street corners, ones we with impairments often flee from more surely than those who imagine themselves as nondisabled.

Activism

The final domain of feminist theory that a disability analysis expands is activism. There are many arenas of what can be seen as feminist disability activism: marches, protests, the Breast Cancer Fund poster campaign I discussed above, action groups such as the Intersex Society of North America (ISNA), and Not Dead Yet, who oppose physician-assisted suicide, or the American Disabled for Accessible Public Transit (ADAPT). What counts as activism cuts a wide swath through U.S. society and the academy. I want to suggest here two unlikely, even quirky, cultural practices that function in activist ways but are seldom considered as potentially transformative. One practice is disabled fashion modeling and the other is academic tolerance. Both are different genres of activism from the more traditional marching-on-Washington or chaining-yourself-to-a-bus modes. Both are less theatrical, but perhaps fresher and more interestingly controversial ways to change the social landscape and to promote equality, which I take to be the goal of activism.

The theologian and sociologist, Nancy Eiesland, has argued that in addition to legislative, economic, and social changes, achieving equality for people with disabilities depends upon cultural "resymbolization" (1994, 98). Eiseland asserts that the way we imagine disability and disabled people must shift in order for real social change to occur. Whereas Eiseland's work resymbolizes our conceptions of disability in religious iconography, my own examinations of disabled fashion models do similar cultural work in the popular sphere, introducing some interesting complications into her notion of resymbolization.

Images of disabled fashion models in the media can shake up established categories and expectations. Because commercial visual media are the most widespread and commanding source of images in modern, image-saturated culture, they have great potential for shaping public consciousness–as feminist cultural critics are well aware. Fashion imagery is the visual distillation of the normative, gilded with the chic and the luxurious to render it desirable. The commercial sphere is completely amoral, driven as it is by the single logic of the bottom line. As we know, it sweeps through culture seizing with alarming neutrality anything it senses will sell. This value-free aspect of advertising produces a kind of pliable potency that sometimes can yield unexpected results.

Take, for example, a shot from the monthly fashion feature in *WE Magazine*, a *Cosmopolitan* knock-off targeted toward the disabled consumer market. In this conventional, stylized, high fashion shot, a typical female model–slender, white, blond, clad in a black evening gown—is accompanied by her service dog. My argument is that public images such as this are radical because they fuse two previously antithetical visual discourses—the chic high fashion shot and the earnest charity campaign. Public representations of disability have traditionally been contained within the conventions of sentimental charity images, exotic freak show portraits, medical illustrations, or sensational and forbidden pictures. Indeed, people with disabilities have been excluded most fully from the dominant, public world of the marketplace. Before the civil rights initiatives of the mid-twentieth century began to transform the public architectural and institutional environment, disabled people were segregated to the private and the medical spheres. Until recently, the only available public image of a woman with a service dog that shaped the public imagination was street-corner beggar or a charity poster. By juxtaposing the elite body of a visually normative fashion model with the mark of disability, this image shakes up our assumptions about the normal and the abnormal, the public and the private, the chic and the desolate, the compelling and the repelling. Introducing a service dog—a standard prop of indigents and poster children—into the conventional composition of an upscale fashion photo forces the viewer to reconfigure assumptions about what constitutes the attractive and the desirable.

I am arguing that the emergence of disabled fashion models is inadvertent activism without any legitimate agent for positive social change. Their appearance is simply a result of market forces. This both troubling and empowering form of entry into democratic capitalism produces a kind of instrumental form of equality: the freedom to be appropriated by consumer culture. In a democracy, to reject this paradoxical liberty is one thing; not to be granted it is another. Ever straining for novelty and capitalizing on titillation, the fashion advertising world promptly appropriated the power of disabled figures to provoke responses. Diversity appeals to an upscale liberal sensibility these days, making consumers feel good about buying from companies that are charitable toward the traditionally disadvantaged. More important, the disability market is burgeoning. At 54 million people and growing fast as the baby boomers age, their spending power was estimated to have reached the trillion-dollar mark in 2000 (Williams).

For the most part, commercial advertising that features disabled models are presented the same as nondisabled models, simply because all models look essentially the same. The physical markings of gender, race, ethnicity, and disability are muted to the level of gesture, subordinated to the overall normativity of the models' appearance. Thus, commercial visual media cast disabled consumers as simply one of many variations that compose the market to which they appeal. Such routinization of disability imagery—however stylized and unrealistic it may be—nevertheless brings disability as a human experience out of the closet and into the normative public sphere. Images of disabled fashion models enable people with disabilities, especially those who acquire impairments as adults, to imagine themselves as a part of the ordinary, albeit consumerist, world rather than as in a special class of excluded untouchables and unviewables. Images of impairment as a familiar, even mundane, experience in the lives of seemingly successful, happy, well-adjusted people can reduce the identifying against oneself that is the overwhelming effect of oppressive and discriminatory attitudes toward people with disabilities. Such images, then, are at once liberatory and oppressive. They do the cultural work of integrating a previously excluded group into the dominant order—for better or worse—much like the inclusion of women in the military.

This form of popular resymbolization produces counterimages that have activist potential. A clearer example of disability activism might be Aimee Mullins, who is a fashion model, celebrity, champion runner, a Georgetown University student, and double amputee. Mullins was also one of People Magazine's 50 Most Beautiful people of 1999. An icon of disability pride and equality, Mullins exposes—in fact calls attention to—the mark of her disability in most photos, refusing to normalize or hide her disability in order to pass for nondisabled. Indeed, her public version of her career is that her disability has been a benefit: she has several sets of legs, both cosmetic and functional, and so is able to choose how tall she wants to be. Photographed in her prosthetic legs, she embodies the sexualized jock look that demands women be both slender and fit. In her cosmetic legs, she captures the look of the high fashion beauty in the controversial shoot by Nick Knight called "Accessible," showcasing outfits created by designers such as Alexander McQueen. But this is high fashion with a difference. In the jock shot her functional legs are brazenly displayed, and even in the voguishly costumed shot, the knee joints of her artificial legs are exposed. Never is there an attempt to disguise her prosthetic legs; rather the entire photos thematically echo her prostheses and render the whole image chic. Mullins' prosthetic legs—whether cosmetic or functional—parody, indeed proudly mock, the fantasy of the perfect body that is the mark of fashion, even while the rest of her body conforms precisely to fashion's impossible standards. So rather than concealing, normalizing, or erasing disability, these photos use the hyperbole and stigmata traditionally associated with disability to quench postmodernity's perpetual search for the new and arresting image. Such a narrative of advantage works against oppressive narratives and practices usually invoked about disabilities. First, Mullins counters the insistent narrative that one must overcome an impairment rather than incorporating it into one's life and self, even perhaps as a benefit. Second, Mullins counters the practice of passing for non-disabled that people with disabilities are often obliged to enact in the public sphere. So Mullins uses her conformity with beauty standards to assert her disability's violation of those very standards. As legless and beautiful, she is an embodied paradox, asserting an inherently disruptive potential.

What my analysis of these images reveals is that feminist cultural critiques are complex. On the one hand, feminists have rightly unmasked consumer capitalism's appropriation of women as sexual objects for male gratification. On the other hand, these images imply that the same capitalist system in its drive to harvest new markets can produce politically progressive counter images and counternarratives, however fraught they may be in their entanglement with consumer culture. Images of disabled fashion models are both complicit and critical of the beauty system that oppresses all women. Nevertheless, they suggest that consumer culture can provide the raw material for its own critique.

The concluding version of activism I offer is less controversial and more subtle than glitzy fashion spreads. It is what I call academic activism—the activism of integrating education—in the very broadest sense of that term. The academy is no ivory tower but rather it is the grass roots of the educational enterprise. Scholars and teachers shape the communal knowledge and the archive that is disseminated from kindergarten to the university. Academic activism is most self-consciously vibrant in the aggregate of interdisciplinary identity studies—of which women's studies is exemplary—that strive to expose the workings of oppression, examine subject formation, and offer counter-narratives for subjugated groups. Their cultural work is building an archive through historical and textual retrieval, canon reformation, role modeling, mentoring, curricular reform, and course and program development.

A specific form of feminist academic activism I elaborate here can be deepened through the complication of a disability analysis. I call it the methodology of intellectual tolerance. By this I don't mean tolerance in the more usual sense of tolerating each other—although that would be useful as well. What I mean is the intellectual position of tolerating what has previously been thought of as incoherence. As feminism has embraced the paradoxes that have emerged from its challenge to the gender system, it has not collapsed into chaos, but rather it developed a methodology that tolerates internal conflict and contradiction. This method asks difficult questions, but accepts provisional answers. This method recognizes the power of identity at the same time that it reveals identity as a fiction. This method both seeks equality, and it claims difference. This method allows us to teach with authority at the same time that we reject notions of pedagogical mastery. This method establishes institutional presences even while it acknowledges the limitations of institutions. This method validates the personal but implements disinterested inquiry. This method both writes new stories and recovers traditional ones. Considering disability as a vector of identity that intersects gender is one more internal challenge that threatens the coherence of woman, of course. But feminism can accommodate such complication and the contradictions it cultivates. Indeed the intellectual tolerance I am arguing for espouses the partial, the provisional, the particular. Such an intellectual habit can be informed by disability experience and acceptance. To embrace the supposedly flawed body of disability is to critique the normalizing, phallic fantasies of wholeness, unity, coherence, and completeness. The disabled body is contradiction, ambiguity, and partiality incarnate.

My claim here has been that integrating disability as a category of analysis, a historical community, a set of material practices, a social identity, a political position, and a representational system into the content of feminist—indeed into all-- inquiry can strengthen the critique that is feminism. Disability, like gender and race, is everywhere, once we know how to look for it. Integrating disability analyses will enrich and deepen all our teaching and scholarship. Moreover, such critical intellectual work facilitates a fuller integration of the sociopolitical world—for the benefit of everyone. As with gender, race, sexuality, and class: to understand how disability operates is to understand what it is to be fully human.

Notes

1. Interestingly, in Fiske's study, feminists, businesswomen, Asians, Northerners, and Black professionals were stereotyped as highly competent, thus envied. In addition to having very low competence, housewives, disabled people, blind people, so-called retarded people, and the elderly were rated as warm, thus pitied.
2. Personal conversation with Paul Longmore, San Francisco, CA, June 2000.

Works Cited

Americans with Disabilities Act of 1990. Retrieved 15 August 2002, from http://www.usdoj.gov/crt/ada/pubs/ada.txt.

Aristotle. 1944. *Generation of Animals*. Trans. A.L. Peck. Cambridge: Harvard UP.

Asch, Adrienne, and Gail Geller. 1996. "Feminism, Bioethics and Genetics." In *Feminism, Bioethics: Beyond Reproduction*, ed. S.M. Wolf, 318–50. Oxford: Oxford UP.

Battin, Margaret P., Rosamond Rhodes, and Anita Silvers, eds. 1998. *Physician Assisted Suicide: Expanding the Debate*. New York: Routledge.

Bordo, Susan. 1994. "Reading the Male Body." In *The Male Body*, ed. Laurence Goldstein, 265–306. Ann Arbor: U of Michigan P.

———. 1993. *Unbearable Weight: Feminism, Western Culture and the Body*. Berkeley: U of California P.

Braidotti, Rosi. 1994. *Nomadic Subjects: Embodiment and Sexual Difference in Contemporary Feminist Thought*. New York: Columbia UP.

Brownsworth, Victoria A., and Susan Raffo, eds. 1999. *Restricted Access: Lesbians on Disability*. Seattle: Seal Press.

Butler, Judith. 1993. *Bodies that Matter*. New York: Routledge.

———. 1990. *Gender Trouble*. New York: Routledge.

Bynum, Caroline Walker. 1999. "Shape and Story: Metamorphosis in the Western Tradition." Paper presented at NEH Jefferson Lecture. 22 March, at Washington, DC.

Clark, David L., and Catherine Myser. 1996. "Being Humaned: Medical Documentaries and the Hyperrealization of Conjoined Twins." In *Freakery: Cultural Spectacles of the Extraordinary Body*, ed. Rosemarie Garland Thomson, 338–55. New York: New York UP.

Davis, Lennard. 1995. *Enforcing Normalcy: Disability, Deafness, and the Body*. New York: Verso.

De Beauvoir, Simone. (1952) 1974. *The Second Sex*. Trans. H.M. Parshley. New York: Vintage Press.

Dreger, Alice Domurat. 1998a. *Hermaphrodites and the Medical Invention of Sex*. Cambridge: Harvard UP.

———. 1998b. "The Limits of the Individuality: Ritual and Sacrifice in the Lives and Medical Treatment of Conjoined Twins." In *Freakery: Cultural Spectacles of the Extraordinary Body*, ed. Rosemarie Garland Thomson, 338–55. New York: New York UP.

Eiesland, Nancy. 1994. *The Disabled God: Toward a Liberatory Theology of Disability*. Nahsville: Abingdon Press.

Fausto-Sterling, Anne. 2000. *Sexing the Body: Gender Politics and the Construction of Sexuality*. New York: Basic Books.

———. 1995. "Gender, Race, and Nation: The Comparative Anatomy of Hottentot Women in Europe, 1815–1817." In *Deviant Bodies: Cultural Perspectives in Science and Popular Culture*, eds. Jennifer Terry and Jacqueline Urla, 19–48. Bloomington: Indiana UP.

Fine, Michelle, and Adrienne Asch, eds. 1988. *Women with Disabilities: Essays in Psychology, Culture, and Politics*. Philadelphia: Temple UP.

Finger, Anne. 1990. *Past Due: A Story of Disability, Pregnancy, and Birth*. Seattle: Seal Press.

Fiske, Susan T., Amy J. C. Cuddy, and Peter Glick. 2001. "A Model of (Often Mixed) Stereotype Content: Competence and Warmth Respectively Follow from Perceived Status and Competition." Unpublished study.

Foucault, Michel. 1979. *Discipline and Punish: The Birth of the Prison*. Trans. Alan M. Sheridan-Smith. New York: Vintage Books.

Gilman, Sander L. 1999. *Making the Body Beautiful*. Princeton: Princeton UP.

———. 1998. *Creating Beauty to Cure the Soul*. Durham: Duke UP.

———. 1985. *Difference and Pathology: Stereotypes of Sexuality, Race, and Madness*. Ithaca: Cornell UP.

Hahn, Harlan. 1988. "Can Disability Be Beautiful?" *Social Policy* 18 (Winter): 26–31.

Haiken, Elizabeth. 1997. *Venus Envy: A History of Cosmetic Surgery*. Baltimore: Johns Hopkins UP.

Haraway, Donna. 1991. *Simians, Cyborgs, and Women*. New York: Routledge.

Harstock, Nancy. 1983. "The Feminist Standpoint: Developing the Ground for a Specifically Feminist Historical Materialism." In *Discovering Reality*, eds. Sandra Harding and Merrell Hintikka, 283–305. Dortrecht, Holland: Reidel Publishing.

Herndl, Diane Price. 2002. "Reconstructing the Posthuman Feminist Body: Twenty Years after Audre Lorde's *Cancer Journals*." In *Disability Studies: Enabling the Humanities*, eds. Sharon Snyder, Brenda Brueggemann, and Rosemarie Garland-Thomson, 144–55. New York: MLA Press.

Hillyer, Barbara. 1993. *Feminism and Disability*. Norman: U of Oklahoma P.

Hubbard, Ruth. 1990. "Who Should and Who Should Not Inhabit the World?" In *The Politics of Women's Biology*, 179–98. New Brunswick: Rutgers UP.

Keller, Evelyn Fox. 1992. "Nature, Nurture and the Human Genome Project." In *The Code of Codes: Scientific and Social Issues in the Human Genome Project*, eds. Daniel J. Kevles and Leroy Hood, 281–99. Cambridge: Harvard UP.

Kessler, Suzanne J. 1990. *Lessons from the Intersexed*. New Brunswick: Rutgers UP.

Kittay, Eva Feder. 1999. *Love's Labor: Essays on Women, Equality, and Dependency*. New York: Routledge.

Kittay, Eva, with Leo Kittay. 2000. "On the Expressivity and Ethics of Selective Abortion for Disability: Conversations with My Son." In *Prenatal Testing and Disability Rights*, eds. Erik Parens and Adrienne Asch, 165–95. Georgetown: Georgetown UP.

Linton, Simi. 1998. *Claiming Disability: Knowledge and Identity*. New York: New York UP.

Longmore, Paul K. 1997. "Conspicuous Contribution and American Cultural Dilemmas: Telethon Rituals of Cleansing and Renewal." In *The Body and Physical Difference: Discourses of Disability*, eds. David Mitchell and Sharon Snyder, 134–58. Ann Arbor: U of Michigan P.

Lorde, Audre. 1980. *The Cancer Journals*. San Francisco: Spinsters Ink.

Mairs, Nancy. 1996. *Waist High in the World: A Life Among the Disabled*. Boston: Beacon Press.

McRuer, Robert. 1999. "Compulsory Able-Bodiedness and Queer/Disabled Existence." Paper presented at MLA Convention, 28 December, at Chicago, IL.

"Meet Ellen Stohl." 1987. *Playboy*. July: 68–74

Morrison, Toni. 1992. *Playing in the Dark: Whiteness and the Literary Imagination*. Cambridge: Harvard UP.

Parens, Erik, and Adrienne Asch. 2000. *Prenatal Testing and Disability Rights*. Georgetown: Georgetown UP.

Piercy, Marge. 1969. "Unlearning Not to Speak." In *Circles on Water, 97*. New York: Doubleday.

Rand, Erica. 1995. *Barbie's Queer Accessories*. Durham: Duke UP.

Rapp, Rayna. 1999. *Testing Women, Testing the Fetus: The Social Impact of Amniocentesis in America*. New York: Routledge.

Rich, Adrienne. 1986. "Compulsory Heterosexuality and Lesbian Existence." In *Blood, Bread, and Poetry*, 23–75. New York: Norton.

Riley, Denise. 1999. "Bodies, Identities, Feminisms." In *Feminist Theory and the Body: A Reader*, eds. Janet Price and Margrit Shildrick, 220–6. Edinburgh, Scotland: Edinburgh UP.

Russo, Mary. 1994. *The Female Grotesque: Risk, Excess, and Modernity*. New York: Routledge.

Saxton, Marsha. 1998. "Disability Rights and Selective Abortion." In *Abortion Wars: A Half Century of Struggle (1950-2000)*, ed. Ricky Solinger, 374–93. Berkeley: U of California P.

Scott, Joan Wallach. 1988. "Gender as Useful Category of Analysis." In *Gender and the Politics of History*, 29–50. New York: Columbia UP.

Sedgwick, Eve Kosofsky. 1990. *Epistemology of the Closet*. Berkeley: U of California P.

Silvers, Anita. 1995. "Reconciling Equality to Difference: Caring (f)or Justice for People with Disabilities." *Hypatia* 10(1): 30–55.

Spelman, Elizabeth, V. 1988. *Inessential Woman: Problems of Exclusion in Feminist Thought*. Boston: Beacon Press.

Thomson, Rosemarie Garland. 1999. "Narratives of Deviance and Delight: Staring at Julia Pastrana, 'The Extraordinary Lady.'" In *Beyond the Binary*, ed. Timothy Powell, 81–106. New Brunswick: Rutgers UP.

———. 1997. *Extraordinary Bodies: Figuring Physical Disability in American Culture and Literature*. New York: Columbia UP.

Tuana, Nancy. 1993. *The Less Noble Sex: Scientific, Religious and Philosophical Conceptions of Woman's Nature*. Indianapolis: Indiana UP.

Wald, Priscilla. 2000. "Future Perfect: Grammar, Genes, and Geography." *New Literary History* 31(4): 681–708.

Williams, John M. 1999. "And Here's the Pitch: Madison Avenue Discovers the 'Invisible Consumer.'" *WE Magazine*, July/August: 28–31.

Wolf, Naomi. 1991. *The Beauty Myth: How Images of Beauty Are Used Against Women*. New York: William Morrow and Co.

Young, Iris Marion. 1990a. "Breasted Experience." In *Throwing Like a Girl and Other Essays in Feminist Philosophy and Social Theory*, 189–209. Bloomington: Indiana UP.

———. 1990b. "Throwing Like a Girl." In *Throwing Like a Girl and Other Essays in Feminist Philosophy and Social Theory*, 141–59. Bloomington: Indiana UP.

22

Introducing White Disability Studies
A Modest Proposal

Chris Bell

My modest proposal is inspired by a popular television program airing on the Chicago PBS affiliate. "Check, Please!" gathers three "ordinary" residents who, after selecting their favorite restaurant, anonymously dine at all three establishments, then gather in a studio to debate the relative merits and shortfalls of each culinary venue. During one episode, the trio included a self-styled *bon vivant* whom I will call Dorian Gray. Dorian, while sharing his observations about a Chinese restaurant in a south Chicago suburb, expressed his unadulterated amazement at the composition of one particular entrée. "The shrimp were *artificial!*" he bemoaned, dread contorting his facial features into an expression of unrecoverable distress. The individual selecting said restaurant as his favorite—I'll call him Bubba Gump—blinked nary an eye at this revelation. Instead, Bubba stoically intoned, "If it looks like a shrimp, and it smells and tastes like a shrimp, it's a shrimp."

Bubba Gump's matter-of-fact rejoinder to Dorian Gray is, I think, indicative of the whiteness of Disability Studies in its present incarnation. The fact that Disability Studies is marketed as such when it is in actuality an artificial (read: limited and limiting) version of the field does nothing to prevent it from being understood as Disability Studies, which is what Bubba, by extension, apprised Dorian of. I contend that it is disingenuous to keep up the pretense that the field is an inclusive one when it is not. On that score, I would like to concede the failure of Disability Studies to engage issues of race and ethnicity in a substantive capacity, thereby entrenching whiteness as its constitutive underpinning. In short, I want to call a shrimp a shrimp and acknowledge Disability Studies for what it is, White Disability Studies.

In contradistinction to Disability Studies, White Disability Studies recognizes its tendency to whitewash disability history, ontology and phenomenology. White Disability Studies, while not wholeheartedly excluding people of color from its critique,[1] by and large focuses on the work of white individuals and is itself largely produced by a corps of white scholars and activists. White Disability Studies envisions nothing ill-advised with this leaning because it is innocently done and far too difficult to remedy. A synoptic review of some of the literature and related aspects of Disability Studies bears this out.

"Vital Signs: Crip Culture Talks Back"

This documentary was filmed during a conference on Disability and the Arts on the campus of the University of Michigan. The film is distressing because of its absence of non-white individuals. Given the absence of people of color, I suggest that a significant number of myths and misconceptions about who/what is constitutive of disability or "crip" culture are bolstered and reinforced in the film.

No Pity: People with Disabilities Forging a New Civil Rights Movement

In his introduction, author Joseph Shapiro refers to the disabled community as the largest minority community in the United States, with more members than communities tallied by race, ethnicity, or sexual orientation amongst other socially-constructed identity categories(7). What interests me is Shapiro's obfuscation of divisions within this ostensibly-largest minority community and his insinuation that the disabled community is a monolithic one, struggling against the same oppressors, striving for identical degrees of dignity, recognition and cultural representation. Such a characterization is a limited one that does not consider or address the rich diversity within disability communities—racial and ethnic diversity, for example.

A Matter of Dignity: Changing the Lives of the Disabled

Comprised of a series of interviews with disabled people from various life strata, the dearth of people of color in the text is as undeniable as it is flagrant. In order to prevent this text from surprising the unexpecting reader, it might be a good idea to acknowledge that whiteness is positioned as its center. Doing so would make for a much more accurate description of who/what is represented.

Claiming Disability: Knowledge and Identity

In her well-known text, Simi Linton describes Disability Studies by stating, "The field explores the critical divisions our society makes in creating the normal versus the pathological, the insider versus the outsider, or the competent citizen versus the ward of the state"(2). The reader should recognize the dichotomous line of thought here, the binary fashion with which Linton makes her critique. At the very least, it should be understood that many white disabled people have cultural capital by virtue of their race and are, therefore, more on the inside than they are on the outside. As an insider, Linton appears unaware of her positioning, and it is that unawareness that is one of the hallmarks of White Disability Studies.

Enforcing Normalcy: Disability, Deafness and the Body

Throughout this text, Davis takes whiteness as a norm. From his discussion of the desirability of the Venus de Milo to his examination of the protagonist in "Born on the Fourth of July," Davis's emphasis on whiteness is undeniable. There is, to be sure, nothing wrong with this focus (aside from being egregiously misleading with regard to which communities and subjectivities are constitutive of "disability"). I only wish Davis had broadened his source materials, or at the very least opted for a more accurate title e.g., *Enforcing Normalcy: Disability, Deafness and the White Body*. Moreover, it matters that an excerpt from this text is reprinted in *The Norton Anthology of Literary Criticism*, the ostensible Bible of literary studies. Those readers coming across this excerpt will necessarily receive a distorted view of Disability Studies as a result of Davis's focus on whiteness.

Queer Disability Conference

Near the conclusion of the first day of this conference that convened in San Francisco in June 2002, I met with approximately thirteen other self-identified queer and disabled people of color during a caucus session. Our conversation focused on our individual and collective sense of exclusion based on race and ethnicity.[2] We could not fathom how the conference organizers—every one of them a white person—could publicize this conference in numerous international contexts and venues—drawing participants from Finland, Australia, and the United Kingdom among other nations—but fail to devise and implement an outreach plan that would attract people of color and other marginalized groups within the queer and disabled communities in the local Bay Area. We also could not understand the overarching mentality of many of the attendees, perhaps best expressed by a remark made in a breakout session: "Being disabled is just like being black, so society should stop hating us and give us our rights."

Society for Disability Studies Annual Conference, 2005

During the business meeting at the conference's conclusion, the people of color caucus presented a list of action items to the membership in an effort to shore up the marginal presence race and ethnicity had at the conference (despite the fact that the conference was themed "Conversations and Connections Across Race and Disability"). Although the hour-long conversation that ensued was collegial and productive, I cannot help wondering, drawing on my experience at the Queer Disability Conference,[3] how many times these questions of inclusion and exclusion have to be raised by people of color to white individuals? As I averred during the business meeting, "I'm tired of being one of the few to point out what should be obvious."

Modern Language Association (MLA) Conference on Disability Studies and the University

Convened on the campus of Emory University March 5–7, 2004, the conference is notable at the outset for the sheer whiteness of those who presented. A quick glance down the list of presenters (as published in *PMLA* in 2005)[4] bears this out. An additional concern is the content of what was shared during this conference.

In his address, "Disability: The Next Wave or Twilight of the Gods?," Lennard Davis, thankfully, speaks to the white nature of Disability Studies: "Disability studies has by and large been carried out by white people" (530). He is grossly incorrect, however, in the follow-up assertion that the field will benefit from "the disability studies book about the African American experience of disability" (ibid). To be sure, there is no singular, structuralist African American experience of disability and it is imprudent to advocate for one. Davis is further incorrect when he insists that said text must incorporate the recent "post-race" debate. Placing strictures on a text is foolish, especially when the strictures themselves lack intellectual value and integrity.[5]

In "What Is Disability Studies?," Simi Linton includes an instructive albeit telling example to illustrate the difficulty of answering the titular question:

> A few years ago, a controversy about the golfer Casey Martin and the golf cart captured a great deal of attention. Martin petitioned the PGA—the Professional Golfers' Association—for permission to ride a golf cart in pro tournaments as an accommodation for a mobility impairment. When the PGA turned him down, Martin took the case to court. It was eventually deliberated in the Supreme Court, where Martin prevailed. The most significant outcome of the debate, I think, is that the discussion came down to the question, What *is* the game of golf? Some people said, If he rides a cart, that's not golf. I'd like to know, then, what golf is and who has decided. (519)

As I mentioned, the example is instructive, but also rather telling: GOLF?! Come on! I challenge the reader to name one non-white golfer... Okay, now name one non-white golfer *besides* Tiger and Vijay.

On a more serious note, as I read through the collection of essays and presentations from the Emory conference I am concerned with how often each scholar cites the other, revealing an uncomfortable incestuousness about Disability Studies. These individuals seem unwilling to step aside even briefly and let someone else have the (proverbial) microphone for a moment. Granted, if the MLA calls, there is appeal in the form of professional legitimacy. But I also suggest that there is appeal in giving someone else a chance to speak to the issues embedded in and examined by Disability Studies, in asking who will be there and figuring out who *should* be there, as well as who has not been asked and why. The failure to do so practically ensures that the silences, namely those concerning race and ethnicity, will not be addressed and will continue.

*　*　*　*　*

If Disability Studies as a field had taken a reflexive look at itself at some point, particularly with regard to its failings in examining issues of race and ethnicity, there might not be such a glaring dearth of disability-related scholarship by and about disabled people of color. As it stands, Disability Studies has a tenuous relationship with race and ethnicity: while the field readily acknowledges its debt to and inspiration by inquiries such as Black Studies, its efforts at addressing intersections between disability, race, and ethnicity are, at best, wanting. Disability Studies claims to examine the experiences of a vast number of disabled people, yet the form that representation takes is, far too often, a white one. This is by no means a sporadic occurrence. Quite the contrary, the slights occur habitually and, as the preceding examples prove, in various contexts, from published works to conferences. I think it is essential to illuminate the fragile relationship between disability, race, and ethnicity in extant Disability Studies, arguing not so much for a sea-change in this formulation, rather for a more definitive and accurate identification of the happening.

What follows then is my ten-point scheme (*pace,* Mr. Letterman) on how to keep White Disability Studies in vogue and instantiated as disability praxis. Given the fact that well-intentioned individuals are inclined to ask what can be done to "make things more diverse," I have purposely crafted the following as a series of "do nots." By doing so, I hope to shore up how presumptuous it is to position the subaltern as the all-knowing savant insofar as issues of diversity; requesting definitive answers from that person when the answers might best come from within, following an extended period of rumination.

10. **Do not change a thing.** Let's keep doing what we're doing. Let's remain firmly rooted in *this* wave of disability, consciously opting not to move to the next. Let's continue to acknowledge white individuals as the Disability Studies core constituency.[6] Do not outreach to communities of color or participate in their events when the opportunity to forge connections arises. Do not solicit for a themed issue of *Disability Studies Quarterly* on race, ethnicity and disability[7] and if by chance said issue should be produced, make sure that it occurs only once; that there are no efforts to ensure that these intersections are spoken to throughout future iterations of the journal in a non-"special issue" context. In sum, do not change a thing. Continue to fetishize and exoticize people of color as subalterns by constantly focusing on *their* race and ethnicity, but not that of the white subject.

9. **Do not address ethnicity, rather continually focus on race.** Many Disability Studies scholars—and people in general—are unwilling or unable to pick up on the cultural significance of ethnicity in contraposition to what some are (erroneously) convinced is the biological foundation of race. Regardless of where the two concepts spring from, the fact is that they are distinct. It becomes problematic then when all that comprises ethnicity gets collapsed under the umbrella term of race. As a field White Disability Studies has no stake in this process and therefore should do nothing to address it.

8. **Do not consider that, as Stuart Hall has explained, "Cultural identity is not an essence but a positioning"** (229). Generally speaking, the same people who hold power in the community of scholars known as Disability Studies are a mimetic rendering of those holding power in non-disabled communities: white people. Despite the fact that people of color outnumber white people in the world, white people harbor hegemony and cultural capital. Whether or not

disabled people of color outnumber disabled white individuals—or whether people of color interested in Disability Studies outnumber whites interested in the same—the fact is Disability Studies is conceived of as a white field (recall Davis's comments from the Emory conference). White Disability Studies should pay no attention to this, doing nothing to change this conception, this positioning. It does not matter that whiteness is not an essentialist prerequisite for a disability identity. We can just pretend that it is.

7. **Pay no attention to Ann duCille's recognition that "[O]ne of the dangers of standing at an intersection...is the likelihood of being run over"** (593). When you come across a non-white disabled person, focus on the disability, eliding the race and ethnicity, letting them be run over, forgotten. Do not consider how the intersection in which this subject lives influences her actions and the way she is seen. Choose not to see that intersection and quickly move on down the road of disability, away from the "perpendicular" roads of race and ethnicity. The fact that the intersection exists is not your fault. It is a prime example of poor engineering.

6. **Disregard Evelynn Hammonds's idea that "visibility in and of itself does not erase a history of silence nor does it challenge the structure of power and domination, symbolic and material, that determines what can and cannot be seen"** (141). Do not forgot to revel in the idea that as more and more disabled people enter the mainstream, all disabled people, irrespective of their racial and ethnic subjectivity, occupy the same place at the table. Equate visibility with inclusivity. Sit back and be satisfied, and do not allow yourself to be troubled by those who carp about their invisibility within disability communities.

5. **Ignore Horkheimer and Adorno's augury that failure to conform to the culture industry results in the individual being "left behind"** (37). The two theorists warn of the perils of living in a culture industry whereby one must subscribe to the right magazines and watch the correct films in order to be accepted in the culture. White Disability Studies is nothing like this; there is nothing even remotely similar to a "disability industry." Thus, it is not true that if you make a film about "crip culture" and you populate that film with only white people, you will be left behind. Quite the contrary, you will receive awards and plaudits, kudos and huzzahs, for this. It is not true that if you enter a room that purports to gather together those interested and engaged in Disability Studies and see not a single person of color present, those people have been left behind or otherwise disinvited. Be still; speak not. Do not draw attention to their absence. Let them be remaindered out. They always have been, and besides, they have probably chosen not to enter the space.

4. **Make no allowances for liminality and hybridity.** Instead, continue the pretence of normality, the idea that everything's just fine and that the disability community is one happy family with no diversity, no multivalence, only a collective sameness. Do not conceive of the silences that are imbricated in extant Disability Studies. Likewise, do not conceive of the concerted efforts to counter those silences, to advocate for liminality and hybridity, as described, in a different context, in Abena Busia's "Silencing Sycorax: On African Colonial Discourse and the Unvoiced Female":

> The systematic refusal to hear our [African American females] speech is not the same thing as our silence. That we have hitherto been spoken of as absent of silenced does not mean we have been so...The systematic refusal to hear our speech which colonial literature mirrors, though it has historically removed us from the nexus of certain kinds of power, does not and never actually could render us silent. In unmasking the dispossessions of the silences of fiction and the fictions of silence, we (re)construct self-understanding. Furthermore, for women, "Narrative" is not always and only, or even necessarily a speech act. We women signify: we have many modes of (re)dress. (103–4)

Do not consider how minority discourse from within a minority discourse is in and of itself counter-hegemonic. Do not encourage the proliferation of that discourse even though it is resistive and liberating. As we all know, the presence of too many voices results in senseless cacophony and what good is that?

3. **Do whatever you can *not* to discuss those texts rife with possibilities insofar as parsing out intersections between disability, race, and ethnicity, namely:**

The Souls of Black Folk

In 1903, W.E.B. DuBois introduced his concept of double consciousness that speaks to the black American's irreconcilable sense of self as "an African" and "an American." Since there is nothing to be gained by applying this theory to black disabled subjects (triple consciousness?), it is best not to consider this text as having any bearing on Disability Studies.

Up From Slavery

Published around the same time as DuBois's text, *Up From Slavery* is frequently taught alongside *The Souls of Black Folk*. Washington takes a much more assimilationist approach to black subjectivity in contraposition to DuBois. Perhaps a Disability Studies scholar might draw parallels between the Washington/DuBois ideas of black subjectivity and the difference between those disabled subjects who want to advocate for peaceful resistance and mainstreaming in juxtaposition to those who take a more activist, resistant stance. But then again, that would be an utter waste of the scholar's time.

Invisible Man

I am an invisible man…I am invisible, understand, simply because people refuse to see me. (3)

The first lines of Ellison's text speak to the difficulty of black ontology in the United States. Ellison's protagonist, of course, is not speaking of a literal invisibility so much as he is drawing light to how it is that others (read: whites with hegemonic power) choose not to see him in totality. If this characterization does not seem applicable to Disability Studies—wherein the racialized subaltern is remembered and considered solely as a matter of convenience more often than not—I don't know what would be. Yet it would be foolish to illuminate this text's applicability to Disability Studies, or, furthermore, to consider the prophetic final lines of the novel—"who know but that, on the lower frequencies, I speak for you?" (581)—wherein the protagonist considers the complexities of representing and/or embodying communal univocality. I do not recommend examining this.

Roots

A Disability Studies scholar might examine aspects of disability throughout the text, namely those that are linked to racial positioning e.g. the causes and effects of Kunta Kinte's "crippling.") Then again, she might not.

Beauty: When the Other Dancer Is the Self

This widely-anthologized personal narrative describes Alice Walker's sense of self as a disabled subject after she is blinded as a child. "I didn't pray for sight," she writes, "I prayed for beauty." Any Disability Studies scholar worth her salt should immediately discern the implications of this statement, but that does not mean that she must act upon it in her scholarship. Likewise, the scholar might pay attention to Walker's intentional use of language, e.g., the allusion to Stevie Wonder towards the end of the narrative. Alas, she might pay attention to it, but there is absolutely nothing to be gained from explicating it.

The Cure

Ginu Kamani's short story is set in contemporary India. The protagonist must deal with living in a culture that has deemed her "too-tall." What is interesting is that the reader never learns just how tall she is, evidentiary of a societal code that is unspoken and yet accepted. Unfortunately, since the story is set in India, where whites are the minority, it cannot be of interest to a Disability Studies scholar.

"The Adventures of Felix"

Race is usually considered a black and white issue. This film complicates that assessment. The protagonist, the titular Felix, is a multiracial French gay man with HIV who sets out to find the father he never knew. Although many critics and individuals familiar with AIDS narratives herald the film for its portrayal of a person with AIDS who is effortlessly "handling" his disease, a disability theorist might pay particular attention to how easily AIDS is removed from the narrative in favor of other concerns. But I doubt that would ever happen.

"Birth of a Nation, or The Clansman"

Long before "Triumph of the Will" was unleashed on the populace, this legendary slice of propaganda was released and heralded. The issues of performativity at play here are rife for discussion, as are their implications insofar as who gets to represent race and/or disability. A Disability Studies scholar might link the use of blackface in this film with the use of non-disabled actors to play disabled figures in contemporary films. But, again, I doubt that would ever happen.

In sum, continue thinking that these texts are too long (e.g., *Invisible Man*) and that the disability perspective is too tangential (e.g., "The Adventures of Felix") to warrant devoting time to. Do not select key scenes to analyze and discuss. Ignore the texts altogether. Continue to herald the overt elisions and missed opportunities.

2. **Do not note how odd "White Disability Studies" looks on this page,** how much effort it requires (or does it?) to contort one's tongue in order to articulate it. Do not take into account how foreign a phrase it seems (although just because something is foreign doesn't necessarily mean that it is incomprehensible…).

1. **Do not change a thing.** Keep doing what *you're* doing. Do so because what you're doing is fine, more than enough to keep White Disability Studies firmly instantiated as the norm. Make no effort to be more inclusive in your scholarship. Do not start today, do not start tomorrow. Wait for someone else to do inclusive work. Wait for however long it takes.

*   *   *   *   *

By way of conclusion, I want to stress that Disability Studies is not the only field of inquiry wherein individuals of color are treated as second-class citizens. If anything, Disability Studies is merely aping the ideology of the vast majority of academic disciplines and ways of thinking that preceded it and which it now sits alongside of. While I could have devoted this modest proposal to advocating for a more hybrid Disability Studies, a liminal version, the fact is I am not certain that advocating for such an idea is a worthwhile undertaking. I deem it far more instructive to acknowledge that we are positioned in the realm of "White Disability Studies" and continue along with the truth of this positioning in mind.

Moreover, offering White Disability Studies, even in the form of a tongue-in-cheek modest proposal, is bound to unnerve many of the individuals who consider themselves engaged in Disability Studies. White Disability Studies will most likely strike these individuals as a hyperbolic and counterintuitive claim. Perhaps my actions might be deemed impolitic and offensive. That is the point. I think it is tactless to dismiss a message solely because of its ostensible unpopularity or because the individual bearing the message seems undesirable. Such a process is itself counterintuitive, intended to draw attention away from a message that, while perhaps unpopular, might contain more than a modicum of validity. Because Disability Studies in its current incarnation *is* White Disability Studies, proposing we honor that creates no crisis of conscience for me. If anything, I take heart in remembering what Bubba Gump declared to Dorian Gray on "Check, Please!": "If it looks like a shrimp, and it smells and tastes like a shrimp, it's a shrimp."

Notes

1. Far from excluding people of color, White Disability Studies treats people of color as if they were white people; as if there are no critical exigencies involved in being people of color that might necessitate these individuals understanding and negotiating disability in a different way from their white counterparts.
2. Reader: If you think it odd that our feelings of solidarity were premised on disinvitation, realize that this is a reality of many people of color engaged in White Disability Studies.
3. Coincidentally, the people of color caucuses at both conferences presented their list of action items in the exact same space, the Mary Ward Hall at San Francisco State University.
4. The pagination to follow is from this issue of *PMLA*.
5. Briefly, the "post-race debate" argues that race is no longer a valid social construct or marker. By that light, the culture as a whole should move on and focus on other, purportedly more pressing issues e.g., class. I can deconstruct the entire post-race argument by simply pointing out that in a culture where racism exists and is pervasive, the casual dismissal of race is specious.
6. I offer AIDS as a precedent here. From the early 1980s until fairly recently, the conception of the AIDS afflicted subject was a gay white man. Indeed, the legacy still retains purchase on mainstream cultural consciousness. Of course, if there were only a few overtures to assess how the disease was impacting women and people of color—and when you think about the history of AIDS, you realize that up until quite recently this was the case—then it becomes obvious how gay white men became equated with AIDS. It is difficult to offer a counternarrative when the structures of power determining which identities comprise a subject are unyielding in their conception.
7. A cursory glance of the past few years of *DSQ*'s topical issues is rather enlightening in this regard. There is an abundance of special topics, none of which verge on what is, to me, one of the more obvious absences in the discourse.

Works Cited

The Adventures of Felix. Dir. Olivier Ducastel and Jacques Martineau. DVD. Perf. Sami Bouajila. Fox Lorber, 2000.

Birth of a Nation, or The Clansman. Dir. D.W. Griffiths. 1915. DVD. Perf. Lillian Gish. Image Entertainment, 2002.

Busia, Abena P. A. "Silencing Sycorax: On African Colonial Discourse and the Unvoiced Female." *Cultural Critique* 14 (Winter 1989–90): 81–104.

Du Bois, W.E.B. *The Souls of Black Folk*. 1903. New York: Penguin, 1996.

duCille, Ann. "The Occult of True Black Womanhood: Critical Demeanor and Black Feminist Studies." *Signs* 19, 3 (Spring 1994): 591–629.

Davis, Lennard. "Disability: The Next Wave or Twilight of the Gods?" Conference on Disability Studies and the University. *PMLA* 120, 2 (March/April 2005): 527–532.

———. *Enforcing Disability: Disability, Deafness and the Body*. London: Verso, 1995.

Ellison, Ralph. *Invisible Man*. New York: Random House, 1952.

Haley, Alex. *Roots*. New York: Doubleday, 1976.

Hall, Stuart. "Cultural Studies and Its Theoretical Legacies." In *Cultural Studies*, edited by Lawrence Grossberg, Cary Nelson, and Paula Treichler et al., 227–234. New York: Routledge, 1992.

Hammonds, Evelynn. "Black (W)holes and the Geometry of Black Female Sexuality." *differences* 6, 2–3 (1994): 126–145.

Horkheimer, Max, and Theodor Adorno. "The Culture Industry: Enlightenment as Mass Deception." *The Dialectic of Enlightenment* (originally published as Dialektik der Aufklarung, 1944). New York: Continuum, 1993.

Kamani, Ginu. "The Cure." *Junglee Girl*. San Francisco: Aunt Lute, 1995.

Leitch, Vincent et al. *The Norton Anthology of Theory and Criticism*. New York: W.W. Norton and Company, 2001.

Linton, Simi. *Claiming Disability: Knowledge and Identity*. New York: NYU Press, 1998.

———. "What Is Disability Studies?" Conference on Disability Studies and the University. *PMLA*. 120, 2 (March/April 2005): 518–522.

Potok, Andrew. *A Matter of Dignity: Changing the Lives of the Disabled*. New York: Bantam, 2003.

Shapiro, Joseph. *No Pity: People with Disabilities Forging a New Civil Rights Movement*. New York: Times Books, 1993.

Vital Signs: Crip Culture Talks Back. Dir. David Mitchell and Sharon Snyder. DVD. Brace Yourselves Productions, 1996.

Walker, Alice. "Beauty: When the Other Dancer Is the Self." *In Search of Our Mother's Gardens: Womanist Prose*, 361–370. New York: Harcourt, Brace and Jovanovich, 1983.

Washington, Booker T. *Up From Slavery*. 1900. New York: Dover, 1995.

23

"When *Black* Women Start Going on Prozac…"

The Politics of Race, Gender, and Emotional Distress in Meri Nana-Ama Danquah's *Willow Weep for Me*

Anna Mollow

Introduction: Disability Essentialism; Or, What Counts?

Meri Nana-Ama Danquah's *Willow Weep for Me: A Black Woman's Journey Through Depression* is a first-person narrative by an author who, without identifying as "disabled" or signaling any alliance with the disability rights movement, instead describes the "suffering" her "illness" caused and recounts her "triumph" over it, an overcoming achieved through a combination of "courage," "resilience," prescription drugs, and other medical interventions (237; 18; 262). As such, Danquah's memoir is precisely the kind of text that much disability scholarship in the humanities has taught us to critique. Foundational work in this field has stressed the formation and assertion of positive disability identities. It has also underscored the distinction between illness and disability, discribing disability in terms of visible bodily difference rather than sickness or suffering. Moreover, disability scholars have criticized personal narratives that highlight disabled people's courage or show them "overcoming" their impairments; framing disability in terms of an individual's struggle against adversity, they have argued, deflects attention from the political realities of disability oppression.[1] These arguments have enormous importance. They form the basis of a scholarship that has redefined disability, demonstrating that it is best understood not as a biological given, but rather as a social process requiring sustained intellectual and political attention.

Yet Danquah's memoir, in its deep engagement with the politics of race, gender, class, and mental illness, forces a reconsideration of several of these tenets of disability studies. Most important, *Willow Weep for Me* makes it clear that disability studies, which has tended to define disability as a visual, objectively observable phenomenon, must also carefully attend to the phenomenological aspects of impairment, particularly those that involve suffering and illness. Such attention will necessitate developing more nuanced ways of describing intersections of multiple forms of oppression than have predominated in the most influential disability scholarship. Examining such intersectionality in Danquah's memoir complicates aspects of some disabled people's critiques of the medical or psychiatric model of mental illness; for many Black women with depression, lack of access to health care, rather than involuntary administration of it, is the most oppressive aspect of the contemporary politics of mental illness.[2] Danquah's memoir may also be the basis for a critique of a tendency, within much disability scholarship, to avoid representing impairments in terms of sickness or suffering. The social model's impairment-disability binary, which has often lead to a de-politicization of impairments, cannot be upheld in *Willow Weep for Me*, which illuminates both the suffering that impairments can cause and the role of politics in producing them. But on the other hand, Danquah's narrative also complicates some disability theorists' deconstructions of the impairment-disability distinction. These postmodern analyses of impairment tend to see individuals' reliance upon impairment categories as invariably serving to buttress hegemonic constructions of disability; but Danquah's autopathography demonstrates that such categories can be mobilized in ways that are politically resistant. Finally, *Willow Weep for Me* presents challenges to disability studies' critique of "stories of overcoming"; by highlighting individuals' power in relation to oppressive political and economic structures, Danquah's narrative offers a powerful antidote to despair.

In order apprehend the significance of *Willow Weep for Me*, a critical method that can account for intersections of multiple forms of oppression is crucial. "I am black; I am female; I am an immigrant," Danquah writes. "Every one of these labels plays an equally significant part in my perception of myself and the world around me" (225).[3] Unfortunately, disability studies has been slow to theorize such intersectionality, particularly when it comes to race. While works like Bonnie G. Smith and Beth Hutchinson's 2004 anthology, *Gendering Disability*, testify to a growing interest in exploring connections between gender and disability, many of the most foundational works in disability studies have analyzed race and disability, not in tandem, but in opposition to each other.[4] In their efforts to stake out a claim for disability as worthy of intellectual and political attention, disability scholars often represent the relationship between people with disabilities and other political minorities in hierarchical terms.[5] In a more subtle way, the frequent use of "like race" analogies in disability scholarship may also have the effect of opposing the interests of disabled people and people of color. When Rosemarie Garland-Thomson characterizes disability as a "form of ethnicity," or when Lennard J. Davis compares "the disabled figure" to "the body marked as differently pigmented," it's clear that neither intends to place race or ethnicity in opposition to disability; rather, they each seek to establish a likeness between two categories, and thus to gain recognition of disabled people as members of a political minority (Thomson, 6; Davis, EN, 80). But as Trina Grillo and Stephanie M. Wildman have argued, "like race" analogies often have the effect of "obscuring the importance of race," enabling the group making the analogy to take "center stage from people of color" (621). Moreover, such analogies assume a false separation between the forms of oppression being compared. As Grillo and Wildman point out in their discussion of analogies between race and gender, "[a]nalogizing sex discrimination to race discrimination makes it seem that all the women are white and all the men are African-American"; thus, they observe, "the experience of women of color ... is rendered invisible" (623). The dangers of "like race" analogies in disability studies are similar: if race and disability are conceived of as discrete categories to be compared, contrasted, or arranged in order of priority, it becomes impossible to think through complex intersections of racism and ableism in the lives of disabled people of color.[6] This is not, of course, to deny that analogies can be useful; I share Ellen Samuel's sense that rather than attempting "somehow to escape from analogy," we might "seek to employ it more critically than in the past" (4).

These intersections must be understood in ways that are more than merely additive, as Angela P. Harris argues in her critique of "gender essentialism—the notion that a unitary, 'essential' women's experience can be isolated and described independently of race, class, sexual orientation, and other realities of experience" (585). According to an additive model of multiple oppressions, Harris argues, "black women will never be anything more than a crossroads between two kinds of domination, or at the bottom of a hierarchy of oppressions" (589).[7] I would therefore suggest that, in examining intersections of forms of oppression, we guard against the dangers of a "disability essentialism," in which the experiences, needs, desires, and aims of all disabled people are assumed to be the same and those with "different" experiences are accommodated only if they do not make claims that undermine the movement's foundational arguments. Many of these arguments have been developed primarily with physical disability in mind. Cognitive and psychiatric impairments, although they are gaining more attention, nonetheless remain marginalized, both within disability studies and in the broader culture. I was recently reminded of the extent of this marginalization when I mentioned to a colleague that I was writing an essay on Black women and depression; she responded by asking, "Does depression count as a disability?" Her question is crucial. "The short answer," I told my colleague, "is 'yes.'" The longer answer would have involved a discussion of the ways in which truly "counting" the experiences of people with mental illness might necessitate revising some of disability studies' most frequently cited claims.

While the necessity of such revisions becomes particularly evident when the politics of race, gender, and mental illness are analyzed together, the arguments that follow should not be taken as part of an unitary account of such intersections: I wish to be clear that I am not suggesting any intrinsic relationship among Blackness, femininity, and mental illness; nor do I propose to read Danquah's memoir as representative of a monolithic "Black women's perspective on depression."[8] I do hope to show, however, that examining the converging effects of multiple forms of oppression can have profound implications for disability studies. Reading *Willow Weep for Me* with such effects in mind will require the rethinking of some of the field's most central tenets: its reluctance to understand disability in terms of sickness or suffering, its tendency to define disability in visual terms, and its resistance to stories of overcoming. If we avoid this critical reevaluation, we risk misreading as naïve or politically disengaged the work of Danquah and others whose perspectives diverge from disability studies' entrenched ideas.

Going on Prozac

Among people with depression, the politics of mental illness are complex and highly contested. In particular, much controversy surrounds questions about whether people who experience emotional distress are sick. Throughout her memoir, Danquah emphasizes that her depression is an "illness"; by doing so, she adopts a strategy that diverges from that of the psychiatric survivor movement (18). Members of this movement define themselves as "survivors," not of mental illness, but rather of institutionalization in psychiatric hospitals.[9] Indeed, they often reject the very category of "mental illness," which they view as a largely meaningless invention of modern psychiatry that serves to enforce conformity to social norms and to derive money and power for mental health "experts." Protesting doctors' excessive control over the lives of people we diagnose as "mentally ill," psychiatric survivors describe incarceration in mental institutions that are often run like prisons, as well as nonconsensual administration of "therapies" that resemble punishments or even torture.[10] Moreover, they note that psychiatrists themselves are unable to define mental illness; that no biological or genetic cause of any putative mental disorder has ever been demonstrated; and that the most common treatments—psychoactive medications, electroconvulsive therapy (ECT), seclusion, and physical restraints—have no proven benefits and cause debilitating side effects, including brain damage.[11] Survivors' testimonies demonstrate the appalling extent to which the label of "mental illness" has been used to deprive people of autonomy, respect, and human rights.[12]

What, then, do we make of Danquah's definition of her depression as a "mental illness" (20)? In what context do we understand her emphasis upon the necessity of taking antidepressant medication? "I have tried to deny my need for medication and stopped taking it," Danquah explains. "Each time, at the slightest provocation, I have fallen, fast and hard, deeper into the depression" (220; 258). However, Danquah does not regard depression as purely a medical phenomenon. "The illness exists somewhere in that ghost space between consciousness and chemistry," she writes (257–58). She takes her Paxil "reluctantly," observing that "there is something that seems really wrong with the fact that Prozac is one of the most prescribed drugs in this country" (258).[13]

But for Danquah, in contrast to members of the psychiatric survivor movement, lack of access to health care, rather than involuntary imposition of it, is the most salient aspect of her interactions with the medical profession. Danquah sees adequate medical treatment for her depression as a necessity, to which poverty, racism, and gender bias have created almost insurmountable barriers. Her obstetrician dismisses one of her first episodes of severe depression as the effect of "hormones" (36). Years later, she seeks treatment but has great difficulty locating a mental health clinic she can afford. Danquah is able to pay for only one of the medications she is prescribed, Zoloft, an antidepressant. Anxiety is a side effect of Zoloft, so her doctor writes her a prescription for BuSpar, an anxiety controllant. This drug, however, is prohibitively expensive, so Danquah resorts to alcohol to manage the side effects of her antidepressant. Indeed, the Zoloft seems to cause an insatiable craving for alcohol, which disappears when she discontinues the medication (221). Danquah is forced to figure most of this out without any medical supervision. Most of the practitioners at the mental health clinic she goes to are therapists-in-training, and hers leaves abruptly once she has completed her certification process. Rather than being "reassigned" at random to another therapist, Danquah suspends psychotherapy (208).

In addition to economic obstacles, Danquah faces cultural barriers to appropriate health care. Her psychiatrist, Dr. Fitzgerald, is a white man who describes at length his inability to "even fathom" the racism with which she routinely copes (224). Experiences like this are commonplace for African American women seeking mental health care. Julia A. Boyd, an African American psychotherapist, observes that many white mental health practitioners "remain in a passive state of denial concerning the therapeutic needs of black women" ("Ethnic," 232). In addition, people of color, especially African Americans, are less likely to be diagnosed with depression or prescribed medication when they report their symptoms to a doctor; even in studies controlling for income level and health insurance status, the disparities are great.[14]

The contrast between Danquah's experience and that of many members of the psychiatric survivor movement highlights a conundrum facing people with depression or other mental illnesses. The enormous power that the psychiatric profession wields in modern Western societies creates a double bind, in which both diagnosis with a mental illness or, alternatively, the lack of such a diagnosis, brings with it serious negative social consequences for people experiencing emotional distress.[15] Being diagnosed with a mental illness means risking social stigmatization, involuntary institutionalization, and treatment with dangerous medications. On the other hand, those who are not deemed truly mentally ill are often regarded as merely malingering. Depression, Danquah observes, is "not looked upon as a legitimate illness. Most employers really don't give a damn if you're depressed, and neither do landlords or bill collectors" (144).

This lack of social validation and support is exacerbated by racism. The symptoms of depression, Boyd points out, often "mirror the stereotypes that have been projected onto Black women"; before she was diagnosed with the disorder herself, Boyd thought that "being depressed meant that you were crazy, lazy, unmotivated" (8; 15). Moreover, as Danquah notes, depression is "still viewed as a predominantly 'white' illness"; when Black people become depressed, the symptoms and coping strategies usually go unrecognized (184).[16] Pervasive social denial and lack of access to necessary medical care are the political realities that Danquah highlights in her account of her struggles with depression. While these realities are inextricable from the politics of race, I do not wish to suggest that all Black women with depression share Danquah's perspective on the medicalization of emotional distress.[17]

In addition, it is important to remember that the other aspect of the double bind I have described—i.e., diagnosis of a mental illness as the justification for involuntary confinement and forcible "treatment"—also carries additional risks for Black people. While white people are more often diagnosed with depression and prescribed antidepressants, African Americans are diagnosed with schizophrenia at much higher rates and are also given antipsychotic medications more frequently and in higher doses. They are also more often institutionalized involuntarily, in part because racial stereotypes affect psychiatrists' assessments of their "dangerousness."[18] The pathologization of Black people is also built into what Danquah terms "the oppressive nature of the existing language surrounding depression," the commonplace metaphors of depression as darkness and blackness (21–22).[19]

Danquah's critique of the politics of race and mental illness exposes and protests linguistic, social, cultural, and economic barriers that impede Black women with depression from accessing health care. In contrast to the psychiatric survivor movement, her primary focus is on this lack of access, rather than the effects of involuntary treatment. But she shares with psychiatric survivors a profound sense of the importance of self-determination and control over one's own medical treatment. Danquah begins to see significant improvement in her depression when, as she puts it, "I took control of my own healing" (225). Recognizing that her own role in her treatment is more important than that of her psychiatrist, she realizes, "it did not make that much of a difference to me if Dr. Fitzgerald was listening or not, if he cared or not, if he understood or not. *I* was listening. *I* was hearing. *I* was understanding. *I* cared" (225–26).

Disability or Impairment?: Depression and the Social Model

Danquah's understanding of her depression as a "disease" not only adds another dimension to the psychiatric survivor movement's critique of the mental health profession, but also complicates what has come to be known as the "social model" of disability. The social model was developed in Britain in the 1970s; a key moment in its emergence occurred in 1976, when the Union of the Physically Impaired Against Segregation (UPIAS) published its *Fundamental Principles of Disability*. Perhaps the most important of these "fundamental principles" was the crucial distinction the document made between "impairment" and "disability":

> In our view it is society which disables physically impaired people. Disability is something imposed on top of our impairments, by the way we are unnecessarily isolated and excluded from full participation in society...(3)

UPIAS's differentiation between the bodily (impairment) and the social (disability) formed the basis of what Mike Oliver subsequently presented as the "social model of disability."[20] The social model, like the minority group model that emerged in the United States, has enabled major transformations in the conceptualization of disability; rather than accepting traditional definitions of disability as a personal misfortune, this new paradigm frames disability in terms of social oppression.

What the social model may sacrifice, however, is a way of thinking in political terms about the suffering that some impairments cause. As Liz Crow points out, the social model sometimes has the effect of obscuring the reality that "[P]ain, fatigue, depression and chronic illness are constant facts of life" for many people with disabilities (58). This problem is pervasive not only in applications of Britain's social model, but also in disability studies in the United States, where the "critique of the medical model" is a fundamental principle. Critiquing the medical model does not necessarily preclude recognition of chronic and terminal illnesses as disabling forms of impairment. However, in practice this critique often functions to differentiate people with disabilities from those who are ill.[21] Arguing for greater inclusion of people with chronic illness in the disability community, Susan Wendell takes issue with Eli Clare's contention that people with disabilities should not be regarded as "sick, diseased, ill people" hoping to be cured (Wendell 18; Clare 105). As Wendell points out, "some people with disabilities *are* sick, diseased, and ill"; moreover, she observes, some disabled people "very much want" to be cured (18). Danquah expresses this wish at the end of her memoir: "I choose to believe that somewhere, somehow, there is a cure for depression" (257).

If the experiences of those who define themselves as ill and hope to be cured are elided in much disability scholarship, this may be due in part to the field's emphasis on visible aspects of disability. Garland-Thomson's definition of disability as a process that emerges through "a complex relation between seer and seen" is of great value in thinking about the "extraordinary bodies" she discusses, but the framing of disability in terms of outward appearance is less useful for analyzing depression and other invisible impairments, particularly those that involve sickness and suffering (136). Similarly, Harlan Hahn's positing of a "correlation between the visibility of disabilities and the amount of discrimination which they might elicit" has little to do with Danquah' experience."[22] Danquah loses friends and jobs precisely because her disability is *not* visible and therefore is not recognized as a "legitimate illness" (144; 30).

Indeed, disability studies' emphasis upon observable manifestations of impairments makes it difficult to know how to begin thinking about a condition like depression, which is primarily a subjective experience. Moreover, it is an experience characterized by suffering: "Suffering...was what depression was all about," Danquah reflects (237).[23] The issue of suffering has been vexed within disability studies. As Bill Hughes and Kevin Paterson observe, "Disabled people...feel uncomfortable with the concept of suffering because...it seems inextricably bound to a personal tragedy model of disability" (336). As Oliver states, "the social model is not about the personal experience of impairment but the collective experience of disablement" ("Social," 22). However, the strategy of maintaining a focus on social oppression rather than personal suffering—or on "disability" as opposed to "impairment"—risks reifying a dichotomy that does not easily apply to disorders like depression. While impairments ranging from cerebral palsy to blindness, spinal cord injury, or autism do not always cause suffering in and of themselves, it makes little sense for a person to say she is clinically depressed but does not suffer. And whereas it's illuminating, when discussing the politics surrounding mobility impairments, to observe that disability results from inaccessible architectural structures rather than from bodily deficiency, it's difficult to use this paradigm to understand depression. It is true that, to a certain extent, one could apply the impairment-disability distinction to Danquah's experience. Arguably, Danquah's impairment, depression, becomes disabling because of a societal unwillingness to accommodate it: "I lost my job because the temp agencies where I was registered could no longer tolerate my lengthy absences," she recounts (30). "I lost my friends. Most of them found it too troublesome to deal with my sudden moodiness and passivity" (30). These social pressures correspond to UPIAS's definition of "disability" as "something imposed on top of our impairments" (3).

But an analysis of Danquah's text that privileges "the collective experience" of disability over "the personal experience" of impairment would greatly distort her account of her struggles with depression (Oliver, 22). A lack of social validation or understanding, although a persistent facet of her experience, seems to recede into the background of the intense and prolonged suffering in which her depression immerses her. Throughout *Willow Weep for Me*, Danquah describes this suffering in vivid and often metaphorical language, which contrasts with her matter-of-fact reports of lost friends and career opportunities. She writes that her life "disintegrated; first, into a strange and terrifying space of sadness and then, into a cobweb of fatigue" (27). She describes "nails of despair...digging...deeply into my skin" and "a dense cloud of melancholy [that] hung over my head" (30). As her depression worsens, she writes, "It seemed as if the world was closing in on me, squeezing me dry" (32). She remembers "absolute terror" and "despair [that] cut so deeply, I thought it would slice me in half" (42; 106). As such stark descriptions of suffering make clear, relegating "impairment" to a secondary status within an impairment-disability binary elides the phenomenological aspects of depression as a state of suffering.

Moreover, analyses that privilege disability over impairment deflect attention from the political nature of impairment itself. In Danquah's narrative, the social environment is important less for its imposition of an additional burden "on top of" a pre-existing impairment than for its role in producing her depression (UPIAS, 3). When Danquah is a child, her schoolmates ostracize her, mocking her accent and calling her "the African Monkey" (104). She recalls that the "host of...horrid epithets" to which she was subjected "shattered any personal pride I felt and replaced it with uncertainty and self-hatred" (105). When her father abandons the family, Danquah begins to think of herself as "the ugly little girl, the 'monkey,' the fatherless child" (109). In junior high, she is raped by a recent high school graduate she has a crush on (120). When she confides in her stepfather about the incident, he rapes her, too; the sexual abuse continues throughout her adolescence (124). As a young adult, undiagnosed postpartum depression coupled with physical abuse by the father of her child contribute to an episode of serious depression. A subsequent episode is triggered by the "not guilty" verdict in the Rodney King trial: "We, all black people, had just been told that our lives were of no value," Danquah remembers (42).

Distress or Disease?: Deconstructing the Social Model

As Danquah's story illustrates, the oppression of disabled people is not merely "something imposed on top of" a pre-existing impairment; rather, the production of some impairments is itself a political process (UPIAS, 3). Therefore, *Willow Weep for Me* might at first seem to accord with the arguments of some disability scholars who, deconstructing the impairment-disability binary, claim that impairment is a discursive production.[24] Shelley Tremain argues that a Foucaultian analysis will reveal "that impairment and its materiality are naturalized *effects* of disciplinary knowledge/power" (SI, 34). Locating the origins of modern-day categorizations of bodies as normal or impaired in the nineteenth-century bio-medical discourses whose genealogies Foucault traces, Tremain observes that impairment is neither a "'prediscursive' antecedent" nor a set of "essential, biological characteristics of a 'real' body" (SI, 42).

Indeed, Tremain's theorization of impairment is *à propos* to any discussion of depression, whose constructedness as a disease entity is easily apparent. While the term "melancholy" is as old as ancient Greek medicine, its defining features have been broad and shifting, never corresponding to the present-day disease category of "clinical depression." The instability of depression as a discrete medical phenomenon is further evident in the extent to which those who wish to establish it as such must continually define it by differentiating it from ordinary states of sadness. "Depression isn't the same as ordinary sadness, it is hell," Danquah's friend Scott says (260). Or, as Danquah explains, "We have all, to some degree, experienced days of depression...But for some, such as myself, the depression doesn't lift at the end of the day...And when depression reaches clinical proportions, it *is* truly an illness" (18).[25]

Moreover, whereas most people in our culture would not question the validity of diseases like diabetes, cancer, or rheumatoid arthritis, skeptics abound when it comes to depression. Eboni, one of several African American woman with whom Boyd engages in a dialogue about depression, says, "look at what our mothers and grandmothers went through in their lives and we don't hear them whining about depression" (CI, 21). Eboni's comments not only underscore the constructedness of depression as a clinical entity, but also raise another set of questions. While it's relatively easy to observe that depression cannot be regarded as a prediscursive bodily or mental "given," what remains unclear are the possible effects of the processes by which it is currently being consolidated as a definable and describable disease. For example, does the construction of depression as an illness enable a potentially emancipatory reinterpretation of behaviors traditionally regarded as moral weakness, such as the "whining" that Eboni dismisses? It is in part to distinguish depression from "a character flaw" that Danquah insists that depression "*is* truly an illness" (18). But Tremain's analysis of the constructedness of impairments raises the possibility that Danquah's self-construction as a "depressive" might have "insidious" effects (Danquah, 18; Tremain, SI, 37). Reliance on biomedicine's constructions of bodily and mental difference, Tremain argues, may only further consolidate the pervasive power of disciplinary regimes (SI, 42).

Tremain's characterization of impairments as discursively produced is cogent and insightful. However, as I will argue, *Willow Weep for Me* demonstrates that impairment categories can be cited in ways that, rather than merely "meet[ing] requirements of contemporary political arrangements," instead also serve to undermine them (Tremain, SI, 42; FG, 10). To elucidate this process, it will be helpful to reflect upon the epistemic shift that Foucault and other historians have documented in late eighteenth- and early nineteenth-century medicine. With the rise of clinical medicine in the nineteenth century, the physical examination and the dissection of corpses supplanted patients' stories as the privileged modes of generating medical knowledge.[26] The dominant medical epistemology became visual rather than narrative: the patient came to be seen as a passive body, manifesting visible signs of disease which could be interpreted by the doctor's detached "gaze."[27] These visible "signs," or objective manifestations of disease, were privileged over "symptoms," which referred to subjective sensations the patient reported (Porter, 313). The sign-symptom binary remains a centerpiece of contemporary medical epistemology, and its continued importance helps explain why depression has not been regarded as a "real" disease in the same way as illnesses such as arthritis or multiple sclerosis, which can be visualized on X-rays or MRIs. Whereas the careful observation of bodily changes, the dissection of cadavers, and eventually the emerging science of bacteriology enabled nineteenth-century physicians to define diseases like tuberculosis as distinct clinical entities, the same cannot be said of depression. Indeed, the project of solidifying depression as a bona fide medical condition is grounded in the expectation that it will one day be possible to identify specific biological markers of the disorder and thus to demonstrate that depression is an organic disease of the brain.

Because such signs remain elusive, the construction of depression as a disease is presently occurring in ways that differ significantly from the discursive materialization of most of the impairments that receive attention in disability studies; that is, from most visible impairments.[28] Western medicine has obtained significant knowledge about impairments such as cataracts, colitis, and heart disease, all of which manifest visible signs, without much active participation on the part of the patient; but a depressed person, to be understood as such, must be a subject who communicates.[29] Moreover, he or she must have a degree of psychological depth that a patient being examined for signs of a physical ailment need not be recognized as possessing. Instead of simply reporting a pain or displaying a rash, a fever, or a tremor, the depressed patient is most often subjectivized as such through the production of a narrative.[30] It is perhaps for this reason that, as Danquah observes, our culture is so reluctant to recognize depression in Black women. It is "hard," she remarks, "for black women to be seen as...emotionally complex" (21).

Yet it would certainly be a mistake to romanticize medicine's inclusion of subjects' accounts of their distress in its process of consolidating depression as a disease entity. The incorporation of patients' stories into medical discourses on depression or other forms of "mental illness" is shaped by a profound power imbalance between doctors and patients. While a diagnosis of depression is rarely made without the participation of the patient as a speaking subject, once one is labeled "mentally ill," one is often treated as less than a full subject, denied the right to choose a course of treatment or decline medical intervention altogether.[31] Moreover, as Anne Wilson and Peter Beresford point out, patients defined as "mentally ill" have little control over the ways in which their words are presented and interpreted in their medical records. Wilson and Beresford, who are themselves psychiatric system survivors, recall that "it can feel as if everything you say or do is being taken down and recorded to be used in evidence against you" (148). In addition, they point out, "as medical records are ineradicable, they also serve to make permanent and immutable the ostensible psychopathological difference or 'disorder' of those diagnosed 'mentally ill'" (149).

This power imbalance between doctors and "mentally ill" subjects exerts itself in more subtle ways as well. Wilson and Beresford relate that "it can be difficult even to begin to make sense of our experience outside of frameworks provided by 'experts,' whose theories and powers may extend to every aspect of our lives, not least our identity as 'mentally ill' (non-)persons" (145). This observation seems to illustrate Foucault's claim that the "individual is an effect of power" (TL, 98). And indeed, Foucault's arguments about subject formation raise questions about the relation of Danquah's narrative to dominant psychiatric discourses. Does Danquah, by defining herself as a "depressive," merely reinscribe the dictates of psychiatric medicine (18)? According to Tremain, "a Foucauldian approach to disability" shows that "the category of impairment...in part persists in order to legitimize the disciplinary regime that generated it" (FG,11; SI, 43). Tremain does not explore the possibility, however, that the production of specific impairment categories might have multiple, competing effects, including, paradoxically, the contestation of the assumptions on which these categories are based.

Such a contestation takes shape in Danquah's autopathography, which depends upon biomedicine's construction of depression as a disease entity but at the same time resists the normalizing effects of this construction. Danquah articulates her resistance to the disciplinary uses of depression as a medical category in ways that Foucault's concept of a "reverse discourse" can illuminate. Foucault argues that the nineteenth-century emergence of psychiatric and other discourses that brought into being "the homosexual"as a "species" had the effect, not only of enabling "a strong advance of social controls into this area of 'perversity,'" but also of making "possible the formation of a 'reverse' discourse: homosexuality began to speak on its own behalf, to demand that its legitimacy...be acknowledged, often in the same vocabulary, using the same categories by which it was medically disqualified" (HS, 101–02). Danquah's narrative might be understood as participating in a "reverse discourse" regarding depression. As we have seen, it employs the categories of psychiatric medicine in order to demand that depression's "legitimacy...be acknowledged" (HS, 101). Depression, Danquah maintains, is "a legitimate illness"; she is not "a flake or a fraud" (144).[32]

Additionally, at the same time that she emphasizes that depression is an authentic medical condition, Danquah also subverts some of psychiatry's most fundamental assumptions about what it means to be mentally ill. If today's "depressive" is "disqualified" in ways analogous to the disqualification of Foucault's nineteenth-century "homosexual," Danquah's narrative perhaps mobilizes a reverse discourse that resists this disqualification while nonetheless retaining the vocabulary and diagnostic categories that enable it. This can be seen in Danquah's emphasis on the imbrication of her illness with political oppression. A common mode of discrediting people with depression effects a discursive separation of symptoms from politics: depression is said to arise from feelings, beliefs, and attitudes which are disproportionately "negative" in relation to the afflicted person's actual circumstances.[33] Indeed, this is Eboni's critique of psychiatric constructions of depression: "I didn't hear where any of those big-time researchers were lookin' at things like racism or sexism," she points out (21). But this, of course, is exactly what Danquah does look at. By showing how the convergence of racism, sexual violence, and poverty literally made her ill, Danquah insists upon the validity of depression as a diagnostic category while at the same time contesting hegemonic accounts of its etiology.

Moreover, even as Danquah accepts the designation of her emotional distress as a "disease," she also undermines one of psychiatric medicine's most fundamental claims (18). As Wilson and Beresford point out, psychiatry's justification as an institution relies in large part upon "its construction of users of mental health services as Other—a separate and distinct group" (144). Interestingly, however, Danquah's gradual process of accepting that she is ill and needs medical treatment paradoxically culminates in her deconstruction of the normal/mentally ill binary upon which psychiatry's authority depends:

> I had always only thought of therapy in stark, clinical terms: an old bespectacled grey-haired white man with a couch in his office listening to the confessions of crazies.... What if, I asked myself, those "crazies" are no different than me? What if they are like me, ordinary people leading ordinary lives who woke up one day and discovered they couldn't get out of bed, no matter how much they wanted to or how hard they tried? (167–68)

Danquah decides to enter psychotherapy, then, not because she comes to define herself as "Other," but because she is able to imagine the dissolution of what Wilson and Beresford call psychiatry's "opposition between 'the mad' and 'the not-mad'" (154). Indeed, her sense that the depressive is not a distinct species, but rather a member of a community of "ordinary people," finds echo in Wilson and Beresford's assertion that "the world does not consist of 'normals' and 'the mentally ill'; it consists of *people*" (Danquah 167–68; Beresford and Wilson, 144).

Like the arguments of critics who use Foucaultian paradigms to analyze disability, Danquah's work demands a deconstruction of the impairment-disability distinction, forcing a theorization of impairment as itself a social process. Yet Danquah nonetheless accepts the category of mental illness and makes it integral to her self-conception. For this reason, an application of Tremain's or Wilson and Beresford's analyses of the constructedness of impairment categories might seem to authorize a reading of Danquah's narrative as "naïve," unaware of how the category of impairment operates within what Tremain, following Foucault, calls the "insidious" production of "an ever-expanding and increasingly totalizing web of social control" (SI, 34; 37; FG, 6).[34] But as we have seen, Foucault's understanding of power is more flexible than Tremain's characterization of it here suggests.[35] Rather than "a general system of domination" whose "effects...pervade the entire social body," Foucault describes a "multiple and mobile field of force relations, wherein far-reaching, but *never completely stable* effects of domination are produced" (HS, 92; 101–02; emphasis mine). "Discourse," he explains, "reinforces" power "but also undermines and exposes it" (HS, 101).

Foucault's conception of discourse as reversible points to the possibility that individuals might invoke discursive constructions such as "depression" so as to do more than merely, as Tremain puts it, "identify themselves in ways that make them governable" (SI, 37; FG, 6). It is true that, as David Halperin remarks, Foucault is critical "of discursive reversal...as a political strategy" in contemporary Western societies (58). Nevertheless, for Foucault a "reverse discourse" can constitute "a significant act of political resistance"; it is by no means "one and the same as the discourse it reverses" (Halperin, 59). Foucault explains that although reverse discourses and other forms of resistance cannot be deployed "outside" of power, "this does not mean that they are only a reaction or rebound... doomed to perpetual defeat" (HS, 95; 96).

Tremain accurately observes that the institutionalization of reverse discourses as identity politics movements poses significant dangers. [36] However, I wish to challenge what seems in her argument to be a global suspicion of any and all processes of "iteration and reiteration of regulatory norms and ideals about human function and structure, competency, intelligence and ability" (SI, 42). This suspicion seems to derive in part from Tremain's mapping of Judith Butler's deconstruction of the sex-gender binary onto the social model's distinction between impairment and disability (SI, 38–41). But the "reiteration" that Tremain regards as functioning to "sustain, and even augment, current social arrangements," is precisely the process in which Butler finds potential for revision of cultural norms and identity categories (SI, 42). Butler argues that "'sex'" is materialized "through a forcible reiteration" of "regulatory norms"; however, this process produces "instabilities" and "possibilities for rematerialization," in which "the force of the regulatory law can be turned against itself" (4). This turning of the regulatory law against itself, Butler suggests, might be achieved through what she calls a "citational politics," which entails a "reworking of abjection into political agency" (21).

Butler's discussion of "citational politics" focuses primarily upon instances in which "the public assertion of queerness" has the effect of "resignifying the abjection of homosexuality into defiance and legitimacy" (21). Although Danquah does not treat race, gender, or mental illness in ways that correspond exactly to Butler's description of queerness as performativity, one can nonetheless discern in *Willow Weep for Me* a "reworking of abjection into political agency" (Butler, 21).[37] Throughout her memoir, Danquah foregrounds abjection in the form of "weakness" (20). She observes that although mental illness is often regarded as a sign of "genius" in white men, of hysteria in white women, and of pathology in Black men, "when a black woman suffers from a mental disorder, the overwhelming opinion is that she is weak. And weakness in black women is intolerable" (20).

It is perhaps also unthinkable: "Clinical depression simply did not exist... within the realm of possibilities for any of the black women in my world," Danquah explains (18–19). "Emotional hardship is *supposed* to be built into the structure of our lives" (19). Indeed, when Danquah tells a white woman she meets at a dinner party that she's writing a book on Black women and depression, the woman responds sarcastically: "*Black* women and depression? Isn't that kinda redundant?... [W]hen *black* women start going on Prozac, you know the whole world is falling apart" (19–20). The foreclosure of depression as a possible diagnosis for Black women, Danquah argues, derives from the "myth" of Black women's "supposed birthright to strength" (19). "Black women are *supposed* to be strong—caretakers, nurturers, healers of other people—any of the twelve dozen variations of Mammy (19).[38]

By linking the image of the strong Black woman to the stereotype of the "mammy," Danquah points to the history of slavery in the United States as one of its possible origins. As Patricia Hill Collins observes, the figure of the "mammy," or the "faithful, obedient domestic servant," was invented in order to "justify the economic exploitation of house slaves" (71). Danquah's contestation of the ideal of an inherently strong Black womanhood thus resists the social demand that Black women deny their own emotional and material needs in order to attend to those of others.[39] As Evelyn C. White writes, "the vulnerability exposed in *Willow Weep for Me* ... will do much to transform society's image of Black women as sturdy bridges to everyone's healing except their own" (Danquah NP).

Paradoxically, while the notion that Black women are uniquely equipped to endure hardship has historically served as a justification for their oppression, it may also have enabled their survival. "Given the history of black women in this country," Danquah argues, "one can easily understand how this pretense of strength was at one time necessary for survival" (NP). The belief that strength is a legacy of slavery persists in Black communities, Danquah remarks, pointing out that it is not only white people who dismiss Black women's depression. "If our people could make it through slavery, we can make it through anything," Black men and women have told Danquah (21). But what this "stereotypic image of strength… requires" of Black women, Danquah emphasizes, "is not really strength at all. It is stoicism. It is denial. It is a complete negation of their pain" (NP).[40]

Because Black women's emotional suffering is generally regarded as normative and unproblematic—"part of the package," as Danquah puts it—rather than symptomatic of a condition in need of a remedy, Danquah's pathologization of her distress cannot be seen as merely an accession to the social norms upon which the category of "mental illness" depends; rather, by defining her suffering as sickness, Danquah transgresses the expectation that when Black women suffer, they do so silently and stoically (19). Refusing any denial of her pain, Danquah unflinchingly describes the shame and self-loathing that are both symptoms and sources of her depression. She relates that amid a severe episode of depression she stopped bathing and cleaning her house, leaving "a trail of undergarments and other articles of clothing" on the floor, "dishes with decaying food" on "every counter and tabletop" (28). She recalls feeling "truly pitiful," "hating myself so much I wanted to die" (219; 106). "Something had gone wrong with me," she realizes (29).

This conclusion may seem at odds with one of the central messages of the disability rights movement. Oliver's critique of the medical model on the grounds that it "tends to regard disabled people as 'having something wrong with them' and hence [being] the source of the problem" is a tenet of disability studies ("Social," 20). And while I certainly do not wish to reinstall hegemonic constructions of disability as a form of individual weakness or inferiority, I would suggest that in Danquah's narrative it's more complicated than a simple opposition between an individual and a social problem. Rather than imagining a wall of immunity between self and society, Danquah dramatizes the impossibility of ever remaining untouched by all that is wrong in the world (29). And her recognition that something has "gone wrong" with her is neither an indictment of herself as "the source of the problem" nor a cause of shame; instead, it is the impetus for her decision to make "a commitment to being alive" (Oliver, 20; Danquah, 230).

This commitment requires a valuing of herself that contrasts sharply with the "stereotypic image of strength" with which "African American women who are battling depression must, unfortunately, contend" (Danquah NP). The strength that Danquah displays—and it would be impossible to come away from her book without feeling the magnitude of that strength—is neither endurance nor self-sacrifice; rather, it is what Danquah describes as a readiness "to claim the life that I want" (266).

Shall We Overcome?

Danquah's memoir about depression ends on a hopeful note. "Having lived with the pain," she writes, "I know now that when you pass through it, there is beauty on the other side" (266). Indeed, as her book's subtitle indicates, hers is a "Black woman's journey *through* depression" (emphasis mine). As such, *Willow Weep for Me* could be read as a story of overcoming. The blurb on the back cover of the paperback edition promises "an inspirational story of healing," and Danquah herself employs many of the linguistic conventions associated with overcoming narratives. It takes "courage, devotion, and resilience" to "contend with depression" and to "triumph" over the illness, she writes (262). Such an emphasis on individual strength is at the crux of what many disability scholars critique in narratives of overcoming. As Simi Linton argues, "the ideas embedded in the *overcoming* rhetoric are of personal triumph over a personal condition," rather than a collective demand for "social change" (18). There is enormous value in this observation, and I wholeheartedly concur with Linton's objections to representations of disability that make "the individual's responsibility for her or his own success… paramount" (19). But as we have seen, the opposition between disability as personal misfortune and as social problem is not tenable in Danquah's autopathography, which understands depression as inextricably both of these things. And if despair is both a cause and a symptom of depression, then perhaps part of its solution is a hope that is both personal and political.[41] As Danquah explains, "The social and economic realities of women, blacks, single parents, or any combination of the three" make "my

[margin handwritten note: not always]

chances for a life that is free of depression appear to be slim…While I recognize the importance of such information, I regard most of the data as blather and refuse to embrace it" (257). This refusal is not a denial of political realities; rather, it is an unwillingness to accept defeat, an assertion of personal strength amid overwhelming social oppression. As Danquah puts it, it is a "standing up in defiance of those things which had kept me silent and suffering to say that I, an African American woman, have made this journey through depression" (NP).

Notes

I would like to thank Richard Ingram, Robert McRuer, and Sue Schweik for their feedback on earlier versions of this essay.

1. See Garland-Thomson 135–37; Linton 17–19; and Mitchell and Snyder 9–11. See also note 21 below.
2. Lack of access to health care is tied to the politics of both race and class. Cultural, linguistic, and geographical barriers, as well as racist stereotypes, present specific impediments for African American, Latino/a, Asian American, and Native American people seeking medical treatment for depression, regardless of income level and health insurance status ("Mental"). Access to health care has received less attention in disability studies than in the disability rights movement, where it has often been the focus of organizing.
3. Born in Ghana, Danquah emigrates to the United States when she is six years old (103). Although being an immigrant is of great importance to Danquah's self-definition, this aspect of her identity receives far less attention in her memoir than race, gender, class, or mental illness.
4. A special issue of *GLQ*, *Desiring Disability: Queer Theory Meets Disability Studies* (2003), edited by Robert McRuer and Abby Wilkerson, is devoted to the topic of queerness and disability.
5. In the introduction to *The Body and Physical Difference*, David T. Mitchell and Sharon L. Snyder write that "while literary and cultural studies have resurrected social identities such as gender, sexuality, class, and race from…obscurity and neglect…disability has suffered a distinctly different disciplinary fate" (1–2). Barnes and Mercer draw a "sharp contrast" between the reception of disability studies in academia and that of "radical analyses of racism and sexism that quickly won favor" (IS, 4). Recently, leading disability scholars and activists have made similar comparisons between race and disability in their discussions of Clint Eastwood's 2005 film, *Million Dollar Baby* (Drake and Johnson, 1; Davis "Why," 2;). And the chairman of Britain's Disability Rights Commission, Bert Massie, recently stated that "neglect and institutionalized exclusion" of disabled people is "more profound" than that of Black people ("Massie," 1).
6. Samuels's suggestion is part of her extended analysis of the dynamics of "passing" and "coming out" for queer people, racial minorities, and people with disabilities. For critiques of the "like race" analogy in queer theory and activism, see Janet E. Halley and Janet R. Jakobsen.
7. For critiques of additive models of racism and sexism, see Barbara Smith and Elizabeth Spelman. An example of an additive representation of intersectionality in disability studies is Davis's assertion that "the most oppressed person in the world is a disabled female, Third World, homosexual, woman of color" (BOB, 29). This formulation, while a useful beginning, leaves untheorized the specific ways in which various forms of oppression come together in individual lives.
8. The Surgeon General reports that "the prevalence of mental disorders for racial and ethnic minorities in the United States is similar to that for whites." These statistics, however, apply only to those "living in the community"; people who are "homeless, incarcerated, or institutionalized" have higher rates of all forms of mental illness ("Mental" 1). According to the American Psychological Association, women are twice as likely as men to suffer from depression; the reasons for this discrepancy remain controversial ("New," 1).
9. Information about the psychiatric survivor movement can be found at the Mind Freedom Support Coalition International Web site: http://www.mindfreedom.org/
10. Courts have long recognized that patients with physical illnesses or disabilities have the right to refuse medical treatment. This constitutional protection, however, has often been denied to people diagnosed with mental illness, who can be committed to mental institutions and treated involuntarily with toxic drugs and other potentially harmful therapies. In many states, involuntary outpatient treatment is also authorized by the courts. For more on this, see Jackson and Winick.
11. The side effects of ECT can be severe and permanent, as can those of neuroleptics, the medications most commonly prescribed for schizophrenia and other "psychotic" illnesses. The chemical effects of neuroleptic drugs are similar to those produced by lobotomies (Breggin, TP, 68–91).
12. Jeanine Grobe aptly compares the most common modern-day psychiatric practices to medieval treatments for "insanity": "[M]ore often than not, [contemporary psychiatric] "medicine" is a complete atrocity—comparable only to the history out of which it grew: is four-point restraint—being tied down at the wrists and ankles—an improvement over being bound with chains? Is the cage inhumane whereas the seclusion room is not? Are the deaths that result from the use of neuroleptic drugs better than the deaths that resulted from bloodletting? Is the terror inspired by the passing of electric current through the brain an improvement over the shock of being submerged in ice water?" (103).
13. The back of *Willow Weep for Me* includes the transcript of an interview of Danquah by Dr. Freda C. Lewis-Hall, director of the Lilly Center for Women's Health, which is part of Eli Lilly, the pharmaceutical company that manufactures Prozac.

Danquah has also given book tours in conjunction with the National Mental Health Association's Campaign on Clinical Depression, which is funded by Eli Lilly (http://www.psych.org/pnews/98-05-15/nmha.html). This may raise concerns about bias in Danquah's representations of the benefits of psychoactive medications. However, *Willow Weep for Me* can hardly be said to read like an advertisement for antidepressants. As noted, Danquah expresses concern about their widespread use. In addition, she details the debilitating side effects she experienced from taking Zoloft. Most important, Danquah's memoir certainly does not understand depression as simply a biological illness that can be cured with drug therapy. If, as she claims, depression "exists somewhere in that ghost space between consciousness and chemistry," her interest in the former greatly exceeds her attention to the latter; describing only briefly her experiences with various medications, Danquah foregrounds her personal struggles and the political contexts in which they take place. I would like to thank Jonathan Metzl for bringing Danquah's relationship with Eli Lilly to my attention.

14. A 2001 Surgeon General's report on these disparities indicates that "racial and ethnic minorities" in the U.S. receive "less care and poorer quality of care" than white people ("Mental"). And a 2000 study of the treatment of people already diagnosed with depression—controlled for age, gender, health insurance status, and other factors—found a striking disparity: 44 percent of white patients and 27.8 percent of Black patients were given antidepressant medication (UT, 70).

15. Anne Wilson and Peter Beresford describe this double bind as an "increasing polarization of madness and distress into two categories—of the 'threateningly mad' and the 'worried well'" (153). Reflecting psychiatry's distinction between "psychoses" and "neuroses," these categories "serve both to dismiss and to devalue the experience and distress of those of us not seen as 'ill' enough to require public resources for support, and to reinforce assumptions about a discrete and separate group of mad people that constitutes a threat to the rest of society" (154; 153).

16. For discussions of the misperception of depression as an illness affecting only white people, see Boyd (5–7) and Marano (2).

17. In Rhonda Collins's documentary film, *We Don't Live under Normal Conditions*, people of various races and ethnicities discuss what it means to them to be depressed; most, but not all, see the origins of their distress as primarily social. Most of the depression memoirs published in the last decade in the United States are authored by white people, many of whom describe the benefits of antidepressants. See Styron, Wurtzel, Solomon, and Jamison.

18. See *Unequal Treatment* 611–21. These discrepancies are well documented and alarming. For example, a 1993 study "found that 79 percent of African Americans in a public-sector hospital were diagnosed with schizophrenia, compared with 43 percent of whites" (613). In another study, "28 percent of African Americans in a university hospital emergency room were given such a diagnosis, compared with 20 percent of whites." A 1996 study found that "African American patients seen in an emergency room received 50 percent higher doses of antipsychotic medications than patients of other ethnic groups, while their doctors devoted less time to assessing them" (613). In a 1998 study, researchers asked psychiatrists to provide diagnoses of patients based upon written case histories. The psychiatrists each reviewed identical case histories, but their diagnoses varied widely, depending on what they were told the patients' race and gender were. The diagnosis of "paranoid schizophrenic disorder," which, the authors of the study note, is associated with "violence, suspiciousness, and dangerousness," was applied to patients believed to be Black men at a rate of 43 percent, compared with 6 percent for white men, 10 percent for white women, and 12 percent for Black women (615).

19. An awareness of the medical profession's pathologizing attitudes toward Black people deters many African Americans from seeking health care, especially for symptoms of mental illness. Psychological studies in reputable journals in the 1950s compared average Africans to "the white mental patient," "the lobotomized West European," and the "traditional psychopath" (L.R.C. Haward and W.A. Roland, "Some inter-cultural differences on the Draw-A-Person Test: Part I, Goodenough scores," *Man* 54 [1954], p. 87, qtd. in Bulhan, 83–84; J.C. Carothers, "The African mind in health and disease," Geneva, World Health Organization, 1953, qtd. in Bulhan, 84). The 1965 Moynihan Report claimed that African American families were disintegrating because of their putatively "matriarchal" structure (Boyd, "Ethnic," 230). In the 1960s and 1970s, respected neurosurgeons and psychiatrists publishing in venues such as the *Journal of the American Medical Association* advocated psychosurgery to treat the "brain disease" they claimed caused "riots and urban violence" (Breggin, WA, 117). In the early 1990s, Frederick Goodwin, the chief scientist at the National Institute of Mental Health, proposed a "violence initiative," which would identify among "inner-city" adolescents—whom Goodwin compared to monkeys in a jungle—those with a genetic predisposition to violence and then subject them to psychiatric interventions (Breggin, WA 8).

20. See Barnes and Mercer (IS, 2) and Oliver (PD, 11). Although the social model's authors intended it to serve primarily as a "heuristic device," rather than a comprehensive theory of disability, its distinction between impairment and disability remains fundamental to disability scholarship in both the UK and the United States (Barnes and Mercer, IS, 3).

21. The concluding chapter of Garland-Thomson's *Extraordinary Bodies* calls for a shift in understanding disability, "From Pathology to Identity." Steven Taylor argues that "a Disability Studies perspective questions the medical model and challenges" the equation of disability with "sickness and pathology" ("Guidelines," 4). Steven E. Brown states that "a person with a disability is not sick" (11). Barnes and Mercer criticize representations of people with disabilities as "sick" or "suffering" (*Disability*, 9; 10). And Simon Brisenden urges a differentiation "between a disability and a disease" (25). Asserting that "disability is not illness," Anita Silvers acknowledges that chronic illnesses can be disabling but insists that "persons with paradigmatic disabilities—paraplegia, blindness, deafness, and others" must be distinguished from "people suffering from illness" (77). David Pfeiffer also emphasizes that "disability is not sickness" and claims that "for a half to three quarters of the disability community there is no present sickness which disables them" (6). Pfeiffer doesn't make

clear, in his estimate of the statistical prevalence of illness among people with disabilities, how he defines the "disability community."

22. See Harlan Hahn, *The Issue of Equality: European Perceptions of Employment Policy for Disabled Persons* [New York: World Rehabilitation Fund, 1984], 14, qtd. in Hahn, "Advertising," 175.

23. This is not to suggest that suffering is the most important aspect of depression for everyone who experiences it. Jane Phillips describes her depression as a "dark and dangerous illness," but also as an experience that "seemed to serve a function," facilitating her emergence "into an utterly new spring" (140–41). I am grateful to Richard Ingram for bringing this passage to my attention.

24. Deconstructions of the social model share similarities with "universalizing" approaches to disability in the United States, which, rather than conceiving of people with disabilities as members of a distinct minority group, instead highlight the fluidity of disability as an identity category and describe bodily difference as existing on a continuum of human variation.

25. Danquah's assertion is tautological (illnesses, by definition, are conditions that "reach clinical proportions"); however, I am concerned here, not with establishing the "truth" or "falsity" of the claim that depression is an illness, but rather with delineating the tactical and strategic uses to which its construction as such is put. I would like to thank Richard Ingram for pointing out to me the tautological nature of Danquah's statement.

26. In the eighteenth century the physical examination was regarded as so unimportant that doctors often practiced medicine by mail, relying on patients' lengthy narratives to make diagnoses (Reiser, 5–6).

27. For detailed accounts of the history of clinical medicine, see Foucault (BC), Ackernecht, and Jewson.

28. There are exceptions to this trend, most of which are also invisible disabilities: "mental illnesses"; some cognitive disabilities; and physical conditions such as chronic fatigue syndrome, repetitive strain injury, Environmental Illness, and fibromyalgia, which don't produce objectively observable bodily changes. But most of these conditions, like depression, are "controversial"; they will be defined as "syndromes" rather than actual "diseases" until they can be correlated with measurable physiological abnormalities.

29. Disorders such as these illustrate the impossibility of any absolute binary between "visible" and "invisible" disabilities. These conditions may often be invisible to the casual observer, but their signs can be seen on medical tests. Notwithstanding medical technologies that rely on senses other than sight, the visual bias of modern medical epistemology is pronounced; it can be discerned even the word "stethoscope," which combines the Greek words for "chest" and "I view" (Reiser, 25).

30. Nonverbal people with disabilities can also be diagnosed with depression, but the formation of depression as an impairment category has depended in large part upon patients' verbal articulations of their distress.

31. I would like to thank Richard Ingram for pointing this out to me.

32. My comparison between Danquah's political strategy and that of the nineteenth-century "homosexual" Foucault describes illustrates the limits of analogies between different subject positions. Despite the similarities I will discuss, Danquah's desire to be cured contrasts with the nineteenth-century "homosexual"'s demands to be accepted as such. I would like to thank Sue Schweik for pointing this difference out to me.

33. For example, see "Cognitive" (3).

34. While I share Tremain's sense that it is "politically naïve to suggest that the term 'impairment' is value-neutral," I nonetheless hope to show that it is possible to cite impairment categories without merely reinforcing normalizing discourses (SI, 34).

35. This characterization is consistent with the overall thrust of Tremain's argument. In "On the Subject of Impairment" (2002), Tremain touches briefly on Foucault's concept of discursive reversibility, noting that the "disciplinary apparatus of the state . . . brings into discourse the very conditions for subverting that apparatus" (44). She maintains, however, that by "articulating our lived experiences" in ways that "continue to animate the regulatory fictions of 'impairment,'" disabled people risk merely augmenting normalizing and homogenizing social processes (44; 45). Similarly, in one paragraph of her introduction to *Foucault and the Government of Disability* (2005), Tremain notes Foucault's interest in the "strategic reversibility" engendered by hegemonic discourses but nonetheless reiterates the central claims of her earlier essay.

36. I strongly concur with Tremain's argument for a disability theory that will "expose the disciplinary character of . . . identity," rather than "ground[ing] its claims to entitlement in that identity" (SI, 44; FG, 10). In fact, Tremain's criticisms of identity-based movements parallel arguments I make in my essay, "Disability Studies and Identity Politics: A Critique of Recent Theory." I share Tremain's view that identity politics risks reifying identity categories that might better be contested, is almost inevitably exclusionary and productive of hierarchies, and impedes alliances with other political minorities. Indeed, I am trying to make these problems apparent in my discussion of the ways in which entrenched ideas within disability studies exclude experiences such as Danquah describes in her memoir. But I am also attempting to demonstrate that Danquah utilizes her self-definition as a "depressive" in ways that do not replicate these dynamics of identity politics movements (18).

37. This discrepancy again exemplifies the limitations of analogies between different forms of oppression. Butler asks, "When and how does a term like 'queer' become subject to an affirmative resignification for some when a term like 'nigger,' despite some recent efforts at reclamation, appears capable of only reinscribing its pain?" (223). For Danquah, such reinscription is also the inevitable effect of hearing this word repeated. She remembers the first time she was called a 'nigger' to her face, by a high school boy she had asked to dance: "Even now when I hear that word—*nigger*—whether it is spoken by a black person or a white person, it is the simple tone and disgust of that boy's voice that I hear" (43).

38.   Boyd also observes that it can be difficult to reconcile "beliefs about being strong Black women" with "having an illness that we've long associated with weakness of the lowest kind" (CI, 5). Similarly, Angela Mitchell observes that "one reason Black women don't get treated for depression is that we often expect to feel sad, tired, and unable to think straight" (47). She reminds her readers that "Black women do not have to be depressed. It is not our lot in life" (47). The perception that depression is a form of weakness that Black women cannot "afford" is addressed on numerous web sites about Black women and depression (Marano, 2). See Rouse, 6.

39.   Mitchell also connects the "mammy stereotype," which is "rooted in the history of slavery," to Black women's depression, arguing that this stereotype creates an imperative for Black women to prioritize other others' needs over their own (53; 56).

40.   Similarly, bell hooks has asserted that "to be strong in the face of oppression is not the same as overcoming oppression... endurance is not be confused with transformation" (qtd. in Mitchell, 69). Mitchell makes this point as well: Black women's endurance of "suffering and hardship," she argues, should not be confused with "strength" (69).

41.   Wilson and Beresford describe the damaging repercussions of constructions of mental illness that "leave the holder of the diagnosis feeling utterly hopeless" and create a social expectation that those who have been diagnosed with mental illness "can never fully recover" (150). In addition, numerous African American feminists, activists, and critical race theorists have argued for the importance of hope and optimism, on both an individual and a collective level. Alex Mercedes, an African American woman who is a subject of Collins's documentary, argues that "it's important to focus on the individual... because the revolution will not happen overnight... so in the meantime, I, as an individual, must walk through this sexist, patriarchal hell." Harris criticizes white feminism for its focus on "victimization and misery" and insists upon women's ability to "shape their own lives" (613). Warning against the danger of a "capitulation to a sense of inevitable doom," Patricia Williams expresses an "optimistic conviction" of the possibility of both "institutional power to make change" and "the individual will to change" (64; 65; 68). And in the introduction to *The Black Women's Health Book*, White is hopeful about Black women's power to "address and overcome the numerous issues that have damaged" their health, in part through individual "resilience and stalwart determination" (xiv; xvi).

Works Cited

Ackernecht, Erwin M. *Medicine at the Paris Hospital 1794–1848*. Baltimore: Johns Hopkins University Press, 1976.

Barnes, Colin, and Geof Mercer, eds. *Implementing the Social Model of Disability: Theory and Research*. Leeds, UK: The Disability Press, 2004. Cited within the text as IS.

———. *Disability*. Cambridge, UK: Blackwell, 2003.

Boyd, Julia A. *Can I Get a Witness?: Black Women and Depression*. New York: Penguin, 1999. Cited within the text as CI.

———. "Ethnic and Cultural Diversity in Feminist Therapy: Keys to Power." In *The Black Women's Health Book: Speaking for Ourselves*, edited by Evelyn C. White, 226–34. Seattle, Washington: Seal Press, 1990. Cited within the text as "Ethnic."

Breggin, Peter R., M.D. *Toxic Psychiatry: Why Therapy, Empathy, and Love Must Replace the Drugs, Electroshock, and Biochemical Theories of the "New Psychiatry."* New York: St. Martin's Press, 1991. Cited within the text as TP.

Breggin, Peter R., M.D., and Ginger Ross Breggin. *The War against Children*. New York: St. Martin's Press, 1994. Cited within the text as WA.

Brisenden, Simon. "Independent Living and the Medical Model." In *The Disability Reader: Social Science Perspectives*, edited by Tom Shakespeare, 20–7. London and New York: Cassell, 1998.

Brown, Steven. "Freedom of Movement: Independent Living History and Philosophy." Independent Living Research Utilization. Available online at http://www.ilru.org/html/publications/bookshelf/freedom_movement.html (1–20).

Bulhan, Hussein Abdilahi. *Frantz Fanon and the Psychology of Oppression*. New York and London: Plenum Press, 1985.

Clare, Eli. *Exile and Pride: Disability, Queerness, and Liberation*. Cambridge, Massachusetts: South End Press, 1999.

Collins, Rhonda, dir. *We Don't Live under Normal Conditions*. Videocassette. Boston, Massachusetts: Fanlight Productions, 2000.

Collins, Patricia Hill. *Black Feminist Thought: Knowledge, Consciousness, and the Politics of Empowerment*. New York and London: Routledge, 1991.

"Cognitive Therapy for Depression." Available online at *Psychology Information Online* http://www.psychologyinfo.com/depression/cognitive.htm#lifeexperiences (1–7). Cited within the text as "Cognitive."

Crow, Liz. "Including All of Our Lives: Renewing the Social Model of Disability." In *Exploring the Divide: Illness and Disability*, edited by Colin Barnes and Geof Mercer, 55–73. Leeds, UK: The Disability Press, 1996.

Danquah, Meri Nana-Ama. *Willow Weep for Me: A Black Woman's Journey Through Depression*. New York: Ballantine, 1998.

Davis, Lennard J.. *Enforcing Normalcy: Disability, Deafness, and the Body*. London and New York: Verso, 1995. Cited within the text as EN.

———. *Bending Over Backwards: Disability, Dismodernism and Other Difficult Positions*. Foreword Michael Bérubé. New York: New York University Press, 2002. Cited within the text as BOB.

———. "Why 'Million Dollar Baby' infuriates the disabled." *The Chicago Tribune*. February 2, 2005. Available online at http://metromix.chicagotribune.com/movies/mmx-0502020017feb02,0,6865906.story (1–3). Cited within the text as "Why."

Drake, Stephen and Mary Johnson. "Movies about disabled keep myths alive." *Chicago Sun-Times*. February 12, 2005. Available online at http://www.suntimes.com/output/otherviews/cst-edt-ref12.html (1–2).

Foucault, Michel. *The Birth of the Clinic: An Archeology of Medical Perception*. Translated by A. M. Sheridan Smith. New York: Random House, 1973. Cited within the text as BC.

———. *The History of Sexuality*. Volume I: An Introduction. Translated by Robert Hurley. New York: Random House, 1978. Cited within the text as HS.

———. "Two Lectures." *Power/Knowledge: Selected Interviews and Other Writings, 1972–1977*. Pantheon Books, 1980. Cited within the text as TL.

Garland-Thomson, Rosemarie. *Extraordinary Bodies: Figuring Physical Disability in American Culture in Literature*. New York: Columbia University Press, 1997.

Grillo, Trina and Stephanie M. Wildman. "Obscuring the Importance of Race: The Implications of Making Comparisons between Racism and Sexism (or Other Isms)." In *Critical White Studies: Looking Behind the Mirror*, edited by Richard Delgado and Jean Stefancic, 619–626. Philadelphia: Temple University Press, 1997.

Grobe, Jeanine, ed. *Beyond Bedlam: Contemporary Women Psychiatric Survivors Speak Out*. Chicago: Third Side Press, 1995.

"Guidelines for Disability Studies: Highlights of a 2004 SDS Listserv Discussion." *Disability Studies Quarterly* 24.4 (Fall 2004). Available online at http://www.dsq-sds.org/_articles_html/2004/fall/dsq_fall04_listserv.asp (1–14). Cited within the text as "Guidelines."

Hahn, Harlan. "Advertising the Acceptably Employable Image: Disability and Capitalism." In *The Disability Studies Reader*, edited by. Lennard J. Davis, 172–86. New York: Routledge, 1997. Cited within the text as "Advertising."

Halley, Janet E. "'Like Race' Arguments." In *What's Left of Theory?: New Work on the Politics of Literary Theory*, edited by Judith Butler, John Guillory, and Kendall Thomas, 40–74. New York: Routledge, 2000.

Halperin, David M. *Saint Foucault: Towards a Gay Hagiography*. New York and Oxford: Oxford UP, 1995.

Harris, Angela P. "Race and Essentialism in Feminist Legal Theory." *Stanford Law Review* 42.3 (February, 1990): 581–616.

Hughes, Bill, and Kevin Paterson. "The Social Model of Disability and the Disappearing Body: Towards a Sociology of Impairment." *Disability & Society* 12.3 (1997): 325–40.

Jackson, Grace E., M.D. "The Right to Refuse Treatment." Available online at http://psychrights.org/Articles/rightorefuse.htm

Jakobsen, Janet R. "Queers Are like Jews, Aren't They? Analogy and Alliance Politics." In *Queer Theory and the Jewish Question*, edited by Daniel Boyarin, Daniel Itzkovitz, and Ann Pellegrini, 64–89. New York: Columbia University Press, 2003.

Jamison, Kay Redfield. *An Unquiet Mind: A Memoir of Moods and Madness*. New York: Random House, 1995.

Jewson, N. D. "The Disappearance of the Sick-Man from Medical Cosmology, 1770-1870." *Sociology*. 10.2 (May 1976): 225–244.

Linton, Simi. *Claiming Disability: Knowledge and Identity*. Foreword Michael Bérubé. New York: New York University Press, 1998.

Marano, Hara Estroff. "Race and the Blues." *Psychology Today*. Available online at http://cms.psychologytoday.com/articles/pto-20030930-000001.html

"Massie: exclusion 'more profound' for disabled people." *Ouch!* BBC.co.uk. June 16, 2005. Available online at http://www.bbc.co.uk/ouch/news/btn/massie_exclusion.shtml. Cited within the text as "Massie."

McRuer, Robert and Abby Wilkerson, eds. *GLQ: A Journal of Lesbian and Gay Studies. Desiring Disability: Queer Theory Meets Disability Studies*. 9.1–2 (2003).

"Mental Health: Culture, Race, and Ethnicity Supplement." U. S. Department of Health and Human Services, Office of the Surgeon General. Available online at http://www.mentalhealth.org/cre/execsummary-2.asp (1–4). Cited within the text as "Mental."

Mitchell, Angela. *What the Blues Is All About: Black Women Overcoming Stress and Depression*. With Kennise Herring, Ph.D. New York: Penguin, 1998.

Mitchell, David T. and Sharon L. Snyder, Eds. *The Body and Physical Difference: Discourses of Disability*. Foreword James I. Porter. Ann Arbor: The University of Michigan Press, 1997.

Mollow, Anna. "Disability Studies and Identity Politics: A Critique of Recent Theory." *Michigan Quarterly Review* 43.2 (Spring 2004): 269–96.

"New Report on Women and Depression: Latest Research Findings and Recommendations." Press Release. American Psychological Association. March 15, 2002. Available online at http://www.apa.org/releases/depressionreport.html (1–5). Cited within the text as "New."

Oliver, Michael. *The Politics of Disablement*. London: Macmillan, 1990. Cited within the text as PD.

———. "The Social Model in Action: If I Had a Hammer." *Implementing the Social Model of Disability: Theory and Research*. Ed Colin Barnes and Geof Mercer. Leeds, UK: The Disability Press, 2004. 18–31. Cited within the text as "Social."

Pfeiffer, David. "The ICIDH and the Need for Its Revision." *Disability & Society* 13.4 (September 1998): 503–23.

Phillips, Jane. *The Magic Daughter: A Memoir of Living with Multiple Personality Disorder*. New York: Penguin, 1995.

Porter, Roy. *The Greatest Benefit to Mankind: A Medical History of Humanity*. New York: W. W. Norton & Company, 1997.

Reiser, Stanley Joel. *Medicine and the Reign of Technology*. Cambridge: Cambridge University Press, 1978.

Rouse, Deborah L. "Lives of Women of Color Create Risk for Depression." *Women's ENews*. http://www.womensenews.org/article.cfm/dyn/aid/666, October 1, 2001. 1-6 (web pagination).

Samuels, Ellen. "My Body, My Closet: Invisible Disability and the Limits of Coming-Out Discourse." *GLQ: A Journal of Lesbian and Gay Studies* 9.1–2 (2003): 233–55.

Silvers, Anita. "Formal Justice." In *Disability, Difference, and Discrimination: Perspectives on Justice in Bioethics and Public Policy*, edited by Anita Silvers, David Wasserman, and Mary B. Mahowald, 13–146. Maryland: Rowan & Littlefield, 1998.

Smith, Barbara. "Notes for Yet Another Paper on Black Feminism, or Will the Real Enemy Please Stand Up?" *Conditions* 5 (1979): 123–142.

Smith, Bonnie G., and Beth Hutchinson, Eds. *Gendering Disability*. New Brunswick, New Jersey, and London: Rutgers University Press, 2004.

Solomon, Andrew. *The Noonday Demon: An Atlas of Depression*. New York: Simon & Schuster, 2001.

Spelman, Elizabeth V. *Inessential Woman: Problems of Exclusion in Feminist Thought*. Boston: Beacon Press, 1988.

Styron, William. *Darkness Visible: A Memoir of Madness*. New York: Random House, 1990.

Tremain, Shelley. "On the Subject of Impairment." *Disability/Postmodernity*. Ed. Mairian Corker and Tom Shakespeare. London: Continuum, 2002. 1–24. Cited within the text as SI.

———. "Foucault, Governmentality, and Critical Disability Theory: An Introduction." In *Foucault and the Government of Disability*, edited by Shelley Tremain. Ann Arbor: University of Michigan Press, 2005. Cited within the text as FG.

Unequal Treatment: Confronting Racial and Ethnic Disparities in Health Care. Ed. Brian D. Smedley, Adrienne Y. Stith, and Alan R. Nelson. Committee on Understanding and Ending Racial and Ethnic Disparities in Health Care. Board on the Health Science Policy. Institute of Medicine of the National Academy. Washington, DC: The National Academy Press, 2003. Cited within the text as UT.

UPIAS. *Fundamental Principles of Disability*. London: Union of Physically Impaired against Segregation, 1976. Available online at http://www.leeds.ac.uk/disability-studies/archiveuk/UPIAS/fundamental%20principles.pdf

Wendell, Susan. "Unhealthy Disabled: Treating Chronic Illnesses as Disabilities." *Hypatia* 16.4 (2001) 17–33.

White, Evelyn C., ed. *The Black Women's Health Book: Speaking for Ourselves*, 226–34. Seattle, Washington: Seal Press, 1990.

Williams, Patricia J. *Seeing a Color-Blind Future: The Paradox of Race*. The 1997 BBC Reith Lectures. New York: Farrar, Straus and Giroux, 1997.

Wilson, Anne and Peter Beresford. "Madness, Distress and Postmodernity: Putting the Record Straight." In *Disability/Postmodernity*, edited by Mairian Corker and Tom Shakespeare, 143–58. London: Continuum, 2002.

Winick, Bruce J. *The Right to Refuse Mental Health Treatment*. Washington, DC: American Psychological Association, 1997.

Wurtzel, Elizabeth. *Prozac Nation: Young and Depressed in America*. Second edition. New York: Riverhead Books, 1995.

24

Compulsory Able-Bodiedness and Queer/Disabled Existence

Robert McRuer

Contextualizing Disability

In her famous critique of compulsory heterosexuality Adrienne Rich opens with the suggestion that lesbian existence has often been "simply rendered invisible" (178), but the bulk of her analysis belies that rendering. In fact, throughout "Compulsory Heterosexuality and Lesbian Existence," one of Rich's points seems to be that compulsory heterosexuality depends as much on the ways in which lesbian identities are made visible (or, we might say, comprehensible) as on the ways in which they are made invisible or incomprehensible. She writes:

> Any theory of cultural/political creation that treats lesbian existence as a marginal or less "natural" phenomenon, as mere "sexual preference," or as the mirror image of either heterosexual or male homo-sexual relations is profoundly weakened thereby, whatever its other contributions. Feminist theory can no longer afford merely to voice a toleration of "lesbianism" as an "alternative life-style," or make token allusion to lesbians. A feminist critique of compulsory heterosexual orientation for women is long overdue. (178)

The critique that Rich calls for proceeds not through a simple recognition or even valuation of "lesbian existence" but rather through an interrogation of how the system of compulsory heterosexuality utilizes that existence. Indeed, I would extract from her suspicion of mere "toleration" confirmation for the idea that one of the ways in which heterosexuality is currently constituted or founded, established as the foundational sexual identity for women, is precisely through the deployment of lesbian existence as always and everywhere supplementary—the margin to heterosexuality's center, the mere reflection of (straight and gay) patriarchal realities. Compulsory heterosexuality's casting of some identities as alternatives ironically buttresses the ideological notion that dominant identities are not really alternatives but rather the natural order of things.[1]

More than twenty years after it was initially published, Rich's critique of compulsory heterosexuality is indispensable, the criticisms of her ahistorical notion of a "lesbian continuum" notwithstanding.[2] Despite its continued relevance, however, the realm of compulsory heterosexuality might seem to be an unlikely place to begin contextualizing disability.[3] I want to challenge that by considering what might be gained by understanding "compulsory heterosexuality" as a key concept in disability studies. Through a reading of compulsory heterosexuality, I want to put forward a theory of what I call compulsory able-bodiedness. The Latin root for *contextualize* denotes the act of weaving together, interweaving, joining together, or composing. This chapter thus contextualizes disability in the root sense of the word, because I argue that the system of compulsory able-bodiedness that produces disability is thoroughly interwoven with the system of compulsory heterosexuality that produces queerness, that—in fact—compulsory heterosexuality is contingent on compulsory able-bodiedness and vice versa. And, although I reiterate it in my conclusion, I want to make it clear at the outset that this particular contextualizing of disability is offered as part of a much larger and collective project of unraveling and decomposing both systems.[4]

The idea of imbricated systems is, of course, not new—Rich's own analysis repeatedly stresses the imbrication of compulsory heterosexuality and patriarchy. I would argue, however, as others have, that feminist and queer theories (and cultural theories generally) are not yet accustomed to figuring ability/disability into the equation, and thus this theory of compulsory able-bodiedness is offered as a preliminary contribution to that much-needed conversation.[5]

Able-Bodied Heterosexuality

In his introduction to *Keywords: A Vocabulary of Culture and Society*, Raymond Williams describes his project as

> the record of an inquiry into a *vocabulary*: a shared body of words and meanings in our most general discussions, in English, of the practices and institutions which we group as *culture* and *society*. Every word which I have included has at some time, in the course of some argument, virtually forced itself on my attention because the problems of its meaning seemed to me inextricably bound up with the problems it was being used to discuss. (15)

Although Williams is not particularly concerned in *Keywords* with feminism or gay and lesbian liberation, the processes he describes should be recognizable to feminists and queer theorists, as well as to scholars and activists in other contemporary movements, such as African American studies or critical race theory. As these movements have developed, increasing numbers of words have indeed forced themselves on our attention, so that an inquiry into not just the marginalized identity but also the dominant identity has become necessary. The problem of the meaning of masculinity (or even maleness), of whiteness, of heterosexuality has increasingly been understood as inextricably bound up with the problems the term is being used to discuss.

One need go no further than the *Oxford English Dictionary* to locate problems with the meaning of heterosexuality. In 1971 the *OED Supplement* defined *heterosexual* as "pertaining to or characterized by the normal relations of the sexes; opp. to *homosexual*." At this point, of course, a few decades of critical work by feminists and queer theorists have made it possible to acknowledge quite readily that heterosexual and homosexual are in fact not equal and opposite identities. Rather, the ongoing subordination of homosexuality (and bisexuality) to heterosexuality allows for heterosexuality to be institutionalized as "the normal relations of the sexes," while the institutionalization of heterosexuality as the "normal relations of the sexes" allows for homosexuality (and bisexuality) to be subordinated. And, as queer theory continues to demonstrate, it is precisely the introduction of normalcy into the system that introduces compulsion: "Nearly everyone," Michael Warner writes in *The Trouble with Normal: Sex, Politics, and the Ethics of Queer Life*, "wants to be normal. And who can blame them, if the alternative is being abnormal, or deviant, or not being one of the rest of us? Put in those terms, there doesn't seem to be a choice at all. Especially in America where [being] normal probably outranks all other social aspirations" (53). Compulsion is here produced and covered over, with the appearance of choice (sexual preference) mystifying a system in which there actually is no choice.

A critique of normalcy has similarly been central to the disability rights movement and to disability studies, with—for example—Lennard Davis's overview and critique of the historical emergence of normalcy or Rosemarie Garland-Thomson's introduction of the concept of the "normate" (Davis, 23–49; Thomson, 8–9). Such scholarly and activist work positions us to locate the problems of able-bodied identity, to see the problem of the meaning of able-bodiedness as bound up with the problems it is being used to discuss. Arguably, able-bodied identity is at this juncture even more naturalized than heterosexual identity. At the very least, many people not sympathetic to queer theory will concede that ways of being heterosexual are culturally produced and culturally variable, even if and even as they understood heterosexual identity itself to be entirely natural. The same cannot be said, on the whole, for able-bodied identity. An extreme example that nonetheless encapsulates currently hegemonic thought on ability and disability is a notorious *Salon* article by Norah Vincent attacking disability studies that appeared online in the summer of 1999. Vincent writes, "It's hard to deny that something called normalcy exists. The human body is a machine, after all—one that has evolved functional parts: lungs for breathing, legs for walking, eyes for seeing, ears for hearing, a tongue for speaking and most crucially for all the academics concerned, a brain for thinking. This is science, not culture."[6] In a nutshell, you either have an able body, or you don't.

Yet the desire for definitional clarity might unleash more problems than it contains; if it's hard to deny that something called normalcy exists, it's even harder to pinpoint what that something is. The *OED* defines *able-bodied* redundantly and negatively as "having an able body, i.e. one free from physical disability, and capable of the physical exertions required of it; in bodily health; robust." Able-bodiedness, in turn, is defined vaguely as "soundness of health; ability to work; robustness." The parallel structure of the definitions of ability and sexuality is quite striking: first, to be able-bodied is to be "free from physical disability," just as to be heterosexual is to be "the opposite of homosexual." Second, even though the language of "the normal relations" expected of human beings is not present in the definition of able-bodied, the sense of "normal relations" is, especially with the emphasis on work: being able-bodied means being capable of the normal physical exertions required in a particular system of labor. It is here, in fact, that both able-bodied identity and the *Oxford English Dictionary* betray their origins in the nineteenth century and the rise of industrial capitalism. It is here as well that we can begin to understand the compulsory nature of able-bodiedness: in the emergent industrial capitalist system, free to sell one's labor but not free to do anything else effectively meant free to have an able body but not particularly free to have anything else.

Like compulsory heterosexuality, then, compulsory able-bodiedness functions by covering over, with the appearance of choice, a system in which there actually is no choice. I would not locate this compulsion, moreover, solely in the past, with the rise of industrial capitalism. Just as the origins of heterosexual/homosexual identity are now obscured for most people so that compulsory hetero-sexuality functions as a disciplinary formation seemingly emanating from everywhere and nowhere, so too are the origins of able-bodied/disabled identity obscured, allowing what Susan Wendell calls "the disciplines of normality" (87) to cohere in a system of compulsory able-bodiedness that similarly emanates from everywhere and nowhere. Able-bodied dilutions and misunderstandings of the mi-nority thesis put forward in the disability rights movement and disability studies have even, in some ways, strengthened the system: the dutiful (or docile) able-bodied subject now recognizes that some groups of people have chosen to adjust to or even take pride in their "condition," but that recognition, and the tolerance that undergirds it, covers over the compulsory nature of the able-bodied subject's own identity.[7]

Michael Bérubé's memoir about his son Jamie, who has Down syndrome, helps exemplify some of the ideological demands currently sustaining compulsory able-bodiedness. Bérubé writes of how he "sometimes feel[s] cornered by talking about Jamie's intelligence, as if the burden of proof is on me, official spokesman on his behalf." The subtext of these encounters always seems to be the same: "*In the end, aren't you disappointed to have a retarded child?* [. . .] *Do we really have to give this person our full attention?*" (180). Bérubé's excavation of this subtext pinpoints an important common ex-perience that links all people with disabilities under a system of compulsory able-bodiedness—the experience of the able-bodied need for an agreed-on common ground. I can imagine that answers might be incredibly varied to similar questions—"In the end, wouldn't you rather be hearing?" and "In the end, wouldn't you rather not be HIV positive?" would seem, after all, to be very different questions, the first (with its thinly veiled desire for Deafness not to exist) more obviously genocidal than the second. But they are not really different questions, in that their constant repetition (or their presence as ongoing subtexts) reveals more about the able-bodied culture doing the asking than about the bodies being interrogated. The culture asking such questions assumes in advance that we all agree: able-bodied identities, able-bodied perspectives are preferable and what we all, collectively, are aiming for. A system of compulsory able-bodiedness repeatedly demands that people with disabilities embody for others an affirmative answer to the unspoken question, Yes, but in the end, wouldn't you rather be more like me?

It is with this repetition that we can begin to locate both the ways in which compulsory able-bodiedness and compulsory heterosexuality are interwoven and the ways in which they might be contested. In queer theory, Judith Butler is most famous for identifying the repetitions required to maintain heterosexual hegemony:

> The "reality" of heterosexual identities is performatively constituted through an imitation that sets itself up as the origin and the ground of all imitations. In other words, heterosexuality is always in the process of imitating and approximating its own phantasmatic idealization of itself—*and failing*. Precisely because it is bound to fail, and yet endeavors to succeed, the project of heterosexual identity is propelled into an endless repetition of itself. ("Imitation," 21)

If anything, the emphasis on identities that are constituted through repetitive performances is even more central to compulsory able-bodiedness—think, after all, of how many institutions in our culture are showcases for able-bodied performance. Moreover, as with heterosexuality, this repetition is bound to fail, as the ideal able-bodied identity can never, once and for all, be achieved. Able-bodied identity and heterosexual identity are linked in their mutual impossibility and in their mutual incomprehensibility—they are incomprehensible in that each is an identity that is simultaneously the ground on which all identities supposedly rest and an impressive achievement that is always deferred and thus never really guaranteed. Hence Butler's queer theories of gender performativity could be easily extended to disability studies, as this slightly paraphrased excerpt from *Gender Trouble* might suggest (I substitute, by bracketing, terms having to do literally with embodiment for Butler's terms of gender and sexuality):

> [Able-bodiedness] offers normative...positions that are intrinsically impossible to embody, and the persistent failure to identify fully and without incoherence with these positions reveals [able-bodiedness] itself not only as a compulsory law, but as an inevitable comedy. Indeed, I would offer this insight into [able-bodied identity] as both a compulsory system and an intrinsic comedy, a constant parody of itself, as an alternative [disabled] perspective. (122)

In short, Butler's theory of gender trouble might be resignified in the context of queer/disability studies to highlight what we could call "ability trouble"—meaning not the so-called problem of disability but the inevitable impossibility, even as it is made compulsory, of an able-bodied identity.

Queer/Disabled Existence

The cultural management of the endemic crises surrounding the performance of heterosexual and able-bodied identity effects a panicked consolidation of hegemonic identities. The most successful heterosexual subject is the one whose sexuality is not compromised by disability (metaphorized as queerness); the most successful able-bodied subject is the one whose ability is not compromised by queerness (metaphorized as disability). This consolidation occurs through complex processes of conflation and stereotype: people with disabilities are often understood as somehow queer (as paradoxical stereotypes of the asexual or oversexual person with disabilities would suggest), while queers are often understood as somehow disabled (as ongoing medicalization of identity, similar to what people with disabilities more generally encounter, would suggest). Once these conflations are available in the popular imagination, queer/disabled figures can be tolerated and, in fact, utilized in order to maintain the fiction that able-bodied heterosexuality is not in crisis. As lesbian existence is deployed, in Rich's analysis, to reflect back heterosexual and patriarchal "realities," queer/disabled existence can be deployed to buttress compulsory able-bodiedness. Since queerness and disability both have the potential to disrupt the performance of able-bodied heterosexuality, both must be safely contained—embodied—in such figures.

In the 1997 film *As Good As It Gets*, for example, although Melvin Udall (Jack Nicholson), who is diagnosed in the film as obsessive-compulsive, is represented visually in many ways that initally position him in what Martin F. Norden calls "the cinema of isolation" (i.e., Melvin is represented in ways that link him to other representations of people with disabilities), the trajectory of the film is toward able-bodied heterosexuality. To effect the consolidation of heterosexual and able-bodied norms, disability and queerness in the film are visibly located elsewhere, in the gay character Simon Bishop (Greg Kinnear). Over the course of the film, Melvin progressively sheds his own sense of inhabiting an anomalous body, and disability is firmly located in the non-heterosexual character, who is initially represented as able-bodied, but who ends up, after he is attacked and beaten by a group of burglars, using a wheelchair and cane for most of the film. More important, the disabled/queer figure, as in many other contemporary cultural representations, facilitates the heterosexual romance: Melvin first learns to accept the differences Simon comes to embody, and Simon then encourages Melvin to reconcile with his girlfriend, Carol Connelly (Helen Hunt). Having served their purpose, Simon, disability, and queerness are all hustled offstage together. The film concludes with a fairly traditional romantic reunion between the (able-bodied) male and female leads.[8]

Critically Queer, Severely Disabled

The crisis surrounding heterosexual identity and able-bodied identity does not automatically lead to their undoing. Indeed, as this brief consideration of *As Good As It Gets* should suggest, this crisis and the anxieties that accompany it can be invoked in a wide range of cultural texts precisely to be (temporarily) resolved or alleviated. Neither gender trouble nor ability trouble is sufficient in and of itself to unravel compulsory heterosexuality or compulsory able-bodiedness. Butler acknowledges this problem: "This failure to approximate the norm [...] is not the same as the subversion of the norm. There is no promise that subversion will follow from the reiteration of constitutive norms; there is no guarantee that exposing the naturalized status of heterosexuality will lead to its subversion" ("Critically Queer," 22; qtd. in Warner, "Normal and Normaller" 168–169, n. 87). For Warner, this acknowledgment in Butler locates a potential gap in her theory, "let us say, between virtually queer and critically queer" (Warner, "Normal and Normaller," 168–169, n. 87). In contrast to a virtually queer identity, which would be experienced by anyone who failed to perform heterosexuality without contradiction and incoherence (i.e., everyone), a critically queer perspective could presumably mobilize the inevitable failure to approximate the norm, collectively "working the weakness in the norm," to use Butler's phrase ("Critically Queer," 26).[9]

A similar gap could be located if we appropriate Butler's theories for disability studies. Everyone is virtually disabled, both in the sense that able-bodied norms are "intrinsically impossible to embody" fully, and in the sense that able-bodied status is always temporary, disability being the one identity category that all people will embody if they live long enough. What we might call a critically disabled position, however, would differ from such a virtually disabled position; it would call attention to the ways in which the disability rights movement and disability studies have resisted the demands of compulsory able-bodiedness and have demanded access to a newly imagined and newly configured public sphere where full participation is not contingent on an able body.

We might, in fact, extend the concept and see such a perspective not as critically disabled but rather as severely disabled, with *severe* performing work similar to the critically queer work of *fabulous*. Tony Kushner writes:

Fabulous became a popular word in the queer community—well, it was never *un*popular, but for a while it became a battle cry of a new queer politics, carnival and camp, aggressively fruity, celebratory and tough like a streetwise drag queen: *"FAAAAABULOUS!"* […] *Fabulous* is one of those words that provide a measure of the degree to which a person or event manifests a particular, usually oppressed, subculture's most distinctive, invigorating features. (vii)

Severe, though less common than *fabulous*, has a similar queer history: a severe critique is a fierce critique, a defiant critique, one that thoroughly and carefully reads a situation—and I mean reading in the street sense of loudly calling out the inadequacies of a given situation, person, text, or ideology. "Severely disabled," according to such a queer conception, would reverse the able-bodied understanding of severely disabled bodies as the most marginalized, the most excluded from a privileged and always elusive normalcy, and would instead suggest that it is precisely those bodies that are best positioned to refuse "mere toleration" and to call out the inadequacies of compulsory able-bodiedness. Whether it is the "army of one-breasted women" Audre Lorde imagines descending on the Capitol; the Rolling Quads, whose resistance sparked the independent living movement in Berkeley, California; Deaf students shutting down Gallaudet University in the Deaf President Now action; or ACT UP storming the National Institutes of Health or the Food and Drug Administration, severely disabled/critically queer bodies have already generated ability trouble that remaps the public sphere and reimagines and reshapes the limited forms of embodiment and desire proffered by the systems that would contain us all.[10]

Compulsory heterosexuality is intertwined with compulsory able-bodiedness; both systems work to (re)produce the able body and heterosexuality. But precisely because these systems depend on a queer/disabled existence that can never quite be contained, able-bodied heterosexuality's hegemony is always in danger of being disrupted. I draw attention to critically queer, severely disabled possibilities to further an incorporation of the two fields, queer theory and disability studies, in the hope that such a collaboration (which in some cases is already occurring, even when it is not acknowledged or explicitly named as such) will exacerbate, in more productive ways, the crisis of authority that currently besets heterosexual/able-bodied norms. Instead of invoking the crisis in order to resolve it (as in a film like *As Good As It Gets*), I would argue that a queer/disability studies (in productive conversations with disabled/queer movements outside the academy) can continuously invoke, in order to further the crisis, the inadequate resolutions that compulsory heterosexuality and compulsory able-bodiedness offer us. And in contrast to an able-bodied culture that holds out the promise of a substantive (but paradoxically always elusive) ideal, a queer/disabled perspective would resist delimiting the kinds of bodies and abilities that are acceptable or that will bring about change. Ideally, a queer/disability studies—like the term *queer* itself—might function "oppositionally and relationally but not necessarily substantively, not as a positivity but as a positionality, not as a thing, but as a resistance to the norm" (Halperin, 66). Of course, in calling for a queer/disability studies without a necessary substance, I hope it is clear that I do not mean to deny the materiality of queer/disabled bodies, as it is precisely those material bodies that have populated the movements and brought about the changes detailed above. Rather, I mean to argue that critical queerness and severe disability are about collectively transforming (in ways that cannot necessarily be predicted in advance) the substantive uses to which queer/disabled existence has been put by a system of compulsory able-bodiedness, about insisting that such a system is never as good as it gets, and about imagining bodies and desires otherwise.

Notes

1. In 1976, the Brussels Tribunal on Crimes against Women identified "compulsory heterosexuality" as one such crime (Katz, 26). A year earlier, in her important article "The Traffic in Women: Notes on the 'Political Economy' of Sex," Gayle Rubin examined the ways in which "obligatory heterosexuality" and "compulsory heterosexuality" function in what she theorized as a larger sex/gender system (179, 198; cited in Katz, 132). Rich's 1980 article, which has been widely cited and reproduced since its initial publication, was one of the most extensive analyses of compulsory heterosexuality in feminism. I agree with Jonathan Ned Katz's insistence that the concept is redundant because "any society split between

heterosexual and homosexual is compulsory" (164), but I also acknowledge the historical and critical usefulness of the phrase. It is easier to understand the ways in which a society split between heterosexual and homosexual is compulsory precisely because of feminist deployments of the redundancy of compulsory heterosexuality. I would also suggest that popular queer theorizing outside of the academy (from drag performances to activist street theater) has often employed redundancy performatively to make a critical point.

2. In an effort to forge a political connection between all women, Rich uses the terms "lesbian" and "lesbian continuum" to describe a vast array of sexual and affectional connections throughout history, many of which emerge from historical and cultural conditions quite different from those that have made possible the identity of lesbian (192–199). Moreover, by using "lesbian continuum" to affirm the connection between lesbian and heterosexual women, Rich effaces the cultural and sexual specificity of contemporary lesbian existence.

3. The incorporation of queer theory and disability studies that I argue for here is still in its infancy. It is in cultural activism and cultural theory about AIDS (such as John Nguyet Erni's *Unstable Frontiers* or Cindy Patton's *Fatal Advice*) that a collaboration between queer theory and disability studies is already proceeding and has been for some time, even though it is not yet acknowledged or explicitly named as such. Michael Davidson's "Strange Blood: Hemophobia and the Unexplored Boundaries of Queer Nation" is one of the finest analyses to date of the connections between disability studies and queer theory.

4. The collective projects that I refer to are, of course, the projects of gay liberation and queer studies in the academy and the disability rights movement and disability studies in the academy. This chapter is part of my own contribution to these projects and is part of my longer work in progress, titled *Crip Theory: Cultural Signs of Queerness and Disability*.

5. David Mitchell and Sharon Snyder are in line with many scholars working in disability studies when they point out the "ominous silence in the humanities" on the subject of disability (1). See, for other examples, Simi Linton's discussion of the "divided curriculum" (71–116), and assertions by Rosemarie Garland-Thomson and by Lennard Davis about the necessity of examining disability alongside other categories of difference such as race, class, gender, and sexuality (Garland-Thomson, 5; Davis, xi).

6. Disability studies is not the only field Vincent has attacked in the mainstream media; see her article "The Future of Queer: Wedded to Orthodoxy," which mocks academic queer theory. Neither being disabled nor being gay or lesbian in and of itself guarantees the critical consciousness generated in the disability rights or queer movements, or in queer theory or disability studies: Vincent herself is a lesbian journalist, but her writing clearly supports both able-bodied and heterosexual norms. Instead of a stigmaphilic response to queer/disabled existence, finding "a commonality with those who suffer from stigma, and in this alternative realm [learning] to value the very things the rest of the world despises" (Warner, *Trouble*, 43), Vincent reproduces the dominant culture's stigmaphobic response. See Warner's discussion of Erving Goffman's concepts of stigmaphobe and stigmaphile (41–45).

7. Michel Foucault's discussion of "docile bodies" and his theories of disciplinary practices are in the background of much of my analysis here (135–169).

8. The consolidation of able-bodied and heterosexuality identity is probably most common in mainstream films and television movies about AIDS, even—or perhaps especially—when those films are marketed as new and daring." The 1997 Christopher Reeve-directed HBO film *In the Gloaming* is an example. In the film, the disabled/queer character (yet again, in a tradition that reaches back to *An Early Frost* [1985]), is eliminated at the end but not before effecting a healing of the heteronormative family. As Simon Watney writes about *An Early Frost*, "The closing shot [...] shows a 'family album' picture. [...] A traumatic episode is over. The family closes ranks, with the problem son conveniently dispatched, and life getting back to normal" (114). I am focusing on a non-AIDS-related film about disability and homosexuality, because I think the processes I theorize here have a much wider currency and can be found in many cultural texts that attempt to represent queerness or disability. There is not space here to analyze *As Good As It Gets* fully; for a more comprehensive close reading of how heterosexual/able-bodied consolidation works in the film and other cultural texts, see my article "As Good As It Gets: Queer Theory and Critical Disability." I do not, incidentally, think that these processes are unique to fictional texts: the MLA's annual *Job Information List*, for instance, provides evidence of other locations where heterosexual and able-bodied norms support each other while ostensibly allowing for tolerance of queerness and disability. The recent high visibility of queer studies and disability studies on university press lists, conference proceedings, and even syllabi has not necessarily translated into more jobs for disabled/queer scholars.

9. See my discussion of Butler, Gloria Anzaldua, and critical queerness in *The Queer Renaissance: Contemporary American Literature and the Reinvention of Lesbian and Gay Identities* (149–153).

10. On the history of the AIDS Coalition to Unleash Power (ACT UP), see Douglas Crimp and Adam Rolston's *AIDS Demo-Graphics*. Lorde recounts her experiences with breast cancer and imagines a movement of one-breasted women in *The Cancer Journals*. Joseph P. Shapiro recounts both the history of the Rolling Quads and the Independent Living Movement and the Deaf President Now action in *No Pity: People with Disabilities Forging a New Civil Rights Movement* (41–58; 74–85). Deaf activists have insisted for some time that deafness should not be understood as a disability and that people living with deafness, instead, should be seen as having a distinct language and culture. As the disability rights movement has matured, however, some Deaf activists and scholars in Deaf studies have rethought this position and have claimed disability (that is, disability revalued by a disability rights movement and disability studies) in an attempt to affirm a coalition with other people with disabilities. It is precisely such a reclaiming of disability that I want to stress here with my emphasis on severe disability.

Works Cited

As Good As It Gets. Dir. James L. Brooks. Perf. Jack Nicholson, Helen Hunt, and Greg Kinnear. TriStar, 1997.

Berube, Michael. *Life As We Know It: A Father, a Family, and an Exceptional Child*. New York: Vintage-Random House, 1996.

Butler, Judith. "Critically Queer." *GLQ: A Journal of Lesbian and Gay Studies* 1.1 (1993): 17–32

———. *Gender Trouble: Feminism and the Subversion of Identity*. New York: Routledge, 1990.

———. "Imitation and Gender Insubordination." In *Inside/Out: Lesbian Theories, Gay Theories*, edited by Diana Fuss, (13–31). New York: Routledge, 1991.

Crimp, Douglas, and Adam Rolston. *AIDS DemoGraphics*. Seattle: Bay Press, 1990.

Davidson, Michael. "Strange Blood: Hemophobia and the Unexplored Boundaries of Queer Nation." In *Beyond the Binary: Reconstructing Cultural Identity in a Multicultural Context*, edited by Timothy Powell (39–60). New Brunswick: Rutgers UP, 1999.

Davis, Lennard J. *Enforcing Normalcy: Disability, Deafness, and the Body*. London: Verso, 1995.

Erni, John Nguyet. *Unstable Frontiers: Technomedicine and the Cultural Politics of "Curing" AIDS*. Minneapolis: U of Minnesota P, 1994.

In the Gloaming. Dir. Christopher Reeve. Perf. Glenn Close, Robert Sean Leonard, and David Strathairn. HBO, 1997.

Foucault, Michel. *Discipline and Punish: The Birth of the Prison*. Translated by Alan Sheridan. New York: Vintage-Random House, 1977.

Garland-Thomson, Rosemarie. *Extraordinary Bodies: Figuring Physical Disability in American Culture and Literature*. New York: Columbia UP, 1997.

Katz, Jonathan Ned. *The Invention of Heterosexuality*. New York: Dutton, 1995.

Kushner, Tony. "Foreword: Notes Toward a Theater of the Fabulous." In *Staging Lives: An Anthology of Contemporary Gay Theater*, edited by John M. Clum, vii–ix. Boulder: Westview Press, 1996.

Linton, Simi. *Claiming Disability: Knowledge and Identity*. New York: NYU Press, 1998.

Lorde, Audre. *The Cancer Journals*. San Francisco: Aunt Lute Books, 1980.

McRuer, Robert. "As Good As It Gets: Queer Theory and Critical Disability." *GLQ: A Journal of Lesbian and Gay Studies* 9.1–2 (2003): 79–105.

———. *Crip Theory: Cultural Signs of Queerness and Disability*. New York: NYU Press, 2006.

———. *The Queer Renaissance: Contemporary American Literature and the Reinvention of Lesbian and Gay Identities*. New York: NYU Press, 1997.

Mitchell, David T., and Sharon L. Snyder. "Introduction: Disability Studies and the Double Bind of Representation." In *The Body and Physical Difference: Discourses of Disability*, edited by Mitchell and Snyder, 1–31. Ann Arbor: U of Michigan P, 1997.

Norden, Martin F. *The Cinema of Isolation: A History of Physical Disability in the Movies*. New Brunswick: Rutgers UP, 1994.

Patton, Cindy. *Fatal Advice: How Safe-Sex Education Went Wrong*. Durham: Duke UP, 1997.

Rich, Adrienne. "Compulsory Heterosexuality and Lesbian Existence." In *Powers of Desire: The Politics of Sexuality*, edited by Ann Snitow, Christine Stansell, and Sharon Thompson, 177–205. New York: Monthly Review Press, 1983.

Rubin, Gayle. "The Traffic in Women: Notes on the 'Political Economy' of Sex." In *Toward an Anthropology of Women*, edited by Rayna R. Reiter, 157–210. New York: Monthly Review Press, 1975. .

Shapiro, Joseph P. *No Pity: People with Disabilities Forging a New Civil Rights Movement*. New York: Times Books-Random House, 1993.

Vincent, Norah. "Enabling Disabled Scholarship." *Salon*. Aug. 18, 1999. Available at http://www.salon.com/books/it/1999/08/18/disability

———. "The Future of Queer: Wedded to Orthodoxy." *The Village Voice* 22 Feb. 2000: 16.

Warner, Michael. "Normal and Normaller: Beyond Gay Marriage." *GLQ: A Journal of Lesbian and Gay Studies* 5.2 (1999): 119–171.

———. *The Trouble with Normal: Sex, Politics, and the Ethics of Queer Life*. New York: The Free Press, 1999.

Watney, Simon. *Policing Desire: Pornography, AIDS, and the Media*. 2nd ed. Minneapolis: U of Minnesota P, 1989.

Wendell, Susan. *The Rejected Body: Feminist Philosophical Reflections on Disability*. New York: Routledge, 1996.

Williams, Raymond. *Keywords: A Vocabulary of Culture and Society*. Rev. ed. New York: Oxford UP, 1983.

25

The Vulnerable Articulate
James Gillingham, Aimee Mullins, and Matthew Barney[1]

Marquard Smith

Prosthetics, Aesthetics, Erotics

This chapter circles around a particular question: what kinds of erotic fantasies are being played out across medical, commercial, and later avant-garde images of the body of the female amputee in our Western visual culture? In attending to this question, my aim is to consider how and why these images articulate *the subject of prosthesis* in academic discourse with regards to what Vivian Sobchack has called "a tropological currency for describing a vague and shifting constellation of relationships between bodies, technologies, and subjectivities."[2] Although these images that point towards the confluence of prosthetics, aesthetics, and erotics are often problematic in the extreme, and the arguments that fasten themselves to and emanate from them are similarly somewhat awkward, it is my hope that asking this question will make certain previously unthinkable possibilities available.

Flirting with Techno-fetishism[3]

I have of late been flirting with techno-fetishism. By techno-fetishism I refer simply to that well-known and wide spread series of cultural practices acted out by academics, writers, artists, and others who fetishize technology in their writings and art-making both within the confines of their intellectual communities and in everyday life. From the start, I'm happy to acknowledge that techno-fetishism is a practice of a "perverse" kind.[4] Fetishes always are in the West, seeing as how, since at least the late nineteenth-century's epistemological explosion of perversions, the presence of fetishistic practices and objects marks the distinction between the "normal" and the "abnormal," the normative and the pathological, the well hinged and the unhinged, the "straight" and the "perverse." We will remember that for Michel Foucault in volume 1 of *The History of Sexuality* fetishism was the "master perversion."[5]

This chapter is well disposed toward perverse, fetishistic practices and objects in general. But it is wary of the idea of techno-fetishism, a pernicious notion whose cause for concern is its dangerously implicit metaphorical opportunism. Philosophers of technology are prone to take advantage of metaphorical *opportunities* that are made available by thinking and writing about technology, and about the technologization of being. They tend to indulge in a metaphorical poetics of technologization at the expense of the more mundane reality of material lives that are lived through technology and the body *as it is experienced* through the technology that it must employ—to the extent, for instance, that the figure of the disabled body has for them become a living, shining embodiment of post-human existence in prosthetic times.[6] Even so, or perhaps because of this, this chapter must become intimate with techno-fetishism to gauge its impact on the constellation of bodies, technologies, and subjectivities—without ever losing sight of its potential dangers or my complicity with it.

Maintaining this fraught dialectic between material and the metaphorical, the literal and the fig-
ural, flesh and poetics, is the most productive way of engaging with the central concerns of this essay,
the "constellation...of bodies, technologies, and subjectivities" in all of their real and phantasmatic,
grounded and *un*grounded possibilities. Maintaining this dialectic becomes so pressing because it
is only in attending to both the literal, material, and fleshy nature of things *and* flirting with techno-
fetishism as a practice that involves an aestheticization, a poeticization, and a metaphorization of "the
prosthetic"—as what Sobchack calls an "unfleshed" out catchword—that one can make use of such
possibilities without becoming unduly sympathetic towards the very things one admonishes.

To this end, the following speculations are staged in two parts. Part 1 considers the role that "passing"
plays in the discourse of prosthesis, and how the challenge that the amputee faces in trying to "pass" for
something that they are not turns on questions of visibility and invisibility. To demonstrate this I draw
on photographs from the early twentieth century that both follow a precedent set in medical imagery in
the nineteenth century and pursue commercial ends that they offer us ways to take in the intermittent
oscillation between the visible and the invisible that engenders a fetishistic eroticization of the female
amputees represented in the images. Part 2 focuses on the American double amputee paralympian
athlete Aimee Mullins. Mullins appeared provocatively in a Nick Knight photo shoot for an issue of
the fashion magazine *Dazed and Confuse,* guest edited by fashion designer Alexander McQueen in
1998; adorned the catwalk, Barbie doll-like on a revolving pedestal in McQueen's 1999 Spring-Summer
Collection in London; and sprinted through the desert landscape of a television advertisement for the
British Internet service provider Freeserve in 2000 on her carbon-graphite "cheetah" legs designed
by Van Phillips. Here I shall be concentrating on Mullins in a more recent fine art context—the latest
episode of American artist and filmmaker Matthew Barney's *Cremaster* cycle released in 2002—in
order to consider how she is drawn on here to both re-affirm the mechanisms and the fantasies of
techno-fetishism and at the same time offer some other nicely surprising possibilities.

Overall, then, I look to account for how these two historically distinct yet conceptually linked visual
renderings of the confluences of bodies, technologies, and subjectivities as they are spun through the
prism of prosthetics, aesthetics, and erotics makes it possible for us to begin to articulate something
neglected and thus worthy of note in the etymology of perversion. This is to say that an etymology of
perversion makes it possible to acknowledge, open up, and seek to separate the more obvious perverse
practices of techno-fetishism as practices of an erotic kind from a far more fascinating thread of the
genealogy of perversion—that is already apparent in Haverlock Ellis's sexology, Max Nordau's studies
in degeneration, and Sigmund Freud's psychoanalysis—in which the matter of sexuality is but one
part of perversion's desire to, in fact, mimic a "turning away" from such sexuality.[7]

The reason to insist upon the prospect of this separation—between the feat of perverting itself and
perversions of a sexual kind—is founded on the need to preserve the promise of the former and to
be wary of the sleight of hand of the latter. That is, to be wary of perversion's fetishizing in general, its
fetishizing of technology in particular, its techno-fetishism, its ability to make things disappear, its
imperative to loss. To put it another way, my endeavor here is to trace and rub up against the points of
articulation between fetishistic practices, fetishistic objects, and perversion itself. To do so is to question some of the ways that—following the three primary models of fetishism; the anthropological, the
Marxian, and the Freudian—the matter of fetishism and its supplementary nature turns on or hints
at a disavowal, a displacement, a replacement of or a compensation for *something else*, a substitute
or surrogate for *other things*, now lost, that are magical, mysterious, horrific. Although I am deeply
suspicious of fetishism's role in the patterning of human sexuality and subjectivity, what interests me
is the prospect of the perverting (but nonsexualizing) thread of the etymology of this genealogy of
perversion in which it becomes possible to begin to understand the implications of how, as Emily
Apter has put it so succinctly, fetishism necessitates "*inanimate* or *non-human objects*, [and] living
part[s] of the body [that are] treated as dead or partial objects substituted for the whole" and how these
inanimate, non-human, or partial objects are surinvested [or overvalued] to the exclusion of all other
targets of desire" [emphasis mine].[8] To put it more simply, what fascinates me is a decision to "turn

away" from perverse and fetishistic practices as being exclusively sexual and to turn toward the way in which fetishistic objects, including the possibility of animat*ed* and animat*ing* objects as replacing our phantasmatic desire for the human body as a totalized union and instead lead us into a malignant, which is to say enduring investment in things that are not wholly human. For Apter, following Jacques Lacan, a body is thus "composed of prosthetic parts...rather than [being] at risk of...loss."

I believe, then, that certain discourses on prosthesis have something provocative to tell us about the nature of fetishistic practices and fetishistic objects—especially given the *supplementary* nature of these fetishistic objects, that, for Freud at any rate, are only ever body parts or inanimate objects substituted inappropriately for the sexual object proper, ultimately taking its place and thereby encouraging us further to abandon this so called "proper" sexual aim. Since this is in essence the definition of perversion, *so by extension* the discourse on prosthesis also has the chance to tell us something unexpected about perversion—the very pathology *spawning* fetishistic practices. For me, something in the *material* and *metaphorical* articulations of the body and its prosthetic technologies is mirrored in the historical, theoretical, and morphological structure that we see unfolding in questions of fetishism and perversion, and as a consequence questions of the emergence of sexuality and eroticism.

Part 1

Passing: Commercial Photography And "Evidence of a New Invisibility"

> I really cannot tell you what my friends thought of your work, I believe there was only one word and that was "marvellous," and when I had the leg on and began to walk about, *I don't think they fully realised it was me*, after walking with a crutch all these years.

> I must tell you I had a good deal of practice while at home, I had a mile walk two days after I left you and I did not feel any inconvenience after and on Sunday I had the leg on nearly all day, and I only had the backache' a little. [emphasis mine]

This letter dated July 19, 1907 is one of a number of such patient testimonies that can be found in the Osteogenesis Collection at the Science Museum, London. It is attached to an archive of photographs of products manufactured by James Gillingham of Chard, a maker of artificial limbs since around 1866. These testimonies and images draw attention to the fact that at the heart of the modern discourse of prosthesis is the realization that the joining together of bodies and machines is not just a manufacturing process, or even just an art and a craft. An ethic is in play here that seeks to answer a challenge of presentation and utility: how an item of prosthetic technology is fashioned industrially, and also how this piece of machinery is experienced. At stake, then, is how a particular prosthesis is sculpted and utilized, how it looks and how it works, and how its aesthetic success and its practical success affect the ontology of its wearer, the body's experience of itself. These are matters of aesthetics, ergonomics, and sentience.

Most interesting for my purposes is the quality of *in*visibility that circles around the presence of the prosthesis in the late nineteenth and early twentieth centuries: as the patient says, *when they put on their leg and began to walk about, they didn't think their friends fully realised who they were*. Like an uncanny inversion of the phenomenon of the spectral phantom limb which is experienced by many amputees, here the identity of the patient has been disguised by the prosthetic device, and at the same time has transformed the patient into someone else by its material existence. This is a perfect instance of the history of the development of prosthetic technology as it stands, and falls, on its ability to play hide-and-seek with the truth. This is simultaneously a humanitarian success story and a story of inevitable failure. One story is about curative therapeutics, a pragmatic episteme of how medicine and technology come together with a shared compassion for the integrity of the human being to begin a process of reparation, to turn the *dis*abled into the *able*-bodied. Another story is about an ever more frantic effort to seek to conceal missing body parts, loss itself, by replacing them with artificial substitutes or surrogates, to replicate or imitate that lost object, an irreconcilable quest, to make the human body whole again, a will to verisimilitude that, in the end, simply draws attention to its own inability to approximate the real.[9]

In this patient testimony, then, success and failure turn on the edge between invisibility and visibility. Success is gauged in terms of invisibility, in terms of *not* being able to see the prosthetic device or its consequences. Given this, it is ironic that the success story of prosthesis is legitimated by its adherence to the truth of reparation when it is in fact determined by *hiding* the truth, making *invisible* the body's "disability" and the very thing that makes it "able-bodied" again. This sleight of hand allows the prosthetic wearer to carry out a so-called normal life safe in the knowledge that the rest of the world is unaware of their disability. But of course, the point is that as effective as evidence of this new invisibility might be in principle and *from a distance*, much like aesthetic surgery, so it is for prosthetic technology. In practice, our eyes can be deceiving. Once you get closer, intimate, there is always a small scar tucked away behind the ear or under the breast, or, in the case of prosthetic technology, a slightly irregular gait, or, as the letter indicates, a little bit of backache suffered by the patient, that evokes a memory, sometimes visible sometimes invisible, that is both a reminder of success and an admission of the failure to hide this truth.

This discourse of prosthesis as one of invisibility and visibility, success and failure, reparation and imitation, deceit and display, can be located in debates around aesthetic and cosmetic surgery especially towards the end of the nineteenth century, although its genealogy goes back much further than this, and in particular within the deeply ideological subject of "passing." While "passing" has been discussed recently by Judith Butler and Judith Halberstam in relation to questions of gender identity, performativity, and queer sexual practices, it is a topic that has also been revitalized by Sander L. Gilman in his cultural history of aesthetic surgery.[10] In *Making the Body Beautiful: A Cultural History of Aesthetic Surgery*, Gilman explores "passing," an aesthetic and, as I have already suggested, ideological undertaking, emerging directly out of the racialization of nineteenth-century culture, as a challenge by which an individual seeks to "pass" for something that they are not. This "passing" has historically assumed a variety of forms as an individual employs all kinds of aesthetic and medical deceits to become something other than what we are. This is not just a question of masquerading, then, but rather of actually *becoming* something other than what we are, looking to pass *as*, or pass *from*, say, being a man to being a woman, or vice versa, from being straight to being gay, or vice versa, from being black to being white, or vice versa, and so on. (One can see why theorists of gender subversion such as Butler and Halberstam would find this trope so productive.) Through this operation of passing, the individual passes from one category to another, for the most part moving in a not unexpected direction: from a category of exclusion to a community of inclusion, from being an abject pariah to an object of desire, from being anomalous to being something else more enviable.[11] And while it must be kept in mind that "passing" is inherently conservative because, as Gilman reminds us, unlike reconstructive surgery it is premised on a purely physical metamorphosis in which signs of physical difference, so called pathological signs, are camouflaged through modification, the *consequences* are none the less very real.[12] As Gilman makes clear, such acts of "passing" do have a profound effect on the correlation between an individual's desire to overcome their physical stigmatization and their psychological unhappiness, or, to put it differently, the *visible* efforts at redesign will have a direct impact on an individual's *invisible* interior emotional architecture.

Much like Gilman's account of aesthetic surgery in which "techniques must constantly evolve so as to perfect the illusion that the boundary between the patient and the group [that they wish to join] never existed,"[13] developments in prosthetic technology, as I have already indicated, are *in principle* committed to the same evolutionary imperative: working seamlessly in such a way as to make themselves invisible. Similar to the narrative that takes place in the discourse of aesthetic surgery,[14] an account of the development of prosthetic technology is caught up in ideological concerns that are similar to those embedded in "passing" and thus might be characterized, as does Gilman for aesthetic surgery, as "evidence of a new invisibility."[15]

Given the importance of this evidence of the new invisibility, that the truth and success of the discourse of prosthesis are premised on hiding the presence of the amputee's disability, their physical otherness, and that visibility makes failure all too evident, it is ironic that the photographs of female amputees produced by James Gillingham do the exact opposite. They *reveal* their prosthetic devices to show the virtuosity of their maker, the triumph of the technology itself, the possibility of their machinic articulations, and the impact that they will have on their user, the purchaser. Let us not forget that the photographs are serving a commercial purpose. Because of this, the wearer, the patient, the model is obliged to display, at the expense of their refusal to disclose, the technology in such a way as to draw attention to the very disability that the technology has been developed to disguise. While male amputees are often presented utilizing their prosthetic limbs as model examples of the enhancing potential of human-machine synergy, and are shown fully integrated in the world of both work and leisure activity, letters in the archives of the Science Museum and elsewhere from *female* amputees emphasize a need for continued disguise, and a pleasure in such disguise, a pleasure in modestly and discreetly being able to pass for something other than dis-abled, in this case to be able to pass for being able-bodied.[16]

This is why the *exposure* of James Gillingham's patients in his catalogues is particularly troubling. In playing this game of hide and seek, the models, the photographer, the photographs themselves, the people using the ads to select prosthetic machinery for themselves, and we viewers as competent interpreters of images are obviously aware of this pivot between invisibility and visibility, hiding and revealing, concealment and revelation, and the assault to modesty that this exposure entails. This play between concealing and disclosure, secrets and their confession, also of course lies at the heart of debates in the discourse of fetishism, and it is writ large here, literally, in the complex way in which the revealing of the fetishistic substitute, the artificial limb, acts as both a desire to overcome loss and a exposure of that very loss itself. It is no wonder, then, that a consequent sexualization of the figure of the female amputee ensues. It is also worthwhile pointing out that because these photographs are images of female amputees displaying their wares for commercial purposes, this display, this exhibition, is a dual seduction that is at once commercial and erotic. Certainly one needs to keep in mind that these images are ads, the purpose of which is to sell Gillingham's products. But at the same time, the interior setting, the studio, the lighting, the painted backdrops, the props, the drapery, the staged quality of the images, and the carefully posed figures of the women themselves, certainly imply that an effort has been made to employ the accoutrements of portraiture—as commercial imperatives themselves maybe—to both humanize and individualize. Perhaps these very aspects of portraiture, coupled with the "theatricized or narritivized tableaux" further eroticises.[17] Some of these women have been invited to lift up their shirts, others to remove their over-garments, so that a potential customer might see more precisely the quality of the products crafted by Gillingham. In giving in to this request to disrobe, the amputees assist in the selling of the calipers, body supports with underarm stirrups, leather bodices, corsetry, and artificial limbs that are Gillingham's speciality. In so doing, they expose their arms, the napes of their neck, the tops of their thighs, the shadow effected by the point at which the tops of their thighs and buttocks meet, revealing skin that has been trussed up by the confines of straps, (garter) belts, and buckles. Skin is squeezed and molded by the bondaged tautness of its restricted lacing, the back-straightening contraptions have a sadistic edge, and the hints of undergarment betray a less than prudent photographer inviting our voyeuristic gaze. With a twist of the hips, the women turn away from the camera, to obscure their faces, to remain anonymous and disguised, to keep their modesty intact and their identity a secret. By averting their gazes, they also endeavor to frustrate the attention that we might lavish on them, which could, in turn, distract our eye from more properly consumerist desires.

Part 2

Matthew Barney's Aimee Mullins:
Intimacy, Between Me and the Ground There Was Nothing

Aimee Mullins appears very differently in the final installment of American artist and filmmaker Matthew Barney's five-part *Cremaster* Cycle, begun in 1994. In this most recent episode that opened in 2002, unlike for Nick Knight, *Dazed and Confused*, Alexander McQueen, or Freeserve, Mullins is no longer the generic if individualized figure of sexual athleticism, the cyborgian sex kitten, or the eroticized amputee. Well, she is still all of these things, and explicitly so, but she is also somehow more. This may have something to do with the numerous guises that she slips into in Barney's *Cremaster 3*, the fictional parts that she takes on. These include: the character of Oonagh, the wife of the Irish giant Fionn MacCumhail; the role of Moll to Matthew Barney's Entered Apprentice; a unnamed woman sitting in a white room in the Cloud Club bar cutting potatoes with a device attached to the sole of her prosthetic legs; a figure known as Entered Novitiate, who quickly morphs into a cheetah divinity, languid one moment and fierce the next; and finally, at the very end of *Cremaster 3*, a dying, bleeding, blindfolded Madonna with a noose around her neck—which may or may not indicate sexual asphyxiation—who is sitting astride a flexi-glass sled tethered to five lambs and wearing clear prosthetic legs that end in man-o'-war tentacles. (And I shall return to this final image in a moment.)

To engage with these current incarnations of Aimee Mullins, and to distinguish them from her earlier phantasmatic, fetishized, and narcissistic manifestations, it is worthwhile focusing on the line of reasoning proposed by Nancy Spector, the curator of the Matthew Barney exhibition that toured the Museum Ludwig, Cologne; the Museum of Modern Art of the City of Paris; and the Solomon R. Guggenheim Museum, New York. As the first, and as far as I can tell the only person so far to discuss, to any great extent, Mullins in the context of Barney's artwork, Spector gives us a way into the figures of Aimee Mullins in her extended catalogue essay "Only the Perverse Fantasy Can Still Save Us."[18] For Spector, the whole of Barney's five-part *Cremaster* film cycle has developed as a project that is, as she says, "a self-enclosed aesthetic system" in which the body "with its psychic drives and physical thresholds—symbolizes the potential of sheer creative force." For Spector, Barney's "perverse imagination" takes us on a journey, a rite of passage, through his physical, psychological, and geographical landscape of "digestion, repression, and morphing," a landscape that emerges from and is carved out of the psychosexual and the libidinal, and is for her narcissistic, anally sadistic, and at one and the same time a masturbatory machine—much like Marcel Duchamp's *Bride Stripped Bare by her Bachelors, Even* (1934) to which she refers.[19] Always meticulous, Barney's *Cremaster* cycle has for Spector "an attention to detail that can only be described as fetishistic"[20] while overall its "creative potential of perversion pervades [its] very genetic code."[21] It is clear that for Spector to be in Matthew Barney's *Cremaster* cycle is to be enveloped in the perverse and fetishistic folds of psychoanalysis.

There is much to debate and much to disagree with in Spector's catalogue essay as well as in the exhibition itself. Nonetheless, for my purposes, the most straightforward way to engage with the roles of Aimee Mullins in *Cremaster 3* is to pit Spector's essay with and against another part of her catalogue entitled "Personal Perspectives" in which a number of the individuals involved in Barney's *Cremaster* cycle—including Gabe Bartalos, the prosthetic makeup and special effects expert;[22] Norman Mailer, a protagonist in *Cremaster 2*; Richard Serra, a character in *Cremaster 3*; Ursula Andress, a star of *Cremaster 5*; and Aimee Mullins herself—are given a chance to speak about their pleasures of working on it.

Having already appeared in a number of early scenes in various guises, Mullins's central performance is at the heart of *Cremaster 3* in a section of the film entitled "The Order" which 'rehearses the secret initiation rites of the Masonic fraternity.'[23] This section is made up of five scenes or degrees as they are called in the film, and each scene reveals Matthew Barney's character, a modification of his earlier incarnation, the Entered Apprentice, as a cross between Odysseus, Lara Croft, and Donkey

Kong, facing a challenge. This challenge is played out as a semi-comedic journey in which he scales the interior walls of the Guggenheim Museum, encountering combative obstacles as he progresses first up and then down the interior levels of the building's spiraling architecture. Each of the five Degrees of "The Order" is representative of one of the five episodes of the *Cremaster* cycle. Aimee Mullins comes into view in the third degree of "The Order," and thus personifies the third episode of the *Cremaster* cycle, *Cremaster 3* itself. She is a personification of the very film in which she acts, of which she is a part, and is thus for Spector the "narcissistic center of the cycle." Positioning Mullins in this way licenses Spector to claim that Mullins, as a character known as Entered Novitiate, a "couture model dressed in white gown with crystal legs," although I have always felt that her outfit is more naughty nurses uniform that couture, will mutate into "a hybrid Egyptian warrior whose lower body is that of a cheetah." For Spector, in this key role at the center of *Cremaster 3* Mullins "is, in essence, the Apprentice's [that is, Barney's] alter ego." Thus when Mullins and Barney confront one another face to face, Spector says that he is "facing himself in all his guises." She continues:

> Looking into the mirror of his own soul, he is transformed into an apparition of his female element. They embrace each other with the FIVE Points of Fellowship in a moment of exquisite oneness, and the model whispers the divine words *Maha byn*[24] into his ear. But she then abruptly transmutes into the cheetah and attacks. An intense struggle ensues, which continues intermittently throughout the Order, until the Apprentice uses the stonemason's tools to slay the hybrid creature; with a blow to the plumb of her temple, she drops to one knee; hit with the level in the other, she drops to both knees; and struck in the forehead with the maul, she falls dead. Having ceremonially killed off his own reflection, the Apprentice achieves the level of Master Mason…[25]

At the end of *Cremaster 3*, we are given a final image of Aimee Mullins, presented to us by Nancy Spector thus:

> The final image of the Order shows Mullins seated on a sleigh drawn by five baby lambs. She is dressed in the costume of the First Degree Masonic initiate. Blindfolded, she wears a noose around her neck. Blood spills from her temple and forehead, where she had endured the fatal wounds of the Mason's tools.[26]

I am less concerned than Spector is with Mullins as the narcissistic center of the cycle, as the Apprentice's/Barney's alter ego, the mirror of his soul, his feminine element, another wise, dead woman whose passing confirms the ascension of Barney's character to greatness. What interests me more is what Mullins has to say about this final scene in her "Personal Perspectives" section of Spector's catalogue. Mullins is well versed in the acknowledged and regulative symbolism of the *Cremaster* cycle. But while she is all too aware, confirming Spector's analysis, that her character is "essentially a reflection of Matthew's character,"[27] she also gives two alternative insights, political and personal, into this specific scene, neither of which is readily available in either Spector's text or Barney's *Cremaster 3*. The political insight is that when Barney "first told [her] about the Entered Novitiate character dressed as a candidate with the Masonic First Degree—with the left pant leg and right sleeve rolled up, the left breast exposed, blindfolded and wearing a noose— [she] thought, "I can't do that", [She] remember[s] thinking how many disability-rights activists were going to be calling [her], outraged."[28] The personal insight is even more telling:

> **The clear legs ending in man-of-war tentacles worn by the Entered Novitiate [in this final scene] evolved as a compromise. Originally Matthew had wanted me to do that scene without prosthetics. He saw this as a way to express the Masonic theory that you have to lose your lower self in order to reach a higher level. I guess the literal representation of that would have been for me to sit on the sled without any limbs below the knee, but that would have been difficult for me because it's very, very intimate. We had a long dialogue about what we could do instead, and Matthew came up with the idea of making the legs appear like jellyfish tentacles because they're not a human form and they're clear. It worked for me because I don't feel so bare where there's something between me and the ground.**[29]

I'm certainly not accusing Barney of being an amputee devotee. His desire to strip Mullins of her prosthetic legs so that he can make some spurious symbolic point is an act that on first viewing strikes me as *far more* disingenuous and boorish than that. In a sense, stripping her of her literal legs so that she can be seen to rise to a higher level replicates some of the most careless and ill-thought-through philosophies of disembodied techno-fetishism in which discussions of *post*-humanism are really little more than celebrations of *de*-humanization. This is what I earlier referred to as metaphorical opportunism. But if we put Barney's Masonic foolishness to one side, and listen carefully to what Mullins has to say, something quite surprising emerges. Hearing her say that to be without one's prosthetic limbs is to be exposed, to be laid bare, and that these prosthetic limbs are an emotional crutch as well as a corporeal support is not surprising. But learning that they are *a guard against intimacy* is unexpected. Or, rather, she tells us that it would have been too, too intimate to have appeared in *Cremaster 3 without* some kind of prosthetic machinery, even if the prosthetic takes the non-human anthropomorphic form of the tentacles of a large coelenterate hydrozoan, and even if it would not permit her to stand by herself, let alone to walk on her own. Anything, as long as there is something to stop her feeling the bareness between her self and the ground, to make sure that there is something, even if it is impossibly shaky and unstable, and makes you all the more vulnerable.

Although unrealized, in hoping to have Aimee Mullins appearing without her legs, her "cheetah legs," her "pretty legs," or even her man-of-war legs, Barney provides us with the chance to make out something very intimate, *too* intimate about the subject of prosthesis. And if you watch Mullins, you realize that there are, in fact, numerous moments of awkwardness throughout *Cremaster 3* in which we see her staggering around the set with her transparent legs, wobbly on her feet, walking backwards unsteadily, often on the brink of toppling over, holding onto the balustrade of the Guggenheim Museum for support, always trying to keep her balance on the oblique angle of the museum's run-way.

These uncomfortable movements, along with the far too intimate image of Mullins without her prosthetic legs, are redolent with a vulnerability that is not a ready part of the discourse of prosthesis with its overwhelming imperatives of rehabilitation, empowering, and resolute unshakability. And yet, here we have many scenes in which Mullins is truly perverse, but in a properly etymological sense of that word. She "twists" and "turns the wrong way" which is to say away from her figuration as a perverse erotic fetishistic object and towards an almost desperate celebration of the relative failure of movement wherein her prosthetic legs are not a *metaphor* of lack, but a *metonymy* of movement, a substitute for nothing, for the space between her self and the ground, that otherwise unbridgeable gap between immobility and touching the ground, undoubtedly an incitement to movement.[30]

*

In this chapter I have tried to say something about the tensions and contradictions between stillness and movement, between the stillness of photographic stills and the movement of moving image culture. Many of the questions that make up a provocative engagement with the discourse of prosthesis lie in the variegated gaps *between* stillness and movement, the hinge between the inanimate and the animate, the so called disabled body that is rendered somewhat inoperative and the ways in which that body is jump-started into all kinds of mobile modifications, however unstable some of these experiences might be. This is very much the position that Aimee Mullins finds herself in, in Matthew Barney's *Cremaster 3*. So while I am all too aware of some of the naïve assumptions I am making about differently-abled bodies in our visual culture, I am more acutely aware that it is necessary to be attentive to the danger that the stillness of images can cause to bodies already often either rendered immobile or overly technologized by metaphorical opportunism. For it is this stillness, such an integral part of the fixity of the process of stereotyping, eroticizing, and objectifying that has played such a destructive part in the history of disability and in the discourse of fetishism. It seems to me, at least in a provisional way, that fetishism, the practice of making an object a fixture, a mark of the recognition of disavowal, an inflexible substitute, a replacement for other things that have moved on for one reason or another, might be affected by the moving part of moving image culture. And at the same time, the discourse of *prosthesis* might wish to focus on the grey area between the inanimate and the animate, on the brink of articulation, which is precisely where we can best attend to the point of convergence between the metaphorization of the prosthetic body *and* its materiality; its moving flesh, as well as its wood, plastic, leather, metal, and hydraulic systems, because it is well worth remembering that the prostheticization of the human body does not mean a necessary material displacement of that body.[31]

While attending to this hinge between stillness and movement, between inanimate and animate, and to its effect on our understanding of both the material and metaphorical prosthetic body, I planned to move backward and forward across the question with which I began this essay: what kinds of erotic fantasies are being played out across medical, commercial, and avant-garde of the body of the female amputee in Western visual culture? In so doing, I did my best to keep two ideas in mind. The first idea was a need to be attentive to how two domains of visual imagery—medical/commercial photography and moving image culture—over the period of almost a hundred years offer almost identical instances of techno-fetishism. Having said that, I hope I have also begun to draw out some of the ways that these two instances of metaphorical opportunism are trying, intentionally or otherwise, to propose an alternative to such techno-fetishism, even if more often than not they fail to deliver in the end. (It is hard to envisage thinking fetishism through the movements of metonymy rather than through its structuring metaphorical dynamics.) The second idea was to consider how the discourse of prosthesis in its facility to articulate the confluence of bodies, technologies, and subjectivities, draws attention both to the role that perversion and fetishism play in the eroticization of visual imagery and some of the reasons why this might be so, and to the ways that we might be able to begin to think about perversion and fetishism, perverse practices and fetishistic objects, in ways that are resoundingly not sexual at all. In the end, I hope to have intimated that the discourse of prosthesis in fact makes it possible for us to begin to speak of fetishism and perversion in a way that is stripped of sexuality and eroticism, that exists beyond an economy of lack and, that endures in other kinds of productive practices, if one can imagine such a thing.

Notes

1. The word "articulate" is being used here to mean "having joints" rather than "to be able to speak fluently and coherently." (*Oxford English Dictionary*.) A longer version of this chapter appeared as Marquard Smith, "The Vulnerable Articulate: James Gillingham, Aimee Mullins, and Matthew Barney," in *The Prosthetic Impulse: From a Posthuman Present to a Biocultural Future*, ed. Marquard Smith and Joanne Morra, Cambridge, MA: The MIT Press, 2005. Earlier versions of this chapter were presented at the Courtauld Institute of Art in October 2002 at the invitation of Caroline Arscott and Gavin Parkinson, and at the Association of Art Historians annual conference at UCL/Birkbeck College in April 2003 at the invitation of John Wood, Aura Satz, and Helen Weston. Thanks to them for the invitations, and to the many interesting questions thrown from the floor during both events. Thanks also to Tim Boon and Craig Brierly at the Science Museum, London, and special thanks to Jean-Baptiste Decavèle, Vivian Rehberg, and, of course, to Joanne Morra.

2. See Vivian Sobchack, "A Leg to Stand On: Prosthetics, Metaphor, and Materiality," in Marquard Smith and Joanne Morra, eds., *The Prosthetic Impulse: From a Posthuman Present to a Biocultural Future*, Cambridge: Massachusetts, The MIT Press, 2005. For a background to the kinds of discussions developed in my essay see also: Katherine Ott, David Serlin, and Stephen Mihm, eds., *Artificial Parts, Practical Lives: Modern Histories of Prosthetics* (New York: New York University Press, 2002); David T. Mitchell and Sharon L. Snyder, *Narrative Prosthesis: Disability and the Dependencies of Discourse* (Ann Arbor: The University of Michigan Press, 2000); David Wills, *Prosthesis* (Stanford: Stanford University Press, 1995); Jacques Derrida, passim; Marquard Smith, "The Uncertainty of Placing: Prosthetic Bodies, Sculptural Design, and Unhomely Dwelling in Marc Quinn, James Gillingham, and Sigmund Freud," *New Formations*, vol. 46, (Summer 2002), 85–102; Marquard Smith and Joanne Morra, *The Prosthetic Aesthetic*, themed issue of *New Formations*, 46, Summer 2002; Allucquère Roseanne Stone, *The War of Desire and Technology at the Close of the Mechanical Age* (Cambridge, MA: The MIT Press, 1995).

3. This chaptr is in certain ways a kind of flirtatious "thinking through," an effort to be curious, skeptical, and hesitant, to display a certain lack of commitment to certain ideas in order to sustain their speculative promise. To avoid making categorical judgments. Here I follow Adam Phillips' book *On Flirtation*, in which he notes, following George Simmel's essay "Flirtation," that "every conclusive decision brings flirtation to an end." See Adam Phillips, *On Flirtation* (London: Faber and Faber, 1994), xxi.

4. See Sigmund Freud, *Three Essays on the Theory of Sexuality* (Harmondsworth: Penguin Books, 1977). For Freud perversions are largely (so called) "non-productive" sexual practices that *deviate* for goal-directed sexual practices. Instances

of this might involve an individual being interested in extended fore-pleasure or the deferral of coitus. The nineteenth century largely reserves perversion for men, women are rarely perverse, and are defined as anything other than perverse; hysterical, frigid, narcissistic, melancholic, psychotic, and so forth.

5. Michel Foucault, *The History of Sexuality, Volume I, An Introduction*, trans. Robert Hurley, (New York: Vintage/Random House, 1980). See also Robert A. Nye, "Medical origins of Sexual Fetishism," in *Fetishism as Cultural Discourse*, eds., Emily Apter and William Pietz, (Ithaca: Cornell University Press, 1993), 13–30, 19. Apter and Pietz's collection is still the most engaging edited volume on fetishism available.

6. In addition to Sobchack's essay, for other criticisms of this state of affairs see: Sarah S. Jain, "The Prosthetic Imagination: Enabling and Disabling the Prosthesis Trope," *Science, Technology, & Human Values*, vol 24, no. 1 (Winter 1999), 31–54; Rosemarie Garland-Thomson, *Extraordinary Bodies: Figuring Physical Disability in American Culture and Literature* (New York: Columbia University Press, 1997); David T. Mitchell and Sharon L. Snyder, "Introduction: Disability Studies and the Double Bind of Representation," in *The Body and Physical Difference: Discourses of Disability*, eds., Mitchell and Snyder, (Ann Arbor, MI: The University of Michigan Press, 1997), 1–31, 7, ftnt. 32. Mitchell and Snyder's "Introduction" includes a very useful overview of many of the issues at stake in techno-fetishism, ranging from a critique of Paul Virilio's writing on the subject to an embrace of N. Catherine Hayles's thought.

7. The Latin etymology of perversion, *pervertere*, means "to twist," "to turn the wrong way." This non-sexual etymology will have a profound impact on my later engagement with the art of Matthew Barney, and Aimee Mullins's place in it.

8. See Emily Apter, "Perversion," *Feminism and Psychoanalysis: A Critical Dictionary*, ed. Elizabeth Wright, (Oxford: Blackwell, 1992), 311–314. As Apter goes on to say: "The dismantled, disembodied body (Lacan's *corps morcelé*) is preferred to the integral or totalised corpus because it presents, as it were, a body composed of prosthetic parts (already split or symbolically castrated) rather than a body at risk of phallic loss. In each of these instances the choice of love-object is neither arbitrary nor convertible. Functioning as an ambient fetish or prosthesis, figured as an *idée fixe*, this object-type both motivates the fantasm and directs the questing of the subject of perversion" (312).

9. One needs to keep in mind the importance of the ideological differences between the discourses of reconstructive surgery (utility, rehabilitation, empowerment) and aesthetic/cosmetic surgery (beauty, passing).

10. Sander L. Gilman, *Making the Body Beautiful: A Cultural History of Aesthetic Surgery* (Princeton, NJ: Princeton University Press, 1999), esp. 21–42.

11. And of course, as Gilman makes clear, historically, there is a direct correlation between an individual's physical stigmatization and their psychological unhappiness. As successful aesthetic surgery after successful aesthetic surgery has shown, the removal of said stigma brings about psychological happiness.

12. For Gilman, this dialectical (or rather binary) process of passing is inherently debilitating because it is premised on the fact that passing is a purely, *and need only be a purely* physical metamorphosis in which signs of physical difference, so called pathological signs, are disguised through modification. (This is, of course, why "passing" is so important an idea for Gilman, because the desire to "pass" is the very foundation upon which aesthetic surgery is built, is the way in which purely cosmetic [which is to say deeply ideological] aesthetic surgery is distinguished from the necessary, utilitarian practice of reconstructive surgery.)

13. Ibid., 37.

14. This narrative is best exemplified in the "before and after" photographs that began (as an initiative, although not directly in relation to aesthetic surgery) in the 1840s and reached their point of saturation in the decades to come, notably, in images of the rebuilt faces of Civil War soldiers in the 1860s.

15. Ibid., 39.

16. As Katherine Ott has said on these matters more generally, "[c]onventions of female modesty, as well as ignorance about and public reluctance to discuss female anatomy" accounts for the relative scarcity of disabled female bodies appearing in medical textbooks at this time. See Katherine Ott, David Serlin and Stephen Mihm, eds., *Artificial Parts, Practical Lives* (New York: New York University Press, 2002), 11. A need for modesty and anonymity may have something to do with why all of the figures of female amputees are turned away, while the majority of the photographs of male amputees are not.

17. This phrase is used by Abigail Solomon-Godeau in "The Legs of the Countess," reprinted in Apter and Pietz, eds. *Fetishism*, 274, originally published in *October*, 39 (Winter 1986), 65–108.

18. Nancy Spector, *Matthew Barney: The Cremaster Cycle* (New York: Guggenheim Museum Publications, 2002).

19. Ibid., 25.

20. Ibid., xii.

21. Ibid., 25.

22. Of working with Bartalos, Mullins says: "It was fascinating working with Gabe because his whole world is the aesthetic prosthetic realm and mine is the mechanics of prosthetics," in *Matthew Barney: The Cremaster Cycle* (New York: Guggenheim Museum Publications, 2002).

23. Spector, *Matthew Barney*, 53

24. Earlier Spector says that *Maha byn* is "an untranslatable term that stands as a surrogate for the words of divine knowledge lost in Abiff's [the architect, played by Richard Serra] death, much as the Hebrew word "Jahweh" is a surrogate for the name of God" (Ibid., 44).

25. Ibid., 57.
26. Ibid.
27. Mullins, "Personal Perspective," in *Matthew Barney: The Cremaster Cycle* (New York: Guggenheim Museum Publications, 2002), 492–493.
28. Ibid., 493.
29. Ibid, 493.
30. At its most basic, and most significant, the point here is that as a metaphor, prosthesis is simply a symbol of something else—whether castration, emasculation, nationhood, body-machine interfaces, and so on. Spoken of as a metaphor—and this is an argument made well by Ott in her introduction to *Artificial Parts, Practical Lives*, and by Jain, and Sobchack—the discourse of prosthesis misses the fact that prosthesis is something incredibly complex in itself.
31. This is not about the autonomy or independent life of the fetishstic object—something both Freud and Marx comment upon.

26

Interlude 1

On (Almost) Passing

Brenda Brueggemann

3. Reasons you cannot be deaf

> *You don't sound funny.*
> *You don't talk too loud.*
> *You have such a nice voice.*
> *You're so normal.*
> *You can wear hearing aids.*
> *You can turn up your hearing aids.*
> *You can try harder.*
> *You don't have any trouble hearing me.*
> *You can do better if you try.*
> *You can hear anything you want to hear.*
> *You can try harder.*
> *You can never really learn sign language.*
> *You didn't grow up deaf.*
> *You didn't go to a deaf school.*
> *You tried to pass as hearing.*
> *You try to pass as hearing.*
> *You don't fit in.*
> *You don't get the jokes.*
> *You don't understand the language.*
> *You don't understand the language.*
> *You just don't understand*
> *the language.*
> *Reasons you can't be hearing:*
> *You can't hear.*
>
> —Ilene C. Caroom, *"Like Love, This Choice of a Language"*

It is much easier to pass as hearing than it is to feign deafness. To be hearing, you can try hard and harder, sound a little funny, talk a little too loud (and often, and fast), wear hearing aids (and hide them)—and you will, for the most part, pass well enough. I should know; I've done it all my life. If I were to write it, my brief biography would read much like Ilene Caroom's, the author of my epigraph: "Although she has a progressive hearing loss, Ilene C. Caroom was raised hearing, with hearing aids, and taught to lipread. She has a B.A. in English from Hollins College and a J.D. from the University of Maryland Law School."[1] While some particulars part us, the sum of our experience looks much the same: to hide my deafness, to pass as hearing, I've tried hard and done quite well. The reasons, as

321

Caroom herself outlines them and unreasonable as they may seem to the hearing world, abound for why I cannot be d/Deaf.

It was not until I had embarked on my "coming out" as a deaf person that I considered my rites of passage and dwelled on my acts, both deliberate and unconscious, both past and present, of passing. Because my coming out was a midlife event, I had much to reflect back on and much to illuminate ahead of me. This passing through an identity crisis, and the rites of passage involved in uncovering the paths of my lifelong passing as "hearing," took place in a hall of mirrors. Later I would come to know this place as the art and act of rhetoric.

I think I first saw myself mirrored in several students I met at Gallaudet University. I was thirty-two and finishing my Ph.D., writing a dissertation—that quintessential act of literate passing. What's more, I was finishing it by doing an ethnographic sort of study on deaf student writers at Gallaudet University; thus, I was using the guise of an academic grant and a Ph.D.—producing project as a professional foil to make a personal journey to the center of Deaf culture.

I was always good at finding a way to pass into places I shouldn't "normally" be.

So, there I was, doing time as a teacher and researcher at Gallaudet, collecting data for my study, taking a sign language class, living with a d/Deaf woman and faculty member at Gallaudet, going to Deaf gatherings, tutoring some of the students. Mostly, I was just trying to pass in ways that were both familiar and unfamiliar to me: to pass (unfamiliarly) as d/Deaf—and doing a lousy job of it—and to pass (more familiarly) as h/Hearing and thereby pass through this last of major academic hoops.

In this passing, I spent a good deal of time watching—an act for which I had, as a hard-of-hearing person, lifelong experience and impeccable credentials—watching myself, watching the students I was doing case studies of, watching everything in the ethnographic scene of Gallaudet Deaf culture before me. I kept seeing myself in and through many of the students I worked with in the "basic English" classrooms. They were the mirror in my ears. These students often had volatile, if not violent, histories of passing—especially academically. Most of them, by virtue of finding themselves "stuck" (there is a powerful sign for that—two fingers jammed into the throat, a desperate look on the face) in English 050, were still floundering mightily, struggling violently, to pass at basic English literacy. Having negotiated that passage rather adeptly I now, oddly enough, found myself struggling to squeeze through another doorway as I was myself engaged in a mighty, violent struggle to pass in basic d/Deaf literacy.

I don't think I ever got it right. Almost, but not quite. I couldn't be deaf any more than I could be hearing. I was hard-of-hearing; and therein I was as confused and displaced, in either Deaf or Hearing culture, as this multiply-hyphenated term indicates.

The mirror in my ears threw back odd images—distorted, illuminating, disturbing, fantastic, funny—but all somehow reflecting parts of me. It put my passing in various perspectives: perspectives of tense and time (past, present, future); perspectives of repeated situations and relationships in my personal and academic life; and perspectives about the ways that stories are told, identities forged, arguments made. These are but some of the things I saw as I passed through, by, on.

*   *   *

For some twenty-five years of my life, from age five on, I went to the movies. And while I think I always more or less got the plot, I missed everything in the dialogue. For twenty-five years I sat, passing time with a Three Musketeers candy bar, some popcorn, a Coke. I sat with my sisters as a grade school child on weeknights when my Mom had to work and my Dad was running the film from up in the little booth (both my parents had two jobs). To be sure, we often didn't sit so much as we crawled the aisles, playing hide-and-seek quietly in an always near-empty theater. Sometimes, more sensibly, I went to the lobby to do some homework. Through some films, though—the Disney classics and the cartoons that opened and closed each feature film—I did try to sit, to listen and watch. I don't think I had a conscious knowledge of it then, but now I know that I heard nothing, that I was a pro at passing even back then.

I got better, too, with age and the requisite social agility that becomes most junior high and high school girls. On weekends in my very small, very rural western Kansas town, the theater was the only place to go, the only thing to do. Past the Friday night football or basketball game, the movies beckoned; we'd often go to the same film both Saturday and Sunday night. Going to the movies was the only date possible in Tribune, Kansas.

I dated. They took me to countless movies, and I never heard a word. What's more, in the dark of the movie theater, with no hope of reading my date's lips as he struck up conversations with me, I nodded and feigned attention, agreement, acceptance all the more.

It now all seems so ludicrous, if not painful. For years I have listened to my friends—especially my academic friends—rave about movies, past and present. For years I have shifted back and forth on my feet at parties, smiling, nodding, looking genuinely interested in the discussion of this film or that. Not that I felt left out of their discussions. I just felt somehow disoriented, out of step—not quite passing. Like many deaf people, I not only saw films but enjoyed them. What I didn't know in all those years of adolescent pretense, but know so well now, is that I tend to enjoy films differently than hearing spectators do. I came to know that while they were concentrating on clues to solve the mystery, say, in the dialogue between characters, my eyes, a little more attuned to detail than theirs, would see in the background the weapon of death or notice the facial tension and odd mannerisms of the guilty party.

Take one example: in my early years of graduate school, one of the last years I still let dates take me to movies, I saw David Lynch's *Blue Velvet*. Just recently I had a conversation with my husband about that movie; it was a conversation based on memory, and on memory in different contexts since we had not seen the film together or even remotely in the same place. What I remembered, what I talked about, were vivid visual details of the movie: the ear lying in the grass that opens the movie, the color of Isabella Rossellini's lips and the way they pouted and quivered, the tenseness in her body, the vivid surreal scenes splashed like canvases in a museum of modern art. And while he himself pointed out how visual the movie was (as indeed most movies are), what my husband remembered most clearly were the conversations. He knew that the severed ear in the grass belonged to Rossellini's husband, that the husband had been kidnapped, and that her actions throughout the movie were done as ransom to keep her husband alive (plenty of reason for body tension and quivering lips). My husband knew this, of course, because they talk about it in the movie.

But I didn't know this. I thought the ear was a symbol of all the scenes of eavesdropping that appear in the film, nothing more, nothing less. I thought the severed ear and the blue velvet forged some artistic link to van Gogh and to Picasso's blue period. This was the sense I made with one sense missing.

So, when the pieces began to fit together and I began, late in my twenties, to understand that I understood precious little of movies beyond the roar of the dinosaurs in *Jurassic Park* or the catchy little tunes of the latest animated Disney "classic," I just stopped going. I had better things to do with my time than hog down a Three Musketeers and bad popcorn. There were other options for dates—especially since my dates now preferred to actually talk about the movie after it was over with, trying out their latest readings in critical theory on the poor, defenseless film over coffee, a drink, dessert. I couldn't hold up my end of the conversation, so I let it stop before it could begin.

I could not always stop conversations before they began, though. (If a genie were ever to grant me three wishes, this would definitely be one of them.) And more times than enough, I found myself pressured into passing and then greatly pressured by my passing. Some days, you see, I could pass; some days I could *almost* pass; some other days the rug almost got yanked out from under me.

My first high school sweetheart was, now that I look back, a real sweetheart; when he could have yanked, he didn't. He let me pass, and he let me do so with grace, saving my hidden deaf face, as it were.

What first attracted me to him was his gentle manner, his quiet, soft-spoken demeanor. It was that demeanor, of course, that doomed our relationship. He was a senior, I only a sophomore—and although I felt enormously comfortable around him (maybe because he didn't talk much, so I didn't have to listen much?), I wanted greatly to impress him. Apparently I did so, because a short month after dating several times, we were cruising main (the only option in Tribune besides "parking"—which only bad girls or longtime steadies did—or going to the movies) and Steve asked me to go steady with him, to wear his gigantic senior class ring. Actually, he asked three times. I didn't hear a one of them. But by the third time—even across the cavernous distance of his big Buick's front seat in the dark of a December night—I could *see* that he was saying something, trying *hard* to say something.

So I said the words that are surely the most common in my vocabulary: "What? Hmmmmm? Pardon me?" (I don't recall exactly which variation it was.)

Now Steve could have been mighty frustrated, out-and-out angry (and I would have not been surprised, since this response is all too common when we are asked to repeat something)—but instead he smiled in his gentle way, the way that had attracted me to him in the first place. He pulled the car over to the curb on main street right then and there, and he shut it off. He turned to face me directly and I could read his lips then. "I said," he still barely whispered, "would you wear my class ring?"

It was a bitter cold, blustery, snowy December night on the western Kansas plains. But I was hot, my face burning. Shamed. And shamed not so much at having not heard the question the first three times, but also in having myself, my deafness, so thoroughly unmasked. It felt as if someone were holding a mirror up to the sun with the reflected sunlight piercing through me. The mirror in my ears hurt. And it hurt even more because in that one fleeting instant in that big Buick at the age of fifteen, I realized, too, how DEAF I was. And I knew I would have to say "no" to soft-spoken Steve, his gentle ways, his giant class ring. I was not hearing enough; he was not deaf enough. And although I couldn't voice it at the time, I knew even then that this was more than just a sheet of glass between us, more than a barrier we could "talk" to each other through.

And I think—in fact, I'm sure—that he knew this, too. But still, instead of saying "never mind" or "oh, nothing" to my "What?" (the other most frequent responses) he let the moment play through, let me have the benefit of the words I had missed. He let me play at passing, let me play it as if it could really be, our going steady, our promise as a couple. He could have ridiculed me with taunts of "Gee, you just don't hear *anything*," or worse, in its "innocent" ignorance, "What's wrong, are you DEAF?" Those, too, are all-too-common responses to my requests that statements be repeated.

So, the moment passed. Steve and I didn't go steady. Nearly a decade later, when he and I were both married (to different persons, of course) we recounted this scene for our spouses; we laughed, they laughed. For a moment, Steve and I locked eyes—and I read it all there: he had known then, as he knew now, that I was indeed deaf. But neither he nor I, then nor at the present moment, would say the word. We let it pass. The conversation went on elsewhere.

*   *   *

When I began talking and working with deaf students at Gallaudet University as part of my dissertation research project, however, the conversation always went there directly: how I, how they, how we, coped with our deafness in personal relationships, especially with lovers and other significant others. We were trying out our mirrors on each other, trying to see if these multiple mirrors would help us negotiate the difficult passages we always encountered in relationships.

One student, David, an older nontraditional student, had mentioned several times in the course of his interview with me that his wife was far more deaf (in strict audiological terms) than he. It came up most strongly when I asked him directly about how much time he spent with hearing people and in "Hearing culture" as opposed to with deaf people and in "Deaf culture." His answer hinged on his relationship with his wife: "I have a little bit of a struggle with my wife over this issue. She isn't comfortable socializing with hearing people she doesn't know or with my hearing friends who don't sign. So I would end up having to interpret for her or stay right with her to keep her company. So I would either go alone, or go with her with a group of deaf people. I didn't have problems with either group [deaf or hearing], but she did have a problem with the hearing group." I mentioned, smiling, that were he asked, my husband might say some of the same things. We left the issue at that, and I went on to other questions. But at the end of the interview, when the videotape was off and the interpreter we used had left the room, David turned directly to me and in both spoken English and sign language, asked, "I'm curious. You said that you and your husband have similar communication problems in hearing situations since you are hard-of-hearing and he isn't. How," David paused, with genuine pain on his face, "do you work around this?" I could see that this was a sore spot, a blemish on both our mirrors. And unfortunately, I didn't have any particularly inspiring answers—no secret passageways to divulge and to help us both thereby solve this mystery more neatly, more quickly. We were (and are) both just stumbling and groping, looking for light switches in the often dark hallways of our deafness within relationships.

In the past, too, I had looked to others, more deaf than I, to help illuminate my way through the relationship with my new husband. When I first came to Gallaudet in 1991, I became good friends with a woman some ten years older than I. She had become late-deafened; her gradual deafness was probably genetic and the result of auditory nerve degeneration; her intellect, acumen, wit, and passion amazed me; she liked simple food and good beer and wine; she was the heroic single mother of four teenagers; and she enjoyed the company of men thoroughly. In the fantasizing way, I think, of adopted children who often feel as if they never quite fit with their own parents, and in this time of substantial identity shifting for myself (I was, you see, trying to come out in my deafness), I fantasized her as potential role model, a mentor, a long-lost mother—or maybe sister—of sorts. I held up the mirror to myself and saw her in it; I held up the mirror to her and saw myself in it.

What I watched most carefully in that mirror was my own just-married relationship with a hearing man and the various reflections of my newfound friend, whom I'll call Lynn, in her relationships with men, both deaf and hearing, past and present. It was not always a pretty sight—on either side of the mirror. What I saw in watching Lynn and in sharing many conversations with her about the dilemmas of life with a hearing man or life with a deaf man was as inspiring as often as it was scary. Either way, the specter of dependence, never really tangible in that mirror, always lurked: to marry a deaf man meant she (we) would be the one(s) that might be most depended on (especially because as late-deafened and exquisitely literate persons we had skills and experience well worth depending on)—and this, then, would leave us little room for the sometimes necessary dependence of our own; but on the flip side (the magnified side of that mirror?), marrying a hearing man might well mean we would come to be too dependent and would, therefore, put at risk our ability to pass on our own, as our own.

When the woman is deaf, in a culture in which the woman is still seen as typically more "dependent" in a male–female relationship, her further dependence on a hearing partner can dangerously diminish her autonomy. Yet at the same time men typically depend on women in certain specialized areas; as Bonnie Tucker has written in *The Feel of Silence,* her controversial autobiography about her deafness, men expect their female partners to carry out an array of social functions that demand precisely the kind of communicative competence that is challenging for the deaf. Women generally mediate between the home and the world in arranging the social obligations and daily domestic duties of (heterosexual) coupled and family life. This calls for speaking with many people, a high proportion of them strangers, both in person and by telephone (in stores, offices, schools . . .), in contexts in which the conversations can't be carefully anticipated or controlled. Discussing her own earlier marriage to a hearing man, Tucker sees the disruption of these cultural norms in the social parameters of male–female relationships as largely responsible for the fact that successful relationships between hearing men and deaf women are few and far between.

Within Deaf culture, there is more at stake than the bounds of the intimate relationship: to marry either deaf or hearing marks one, proffers one a pass, in the eyes of Deaf culture. Often immediately after the initial identity-confronting question that greets one—"Are you deaf or hearing?"—comes the next test: "Is your spouse deaf or hearing?" In the strictest of cultural terms, to marry deaf is to be Deaf; to marry hearing is to be Hearing. Of course, these strict terms constitute far more an ideal than a reality. Many deaf—and even Deaf—persons I know have nondeaf partners. Still, according to surveys conducted by Jerome Schein and Marcus Delk, over 68 percent of deaf people marry endogamously, with 86 percent expressing a desire to do so.[2]

To marry one or the other, then, is to pass as one or the other. Yet another reason why I have *al-*

most, but not quite, passed: when Deaf culture seeks to identify me, it holds up the mirror and sees my husband, a hearing man. He is a gentle man, a generally soft-spoken man—like the Steve I didn't go steady with. And yes, I must often depend on him in ways I'd much rather not—asking him to make phone calls for me, asking him to interpret or relay bits of conversation I've missed in social settings, asking him to repeat what one of my own children has said, asking him to help me bow out of uncomfortable social situations, asking him to order for me at restaurants, asking him to pronounce with exaggeration words I'm not sure of, and often, most difficult of all, asking him to just intuitively know when I want to pass on my own and when I want to depend upon him.

It isn't easy. Sometimes I feel like shattering the mirror: it shows me as "crippled," as "disabled" in my dependence.

*   *   *

It was a young woman, a new and very much struggling student, that I met at Gallaudet when I first went there and was so engrossed in my own coming out, so obsessed with my own identity, who first showed me and let me feel the shards of that mirror. She had been a student in the English 50 class I was a teaching assistant in; I had also tutored her individually and she had served as one of my in-depth case studies, meeting with me weekly for interviews and videotapes of her in the process of writing. We had come to know each other well. And although she looked, figuratively or literally, nothing like Lynn, the older deaf woman I now know I fetishized, I think the mirror drew us to each other—in the way most of us can hardly resist glimpsing ourselves, can hardly resist turning to stare at ourselves, when we pass by any reflective glass. This younger woman (whom, interestingly or conveniently enough, I had assigned the pseudonym "Lynne") turned to me as her model and mentor—me the mainstreamed, academically and somewhat socially successful woman, who had married a hearing man and got along, so it seemed, rather well in the Hearing world.

I hadn't realized how much she had turned to see me in her mirror (and I, in that way that we do when the mirror flatters us, not only had let her but had probably encouraged her)—I hadn't realized until toward the end of the semester I received several desperate long-distance phone calls from her mother in Nebraska. Lynne was not doing well at Gallaudet. It wasn't just her grades, although those were bad enough, to be sure. (Lynne was one of those lifelong products of mainstreaming—now found in abundance at Gallaudet—who arrived as a college freshman with little sign language skills and found herself immersed, even drowning, in Deaf culture and the precedence of sign language—yet another language now, in addition to English, that she didn't quite get.) Lynne was failing miserably in the Gallaudet social arena: she was lonely, depressed, even cast out. She just didn't fit. And her mother suffered for her, with her.

Back home, it turns out, Lynne had a hearing boyfriend. In righteous anger, her mother wanted her out of the "meanness" of Gallaudet, and so she had begun contacting me to seek my counsel on both the meanness and on getting Lynne out. Essentially, she wanted me to talk to Lynne and encourage her to abandon her long dream of studying at Gallaudet. Lynn's mother, understandably, wanted her back in the hearing world. It was mean there, too—but I think her mother had forgotten about that for the moment. What's more, she wanted Lynne married to a hearing man.

In a bit of conversation that jarred my very bones, her mother asked me if I was married. "Yes," I replied tentatively, not sure why this question had come up.

"Is he hearing?" she probed further. And then I knew just why the question had come up and where it was headed.

"Yes, he is," I confirmed.

"Are you happy—married to him?"

I sputtered a little, I remember, not quite comfortable with the suddenly personal tack that this conversation with a stranger some thousand miles away had taken. But I didn't know how to turn either back or away (mirrors are like this). "Yes," I answered simply.

"Well, good—then there's hope for Lynne, too. Would you tell her that? Could you tell her that she could be married—and happy—with a hearing man?"

I don't know what I said then. Stories and memories are selective, and, as Benedict Anderson has written, "all profound changes in consciousness, by their very nature, bring with them characteristic amnesias";[3] mirrors simply cannot say and show it all. But I do know that I felt deeply the pain of a shattered mirror—the pain of trying to be Lynne's inspiration, her role model, her fetish, her whatever. I could barely get it right for myself, could barely pass either as clearly and securely "d/Deaf" or as "h/Hearing"—how could I ever show someone like Lynne which, if any of those, to be?

I felt very much nailed to the threshold with several tons of doors, from both sides, closing on me.

*   *   *

When I get to feeling this way—trapped, nailed, stuck in between overwhelming options—I tend to get frantic, nervously energized, even mean. And my will to pass, to get through and beyond at all costs, kicks in ferociously. Some animals freeze in fear, shut down in fright; I run—harder, faster, longer. I run until I pass—until I pass on, or out.

And that running always seems to lead me to stories. I have always been a storyteller, a writer, a talker. These "talents" pass me off as "hearing" even as they connect me to "the Deaf way." "The Deaf way" revolves around narrative, around sharing stories—and the narration itself is, in Deaf culture, far more than incidental to the experience. Using sign language, Deaf culture prides itself on its "oral" and "narrative" nature. And for Deaf people, *who* tells the story and *how* they tell it is every bit as important as *what* the story is. The narrator, then, is in control of the experience instead of vice versa.

I tend to control conversations. This is not always a truth I am proud of, but it is the experience I present, the face I show in the mirror. I can talk a lot. I ramble, I chatter—especially on the phone and in one-on-one conversations. It is safer this way: if I don't shut up, if I keep talking, then voilà, I don't have to listen. And if I don't have to listen, I don't have to struggle, don't have to ask for repeats, don't have to assume any of the various appearances that I and other deaf/hard-of-hearing people often appear as—stupid, aloof, disapproving, suspicious. If I keep talking, I pass. I thrive and survive in perpetual animation.

But in situations in which animation affords me no control—in social settings with more than two in the conversation, for example, or as a student in the classroom—I resort quite rhetorically to another strategy: I disappear to what my mother and sisters called "Brenda's La-La Land." I just fade away, withdraw from the conversation. Here it is safer not to speak at all. For if I do, I am sure to be off-topic, three steps behind, completely out of sync with the others. Or even worse, if I speak, some-one might ask me a question—a question I would struggle to hear, would have to ask to be repeated (probably more than once), would fail then to answer with wit, intelligence, clarity, quickness. Passing is treacherous going here, so I usually choose not to even venture out, not to cross over the mythical yellow line that marks the divide between d/Deaf and h/Hearing.

When I do venture out or across, I've been trapped more than once—have talked myself right back into the deaf corner. You see, when I talk, people sometimes wonder. "Where are you from? You have quite an accent," I have heard times too innumerable to count—and usually from near strangers. The question is, I suppose, innocent enough. But my answer apparently isn't. For many years I used to pass myself off as German; it was easy enough since my grandparents were quite German and I, as the child of an army family in the 1950s, was born in Germany. Of course, having grandparents who once spoke the language and having lived there, attached to the U.S. Army, for only the first four years of my life didn't really qualify me as a native speaker, complete with an accent. But my interlocutors didn't need to know any of that; when I said "German," they were satisfied. "Oh yes," they nodded, completely in understanding.

But some years ago, as another act of coming out, I stopped answering "German." First I tried out a simple, direct, "I'm deaf." But the result was too startling—it rendered my audience deaf and dumb. They sputtered, they stared at me speechlessly, they went away—fast. It quite unhinged them.

So I have softened the blow a bit and begun to respond, "I'm quite hard-of-hearing." To this I get a split response, which probably fits those multiple hyphens in my identity—they will both smile and nod an affirmative, "Oh yes, I understand now" (although I know that they really *don't* understand the connections between hearing loss and having an "accent"), and they will also back away rather quickly, still reluctant to continue a conversation under these circumstances.

I didn't like passing as German, but I'm never sure I like their response to my real answer any better. When I see the fright in their eyes, the "oh-my-god-what-should-I-say-now?" look that freezes their face into that patronizing smile, I feel cornered again. I feel scared, too, for the way it reflects back on the way I saw myself for many years. I wish I had just stayed mute.

For all that it frightens me, though, when I get cornered and I see my scared, caught-between-the-hyphens, hard-of-hearing face in the mirror, something comes of it. This happened to me first, and I think most significantly, at my first successful academic conference. I had just finished my first year of graduate school and had journeyed to give a paper at the Wyoming Conference on English. I had attended the conference the summer before as well, but I had been in my silently passing mode. This year, however, I was animated by everything from a very positive response to my own paper on the first day, to the glitter of the featured speakers, to a headful of theory-stuff mixed near explosively with my first year of teaching college freshman in a university principally composed of minority and Appalachian, first-generation college students. I was primed. I was talking a lot.

On the third day of the conference we were having a picnic lunch up in the mountains; at a table with one of the conference's biggest stars, I was feeling lit up, I guess by the glitter he was sprinkling on me by showing genuine interest in my own projects and things I had said in earlier sessions. I was telling stories about growing up in western Kansas. Everyone was listening, engaged, laughing.

Then a woman across the table, slightly to the left of me, wearing a tag from some small place in Louisiana, I remember, asked me, point-blank, "So, how long have you been DEAF?" (And that word, especially, went echoing off the mountain walls, I swear.) The question did not fall on deaf ears. The table, full of some sixteen people, went silent—awfully, awesomely silent. They waited.

"A-a-all my life." Silence again. Eons of silence. Echoes of silence.

"Wow," said the star, and he touched my arm—a genuine touch, a caring touch, a you-don't-have-to-feel-bad touch.

But I felt plenty bad. I excused myself under pretense of wanting some more potato salad. Instead I went behind a giant pine tree on the other side of the chow table and tried to breathe, tried to think of how I could make it past those people, to my car, out of here, out of here, out of here.

I know that in this telling the incident may all sound quite melodramatic. But in that moment, I learned, if nothing else and quite melodramatically, that I am the narrator of my experience. I learned that there was a price for passing, that the ticket cost more than just a pretty penny, that the fear of always, at any moment, being "found out" was far worse than just telling at the outset. (Like telling a lie and having to remember who you told it to, who you didn't.)

And what was I so afraid of in the first place?

That moment in Wyoming, at the dawn of my academic career, shortly before I entered my thirties, was the first time I think I asked myself that question. And when I began asking it, I also began taking care and charge of narrating my own experience and identity. I began coming out. At the age of thirty, I took my first sign language class. And I cried mightily on the first night at the sheer thrill of not having to sit in the chair at the front and center of the classroom so I could "hear" the instructor—cried for the simple freedom of choosing my own seat. I also dreamed up a dissertation project, rhetorician that I was, that would take me into "deafness"—my own and others—and to Gallaudet University, to the "heart" of Deaf culture.

If nothing else, I could always write about it, read about it. I had been doing literacy, and doing it well, all my life as yet another supremely successful act of passing. In all those classrooms I disappeared from as I drifted off, when my ability to attend carefully was used up and I wafted away to Brenda's La-La Land, I made up my absence by reading and writing on my own. If nothing else, I could always write about it, read about it.

At Grandma's family gatherings for the holidays, Brenda was always in the other room, away from the crowds, reading. Nine times out of ten, when Brenda's high school friends went out for lunch and to quickly cruise main, Brenda went to the high school library and read (or wrote one of her crummy poems). The summer before she was to start college, Brenda spent her lifeguard breaks at the noisy pool in the corner of the office, plowing through a used introduction to psychology textbook she'd gotten from another older friend who was already at college. As it turns out, this plowing was what saved her when that fall she found herself in the cavernous intro to psych lecture hall with some three hundred other students—thankful that her name alphabetically allowed her to sit near the front, but still yearning to be an A so she could optimize the lecture from the choicest chair.

And she read. She bought or checked out a dozen more texts on psychology, biology, the skills of writing an essay. She took copious notes from each of them, recorded and memorized key vocabulary from them, read over those notes and her own in-class lecture notes (which she didn't trust) carefully each week, adding notes on top of those notes.

She spent most of her freshman year in the all-girl dorm holed up in her room, writing, reading, taking notes, passing. She went swimming—a silent, individual sport—for a "social" life. After that first frightful year of college it got better. The initial panic of failing, of being found out, subsided. She even skipped class now and then, forgot to study scrupulously for each and every test. She still passed quite well. She took a job—a safe one—lifeguarding in a tall, antisocial chair at the university pool on nights and weekends. She kept writing and reading, but now found her interests were far beyond ingesting college textbooks and taking careful notes; outside of her homework, she started working her way through Russian literature (don't ask me why) and writing short stories.

She avoided bars and parties—sooner or later a young man would come slosh a beer on her, ask her something, and not having heard him, but not wanting to appear any of those dreaded things, she would just nod "yes." It was not always the answer she meant to give.

Books were far easier to control. When she didn't understand a text, it didn't seem to mind her asking for a repeat. She could stare hard, be aloof, acquiesce without embarrassing consequences, speak out of turn, and question a book again and again. It didn't seem to mind. She wasn't deaf when she was reading or writing. In fact, she came to realize that we are all quite deaf when we read or write—engaged in a signing system that is not oral/aural and is removed from the present.

How many times must she have written—to herself or to someone else—"it's easier for me to write this than it is to say it; I find the words easier on paper." On paper she didn't sound deaf, she could be someone other than herself—an artificer (thus fulfilling Plato's worst nightmare about the rhetorical potential in writing). On paper she passed.

*   *   *

Through the years, although I've become more confident in public speaking and far more willing to unmask myself, my deafness, before others have a chance to, I've always been better at writing and reading than I have at speaking. In graduate school, I was given a prestigious fellowship—principally for my writing skills—and thus my colleagues, both the faculty and other graduate students, expected me, I think, to be a class leader, to speak often and well. I didn't. In fact, I later came to know that many interpreted my silence in the classroom as negligence about the reading, or just arrogant indifference. Negligence about reading was never a crime I was guilty of, although I might own up to some indifference. How could it be otherwise, when only two of my graduate school professors spoke loudly and clearly enough for me to understand more than half of their mumbled, head-down, lifeless, eyes-stuck-on-the-page lectures?

Mostly I was still afraid of myself—still scared of what I saw when I stood in front of the mirror and spoke. As long as I had a written text—something I had worked on and rehearsed in order to smooth out my odd "accent," my tendency for fast talk and illogical progression, and my tonal infelicities—I could be comfortable speaking from and through it. But just to speak well extemporaneously—this was risking breaking the mirror, seven years' bad luck. Writing smoothed the blemishes, softened the sharp edges.

Even when I teach, I teach from and with writing, thereby maintaining control. I avoid, at all costs, leading large group discussions that involve the whole class, discussions in which students might speak from the back of the room—from the places where even my hearing aids on the highest setting won't go. I put them in small groups for discussion and then I walk around, lean over their shoulders, sit down with a small group for a short time. Then I bring one group to the front of the class to help me lead the whole class through discussion, branching out from what they were talking about in their smaller groups. In this way, the students take charge of receiving the questions and become interpreters for me and each other. I like to argue that in this process they gain a new kind of responsibility and learning that they might not have had before; but I know, truth be told, that it's mostly just a matter of getting *me* past some of the more difficult parts of teaching.

My premier pedagogy for passing is, of course, writing. My students, even in the more literature-based classes, write a lot. They always keep journals; they always write too many papers (or so it seems when I'm reading and responding to all of them). And my students, for sixteen years now, are always amazed at how much I write in responding to their journals and papers. For here is a place where I can have a conversation, unthreatened and unstressed by my listening limitations. They write, and I write back.

Writing is my passageway; writing is my pass; through writing, I pass.

Notes

1. Ilene Caroom's poem and her brief biography appear in Garretson, *Deafness,* p. 8.
2. These figures, to be sure, are likely somewhat outdated; see Schein and Delk, *Deaf Population of the United States,* pp. 15–34.
3. Anderson, *Imagined Communities,* p. 204.

27

Deaf People
A Different Center

Carol Padden and Tom Humphries

In Chapter 1 we quoted our friend Howard, who said "I never knew I was deaf until I went to school." Howard's statement shows that the meanings of DEAF and "deaf are, at the very least, not the same. DEAF is a means of identifying the group and one's connection to it, and "deaf " is a means of commenting on one's inability to speak and hear. During a conversation with another friend, we began to understand that behind the two supposedly straightforward terms "deaf " and DEAF lie worlds of meaning that are rarely described.

The subject was whether a mutual acquaintance could use the telephone. She couldn't use the phone, our friend told us, because she was only "A-LITTLE HARD-OF-HEARING." We understood this to mean that the woman could hear only a little, not well enough to use the telephone.

On another occasion, another Deaf friend brought up the name of a woman we did not know, and explained that she had many of the recognizable characteristics of a person who could hear well, because she was VERY HARD-OF-HEARING. Our friend added that this woman regularly used the telephone to conduct business.

At the time, we did not recognize the conversations as strange; we did not think about the fact that these ASL terms, if translated literally into English, would mean the opposite of what they mean in English. Instead of using A-LITTLE HARD-OF-HEARING to mean someone whose hearing is only slightly impaired, and VERY HARD-OF-HEARING to mean someone who doesn't hear well, we and our friends used the signs to express exactly the opposite of their English meanings.

It was not until much later, when an older member of our community, Dan, asked if we realized that the signs A-LITTLE HARD-OF-HEARING and VERY HARD-OF-HEARING were being used incorrectly by some Deaf people, that we began to understand. Dan offered an explanation for these "errors": he said they were the kinds of mistakes Deaf people are inclined to make because they lack skill in the English language. We were not surprised by the explanation; at one time it would probably have occurred to us to say the same thing. Deaf people cannot hear English, so they learn it imperfectly. In this case, it was simply a matter of getting the meanings backward. Deaf people ought to be made aware of these kinds of incorrect uses of signs, Dan told us.

But if they were mistakes, we wondered, why did so many Deaf people, including those fluent in English, use them in this way? Perhaps these were not errors at all, but simply a different set of meanings. Signs from ASL are often thought to be direct representations of spoken words, but in fact they are independent of English. Although signs and their translations may have overlapping meanings, signs are not simply codes for English words. We told Dan he should describe signs in terms independent of the English words used to translate them.

But Dan was ready with his next argument. Surely we had noticed that not all Deaf people use the terms in the "wrong" way. Some, in fact many, Deaf people use the signed phrase A-LITTLE HARD-OF-HEARING to mean a person who can hear quite well and VERY HARD-OF-HEARING for someone who cannot hear well at all. What explanation did we have for that? We had to agree that these terms were also being used according to the "correct" English definitions.

Faced with two opposite sets of meanings, Dan decided that the way to resolve the contradiction was to assign a "correct" definition for HARD-OF-HEARING, and for that he chose the one that conformed to the English meaning. The other use of the term was simply incorrect in his eyes, and no amount of arguing could sway him. There must be one official definition, and any others must be simply wrong.

Our first clue to an explanation for these backward definitions came from a story another friend told us. At a football game between two Deaf schools, he saw members of the home team refer to the opposing team as HEARING. Even though the name of the opponents' school was prominently displayed on the scoreboard, the home team had strangely "forgotten" that the opponents were also Deaf. We exchanged laughs. But it occurred to us that this "error" brought out a key concept in defining HEARING: HEARING means the opposite of what we are.

The sign HEARING has an official English translation, "can hear," but in ASL HEARING is aligned in interesting ways with respect to DEAF and HARD-OF-HEARING. In ASL, as in English, HARD-OF-HEARING represents a deviation of some kind. Someone who is A-LITTLE HARD-OF-HEARING has a smaller deviation than someone who is VERY HARD-OF-HEARING. In this way, ASL and English are similar—and yet the terms have opposite meanings in the two languages. The reason for this is clear: for Deaf people, the greatest deviation is HEARING.

This is the crucial element in understanding these "backward" definitions: there is a different center, a different point from which one deviates. In this case, DEAF, not HEARING, is taken as the central point of reference. A-LITTLE HARD-OF-HEARING is a small deviation from DEAF, and thus is used for someone who is only slightly hearing. VERY HARD-OF-HEARING is someone who departs from the center greatly, thus someone who can hear quite well.

Once we had noticed the different meanings, we began to watch how these terms were used. Many of our friends, like us, did not use one definition exclusively, but often switched meanings according to context and situation. The switching never seemed awkward or confusing, but was normal and expected; the shifts were unconscious. Until our friend brought them to our attention, we had never thought about how we used the terms.

These definitions of DEAF and HARD-OF-HEARING are not remarkable and isolated examples, but are indications of a larger world of meaning where there are conventions for describing relationships between conditions and identities. Within this world of meaning—compared to that of English and the world of others—there is a different alignment, toward a different center.

We knew from our conversations with friends and colleagues that these labels and definitions and many more that Deaf people give themselves and others would compose a rich area of study, one often overlooked in favor of "official" or literal English meanings. When we began writing this book, people often asked us about whose lives we would describe. One friend asked if we would only write about our professional friends, or if we would also include "the average Deaf person." He reminded us that there were a lot of "average Deaf people" out there and we couldn't write only about "exceptional" Deaf people. Not all Deaf people were like us, and he wanted us to be sure to address the problems of those victimized by poor education.

Another friend, testing us, asked if we planned to write about "peddlers," the itinerant vendors who make a living by selling tokens and alphabet cards in exchange for donations. Would our book be about only the "hard-working, honest Deaf person," he asked with a hint of irony, or about all Deaf people, including the seamier types? Other friends suggested we write a book that would set "a good example" to the "hearing world" by focusing on "the intelligent Deaf."

Each recommendation, each label, points to a group within the central category of DEAF, but more clearly to us, the recommendations taken together reveal a rarely described world of meaning used by people who refer to themselves as DEAF. As we began to sort out the different categories, we focused not so much on who was in each category as on how each category was used as a way of talking about the self and about relationships with other people.

Some of the labels we came across are not used to establish commonality, but are used to label certain people as having lesser status—to marginalize them. To ignore the ways that Deaf people use a variety of labels, those which mock and tease as well as those which praise and respect, not only would paint an overly romantic picture but would make our description less rich. Each label, however petty or harsh some might seem, in its own way helps us to understand the group's deep beliefs and fears.

We started with what seemed to be the most straightforward distinction, that between DEAF and HEARING. What is DEAF? DEAF is first and foremost the group's official name for itself. Deaf organizations take care to specify "of the Deaf" in their names, as in the American Athletic Association of the Deaf, the National Fraternal Society of the Deaf, and the National Association of the Deaf (NAD). These official names contrast with that of an organization recently founded to meet the needs of adults who have lost their hearing at later ages: Self-Help for the Hard of Hearing (SHHH). Although this group's membership includes people who are deaf, its social and political agenda is distinctly different from those of the other organizations. A look at the programs for recent national conventions makes the differences clear. The NAD regularly features workshops on sign language, on improving the image of Deaf people in the media, and on how to lobby for local social service agencies "of, by and for the deaf." In contrast, SHHH offers workshops on promising new medical treatments for hearing impairment, on improving lipreading skills, and on how to use assistive devices such as amplifiers. Although in recent years the term "hearing impaired" has been proposed by many in an attempt to include both Deaf people and other people who do not hear, Deaf people still refer to themselves as DEAF.

A chance meeting with a Deaf acquaintance on the San Francisco subway (the BART) told us something about what DEAF is not. After the usual greetings, we began to make conversation: Did he work in San Francisco? Did he enjoy riding the subway? He did, and he told us he always rode the Bart because he could take advantage of a "handicapped" discount that made the subway much cheaper than driving to work. But then, quickly, he added, "I don't like using this disabled discount." We nodded sympathetically, and he continued, "But, hey, they offered it to me anyway, and look at how much money I'm saving." We congratulated him on his effective use of public funds. But we took note of his uneasiness and understood that for him the term "disabled" describes those who are blind or physically handicapped, not Deaf people.

"Disabled" is a label that historically has not belonged to Deaf people. It suggests political self-representations and goals unfamiliar to the group. When Deaf people discuss their deafness, they use terms deeply related to their language, their past, and their community. Their enduring concerns have been the preservation of their language, policies for educating deaf children, and maintenance of their social and political organizations. The modern language of "access" and "civil rights," as unfamiliar as it is to Deaf people, has been used by Deaf leaders because the public understands these concerns more readily than ones specific to the Deaf community. Knowing well the special benefits, economic and otherwise, of calling themselves disabled, Deaf people have a history, albeit an uneasy one, of alignment with other disabled groups. But as our friend on the subway reminded us, "disabled" is not a primary term of self-identification, indeed it is one that requires a disclaimer.

*   *   *

Our friend's uneasiness brought us back to an earlier debate among Deaf people about how they should represent themselves to others. Beginning during World War II, Deaf organizations and political leaders began to complain of an alarming increase in the number of deaf peddlers who were soliciting donations from the public. Although deaf peddlers have existed at least since biblical times, these organizations made it clear that peddling by these "able-bodied louts" would no longer be tolerated by "honest and hard-working" Deaf people.

An older member of the community used the sign BEGGING when he talked about peddlers, but technically, to avoid vagrancy laws, peddlers do not beg but sell inexpensive tokens in exchange for "contributions." After the war years, they sold packets of adhesive bandages with small cards explaining that they were deaf and had trouble finding jobs and feeding themselves and their families. The backs of the cards characteristically had an illustration of the manual alphabet with a short note: "Learn to Communicate with the Deaf!" After the war, railroad stations and downtown bars were favorite places for peddlers. A dime or a quarter was the usual contribution; on a good day, a peddler could make between $25 and $30. Peddlers still make their rounds today, but popular wisdom has it that they are "heavily into drugs." Their places of operation have been upgraded to airports and shopping malls, and they sell not bandages but combs, pens, scissors, or religious bookmarks.

The debate about peddlers probably reached its highest and most emotional point after the war. Along with the subject of sign language, a frequent topic in columns and letters to the editor in popular Deaf newsmagazines was the "problem" of peddlers. Arthur L. Roberts, the president of the National Fraternal Society of the Deaf ("The Frat"), wrote relentlessly against peddlers in the organization's publication. In one editorial he wrote: "Tell citizens they should refuse to contribute a cent to these able-bodied louts who ride around the country in good automobiles, stay at good hotels, 'work' only a few hours daily, and ridicule the gullibility of the public which supports them with their ill-gotten means of livelihood" (Roberts 1948). Roberts also made attempts to confront peddlers personally, including posting a list of names of alleged peddlers in the local Deaf club hall. The hearing son of a reputed "king" peddler, an attorney, threatened to sue him for libel and the list was removed.

The NAD established a Committee for the Suppression of Peddling, and in its official publication, the *Silent Worker,* invited readers to offer suggestions for "wiping out peddlers." Occasionally a minority voice was printed, decrying the leaders for their vicious campaigns:

> How I wish Mr. [Arnold] Daulton and his committee for the suppression of peddling could come down to Arkansas and get a glimpse of the number of unemployed here—men with mouths to feed and no money to feed them with. I just don't have it in my heart to condemn these men when, after months of struggling with their conscience, they take to peddling. I have been loud in my protests against peddling, but I know that to solve a problem you must get to the root of it. Get our Arkansas peddlers jobs! I'll bet my last nickel there wouldn't be any peddling in our town then. (Collums 1950).

The Frat and the NAD, with their new leaders, wanted a visible social and political agenda, and a crackdown on peddling was consistent with their beliefs about how to improve the lives of Deaf people. They believed that Deaf people's economic difficulties stemmed from a public image of them as lazy and ineffective. Each Deaf person was individually responsible for maintaining an appropriate image to the public. Roberts firmly believed that eliminating peddlers would also eliminate the larger society's perception that Deaf people were beggars.

A play set in a fictitious Deaf club, *Tales from a Clubroom* (Bragg and Bergman 1981), brings to the surface the tensions revealed by the controversy about peddling. The club's members snipe about a "flashy well-dressed" peddler who comes to their socials and acts as if he is one of them. But the peddler has a ready answer for those who accuse him of not getting a job and of stealing from the "hearies": "You accuse me of stealing money? Who, me? No, you're wrong. I'm only taking back what hearing people took from me because I'm deaf " (Bragg and Bergman 1981:113). Whatever the justification raised for peddling, it is counter to the way most Deaf people see themselves or want others to see them.

*   *   *

Peddlers are drawn from the ranks of what is often referred to as "the average deaf person." Leo Jacobs, in *A Deaf Adult Speaks Out* (1974), identifies nine categories of deaf people: the average deaf adult, prelingually deaf adults who come from deaf families, other prelingually deaf adults, low-verbal deaf adults, uneducated deaf adults, products of oral programs, products of public schools, deafened adults, and hard-of-hearing adults.

The first category is an important one for Jacobs. In English one might say "I'm just your average American," but in ASL the phrase "average deaf person" does not have the same quality of normality; instead it suggests someone "simple" or lacking in knowledge of the world. Deaf people who are competent in the English language and have a reasonably good knowledge of others' world are not "average" but "educated." Jacobs rails against the victimization of Deaf people that has resulted in a large group of those called "average," those who suffer because of ignorance, poor education, or poor childrearing practices. The term acknowledges the common belief that the average deaf person is more likely than not to have been victimized in this way.

The label L-V ("low-verbal") is used for educational unfortunates, but often also as a blanket term for low-income ethnic minorities. A common alternative term for L-V is "not smart." Jacobs describes these people as having "missed for various reasons a great deal of education that they should have received," so that they are almost illiterate. When we once inquired about attending a Deaf club in an urban area, we were told that we would not find it useful to go because members of the club were mostly L-V. Carol was told as a child that many Deaf peddlers were L-V, manipulated into working for unscrupulous king peddlers. More informal terms include, loosely translated, "those out of it," "locals," and "those who do drugs." Again, although these distinctions primarily refer to educational features, they are ways of labeling the uneducated, the working poor, and the chronically unemployed.

With his use of the term "prelingually," Jacobs acknowledges the official distinctions others use for the Deaf population. Those who "lost their hearing before the acquisition of language" are called "prelingually" Deaf, while "postlingually" Deaf is used for those who lost their hearing after having acquired "language." "Language" in this sense, of course, is used to mean English, not sign language. The distinction ignores those who have learned sign language as a first language, and who hence are native users of a human language, like those who are "postlingually deaf." The terms, as would be expected within an official frame with HEARING at the center, emphasize the role of onset of hearing loss and the presence of English, rather than the age at which any human language, including ASL, is acquired.

But Jacobs modifies this distinction and incorporates another; working around the official frame, he adds a new category: "prelingually deaf adults who come from deaf families." He writes that members of this category are "more outgoing and at ease with other deaf persons" and are less likely to have feelings of inferiority. "Other prelingually deaf adults," that is, those who do not have deaf families, form "the bulk of the deaf community," and "come from hearing families who have had trouble communicating with them when they were little." Jacobs adds the unfair generalization that "they are for the most part less aggressive and confident" than those "prelingually deaf adults who come from deaf families" (1974:56–57).

* * *

Deaf children of Deaf parents may have a respected status among Deaf people because they display effortless facility in the language of the group. But like all the distinctions we have been discussing, this one is not simple. For one thing, outside the group, the notion that parents knowingly gave birth to children when there was a good possibility that the children might be deaf is not an acceptable one. This opinion of others has insidiously affected the way Deaf people view their own Deaf children. On the one hand they are respected and on the other stigmatized.

Out of this deep contradiction, the two groups, Deaf children of Deaf families and Deaf children of hearing families, play out their public images and respond to this tension in different ways. The husband of a Deaf couple told us that for a long time he harbored feelings of superiority over his wife when he introduced himself as having lost his hearing in childhood. His wife, on the other hand, introduced herself as having Deaf parents. By explaining that he had lost his hearing, he could avoid the silent condemnation he believed hearing people directed toward his wife, who had inherited her deafness. He himself could not be held responsible for his condition because he had become deaf "by accident," that is, through illness.

Stories we have heard about hearing children born to Deaf families also involve conflicting sentiments that reveal the complexity of the rules for categorization and identity. For example, a friend told us about a recent dispute at a local Deaf basketball club over a hearing son of Deaf parents who wanted to play for the club. Because this young man could hear, he would have been automatically barred from playing in any games sanctioned by the American Athletic Association of the Deaf (AAAD). Sports organizations like these are one of the few places where Deaf people exercise almost total control over their own affairs, from deciding their own rules to determining who qualifies as a member. And one of the inviolable rules is that hearing players cannot play, on grounds of "unfair" competition. But in this particular case, the club's officers wavered and delayed action that would have removed the player. When the officers of the regional organization learned that the club had a player who was not "legally" Deaf, they pressed the club to act. Recognizing that the hearing player was in all other respects a member of the group, behaved as a Deaf person, and was virtually indistinguishable from his teammates, the club tried labeling him HARD-OF-HEARING. When the regional officers insisted on an audiological test, the club's officers knew they had played their last card and regretfully asked him to leave the team.

The club probably would not have tried to violate the rules if the hearing player had not had Deaf parents. There would have been no question of his being allowed to play. Despite the national organization's watchfulness, there are stories of other basketball clubs where "arrangements" are made allowing hearing children of Deaf parents to play, either "illegally" or at non-AAAD-sanctioned games. No such allowance is ever made for genuine outsiders.

Hearing children of Deaf parents represent a special problem. They have blood ties to Deaf people as well as knowledge of the customs and language of the group. The club officials knew their efforts to keep the player would be supported by the members, and their attempt to label him HARD-OF-HEARING was a desperate but not impossible move to keep him within the category of DEAF. When that move failed, they had no choice but to remove him. In matters where these labels count, such as competing fairly for a prize, the boundaries between DEAF and HEARING are firm.

*   *   *

Real HARD-OF-HEARING people walk a thin line between being Deaf people who can be like hearing people and Deaf people who are too much like hearing people. They can be admired for their ability to seem like others for specific purposes, but they are viewed with suspicion when they begin to display behaviors of the others when there is no apparent need to, such as when there are no hearing people present. A friend who uses the telephone "without effort" confided that in the presence of new Deaf acquaintances she finds herself feigning difficulty on the telephone to avoid being categorized toward the hearing end of the HARD-OF-HEARING continuum. Another Deaf woman whose Deaf parents and friends call her HARD-OF-HEARING remembers that in her adolescence her parents showed surprise and disbelief when she described having problems communicating with her hearing co-workers. "But you can hear and talk," they told her. Since she was more like hearing people, she was not entitled to make the kinds of complaints Deaf people use about the difficulty of communicating with hearing people.

A hard-of-hearing friend who successfully walks this line was described as "DEAF but really HARD-OF-HEARING," an acknowledgment of his ability to use his skills selectively. HARD-OF-HEARING people can also be DEAF, but there is an imaginary asterisk by their label, qualifying them from time to time.

The label HARD-OF-HEARING involves discussion about having characteristics like hearing people, but being called ORAL is a stronger accusation. A Deaf man reported that though he had no hearing and his voice was barely intelligible, he had become used to being called HARD-OF-HEARING because his mouthing behavior was very "hearing-like." He had lost his hearing at six years of age and did not mind being called "deafened," but he drew the line at being called ORAL. Because ORAL represents a misaligned center, the results of having made wrong choices in life, it is an unacceptable insinuation to someone who considers himself DEAF.

The sign ORAL incorporates a long social and political history of the role of the school in the community. "Oral" schools promote ideologies counter to those of Deaf people; "manual" schools, which allow use of signed language in the schools, are ideologically appealing to Deaf people. Although the term "oral" is slowly losing its traditional context—many schools are no longer represented as either "oral" or "manual," the labels having been replaced by newer terms such as "total communication"—it is still used to represent an ever-present threat, the malevolent opposition.

At a conference for teachers of ASL, a woman stood before her peers and warned that while teachers squabble among themselves about signed language and the different "sign systems," there are "oralists" out there hatching new plots to remove signed language from the education of Deaf children. Let us not forget our true enemy, she proclaimed.

ORAL recalls many extreme stereotypes; our friends gave us two: MIND RICH and ALWAYS PLAN. ORAL individuals are stereotypically represented as members of the establishment, as coming from hearing families that are inflexible about their children's behavior. As the belief goes, the richer the family, the more likely the family will embrace oralism (MIND RICH). The second stereotype portrays a typical ORAL person as one who actively tries to pass as hearing, and must be alert to every possible situation in order to pass successfully (ALWAYS PLAN). In its strongest connotations, ORAL means one who "cozies up to the opposition" and uncritically embraces the world of others.

ORA FAIL ("oral failure") is a term used for those who are products of oppressive educational programs. Deaf teachers talk of having to take in "oral failures" in their "manual" classrooms, of having to take care of others' "rejects." One example appears in *A Deaf Adult Speaks Out*:

> The deaf pupils were only allowed to change to "manual classes" when they proved to be failures in the oral method, usually during their adolescence. These older pupils were generally considered to be brain damaged, aphasic or "slow" by their teachers. Thus many bright and capable youngsters were labeled failures in everything else. Thus incalculable damage was done not only to their self-image but also to their capabilities for optimum achievement toward desirable careers. (Jacobs 1974:34)

"Oral failures" are, like ORALS, those who pay the price for wrong life choices, but they can be redeemed and become #EX ORAL. (The symbol # is a convention used to represent vocabulary borrowed from fingerspelling.) Jacobs recounts stories of "oral failures" who recover from the damage done to them in their early years and, with the help of instruction in signed language, regain their hidden abilities: "Ted found himself when he discovered manual communication, and was soon making astonishing progress. He caught up with his age level, and displayed an extraordinary bent for mathematics. His language developed at such a rate that he was writing fairly adequate English at the time of his graduation from the school" (p. 36).

In *Tales from a Clubroom,* members of the club charitably call their resident oralist, Spencer Collins, an #EX ORAL because he has repented and joined their ranks. But his slow, lumbering manner remains a comfortable symbol to the others of his past and their own good luck in not being ORAL themselves.

Stories about people like Collins are popular. They are defectors from others' world, those oralists who, when they come of age and are free to make their own choices, join the world of Deaf people as adults and learn signed language. Carol remembers as a child attending an evening at a local Deaf bowling league where a friend pointed out a woman several alleys down. This woman's father was a prominent leader of oral education, the friend said, and yet here she was, mixing and signing with us like a regular. She had rebelled against her father and married a Deaf man! The defection was as significant as that of a daughter of a prominent Soviet party official. All it takes, Carol's friend explained, is a taste of our world and they want to leave the old one behind.

In fantasy storytelling, an ORAL is a powerful symbol of one in need of being rescued. At a party, a man told a variation on a Cinderella story with an impoverished ORAL girl. The simple structure of the fairy tale highlighted the idealized difference between those who are ORAL and those who are DEAF. This deaf Cinderella is given a pair of glass gloves by her fairy godmother, allowing her to sign effortlessly and gracefully. Her ragged clothing disappears under her godmother's wand, and she finds herself wearing jewelry made by Deaf artists. She goes to the Deaf club and falls in love with the son of the club president. With her glass gloves, she captivates the "prince" of the club. At midnight, true to the original story, she flees, leaving behind one of the glass gloves. The story ends as predicted: the "prince" finds the girl of his dreams, and she becomes his "princess," her magic gloves allowing her to erase her many years as an ORAL person and gain the difficult but admired skill of signing like a native.

A trendier accusation that one Deaf person can make of another, one some older members of the community find confusing, is THINK-HEARING. Its literal meaning is "to think and act like a hearing person," but a more accurate translation is "to embrace uncritically the ideology of others." The term's range of meaning is similar to that of ORAL, except that the accusation can be made against any Deaf person, including those who are not ORAL, that is, not orally trained.

THINK-HEARING illustrates the present generation's sophistication with sign structure (which we describe in Chapter 5). Instead of an adaptation of an existing sign, as with ORAL which also means SPEECH or MOVING-LIPS, THINK-HEARING is a novel creation formed by combining selected elements from the two signs THINK and HEARING. THINK-HEARING goes beyond ORAL to include other unacceptable choices such as voicing opposition to ASL, or insisting that signers should use among themselves invented sign vocabulary developed for teaching English to deaf children. Older members of the community, more comfortable with the distinction between "oral" and "manual," or between not signing and signing, find accusations based on what kind of signing one uses unfamiliar. THINK-HEARING, through its self-conscious analysis of signs, emphasizes a modern realignment of the center.

*　*　*

As we have said, to understand how these categorizations and labels work one must begin from a different center. Deaf people work around different assumptions about deafness and hearing from those of hearing people. The condition of not hearing, or of being hard of hearing, cannot be described apart from its placement in the context of categories of cultural meaning. Names applied to one another are labels that define relationships. The relationships Deaf people have defined include their struggles with those who are more powerful than they, such as hearing others.

A person who is "DEAF but really HARD-OF-HEARING" has skillfully managed his relationships across groups. Deaf people may use a politically advantageous label such as "disabled," but they must apologize for it among themselves. Jacobs borrows the supposedly scientific distinction between "prelingually deaf" and "postlingually deaf" and adds modifiers that readjust the relationships in ways that are more compatible with group knowledge. All of these adjustments indicate how well the center accommodates and, at the same time, how tightly it holds.

Works Cited

Bragg, Bernard. *Lessons in Laughter: The Autobiography of a Deaf Actor.* Bernard Bragg as signed to Eugene Bergman. Washington, D.C.: Gallaudet UP, 1989.

Collums, C. 1950. "Letter to the Open Forum." *Silent Worker* 2:31.

Jacobs, Leo. *A Deaf Adult Speaks Out.* Washington, D.C.: Gallaudet College Press, 1974.

28

A Mad Fight
Psychiatry and Disability Activism

Bradley Lewis

In the late summer of 2003, six people gathered at a small building in Pasadena, California and starved themselves for twenty-two days. The small group of hunger strikers were later joined by over a dozen "solidarity strikers" around the world. Their strike was about "human rights in mental health" and, in particular, it sought to protest the "international domination" of biological approaches to psychiatry and the ever-increasing and widespread use of prescription drugs to treat "mental and emotional crises" (Mindfreedom, July 28, 2003).

The hunger strike caught the attention of the *LA Times*, *The Washington Post* and, most important for those involved, the attention of the American Psychiatric Association (APA). One of the central aims of the strike was to challenge the main institutions in psychiatry—namely the American Psychiatric Association, the National Alliance of the Mentally Ill (NAMI) and the U.S Surgeon General—and to rouse them into providing "evidence that clearly establishes the validity of 'schizophrenia,' 'depression' or other 'major mental illnesses' as biologically-based brain diseases" (Mindfreedom, July 28, 2003). The fasters demanded evidence that mental and emotional distress results from "chemical imbalances" in the brain; a view that underpins the biopsychiatric medical model and which currently dominates mental health treatment in the West.

In demanding this evidence, the strikers were taking a risk. Using a hunger strike to challenge psychiatry and its scientific findings (which are now almost ubiquitously accepted throughout the medical world and wider culture), the protestors faced the possibility of being labeled "mad"—after all, isn't psychiatry a science? Shouldn't scientific questions be decided in laboratories and in peer-reviewed articles filled with graphs and statistical analysis? What sense does it make to hold a hunger strike to challenge contemporary scientific beliefs?

The hunger strikers took the risk because, indeed, they are mad. They are all members of a psychiatry disability activist group known among their friends and allies as "Mad Pride." This activist group is an international coalition devoted to resisting and critiquing clinician-centered psychiatric systems, finding alternative and peer-run approaches to mental health recovery, and helping those who wish to do so minimize their involvement with current psychiatric institutions. They affectionately call themselves "Mad Pride" because they believe mainstream psychiatry over exaggerates psychic pathology and over enforces psychic conformity in the guise of diagnostic labeling and treatment—which all too often comes in the form of forced or manipulated hospitalizations, restraints, seclusions, and medications. Like the celebratory and reappropriative uses of the terms "Crip," "Queer," and "Black Pride," the term "Mad Pride" overturns traditional distinctions and hierarchies. It signifies a reversal of standard pathological connotations of "madness." Rather than pathologizing mental difference, Mad Pride signifies a stance of respect, appreciation, and affirmation.

In this chapter, I discuss the relation of Mad Pride to disability studies, review the history the movement, and work through its contemporary struggles with psychiatry. Throughout the discussion, I highlight the importance of Mad Pride's efforts to go beyond "politics-as-usual." Mad Pride, like other forms of "biocultural" activisms (such as Women's Health Movement and AIDS Coalition to Unleash Power), is located at the interface of bioscience and politics. As such, Mad Pride continuously struggles with epistemological issues along with more typical political issues. In short, the people in Mad Pride struggle over *both* truth and values.

This commingling of politics, power, and truth is familiar ground for disability studies. Similar to Mad Pride, disability studies unpacks and undermines stereotyped representations of disability in science and popular culture to understand and intervene in how "representation attaches meanings to bodies" (Garland-Thomson 1997, 5). Michael Oliver gives a good sense of these stereotyped disability representations by dividing them into key themes of "individualism," "medicalization," and "normality" (Oliver 1990, 56, 58). *Individualism* refers to the perspective that disability is a "personal tragedy." This frame undergirds a "hegemony of disability" which views disability as "pathological and problem-oriented" (Oliver 1996, 129). It leads to a ubiquitous *medicalization* that legitimizes the medical infrastructure for acquiring knowledge about the disabled individual. The logic of this medical infrastructure rests on notions *normality* and the dichotomy between normal and pathological. The able-bodied and the disabled, the valued and the devalued, become co-constituted cultural divisions which structure medical and cultural preoccupations (Davis 1995). One side of the binary defines the other and both operate together as "opposing twin figures that legitimate a system of social, economic, and political empowerment justified by physiological differences" (Garland-Thomson 1997, 8).

Together, these stereotyped disability representations direct the health care industry toward a near exclusive focus on individual biomedical cures. Rather than adjust social environments to meet differing bodily needs, medical interventions seek to cure the individual "abnormal" body. Disability activists resist these individualizing and medicalizing approaches by reframing disability as a social restriction and oppression rather than simply a medical problem. Emphasizing a social model rather than a medical model they call attention to the fact that much of the suffering of different bodies comes from social exclusion, isolation, and lack of opportunity, along with the often pernicious side effects of a medical industry bent on aggressive intervention to achieve "normal" bodies.[1]

The task of undermining stereotyped representations of individualism, medicalization, and normality are also central to the Mad Pride movement. Individualistic approaches to mental difference and distress blame and punish the victim for structural problems that are often better understood as located in families, communities, and society. Medicalization, or psychiatrization, legitimizes the medical community's expert authority over the domain of mental difference. And the binary between normal and abnormal shores up this psychiatrization by providing tremendous social and psychological pressure to stay on the side of normality, or sanity. Disability studies scholars refer to social stigma and oppression against the physically different as "ableism;" those in Mad Pride refer to social stigma and oppression against mental difference as "mentalism" or "sanism" (Chamberlin 1977, 219, Perlin 2000, 21).

Despite these similarities, disability activists and Mad Pride members have had difficulty forming a sustained coalition. Part of this difficulty involves the simple fact that two groups are composed of different subcultures—with different histories, different cultural artifacts, and different networks of association. But, beyond this, there are other, deeper reasons. Some disability advocates continue to harbor sanist style associations toward mental difference and do not wish to be associated or "tarnished" by Mad Pride. Likewise, many in Mad Pride (like many in the Deaf community) express discomfort with the "disability" label. They do not see their mental difference as a disability, but rather as a valued capacity. In addition, many in Mad Pride feel that disability struggles are separate from their concerns because physical disability does not involve the same level of state coercion. People with physical differences are often inappropriately confined (through limited choices and multiple manipulations), but Mad Pride activists must deal with an additional layer of state sponsored coercion in the forms of involuntary commitment and forced medication laws.[2]

Like many in both movements, however, I believe it is wise to foreground the similarities between disability activism and Mad Pride. Clearly, all of the new social movements, in one way or another, have to struggle with both truth and values—largely because biomedical science has been used to justify such a broad range of subordination practices. But, more than most, Mad Pride and disability activism face a combined political and epistemological struggle. The very heart of these activisms begins with expressly biomedical assignments of impairment. This comes not in the form of a general pronouncement of inferiority, but in a direct and specific diagnosis and treatment process. Because of this, Mad Pride and disability activist efforts to reduce individualization, medicalization, and ableism require a dual struggle that goes beyond politics-as-usual. The challenge of this dual epistemological and political struggle requires all the allies you can get. When disability activist and Mad Pride work together, they can form a formidable coalition.

The Birth of Mad Pride Movement

Mad Pride activists have had extensive experience going beyond politics-as-usual. Their lesson of dual engagement goes back to the nineteenth century efforts of Mrs. Elizabeth Ware Packard, an early precursor to today's Mad Pride movement. In 1886, Packard, a former mental hospital patient and founder of the Anti-Insane Asylum Society, began publishing a series of books and pamphlets critical of psychiatry. Packard's writings challenged the subordination of women to their husbands and the remarkable complicity of the political and psychiatric establishment to this subordination (Packard 1868, 1874). As Gerald Grob explains, "When Packard refused to play the role of obedient [minister's] wife and expressed religious ideas bordering on mysticism, her husband had her committed in 1860 to the Illinois State Hospital for the Insane" (Grob 1994, 84). Packard remained incarcerated for three years and only won her freedom by going to court to challenge her confinement. The trial received national publicity and eventually led to Packard being declared sane by the court and released from the asylum. She spent the next twenty years campaigning for personal liberty laws that would protect individuals from wrongful commitment and retention in the asylums.

Even in this early precursor to today's movement, the issues of epistemological struggle and political struggle are inseparably intertwined. Packard challenged pathologizing diagnostic practices that would treat people as insane "simply for the expression of opinions, no matter how absurd these opinions may appear for others" (quoted in Geller & Harris 1994, 66). And she challenged the political abuses that occurred once the insanity diagnosis had been made. Lunatic asylums, she argued, too often left people at the complete mercy of hospital despotism where they were treated worse than convicts or criminals. Packard's dual stress on both the "facts" of insanity and the inhumane treatment of those considered to be insane reverberate into today's resistance to psychiatry.

The more proximate antecedents to today's Mad Pride movement began in the 1970's. Mad Pride activists, during these years, gained momentum from the black civil rights movement, the women's movement, and from the early stages of lesbian and gay movement and the disability movement. Like Elizabeth Packard almost a century before, the key experience that motivated Mad Pride activists was their negative treatment within the psychiatric system. Early founders of the movement shared common experiences of being treated with disrespect, disregard, and discrimination at the hands of psychiatry. Many also suffered from unjustified confinement, verbal and physical abuse, and exclusion from treatment planning.

The testimony of Leonard Roy Frank, co-founder of the Network Against Psychiatric Assault (1972), provides a helpful glimpse into the experiences of many. After graduating from Wharton, Frank moved to San Francisco to sell commercial real estate. He was in his own words "an extraordinarily conventional person" (Farber 1993, 191). Gradually, during his late twenties, he started discovering a new world within himself and began going through an "obvious clash between ... my emerging self and that of my old self" (191). He later thought of this as a "spiritual transformation." But, at the time, he responded by doing serious reading and reflection on his emerging insights. He ended up rethinking everything in his life: "what was happening to me was that I was busy being born" (191).

A key text for Frank during his transformation was Mohandas Gandhi's autobiography. Frank took seriously Gandhi's message that one's inner life and outer life should interact and compliment each other. Reading Gandhi opened his eyes to the violence of political injustice and to the power of non-violent resistance. It also raised his awareness that animals had feelings and could suffer. The more Frank thought about Gandhi's writings on meat-eating, the more he concluded it was inescapably cruel to both animals and to humans: "We can't avoid harming ourselves when we harm other beings, whether human or animal. Meat-eating was an excellent example of how this principle played out in real life...Because it was inherently cruel to animals and morally wrong, it affected the wrong doers by causing them to become sick and cutting short their lives" (206). This combination of insights made it difficult for Frank to continue his previous lifestyle and his work selling commercial real estate; he soon lost his job, grew a beard, became vegetarian, and devoted himself to full time spiritual exploration.

Frank was exhilarated by the process, but his parents were deeply concerned. Seeing Frank's transition through the stereotyped frames of individualization, psychiatrization, and sanism, they thought he was having a "breakdown." They tried to persuade him to see a psychiatrist, but Frank resisted. They responded by arranging an involuntary commitment. The hospital records show that Frank's psychiatrists document symptoms of "not working, withdrawal, growing a beard, becoming a vegetarian, bizarre behavior, negativism, strong beliefs, piercing eyes, and religious preoccupations" (193). The psychiatrists diagnosed him as "paranoid schizophrenia," and they started a sustained course of court authorized insulin-electroshock treatments that lasted nine months and included fifty insulin comas and thirty-five electroshocks.

When the psychiatrists were not giving him shock treatments, their "therapeutic" interactions with Frank revolved around his behavior: particularly his refusal to shave or eat meat. There was never any discussion of his emerging beliefs or his spirituality. Instead, Frank's psychiatrists focused on changing overt signs of "abnormality." They even went so far as to shave his beard while he was unconscious from an insulin treatment. Frank eventually came to realize that his hospital resistance was futile, and, with the ever increasing numbers of shock treatments, he also came to fear he was in a "life or death" situation: "These so-called [shock] treatments literally wiped out all my memory for the [previous] two-year period...I realized that my high-school and college were all but gone; educationally, I was at about the eighth-grade level" (196).

Rather than risk more "treatments," Frank surrendered. He played the psychiatrists' game and did what they wanted: "I shaved voluntarily, ate some non vegetarian foods like clam chowder and eggs, was somewhat sociable, and smiled 'appropriately' at my jailers" (196). After his release, it took six years to recover from his treatment. But, throughout it all, he never gave up on his beliefs, and he never saw another psychiatrist for treatment. He went on to become a major figure in early Mad Pride activism.

During the early 1970's, people like Frank began to recognize they were not alone and started organizing local consciousness-raising groups. In the United States this includes such organization as the Insane Liberation Front in Portland Oregon (1970), the Mental Patient's Liberation Project in New York City (1971), and the Mental Patients' Liberation Front in Boston (1971). These groups built support programs, advocated for hospitalized patients, lobbied for changes in the laws, and educated the public through guest lectures and newsletters. In addition, they began the process of developing alternative, creative, and artistic ways of dealing with emotional suffering and psychological difference outside the medical models of psychiatry. The publication of Mad Pride activist Judi Chamberlin's book *On Our Own* (1977) in the mainstream press was a milestone in the development of peer run alternatives (Van Tosh & del Vecchio 2000, 9). Chamberlin used the book to expose her own abuse at the hands of psychiatry and to give a detailed account of burgeoning consumer run alternatives. The eloquence, optimism, and timing of the book was a critical catalyst for many in the movement. As ex-patient Mary O'Hagan puts it: "When my mood swings died away I was angry and amazed at how the mental health system could be so ineffective. There had to be a better way. I searched the library not quite knowing what I was looking for. And there it was, a book called *On Our Own* by Judi Chamberlin. It was all about ex-patients who set up their own alternatives to the mental health system and it set me on my journey in to the psychiatric survivor movement" (quoted in Chamberlin, 1977, back cover).

The newly formed local Mad Pride groups also organized an annual Conference on Human Rights and Psychiatric Oppression to help connect local members with the wider movement. At these meetings, activists from across the country gathered to socialize, strategize, and share experiences. They gained solidarity and increasing momentum from the experience of being with like minded activists. Between meetings local groups communicated through a newspaper forum. The San Francisco local newsletter, *Madness Network News*, evolved into a newspaper format which covered ex-patient activities across North America and around the world. This publication became the major voice of the movement, with each issue containing a rich selection of personal memoirs, creative writing, cartoons, humor, art, political commentary, and factual reporting—all from the ex-patient point of view (Hirsch 1974; Chamberlin 1990, 327).

This early period of the Mad Pride movement was also the most radical in its epistemological critique. Early leaders of the movement drew philosophical support from high-profile critical writers that, as a group, came to be known as "anti-psychiatry." Writers such as Erving Goffman (1961), R. D. Laing (1967), Thomas Scheff (1966), and Thomas Szasz (1961) may have differed widely in their philosophies, but collectively their main tenets were clear. Mental illness is not an objective medical reality but rather either a negative label or a strategy for coping in a mad world. As Laing put it, "the apparent irrationality of the single 'psychotic' individual" may often be understood "within the context of the family." And, in turn, the irrationality of the family can be understood if it is placed "within the context of yet larger organizations and institutions" (Laing 1968,15). Put in context in this way, madness has a legitimacy of its own which is erased by medical-model approaches that can only pathologize it. For many anti-psychiatry writers, mental suffering can be the beginning of a healing process and should not be suppressed through aggressive behavioral or biological interventions.

The most epistemologically radical of the anti-psychiatry writers, Thomas Szasz, had the most influence on U.S. activists. Szasz, a dissident psychiatrist, was shunned within his own field, but his prolific writings (over twenty-five books) and forceful prose gave him tremendous influence outside psychiatry (Leifer 1997). Throughout his work, Szasz's argument was always two-fold: (1) mental illness is a myth and (2) there should be complete separation between psychiatry and the state. As Szasz put it in a summary statement, "Involuntary mental hospitalization is imprisonment under the guise of treatment; it is a covert form of social control that subverts the rule of law. No one ought to be deprived of liberty except for a criminal offense, after a trial by jury guided by legal rules of evidence. No one ought to be detained against their will in a building called 'hospital,' or any other medical institution, on the basis of expert opinion" (Szasz 1998).

Consistent with others in the Mad Pride movement, Szasz combined his epistemology and his politics. Szasz's insistence on the autonomy of mental health clients rested directly on his epistemology, which he based on a strong positivist philosophy of science that emphasized a sharp demarcation between observation and conjecture. For Szasz, *physical illness* was real because it was based on actual observation, but *mental illness* was at best a metaphor. A broken leg is real because you can see the x-ray, but a "broken brain" is a myth because there is no x-ray that will show it. For Szasz, to see mental illness as "real" rather than as a metaphor was to make a serious category mistake. "Mental illness" is not objectively observable; it is a myth.

Mad Pride Today

During the last thirty years of their struggle, Mad Pride has increasingly infiltrated the mental health system rather than simply criticizing it from outside. Despite the fact that institutional psychiatry continues to ignore and denigrate their efforts, important government agencies involved in mental health policy have begun to pay attention. Mad Pride activists have been particularly successful in increasing consumer participation in treatment planning and facility governance. In addition, they have gained increasing respect for the work developing peer run treatment alternatives.

The most important agency to pay attention to Mad Pride perspectives has been the national Center for Mental Health Services (CMHS). This little known public agency is "charged with leading the national system that delivers mental health services" (Center for Mental Health Services 2002). Following on the success of Chamberlin's *On Our Own*, the agency worked with a local California peer group to publish *Reaching Across: Mental Health Clients Helping Each Other*, a "how to" manual for peer run services (Zinnman, Harp, and Budd 1987). For too long, CMHS explains, "decisions about mental health policies and services were made without any input from people who have mental illnesses or their families. As a result, some policies and programs failed to meet the needs of the people they were intended to serve" (Center for Mental Health Services 2004) CMHS worked to change this by sponsoring peer-run research, training, and technical assistance centers, and producing federally mandated documents encouraging states to include consumer-operated alternatives to traditional treatment programs. Since 1985, CMHS has also sponsored an annual, national level, Alternatives Conference that brings together consumers and ex-patients to network and to share the results of their scholarship and program development.

These political successes have gradually necessitated a change in Mad Pride's epistemological critique. Szasz's strong epistemological critique of psychiatry was useful in the early days of the movement, but it became less so as Mad Pride shifted into its more contemporary formations. The early anti-psychiatry literature set up an either/or relation between consumers and providers. People had to either be with psychiatry or against it. Szasz's rigid positivist epistemology left little room for contradiction and coalition politics. As sociologist and Mad Pride activist Linda Morrison points out, with increasing infiltration of the mental health system, many members no longer took a hard-line approach to psychiatry. These members identified themselves more as "consumers" than "survivors" or "ex-patients." Consumers, by definition, were critical of aspects of psychiatry but were willing to legitimize and participate in other aspects (Morrison 2005). Mad Pride needed to embrace these contradictions and adopt coalition politics to avoid losing these members.

Contemporary Mad Pride members have made just this kind of epistemological shift. Though activists still reference Szasz favorably, they now draw more on his political values (of autonomy and separation of psychiatry and state) than on his epistemology. Mad Pride members mark this shifting epistemology by referring to themselves as "consumer/survivor/ex-patient" groups. This hyphenated designation, usually shortened to "c/s/x" or "consumer/survivors," highlights that today's Mad Pride is a coalition of critical activists—some whom have a more radical epistemological critique than others (Morrison 2005).

This shift has set the stage for additional coalitional possibilities between Mad Pride and critical psychiatrists. Increasingly, critical psychiatrists are moving beyond the narrow approaches of their training and drawing from interdisciplinary theory in science studies, disability studies, and the humanities. Like Mad Pride, they are developing alternative perspectives on psychiatry that emphasizes the importance of social models and of democratic research and treatment. In Britain, an influential Critical Psychiatry Network (www.critpsynet.freeuk.com/critpsynet.htm) has recently formed, bringing together a coalition of critical providers and consumer/survivors (Double 2002).[3]

Contemporary Mad Pride's political success at getting a seat at the table of mental health policy has also necessitated a change in the more radical infrastructure of the movement. The Conference on Human Rights and Psychiatric Oppression no longer meets and has now been replaced by the Alternatives Conference sponsored by CMHS. The different name of the conference is consistent with a shift in emphasis from psychiatric oppression to peer-run support and service involvement. The change is subtle as both oppression and support remain paramount for Mad Pride, but the change does mark a shift of the emphasis within the movement.

In addition, the newspaper *Madness Network News* is no longer being published. Today's Mad Pride connects its members largely through the activities of the Support Coalitions International (SCI) which brings together one hundred international local groups. Under the leadership of David Oaks, SCI has become "the epicenter of the Mad Movement" ("Windows into madness," 2002). It runs a Web site (www.mindfreedom.com), an e-mail list, a magazine (*Mindfreedom Journal*), and an online "Mad Market" (where interested parties can find "a little library of dangerous books"). Much of the success of the center comes from Oaks' capacity to build a coalition of consumers, survivors, and ex-patients. Like Packard, Frank, and Chamberlin before him, Oaks' motivation for mental health activism comes from his experiences of psychiatric abuse: including forced hospitalization and forced treatment. Like so many others, he has taken those experiences and turned them into political action.

Recent Struggles with Psychiatry

Despite the successes Mad Pride has had within the mental health system, their epistemological and political struggle with psychiatry continues. These struggles are often complicated, and they require impressive political savvy. In this section, I work through some examples of these struggles to give a sense of the political terrain and the critical importance of today's consumer/survivor activism. The 2003 hunger strike is a good example of Mad Pride's contemporary epistemological battles. To understand the context of the strike, it is important to note that during the same time Mad Pride has complicated its epistemology, psychiatry has gone in the exact opposite direction. The last thirty years have seen a "scientific revolution" in psychiatry that primarily values quantitative, positivistic protocols for research (Lewis, 2006). The emphasis on "objective" data has created a preference for neuroscience and genetics at the expense of an array of cultural and humanistic styles of inquiry. This new scientific psychiatry, working in tandem with pharmaceutical funding, has gone on to create today's dominant clinical model of psychiatry, "biopsychiatry"—whose emphasis is almost exclusively biomedical style diagnoses and pharmacological treatments.

The blockbuster medication, Prozac, gives a window into biopsychiatry's dominance. Between 1987 and 2002 (the year Prozac came off patent), over 27 million new prescriptions for the drug were written. Combined with the multiple "me too" drugs it inspired—the class of antidepressants known as "selective serotonin inhibitors" (SSRI)—that total reached 67.5 million in the United States alone (Aldred 2004). That means almost one in every four people in the United States were started on a Prozac-type drug between 1987 and 2002. These same one in four people were dealing with sufficient emotional issues that someone thought they needed help.

For some of these people, the SSRIs may have been the best choice. But was it the best choice for 67.5 million people? Psychiatry's professional literature, its patient hand-outs, and the popular press all tell us "yes." They tout "scientific progress in the treatment of depression" as the main reason for the SSRIs extensive use (Gardner 2003; Lewis 2006; Metzl 2003). But, if we scratch the surface, we find that the SSRIs are highly controversial, and researchers have not been able to agree on even simple questions like: Do the drugs work? Or, are they safe? The *Handbook of Psychiatric Drug Therapy*, typical of most clinical reviews, claims with great authority that the SSRIs are highly effective and that they have a mild side effect profile (Arana and Rosenbaum 2000, 57, 76). But critical analysts conclude just the opposite: that the SSRIs are not much better than sugar pills and that they have major side effects—including sexual dysfunction, suicidality, and even violence (Breggin 1994, 65; Fisher and Fisher 1996; Glenmullen 2000; Healy 2004; Kirsch and Sapirstein 1998). Going further, scientific opinion is also at odds regarding the question of explanation. Some argue that the SSRIs have effects because they treat biological disease. But others argue these drugs are simply stimulants like cocaine and amphetamines. These researchers conclude that SSRIs are mood brighteners and psychic energizers because they work on the same neurotransmitters as other stimulants (Breggin 1994; Glenmullen 2000).

When we take these controversies surrounding the Prozac-type drugs into account, it seems highly questionable that the SSRIs were the best choice for 67.5 million people. For most of these people, alternatives like psychotherapy, peer-support, and personal and political activism would have likely been better options than taking drugs that are expensive, are possibly no better than placebo, have multiple side effects, and may be little more than a dressed up version speed. But, because of the hype of biopsychiatry, these controversies are not well known and alternatives are not given a chance. The SSRIs are seen as quick and easy solutions backed by advances in psychiatric science and individual medical recommendations. For most people thrown in that situation, they are seen as the only viable option.

Mad Pride's hunger strike was directed squarely at this so-called "biological revolution" in psychiatry. The fasters, organized by David Oaks and Support Coalition International, demanded evidence that emotional and mental distress can be deemed "biologically-based" brain diseases, and also evidence that psychopharmaceutical treatments can correct those "chemical imbalances" attributed to a psychiatric diagnoses (MindFreedom, July 28, 2003).

The strikers were not trying to show that the biopsychiatric model of mental illness is myth, and they were not touting another model of mental distress as better or more accurate. The protestors stated from the outset that they were aware that psychopharmaceuticals work for some people, and that they were not judging individuals who choose to employ biopsychiatric approaches in an effort to seek relief. For Oaks and his fellow protestors, there are "many ways to help people experiencing severe mental and emotional crises... We respect the right of people to choose the option of prescribed psychiatric drugs. Many of us have made this personal choice.... However, choice in the mental health field is severely limited. One approach dominates, and that is a belief in chemical imbalances, genetic determinism and psychiatric drugs as the treatment of choice. Far too often this limited choice has been exceedingly harmful to both the body and the spirit" (MindFreedom, July 28, 2003). In demanding evidence, the strikers hoped to show that the "chemical imbalance" theory of mental distress is not watertight, and to therefore challenge the overinvestment in this "biopsychiatric approach" by the mental health institutions.

In the early days of the strike, the APA brushed off the strikers demands for evidence and told them to consult introductory textbooks on psychiatry. The strikers responded by persisting in their demands and by sending a letter to the APA written by a panel of fourteen critical scholars. The letter showed that within the very textbooks that the APA had recommended there were numerous statements that invalidated the notion that mental illnesses have specific biological bases (MindFreedom, August 22, 2003). Using psychiatry's own knowledge against itself, the hunger strikers prompted the APA to respond more fully, and a follow up communiqué from APA finally conceded that "brain science has not advanced to the point where scientists or clinicians can point to readily discernible pathological lesions or genetic abnormalities that in and of themselves serve as a reliable or predictive biomarkers of a given mental disorder" (APA 2003). This reluctant admission from the APA marked an important epistemological victory for Mad Pride. In an interview, Oaks said: "They acknowledged that they didn't have the biological evidence [of mental illness], so that's on the record" (Davis 2003). The hunger strike vividly demonstrated how problematic it is to accept without question the "truths" of biopsychiatry.[4]

Despite this small success, Mad Pride's epistemological struggle continues to be a tough one. They are battling against a veritable superpower whose main ally is the hugely profitable and very influential pharmaceutical industry. As David Davis reports in his *LA Times* article on the hunger strike, Mad Pride is up against both an American Psychiatric Association, whose conventions bustle with "brightly colored" booths of the drug companies, and a booming pharmaceutical industry whose "sales of psychotherapeutics reached $21 billion in 2002, almost double the $11 billion in sales in 1998" (Davis 2003).[5]

Because of the influence and clout of biopsychiatry, Mad Pride knows all too well that skirmishes over epistemology are only part of the struggle. While it is vital to strike at the heart of mainstream psychiatry's "knowledge" and "truths," it is just as vital to realize that the epistemology game is hard to win. Science studies scholar Bruno Latour explains that dissenters of science can only go so far by using scientific literature against itself. For alternative perspectives to successfully join in the process of science (and truth) in the making, they must build their own "counter-laboratories," which of course requires tremendous resources (Latour 1987, 79). Mad Pride clearly does not have the resources to compete laboratory for laboratory with the institutions of psychiatry and their pharmaceutical supporters. Thus, while Mad Pride continues to play the game of epistemology, and continues to have some successes destabilizing psychiatry's biomedical model, it also struggles with psychiatry on the more typically political and economic terrain.

This was particularly evident in 2002 when President George W. Bush's administration initiated what David Oaks dubbed "the Bush triple play," which prompted Mad Pride to mobilize swiftly and energetically to fight on the political front (Oaks, 2002–2003). The triple play included:

1. The planned appointment of a controversial conservative psychiatrist, Dr. Sally Satel, to the important National Advisory Council for Mental Health.
2. The announcement of budget cuts to key government sponsored consumer/survivor technical support centers.
3. The creation of a New Freedom Commission to study U.S. mental health services.

All aspects of this triple play posed direct threats to Mad Pride and to the consumer/survivor movement, and they threatened the freedoms and rights of those suffering mental and emotional crises.

The first part of the triple play began with a White House leak, with word coming out that Dr. Sally Satel was being selected by the Bush administration for a position on the advisory council for the CMHS (the very organization which has been most receptive to consumer/survivor initiatives). Dr. Satel—a fellow at the American Enterprise Institute (a conservative political think tank)—is the author of the controversial book *P. C., M.D.: How Political Correctness is Corrupting Medicine*. She is not only a vociferous advocate of the biopsychiatric model of mental illness, she is also an outspoken critic of the consumer survivor movement, and an insistent lobbyist for involuntary commitment and treatment laws. In *P.C., M.D.*, under a chapter titled "Inmates Take Over the Asylum," Satel names the leaders of the Mad Pride movement and attacks their hard fought efforts to increase peer run services and reduce involuntary treatments. She denigrates mental health administrators who have taken Mad Pride seriously: "Tragically, they [mental health administrators] seem to be willing to sacrifice the needs of those with the most severe illnesses to political correctness and to the expediency of placating the vocal and annoying consumer/survivor lobby" (76). And she even goes so far as to describe the Alternatives Conference as the "guinea pig rebellion" (50).

For Mad Pride, Satel's appointment and her public vilification of consumer-run organizations signaled an overall Bush administration strategy to aggressively push a controversial biopsychiatry paradigm, to abandon consumer run self-help and peer support programs, and to increase forced psychiatric medication.

These concerns were reinforced by the second part of the Bush triple play. Soon after the leak about Dr. Satel, the Bush administration announced budget cuts for CMHS sponsored consumer/survivor technical assistance centers. Although the cuts totaled only $2 million out of the total CMHS budget, they were targeted directly at consumer/survivors. Three out of five of these centers were consumer run, which represented a clear about face for CMHS. Joseph Rogers, director of one of the programs to be cut, the National Mental Health Consumer Self-Help Clearinghouse, commented that "We had no warning. The cuts just came out of the blue, and we've had no explanation since that makes any sense" (Mulligan 2002).

The third part of the Bush triple play was the creation of a New Freedom Commission on mental health. Bush hailed the commission as a major step toward improving mental health services, and he charged it with the ambitious goals of reviewing the quality of mental health services, identifying innovative programs, and formulating federal, state, and local level policy options. The administration stipulated that the commission be composed of fifteen members and that these members be selected from a range of stakeholder groups: including providers, payers, administrators, consumers, and family members (Bush 2002). Although all of this sounded laudable enough, but true to Mad Pride concerns, when the New Freedom Commission's fifteen members were made public, only one person self-identified as having personally experienced the mental health system or as involved in the consumer/survivor movement. The New Freedom Commission's choice of members appeared not to be about true stakeholder inclusion, but only a crude form of tokenism.

For many consumer/survivors, the Bush triple play was not only an outrage, it was a serious danger. These three deft moves threatened to undo all the gains consumer/survivors had made over the past thirty years. Oaks put it this way: "Mental health consumers and psychiatric survivors have experienced fierce repression. But to have a well-funded think tank unite with a Presidential administration to openly attack our movement in such a way is unprecedented. As the enormity of the attacks set in, several activists said they were numb with disbelief" (Oaks 2002–2003).

Mad Pride activists could have reasonably given up at this juncture. Instead, they held a strategy meeting with colleagues from the international movement, and they decided to directly oppose each part of the Bush triple play. Opposition to Dr. Satel's appointment and the cuts to CHMS programs took the form of a blitz of emails to consumer/survivor list-servs, active lobbying of mental health administrators, and a barrage of critical faxes to Secretary Tommy Thompson of the US Dept. of Health & Human Services. And, rather than being dismayed by the non-democratic message of the New Freedom Commission's selection process, consumer/survivors took full advantage of the Commission's plan to hold public hearings on psychiatric services. Four days before the first scheduled hearing, consumer/survivors gathered for an emergency meeting with a network of physical disability activists. Judi Chamberlin, who has been a long-time advocate of disability and Mad Pride coalitions, explained the rationale for involving the larger disability movement, "When a wolf wants to target a whole flock, it looks for the most vulnerable lamb. The Bush administration is targeting psychiatric survivors today, but the whole disability movement is the target tomorrow" (Oaks 2002–2003).

The meeting turned out to be a major inspiration for consumer/survivors. The first speaker that night was Justin Dart, who many call the "Martin Luther King" of the disability movement. Dart, struggling with the last stages of terminal illness (he died just eight days later), gave a rousing speech which set the tone for the meeting. Dart proposed that,

> ....we in the disability communities must unite with all who love justice to lead a revolution of empowerment. A revolution, to create a culture that will empower every single individual including all people with psychiatric disabilities, to live his or her God given potential for self determination, productivity and quality of life.
> Empowerment means choices—individual choices about where we live, how we live, where we work, choices about health care. We have a right to complete quality health care of our own choosing.
> NO FORCED TREATMENT EVER.
> We choose our own doctors and medication. We choose the places of care. No denial of treatment ever.
> NO FORCED TREATMENT EVER. (Oaks 2002)

The combined presence of Dart and several other disability representatives created the strategic capacity to get the word out and rally support and resistance far beyond the usual consumer/survivor community. It also further advanced a cross-disability activist connection between the disability movement and consumer/survivors.

On the day of the New Freedom Commission's first public meeting, consumer/survivor activists and their disability activist comrades, made their presence known. Not only did they hand out their own press release and talk individually to members of the Bush Commission, they also made public announcements. Judi Chamberlin's testimony was typical. Announcing that she was a "psychiatric survivor" and "an advocate" on consumer/survivor issues for more than thirty years," she pointed out:

> A basic premise of the disability rights movement is simply this: Nothing About Us Without Us. The makeup of the Commission violates this basic principle. Just as women would not accept the legitimacy of a commission of "expert" men to define women's needs, or ethnic and racial minorities would not accept a panel of "expert" white people to define their needs, we similarly see the Commission as basically irrelevant to our struggle to define our own needs. (Chamberlin 2002)

Chamberlin argued that the New Freedom Commission lacked the "expertise on the consumer/survivor experience" as well as the "expertise of disability rights activists, those knowledgeable about the legal and civil rights of people diagnosed with mental illness, and experts in community integration." And she went on to detail how that expertise could be provided.

Unlike the results of the hunger strike, however, the results of Mad Pride's efforts to resist the Bush triple play can only be described as mixed. With regard to part one of the triple play, Mad Pride was unable to stop Sally Satel's appointment to the advisory board. Once on the board, she predictably advocated for more forced treatment and for discontinuation of consumer-run programs. But part two of the triple play, the planned budget cuts to peer support programs, never materialized. The three technical centers sponsored by CMHS continued to be funded.

The New Freedom Commission results were also contradictory. On the one hand, the commission was quite responsive to Mad Pride concerns. It agreed with Mad Pride that the mental health system is fundamentally broken, that it needs extensive overhaul (not just piecemeal reform), that mental health services must consumer and family centered, that modern psychiatry over emphasizes reductionist biomedical approaches, and that consumers must be protected from unjust incarceration and the use of seclusion and restraints. Together these recommendations signified an impressive success for Mad Pride's (and their disability allies) efforts to reach the commission and have their voices included in the report.

But, on the other hand, all was not rosy with the commission's report. In addition to the above recommendations, the New Freedom Commission also recommended nationwide mental health screenings in schools, primary care offices, prisons, and the welfare system. The ominous dimension of this plan was pointed out the *British Medical Journal* (*BMJ*) in an exposé titled "Bush plans to screen whole US population for mental illness." The *BMJ* explained that the New Freedom Commission recommendation for nationwide screening was linked to their recommendation for "evidence-based" treatment protocols. In psychiatry, these protocols are code words for the Texas Medication Algorithm Project (TMAP). TMAP was started in 1995 as an alliance between the pharmaceutical industry, the University of Texas, and the mental health system to set up expert guidelines for psychiatric practices. But a whistle blower at TMAP, Allen Jones, revealed that key officials received money and perks from the drug companies to unnecessarily promote expensive on-patent drugs. As Jones explained, "the same political/pharmaceutical alliance" behind TMAP are also behind the New Freedom Commission. This alliance is "poised to consolidate the TMAP effort into a comprehensive national policy" of over-treating mental illness with expensive medications (Lenzer 2004). When you add to this state of affairs the recent National Institute of Health conclusion that half of all Americans will meet the criteria for a *DSM-IV* disorder some time in their life, the profiteering possibilities of the New Freedom Commission's political/pharmaceutical alliance is easy to imagine (Kessler 2005).

Of course, none of this screening will go forward without resistance. In quick response to the *BMJ* exposé, Mindfreedom sent out a news release "What You Gonna Do When They Screen For You" and set up a section of its Web site titled "President Bush and the Shrinking of the USA" (see http://www.mindfreedom.org/mindfreedom/bush_psychiatry.shtml). This news board gives access to breaking stories and commentary, plus it provides answers to frequently asked questions concerning the controversy. In addition, the Mad Pride advocacy group, Alliance for Human Research Protection (AHRP), has begun to monitor closely the outcomes of the New Freedom Commission (see http://www.ahrp.org/about/about.php). At the time of this writing, AHRP reports that lawsuits are already being filed in Indiana to resist the effects of "TeenScreen Depression"—a program funded partly with new federal grants initiated by the New Freedom Commission.[6]

Conclusion

These recent conflicts with psychiatry provide an important window into Mad Pride's ongoing episte-mological and political struggles. Against tremendous odds, the movement has worked impressively to expose psychiatry as a limited field of inquiry, to open up its clinical services to more peer-run alternatives, and to reduce coercive connections between psychiatry and the state. Their fight to re-duce indivualization, psychiatrization, and sanist approaches to psychic life is arduous, and at times a little "mad." But the stakes are high and the struggle must continue. With the increasing coalition with the broader disability movement and the emergence of a critical psychiatry network, the fight is becoming more and more mainstream. Soon the battle will be one about which we all know and in which we can all participate. Active biocultural citizenship regarding mental difference and distress requires nothing less.

As the editors of *Adbusters* sum up in their issue on Mad Pride, in a culture of hardening isola-tion, status, materialism, and environmental degradation, "Mad Pride can be a broad embrace. It is a signal that we will allow ourselves our deep sorrow, our manic hope, or fierce anxiety, our imperfect rage. These will be our feedback into the system. We reserve the right to seek relief from both our most troubling symptoms and from society's most punitive norms. The sickness runs deep; without madness, there is no hope of cure" ("Deep sadness, manic hope," 2002).

Notes

1. Public health scholar Barbara Starfield estimates that the combined effect of medical adverse effects in the United States are as follows:
   - 12,000 deaths/year from unnecessary surgery
   - 7,000 deaths/year from medication errors in hospitals
   - 20,000 deaths/year from other errors in hospitals
   - 80,000 deaths/year from nosocomial infections in hospitals
   - 106,000 deaths/year from nonerror, adverse effects of medications

   That comes to a total to 225,000 deaths per year from iatrogenic causes—which constitutes the third leading cause of death in the United States. Just after heart disease and cancer (Starfield 2000, 484).
2. For an extended discussion of confinement and disability see the "Confinement" entry in the *Encyclopedia of Disability Studies* (Lewis 2005).
3. The Critical Psychiatry Network organizes its members less under the banner of "anti-psychiatry" and more under the banner of "post-psychiatry" (Thomas and Bracken 2004). The epistemological underpinning of post-psychiatry avoids the either/or problems of anti-psychiatry. Relying on the philosophy of Michel Foucault, a post-psychiatric perspective blurs the binary between truth and myth as all forms of human knowledge making are understand to be both material and semantic, (Bracken and Thomas 2001; Foucault 1965 and 2003; Lewis 2006). This shift moves the legitimacy ques-tion of psychiatric knowledge from "truth" to "consequences." The issue is not whether psychiatric knowledge magically mirrors the world, but who is allowed to participate in making the knowledge? What kinds of consequences (and for whom) will follow from the knowledge?
4. For an extended analysis of the exchange between Mad Pride and the APA see critical psychiatrists Duncan Double's review: "Biomedical Bias of the American Psychiatric Association" (Double 2004).
5. See former editor-in-chief of the *New England Journal of Medicine* Marcia Angell's book, *The Truth about Drug Companies: How They Deceive Us and What to do About It* (2004), for an extended discussion of the influence of the pharmaceuticals on medical research and practice. Also see Pulitzer Prize finalist Robert Whitaker's book, *Mad in America: Bad Science, Bad Medicine, and the Enduring Mistreatment of the Mentally Ill* (2002) for an historical perspective specific to psychiatry.
6. Theresa and Michael Rhoades, who filed the first suit, claim that TeenScreen sent their daughter home from school tell-ing her she had been diagnosed with obsessive compulsive disorder and social anxiety disorder. The Rhoades "claim that the survey was erroneous, improper, and done with reckless disregard for their daughter's welfare and that they did not give the school permission to give the test" (Pringle, 2005). High profile attorney John Whitehead calls the situation an "Orwellian Nightmare" and has agreed to take on the Rhoades case. However, "because of the financial backing of phar-maceutical companies and the Bush administration's support through the New Freedom Commission," even Whitehead is concerned and considers his opposition to be formidable foes (Alliance for Human Research Protection, 2005).

References

Aldred, G. (2004). "An Analysis of the Use of Prozac, Paxil, and Zoloft in USA 1988–2002." Retrieved on June 2, 2005 from the Alliance for Research Protection, http://www.ahrp.org/risks/usSSRIuse0604.pdf.

Alliance for Human Research Protection (2005). "The Rutherford Institute takes on TeenScreen case in Indiana." Retrieved on July 25 from http://www.ahrp.org/infomail/05/06/13.php.

American Psychiatric Association (2003). *Statement on Diagnosis and Treatment of Mental Disorders*. Release no. 03-39, September 25, 2003. Retrieved on July 15, 2005 from http://www.psych.org/news_room/press_releases/mentaldisorders0339.pdf.

Angell, M. (2004). *The truth about drug companies: How they deceive us and what to do about it*. New York: Random House.

Arana, G., and Rosenbaum, J. (2000). *Handbook of psychiatric drug therapy*, 4th ed. Philadelphia: Lippincott Williams and Wilkins.

Braken, P., and Thomas, P. (2001). Postpsychiatry: a new direction for mental health. *British Medical Journal* 322:724–727.

Breggin, P. (1994). *Talking back to Prozac: What doctors aren't telling you about today's most controversial drugs*. New York: St. Martins Press.

Bush, G. W. (2002). "President's New Freedom Commission on Mental Health: Executive Order." The White House. President George W. Bush On line. Released on April, 29, 2002. Retrieved on June 17, 2005 from http://www.whitehouse.gov/news/releases/2002/04/20020429-2.html.

Center for Mental Health Services (2002). "About CMHS." Retrieved on July 20, 2005 from http://www.mentalhealth.samhsa.gov/cmhs/about.asp.

Center for Mental Health Services (2004). "Consumer affairs program." Retrieved on July 20, 2005 from http://www.mentalhealth.samhsa.gov/consumersurvivor/about.asp.

Chamberlin, J. (1977). *On our own: Patient-controlled alternatives to the mental health system*. Lawrence, MA: National Empowerment Center, Inc.

Chamberlin, J. (1990). The ex-patients' movement: Where we've been and where we are going. *Journal of Mind and Behavior* 11 (3&4): 323–336.

Chamberlin, J. (2002). "Testimony of Judi Chamberlin." American Association of People with Disabilities On line. Retrieved on June 17, 2005 from http://www.aapd-dc.org/News/disability/testjudichamberlin.html.

Davis, D. (2003). David Oaks and others in the "Mad Pride" movement believe drugs are being overused in treating mental illness, and they want the abuse stopped. *L.A. Times Magazine*, Sunday, October 23, 2003 .Retrieved on July 20, 2005 from http://www.latimes.com.

Davis, L. (1995). *Enforcing normalcy: Disability, deafness, and the body*. London: Verso.

"Deep sadness, manic hope: A movement for liberty, and the pursuit of madness." (2002). *Adbusters* (10) 3.

Double, D (2002).The limits of psychiatry. *British Medical Journal* 324: 900-904.

Double, D. (2004). "Biomedical bias of the American Psychiatric Association." Critical Psychiatry Web site. Retrieved on June 22, 2005 from http://www.critpsynet.freeuk.com/biomedicalbias.htm.

Farber, S. (1993). From victim to revolutionary: An interview with Lennard Frank.In *Madness, heresy, and the rumor of angels: The revolt against the mental health system*. Chicago: Open Court.

Fisher, R., and Fisher, S., (1996). Antidepressants for children: Is scientific support necessary? *Journal of nervous and mental disease* 184:99–102.

Foucault, M.(1965). *Madness and civilization: A history of insanity in the age of reason*. New York: Vintage Books.

Foucault, M. (2003). *Abnormal: Lectures at the College of France 1974–1975*. New York: Picador.

Gardner, P. (2003). Distorted packaging: Marketing depression as illness, drugs as cures. *Journal of medical humanities* 24 (1/2):105–130.

Garland-Thomson, R. (1997). *Extraordinary bodies: figuring physical disability in American culture and literature*. New York: Columbia University Press.

Geller, J., and Harris, M. (1994). *Women of asylum: Voices from behind the walls 1840–1945*. New York: Doubleday.

Glenmullen, J. (2000). *Prozac backlash: Overcoming the dangers of Prozac, Zoloft, Paxil, and other antidepressants with save, effective alternatives*. New York. Touchstone.

Goffman, E. (1961). *Asylums: Essays on the social situation of mental patients and other inmates*. New York: Doubleday.

Grob, G. (1994). *The mad among us: A history of the care of America's mentally ill*. Cambridge, MA: Harvard University Press.

Healy, D. (2004). *Let them eat Prozac: The unhealthy relationship between the pharmaceutical industry and depression*. New York: New York University Press.

Hirsch, S. (Ed.) (1974) *Madness Network News Reader*. San Francisco: Glide Publications.

Hogan, M. (2003) "Cover letter: Presidents New Freedom Commission on Mental Health." Retrieved on June 17, 2005 from http://www.mentalhealthcommission.gov/reports/FinalReport/CoverLetter.htm.

Kessler, R. et al. (2005). Lifetime prevalence and age-of-onset distributions of *DSM-IV* disorders in the national comorbidity survey replication. *Archives of General Psychiatry* Vol. 62. Retrieved on July 25, 2005 from http://www.archgenpsychiatry.com.

Kirsch, I., and Sapirstein, G. (1998). Listening to Prozac but hearing placebo: A meta-analysis of antidepressant medications. *Prevention and treatment.* Retrieved on July 25, 2005 from http://journals.apa.org/prevention/volume1.

Leifer, R. (1997). The psychiatric repression of Dr. Thomas Szasz: Its social and political significance. *Review of Existential Psychology and Psychiatry* XXIII (1, 2 & 3):85 –107.

Laing, R. (1967). *The politics of experience.* New York: Ballantine.

Laing, R..D. (1968) "The obvious." In D. Cooper (Ed.). *The dialectics of liberation.* Harmondsworth. Penguin.

Latour, B. (1987). *Science in action.* Cambridge, MA: Harvard University Press.

Lenzer, J. (2004) "Bush plans to screen whole US population for mental illness." *British Medical Journal.* Vol 328. June 19, 2004. Retrieved on August 10, 2004 from http://www.bmj.com.

Lewis, B. (2005). "Confinement." In G. Albrect (Ed.). *The encyclopedia of disability.* Thousand Oaks, CA: Sage Publications.

Lewis, B. (2006). *Moving beyond Prozac, DSM, and the new psychiatry: The birth of postpsychiatry.* Ann Arbor: University of Michigan Press.

Metzl, J. (2003). Selling sanity through gender: The psychodynamics of psychotropic advertising. *Journal of Medical Humanities* 24 (1/2):79–105.

MindFreedom (July 28, 2003). "Original statement by the Fast for Freedom in Mental Health to the American Psychiatric Association, National Alliance for the Mentally Ill, and the US Office of the Surgeon General." Retrieved on July 10, 2005 from http://www.mindfreedom.org/mindfreedom/hungerstrike1.shtml#original.

Morrison, L. (2005). *Talking back to psychiatry: The consumer/survior/ex-patient movement.* New York. Routledge.

Mulligan, K. (2002). CMHS budget cuts harm consumer involvement. *Psychiatric News* 37(6):17.

Oaks, D. (2002). "From patients to passion: A call for nonviolent revolution in the mental health system. Plenary Address Alternatives 2002 Convention. Retrieved on March 3, 2003 from http://www.mindfreedom.org/mindfreedom/conference.shtml.

Oaks, D. (2002–2003). "President Bush's position on people with psychiatric labels." *Mindfreedom Journal* (Winter): 4–6.

Oliver, M. (1990). *The politics of disablement: A sociological approach.* New York: St. Martin's Press.

Oliver, M. (1996). *Understanding disability: From theory to practice.* London: Macmillan.

Packard, E. (1868). *The prisoner's hidden life, or insane asylums unveiled: As demonstrated by the report of the investigating committee of the legislature of Illinois.* Chicago: Published by the Author, A.B. Case.

Packard, E. (1874). *Modern persecutions, or married woman's liabilities.* Hartford, CT: Case, Lockwood and Brainard.

Perlin, M. (2000). *The hidden prejudice: Mental disability on trial.* Washington, DC: American Psychological Association.

President's New Freedom Commission (2003). "Executive Summary." Retrieved on June 17, 2005 from http://www.mentalhealthcommission.gov/reports/FinalReport/FullReport.htm.

Pringle, E. (2005). TeenScreen: The lawsuits begin. *CounterPunch.* June 13, 2005. Retrieved July 25, 2005 from http://www.counterpunch.org/pringle06132005.html.

Richman, S. (2004) "Bush's brave new world." *The Washington Times.* October 17, 2004. Retrieved on July 25, 2005 from http://www.washingtontimes.com/commentary/20041016-115126-9840r.htm.

Satel, S. (2000). *P.C., M.D.: How political correctness is corrupting medicine.* New York: Basic Books.

Scheff, T. (1966). *Being mentally ill.* Chicago: Aldine.

Starfield, B. 2000. Is US health really the best in the world? *Journal of the American Medical Association* 284 (4): 483–-485.

Support Coalition News (May 15, 2002). "Stop the appointment of extremist psychiatrist Sally Satel!" Retrieved on June 15, 2005 from http://www.mindfreedom.org/mindfreedom/satel_f.shtml.

Szasz, T. (1961). *The myth of mental illness: Foundations of a theory of personal conduct.* New York: Hoeber-Harper.

Szasz, T. (1998). "Thomas Szasz's summary statement and manifesto." Retrieved on July 20, 2005 from http://www.szasz.com/manifesto.html.

Thomas, P., and Bracken, P. (2004). Critical psychiatry in practice. *Advances in Psychiatric Treatment* 10:361–370.

Van Tosh, L., and del Vecchio, P. (2000). *Consumer-operated and self-help programs: A technical report.* Rockville, MD: U.S. Center for Mental Health Services.

Whitaker, R. (2002). *Mad in America: Bad science, bad medicine, and the enduring mistreatment of the mentally ill.* Cambridge, MA: Perseus Publishing.

"Windows into madness" (2002). *Adbusters* (10) 3.

Zinnman, S., Howie the Harp, and Budd, S. (Eds.) (1987). *Reaching across: Mental health clients helping each other.* Sacramento, CA: California Network of Mental Health Clients.

Part VI

Disability and Culture

29

Toward a Poetics of Vision, Space, and the Body
Sign Language and Literary Theory[1]

H-Dirksen L. Bauman

Suppose that we had no voice or tongue, and wanted to communicate with one another, should we not, like the deaf…make signs with the hands and head and the rest of the body?

—Plato *The Cratylus* (212)

An exchange between literary theory and sign languages is long overdue. Centuries overdue: for as early as Plato's *Cratylus*, Western "hearing" intellectuals have been aware of the manual languages of Deaf[2] communities, but twenty-five centuries since Plato, we remain largely ignorant that our concepts of language and literature have evolved within a false dualism of speech and writing. Only as recently as William Stokoe's linguistic research in the 1960s, have we realized that Sign[3] is an "official" human language with the capacity to generate a nearly infinite number of propositions from a vast lexicon. Yet, while linguists have been exploring this revolution in language, literary critics remain largely unaware that Sign is a natural linguistic mode capable of producing a body of literature.[4] This body of literature is, rather, a literature of the body that transforms the linear model of speech and writing into an open linguistic field of vision, time, space, and the body.

As Sign literature emerges in the late twentieth century, we can only wonder how its absence has helped to shape our ideas about language, literature, and the world. We must wonder if Sign's absence has lead to hidden limits and desires in our relationship to language. One could, perhaps, argue that speech and writing have been searching for their visual/spatial counterpart since Simonides of Keos' formulation that "poetry is speaking painting" while "painting is mute poetry," and extending through, among others, Horace's dictum *ut pictura poesis*, centuries of religious "pattern poetry,"[5] Blake's illustrations, Stein's cubism, Pound's ideograms, Olson's hieroglyphics, concrete poetry, performance poetry, ethnopoetics, video-texts, and virtual texts. These experiments have, in their various ways, sought to imbue speech and writing with the visual and spatial dimensions of images and the body. Have these experiments emerged out of a phantom-limb phenomenon where writers have sensed language's severed visual-spatial mode and went groping after it?[6] If the Deaf poet had been mythologized as the blind poet has been, would literature have developed differently? Would the map which draws the historical relation between visual and literary arts have to be redrawn? What sorts of genres would have emerged? Would our metaphysical heritage have been different if we were not only the speaking but also the "signing animal"?

While these questions are beyond the scope of the present essay, they lead toward its general purpose: to show that what many scholars would consider the marginal literary practices (if you can even call them "literary") of "disabled" persons is, on the contrary, of central importance to any one, hearing or Deaf, who is interested in the relations of language and literature to culture, identity, and being. In order to recognize Sign as a medium for literature, we must open an exchange between Sign and theory by exploring ways that theory enhances our understanding of Sign and ways that Sign enhances—and challenges—our understanding of theory and literature. This opening exchange will ask numerous questions that will gesture toward a more in-depth study of Sign literature.

The following dialogue between Sign and theory is more like a conference call between Sign and interconnected and contradictory areas of criticism: deconstruction, cultural studies (at the intersection of feminism/postcolonialism/multiculturalism), semiotics, and phenomenology. Rather than applying a monolithic paradigm, I hope to assemble a collection of perspectives that will offer the best vantage points from which to explore a nonwritten, spatial form of literature. This eclectic approach is especially important as the small body of criticism of Sign literature remains rooted in one-dimensional approaches. The formalist analyses of Clayton Valli and Edward Klima and Ursula Bellugi and the semiotic approaches of Jim Cohn and Heidi Rose are much needed contributions to their field, but are unable to place Sign literature in its proper historical, political, metaphysical perspective—which is the goal of this present study. My intent, though, is ultimately not to feed Sign poems through a convoluted critical machine to produce insightful "readings" or rather, "viewings"; instead, one hopes these concepts and connections will eventually develop dialogically with Sign poetic practices themselves.

Deconstruction and Deafness: Phonocentrism, Audism, and Sign Language

The exchange between theory and Sign should open, appropriately, with Jacques Derrida, for it is he who has brought the importance of nonphonetic linguistic modalities to the forefront of twentieth-century thought by severing the "natural" connection between the voice and language. The voice, Derrida believes, is more than a means of communicating—it is the source for Western ideas of truth, being, and presence. The system of "hearing-oneself-speak," Derrida contends, "has necessarily dominated the history of the world during an entire epoch, and has even produced the idea of the world, the idea of world-origin" (8). This constitutive role of the voice results from the self-presence created by hearing-oneself-speak. One's own voice is completely interior, fully present to the speaker; it is the source of self-identity, of self-presence. Meaning constituted within this full-presence then becomes the standard for notions of identity, precipitating a metaphysics based on the full-presence of self, meaning, and identity. The privileging of the voice, which Derrida calls "phonocentrism," is the linguistic phenomenon that leads toward "logocentrism," the Western metaphysical orientation which perceives meaning to be anchored by the self-presence of identity. Against this tradition, Derrida recognizes that the voice has no natural primacy over nonphonetic forms of language and that the metaphysics of presence is infused with the free-play and undecidability of language. Seeking to deconstruct phonocentric metaphysics, Derrida explores nonphonetic forms of language—hieroglyphics, ideograms, algebraic notations, and nonlinear writing. His explorations lead beyond phonocentric linguistics toward "grammatology," a science of writing and textuality.

When seen through deconstructive lenses, Sign dilates its sphere of influence from the socio-political site of the Deaf community to the entire history of Western "hearing" metaphysics. With its deconstruction of the voice-centered tradition, grammatology, one might say, initiates a "Deaf philosophy"—if it weren't for the fact that Derrida fails to engage theoretical issues of deafness or signing to any significant degree. The exchange between Sign and deconstruction, then, recognizes the metaphysical implications of Sign while Sign, in turn, extends the project of deconstruction beyond its own limitations drawn by the exclusion of Sign and Deaf history.

The theoretical significance of "deafness," in this sense, takes on new historical and metaphysical importance that pathologized "deafness" cannot. If nonphonetic writing interrupts the primacy of the voice, deafness signifies the consummate moment of disruption. Deafness exiles the voice from the body, from meaning, from being; it sabotages its interiority from within, corrupting the system which has produced the "hearing" idea of the world. Deafness, then, occupies a consummate moment in the deconstruction of Western ontology. Further, deafness does more than disrupt the system of "hearing-oneself-speak"; it creates an embodied linguistic system which, unlike speech, is not fully present to itself. Signers, unless gazing into the mirror, do not fully see themselves signify. While they may see their hands, they cannot see their own face perform much of Sign's grammatical nuances. The eye, unlike the ear in the system of "hearing-oneself-speak," can only partially "see-oneself-sign." There is always a trace of nonpresence in the system of signing.

One wonders, then, if Derrida had engaged the theoretical implications of deafness and Sign further, might he have expanded the term "Sign" as he did "Writing" to signify *differance*, Derrida's neologism that cannot be spoken but only seen, signifying that phonetic writing is not simply a copy of speech. At this point, we can only begin to conjecture what sort of different philosophical resonance would occur by re-reading deconstruction with regards to Sign in the place of—or in addition to—writing.

While Derrida does not engage the theoretical implications of deafness or Sign in any depth, he does entertain Rousseau's contradictory relation to the language of gesture, which Rousseau attributes to Deaf persons on occasion. Early in the *Essay on the Origin of Human Languages* when Rousseau imagines that a society could develop arts, commerce, government—all without recourse to speech. After all, Rousseau writes, "The mutes of great nobles understand each other and understand everything that is said to them by means of signs, just as well as one can understand anything said in discourse" (*Essay* 9). This observation leads Rousseau to muse that "the art of communicating our ideas depends less upon the organs we use in such communication than it does upon a power proper to man, according to which he uses his organs in this way, and which, if he lacked these, would lead him to use others to the same end" (10). Derrida seizes on this nonphonocentric moment in Rousseau to destabilize the primacy of the voice in Western philosophy. "It is once again the power of substituting one organ for another," Derrida writes, "of articulating space and time, sign and voice, hand and spirit, it is this faculty of supplementarity which is the true origin—or nonorigin—of languages" (241). As the condition leading toward the supplement, deafness could be read, ironically, as that which makes the origin of language possible. Deafness summonses up the visual-spatial dimension of language to supplant the voice from within. It sets *differance* in motion.

This inversion of deafness—from linguistic isolation to the precondition of language itself—has political implications for the Deaf community's difficult task of depathologizing Deaf identity within the culture of academia. After considering deafness in relation to deconstruction, one may begin to see the Deaf community—not as a group defined by its pathological relation to language—but rather as an example of a culture flourishing beyond the reaches of logocentrism. The possibility of such a community raises questions. Is resisting phonocentrism tantamount to resisting logocentrism? What are the phenomenological differences between "being-in-the deaf-world" and "being-in-the-hearing-world"? Are Deaf persons—over ninety percent of whom are born in hearing families—really out of reach of logocentrism? By raising issues surrounding Sign to the metaphysical level, could the argument for a Deaf cultural identity be expanded beyond the anthropological and socio-linguistic identifications of distinctly "Deaf " cultural acts—such as Deaf folklore, jokes, attention getting strategies, and social organizations—to encompass a deeper level: a level that Sign and "not-hearing-oneself-speak" creates outside of hearing-dominated metaphysics?

Given the relevance of these questions to grammatology, it is surprising that Derrida never engages signing and deafness as theoretically and historically significant issues.[7] When he does mention deafness it is through the "voices" of others: Hegel, Leibniz, Rousseau, and Saussure. Making others speak about deafness is a strange ventriloquism which demonstrates that Derrida is aware, obviously, of Sign and Deaf communities. One may link this critical oversight as being symptomatic of not really *seeing* Deaf people, of tacitly acknowledging their absence from being. If this is so, this audist oversight reinscribes the very phonocentrism Derrida sets out to deconstruct. At the very least, one may accuse Derrida's grammatology of suffering from an undertheorized sociopolitical site because he neglects Deaf history. While he considers logocentrism to be "the most original and powerful ethnocentrism," (3) he does not follow this statement to its most severe sociopolitical manifestation: audism.

Audism is the most extreme deployment of phonocentrism ranging from incarcerating Deaf persons in mental institutions, to eugenics movements (one sponsored by Alexander Graham Bell in America, another currently practiced in China), to the oppression of sign language in the education of Deaf persons. Many Deaf adults today tell of their violent experiences growing up in oralist schools—their hands slapped or tied behind their backs if they were caught signing.[8] Further, early Deaf schools offered a collection of subjugated bodies on which doctors could develop the science of otology. Acids, needles, and hammers all violated the ears and skulls of Deaf children so that they could be returned to "normal."[9]

While he could have made many relevant connections between phonocentrism and oralist educational practices, Derrida instead labels the condemnation of Leibniz's desire for a nonphonetic, universal script as "the most energetic eighteenth-century *reaction* organizing the defense of phonologism and of logocentric metaphysics" (99). I propose, instead, that the history of deaf education, as it is marked by violent oppression of sign and the subjugation of Deaf persons, is a more "energetic reaction" to phonocentrism. It is where phonocentrism meets social and educational policy. Indeed, nowhere will one find a more vehement declaration of voice-as-presence than by reading the words of oralist educators. Consider, for example, the following declaration from the father of deaf education in German-speaking lands:

> The breath of life resides in the voice.... The voice is a living emanation of that spirit that God breathed into man when he created him a living soul...What stupidity we find in most of these unfortunate deaf...How little they differ from animals. (Lane, 107)

This all too common association between Deaf persons and animals offers arguably the most vivid illustration of Derrida's central connection between voice and human presence. As Douglas Baynton, Harlan Lane, and others have shown, Deaf identity has been publicly constructed through metaphorics of animality, darkness, imprisonment, and isolation, resulting in a relay of hierarchized binary oppositions which divide along the axis of absence and presence: animal/human; prisoner/property owner; foreigner/citizen; darkness/light; normality/pathology. Just as the Deaf voice is exiled from its own body, Deaf persons have been exiled from the phonocentric body-politic.

One hopes these initial ideas point toward a future critical project of exploring a grammatology of Sign that recognizes Sign's historical and metaphysical context while also documenting phonocentrism's political legacy. Such a project, however, would require a broader theoretical base than grammatology itself offers. If Sign criticism is to be an instrumental means of spreading the recognition of Sign literature and Deaf culture, it needs to articulate itself as an oppositional discourse alongside others which oppose oppression in its various forms. For this reason, Sign criticism would benefit from exploring its relation with feminism, postcolonialism, and multiculturalism, in addition to deconstruction.

Feminism/Postcolonialism/Multiculturalism and Sign Literature

Inviting feminism, postcolonialism, and multiculturalism into a dialogue with deconstruction brings together an uneasy alliance. It has become a critical cliche, for example, to accuse deconstruction of decentering the human subject just as disempowered groups were gaining empowered subjectivities. Despite important differences, however, deconstruction may find its greatest alliance with these oppositional discourses in its dismantling of phonocentrism and audism. Instead of exhuming well-documented contentions, therefore, it seems more advantageous to draw together overlapping concerns in order to form a broad textual, social, and political context for the emergence of Deaf/Sign literature.

Forming such a coalition of ideas is based on Audre Lorde's belief that sexism, homophobia, and racism are "particular manifestations of the same disease" (137)—as are ethnocentrism, colonialism, ableism, and audism. "Can any one here," Lorde asks, "still afford to believe that the pursuit of liberation can be the sole and particular province of any one particular race, or sex, or age, or religion, or sexuality, or class?" (140). Indeed, we cannot—nor can we continue to neglect the commonly elided category of "ability" from this "pursuit of liberation."

In clearing a space to talk about Deaf culture and Sign literature, a number of questions arise in the initial dialogue between Deaf studies and each area: feminism, postcolonialism, and multiculturalism; and from those questions, a few overlapping concerns may be identified that will form ways of talking about Sign literature in a political and cultural context. This exchange will, one hopes, begin to build for Deaf studies a strong sociopolitical foundation while Deaf studies, in turn, may expand the "pursuit of liberation" to include ableism and audism which are frequently overlooked by an overdetermination of racism and sexism.

The project of recognizing Deaf identity bears similarities to the feminist project of re-gaining a "body of one's own" through linguistic and literary practices. Sign, in a more graphic way, perhaps, than *l'écriture feminine* is a "writing of/on the body." The relation between Sign and *l'écriture feminine* raises questions that could have interesting implications for feminist performance. Does the antiphonocentric nature of Sign offer a means of averting the essentializing tendency of *l'écriture feminine*? Does the four-dimensional space of performance offer ways of deconstructing phallogocentric linear discourse? How does the gender of the signer influence the reading/viewing of the "text" itself? How does the male gaze construct the female body/text? Can gender ever be bracketed out of a reading of a Sign performance?

Many of these feminist issues anticipate those of postcolonial discourse. At first glance, though, one would not think of Deaf persons as being "colonized"—disciplined, yes, but colonized? However, as Harlan Lane shows, audism is homologous with colonialism, including "the physical subjugation of a disempowered people, the imposition of alien language and mores, and the regulation of education in behalf of the colonizer's goals" (32). How accurate is Lane's position? Could one consider medicine's often brutal experimentation on the ears of Deaf children a form of physical subjugation? Could the controversial surgical procedure used to restore hearing—the cochlear implant—be considered a form of colonizing the Deaf body and eradicating a Deaf culture? Is the effort to impose English-only in Deaf residential schools similar, say, to forcing Native Americans to adopt a nationalized language and identity in residential schools? Is the fact that oral-based pedagogies exclude Deaf persons from deaf education a means of securing hearing dominance over the Deaf community? How does a postcolonial writer/signer resist the hegemony of dominant literature while working within the field of literature?

In addition, if Sign literature is to be considered as an "ethnic" literature, it should inquire into its relation to other minority literatures and their ethnic origins. The very claim that Deaf identity is cultural rather than pathological provokes an interrogation of our assumed "natural" categories of cultural identity. How can Deaf persons share a cultural identity if they do not have a common religion, nationality, race, or ethnicity? Do predominantly "Deaf spaces," such as Deaf residential schools and Deaf clubs, constitute a type of national "homeland"? How does Deaf identity intersect with other simultaneous subject positions—gender, race, nationality, class? Would a Deaf American feel more "at home" with, say, a Deaf Japanese than a hearing American from around the block? Is it possible to acknowledge the strength of Deaf identity but not fall into the trap of hierarchizing identities? Is Deaf culture, as it crosses national, racial, and economic borders, an emblematic postmodern culture? And finally, how does a postmodern theory of Deaf culture influence a theory of Sign literature?

This initial meeting of Deaf studies, Sign literature, and cultural studies helps to identify a few underlying concepts—anti-essentialism, hybridity, and border consciousness—that will be helpful in providing a political context for discussing Sign literature. Because of the relay between logocentrism, phonocentrism, and audism, any critical practice of Sign literature needs to move beyond logocentric ways of looking at identity—that is, basing one's identity on essentialized definitions such as "speech is an *essential* human trait" or "whites are *essentially* more intelligent than other races." Instead, we need to recognize identities as constantly being constructed within a complex network of social, political, and linguistic influences. Such anti-essentialist thinking is important, for, as Edward Said comments, "essentialisms have the power to turn human beings against one another" by allowing us to slide into "an unthinking acceptance of stereotypes, myths, animosities, and traditions encouraged by imperialism" (229). If audism is itself a form of essentialist thinking, then Deaf resistance to it should not be a reinscription of it. We need to recognize, then, that a person cannot be *purely* Deaf apart from the confluence of multiple subject positions—nationality, race, gender, class, disability, sexual preference—just as one cannot be *purely* Female, Mexican, or Asian. Avoiding an essentialist view of Deaf identity would be the equivalent of avoiding what Frantz Fanon calls "the pitfalls of national consciousness" that reinscribes the oppressive essentialism of colonialism.

As opposed to an essentialized "national" or "audist" consciousness, Sign literature might be more effectively approached through a "border consciousness" that recognizes the uniqueness of Deaf culture and Sign literature, but that also acknowledges their social construction. Indeed, the institutional patterns of Deaf cultural transmission offer a particularly postmodern example of the constructed rather than essential nature of identity. Over ninety percent of Deaf persons do not form their cultural identity through their family but through social organizations and institutions. As Carol Padden and Tom Humphries explain, one learns to be Deaf, not through an essential "presence of a common physical condition," but by gaining "access to a certain cultural history, the culture of Deaf people in America" (25). To paraphrase Simone de Beauvoir's famous statement about female identity: one is not born but rather becomes Deaf. Such a perspective of Deaf identity has bearing on the ways we discuss Sign literature; for, as Edward Said reminds us, we need to recognize that all "cultural forms are hybrid, mixed, impure, and the time has come in cultural analysis to reconnect their analysis with their actuality" (14).

In fact, the notion of "Sign literature" is itself a product of hearing/Deaf borderlands. As the term "literature" derives from the Latin *litere*, or "letter," "Sign literature" is oxymoronic in the same sense as "oral literature." Because of the inaccuracy of the label, Heidi Rose has proposed that creative use of American Sign Language be known as "ASL ART" which "should be studied as a distinct phenomenon, not as some sort of hybrid between the written and oral form" ("Critical Methodology," 15). Rose's re-definition raises interesting ontological questions regarding the definition of Sign literature. Yet, rather than establishing a wholesale re-definition, it may be wise to let the question of ASL "literature" remain just that, a question. The desire to define whether creative use of ASL is or is not "literature," I feel, unnecessarily limits the discussion to an essentialized either/or opposition. The issues involved in making such a distinction are far too complex and important to both hearing and Deaf communities to be reduced to such a dichotomy. Rather than offering a totalizing answer, it may be wise to tolerate the ambiguity that ASL "art" both *is* and *is not* "literature," that it is akin to hearing literary practices, but also cannot be contained by those practices.[10]

There are too many political and analytical benefits of discussing creative Sign as literature to banish it from the curricular domain of literature. These benefits have been demonstrated best, perhaps, by Clayton Valli who has defined such techniques as "lines" and "rhymes" in Sign poetry. In his essay, "The Nature of a Line in ASL Poetry," Valli explains how an ASL poet creates signed "lines" through visual rhyme patterns. A signed rhyme is made through a repetition of particular handshapes, movement paths, sign locations, or nonmanual markers such as facial expressions or body postures. For example, in his poem, "Snowflake," Valli employs visual rhyme by repeating the same "five" handshape (palm open, all fingers extended) to sign TREE, then to draw the outline of the leaves on the tree, and then to show the leaves falling to the ground. In addition, Valli and others accept the same genre distinctions for Sign as for hearing literature. Identifying such hearing-centered literary analogues demonstrates that Sign can be explored creatively to produce as linguistically complex "texts" as can speech and writing. That Sign can partake in the literary traditions of the West is an indispensable argument in convincing universities to recognize Sign literature, a move which would continue to depathologize Deaf identity in the minds of hearing persons.

However, uncritically adopting the signifier of "literature" dismisses the fact that "literature has been formed within exclusive practices of spoken and written languages. As the linear model is the structural embodiment of hearing forms of literature, Valli's concept of the "line" places Sign literature directly within a phonocentric/audist tradition. Why even concern ourselves with the discussions of "lines" and "rhymes"? What sort of political, historical, and metaphysical baggage do those terms carry? How well can the terms of an aural/temporal art be applied to a visual-spatial art? In order to discuss Sign as literature, then, one must proceed through the lexicon of hearing criticism and interrogate the terms for their imbedded audist ideologies and their critical accuracy. In some instances, terminology can take on new dimensions when it crosses the inter-semiotic gap to visual/spatial language—or old dimensions, as with "rhythm" which originated, not in the musical arts, but in dance.[11] Within Sign criticism, the concept of rhythm may be restored to its original connection with the movements of the body in time and space.

In fact, there is no reason to confine a lexicon for Sign literature to the literary arts. As a visual performance art, Sign literature may bear more similarity to painting, dance, drama, film, and video than to poetry or fiction. A "line" in Sign poetry, for example, might be more accurately modeled after the concept of the "line" in painting or a choreographed "phrase" in dance. Instead of moving from left to right, the Sign poet draws lines through space in all directions. In addition, given the cinematic nature of ASL,[12] the Sign lexicon must be expanded to include such concepts as "editing," "montage," "panning," "close-up," and "slow-motion." Indeed, why not go so far as to invent a new vocabulary in Sign and then translate that lexicon into written glosses for ASL signs?

This "border theory" asks us to consider ways to avert a reductive either/or response to Sign literature; it asks us how we may refer to it in such a way that always already implies resistance to being called "*literature*"; it asks us to see Sign literature as a hybrid creation, at once unique to Deaf cultural experience, but also crossing over a multitude of national, economic, racial, ethnic, gendered, sexual, linguistic, artistic, and textual borders. Identifying the borders that a particular poem, narrative, or performer crosses over, invites critical dialogue about the relations between minority and dominant literatures, between Deaf and hearing worlds, and between Deaf identity and Sign literature.

One hopes that, as Trinh Minh-ha writes, "this shuttling in-between frontiers is a working out of and an appeal to another sensibility, another consciousness of the condition of marginality: that in which marginality is the condition of the center" (216). The ultimate scope of this project, then, is to recognize the previously marginalized body of Sign literature, and in so doing to expose the false dualism of speech and writing that has helped to structure the hearing "center" of Western civilization.

Toward a "Poetics of Space": From Semiotics to Phenomenology

If Sign literature offers a rare opportunity to reconsider what literature is, then Sign criticism needs to amass the critical breadth for such an undertaking. The first step is to move beyond Sign criticism's preoccupation with formalist linguistic analysis. The writings of Clayton Valli, Edward Klima, and Ursula Bellugi offer a useful vocabulary for describing a Sign's physical and linguistic characteristics, but they are unable to explore the wider metaphysical, sociopolitical, and phenomenological dimensions of Sign literature. As linguists, these writers are more concerned with demonstrating ASL's depth and flexibility than with exploring a fundamental rethinking of the way that literature is produced and perceived.

Heidi Rose is one of the first persons to break away from linguistic formalism to discuss Sign literature in the context of a more contemporary criticism—semiotics. In her essay, "A Semiotic Analysis of Artistic American Sign Language and a Performance of Poetry," Rose makes a significant contribution toward a theory of Sign literature by applying C. S. Peirce's semiotics to a reading of a signed poem. According to Peirce, signs (not ASL "signs," but rather anything that produces meaning) can take three different forms: icon (representation by likeness, e.g., portrait, onomatopoeia), index, (representation by relation, e.g., smoke to fire, temperature to fever) and symbol (representation by arbitrary signifiers, e.g., conventional words.) Unlike speech and writing, Sign is most often associated with iconic signification. Rose agrees that Sign's unique character is its iconicity, but only after demonstrating that a Sign poem is more complex than a series of manual pictures in the air. During the course of a performance, Rose explains, the hands may sign on the iconic or symbolic levels while the non-manual markers (i.e., facial expressions) tend to produce indexical meaning. In the end, though, the noniconic elements of the poem "flesh out the manual signs and complete the message with the final effect highlighting the iconic means of communication" (154). The body signifies differently throughout the course of a poem, though its ultimate goal, according to Rose, is to embody iconic images, to move closer to the thing-itself.

Underlying Rose's analysis (and the existing body of Sign criticism), however, is the assumption that iconicity is an inherent and constant element within the text, independent of the viewer's relationship to the poem. This assumption is closely allied with another: that Peirce's semiotic taxonomy is mutually exclusive and stable. Deaf critic Joseph Grigely, however, demonstrates that semiotics cannot, in the end, produce the predictable science of language that it had hoped. "Peirce's taxonomy of signs," Grigely writes, "is essentially an unstable ontology, and that the attribution of sign values—iconicity, indexicality, and arbitrariness—is part of a dynamic process by which a reader circumscribes frames of reference as part of the act of reading" (243). While Grigely discusses but does not focus on Sign poetry, he helps Sign criticism to move beyond its preoccupation with iconicity to engage the larger process of how iconicity is itself produced and received. In "The Implosion of Iconicity," Grigely writes:

> Every time we claim to discover an iconic presence—be it an onomatope like "moo-cow" or in a visual analogue like the ASL sign for TREE—our discovery is actually a hermeneutic act, an interpretation of certain textual relations.... An interpretive model of iconicity does not require a factual similarity between a sign and its referent, but merely an impression that similitude of some kind or form exists—whether or not it actually does. (246)

Iconicity, therefore, is less an element of the poem itself than a form of perception, less an absolute value than, as Charles Morris has remarked, "a matter of degree" (quoted in Grigely, 246). Taking into account the role of the reader or viewer in the production of meaning, Grigely moves away from the formalized "text-as-object" toward the "text-as-an-event" that takes place somewhere between the poet and the audience. This move is liberating, especially to oral and sign poetics, for it recognizes the inescapable performative nature of literature.

Once we expand our criticism to accommodate the viewer's active role in creating the poem, we are no longer limited to discussing poems as if they took place in objectifiable, linguistic space, for we do not *perceive* that space. Such linguistic space is based on a Newtonian constancy of spatial relations. The poetic space we perceive, however, is of a different nature. Calculating and recording the positions of the hands in relation to the body, for instance, may help to describe the physical properties of text, but leaves us unable to explain our perceptions of embodied images that appear, dissolve, enlarge, shrink, transform, as they shift from close-up to far-away, wide-angle, slow-motion, fast-forward, and freeze-frame. While these spatio-temporal techniques have their basis in Sign's unique linguistic use of four-dimensions, their effect can only be articulated within a theory that remains rooted in the perceptions of the body. For this reason any linguistic or semiotic analysis is incomplete without considering viewer-oriented phenomenological criticism.

Phenomenology takes as its starting point Edmund Husserl's questioning of the "natural attitude" that objects exist independently from our consciousness of them. Human consciousness, according to Husserl and other phenomenologists, is not formed through a passive reception of the ready-made world, but through active constitution of that world. Phenomenological or "reader-response" criticism, then, inquires into the ways that readers are themselves producers of literary texts. Any "viewer-response" criticism of Sign poetry must begin by taking into account the embodied perception of space, vision, and time, and then by considering these in relation to phenomenologies of language and the literary imagination. This confluence of phenomenologies leads toward what may be called the "poetics of space," intentionally borrowing from Gaston Bachelard's book by the same title.

A starting point for the understanding of the poetics of space is Merleau-Ponty's phenomenology of language which applies to Sign as well as to speaking and writing. "The word and speech," Merleau-Ponty writes, must somehow cease to be a way of designating things or thoughts, and become the presence of that thought in the phenomenal world, and, moreover, not its clothing, but its token or *its body....* [W]e find there, beneath the conceptual meaning of the words, an existential meaning which is not only rendered by them, but which inhabits them." (*Phenomenology of Perception*, 182)

In taking on a phenomenal, embodied presence of its own, language is not condemned to the perpetual task of mimesis and referentiality; language is itself the body, flesh, and bone of meaning. When audiences watch Clayton Valli's poem, "Dew on Spiderweb," for example, they may witness the linguistic spinning of a spiderweb as real as any spiderweb seen before. Of course, this is an image of a spiderweb, but as Gaston Bachelard asks, "why should the actions of the imagination not be as real as those of perception?" (158). Valli's image does not so much iconically *refer* to a spiderweb "out-there," but rather brings what Merleau-Ponty has called "a diagram of the life of the actual" ("Eye and Mind," 126) into *being*. As witnesses of this poetic incarnation, we inhabit the poem's four-dimensional topography and find ourselves in the intimate physical and phenomenal presence of image-things.[13]

Such an experience cannot be measured. We do not so much see the text as an object "out there" as we "see according to, or with it" (Merleau-Ponty, 126). We do not so much see a stable volume of linguistic space, but rather a much more volatile volume of poetic space. For "everything, even size, is a human value," Bachelard writes. Just as "miniature can accumulate size... [and become] *vast* in its own way," "the dialectics of inside and outside can no longer be taken in their simple reciprocity" (216). In the poetics of space, the "duality of subject and object is iridescent, shimmering, unceasingly active in its inversions" (xv). Indeed, it would even be difficult to say exactly where any given image *is*; in the "text-as-event," the borders between viewer and text, subject and object, inside and outside, become porous.

We now enter into a whole new field of questions about the nature of perception, body, space, time, Sign, and literature. A few beginning questions must be asked, even if there is not time to answer them: How is (or isn't) "poetic space" different from "everyday" space? How is spatial perception in Sign different from that of speech and writing? Does Sign structure the world differently? What are the poetic and cultural implications of this different 'structure'? How would a phenomenology of Sign change the ways we talk about relations between the viewer and the text, the subject and the object?

In order to demonstrate briefly how the poetics of space may help us to approach Sign poetry, I return to the notion of the poetic "line." As Valli chooses the rhymed line break as the exclusive model for the signed line, this analogy precludes ASL from more contemporary types of line breaks, such as those of free verse. One wonders why Sign criticism would want to coerce ASL's most unique quality—its four dimensions—into the one-dimensional model of the line. Not only is this an inaccurate analogy, it also places ASL literature as a derivative form of poetry.

Instead of forcing the linear model of oral and written poetics on Sign, it may be more beneficial to inquire into the phenomenological reception of a "line." A viewer does not actually perceive line division rhyme as such—for it is a linguistic analogy. What the viewer sees, rather, is a complex assemblage of lines drawn through space by fingers, hand movements, arm movements, or whole body movements. If the afterimage of all the lines were recorded on video throughout the course of a poem, the visual effect would be more like that of a Susan Howe poem than a sonnet.

Take, for example, the opening of Flying Word Project's "Poetry," where performer Peter Cook gestures shooting a gun. He begins the "line" by tracing the direction of the bullet with the index finger. Cook repeats the motion quickly, conveying the speed of the bullet. This line drawn through space then extends and curves as it transforms into signifying a moon circling a planet.

This radical transformation from human to cosmic scale, from straight to circular, threaded together through the same handshape, moves the reader through vastly different experiences of space. From the intimacy of a mid-range shot to the immensity of the distance shot of a whole planet, the producer/viewer's body not only shifts perspectives, but in so doing, *inhabits a new kind of space*. This perceived "line," in other words, cannot be measured as a constant volume, but only in its ability to generate *poetic volume*.

Seeing the line within the full space and time of the body leads Sign literature away from the pho-nocentric literary model, and toward concepts more akin to the visual and performative arts. Indeed, at the hands of Sign poets, the poetic line may resemble a Klee more than a Keats; and like the lines in a Klee, Sign is "a matter of freeing the line, of revivifying its constituting power" (Merleau-Ponty, "Eye and Mind," 143). Such a liberation of the prosaic line may provide an example of the margin freeing the center from its own constraints.

Further phenomenological study of Sign poetry will, one hopes, explore other literary concepts in their visual-spatial quality, as opposed to their linguistic quantity. This approach will keep Sign criticism close to the original site of poetic creation: the meeting of body, time, space, and language. In the end, we may arrive at a viewing practice in which Sign poems are not so much "read" or "seen" as they are *lived* in from the inside.

Conclusion

Drawing out all the possible connections, contradictions, and ambiguities between deconstruction, cultural studies, semiotics, and phenomenology as they apply to Sign literature will be a major critical task. To begin, a few key critical concepts may be isolated: while Sign literature is a minority cultural practice, it nonetheless has profound implications for the dominant group's understanding of language, literature, and culture. These implications manifest at the metaphysical site (the breaking of the he-gemony of speech-writing); the sociopolitical site (the emergence of a postmodern culture outside of phonocentrism); the textual site (the practice of a postmodern bardic tradition recorded only through video-text); and the phenomenological site (the performance of an alternative visual-spatial means of being-in-the-world). Through the performance of a signed text, all these sites operate simultaneously, each within the other. Boundaries give way and become openings. "A narrow gate," Bachelard writes, "opens up an entire world" (185). One hopes the narrow gate of Sign literature and criticism will open up the entire world of experience previously foreclosed by the dominance of speech and writing. If the figure of the blind poet inhabits the origins of poetry, then we may look toward the Deaf poet to explore the future of poetry as it becomes increasingly visual, spatial, and embodied.

Notes

1. Deaf persons, I believe, are first and foremost members of a cultural and linguistic community, bearing more similarity, say, to Hispanics than to persons with cerebral palsy. My publishing this article in a disability studies reader, however, highlights what I feel may be a coalition formed between Deaf studies and disability studies. This coalition must be aware that Deaf persons form a unique linguistic and cultural group, but that both groups may strive in tandem to resist the pathologization of the body by the abled body-politic. Deaf and disability studies, for example, could collaborate to resist China's present eugenics practice of sterilizing "disabled" persons. Only by joining forces and resources may the Deaf and persons with disabilities gain a larger political voice to denounce China's human rights violations as well as America's policy to China.

2. In keeping with conventions within Deaf studies, I use the capitalized *Deaf* to refer to the cultural group of ASL-users while lower case *deaf* and *deafness* refer to the physical phenomena of not hearing.

3. I refer to sign languages collectively as "Sign." Sign includes all native sign languages—British Sign Language, American Sign Language, French Sign Language, Chinese Sign Language, etc. but does not include manual versions of dominant languages such as Signed Exact English. The distinctions between manual versions of dominant languages and the native languages of Deaf communities presents an interesting field of study which may illuminate the constitutive nature of vision in Sign grammar that is at odds with the logic of spoken languages.

4. Since the advent of video publications, a number of Deaf poets and storytellers have achieved national recognition within the Deaf community: Ella Mae Lentz, Dorothy Miles, Bernard Bragg, Debbie Rennie, Patrick Graybill, Gilbert Eastman, Ben Bahan, Sam Supalla and Flying Words Project (Peter Cook and Kenny Lerner). The most accessible videos are pro-duced by Dawn Sign Press which has published the *Poetry in Motion* series featuring Debbie Rennie, Patrick Graybill, and Clayton Valli, the *ASL Literature* series featuring narratives by Ben Bahan and Sam Supalla, and more recently, Clayton Valli's *Selected Works*. In Motion Press has also published a collection of poems by Ella Mae Lentz entitled *The Treasure*.

5. See Dick Higgins's *Pattern Poetry: Guide to an Unknown Literature.*

6. Indeed, some writers tread so close to the poetics of Sign, that it is only their inability to see through the label of disability (and the oppression of Sign in the early part of this century) that precluded recognition of Sign as a medium for literature. Ernest Fenollosa's *The Chinese Written Character as a Medium for Poetry* might have been more accurate had he written about ASL rather than the Chinese ideogram. In addition, Artaud's *The Theater and its Double* praises sign language without ever connecting the language of gesture to the Deaf community. No doubt, Artaud, Fenollosa, and Pound would have been enthralled with the experimental poetics of avant-garde Deaf poets. More recently, only a scattering of contemporary poets and critics have recognized Sign poetry. Jerome and Diane Rothenberg include an article on Sign poetry by Edward Klima and Ursula Bellugi in *Symposium of the Whole: A Range of Discourse Toward an Ethnopoetics*; in 1984, Allen Ginsberg visited the National Technical Institute for the Deaf in Rochester, New York where he met with Deaf poets (cf. Cohn's "Visible Poetics" essay.); and in the *MLA Newsletter*, critic W.J.T. Mitchell wrote that "The poetry of the deaf stages for us in the most vivid possible form the basic shift in literary understanding that has been occurring in the last decade: the movement from a "textual" model (based in the narrowly defined circuit of writing and speech) to a "performance" model." (14).

7. In the thirty years since the publication of *De la Grammatologie*, Derrida continued to overlook deafness and Sign. In those years, Europe and the United States have witnessed the most important years in Deaf history. With the 1988 Gallaudet Revolution, Deaf culture has become recognized in the international media. And yet, Derrida continues to avoid the questions raised by deafness even though he, along with Paul de Man has explored the metaphorics of blindness. Derrida, however, is not the only deconstructionist to miss the metaphysical implications of deafness. In *The Telephone Book*, Avital Ronell is an audist tourist in her brief foray into Deaf culture. In fact, she treats the audist, Alexander Graham Bell, so sympathetically that she fails to see the strong arm of logocentrism reaching through Bell's call for a eugenics movement to eradicate "a deaf variety of the human race." When discussing the work of Bell, Ronell writes, "We are still talking art, and of the poetry diverting a child from the isolation of deafness, saving the child in language, bringing him to the proximity of speech with his father. AGB did this—an act of genuine *poiesis . . .*" (329–30). Is this not, rather, an act of coercing a deaf child into phonocentrism?; is it not a form of violence to deny a child a natural visual language when he cannot hear speech? Would it not be more of an act of genuine *poeisis* to teach the Father to sign? Further, Ronell's worst kind of tourism is evident as she does not bother to understand basic cultural literacy of Deaf persons. She calls the Abbé de l'Epée the "first literate deaf-mute"; the Abbé, however, was a hearing man in his fifties who stumbled upon two deaf women in Paris and subsequently became interested in deaf education.

8. See Bernard Bragg's *Lessons in Laughter: The Autobiography of a Deaf Actor* as signed to Eugene Bergman. Bragg recounts his childhood experiences being taught how to laugh like hearing persons because his teacher was annoyed that his pupils sounded like animals when they laughed.

9. See Harlan Lane, *The Mask of Benevolence* for further discussion, especially p. 212–16. Lane is the first to use the work of Michel Foucault as it applies to deafness. As with Derrida, Foucault's work may be enormously beneficial to Deaf Studies, even though he overlooks the question of Deaf Culture. In fact, the discursive "birth of deafness" is so closely allied to the births of the asylum, the clinic and prisons, it is quite surprising to find no mention of deafness in Foucault. The same years that witnessed the rise of Pinel's asylums for the insane also witnessed Pinel's methods of observation and classification deployed by his student, Jean-Marc Itard, within the newly founded "Asylums for the Deaf and the Dumb"; when the medical gaze penetrated the surface of the body in the age of Bichat, otologists probed the workings of the ear; when *écoles normales* produced disciplinary pedagogies, "oralist" teachers (some of whom were also teachers at *écoles normales*) developed pedagogies to discipline the deaf body into normative language practices. In short, the Asylum for the Deaf and Dumb served as a point of convergence of discourses which, as Foucault demonstrates, all work toward the same goal: to separate the normal from the abnormal, the hearing from the deaf, in order to normalize the transgressive Other, to eradicate all differences—while ironically exacerbating them, perpetuating the subjugation of the abnormal body.

10. The inability to define ASL literature is not unique to ASL; rather, I believe hearing literature itself cannot be defined with any consistency and accuracy. The term *define* originates from the Latin *definare*, meaning to limit; I believe that it is unwise to be overly concerned with limiting the boundaries of creative practices—whether Deaf or hearing.

11. As J. J. Pollitt notes, "[rhythmos] were originally the "positions" that the human body was to assume in the course of a dance in other words the patterns or *schemata* that the body made. In the course of a dance certain obvious patterns or positions, like the raising or lowering of a foot, were naturally repeated, thus marking intervals in the dance. Since music and singing were synchronized with dancing, the recurrent positions taken by the dancer in the course of his movements also marked distinct intervals in the music.... This explains why the basic component of music and poetry was called a...foot" (quoted in Mitchell 280–81).

12. Linguist William Stokoe describes the cinematic properties of ASL, a concept originally developed by Deaf artists Bernard Bragg and Gil Eastman: "In a signed language...narrative is no longer linear and prosaic. Instead, the essence of sign language is to cut from a normal view to a close-up to a distant shot to a close up again, and so on, even including flashback and flash-forward scenes, exactly as a movie editor works.... Not only is signing itself arranged more like edited film than like written narration, but also each signer is placed very much as a camera: the field of vision and angle of view are directed but variable. Not only the signer signing but also the signer watching is aware at all times of the signer's visual orientation to what is being signed about" (quoted in Sacks, 90).

13. While this phenomenology of language could lead toward a type of logocentric self-presence, Merleau-Ponty recognizes the ambiguity of absence/presence which underlies all perception. "The perceived thing exists only insofar as I perceive it, and yet its being is never exhausted by the view I have of it. It is this simultaneous presence and absence that is required for 'something to be perceived at all' " (*Logos and Eidos: The Concept in Phenomenology*, 10). For this reason, Merleau-Ponty refers to the realm of language and the imaginary to be "quasi-present."

Works Cited

Artaud, Antonin. 1958. *The Theater and Its Double*. Trans. Mary Richards. New York: Grove Press.

ASL Literature Series. 1994. Video with Ben Bahan and Sam Supalla. Pro. Joe Dannis. Dir. James. R. DeBee. Sand Diego: DawnSignPress.

Bachelard, Gaston. 1969. *The Poetics of Space*. Trans. Maria Jolas. Boston: Beacon Press.

Baynton, Douglas. 1992. "'Silent Exile on This Earth': The Metaphorical Construction of Deafness in the Nineteenth Century." *American Quarterly* 44.2: 216–43.

Cohn, Jim. 1986. "The New Deaf Poetics: Visible Poetry." *Sign Language Studies* 52: 263–77.

Derrida, Jacques. 1976. *Of Grammatology*. Trans. Gayatri Spivak. Baltimore: The Johns Hopkins Press.

Fanon, Frantz. 1968. *The Wretched of the Earth*. Trans. Constance Farrington. New York: Grove Press.

Fenollosa, Ernest. 1968. *The Chinese Written Character as a Medium for Poetry*. Ed. Ezra Pound. San Francisco: City Lights Books.

Graybill, Patrick. 1990. *Patrick Graybill*. Video. Series *Poetry in Motion: Original Works in ASL*. Burtonsvile, MD: Sign Media.

Grigely, Joseph. 1993. "The Implosion of Iconicity." *Word and Image Interactions A Selection of Papers Given at the Second International Conference on Word and Image*. Ed. Martin Heusser. Wiese Verlag Basel.

Higgins, Dick. 1987. *Pattern Poetry: Guide to an Unknown Literature*. Albany: SUNY Press.

Klima, Edward and Ursula Bellugi. 1983. "Poetry Without Sound." *Symposium of the Whole: A Range of Discourse Toward an Ethnopoetics*. Eds. Jerome and Diane Rothenberg. Berkeley: University of California Press.

Lane, Harlan. 1992. *The Mask of Benevolence*. New York: Alfred Knopf.

Lentz, Ella Mae. 1995. *The Treasure*. Video. In Berkeley, CA: Motion Press.

Lorde, Audre. 1984. "Learning from the 60s." *Sister Outsider*. Freedom, CA: The Crossing Press.

Merleau-Ponty. 1989. *The Phenomenology of Perception*. Trans. Colin Smith. London: Routledge.

———. "Eye and Mind." 1993. *The Merleau-Ponty Aesthetics Reader: Philosophy and Painting*. Ed. Galen Johnson. Evanston, Ill: Northwestern University Press.

Mitchell, W. J. T. 1989. "Gesture, Sign, and Play: ASL Poetry and the Deaf Community." *MLA Newsletter*. Summer (1989): 13–14.

———. 1974. "Spatial Form in Literature: Toward a General Theory." *The Language of Images*. Ed. W. J. T. Mitchell. Chicago: University of Chicago Press.

Padden, Carol and Humphries, Tom. 1988. *Deaf in America: Voices from a Culture*. Cambridge: Harvard University Press.

Plato. 1937. *The Dialogues of Plato*. Vol. 2 Trans. Jowett Benjamin. New York: Random House.

Rennie, Debbie. 1990. *Debbie Rennie*. Video. *Poetry in Motion: Original Works in ASL*. Burtonsvile, MD: Sign Media.

Ronnell, Avital. 1989. *The Telephone Book: Technology—Schizophrenia—Electric Speech*. Lincoln: University of Nebraska Press.

Rose, Heidi. 1993. "A Critical Methodology for Analyzing American Sign Language Literature." Dissertation, Arizona State University.

———. 1992. "A Semiotic Analysis of Artistic American Sign Language and a Performance of Poetry." *Text and Performance Quarterly* 12.2: 146–59.

Rothenberg, Jerome and Rothenberg, Diane, eds. 1983. *Symposium of the Whole: A Range of Discourse Toward an Ethnopoetics*. Berkeley: University of California Press.

Sacks, Oliver. 1990. *Seeing Voices: A Journey into the World of the Deaf*. New York: HarperPerennial.

Said, Edward. 1994. *Culture and Imperialism*. New York: Vintage.

Trinh, Minh-ha. 1995. "No Master Territories." *The Post-Colonial Studies Reader*. Eds. Ashcroft, Bill, Griffiths, Gareth, Tiffin, Helen London: Routledge.

Valli, Clayton. 1995. *ASL Poetry: Selected Works of Clayton Valli*. Video. Pro. Joe Dannis Dir. Clayton Valli. San Diego: DawnSignPress, 1995.

———. 1990. *Clayton Valli*. Video. Series *Poetry in Motion: Original Works in ASL*. Burtonsvile, MD: Sign Media.

———. 1990. "The Nature of the Line in ASL Poetry." *SLR '87 Papers from The Fourth International Symposium on Sign Language Research*. Eds. W.H. Edmondson and F. Karlsson. Hamburg: Signum Press.

30

The Enfreakment of Photography

David Hevey

Before reading this chapter, I feel I must contextualise what lies ahead for the reader. In many ways, charity advertising as oppressive imagery appears to be the *bête noire* of disabled people. Unfortunately, oppressive as it is, it represents colours of a social order tied to a specific mast. Those colours and constructions also exist in other areas of photographic representation. This is demonstrated in this chapter. I ask the reader to join me on a journey into oppressive disability imagery. At times, particularly in the examination of the work of Diane Arbus, it can be depressing. However this chapter is here because I feel we have to take the fight against constructed oppression (whether by non-access or by representation) into the camp of the oppressors.

Apart from charity advertising, when did you last see a picture of a disabled person? It almost certainly wasn't in commercial advertising since disabled people are not thought to constitute a body of consumers and therefore do not generally warrant inclusion. It might have been within an "in-house" health service magazine, in which disabled people are positioned to enflesh the theories of their oppressors. The stories might range from the successes of a toxic drugs company to the latest body armour for people with cerebral palsy, and some person with proverbial "disease" will be shown illustrating the solution and its usefulness. It might have been in an educational magazine, in which a non-disabled "facilitator" will regale in words and text the latest prototype "image-workshop," using disabled people as guinea pigs while developing their "educational" ideas. The text brags about the colonization of disabled people's bodies and identities, while the images show how much "the disabled" enjoyed it. Passive and still and "done to," the images bear a bizarre resemblance to colonial pictures where "the blacks" stand frozen and curious, while "whitey" lounges confident and sure. Whitey knows the purpose of this image, the black people appear not to (or at least, perhaps as employees, have no right to record visual dissent).

The "positive" side of their ultra-minority inclusion, then, is that disabled people are there to demonstrate the successes of their administrators.[1] Apart from the above areas, however, disabled people are almost entirely absent from photographic genres or discussion because they are read as socially dead and as not having a role to play. But although the absence is near absolute, the non-representation of disabled people is not quite total. Taking the structured absence as given, I wanted to discover the terms on which disabled people *were* admitted into photographic representation. As Mary Daly once wrote of feminism, the job entails being a full-time, low-paid researcher of your own destiny.[2]

I visited one of the largest photographic bookshops in London and leafed through the publications. Generally disabled people were absent, but there was a sort of presence. Disabled people are represented but almost exclusively as symbols of "otherness" placed within equations which have no engagement to them and which take their non-integration as a natural by-product of their impairment.

I picked books at random. *The Family of Man; Another Way of Telling; diane arbus; Figments from the Real World*. There were obviously lateral associations but only one, *diane arbus*, I knew to include images of disabled people. In the research for this book, I had begun to uncover sometimes hidden, sometimes open, but always continuous constructions of disabled people as outsiders admitted into culture as symbols of fear or pity. This was particularly true in literature[3] but I wanted to see if it held true in photography, so I picked the books at random. They may have been connected in styles or schools but, as far as I knew, had no connection whatsoever on disability representation. Only Arbus was infamous for having centred disabled people in her work but I felt an uneasy faith that all of them would "use" disabled people somewhere.

The first book examined was entitled *The Family of Man*.[4] The Family of Man exhibition at the Museum of Modern Art, New York, in 1955 is considered the seminal exhibition for humanist-realist photography. It was the photographic height of postwar idealism. It showed the great "positive image" of an unproblematised and noble world—a world from which pain was banished. Where there are images of "working folk," their muscles and their sweat appear to be a part of the great spiritual order of things. Where there are images of black people, the images show poverty; some show harmony, but all are visually poetic. Black life has been harmonised through aesthetics.

However, throughout the catalogue of the show, which contained 503 images show from 68 countries by 273 male and female photographers, there is only one photograph of someone identifiably disabled. This is more than an oversight. Put together ten years after the Second World War, *The Family of Man* was about "positively" forgetting the past and all its misery. Forward into glory, backward into pain! Although this publication and exhibition heralded a brave new world of postwar hope and harmony, on reading it it becomes clear that the inclusion of disabled people—even disabled people tidied up like black people and working people—was not a part of the postwar visual nirvana. Why was this?

The one image of a disabled person appears on the penultimate page of the 192-page publication. It is mixed in among six other images on that page and is part of the final section of the book, which covers children. Children are shown laughing, playing, dancing, crying and so on. Of the thirty-eight images in this section, three buck this trend. The three are all on this penultimate page. In the final section, after five pages of innocent joy, you encounter on the sixth page three that remind you it is not like that always. At the top of these three is a disabled boy who appears to be a below-the-knee amputee. He is racing along the beach with a crutch under his right arm. He is playing and chasing a football. His body tilts to our right as he approaches the ball, while his crutch tilts to our left, to form a shape like an open and upright compass. The ball is situated in the triangle which his left leg and his right-side crutch make on the sand. The triangle shape is completed by a shadow which the boy casts from his right leg to the crutch (and beyond). The ball enters this triangle focusing point but his right leg does not. Its absence is accentuated and impairment here is read as loss. The game he plays is his personal effort to overcome his loss.

The photograph creates a flowing but awkward symmetry and our reading of its flow is continually interrupted by the fact that the triangle's neatness is dependent on the absence of a limb. Two readings occur simultaneously: it is tragic but he is brave. In a book of hope, the disabled person is the symbol of loss. The disabled boy is a reminder that all is not necessarily well in the world but *he* is doing *his* best to sort it out. The image is "positive" in that he is "positively" adjusting to his loss. Because he is "positively" adjusting to his loss, the image is allowed into the exhibition and the catalogue. The image of his disablement has been used not for him but against him. The image's symbolic value is that disability is an issue for the person with an impairment, not an issue for a world being (inaccessibly) reconstructed. In *The Family of Man*, disabled people were almost entirely absented because harmony was seen to rest in the full operation of an idealised working body. The exhibition and catalogue did not admit disabled people (bar one) because it did not see a position for disabled people within the new model army of postwar production or consumption.

Photographically speaking, the decline of this high ground of postwar hope in the "one world, one voice, one leader" humanity was heralded (in historical photographic terms) by an equally influential but far more subversive exhibition, again at the Museum of Modern Art, New York, which was held in 1967. This exhibition was called New Documents and brought into a wide public consciousness reportage portraiture showing the human race as an alienated species bewildered by its existence. New Documents featured the work of Gary Winogrand, Lee Friedlander and Diane Arbus. The importance of these three photographers (and others like Robert Frank) is that their work heralded the breakdown of the universal humanism of *The Family of Man* into a more fragmented, psychic or surrealistic realism. The appalling reverse of the coin is that they anchored the new forms of a fragmented universe (to a greater or lesser extent) in new, even more oppressive images of disabled people.

What is particularly crucial in terms of the representation of disabled people in this photojournalism is a clear (yet still uncritical) emergence of the portrayal of disabled people as the *symbol* of this new (dis)order. Whereas the tucked-away disabled person in *The Family of Man* had been a hidden blemish on the body of humanity, in a world of the Cold War, the Cuban Missile Crisis and Vietnam, disabled people were represented as the inconcealable birthmark of fear and chaos. Diane Arbus was the second photographer whose work I looked at. The monograph that I had pulled from the shelf is from her posthumous retrospective, held at the Museum of Modern Art, New York, in 1972 and entitled *diane arbus*.[5]

Of all photographers who have included or excluded disabled people, Diane Arbus is the most notorious. She was born into an *arriviste* family of immigrants, whose money was made in the fur trade. She became a photographer through her husband, Allan Arbus, and worked with him in fashion photography. She moved away from that (and him) into work which still dealt with the body and its surrounding hyperbole but from a very different angle. It was on her own and in her own work that she became known, unwittingly according to her, as "the photographer of freaks." Whether she liked it or not, there can be no doubt that this is how her work has been received. The monograph contains 81 black-and-white images, of which eleven are of disabled people. These eleven can be divided into three quite critical periods of her work. The first is demonstrated in two portraits of "dwarfs"; the second with the portrait of the "Jewish giant"; and the third with the imagery shot just before her death, that of the "retardees" (her term for people with Down Syndrome).

In any of the material on Arbus, including this monograph, Patricia Bosworth's biography of her entitled *Diane Arbus, A Biography*, and Susan Sontag's discussion of her work in *On Photography*, the stages of her oppressive representations of disabled people are never discussed. Moreover, the "factual" recording of disabled people as freaks is accepted totally without question by major critics like Sontag, who says, "Her work shows people who are pathetic, pitiable, as well as repulsive, but it does not arouse any compassionate feelings."[6] Later, she rhetorically adds, "Do they see themselves, the viewer wonders, like *that*? Do they know how grotesque they are?" (her italics). Sontag brings to the disability imagery of Arbus a complete faith in Arbus's images as unproblematic truth-tellers. Bosworth also colludes by patronising disabled people, telling us of Arbus's "gentle and patient" way with "them." Neither of these critics, it goes without saying, considered asking the observed what *they* felt about the images in which they figured. Once again, the entire discourse has absented the voice of those at its center—disabled people.

Since there is only one other book on Arbus's work, and that deals with her magazine work,[7] it is safe to say that Bosworth and Sontag represent key parts of the Arbus industry. In their validations of Arbus's work, they both miss a central point. Although she was profoundly misguided (as I demonstrate further on), there can be no doubt that her work paradoxically had the effect of problematising, or opening up, the issue of the representation of disabled people. Her critics and defenders have built a wall around her work (and any discussion of disability in her work) by "naturalising" the content. In this, the images of disabled people have been lumped into one label, that of "freaks." Perhaps this has been done because her work appears to buck the contradictory trend of "compassion" in the portrayal of disabled "victims" practised by other photographers. Although Arbus's work can never be "reclaimed," it has to be noted that her work, and the use of "enfreakment" as message and metaphor, is far more complicated than either her defenders or critics acknowledge. The process of analysis is not to rehabilitate her or her work but to break it down once and for all.

She was a part of the "snapshot aesthetic" which grew up beyond the New Documents exhibition and exhibitors. This form attempted to overturn the sophisticated and high-technique processes of the Hollywood fantasy portrait, as well as rejecting the beautiful toning of much of *The Family of Man*. However, more than any of her peers, she took this aesthetic nearer to its roots in the family photograph or album (indeed she intended to shoot a project entitled Family Album).[8] Arbus had experienced, in her own family, the emotional and psychological cost of wealth in terms of the painful subjectivity and isolation of the individual hidden and silenced within the outward signs of bourgeois upward mobility and success. In terms of disability, however, Arbus read the bodily impairment of her disabled subject as a sign of disorder, even chaos; that is, as a physical manifestation of *her* chaos, *her* horror. Despite her relationships with disabled people (often lasting a decade or more) she viewed these not as social and equal relationships but as encounters with souls from an underworld.

There was nothing new in this pattern of "reading" the visual site of a disabled person away from a personal value into a symbolic value which then seals the representational fate of the disabled person. However, at least in the first period of her disability work, Arbus deviated from the Richard III syndrome by reading this "disorder" as the manifestation of a psychic disorder not in the subject but in society. There is no question of Arbus using her subjects "positively"—it is clear that she always intended them and their relationships to themselves and others to symbolise something other than themselves. She saw herself and her "freaks" as fellow travellers into a living oblivion, a social death. There is a perverse sense in which she was right—disabled people are expected to inhabit a living death—but the crucial thing is that she considered her projection to be more important than their reality. She "normalised" subjects like Morales, *The Mexican Dwarf*,[9] or *The Russian Midget Friends*[10] by specifically placing them in that great site of bourgeois culture and consumption, the home. The "horror" of Arbus's work is not that she has created Frankenstein but that she moved him in next door! What is more, the freak had brought his family! The "shock" for the hundreds of thousands of non-disabled viewers was that these portraits revealed a hinter-land existing in spite of the segregationist non-disabled world view.

For Arbus, the family—her own family—represented an abyss. She saw in the bourgeois promise to the immigrant family, her own family, a Faustian contract. Her Mephistopheles, her threat to the bourgeois privilege, was to move a non-disabled fear that dare not speak its name into the family snap. In a sense, this first period of her work (a period not of time but of understanding) is her least oppressive and in some ways complete. The sitters acknowledge her presence and her camera. They stare out from the picture at the viewer. Far from making apologies for their presence, they are distinctly proud, they are committed to their identity. Although the disabled people portrayed existed within subcultures (such as the circus), they were clearly not segregated and it is this which shocked the public who flocked to her posthumous retrospective at the Museum of Modern Art in 1972. It is the *conscious dialogue* between Arbus and the subjects which "horrified" and yet fascinated people more used to compassionate victim images of disabled people obligingly subhuman and obligingly institutionalized as "tragic but brave." Morales, the Mexican "dwarf" in *diane arbus*, is pictured naked but for a towel over his crutch. He wears a trilby at a rakish angle and his elbow leans casually on to the sideboard, resting just in front of a bottle of liquor. It is not clear quite what went on between Arbus and Morales (though Arbus had previously "spent the night" with another disabled subject, Moondance, as part of his agreement to be photographed) but the eroticism of the image cannot be denied. Not only is the so-called "dwarf" distinctly unfreaky in his three-quarters nakedness, he is positively virile! A constant theme of Arbus's work, not just of her disability work, is the relationship between people's bodies and their paraphernalia. While the attire is crisp and clear, the flesh of the subject has been "zombified." This, however, is not the case with her first pictures of "dwarfs." Morales's body is very much alive.

Arbus had attempted to trace the psychic disorder of consumer society back to a primal state of terror within everyday life. That she believed disabled people to be the visual witness of this primal state is clear. That is, she accepted at the level of "common sense" the non-integration of disabled people. However, much of "the Horror, the Horror"[11] with which Arbus's work has been received is in her location of this disabled terror within non-disabled normality. The disabled subjects themselves, at least in this early "freak" work, are treated reverentially. The camera is close. The camera is engaged. The subject has agreed to the session (but agreed in isolation?). The "horror" of the process for nondisabled society is in her placing a disabled normality within a non-disabled normality. The horror is in how she could even think them equivalent. The horror, I repeat, was in Arbus's recording in her constructions of disabled people a double bind of segregation/non-segregation. The "non-segregation," however (and this is where Arbus's crime really lay) did not lead towards integration—the "Russian midgets" were not living down the road as part of an independent living scheme—but towards transgression. It was a spectacle, not a political dialectic (the disability paradox) that Arbus wanted to ensnare. For this she accepted, indeed depended, on the given segregation of disabled people as "common sense."

Things began to disintegrate for Arbus in the second part of her disability work. This is illustrated in the monograph by the image entitled *A Jewish Giant at Home with his Parents in the Bronx, N.Y. 1970*. Again, we see a cosy family setting of a front room with two comfy chairs and a sofa, two elderly and self-respecting pensioners, a lamp by the drawn curtains, a reproduction classic painting in a tasteful frame, and a giant. The "giant" is not given a name in the title but his name was Eddie Carmel.[12] Again, Arbus did not sneak in and sneak out in this shot but got to know and photograph Eddie Carmel over a period of ten years before printing this one which she considered to work. This image of *A Jewish Giant* with its glaring flash-lit room, its portrayal of "the beast" from the womb of the mother, shows less harmony, even a deliberate asymmetry from that of her "dwarf" images. In *A Jewish Giant* she had created an image which took her beyond the reverence in both form and content of her "dwarf" images. Unlike them, Eddie the Jewish "giant" directs his attention away from the presence of the camera, his only acknowledgement that an image is being made is by being on his feet like his parents. His body language appears unclear and unsettled. The flash has cast black halos round the bodies of the subjects and they begin to resemble a Weegee as a found specimen of urban horror. The image of the "giant" as he crouches towards his more formal parents is that of a father over two children. The classic family portrait of parents and child is completely reversed by her use of their size relationship. The body language of the "Jewish giant" is more "out of control" (that is, it diverges more from non-disabled body language signs) than that of the "dwarf." It is all the more "threatening" to the non-disabled family snap because his body is situated with that of his "normal" parents. A clash or a confrontation between styles and discourses is occurring. The alchemy, confrontation and visual disorder of the image bring Arbus closer to avenging the control and repression in her own family. This is the key to her use and manipulation of isolated disabled people. During the ten years of their knowing each other, Eddie Carmel told Arbus about his ambitions, about his job selling insurance, about his acting hopes (and his despair at only being offered "monster" roles), and so on. Arbus dismissed this in her representations. She clearly found his actual day-to-day life irrelevant. Indeed, she appears to have disbelieved him, preferring her own projection of a metaphysical decline. His real tragedy is that he trusted Arbus, and she abused that trust outside of their relationship in an area within her total control, that is, photography.

The visual dialogue within the image between herself and the subject in the "dwarf" works, although decreasing in the imagery of Eddie the "giant," was still prevalent and was important precisely because it created a snapshot family album currency within the imagery. The commonness of this form was a part of its communicative power. As a structure it spoke to millions, while its content, Arbus's enfreakment of disabled people,[13] spoke to the able-bodied fear of millions. Were the subject to disengage, to reject the apparent co-conspiracy (in reality a coercion) or contract between themselves and Arbus, the images would move from the genre of family album currency and understanding of millions, to a reportage subgenre position of one specialist photographer. Arbus's work would then be that of an outsider constructing outsiders which need not be internalised by the viewer. The enfreakment in her disability images was internalised by the non-disabled viewers because the disabled subjects, while chosen for their apparent difference, manifested body language and identity traits recognisable to everyone. Arbus was concerned to show the dichotomy, even the pain, between how people projected themselves and how she thought they "really" were. The projection of this "imagined self" by the subject was through the direct gaze to camera (and therefore direct gaze to viewer). The image of *A Jewish*

Giant, to Arbus, suggested a higher level of fear and chaos than the "dwarf" work. This higher level of discrepancy between order (the setting is still the family at home) and chaos (Eddie outgrowing that which contained him), than that manifested in the "dwarf" work, is also highlighted by the fact that, although the "giant" is on his feet posing with his parents, his dialogue is as much between him and his parents as between him and Arbus/the viewer.

Arbus was reported to have told a journalist at the *New Yorker* of her excitement over this image, the first one that had worked for her in the ten years of photographing Eddie. "You know how every mother has nightmares when she's pregnant that her baby will be born a monster? I think I got that in the mother's face as she glares up at Eddie, thinking, 'OH MY GOD, NO!' "[14] You could be forgiven for imagining that the mother recoils from her Eddie much like Fay Ray recoiled from the horror of King Kong, but this is not the case. Arbus betrayed in her excited phone call to the journalist what she wished the image to say, rather than what it actual does say (though, of course, meanings shift). Arbus's comment about "every mother's nightmare" speaks of her nightmare relationship with her own body, which I believe she viewed as the sole site of her power. It was this loss of control of the body which she saw disability/impairment as meaning. Arbus once quoted a person who defined horror as the relationship between sex and death. She also claimed that she never refused a person who asked her to sleep with them. Furthermore, Bosworth hints that Arbus may have been confused about her bi-sexuality. In any event, the clues suggest that while she viewed her body and sexuality as key points of her power, her sexuality was not clear to her, and sex itself probably failed to resolve her feelings of aloneness and fragmentation. She sought the answer to this dilemma in locating bodily chaos in all her subjects (to varying degrees) and felt she'd found it in its perfect form in disabled people. (That major institutions of American representation, like the Museum of Modern Art, promoted her work shows their willingness to cooperate with this oppressive construction of disabled people.)

The "OH MY GOD, NO!" which she attributes to the mother in *A Jewish Giant* is in reality an "OH MY GOD, YES!" victory call that Arbus herself felt. She had made her psychic vision physical, or so she felt. Diane Arbus's daughter, Doon Arbus, has written that her mother wanted to photograph not what was evil but what was *forbidden*.[15] She believed she had pictured a return of the forbidden and repressed within her own remembered family. In her construction, the awkwardness of *A Jewish Giant* hints at the unwieldiness of her vision as a long-term solution to her own needs and begins to hint at this vision's ultimate destructiveness—not only, and obviously, to disabled people, but to the psychic well-being of Arbus herself.

It is here that the third period in her work on disabled people begins. She starts to photograph "retardees" (as she labels people with Down Syndrome). She moves from observing her subjects at home to observing them in a home; that is, an institution. These images of people with Down Syndrome were practically the last she shot before killing herself. They are clustered, six of them, at the end of the book. In the previous work with "dwarfs" and *A Jewish Giant* Arbus had maintained that she did not photograph anybody who did not agree to be photographed. This was undoubtedly so (although coercion is probably truer than agreement), but the images show a decline in conscious frontal participation of the subject. This decline was also mirrored in the growing discordance on the technical side of her work. The beautiful tones of Morales, the "dwarf," give way to a harsh flash-light in the "Jewish giant." There is no doubt that Arbus, as an ex-fashion photographer, knew what she was doing in using technical disharmony as an underwriting of the narrative disharmony. When we come into the third period, her work on "retardees," Arbus continues to pursue technical discordance. She still uses flash-and-daylight to pick up the figures from their landscape, but the focus is clearly weaker than that of the previous work. The subjects are now barely engaged with Arbus/the viewer *as themselves*.

Arbus finds them not in a position to conspire with her projection. The visual dialogue collapses. The dialectic between body and attire which Arbus had pursued is broken. The chaos of their paper and blanket costumes appears, to her, not to challenge their bodies but to match them. Arbus's order-chaos paradoxical projection has not happened. Instead, Arbus sees zombies in another world. To her they project no illusions of being neighbours to normality. These people are not at home but in a home. The institution of the family give sway to the institution of segregation (in this case, a New Jersey "home" for "retardees"). The people with Down Syndrome are set in a backdrop of large open fields showing only distant woods. For Arbus, their consciousness and activity is arbitrary. She does not know how to make them perform to her psycho-ventriloquist needs. In her career-long attempt to pull the psychic underworld into the physical overworld by manipulating the bodies of disabled people, she has come to the borders in these images. She had met "the limits of her imagination"; she had not found in these images the catharsis necessary for her to continue. Arbus first loved then hated this last work. She entered a crisis of identity because these segregated people with Down Syndrome would not perform as an echo of her despair. Because of this, her despair deepened. In the final image of this series and the final image of her monograph, nine disabled people pass across the view of the camera. Of the nine, only one turns towards the camera. His gaze misses the camera; consequently the possibilities that might have been opened up by a direct gaze are, for Arbus, lost. He joins the rest of this crowd who come into the frame for no purpose. Arbus's camera became irrelevant not only for disabled people, but for Arbus herself. This was her last work before she killed herself.

The next book I looked at was Gary Winogrand's *Figments from the Real World*.[16] Of the 179 black-and-white plates in *Figments from the Real World*, six included the portrayal of disabled people on one level or another. Like Arbus, the inclusion of disabled people, regardless of their role, was that of a significant minority with their oppression unquestioned and constructed as intact. Unlike Arbus's work, however, Winogrand did not produce any images (at least not for public consumption) whose central character was the disabled person or disablement. He did produce bodies of work on women, for example, but where a disabled person appears in the work, it is as a secondary character to the women. Nevertheless, within the "underrepresentation" in *Figments from the Real World*, it becomes clear that, like Arbus and the others from my ersatz list, "the disabled" had a role to play. Nevertheless, Winogrand consciously or otherwise included disabled people with the specific intention of enfreaking disability in order to make available to his visual repertoire a key *destabilising* factor.

With regard to the representation of women by Winogrand, Victor Burgin has critiqued Winogrand's work and has explored the reading of meaning within his imagery and the relationship of this meaning to the wider social and political discourses of his time.[17] Burgin describes and discusses an image of Winogrand from an exhibition in 1976. The image is of four women advancing towards the camera down a city street. The group of women, who are varying degrees of middle age, is the most prominent feature in the right-hand half of the image; equally prominent is a group of huge plastic bags stuffed full of garbage. The introduction to the catalogue of the exhibition makes it clear that this "joke" is intended. The reading of middle-aged women as "old bags" is unavoidable.

Despite the protestations by John Szarkowski in the introduction of *Figments from the Real World* that Winogrand celebrated women (he called the book of this phase of his work, *Women are Beautiful*), it is clear that his construction of women singly or in groups advancing towards the camera from all directions displays an unease, a fear, of what the results of his desire for them might be. Their faces frown by his camera, their eyes bow down to avoid his gaze. Burgin highlighted the dynamics of his "old bag" image. Winogrand's fear at what he reads as a loss of (female) beauty in ageing is registered by his "old bag" image. It is no coincidence that one of the six disability images (and the only one of two showing a wheelchair user) in *Figments from the Real World* involves an almost identical dynamic to that of the "old bags".

The center of the image is three young women. They are lit by a sun behind them and their sharp shadows converge towards the camera. They dominate the center third of the image and they are walking along a ray of light towards the lends. They are dressed in the fashion of the moment. In their movement is recorded an affecting, perhaps transitional beauty. Their symmetry is, however, broken by the gaze of the woman on the right. The symmetry is further challenged by this woman being a step ahead of the other two as she stares down at the presence, in the shadows, of a crouched wheelchair user. The other two women slightly move their heads towards the wheelchair. All of their eyes are tightened and all of their facial expressions "interpret" the presence of the wheelchair user with degrees of controlled horror.

Unlike Winogrand's dumping of middle-aged women into "old bags," he confronts these young women with a warning. He observes them as beautiful but warns them that their beauty and all its "paraphernalia" is all that separates them from the "grotesque" form they are witnessing. Beauty is warned of the beast. Clearly, Winogrand could not assuage his desire for women, whom he spent years photographically accosting on the street. His work harbours a resentment that they do not respond to his aggressive desire and so he implants warnings. The asymmetry of the imagery is anchored in the non-disabled reading (in this instant, Winogrand's) of disabled people as sites of asymmetrical disharmony. The women's body harmony (as Winogrand desires it) is set against the wheelchair user's disharmony (as Winogrand sees it). Winogrand's use of the disabled person, again enfreaked, is to bring out of the underworld and into the shadows a symbol of asymmetry *as fear and decay* which challenges the three women's right to walk "beautifully" down the street.

Like Arbus, Winogrand's use of disability is to warn the "normal" world that their assumptions are fragile. This he does by the use of differentness of many disabled people's bodies as a symbol of the profound asymmetry of consumer society, particularly in the United States. Despite the fact that the American President Roosevelt had been disabled, the enfreakment of disabled people in these new practices became the symbol of the alienation of humanity which these new photographers were trying to record.

The Family of Man exhibition had all but excluded disabled people because they did not represent hope in the new order, so the post New Documents practitioners *included* disabled people for precisely the same reasons. The Family of Man and the New Documents exhibitions, constructed within photographic theories as radically separate, are inextricably linked, in that the inclusion of disabled people does not mean progress, but regression. Disabled people increased their presence in the new reportage of these photographers not as a sign of enlightenment and integration, but as a sign of bedlam.

The fourth book picked at random, I realized afterwards, takes us to a European setting. In *Another Way of Telling*,[18] the inevitable inclusion of a disabled subject comes almost at the very beginning. This book deals heavily with photographs of the countryside and the peasantry of various countries and the first photo-text piece sets this agenda. This is a story of Jean Mohr taking photographs of some cows, while the cow owner jokingly chastises him for taking pictures with permission and without payment. This first part very much sets the geographic and political agenda for the whole book, which explores the three-way relationship between the photographer, the photographed and the different meanings and readings taken from the photographs.

In every image or image-sequence, excluding the second one in the book (that of a blind girl in India) the images are more or less openly problematical. That is, the relationship between the image and its apparent informative or communicative value is put to the test. "Only occasionally is an image self-sufficient," says Jean Mohr. From this assertion, Mohr and Berger explore the image-making processes and what can be taken on or used within the process of photography that might work for both the photographer and the subject. The genesis of the book is to question meaning and use-value of imagery from all points, not just that of the photographer.

In Mohr's eighty-page first part, he illuminates different contexts of his own image-making, from shooting running children from a passing train, to shooting and reshooting working people and directing his work according to their expressed wishes. The theme which pervades the whole book is that of the working process. Moreover, the working process that they have chosen to explore visually is that of people working on the land and their lives and communities. The image-sequences, whether of cow-herders or of wood-cutters, begin with labour and its dignity. Clearly, unlike many "concerned" social realist photographers, Mohr is attempting to inhabit the process from the inside, not just to observe it externally. His method is through the voice, feedback and acknowledgement of the person photographed in their work. Their work is the anchor, the base, from which the story unfolds.

At one point and in one sequence, Mohr turns the camera on himself. He puts himself in the picture. He talks about the fear, the anxiety, even the panic which assails many people when they are the subject of the camera. Am I too fat? Am I too skinny? Is my nose too large? He tells us that he finds the process of putting himself in the picture difficult and talks about how he attempts to lose his image through technical disguises, like deliberately moving the camera during an exposure so as to blur the image, and so on. He anchors this process of putting himself in the picture on the quite valid and narcissistic idea that he used to imagine that he looked like Samuel Beckett. After bringing the story home by saying that he was finally forced to view his own image by being the subject matter of *other* people's lens, rather than his own, he finally finishes it by telling us that a student who photographed him felt that he did indeed resemble Beckett.

His work on other people's images and stories and his work on his own image and self are linked because, in grappling with the process of representation of his self or of others, he tells us and attempts to show us that the meaning of images is rooted in the process and context in which they were made. This is an important assertion but not unique. This book was published in 1982 and came at a time when other photographers and theorists, like Victor Burgin, Allan Sekula, Photography Workshop (Jo Spence/Terry Dennett) *et al.*, were questioning and problematising and naturalist truth-telling assumptions underpinning the left's use of social realist photography. *Another Way of Telling*, then, was a part of this "movement."

However, *Another Way of Telling*, and Jean Mohr's opening piece in particular, is clearly anchored in finding another way of using naturalist reportage, not abandoning it altogether. Mohr explains the use-value of the naturalist image to the subject. He tells stories of how this or that peasant wanted the image to show the whole body—of the person, of the cow, of the tree-cutting process—rather than be "unnaturally" cropped. Naturalism, then, to him, has a purpose *in context*.

Here, we begin to get close to the *purpose* of the blind girl pictures within Jean Mohr's piece and the book as a whole. The realist (time/place) agenda is set in the first image, that of the cowman, but the *underlying agenda of "simple" naturalism* (that is to say, Mohr and Berger's belief in its ability to tell a simple story) is anchored in the hypersimplicity of the blind girl's pleasure. These pictures of a disabled person—a blind Asian girl—form the apex of the book's naturalist thesis that the value of naturalism is in its portrayal of unconscious innocence.

The story is called "The Stranger who Imitated Animals." The "stranger" in question is Jean Mohr. In the 250-odd words which accompany the five images, he tells us of visiting his sister in the university town of Aligarh in India and of his sister's "warning" of the blind girl who comes round and likes to know what is happening. He awakes the next morning unclear of where he is when.

> The young blind girl said Good Morning. The sun had been up for hours. Without reasoning why I replied to her by yapping like a dog. Her face froze for a moment. Then I imitated a cat caterwauling. And the expression on her face behind the netting changed to one of recognition and complicity in my play-acting. I went on to a peacock's cry, a horse whinnying, a large animal growling—like a circus. With each act and according to our mood, her expression changed. Her face was so beautiful that, without stopping our game, I picked up my camera and took some pictures of her. She will never see these photographs. For her I shall simply remain the invisible stranger who imitated animals.[19]

Clearly, despite his simplification of his response ("without reasoning why"), he responded with impersonations precisely because he had observed that she was blind. He objectified her, his first impulse on waking up to see a blind person was to play games with the blindness. Underlying this was the assumption that blind people (whatever the level of visual impairment) have no idea of quantifiable physical reality and would, of course, think that the sound really was of a yapping dog waking up in bed. His joke reveals his disability (un-) consciousness, not hers.

But she responds to this with laughter, she joins in. So, he further objectifies her by again distancing himself. While she laughs along with his imitations, he secretly photographs her, because her laughing but blind face was "so beautiful." Clearly, because she is laughing in his pictures, he presumably continued his imitations while he photographed her. The game for two turned into manipulation by one. The pictures show her leaning against the dark wooden surround of the door. She is framed by this and leans into this frame by pressing her ears to his mimicry. She is kept at a distance and keeps her responses on that surface of the mosquito net which fits into the wooden frame. This framing of her by the door is copied in his framing of her in the camera. Out of the five pictures in the sequence, four clearly show her eyes. Technically, these have been deliberately whitened in the printing to highlight the blindness.

As labour is the anchor in the other series, and as narcissism is the anchor in his self-image series, shooting the whites of her eyes is the anchor in this series. Her blindness is the symbol of innocence and nobility. Her blindness is the anchor of her simplicity. Her blindness is the object of his voyeurism. He has taken and symbolised this disabled person's image, which he says "she will never see" (he obviously didn't consider aural description), as the anchor and beauty of naturalism. The text which accompanies this series of images doesn't quite have the once-upon-a-time-ness of some of the other photo-essays, but it still serves to push the imagery into the magical or metaphysical. The always-to-be natural images of the blind girl are the only set that have no significant time element to them. His work with the cowman spans days, his work with the wood-cutter is over a period of time (enough for the wood-cutter to give an opinion of the finished prints), but the work with the blind girl of beauty and innocence needs saying once, because it is forever. Again, like *The Family of Man*, like Arbus and Winogrand, Mohr has chosen to absent both the three-dimensional disabled person and their social story because it is incongruous to their own disability (un) consciousness. Their images tell us nothing about the actual lives of disabled people, but they add to the history of oppressive representation.

I have just analysed a random selection of four major photographic books, only one of which I knew to have been involved in disability representation. In the event, all four were. In the final analysis, these books which include disabled people in their field of photographic reference do so on the condition that disabled people are, to use Sontag's term for Diane Arbus's work, "borderline" cases. Sontag meant this term in its common reference to psychic or spiritual disorder. However, disabled people in the representations which I have discussed in this and the previous chapters share a commonality in that they live in different camps beyond the border. Whether beauty or the beast, they are outsiders. The basis for this border in society is real. It is physical and it is called segregation. The social absence of disabled people creates a vacuum in which the visual meanings attributable (symbolically, metaphorically, psychically, etc.) to impairment and disablement appear free-floating and devoid of any actual people. In the absence of disabled people, the meaning in the disabled person and their body is made by those who survey. They attempt to shift the disablement on to the impairment, and the impairment into a flaw. The very absence of disabled people in positions of power and representation deepens the use of this "flaw" in their images. The repression of disabled people makes it more likely that the symbolic use of disablement by non-disabled people is a sinister or mythologist one. Disablement re-enters the social world through photographic representation, but in the re-entry its meaning is tied not by the observed, disabled people, but by the non-disabled observers.

It is here that all the work, picked at random, is linked. Disabled people, in these photographic representations, are positioned either as meaningful or meaningless bodies. They are meaningful only as polarised anchors of naturalist humility or psychic terror. Brave but tragic: two sides of the segregated coin? Disabled people are taken into the themes pursued by Arbus, Winogrand, Mohr, and so on, to illustrate the truth of their respective grand narratives. The role of the body of the disabled person is to enflesh the thesis or theme of the photographer's work, despite the fact that most of the photographers had taken no conscious decision to work "on" disability. It is as if the spirit of the photographer's mission can be summed up in their manipulation of a disabled person's image. "The disabled" emerge, like a lost tribe, to fulfil a role for these photographers but not for themselves.

Disabled people appeared either as one image at a time per book or one role per book. The use of disabled people is the anchor of the weird, that is, the fear within. They are used as the symbol of enfreakment or the surrealism of all society. "Reactionary" users of this notion hunt the "crips" down to validate chaos within their own environment (Arbus); "progressive" users of this notion hunt them down within their own environment to find an essential romantic humanity in their own lives (but no question of access). The US "crip" symbol denotes alienation. The impaired body is the site and symbol of all alienation. It is psychic alienation made physical. The "contorted" body is the final process and statement of a painful mind.

While this symbol functions as a "property" of disabled people as viewed by these photographers, it does not function as *the* property of those disabled people observed. Its purpose was not as a role model, or as references for observed people, but as the voyeuristic property of the non-disabled gaze. Moreover, the impairment of the disabled person became the mark, the target for a disavowal, a ridding, of the existential fears and fantasies of non-disabled people. This "symbolic" use of disablement knows no classic political lines, indeed it may be said to become more oppressive the further left you move.[20] The point is clear. If the disability paradox, the disability dialectic, is between impaired people and disabling social conditions, then the photographers we have just examined represent the construction of an "official" history of blame from the disabling society towards disabled people.

The works were selected at random and I fear their randomness proves my point. Wherever I drilled, I would have found the same substance. Were I to continue through modern photographic publications, I have no doubt that the pattern I am describing would continue; the only variation being that some would use disabled people for the purposes described, while others would absent disabled people altogether. A cursory widening of the list, to glance at photographers who have come after those named above, people like Joel-Peter Witkin,[21] Gene Lambert,[22] Bernard F. Stehle,[23] Nicholas Nixon,[24] and others who have all "dealt with" disablement, shows photographers who continued a manipulation of the disability/impairment image but have done so in a manner which depressingly makes the work by, say, Arbus and Mohr (I don't suppose they ever felt they'd be mentioned in the same breath!) seem positively timid! The work of many of the "post New Documentaries" has shifted the ground on the representation of disabled people by making "them" an even more separate category. While the volume of representation is higher, the categorisation, control and manipulation have become deeper. In this sense, the photographic observation of disablement has increasingly become the art of categorisation and surveillance. Also, from a psychological viewpoint, those that appear to have transgressed this commodification of disabled people have only transgressed their own fears of their constructions. The oppression remains the same. The segregated are not being integrated, they are being broken into! The photographic construction of disabled people continues through the use of disabled people in imagery as the site of fear, loss or pity. Those who are prevented by their liberal instincts from "coming out" in their cripple-as-freak, freak-as-warning-of-chaos, circumvent it by attempting to tell the unreconstructed "natural" story of oblivion. Either way, it is a no-win victim position for disabled people within those forms of representation. My intention in this essay is to suggest new forms.

A final note of hope. Diane Arbus was "extremely upset" when she received a reply from "The Little People's Convention" to her request to photograph them. They wrote that, "We have our own little person to photograph us." [25] In terms of disabled people's empowerment, this is the single most important statement in all of the work considered.

Notes

1. Vic Finkelstein has argued that the "administrative model" of disablement has replaced the "medical model" to the extent that it is now the dominant oppressive one. This model, according to Finkelstein, suggests that the move away from the large "phase-two" institutions (which mirrored heavy industrial production) towards the dispersal of "care in the community" has meant that disablement has shifted from a predominantly cure-or-care issue to an administrative one. There is no doubt in my mind that this shift is being echoed in the production of "positive" images within the UK local authorities. They are similar to the functionalist images of the charities third-stage imagery in their portrayal of the administration of service provision to (grinning) disabled people.
2. *GYN/ecology* (1981), by Mary Daly, London: Women's Press.
3. *Images of the Disabled, Disabling Images* (1987), ed. Alan Gartner and Tom Joe, New York: Praeger.
4. *The Family of Man*, exhibition and publication by the Museum of Modern Art, New York, 1955. (Reprinted 1983.)
5. *diane arbus* (1990), London: Bloomsbury Press.

6. *On Photography* (1979), by Susan Sontag, London: Penguin.

7. "Arbus revisited: a review of the monograph," by Paul Wombell, *Portfolio* magazine, no. 10, Spring 1991.

8. Ibid., p. 33.

9. *diane arbus*, op. cit., p. 23. The full title of the photograph is *Mexican Dwarf in his Hotel Room in N.Y.C. 1970*.

10. *diane arbus*, op. cit., p. 16. The full title for this photograph is: *Russian Midget Friends in a Living Room on 100th St. N.Y.C. 1963*.

11. The death cry of Kurtz on discovering the unpronounceable, in Conrad's *Heart of Darkness*.

12. *Diane Arbus: A Biography* (1984), by Patricia Bosworth, New York: Avon Books, p. 226.

13. It is important to remember that the ability of naturalist photographic practice to "enfreak" its subject is not peculiar to the oppressive portrayal of disabled people. For example, the same process of fragmenting and reconstructing oppressed people into the projection of the photographer is particularly marked in the projection of the working classes. See *British Photography from the Thatcher Years* (book and exhibition) by Susan Kismaric, Museum of Modern Art, New York, 1990.

14. *Diane Arbus: A Biography*, op. cit., p. 227.

15. Ibid., p. 153.

16. Gary Winogrand (1988), *Figments from the Real World*, ed. John Szarkowski, New York: Museum of Modern Art.

17. *The End of Art Theory: Criticism and Post-Modernity* (1986), by Victor Burgin, London: Macmillan, p. 63.

18. *Another Way of Telling* (1982), by John Berger and Jean Mohr, London: Writers and Readers.

19. Ibid., p. 11.

20. For the "left" use of disability/impairment as the site of a defense of the welfare state, see "Bath time at St. Lawrence" by Raissa Page in *Ten-8*, nos. 7/8, 1982. Alternatively, for a cross-section of the inclusion of disability imagery within magazines servicing the welfare state, see the King's Fund Centre reference library, London. Finally, see the impairment charity house journals and read the photo credits, i.e., the Spastics Society's *Disability Now*. Network, Format, Report and other left photo agencies regularly supply uncritical impairment imagery.

21. *Masterpieces of Medical Photography: Selections from the Burns Archive* (1987), ed. Joel-Peter Witkin, California: Twelve-tree Press.

22. *Work from a Darkroom* (1985), by Gene Lambert (exhibition and publication), Dublin: Douglas Hyde Gallery.

23. *Incurably Romantic* (1985), by Bernard F. Stehle, Philadelphia: Temple University Press.

24. *Pictures of People* (1988), by Nicholas Nixon, New York: Museum of Modern Art.

25. *Diane Arbus: A Biography* (1984), by Patricia Bosworth, New York: Avon Books, p. 365.

31

Blindness and Art

Nicholas Mirzoeff

Derrida's philosophical investigation of blindness leaves many questions to be answered by art historians. Blindness was and remains a central metaphor in Western art, representing and permitting insight and understanding for the artist, gendered male, over his "female" subject-matter. Here it now seems to suggest that visual representation is the outcome of an interplay between the metaphor of insight and the physiological structures of sight. Following Derrida's provocative comments, I shall now re-examine the canon of the blind and blindness from Poussin via David, Ingres and Delacroix to Paul Strand and Robert Morris. Given the force attached by Merleau-Ponty and Derrida to the physiology of seeing, I shall consider blindness not just as a metaphor but as a condition. For Derrida himself stands within a historical construction of blindness as insight, which is not natural but is less than two hundred years old now. How did depictions of blindness change in accord with changing notions of sight and blindness? In what ways is the metaphor of blindness affected by these changes? And what becomes of the Classical body that is known not through insight metaphorized as blindness but through insight enabled by blindness?

In France the modern period is held to begin with the reign of Louis XIV (1648–1715). For art history, this period marks the foundation of the Academy of Painting and Sculpture and the beginnings of public debate over the nature and accomplishments of art. One central moment in this history came in 1666 when Louis ordered that the Academy should hold conferences on works of art for the edification of an audience composed of their peers, students and, occasionally, government ministers. The Seventh conference was given by the artist Sébastien Bourdon, who chose a painting by Nicolas Poussin (1593–1665), *Christ Healing the Blind at Jericho* (1651), as the springboard for his discussion of light, for Poussin was regarded as the greatest artist of the French school. He emphasized that Poussin had chosen to represent an early morning scene, which cast a strong blue light from the left side of the canvas. Bourdon elaborated upon the advantages of such morning light, which later became so conventional that only the angled fall of light from the left was retained. Bourdon, however, read Poussin's painting as a treatise on luminosity:

> For though all the Parts retain their true Teints, yet the Shade which passes above them, is as it were a Veil to extinguish their Vivacity, and hinder their having so much strength as to fill the View, and thrust out other Objects more considerable, and on which the Painter has laid greater Stress. But in return, he has not failed to fill those Places with Light where he saw it would not hurt the beauty of the Figures. (Bourdon 1740: 132)

His audience, however, were not satisfied with such subtleties and demanded to know where the multitude of witnesses described in the New Testament had gone in Poussin's painting. Bourdon replied that

> We cannot suppose that all the Multitude who followed Christ could be about him at once, and being some steps from him, they were concealed by the Buildings. That there are Witnesses enough of the Action, since by that person cloathed in Red, who appears surprised, the Painter has represented the

Astonishment of the *Jews*; and by him who is looking very near, he shews the desire that Nation had
to see Miracles wrought. A greater Number of Figures would only have occasioned Confusion, and
hindered those of Christ and the blind Men from being seen so distinctly. (145)

This literal reading of the painting belied what now seem to be the obvious metaphorical connotations of the painting, connecting the blindness of the figures to the light being spread by Christ. Just
as the king could heal by his touch, one might argue, so could artists bring vision into being by their
brushstrokes. In this view, the royal artists of the Academy could then claim connection to the sacred
person of the king and imbibe something of his divine essence from his aura. Bourdon, however, also
insisted on a literal interpretation of blindness:

By the Action of the first blind Man, his Faith and Confidence in him who is touching him is expressed;
in the second, the Favour he is asking is likewise shown. It is common for Persons who are deprived
of any one of the five Senses to have the rest better and more subtle; because the Spirits which move in
them, to make them known what they want, move with greater force having fewer Offices to perform;
thus they who have lost their Sight, have a more acute Hearing, and a more sensible Touch. This is
what Mr Poussin has intended to express in the last blind Man, and in which he has wonderfully suc-
ceeded. For by his Face and his Arms one may know he is all Attention to the Voice of the Saviour,
and endeavoring to find him out. This attentive hearkening appears in his Forehead, which is not quite
smooth; the Skin and all the other Parts of which are drawn up. He likewise discovers it, by suspending
all the Motions of his Countenance, which continue in that Posture to give time to his Ear to listen
more attentively, and that he may not be diverted. (164)

Bourdon thus used the new insights of Cartesian science to explain that the blind have sharper hearing
than the average person, a myth that has long out-lasted the medical theory of the spirits from which
it was devised (as the body has a finite number of spirits to enable the senses, the loss of one sense
leaves more spirits available for the others and they are thus enhanced). In fact, the blindness which
is on the verge of being cured in Poussin's image calls attention, then, not to insight but to the human
voice. Bourdon read the rhetoric of Poussin's painting through physical blindness and found it the
key to the expression of the "Voice of the Saviour." He envisaged blindness as a means of intensifying
the tactile and auditory response to the painting, rather than as a signifier of incapacity. Light had to
be arranged by the painter in such a way as to prevent illegibility, creating a balanced visual economy,
which Bourdon described as "a fine Oeconomy of Colours and Lights…which make an agreeable
Concert and Charming Sweetness that never cloys the Sight" (170).

The mute painter's achievement was like that of the blind in calling a sensible world into being,
while deprived of certain sensory tools. For just as there is a moment of blindness inherent in the
act of visual representation, the resulting image was inevitably silent. Throughout the *ancien régime*,
artists turned to the gestural sign language of the deaf as a means of overcoming this deficiency for,
as the French writer du Fresnoy put it:

Mutes have no other way of speaking (or expressing their thoughts) but only by their gesture and their
actions, 'tis certain that they do it in a manner more expressive than those who have the use of Speech,
for which reason the Picture, which is mute ought to imitate them, so as to make itself understood.
(Dryden 1695 [1648]: 129)

The mute picture required the assistance of the deaf in order to signify. For in the early modern period, the simple binary opposition between the able-bodied and the disabled did not exist. Instead,
the human body was perceived as inevitably imperfect, each person having certain skills that others
might not possess. Even Louis XIV had regular bleedings and purgatives before any unusual or tiring
activity to purify his body. If the sacred body of the Sun King could be considered imperfect, then
his subjects were even more vulnerable. The artists of the period were quick to figure blindness and
deafness as complex metaphors in their work, in ways which have been insufficiently recognized.

In the eighteenth century, the sensualist philosophy of the Enlightenment continued this relativ-
ist concept of the body, but gave it a moral connotation. Sensualism held that the mind was formed

directly from sensory experience and that those with differing senses had different minds. In his *Letter on the Blind*, the philosopher and critic Denis Diderot (1713–1784) reflected at length on the distinctions between the blind and the sighted, pursuing his conviction that: "I doubt that anything at all can be explained without the body" (Josephs 1969: 50). He first mused on the morality of the blind, which he found wanting:

> I suspect them of inhumanity. What difference would there be for a blind man between a man who urinates and a man who, without complaining, was spilling blood?...All our virtues depend upon our manner of sensing, and the degree to which things affect us! Ah! Madame, how different the morality of the blind is from our own. How that of a deaf man would differ again from that of the blind, and how a being which had one sense more than us would find our morality imperfect, to say the least. (Diderot 1975–; vol. 4 (1978): 27)

Diderot found the blind different to the sighted but did not pretend that the sighted were perfect. Indeed, he went on to reflect on ways in which the lack of sight could even be an advantage. He argued that the blind have a tactile memory in the same way that the sighted have a visual memory. The sensation of a mouth on the hand of a blind man and the drawing of it amounted to the same thing, as both were secondary representations of the original. But the blind person had an advantage when it came to abstract thought: "The person born blind perceives things in a far more abstract manner than us, and in questions of pure speculation, he is perhaps less subject to making mistakes" (32). Diderot's example was the blind English mathematician Nicholas Saunderson:

> Those who have written about his life say that he was prolific in fortunate expressions...But what do you mean by fortunate expressions, you may perhaps ask? I would reply, Madame, that they are those which are proper to a sense, to touch for example, and which are metaphorical at the same time to another sense, like sight; there was thus a double light for those who spoke to him, the true and direct light of the expression, and the reflected light of the metaphor. (Diderot 1978: 41)

Paradoxically, therefore, the sighted person gained a greater illumination by discussing a topic with a blind person.

The paradox was a central concept in Diderot's thought. In the *Paradox on the Actor* (1773–8). Diderot examined this question at length. Discussing the actress Mlle Clairon, he observed:

> If you were with her while she studied her part, how many times would you cry out: "That is just right!" and how many times would she answer: "You are wrong!" Just so a friend of Le Quesnot's once cried catching him by the arm: "Stop! you will make it worse by bettering it—you will spoil the whole thing!" "What I have done," replied the artist, panting with exertion, "you have seen; what I have got hold of and what I mean to carry out to the end you cannot see." (Lacoue-Labarthe 1989: 262)

The artist's vision was doubled, like that of the *philosopher* conversing with the blind man, seeing what is present, what is implied and what is yet to come. The true blindness was not that of the visually impaired but of those who believed they could see like the artist but could not. Diderot disliked the "false mimetician or abortive genius who simply *mimes the mimetician*." The paradox in question stemmed from Diderot's notion that actors "are fit to play all characters because they have none." In the process, actors step outside their characters: "He must have in himself an unmoved and disinterested onlooker. He must have, consequently, penetration and no sensibility, the art of imitating everything, or, which comes to the same thing, the same aptitude for every sort of character and part" (257). For actors to accurately represent the widest range of emotions, it was essential that they themselves have no emotions. Actors constantly observed their work in order to make it appear natural and unforced. For this reason, the British artist John Opie (1761–1807) refused to paint actors at all. Acting was to be no one in order to be everyone, just as it is the blind spot which permits seeing.

In Jacques-Louis David's *Bélisaire, reconnu par un soldat qui avait servi sous lui au moment qu'une femme lui fait aumône* (Lille: Musée Wicar, 1781), blindness was again used by the artist to express a sense of paradox. Belisarius was a Roman general who, after many successes, lost the confidence of the

Emperor Justinian and was blinded by him. David (1748–1825) showed the now blind general begging for alms, at a moment when he is recognized by one of his former soldiers. Belisarius' blindness thus comes to have a metaphorical meaning, suggestive of his indifferent not merely to his fate but to the potential spectator. This painting of the blinded Roman general has recently been hailed by art historian Michael Fried as the first truly modern painting, in which David can be seen "reinventing the art of painting" (Fried 1983: 160). Fried in effect proposes that the picture itself postulates a certain blindness in that it is constructed without the needs of a spectator in mind. He argues that David followed Diderot's remark in his *Salon of 1767*: "A scene represented on a canvas or on stage does not suppose witnesses" (Fried 1983: 97). Fried discerns a central distinction between such absorption, which is praised, and vulgar theatricality, which is to be condemned. He argues that David constructed an image which refused theatricality, and instead opted to create a pictorial space in which the characters are wholly absorbed and unaware of the possibility of spectatorship.

Such analyses run counter to the notion of the paradox, developed above, and indeed Fried noted that the late publication of the *Paradox* renders it less relevant for eighteenth-century art history. However, this argument cannot apply to the central example of the *Belisarius*, which was exhibited in the Salon of 1781. Fried applies Diderot's comments of 1762 to David's work:

> If, when one makes a painting, one supposes beholders, everything is lost. The painter leaves his canvas, just as the actor who speaks to the audience [*parterre*] steps down from the stage. In supposing hat there is no-one else in the world except the personnages of the painting, Van Dyck's painting is sublime. (Fried 1983: 149)

Certainly the actor addressing the audience destroys the illusion of the performance but the paradox remains that they know the audience is there. Diderot was not afraid that the actor might communicate with the audience in general but that he might speak to the *parterre*, the popular audience standing in front of the stage. This group was never envisaged in the eighteenth century as being equivalent to the entire audience, as Fried translates it, but were disparaged as a rowdy, disruptive group of pleasure seekers. In the eighteenth century the *parterre* were able to disrupt plays to such an extent that one new production by the Comédie Française had to be cut from five acts to only one and a half. It was a cliché of eighteenth-century French aesthetics that, while the public could form accurate judgments of artistic works, the *parterre* and its socially mixed clientele could not be equated with that public.[1]

Fried's analysis of David's painting concentrates upon the use of architecture to create a sense of space, focusing on the plane created by the Arch of Triumph, which makes it plain that the *Belisarius* was "a painting not made to be beheld" (158). Although this architecture did not appear in the Van Dyck print upon which Fried considers it "virtually certain" that David modelled his work, it was not an original motif. The Arch was in fact borrowed from the illustrations to Jean-François Marmontel's wildly successful novel *Belisarius* (1767) (Boime 1987: 175). Many of the other details of David's painting were taken directly from Gravelot's engravings, including the horrified Roman officer, the block of stone upon which Belisarius' cane rests, and the general's outstretched gesture. The original features of David's work were, then, the woman giving alms and the use of an inscription. The inscription reads "Date obolum Belisario" (Give an obol to Belisarius). In the first version of the painting, it is slightly obscured by Belisarius' staff, but it is prominent in the later copy now in the Louvre. This tag does not feature in Marmontel's text, or any of the other painted versions of the Belisarius story before and after David's work. In itself, it requires a beholder, for only a spectator of the image would be in a position to read it. Furthermore, only an outside beholder would need such an inscription for all the figures painted by David are only too aware of the identity of the general. It would be stretching credulity to suggest that the wandering, blind general carved the sign himself to attract alms. The inscription is an interpellation by David which addresses the outside spectator and calls attention to the political message of the painting. In English political satire, Belisarius had been a symbol of government ingratitude and incompetence since 1710, when a pamphlet compared the then disgraced Duke of Marlborough to the Roman general.[2] Ever since, plays and pamphlets had hearkened to Belisarius as a metaphor for the failings of government.[3] In 1768, the leading radical journal the *Political Register*, published a print decrying the "tyrannical" British policy towards the American colonies, in which the dismembered figure of Britannia is captions "Date obolum Belisario" (Wilson 1995). The *Political Register* was well known in Paris and ties between British and French radicals were sufficiently close in the period for Jean-Paul Marat, the future revolutionary leader, to campaign in Newcastle and publish his first book—*The Chains of Slavery* (1774)—in English translation. The caption places David's work as one of his first political statements, and it was no coincidence that he made it more legible in the later version.[4]

David did not simply add a political label to an illustration in Marmontel's novel, but changed the dynamics of the scene with the addition of the woman giving alms. Her presence allows the soldier to drop back and recognize his former leader from a safe distance, but more importantly it gives a gendered dynamic to the painting. Gender roles were similarly important in the British print, contrasting Britannia's virtue with the effeminacy of the British political elite. The horror of the soldier is caused as much by the reduced circumstances of the general, indicated by the woman's act of charity, as by his blindness. The paradox of the *Belisarius* is precisely this opposition of gender roles. In the *Paradox*, Diderot advised his readers to "[t]hink of women, again. They are miles beyond us in sensibility; there is no sort of comparison between their passion and ours. But as much as we are below them in action, so much are they below us in imitation" (Lacoue-Labarthe 1989: 263). The unknown woman who acts out of pity for the fallen general is the counterpoint to the masculine sensibility of the soldier. She is also the inspiration for David's exercise in artistic imitation and it is inspiration that, for Diderot, sets the true artist apart from the crowd. "The beauty of inspiration" was what the artist Le Quesnoy could see and his visitor could not. It is what gives a work its force and enthusiasm. But that moment must be contained and controlled in conscious reflection, the masculine quality which women are held to lack. This paradox is contained in the epigram Diderot wrote for the *Belisarius*: "Every day I see it, and always I believe I am seeing it for the first time." The doubled insight of the witness to the blind is given force and freshness by the differing reactions of the spectators within the frame, according to their gender stereotypes. Only the spectator outside, whether it was the artist observing himself, the Salon spectator or the critic, could fully appreciate and meditate upon these different reactions and insights.

Blindness in *ancien régime* art, then, called attention to the relativism and vulnerability of human sensory perception, and the paradoxical nature of artistic creation. The blind were not used as metaphors beyond the specific limitations of their condition, but constituted an important point of reference for sensualist philosophy, as it strove to understand understanding itself. As Ménuret de Chambaud, a principal contributor to the great *Encyclopedia* of Diderot and d'Alembert, opined: "Perhaps it is true that in order to be a good moralist, one must be an excellent doctor" (Rey 1993: 25). However, not long after these words were written, philosophy took a turn away from sensualism to the more abstracted pursuit of epistemology, and medicine became inseparable from morality. In the second half of the eighteenth century, medical science began to rely on a distinction between the normal states of the body and its pathology, that is, its diseases and abnormalities. Disease, abnormality and immorality became linked in a powerful trinity which is still in force today. Georges Canguilhem has analyzed the spread of a distinction between the normal and the pathological from the first appearance of the terms in the mid-eighteenth century to their widespread acceptance in the nineteenth century:

> In the course of the nineteenth century, the real identity of normal and pathological vital phenomena, apparently so different, and given opposing values by human experience, became a kind of scientifically guaranteed dogma, whose extension into the realms of philosophy and psychology appeared to be dictated by the authority biologists and physicians granted it. (Canguilhem 1991 [1966]: 43)

Sensualist philosophy, which depended upon the authority of sense impressions, was among the first areas to be so affected.

Blindness was at once categorized as a pathological state of the body, in distinction to the normal condition of sight. During the French Revolution the state appropriated the wealth of the Quinze-Vingts, the charitable hospital for the blind in Paris, due to the tradition that patients said prayers for the Church and the King. Moreover, those blind persons who had formerly been in the nobility or clergy received a higher pension than others and there were suspicions of immoral conduct in the hospital. In its place, the revolutionaries proposed to create a national network of "residential assistance for all the blind, public asylums for those who have neither habitation to shelter them, nor family to care for them" (*Observations* An II: 37). In place of royal charity, the Revolution hoped to construct a national, moral and egalitarian system of assistance for the blind, which did not entail any change in the medical care of the blind.

Although there was a seemingly absolute distinction between the pathological blind and the normal sighted, it was soon blurred by further classification among the ranks of the pathological. As the nineteenth century progressed, it became clear that, despite the physical limitations of blindness, it was regarded as less morally debilitating than other sensory loss. In particular, the blind came to be seen as superior to the deaf—in the minds of the hearing and seeing—and to be endowed with special moral qualities. The blind and deaf pupils of the state were initially housed together during the French Revolution, until political discord among their educators forced a separation in 1793. At this time, both the deaf and the blind were seen as pre-civilized beings who required the assistance of the state to render them human. In a pamphlet published in 1783, Perier, a deputy administrator at the Institute for the Deaf, adamantly insisted on the need for such an institution: "The Deaf-Mute is always a savage, always close to ferocity, and always on the point of becoming a monster." Even after birth, the "savage" Deaf could mutate into monstrous forms without the restraining hand of the disciplinary Institute. The language used to describe the deaf was also applied to the blind, as here by one administrator of the blind school in 1817: "The moral world does not exist for this child of nature; most of our ideas are without reality for him: he lives as if he was alone; he relates everything to himself " (Paulson 1987: 95). The initial breakthrough in the education of the blind was the invention of a raised typeface by Valentin Haüy, condensed by Louis Braille (1809–1852) into the code of dots with which we are familiar. As discussions of the old chestnut regarding the preferability of blindness or deafness continued, the issue was decisively resolved (by those who could see and hear) in favour of blindness. For the loss of hearing was held to entail the loss of voice and hence of thought. When the blind read Braille, they converted the dots into the pure medium of sound, which more than compensated for its non-alphabetic character, whereas the deaf used sign language, and thought without sound. By late century, official French government manuals on the care of the abnormal advised that Braille was "an intermediary system between the manuscript and the printed text," but in sign language, "all spiritual ideas will be unhappily materialized" (Couètoux and de Fougeray 1886: 131 and 19). Thomas Arnold (1823–1900), who founded a small school for the deaf in Northampton in 1868, believed that the blind: "mentally, morally and spiritually [are] in a more advantageous condition than the deaf." If the blind could create "a mental language of vibrations and motions" from touch, the deaf were restricted to "a language of mimic gestures…which is destitute of all that phonetic language provides of antecedent progress in thought and knowledge" (Arnold 1894: 9–15). In 1840, Braille was considered arbitrary and deaf sign language had won a certain acceptance, but by 1890 it was Braille that had become acceptable and the deaf were considered pre-civilized. Nothing essential had changed in the nature of sign language and Braille in the intervening fifty years. In Arnold's widely accepted viewpoint, the decisive factor in this change of opinion was the blind's ability to hear. Sight was "much inferior in providing us with available mental images and an organ of expression," indicating that hearing alone was now considered a "pure" sense. Arnold's privileged point of reference was the French neurologist Jean-Martin Charcot (1825–1893), as the "abnormal" became the province of what was termed medico-psychology. By way of contrast, French officials considered that deafness rendered even the sense of sight pathological: "[the deaf person] knows that what he does not see does not exist for him; he does not look, he *devours*" (Denis 1895: 23–6). Medico-psychology thus considered the loss of sight to be far less grievous a blow than deafness. This sense that the blind are more "human" than the deaf has persisted to the present and accounts for the greater sympathy and funding that is available for the blind.

The rise of this perceived morality of blindness from the nineteenth to the early twentieth century can also be traced in the cultural representation of blindness. In Paul De Man's famous essay, "The Rhetoric of Blindness," he advances the case that a writer only gains a certain insight because of his or her blindness to other aspects of the problem.

> Insight could only be gained because the critics were in the grip of this peculiar blindness: their language could grope toward a certain degree of insight only because their method remained oblivious to the perception of this insight. The insight exists only for a reader in the privileged position of being able to observe the blindness as a phenomenon in its own right—the question of his own blindness being one which he is by definition incompetent to ask—and so being able to distinguish between statement and meaning. (De Man 1983: 106)

De Man's argument is central to the modern canon of blindness as outlined in this essay. In the pursuit of clarity, insight and self-expression, successive modernist artists have deployed blindness as a key figure for their work. De Man does not, however, clarify that this relationship of blindness and insight is both historically specific—as opposed to a universal truth about criticism—and gendered. The gendered dimension of the Dibutade myth and David's *Belisarius* came to be transferred to this critical relationship valorizing insight as inevitably and uniquely masculine

In both Romantic and Neo-Classical painting, blindness was used as a figure for insight and morality. Jean-Auguste-Dominique Ingres (1780–1867) was the leader of the French Neo-Classical school from the collapse of Napoleon's Empire in 1815 until his death. Ingres created a series of painted manifestos, setting out the influences and beliefs of a Neo-Classicism which sought to reclaim the French Classical tradition, stemming from Poussin, while bypassing the images of the French Revolution. As a leading student of David, Ingres was well placed to carry out this artistic revision of history painting, in accord with the wider rewriting of history during the Restoration (1816–30). In his vast ceiling painting, *The Apotheosis of Homer*, Ingres reinvented French Neo-Classicism after the Revolution. This painting, installed in the Louvre in 1827, literally put the lid on what can be called the French cultural revolution (Bianchi 1982). It is a history painting, the most important genre of painting in the period, which became the precondition of all French history painting, depicting the appropriate sources and inspirations for this art. At the center of the painting is the figure of Homer being crowned by the Muses, surrounded by those who have followed in his wake. Ingres depicted an artistic lineage which passed from the ancient Greek artists Apelles and Zeuxis, via the Renaissance masters Raphael and Poussin, ending by inference with Ingres himself. At the heart of this artistic pedigree sits the blind poet Homer, author if the *Iliad* and the *Odyssey*. Blindness was thus for Ingres quite literally the origin of representation. Clearly, Homer's blindness cannot be understood in the relativizing sensory tradition of the Enlightenment, for Ingres sought to deify Homer, not to place his work in relation to that of others. His blindness, symbolized by his closed eyes, is metaphorical and suggests instead that, in order to achieve the degree of insight attained by Homer, some sacrifice is necessary. Despite his success, Ingres believed that he too had suffered in his artistic career. His *Jupiter and Thetis* had been a dramatic failure at the Salon of 1811 and after his *Saint Symphorien* suffered a similar fate in 1834, Ingres refused to show his work at the Salon. It is hard not to take the metaphor of blindness a little farther. Ingres excluded his own master David and the other leading French Neo-Classicists, such as Gros, Gérard and Girodet from his vision of painting. Homer's blindness was matched by Ingres' own metaphorical blind spot concerning his own artistic formation in the Neo-Classical school of David, overlooked in his painting in favour of the eternal verities of Homer.

Ingres was haunted by the symbolism of blindness. In 1816, he completed the first of many versions of the theme *Oedipus and the Sphinx*, in which Oedipus is shown answering the Sphinx's riddle. His successful response ensured that the second part of his oracle would be enacted, for having already unwittingly killed his father, Oedipus was not to marry his mother. Oedipus is finally the agent of his own destruction, when he seeks to uncover the causes of a plague and discovers the truth of his own actions. By way of self-punishment, Oedipus blinds himself. The Freudian overtones of this story are only too apparent. For Freud, the Oedipus myth was a representation of the most fundamental masculine desires to kill the father and sleep with the mother, as well as of its most potent fear, namely Oedipus' blindness, equated to the fear of castration. It is in fact arguable that without the nineteenth century construct of blindness as moral sacrifice, Freud would not have been able to use the Oedipus myth as he did. Blindness appears at the centre of Ingres' history paintings precisely because of these new resonances it acquired in the period. The meanings conveyed by blindness as metaphor were, however, complex and irreducible to a single message. It was a short step from the moral insight of Homer to the castrated gaze of Oedipus. Blindness became a complex figure in Ingres' work, standing for representation, for morality and for the construction of the masculine ego itself, always haunted by the fear of castration, itself envisaged as blindness.[5]

For Ingres' depiction of history painting is a striking example of what Donna Harraway has called the patriline. His *Homer* is a homosocial world in which women appear only in non-human form as Muses. The transmission and reproduction of cultural value was envisaged as a purely masculine affair, eliminating the fear of castration and the blind(ed) gaze. A central theme of eighteenth-century painting had been the "fallen father," to use Carol Duncan's insightful phrase. History and genre painting had sought to construct an authoritative father figure in a society widely believed to be unusually susceptible to feminine influence. For many revolutionary leaders, this feminizing of the French state was to blame for the political weaknesses and corruption of the *ancien régime*. Even avowed supporters of the monarchy agreed that, in the words of the painter Elizabeth Vigée Lebrun, "the women reigned then. The Revolution dethroned them" (Vigée Lebrun 1989: 49). Rather than return to this charged political controversy, Ingres elided it by creating an idea of culture as the exclusive province of the white male. From its foundation in 1648, the French Academy of Painting had permitted women to become members in theory, although few in practice were able to gain the necessary training. But in 1776, it was felt to be necessary to limit the number of potential women members to four. Even then, the admission of Vigée Lebrun in 1783 required considerable politicking to evade the censure of the leading Academician Pierre (Vigée Lebrun 1989: 34–5). The reformed nineteenth-century Academy excluded women altogether. In Ingres' representation of civilization, there was no place for women.

Eugène Delacroix (1798–1863), the leader of the Romantic school of painting, also represented blindness as the origin of representation, even though he is usually considered as being directly opposed to Ingres' Neo-Classicism. Delacroix chose as a subject *The Poet Milton Dictating to His Daughters* (1826). For the Romantics, the blind poet Milton occupied the same position of authority as Homer for the Neo-Classicists. The subject had been treated by Henry Fuseli in 1799, but he was so anxious to represent Milton's blindness that the poet has ashen skin and sunken eyes, looking more like Boris Karloff's Frankenstein than an inspired poet. Delacroix represented the scene in quieter but altogether more effective fashion. Just as David used the woman giving alms to give meaning to his *Belisarius*, so did Delacroix highlight the contrast between the active women and their passive father. Milton becomes the supreme embodiment of the superiority of the voice and hearing over sight, as his powers of creativity are contrasted with the women, who although sighted, are fit only to copy down their father's words. The poet's insight is such that it overcomes his physical blindness. Milton retains his patriarchal authority, despite having suffered the loss of his sight, and his potency is doubly attested to by the presence of his daughters. Delacroix's confident embrace of blindness as a gendered metaphor for creativity and morality was to gain ascendancy over Ingres' homosocial vision. While the Neo-Classical Ingres saw blindness as both the origin and the potential annihilation of representation, the modern Romantics bestowed creativity on the individual male and were unconcerned to construct secure artistic genealogies. Indeed the Oedipal gesture of revolt becomes *de rigueur* for any aspiring young artist.

The high point of this moralizing trajectory came with Paul Strand's (1890–1976) photograph *Blind Woman* (1916). Taken as a manifesto for Strand's departure from the gradated tones of the Photo-

Secession movement, his representation of blindness thus embodied revolt and coming of age. The photograph has long been hailed as a modernist masterpiece:

> The portrait conveys *qualities*: endurance, isolation, the curious alertness of the blind or nearly blind, and a surprising beauty in the strong, possible Slavic, head. The whole concept of blindness is aimed like a weapon at those whose privilege of sight permits them to experience the picture, much like the "dramatic irony" in which an all-knowing audience observes a doomed protagonist onstage. Although he excluded bystanders from the picture, Strand included everyone who sees it. This extraordinary device gives the photograph its particular edge, adding new meaning to a simple portrait. (Haworth-Booth 1987: 5)

In this view, Strand's photograph of the blind woman functions as an abstract, moral discourse on perception. The weapon of blindness belonged not to the blind woman but to the photographer. It was no coincidence that Strand photographed a blind woman. In so doing, he collapsed the moral exchange created by David and Delacroix between the blind man and the sighted woman into one figure. Strand's deployment of gender constituted the originality of his work, for photographers had long considered the blind as an intriguing subject. As early as 1858, the photographic journal *La Lumière* reported the placard of a Parisian male beggar: 'Give to the poor blind man, he will not see you (*La Lumière* 1858: 99). In Strand's work, the woman represents the modernist quandary as to the nature of perception, but it is the photographer who has the key to representation rather than the figure within the image. In his quest to deny the woman any specificity, Strand erased her name and any details about her in order to make blindness a more effective symbol. If blindness is to be fully effective as a moral lesson, it cannot be dogged by such trivial details. None the less, the history of the blind, as opposed to the abstract idea of blindness, is present in this photograph. The blind woman wears a brass badge, bearing the legend "Licensed Peddler. New York. 2622." The badge, together with the crudely painted sign reading BLIND, attests to the state's intervention in controlling the "degenerate" population. In order to sell items on the street, the woman has to be registered and classified, involving tests to ensure that she is "really" blind and not simply "idle." These policies were the culmination of over a century of designating the blind as pathological and hence a problem for the body politic. Strand's abstract moral lesson was enabled and given meaning by the classification and labeling of the blind by that nexus of medical and political authority which Michel Foucault has named bio-power. As a meditation on representation, the photograph takes blindness to be the origin of representation, but denies the woman any participation in this process, except as its object.

This interpretation of the role of blindness in representation received ironic confirmation when the American Minimalist artist Robert Morris (b. 1931) set about his series called *Blind Time* in 1973. Morris had pursued a critique of the prevalent modes of art practice, criticism and display in a variety of media since the early 1960s. Now, seeking to move on from his site-specific earth pieces of the early 1970s, Morris undertook a series of works in which he was unable to see. He assigned himself a specific task and a length of time in which to complete it, drawing on paper with his fingers. By so doing, Morris sought to disrupt the modernist obsession with sight and its representation, as Maurice Berger has noted:

> Like being lost in a labyrinth, such drawing processes radically altered the artist's sense of control of his own actions. By undoing the compositional claims of the artist over his work, the *Blind Time* series distanced the artists from the modernist conceits of ego and temperament. Because the artist's masterful control of his process was not rendered irrelevant, such works travestied the obsession of formalist abstraction with compositional balance and harmony. (Berger 1989: 151)

Morris soon decided to take this process one step farther. In 1976, he commenced the series *Blind Time II*, in which he used a woman who had been blind from birth as what he termed as "assistant." The woman, known only as A. A., was recruited from the American Association for the Blind and was asked to carry out similar tasks to those Morris himself had previously performed. The experience was not a success. A. A. quickly became skeptical of the project and confused as to its intentions. Here, for example, Morris commented:

> She had no idea of illusionistic drawing. I described perspective to her and she thought that was abso-
> lutely ridiculous, that things got smaller in the distance. She had no conception of that. She kept asking
> me about criteria, got very involved in what is the right kind of criteria for a thing. And there was no
> way that she could find any and finally that sort of conflict became very dramatic. She was operating
> in a way that she wouldn't have to invoke [these criteria]. And at the same time she was aghast that
> she was not able to. (Berger 1989: 153)

This scene, far from constituting a radical experiment, was a re-enactment of the modernist legend connecting blindness to the origin of representation, as if Morris had tried to find his own Dibutade and recreate the origin of drawing in a woman whom he believed had no concept of visual representation. Like Dibutade, A. A. could not record her own work, but relied on the intercession of the male authority figure for her claim to a place in art history. Whereas Paul Strand had used blindness as a weapon, Morris went one further and used the blind woman as a form of tool. He denied her the chance to formulate her own concepts of art practice and refused to let her establish any rules in her work. In 1856, Théophile Gautier had made this distinction central to his "programme of the modern school" of art for arts sake.

> The artist much search for his alphabet in the visible world, which supplies him with conventional
> signs . . .; but if the idea of the beautiful pre-exists within us, would it pre-exist in a man born blind,
> for example? What image of the beautiful in art could a pensioner of the Quinze Vingts make for
> himself? (Gautier 1856: 157)

The relativistic notions of perception which had so fascinated Enlightenment critics no longer applied. Sight was essential not just for art, as might seem obvious, but for the very notions of art and beauty. The very initials A. A. by which the blind woman is known are indicative of Morris's sense that she was at the origin of art and could have no rules. Soon becoming dissatisfied with her work, Morris discontinued the project, finding it "[s]parer and less controlled than the artist's own blind drawings, they are more about her impressions and feelings" (Fry 1986: 34). Morris withdrew all 52 works created in the *Blind Time II* series from circulation. Modernism had so far abstracted blindness and gender from the body that Morris's encounter with an actual blind woman was bound to end in failure.

When he resumed *Blind Time* in 1985, Morris undertook the works himself. In his version of the project, he added philosophical commentaries on the images produced and the ideas that lay behind them. For example, in one 1985 piece, Morris set about constructing a grid in a seven-minute experiment. As Rosalind Krauss has argued, the grid has been one of the defining motifs of modernism and Morris attached considerable weight to the procedure in his inscription: "Searching for a metaphor for the occupation of that moment between lapsed time and the possibilities spent on the one hand and an imagined but unoccupiable future on the other, both of which issue from that tightly woven nexus of language, tradition and culture which constructs our narrative of time" (Fry 1986: 37). Although *Blind Time III* makes considerable reference to contemporary physics, citing such figures as Einstein, Bohr and Feynman, this passage seems closer to Marcel Proust and his search for lost time. These literary and philosophical comments could hardly be further removed from the excerpts of conversation between the artist and A. A., which accompanied the previous version of the series. The male artist feels able to explore the metaphorical dimensions and wider implications of his "blindness," precisely the avenues he had blocked for the anonymous blind woman. Morris's modernism denied the blind any possibility of participating in visual representation. While this exclusion might seem natural, it did not seem so to early modern blind sculptors or indeed to A. A. Within this metaphorical framework, blindness-as-lack-of-sight affects only women, whereas blindness-as-insight is a particularly male phenomenon. The radical feminist art collective, the Guerilla Girls, would no doubt wish to note that in Derrida's exhibition at the Louvre, for which he was given access to their entire collection of prints and drawings, the philosopher selected no women artists.[6]

Blindness—or more exactly, the interplay between the insightful artist and the blind woman—is only one metaphor for modernism and is not equivalent to it. But the nexus of race, gender and disability created by the triumph of the Dibutade myth of the origin of painting in the mid-eighteenth century forms a crucial point of investigation for the modern representation of the body, which was caught between two difficult alternatives. The Dibutade myth was itself determined by a wider revision of European intellectual history which excluded African and Semitic influences in favour of a pure Aryan model for ancient Greek history. However, the alternative modernist reading of the body, which privileges the fragmentary and dispersed body and argues that culture oscillates between the poles of blindness and insight, is constructed around a notion of originary gender difference. Both readings of the body thus depend upon essential differences of race or gender, which are both necessarily exclusive and ahistorical. It would be equally disingenuous simply to call for an end to the metaphorization of the body, still more so for an end to the representation of the body—even a Minimalist sculpture can be read as a denial of the body. For it is not enough to reveal yet again that cultural products are social constructions, as Michael Taussig has recently argued: "What do we do with this old insight? If life is constructed, how come it appears so immutable? How come culture appears so natural?" (Taussig 1993a: xvi). Rather than concluding by producing the white rabbit of cultural construction from the intellectual's top hat, it is my point of departure that these contradictions produce a necessary and productive disease concerning the bodyscape.

However, this constructed understanding of the modern body does not make it any less real, nor does it allow the modern subject to bypass the limits of body in a quest for identity. The body cannot be known or understood without visual representation, yet both the body itself and its image seem inevitably flawed. An indication of this problem is that there is no way to describe the body as imperfect (disabled, incomplete, virtual, etc.) which does not logically and linguistically imply the existence of a perfect body. In order to extend our understanding, it is therefore necessary to examine the persistence and cultural function of notions of the perfect body.

Notes

1. In Britain, by contrast, the pit was held to be the most important venue for determining public opinion in the theatre.
2. See Anon, *Belisarius and Zariana: A Dialogue* (London, 1709) and the play *Belisarius* by William Philips (London, T. Woodward, 1724), dedicated to General Webb, reprinted in 1758.
3. Plays included: *Belisarius* ascribed to John Phillip Kemble (1778) and *Belisarius* by Hugh Downman (Exeter, 1786); a scene concerning Belisarius was published in *The Oracle* (17 October 1795). Many thanks to Kathleen Wilson for these references.
4. Thomas Crow has suggested that the exile referred to was the minister Turgot, an identification made all the more likely by the English parallel.
5. The polysemicity of blindness in the modern period does not undermine Derrida's interpretation, but rather reinforces it. Derrida has often emphasized that the keywords in his readings, such as deconstruction, glyph, hymen, *différance*, *pharmakon*, and so on, are not to be individually privileged as the key to the Western metaphysic, but are different points of entry to that discourse.
6. In fact, when Derrida discusses sexuality it is male sexuality that is in question, via an examination of representations of the blinding of Samson, read as castration.

Works Cited

Arnold, Thomas. 1894. *The Language of the Senses with Special Reference to the Education of the Deaf, Blind, Deaf & Blind*. Margate, England: *Keble's Gazette*.

Berger, Maurice. 1989. *Labyrinths: Robert Morris, Minimalism, and the 1960s*. New York. Harper and Row.

Bourdon, Sébastien. 1740. "Seventh Conference." In [Anon.] 1740 *Seven Conference Held in the King of France's Cabinet of Paintings*. London: T. Cooper.

Canguilhem, Georges. 1991 [1966]. *The Normal and the Pathological*. Trans. Caroyn R. Fawcettt. New York. Zone.

Couétoux, L. and Hamon de Fougeray. 1886. *Manuel pratique des méthodes d'enseignement spéciales aux enfants anormaux (sourds-muets, aveugles, idiots, bégues, etc.)*. Paris: Félix Alcan.

Denis, Théophile. 1895. "Les Artistes sourds-muets au Salon de 1886." In *Etudes variées concernant les sourds-muets. Histoire—Biographie—Beaux-arts*. Paris: Imprimérie de la Revue Francaise de l'Enseignement de Sourds-muets.

De Man, Paul. 1983. *Blindness and Insight*. Minneapolis: University of Minnesota Press.

Derrida, Jacques. 1993. *Memoirs of the Blind: The Self Portrait and Other Ruins*. Trans. Pascale-Anne Brault and Michael Naas. Chicago. Chicago University Press.

Diderot, Denis. 1975–. *Oeuvres complètes*. Paris: Hermann. 25 vols.

Dryden, John. 1695. *De Arte Graphica: The Art of Painting by C. A. du Fresnoy*. London. J. Hepinstall.

Fried, Michael. 1983. *Absorption and Theatricality*. Chicago: Chicago University Press.

Fry, Edward F. with Donald P. Kuspit. 1986. *Robert Morris: Works of the Eighties*. Chicago. Museum of Contemporary Art.

Gautier, Théophile. 1856. "Du Beau dans l'Art." In *L'Art moderne*. Paris: Michel Levy.

Haworth-Booth, Mark. 1987. *Paul Strand*. New York: Aperture.

Josephs, Herbert. 1969. *Diderot's Dialogue of Language and Gesture: Le Neveu de Rameau*. Columbus: Ohio University Press.

Lacoue-Labarthe, Phillipe. 1989. *Typography*. Cambridge, MA: Harvard University Press.

La Lumière Observations. An II. Anon. *Observations pour les aveugles de l'Hôpital des Quinze-Vingts sur le project décret du comité de secours de la Convention Nationale pour la suppression de cet hopital*, Paris: J. Grand.

Paulson, William R. 1987. *Enlightenment, Romanticism and the Blind in France*. Princeton: Princeton University Press.

Taussig, Michael. 1993a. *Mimesis and Alterity: A Particular History of the Senses*. New York: Routledge.

Vigée Lebrun, Elizabeth. 1989. *Memoirs of Madame Vigée Lebrun*. New York: George Braziller [1903].

32

Blindness and Visual Culture
An Eye Witness Account

Georgina Kleege

In April 2004, I was invited to speak at a conference on visual culture at the University of California, Berkeley. Speakers were asked to respond to an essay by W. J. T. Mitchell titled, "Showing Seeing: A Critique of Visual Culture," which offers a series of definitions of the emergent field of visual studies, distinguishing it from the more established disciplines of art history, aesthetics and media studies. As an admitted outsider to the field of visual studies, I chose to comment on the following statement: "Visual culture entails a meditation on blindness, the invisible, the unseen, the unseeable, and the overlooked" (Mitchell 2002, 170). In my last book, *Sight Unseen*, I attempted to show blindness through my own experience, and a survey of representations of blindness in literature and film. At the same time, I wanted to show seeing, to sketch my understanding of vision, drawn from a lifetime of living among the sighted in this visual culture we share. I started from the premise that the average blind person knows more about what it means to be sighted than the average sighted person knows about what it means to be blind. The blind grow up, attend school, and lead adult lives among sighted people. The language we speak, the literature we read, the architecture we inhabit, were all designed by and for the sighted.

If visual studies entails a meditation on blindness, it is my hope that it will avoid some of the missteps of similar meditations of the past. Specifically, I hope that visual studies can abandon one of the stock characters of the western philosophical tradition—"the Hypothetical Blind Man" (Gitter 2001, 58). The Hypothetical Blind Man—or the Hypothetical as I will call him for the sake of brevity—has long played a useful, though thankless role, as a prop for theories of consciousness. He is the patient subject of endless thought experiments where the experience of the world through four senses can be compared to the experience of the world through five. He is asked to describe his understanding of specific visual phenomena—perspective, reflection, refraction, color, form recognition—as well as visual aids and enhancements—mirrors, lenses, telescopes, microscopes. He is understood to lead a hermit-like existence, so far at the margins of his society, that he has never heard this visual terminology before the philosophers bring it up. Part of the emotional baggage he hauls around with him comes from other cultural representations of blindness, such as Oedipus and the many Biblical figures whose sight is withdrawn by the wrathful God of the Old Testament or restored by the redeemer of the New. His primary function is to highlight the importance of sight and to elicit a frisson of awe and pity which promotes gratitude among the sighted theorists for the vision they possess.

I will not attempt to survey every appearance of the Hypothetical throughout the history of philosophy. It is enough to cite a few of his more memorable performances, and then to suggest what happens when he is brought face-to-face with actual blind people through their own first-hand, eye-witness accounts. Professor Mitchell alludes to the passages in Descartes' *La Dioptrique* where he compares vision to the Hypothetical's use of sticks to grope his way through space. Descartes's references to the Hypothetical are confusing and are often conflated by his readers. In one instance, he compares the way the Hypothetical's stick detects the density and resistance of objects in his path, to the way light acts on objects the eye looks at. In a later passage, Descartes performs a thought experiment, giving the Hypothetical a second stick which he could use to judge the distance between two objects by calculating the angle formed when he touches each object with one of the sticks. Descartes does not explain how the Hypothetical is supposed to make this calculation or how he can avoid running into things while doing so. I doubt that Descartes actually believed that any blind person ever used two sticks in this way. In fact, the image that illustrates his discussion shows the Hypothetical's dog sound asleep on the ground, indicating that the Hypothetical is going nowhere. Even so, Descartes' description of the way a blind person uses one stick reflects a basic misunderstanding. He imagines that the blind use the stick to construct a mental image, or its equivalent, of their surroundings, mapping the location of specifically identified objects. In fact, then as now, a stick or cane is a poor tool for this kind of mental imaging. The stick serves merely to announce the presence of an obstacle, not to determine if it is a rock or a tree root, though there are sound cues—a tap versus a thud—that might help make this distinction. In many situations, the cane is more of an auditory than a tactile tool. It seems that in Descartes' desire to describe vision as an extension of or hypersensitive form of touch, he recreates the blind man in his own image, where the eye must correspond to the hand extended by one or perhaps two sticks.

The most detailed depiction of the Hypothetical came about in 1693, when William Molyneux wrote his famous letter to John Locke. He proposed a thought experiment where a blind man who had learned to recognize geometric forms such as a cube and a sphere by touch, would have his sight restored through an operation. Would he be able to distinguish the two forms merely by looking at them? The Molyneux question continues to be debated today, even though the history of medicine is full of case studies of actual blind people who have had their sight restored by actual operations. Apparently, Molyneux was married to a blind woman, which has always led me to wonder why he did not pose his hypothetical question about her. Perhaps he knew that others would object that marriage to a philosopher might contaminate the experimental data. There was a risk that the philosopher might prime her answers or otherwise rig the results. Certainly in commentary on actual cases of restored sight, debaters of the Molyneux question are quick to disqualify those who were allowed to cast their eyes upon, for instance the faces of loved ones, before directing their gaze at the sphere and the cube.

Denis Diderot's 1749 "Letter on the Blind for the Use of Those Who See" is generally credited with urging a more enlightened, and humane attitude toward the blind. His blind man of Puiseaux and Nicholas Saunderson, the English mathematician, were both real rather than hypothetical blind men. As he introduces the man from Puiseaux, Diderot is at pains to supply details of his family history and early life to persuade his reader that this is a real person. Significantly, the man from Puiseaux is first encountered helping his young son with his studies, demonstrating both that he is a loving family man, and capable of intellectual activity. But the questions Diderot poses generally fall under the pervu of the Hypothetical. Certainly, many of his remarks help support Descartes' theory relating vision to touch:

> One of our company thought to ask our blind man if he would like to have eyes. "If it were not for curiosity," he replied, "I would just as soon have long arms: it seems to me my hands would tell me more of what goes on in the moon than your eyes or your telescopes." (Diderot 1999, 153)

Diderot praises the blind man's ability to make philosophical surmises about vision, but does not have a high opinion of blind people's capacity for empathy:

> As of all the external signs which raise our pity and ideas of pain the blind are affected only by cries, I have in general no high thought of their humanity. What difference is there to a blind man between a man making water and one bleeding in silence? (Diderot 1999, 156)

The phrasing of the question here suggests an afterthought. I imagine Diderot, at his table, conjuring up two men, one pissing, one bleeding. While his visual imagination is practiced in making these sorts of mental images, he is less adept at tuning his mind's ear. He recognizes that for the blood to be spilt at a rate sufficient to create the same sound as the flowing urine, the bleeding man would normally cry out in pain. So he imagines, in effect, a bleeding mute. But he fails to take into account the relative viscosity, not to mention the different odors, of the two fluids. But Diderot cannot think of everything.

Now I imagine a blind man wandering onto the scene. My blind man is not quite the one Diderot imagines. For one thing he is a bit preoccupied; the philosophers have dropped by again. They talk at him and over his head, bandying about names that are now familiar to him: Locke, Molyneux, Descartes. They question him about his ability to conceptualize various things: windows, mirrors, telescopes—and he responds with the quaint and winsome answers he knows they have come for. Anything to get rid of them. Distracted as he is, the sound of the bleeding mute's plashing blood registers on his consciousness. Lacking Diderot's imagination, however, the thought does not occur to him that this sound emanates from a bleeding mute. His reason opts instead for the explanation that the sound comes from some man relieving his bladder—a far more commonplace phenomenon, especially in the means streets where the blind man resides. It is not that the blind man has no fellow feeling for the mute. Come to think of it, the mute would make a good companion. He could act as a guide and keep an eye out for marauding philosophers, while the blind man could do all the talking. But the blind man does not have enough information to recognize the mute's dilemma. The only hope for the bleeding mute is to find some way to attract the blind man's attention, perhaps by throwing something. But surely, such a massive loss of blood must have affected his aim. While the blind man, living as he does at the margins of his society, is accustomed to being spurned by local homeowners and merchants who find his presence unsightly, and so might flee the bleeding mute's missiles without suspecting that his aid is being solicited.

The blind man quickens his pace as best he can. The mute succumbs at last to his mortal wound. And the philosopher shifts to another topic.

I am wrong to make fun of Diderot, since his treatment of blindness was at once far more complex and far more compassionate than that of other philosophers. And it is not as if his low opinion of the blind's ability to empathize with others' pain has ceased to contribute to attitudes about blindness. Consider this anecdote from recent history. Some weeks after September 11, 2001, the blind musician Ray Charles was interviewed about his rendition of "America the Beautiful," which received a good deal of air time during the period of heightened patriotism that followed that event. The interviewer, Jim Gray, commented that Charles should consider himself lucky that his blindness prevented him from viewing the images of the World Trade Center's collapse, and the Pentagon in flames: "Was this maybe one time in your life where not having the ability to see was a relief?" Like Diderot, the interviewer assumed that true horror can only be evinced through the eyes. Many eyewitness accounts of the event however, were strikingly nonvisual. Many people who were in the vicinity of Ground Zero during and soon after the disaster found it hard to put what they saw into words, in part because visibility in the area was obscured by smoke and ash, and in part because what they were seeing did not correspond to any visual experience for which they had language. People described instead the sound of falling bodies hitting the ground, the smell of the burning jet fuel, and the particular texture of the ankle deep dust that filled the streets. But for the majority of television viewers, eye-witnesses from a distance, those events are recalled as images, indelible, powerful, and eloquent. To many, like the reporter interviewing Ray Charles, it is the images rather than the mere fact of the events that produce the emotional response. The assumption seems to be that because the blind are immune to images they must also be immune to the significance of the events, and therefore must be somehow detached from or indifferent to the nation's collective horror and grief.

It is fortunate for anyone interested in dismantling the image of blindness fostered by the Hypothetical Blind Man that we have today a great many first-hand accounts of blindness. In recent decades, memoirs, essays and other texts by actual blind people attempt to loosen the grip the Hypothetical still seems to hold on the sighted imagination. Thanks to work by disability historians, we are also beginning to have older accounts of blindness drawn from archives of institutions and schools for the blind around the world. One such account is a text written in 1825, by a twenty-two-year-old blind French woman named Thérèse-Adèle Husson. Born in Nancy into a petit bourgeois household, Husson became blind at nine months following a bout of smallpox. Her case attracted the attention of the local gentry who sponsored a convent education for her, and encouraged her to cultivate her interests in literature and music. At the age of twenty she left home for Paris where she hoped to pursue a literary career. Her first text, "Reflections on the Moral and Physical Condition of the Blind" seems to have been written as a part of her petition for aid from the Hôpital des Quinze-Vingts, an institution that provided shelter and financial support to the indigent blind of Paris. For the most part, her text follows the example of comportment and educational manuals of the time, offering advice to parents and caretakers on the correct way to raise a blind child, and to young blind people themselves on their role in society. It is by turns, formulaically obsequious and radically assertive, since she writes from the premise—revolutionary for the time—that her first-hand experience of blindness gives her a level of expertise that equals or surpasses that of the institution's sighted administrators. While it is unlikely that Husson's convent education would have exposed her to the work of Descartes or Diderot, she considers some of the same questions previously posed to the Hypothetical. It is possible that the provincial aristocrats, who took up her education, may have engaged in amateurish philosophizing in her presence. For instance, like Diderot's blind man of Puiseaux, she prefers her sense of touch to the sight she lacks. She recounts how, at the time of her first communion, her mother promised her a dress made of chiffon, then, either as a joke or in an attempt to economize, purchased cheaper percale instead. When the young Husson easily detected the difference through touch, her mother persisted in her deception, and even brought in neighbor women to corroborate. Whether playing along with the joke, or as a genuine rebuke of her mother's attempt to deceive her, Husson retorted:

> I prefer my touch to your eyes, because it allows me to appreciate things for what they really are, whereas it seems to me that your sight fools you now and then, for this is percale and not chiffon. (Husson 2001, 25)

In a later discussion of her ability to recognize household objects through touch, her impatience seems out of proportion, unless we imagine that she frequently found herself the object of philosophical speculation by literal-minded practitioners:

> We know full well that a chest of drawers is square, but more long than tall. Again I hear my readers ask what is a square object! I am accommodating enough to satisfy all their questions. Therefore, I would say to them that it is easy enough to know the difference between objects by touching them, for not all of them have the same shape. For example, a dinner plate, a dish, a glass can't begin to be compared with a chest of drawers, for the first two are round, while the other is hollow; but people will probably point out that it is only after having heard the names of the articles that I designate that it became possible for me to acquire the certainty that they were hollow, round, square. I will admit that they are right, but tell me, you with the eyes of Argus, if you had never heard objects described, would you be in any better position to speak of them than I? (Husson 2001, 41)

Her emphasis on square versus round objects as well as her tone and her taunt, "You with the eyes of Argus," suggests an irritation that may come from hearing the Molyneux question one too many times. She is also arguing against the notion that such words as "square" and "round" designate solely visual phenomena, to which the blind have no access and therefore no right to use these words.

Almost a century later, Helen Keller gives vent to a similar irritation at literal-minded readers. In her 1908 book, *The World I Live In*, she gives a detailed phenomenological account of her daily experience of deaf-blindness. Early on, she footnotes her use of the verb "see" in the phrase, "I was taken to see a woman":

> The excellent proof-reader has put a query to my use of the word "see." If I had said "visit," he would have asked no questions, yet what does "visit" mean but "see" (*visitare*)? Later I will try to defend myself for using as much of the English language as I have succeeded in learning. (Keller 2003, 19)

Keller makes good use of her Radcliffe education to show that the more one knows about language the harder it is to find vocabulary that does not have some root in sighted or hearing experience. But, she argues, to deny her the use of seeing-hearing vocabulary would be to deny her the ability to communicate at all.

In their 1995 book, *On Blindness*, two philosophers, one sighted and one blind, conduct an epistolary debate that might seem to put to rest all the old hypothetical questions. Unfortunately, Martin Milligan, the blind philosopher, died before the discussion was fully underway. If he had lived, we can assume not only that he and his sighted colleague, Bryan Magee, would have gotten further with their debate, but also that they would have edited some testy quibbles about which terms to use and which translation of Aristotle is more accurate. Milligan, who worked primarily in moral and political philosophy, and was an activist in blind causes in the United Kingdom, forthrightly resists the impulse to allow the discussion to stray far from the practical and social conditions that affect the lives of real blind people. For instance, he cites an incident from his early life, before he found an academic post, when he was turned down for a job as a telephone typist on a newspaper because the employer assumed that he would not be able to negotiate the stairs in the building. He identifies this as one of thousands of examples of the exaggerated value sighted people place on vision. Any thinking person has to recognize that sight is not required to climb or descend stairs. He asserts that the value of sight would be that it would allow him to move around unfamiliar places with greater ease. He concedes that vision might afford him some aesthetic pleasure while viewing a landscape or painting, but insists that he can know what he wants to know about the visible world from verbal descriptions, and that this knowledge is adequate for his needs, and only minimally different from the knowledge of sighted people. He accuses Magee of voicing "visionist"—or what I might call "sightist"—attitudes that the differences between the sighted and the blind must be almost incomprehensibly vast, and that vision is a fundamental aspect of human existence. Milligan says that these statements seem

> to express the passion, the zeal of a missionary preaching to the heathen in outer darkness. Only, of course, your "gospel" isn't "good" news to us heathens, for the message seems to be that ours is a "darkness" from which we can never come in—not the darkness of course that sighted people can know, but the darkness of never being able to know *that* darkness, or of bridging the vast gulf that separates us from those who do. (Magee and Milligan 1995, 46)

This prompts Magee to cite his own early work on race and homosexuality, as proof of his credentials as a liberal humanist. He also speculates, somewhat sulkily, about whether the first eighteen months of Milligan's life when his vision was presumed to be normal, might disqualify him as a spokesman for the blind, since he might retain some vestige of a visual memory from that period. Later, Magee consults with a neurologist who assures him that the loss of sight at such an early age would make Milligan's brain indistinguishable from that of a person born blind. And so the discussion continues.

Along the way, Magee makes some claims about sight that seem to me to be far from universal. For instance, he states:

> By the sighted, seeing is felt as a *need*. And it is the feeding of this almost ungovernable craving that constitutes the ongoing pleasure of sight. It is as if we were desperately hungry all the time, in such a way that only if we were eating all the time could we be content—so we eat all the time. (Magee and Milligan 1995, 104)

Magee asserts that when sighted people are obliged to keep their eyes closed even for a short time, it induces a kind of panic. To illustrate his point, he notes that a common method of mistreating prisoners is to keep them blindfolded, and this mistreatment can lead them to feel anxious and disoriented. I suspect that his example is influenced by traditional metaphors that equate blindness with a tomb-like imprisonment. Surely a blind prisoner, accustomed to the privation of sight, might still have similar feelings of anxiety and disorientation, due to the threat, whether stated or implied, of pending bodily harm.

To his credit, Magee does allow that some blind experiences are shared by the sighted. Milligan describes how many blind people negotiate new environments, and can feel the presence of large objects even without touching them as "atmosphere-thickening occupants of space." Magee reports that when he

> was a small child I had a vivid nonvisual awareness of the nearness of material objects. I would walk confidently along a pitch black corridor in a strange house and stop dead a few inches short of a closed door, and then put out my hand to grope for the knob. If I woke up in the dark in a strange bedroom and wanted to get to a light-switch on the opposite side of the room I could usually circumnavigate the furniture in between, because I could "feel" where the larger objects in the room were. I might knock small things over, but would almost invariably "feel" the big ones. I say "feel" because the sensation, which I can clearly recall, was as of a feeling-in-the-air with my whole bodily self. Your phrase "atmosphere-thickening occupants of space" describes the apprehension exactly. I suddenly "felt" a certain thickness in the air at a certain point relative to myself in the blackness surrounding me.... This illustrates your point that the blind develop potentialities that the sighted have also been endowed with but do not develop because they have less need of them. (Magee and Milligan 1995, 97–98)

Here, and in a few other places in the correspondence, Magee and Milligan seem to be moving in a new direction. It is not merely that they discover a shared perceptual experience, but one that is not easy to categorize as belonging to one of the five traditional senses. Here, a "feeling" is not the experience of texture or form through physical contact, but an apprehension, of an atmospheric change, experienced kinesthetically, and by the body as a whole. This seems to point toward a need for a theory of multiple senses where each of the traditional five could be subdivided into a number of discrete sensory activities, which function sometimes in concert with and sometimes in counterpoint to others. Helen Keller identified at least three different aspects of touch that she found meaningful: texture, temperature, and vibration. In fact, she understands sound as vibrations that the hearing feel in their ears while the deaf can feel them through other parts of their bodies. Thus she could feel thunder by pressing the palm of her hand against a windowpane, or someone's footsteps by pressing the soles of her feet against floorboards.

What these blind authors have in common is an urgent desire to represent their experiences of blindness as something besides the absence of sight. Unlike the Hypothetical, they do not feel themselves to be deficient or partial—sighted people minus sight—but whole human beings who have learned to attend to their nonvisual senses in different ways. I have deliberately chosen to limit my discussion here to works by people who became blind very early in life. One of the most striking features of the Hypothetical Blind Man is that he is always assumed to be both totally and congenitally blind. Real blindness, today as in the past, rarely fits this profile. Only about 10–20 percent of people designated as legally blind, in countries where there is such a designation, are without any visual perception at all. It is hard to come by statistics on people who are born totally blind, in part because it only becomes an issue when the child, or her parents, seek services for the blind, which tends to occur only when the child reaches school age. We can assume that more infants were born blind in the past, since some of the most prevalent causes of infantile blindness have been eliminated by medical innovations in the nineteenth and twentieth centuries. Nevertheless, in the past, as now, the leading causes of blindness occur later in life, and often leave some residual vision. Some may retain the ability to distinguish light from darkness, while others may continue to perceive light, color, form, and movement to some degree. Some people may retain the acuity to read print or facial expressions, while lacking the peripheral vision that facilitates free movement through space. And regardless of the degree or quality of residual vision, blind people differ widely in the ways they attend to, use or value these perceptions.

Although the situation of the Hypothetical is rare, his defenders are quick to discount anyone with any residual sight or with even the remotest possibility of a visual memory. In traditional discussions of blindness, only total, congenital blindness will do. In a review of my book *Sight Unseen*, Arthur Danto asserted that I had too much sight to claim to be blind (Danto 1999, 35). He quoted a totally blind graduate student he once knew who said that he could not conceptualize a window, and that he was surprised when he learned that when a person's face is said to glow, it does not in fact emit light like an incandescent light bulb. Danto does not tell us what became of this student or even give his name, using him only as a modern-day version of the Hypothetical. He then goes on to relate the history of the Molyneux question.

If only the totally blind can speak of blindness with authority, should we make the same restriction on those who talk about vision? Is there such a thing as total vision? We know that a visual acuity of 20/20 is merely average vision. There are individuals whose acuity measures better than 20/20, 20/15, or even 20/10. Such individuals can read every line of the familiar Snellan eye chart, or, as in the case of Ted Williams, can read the print on a baseball whizzing toward their bat at a speed close to ninety miles per hour. How many scholars of visual culture, I wonder but won't ask, can claim such a level of visual acuity?

What visual studies can bring to these discussions is an interrogation of the binary opposition between blindness and sight. It is clearly more useful to think in terms of a spectrum of variation in visual acuity, as well as a spectrum of variation in terms of visual awareness or skill. The visual studies scholar, highly skilled in understanding images, who loses some or even all her sight, will not lose the ability to analyze images and to communicate her observations. In his essay, "Showing Seeing," W. J. T. Mitchell describes a classroom exercise in which students display or perform some feature of visual culture as if to an audience that has no experience of visual culture. The exercise assumes that some students will be better at the task, while others might improve their performance with practice, and in all cases their aptitude would have little, if anything, to do with their visual acuity. The skill, as I understand it, is in the telling as much as it is in the seeing—the ability to translate images in all their complexity and resonance into words.

And as we move beyond the simple blindness versus sight binary, I hope we can also abandon the clichés that use the word "blindness" as a synonym for inattention, ignorance, or prejudice. If the goal is for others to see what we mean, it helps to say what we mean. Using the word in this way seems a vestigial homage to the Hypothetical, meant to stir the same uncanny frisson of awe and pity. It contributes on some level to the perception of blindness as a tragedy too dire to contemplate, which contributes in turn to lowered expectations among those who educate and employ the blind. It also contributes to the perception among the newly blind themselves that the only response to their new condition is to retire from view.

I will leave you with a futuristic image of blindness. In Deborah Kendrick's story, "20/20 with a Twist," Mary Seymour, chief administrator of the department of visual equality, looks back on her life from the year 2020. In this blind Utopia, the major handicaps of blindness have been eliminated; private automobiles were phased out a decade earlier and technologies to convert print to Braille or voice had become ubiquitous and transparent. Of course, Mary reflects, it was not always like this. Back in the dark ages of the 1980s and '90s, Braille proficiency had ceased to be a requirement for teachers of blind children, Braille production facilities and radio reading services were shut down, and blind children were no longer being educated at all. Mary and other blind people who had grown up in an earlier, slightly more enlightened period, banded together to lead a nonviolent, visionary rebellion to bring down the oppressive regime. They tampered with the power supply—since darkness is no impediment to blind activity—scrambled computer transmissions and disrupted television broadcasts. All across the country, television screens went blank while the audio continued, interrupted periodically by the revolutionary message: "You, too, can function without pictures."

The rebel leaders were captured, however, and forced to undergo implantation of optic sensors, which, the captors reasoned, would transform them into sighted people who would see the error of their ways and abandon the cause. But the rebels persisted. The power supply was shut down completely. The government fell, and the captured leaders were liberated in triumph.

Significantly, the optic sensors did not transform the revolutionary leaders into sighted people. Rather, each acquired only a facet of visual experience. One gained the ability to perceive color. Another developed a sort of telepathic vision, allowing him to form images of places at great distances. Mary's sensor gave her a kind of literal hindsight, making her able to create a detailed mental picture of a room, only after she had left it. These bits and pieces of vision serve as a badge of the former rebels' heroic past, and allow them to perform entertaining parlor tricks, but are otherwise easy to disregard.

This is a far cry from the Hypothetical. In Deborah Kendrick's image of the future, blindness is a simple physical characteristic rather than an ominous mark of otherness. If the Hypothetical Blind Man once helped thinkers form ideas about human consciousness surely his day is done. He does too much damage hanging around. It is time to let him go. Rest in peace.

References

Charles, Ray. Interview. *The Today Show*. NBC Television, October 4, 2001.

Danto, Arthur. 1999. "Blindness and Sight." *The New Republic* 220 (16):34–36.

Diderot, Denis. 1999. *Thoughts on the interpretation of Nature and other philosophical works*. Ed. David Adams. Manchester: Clinaman Press.

Gitter, Elisabeth. 2001. *The Imprisoned Guest: Samuel Howe and Laura Bridgman, the Original Deaf-blind Girl*. New York: Farrar, Straus and Giroux.

Husson, Thérèse-Adèle. 2001. *Reflections: The Life and Writing of a Young Blind Woman in Post-revolutionary France*. Eds. Catherine J. Kudlick and Zina Weygand. New York and London: New York University Press.

Keller, Helen. 2003. *The World I Live In*. Ed. Roger Shattuck. New York: New York Review Books.

Kendrick, Deborah. 1987. 20/20 with a Twist. In *With Wings: An Anthology of Literature by and about Women with Disabilities*, eds. Marsha Saxton and Florence Howe New York: Feminist Press at the City University of New York.

Magee, Bryan and Milligan, Martin. 1995. *On Blindness*. Oxford and New York: Oxford University Press.

Mitchell, W. J. T. 2002. "Showing Seeing: A Critique of Visual Culture." *Journal of Visual Culture* 1 (2):165–181.

33

Disability, Life Narrative, and Representation

G. Thomas Couser

Disability is an inescapable element of human existence and experience. Although it is as fundamental an aspect of human diversity as race, ethnicity, gender, and sexuality, it is rarely acknowledged as such. This is odd, because in practice disability often trumps other minority statuses. That is, for people who differ from the hegemonic identity in more than one way, certain impairments—such as blindness or deafness—may function as their primary defining characteristic, their "master status." In this sense, disability may be *more* fundamental than racial, ethnic, and gender distinctions. Yet until the recent advent of Disability Studies, it escaped the critical scrutiny, theoretical analysis, and recognition accorded other forms of human variation.

At the same time, disability has had a remarkably high profile in both high and popular culture, both of which are pervaded with images of disability. Unlike other marginalized groups, then, disabled people have been *hyper*-represented in mainstream culture; they have not been disregarded so much as they have been subjected to objectifying notice in the form of mediated staring. To use an economic metaphor that is a literal truth, disability has been an extremely valuable cultural commodity for thousands of years. The cultural representation of disability has functioned at the expense of disabled people, in part because they have rarely controlled their own images. In the last several decades, however, this situation has begun to change, most notably in life writing, especially autobiography: in late twentieth century life writing, disabled people have initiated and controlled their own narratives in unprecedented ways and to an extraordinary degree.

Indeed, one of the most significant developments—if not *the* most significant development—in life writing in North America over the last three decades has been the proliferation of book-length accounts (from both first- and third-person points of view) of living with illness and disability. Whereas in the 1970s it was difficult to find *any* representation of most disabling conditions in life writing, today one can find *multiple* representations of many conditions. Equally significant, and more remarkable, one can find *autobiographical* accounts of conditions that would seem to preclude first-person testimony altogether—for example, autism, locked-in syndrome, and early Alzheimer's disease.

A comprehensive history of disability life writing has yet to be written, but it is safe to say that there was not much in the way of published autobiographical literature before World War II. War both produces and valorizes certain forms of disability; not surprisingly, then, disabled veterans produced a substantial number of narratives after the war. Polio generated even more narratives; indeed, polio may be the first disability to have engendered its own substantial autobiographical literature (Wilson). In the 1980s and 1990s, HIV/AIDS and breast cancer provoked significant numbers of narratives; many of these challenge cultural scripts of the conditions (such as that AIDS is an automatic death sentence or that breast cancer negates a woman's sexuality [Couser 1997]). A dramatic example of the generation of autobiographical literature devoted to a particular condition is the advent of autobiographies by people with autism (sometimes referred to as "autiebiographies"). Before 1985 these were virtually nonexistent; since 1985, nearly one hundred have been produced. (This number does not include the many narratives written by parents of autistic children.) Thus, one major post-World

War II cultural phenomenon was the generation of large numbers of narratives about a small number of conditions.

A complementary phenomenon has been the production of small numbers of narratives about a large number of conditions, some quite rare and some only recently recognized. Among these conditions are ALS (also known as Lou Gehrig's disease), Alzheimer's, aphasia, Asperger's syndrome, asthma, cerebral palsy, chronic fatigue syndrome, cystic fibrosis, diabetes, disfigurement, Down syndrome, epilepsy, locked-in syndrome, multiple sclerosis, obesity, obsessive-compulsive disorder, stuttering, stroke, and Tourette syndrome. As the twentieth century drew to a close, then, many disabilities came out of the closet into the living room of life writing.

Like life writing by other marginalized groups—women, African Americans, and gays and lesbian—life writing by disabled people is a cultural manifestation of a human rights movement; significantly, the rise in personal narratives of disability has roughly coincided with the disability rights movement, whose major legal manifestation in the United States is the Americans with Disabilities Act, which was passed in 1990 (but which, some would argue, has never been fully implemented). The first flowering of disability autobiography is also part of a disability renaissance involving other arts and media. Disability autobiography should be seen, then, not as spontaneous "self-expression" but as a response—indeed a retort—to the traditional misrepresentation of disability in Western culture generally.

This rich body of narrative can be approached in a number of ways. One way of getting at the relation between somatic variation and life narrative is through an everyday phenomenon: the way deviations from bodily norms often provoke a demand for explanatory narrative in everyday life. Whereas the unmarked case—the "normal" body—can pass without narration, the marked case—the scar, the limp, the missing limb, or the obvious prosthesis—calls for a story. Entering new situations, or re-entering familiar ones, people with anomalous bodies are often called upon to account for them, sometimes quite explicitly: they may be asked, "What happened to *you*"? Or, worse, they may be addressed as if their stories are already known. Evidence of this is necessarily anecdotal. Let one compelling example suffice. Harriet McBryde Johnson, a Charleston lawyer and disability rights advocate who has a congenital muscle-wasting disease, reports remarks made by strangers she encounters on the street as she drives her power chair to the office:

> "I admire you for being out: most people would give up."

> "God bless you! I'll pray for you."

> "You don't let the pain hold you back, do you?"

> "If I had to live like you, I think I'd kill myself." (2)

One of the social burdens of disability, then, is that it exposes affected individuals to inspection, interrogation, interpretation, and violation of privacy.

In effect, people with extraordinary bodies are held responsible for them, in two senses. First, they are required to account for them, often to complete strangers; second, the expectation is that their accounts will serve to relieve their auditors' discomfort. The elicited narrative is expected to conform to, and thus confirm, a cultural script. For example, people diagnosed with lung cancer or HIV/AIDS are expected to admit to behaviors that have induced the condition in question—to acknowledge having brought it upon themselves. Thus, one fundamental connection between life narrative and somatic anomaly is that to have certain conditions is to have one's life written *for* one. For people with many disabilities, culture inscribes narratives *on* their bodies, willy nilly.

Disability autobiographers typically begin from a position of marginalization, belatedness, and preinscription. Yet one can see why autobiography is a particularly important form of life writing about disability: written from inside the experience in question, it involves *self*-representation by definition and thus offers the best-case scenario for revaluation of that condition. Long the objects of others' classification and examination, disabled people have only recently assumed the initiative in representing themselves; in disability autobiography particularly, disabled people counter their historical subjection by occupying the subject position. In approaching this literature, then, one should attend to the politics and ethics of representation, for the "representation" of disability in such narratives is a political as well as a mimetic act—a matter of speaking *for* as well as speaking *about*.

With particularly severe or debilitating conditions, particularly those affecting the mind or the ability to communicate, the very existence of first-person narratives makes its own point: that people with condition "X" are capable of self-representation. The autobiographical act models the agency and self-determination that the disability rights movement has fought for, even or especially when the text is collaboratively produced. One notable example is *Count Us In: Growing Up with Down Syndrome*, a collaborative narrative by two young men with the syndrome in question. Not only is the title cast in the imperative mood—"count us in"—the subtitle puns on "up" and "down," a bit of verbal play that challenges conventional ideas about mental retardation, such as that those with it never really mature. Autobiography, then, can be an especially powerful medium in which disabled people can demonstrate that they have lives, in defiance of others' common sense perceptions of them. Indeed, disability autobiography is often in effect a post-colonial, indeed an anti-colonial, phenomenon, a form of autoethnography, as Mary Louise Pratt has defined it: "instances in which colonized subjects undertake to represent themselves in ways that engage with [read: contest] the colonizer's own terms" (7).

People with disabilities have become increasingly visible in public spaces and open about their disabilities. But their physical presence in public life represents only a rather limited kind of access. Properly conceived and carried out (admittedly, a large qualifier), life narrative can provide the public with controlled access to lives that might otherwise remain opaque or exotic to them. Further, much disability life writing can be approached as "quality-of-life" writing because it addresses questions discussed under that rubric in philosophy, ethics, and especially biomedical ethics. It should be required reading, then, for citizens in a world with enormous technological capability to sustain life and repair bodies in the case of acute illness and injury but with very little commitment to accommodate and support chronic disability. Because disability life narratives can counter the too often moralizing, objectifying, pathologizing, and marginalizing representations of disability in contemporary culture, they offer an important, if not unique, entree for inquiry into one of the fundamental aspects of human diversity.

Works Cited

Couser, G. Thomas. *Recovering Bodies: Illness, Disability, and Life Writing*. Madison: U of Wisconsin P, 1997.

Johnson, Harriet McBryde. *Too Late to Die Young: Nearly True Tales from a Life*. New York: Henry Holt, 2005.

Kingsley, Jason and Mitchell Levitz. *Count Us In: Growing Up with Down Syndrome*. New York: Harcourt, 1994.

Pratt, Mary Louise. *Imperial Eyes: Travel Writing and Transculturation*. New York: Routledge, 1992.

Wilson, Daniel J. "Covenants of Work and Grace: Themes of Recovery and Redemption in Polio Narratives." *Literature and Medicine* 13, 1 (Spring 1994): 22–41.

Part VII

Fiction, Memoir, and Poetry

34

Helen and Frida

Anne Finger

I'm lying on the couch downstairs in the TV room in the house where I grew up, a farmhouse with sloping floors in upstate New York. I'm nine years old. I've had surgery, and I'm home, my leg in a plaster cast. Everyone else is off at work or school. My mother recovered this couch by hemming a piece of fabric that she bought from a bin at the Woolworth's in Utica ("Bargains! Bargains! Bargains! Remnants Priced as Marked") and laying it over the torn upholstery. Autumn leaves—carrot, jaundice, brick—drift sluggishly across a liver-brown background. I'm watching *The Million Dollar Movie* on our black-and-white television: today it's *Singing in the Rain*. These movies always make me think of the world that my mother lived in before I was born, a world where women wore hats and gloves and had cinched-waist suits with padded shoulders as if they were in the army. My mother told me that in *The Little Colonel*, Shirley Temple had pointed her finger and said, "As red as those roses over there," and then the roses had turned red and everything in the movie was in color after that. I thought that was how it had been when I was born, everything in the world becoming both more vivid and more ordinary, and the black-and-white world, the world of magic and shadows, disappearing forever in my wake.

Now it's the scene where the men in blue-jean coveralls are wheeling props and sweeping the stage, carpenters shouldering boards, moving behind Gene Kelly as Don Lockwood and Donald O'Connor as Cosmo. Cosmo is about to pull his hat down over his forehead and sing, "Make 'em laugh..." and hoof across the stage, pulling open doors that open onto brick walls, careening up what appears to be a lengthy marble-floored corridor but is in fact a painted backdrop.

Suddenly, all the color drains from the room: not just from the mottled sofa I'm lying on, but also from the orange wallpaper that looked so good on the shelf at Streeter's (and was only $1.29 a roll), the chipped blue-willow plate: everything's black and silver now. I'm on a movie set, sitting in the director's chair. I'm grown-up suddenly, eighteen or thirty-five.

Places, please!

Quiet on the set!

Speed, the soundman calls, and I point my index finger at the camera, the clapper claps the board and I see that the movie we are making is called "Helen and Frida." I slice my finger quickly through the air, and the camera rolls slowly forward towards Helen Keller and Frida Kahlo, standing on a veranda, with balustrades that appear to be made of carved stone, but are in fact made of plaster.

The part of Helen Keller isn't played by Patty Duke this time; there's no *Miracle Worker* wild child to spunky rebel in under 100 minutes, no grainy film stock, none of that Alabama sun that bleaches out every soft shadow, leaving only harshness, glare. This time Helen is played by Jean Harlow.

Don't laugh: set pictures of the two of them side by side and you'll see that it's all there, the fair hair lying in looping curls against both faces, the same broad-cheeked bone structure. Imagine that Helen's eyebrows are plucked into a thin arch and penciled, lashes mascaraed top and bottom, lips cloisonné vermillion. Put Helen in pale peach mousseline-de-soie, hand her a white gardenia, bleach her hair from its original honey blonde to platinum, like Harlow's was, recline her on a *Bombshell* chaise with a white swan gliding in front, a palm fan being waved overhead, while an ardent lover presses sweet nothings into her hand.

I play the part of Frida Kahlo.

It isn't so hard to imagine that the two of them might meet. They moved after all, in not so different circles, fashionable and radical: Helen Keller meeting Charlie Chaplin and Mary Pickford, joining the Wobblies, writing in the *New York Times*, "I love the red flag…and if I could I should gladly march it past the offices of the *Times* and let all the reporters and photographers make the most of the spectacle…"; Frida, friend of Henry Ford and Sergei Eisenstein, painting a hammer and sickle on her body cast, leaving her bed in 1954, a few weeks before her death, to march in her wheelchair with a babushka tied under her chin, protesting the overthrow of the Arbenz regime in Guatemala.

Of course, the years are all wrong. But that's the thing about *The Million Dollar Movie*. During Frank Sinatra Week, on Monday Frank would be young and handsome in *It Happened in Brooklyn*, on Tuesday he'd have grey temples and crow's feet, be older than my father, on Wednesday, be even younger than he had been on Monday. You could pour the different decades in a bowl together and give them a single quick fold with the smooth edge of a spatula, the way my mother did when she made black and white marble cake from two Betty Crocker mixes. It would be 1912, and Big Bill Haywood would be waving the check Helen had sent over his head at a rally for the Little Falls strikers, and you, Frida, would be in the crowd, not as a five-year-old child, before the polio, before the bus accident, but as a grown woman, cheering along with the strikers. Half an inch away, it would be August 31, 1932, and both of you would be standing on the roof of the Detroit Institute of the Arts, along with Diego, Frida looking up through smoked glass at the eclipse of the sun, Helen's face turned upwards to feel the chill of night descending, to hear the birds greeting the midday dusk.

Let's get one thing straight right away. This isn't going to be one of those movies where they put their words into our mouths. This isn't *Magnificent Obsession*, blind Jane Wyman isn't going to blink back a tear when the doctors tell her they can't cure her after all, saying, "and I thought I was going to be able to get rid of these," gesturing with her ridiculous rhinestone-studded, catseye dark glasses (and we think, "*Really*, Jane,"); she's not going to tell Rock Hudson she can't marry him: "I won't have you pitied because of me. I love you too much," and "I could only be a burden," and then disappear until the last scene when, lingering on the border between death and cure (the only two acceptable states), Rock saves her life and her sight and they live happily ever after. It's not going to be *A Patch of Blue*: when the sterling young Negro hands us the dark glasses and, in answer to our question: "But what are they for?" says "Never mind, put them on," we're not going to grab them, hide our stone Medusa gaze, grateful for the magic that's made us a pretty girl. This isn't *Johnny Belinda*, we're not sweetly mute, surrounded by an aura of silence. No, in this movie the blind women have milky eyes that make the sighted uncomfortable. The deaf women drag metal against metal, oblivious to the jarring sound, make odd cries of delight at the sight of the ocean, squawk when we are angry.

So now the two female icons of disability have met: Helen, who is nothing but, who swells to fill up the category, sweet Helen with her drooping dresses covering drooping bosom, who is Blind and Deaf, her vocation; and Frida, who lifts her skirt to reveal the gaping, cunt-like wound on her leg, who rips her body open to reveal her back, a broken column, her back corset with its white canvas straps framing her beautiful breasts, her body stuck with nails: but she can't be Disabled, she's Sexual.

Here stands Frida, who this afternoon, in the midst of a row with Diego, cropped off her jet-black hair ("Now see what you've made me do!"), and has schlepped herself to the ball in one of his suits. Nothing Dietrichish and coy about this drag: Diego won't get to parade his beautiful wife. Now she's snatched up Helen and walked with her out here onto the veranda.

In the other room, drunken Diego lurches, his body rolling forward before his feet manage to shuffle themselves ahead on the marble floor, giving himself more than ever the appearance of being one of those children's toys, bottom-weighted with sand, that when punched, roll back and then forward, an eternal red grin painted on their rubber faces. His huge belly shakes with laughter, his laughter a gale that blows above the smoke curling up towards the distant, gilded ceiling, gusting above the knots of men in tuxedos and women with marcelled hair, the black of their satin dresses setting off the glitter of their diamonds.

But the noises of the party, Diego's drunken roar, will be added later by the Foley artists.

Helen's thirty-six. She's just come back from Montgomery. Her mother had dragged her down there after she and Peter Fagan took out a marriage license, and the Boston papers got hold of the story. For so many years, men had been telling her that she was beautiful, that they worshipped her, that when Peter declared himself in the parlor at Wrentham, she had at first thought this was just more palaver about his pure love for her soul. But no, this was the real thing: carnal and thrilling and forbidden. How could you, her mother said. How people will laugh at you! The shame, the shame. Her mother whisked her off to Montgomery, Peter trailing after the two of them. There her brother-in-law chased Peter off the porch with a good old Southern shotgun. Helen's written her poem:

What earthly consolation is there for one like me
Whom fate has denied a husband and the joy of motherhood?. . .
I shall have confidence as always,
That my unfilled longings will be gloriously satisfied
In a world where eyes never grow dim, nor ears dull.
Poor Helen, waiting, waiting to get fucked in heaven.

But not Frida. She's so narcissistic. What a relief to Helen! None of those interrogations passing for conversation she usually has to endure. (After the standard pile of praise is heaped upon her—I've read your book five, ten, twenty times, I've admired you ever since...come the questions: Do you mind if I ask you: Is everything black? Is Mrs. Macy always with you?): no, Frida launches right into the tale of Diego's betrayal "... of course, I have my fun, too, but one doesn't want to have one's nose rubbed in the shit..." she signs into Helen's hand.

Helen is delighted and shocked. In her circles, Free Love is believed in, spoken of solemnly, dutifully. Her ardent young circle of socialists want to do away with the sordid marketplace of prostitution, bourgeois marriage, where women barter their hymens and throw in their souls to sweeten the deal; Helen has read Emma, she has read Isadora; she believes in a holy, golden monogamy, an unfettered, eternal meeting of two souls-in-flesh. And here Frida speaks of the act so casually that Helen, like a timid schoolgirl, stutters,

"You really? I mean, the both of you, you...?"

Frida throws her magnificent head back and laughs.

"Yes, really," Frida strokes gently into her hand. "He fucks other women and I fuck other men—and other women."

"F–U–C–K?" Helen asks. "What is this word?"

Frida explains it to her. "Now I've shocked you," Frida says.

"Yes, you have...I suppose it's your Latin nature..."

I'm not in the director's chair anymore. I'm sitting in the audience of the Castro Theatre in San Francisco watching this unfold. I'm twenty-seven. When I was a kid, I thought being grown up would be like living in the movies, that I'd be Rosalind Russell in *Sister Kenny*, riding a horse through the Australian outback or that I'd dance every night in a sleek satin gown under paper palms at the Coconut Grove. Now I go out to the movies, two, three, four times a week.

The film cuts from the two figures on the balcony to the night sky. It's technicolor: the pale gold stars against midnight blue. We're close to the equator now: there's the Southern Cross, and the Clouds of Magellan, and you feel the press of the stars, the mocking closeness of the heavens as you can only feel it in the tropics. The veranda on which we are now standing is part of a colonial Spanish palace, built in a clearing in a jungle that daily spreads its roots and tendrils closer, closer. A macaw perches atop a broken Mayan statue and calls, "I am queen/I am queen/I am queen." A few yards into the jungle, a spider monkey shits on the face of a dead god.

Wait a minute. What's going on? Is that someone out in the lobby talking? But it's so loud—

Dolores del Rio strides into the film, shouting, "Latin nature! Who wrote this shit?" She's wearing black silk pants and a white linen blouse; she plants her fists on her hips and demands: "Huh? Who wrote this shit?"

I look to my left, my right, shrug, stand up in the audience and say, "I guess I did."

"Latin nature! And a white woman? Playing Frida? *I* should be playing Frida."

"You?"

"Listen, honey." She's striding down the aisle towards me now. "I know I filmed that Hollywood crap. Six movies in one year: crook reformation romance, romantic Klondike melodrama, California romance, costume bedroom farce, passion in a jungle camp among chicle workers, romantic drama of the Russian revolution. I know David Selznick said: 'I don't care what story you use so long as we call it *Bird of Paradise* and Del Rio jumps into a flaming volcano at the finish.' They couldn't tell a Hawaiian from a Mexican from a lesbian. But I loved Frida and she loved me. She painted 'What the Water Gave Me' for me. At the end of her life, we were fighting, and she threatened to send me her amputated leg on a silver tray. If that's not love, I don't know what is—"

I'm still twenty-seven, but now it's the year 2015. The Castro's still there, the organ still rises up out of the floor with the organist playing "San Francisco, open your Golden Gate...." In the lobby now, alongside the photos of the original opening of the Castro in 1927, are photos in black and white of lounging hustlers and leather queens, circa 1979, a photographic reproduction of the door of the women's room a few years later ("If they can send men to the moon, why don't they?") Underneath, in Braille, Spanish, and English: "In the 1960s, the development of the felt-tip pen, combined with a growing philosophy of personal expression caused an explosion of graffiti...sadly unappreciated in its day, this portion of a bathroom stall, believed by many experts to have originated in the women's room right here at the Castro Theater, sold recently at Sotheby's for $5 million...."

Of course, the Castro's now totally accessible, not just integrated wheelchair seating, but every film captioned, a voice loop that interprets the action for blind people, over which now come the words: "As Dolores del Rio argues with the actress playing Frida, Helen Keller waits patiently—"

A woman in the audience stands up and shouts, "Patiently! What the fuck are you talking about, patiently? You can't tell the difference between patience and powerlessness. She's being *ignored*." The stage is stormed by angry women, one of whom leaps into the screen and begins signing to Helen, "Dolores del Rio's just come out and—"

"Enough already!" someone in the audience shouts. "Can't we please just get on with the story!"

Now that Frida is played by Dolores, she's long-haired again, wearing one of her white Tehuana skirts with a deep red shawl. She takes Helen's hand in hers, that hand that has been cradled by so many great men and great women.

"Latin nature?" Frida says, and laughs. "I think perhaps it is rather your cold Yankee nature that causes your reaction...." And before Helen can object to being called a Yankee, Frida says, "But enough about Diego...."

It's the hand that fascinates Frida, in its infinite, unpassive receptivity: she prattles on. When she makes the letters "z" and "j" in sign, she gets to stroke the shape of the letter into Helen's palm. She so likes the sensation that she keeps trying to work words with those letters in them into the conversation. The camera moves in close to Helen's hand as Frida says, "Here on the edge of the Yucatan jungle, one sometimes see jaguars, although never jackals. I understand jackals are sometimes seen in Zanzibar. I have never been there, nor have I been to Zagreb nor Japan nor the Zermatt, nor Java. I have seen the Oaxacan mountain Zempoaltepec. Once in a zoo in Zurich I saw a zebu and a zebra. Afterwards, we sat in a small cafe and ate cherries jubilee and zabaglione, washed down with glasses of zinfandel. Or perhaps my memory is confused: perhaps that day we ate jam on ziewback crusts and drank a juniper tea, while an old Jew played a zither...."

"Oh," says Helen.

Frida falls silent. Frida, you painted those endless self-portraits, but you always looked at yourself level, straight on, in full light. This is different: this time your face is tilted, played over by shadows.

In all those self-portraits, you are simultaneously artist and subject, lover and beloved, the bride of yourself. Now, here, in the movies, it's different: the camera stands in for the eye of the lover. But you're caught in the unforgiving blank stare of a blind woman.

And now, we cut from that face to the face of Helen. Here I don't put in any soothing music, nothing low and sweet with violins, to make the audience more comfortable as the camera moves in for its close-up. You understand why early audiences were frightened by these looming heads. In all the movies with blind women in them—or, let's be real, sighted women playing the role of blind woman—Jane Wyman and Merle Oberon in the different versions of *Magnificent Obsession*, Audrey Hepburn in *Wait Until Dark*, Uma Thurman in *Jennifer 8*, we've never seen a blind woman shot this way before: never seen the camera come in and linger lovingly on her face the way it does here. We gaze at their faces only when bracketed by others, or in moments of terror when beautiful young blind women are being stalked. We've never seen before this frightening blank inward turning of passion, a face that has never seen itself in the mirror, that does not arrange itself for consumption.

Lack = inferiority? Try it right now. Finish reading this paragraph and then close your eyes, push the flaps of your ears shut, and sit. Not just for a minute: give it five or ten. Not in that meditative state, designed to take you out of your mind, your body. Just the opposite. Feel the press of hand crossed over hand: without any distraction, you feel your body with the same distinctness as a lover's touch makes you feel yourself. You fold into yourself, you know the rhythm of your breathing, the beating of your heart, the odd independent twitch of a muscle: now in a shoulder, now in a thigh. Your cunt, in all its patient hunger.

We cut back to Frida in close up. But now Helen's fingers enter the frame, travel across that face, stroking the downy moustache above Frida's upper lip, the fleshy nose, the thick-lobed ears.

Now, it's Frida's turn to be shocked: shocked at the hunger of these hands, at the almost-feral sniff, at the freedom with which Helen blurs the line between knowing and needing.

"May I kiss you?" Helen asks.

"Yes," Frida says.

Helen's hands cup themselves around Frida's face.

I'm not at the Castro anymore. I'm back home on the fold-out sofa in the slapped-together TV room, watching grainy images flickering on the tiny screen set in the wooden console. I'm nine years old again, used to Hays-office kisses, two mouths with teeth clenched, lips held rigid, pressing stonily against each other. I'm not ready for the way that Helen's tongue probes into Frida's mouth, the tongue that seems to be not so much interested in giving pleasure as in finding an answer in the emptiness of her mouth.

I shout, "Cut," but the two of them keep right on. Now we see Helen's face, her wide-open eyes that stare at nothing revealing a passion blank and insatiable, a void into which you could plunge and never, never, never touch bottom. Now she begins to make noises, animal mewlings and cries.

I will the screen to turn to snow, the sound to static. I do not want to watch this, hear this. My leg is in a thick plaster cast, inside of which scars are growing like mushrooms, thick and white in the dark damp. I think that I must be a lesbian, a word I have read once in a book, because I know I am not like the women on television, with their high heels and shapely calves and their firm asses swaying inside of satin dresses waiting, waiting for a man, nor am I like the women I know, the mothers with milky breasts, and what else can there be?

I look at the screen and they are merging into each other, Frida and Helen, the dark-haired and the light, the one who will be disabled and nothing more, the other who will be everything but. I can't yet imagine a world where these two might meet: the face that does not live under the reign of its own reflection with the face that has spent its life looking in the mirror; the woman who turns her rapt face up towards others and the woman who exhibits her scars as talismans, the one who is only, only and the one who is everything but. I will the screen to turn to snow.

35

Poems

Cheryl Marie Wade

I Am Not One of the

I am not one of the physically challenged—

I'm a sock in the eye with a gnarled fist
I'm a French kiss with cleft tongue
I'm orthopedic shoes sewn on a last of your fears

I am not one of the differently abled—

I'm an epitaph for a million imperfect babies left untreated
I'm an ikon carved from bones in a mass grave in Tiergarten, Germany—
I'm withered legs hidden with a blanket

I am not one of the able disabled—

I'm a black panther with green eyes and scars like a picket fence
I'm pink lace panties teasing a stub of milk white thigh
I'm the Evil Eye

I'm the first cell divided
I'm mud that talks
I'm Eve   I'm Kali
I'm The Mountain That Never Moves
I've been forever   I'll be here forever
I'm the Gimp
I'm the Cripple
I'm the Crazy Lady
I'm The Woman With Juice

Cripple Lullaby

I'm trickster coyote in a gnarly-bone suit
I'm a fate worse than death in shit-kickin' boots

I'm the nightmare booga you flirt with in dreams
'Cause I emphatically demonstrate: It ain't what it seems

I'm a whisper, I'm a heartbeat, I'm "that accident," and goodbye
One thing I am not is a reason to die.

I'm homeless in the driveway of your manicured street
I'm Evening Magazine's SuperCrip of the Week

I'm the girl in the doorway with no illusions to spare
I'm a kid dosed on chemo, so who said life is fair

I'm a whisper, I'm a heartbeat, I'm "let's call it suicide," and a sigh
One thing I am not is a reason to die
I'm the poster child with doom-dipped eyes
I'm the ancient remnant set adrift on ice

I'm that Valley girl, you know, dying of thin
I'm all that is left of the Cheshire Cat's grin

I'm the Wheelchair Athlete, I'm every dead Baby Doe
I'm Earth's last volcano, and I am ready to blow

I'm a whisper, I'm a heartbeat, I'm a genocide survivor, and Why?
One thing I am not is a reason to die.

I am not a reason to die.

36

Poems

Kenny Fries

Beauty and Variations

1.

What is it like to be so beautiful? I dip
my hands inside you, come up with—*what?*

Beauty, at birth applied, does not transfer
to my hands. But every night, your hands

touch my scars, raise my twisted limbs to
graze against your lips. Lips that never

form the words—*you are beautiful*—transform
my deformed bones into—*what?*—if not beauty.

Can only one of us be beautiful? Is this your
plan? Are your sculpted thighs more powerful

driving into mine? Your hands find their way
inside me, scrape against my heart. Look

at your hands. Pieces of my skin trail from
your fingers. What do you make of this?

Your hands that know my scars, that lift me to your
lips, now drip my blood. Can blood be beautiful?

2.

I want to break your bones. Make them so
they look like mine. Force you to walk on

twisted legs. Then, will your lips still beg
for mine? Or will that disturb the balance

of our desire? Even as it inspires, your body
terrifies. And once again I find your hands

inside me. Why do you touch my scars? You
can't make them beautiful any more than I can

tear your skin apart. Beneath my scars,
between my twisted bones, hides my heart.

Why don't you let me leave my mark? With no
flaws on your skin—how can I find your heart?

3.

How much beauty can a person bear? Your smooth
skin is no relief from the danger of your eyes.

My hands would leave you scarred. Knead the muscles
of your thighs. I want to tear your skin, reach

inside you—your secrets tightly held. Breathe
deep. Release them. Let them fall into my palms.

My secrets are on my skin. Could this be why
each night I let you deep inside? Is that

where my beauty lies? Your eyes, without secrets,
would be two scars. I want to seal your eyes,

they know my every flaw. Your smooth skin, love's
wounds ignore. My skin won't mend, is calloused, raw.

4.

Who can mend my bones? At night, your hands press
into my skin. My feet against your chest, you mold

my twisted bones. What attracts you to my legs? Not
sex. What brings your fingers to my scars is beyond

desire. Why do you persist? Why do you touch me
as if my skin were yours? Seal your lips. No kiss

can heal these wounds. No words unbend my bones.
Beauty is a two-faced god. As your fingers soothe

my scars, they scrape against my heart. Was this
birth's plan—to tie desire to my pain, to stain

love's touch with blood? If my skin won't heal, how
can I escape? My scars are in the shape of my love.

5.

How else can I quench this thirst? My lips
travel down your spine, drink the smoothness

of your skin. I am searching for the core:
What is beautiful? Who decides? Can the laws

of nature be defied? Your body tells me: come
close. But beauty distances even as it draws

me near. What does my body want from yours?
My twisted legs around your neck. You bend

me back. Even though you can't give the bones
at birth I wasn't given, I let you deep inside.

You give me—*what*? Peeling back my skin, you
expose my missing bones. And my heart, long

before you came, just as broken. I don't know who
to blame. So each night, naked on the bed, my body

doesn't want repair, but longs for innocence. If
innocent, despite the flaws I wear, I am beautiful.

37

Selections from *The Cry of the Gull*

Emmanuelle Laborit

Cry of the Seagull

I let out screams, lots of them, real ones. Not because I was hungry or thirsty, afraid, or in pain, but because I was beginning to want to talk. I wanted to hear myself, but the sounds I was making weren't rebounding back to me.

I could feel the vibrations. I knew I was screaming but the sounds didn't mean a thing to my mother and father. To them, they were like the piercing cries of a sea bird, like a gull gliding over the ocean. So they nick-named me Mouette, which means *seagull* in French.

The little seagull shrieked above an ocean of noises she couldn't hear, and no one understood her cries.

"You were a very beautiful baby," my mother recalls. "It was an easy birth. You weighed 7 pounds 11 ounces. You cried when you were hungry. You laughed and babbled like other babies. You were happy. We didn't realize right away. We just thought you were well-behaved because, on evenings when we had friends over, you'd sleep soundly even with the music blaring in the living room, which was next to the room where you were sleeping. We were proud to have such a good baby. We thought you were 'normal' because you'd turn your head whenever a door slammed. We didn't know it was because you could feel the vibrations and drafts on the floor where you were playing. And when your father put on a record, you'd dance in your playpen, swaying back and forth, swinging your arms and legs."

I was at the age when babies crawl around on all fours and start trying to say "mama" and "dada." But I wasn't saying anything. I sensed vibrations on the floor. I felt them from the music and would join in with my seagull-like sounds. At least that's what I've been told.

I was a perceptive little seagull. I had a secret. A world all to myself.

I come from a seafaring family. My mother's father, grandfather, and brother were among the last of the Cape Horn sailors. That's another reason why they called me their little seagull. But the French words for "seagull" and "mute" look and sound practically the same: *mouette/muette*. So which was I? Today, that strange phonetic similarity makes me smile.

Uncle Fifou, my father's older brother, was the first to say, "Emmanuelle makes shrieking sounds because she can't hear herself." My father claims it was my uncle who "was the first to arouse our suspicions." "The scene is frozen in my mind," says my mother.

My parents didn't want to believe it. To such an extent, in fact, that it was only much later that I found out my paternal grandparents had been married in the chapel of the National Institute for the Deaf in Bordeaux. What's more, the institute's director was my grandmother's stepfather. In an attempt to hide their concern, perhaps, or avoid facing the truth, my parents had forgotten about all that! Basically, they were proud of not having a little brat who would wake them up in the wee hours of the morning. So they got into the habit of jokingly referring to me as their little seagull. It was their way of not admitting they were worried because I was different.

Some people say we end up yelling out what we really want kept silent. In my case, I had to yell to try to hear the difference between my screams and silence, to compensate for the absence of all the words I saw moving on my mother's and father's lips and whose meaning escaped me. And since my parents silenced their anguish, maybe I had to scream for them as well. Who knows?

"The pediatrician thought I was crazy," my mother says. "He didn't believe it either because you seemed to react normally to sounds, but it was the same old story—you were really just feeling vibrations. Yet when we clapped our hands next to you or behind you, you didn't turn your head in the direction of the noise. You didn't respond when you were called. And I could tell it wasn't normal. When I used to walk up to you, you seemed so surprised you would practically jump, as though you had become aware of my presence only a split second before. I started thinking I had psychological problems, especially since the pediatrician still didn't want to believe me even though he saw you for checkups once a month.

"I set up yet another appointment with him to discuss my concerns. That's when he bluntly told me, "Madam, I strongly suggest you get counseling!' Then, he slammed the door on purpose and since you just happened to turn around, maybe because you had felt the vibrations or simply because you found his behavior strange, he said, 'You can clearly see the idea's absurd!'

"I'm angry at him, and at myself for having believed him. After that office visit, your father and I went through a period of real anguish. We observed you constantly. We whistled, called you, slammed doors, watched you clap your hands and sway as though you were dancing to the music. One minute we believed you could hear, the next minute we thought you couldn't. We were totally confused.

"When you were nine months old, I took you to a specialist. He lost no time in telling me you had been born profoundly deaf. It was a tremendous shock. I couldn't accept it and neither could your father. We kept telling ourselves, 'It's a misdiagnosis. There's no way.' We went to see another specialist. I was so hoping he'd grin, reassure us, and send us home.

"Then we went to Trousseau Hospital with your father. During the examination, they made you listen to sounds so loud they practically pierced my eardrums. But you were totally unresponsive to them. You were sitting on my lap and that's when I realized it was true. I asked the specialist three questions.

'Will she talk?'

'Yes but it'll take a long time.'

'What should we do?'

'Have her fitted with a hearing aid and get her into speech therapy as soon as possible. Avoid sign language at all costs.'

'Is there any way I could meet some deaf adults?'

'That wouldn't be a good idea. They belong to a generation that didn't have early training. You'd be disappointed and discouraged.'

"Your father was completely overcome. I cried. Where had this 'curse' come from? Was it genetic? Had it been caused by an illness during pregnancy? I felt guilty and so did your father. We tried, to no avail, to find out who might have been deaf on one side of the family or the other."

I can understand the shock my parents suffered from all that. Parents of deaf children always want to assign guilt. They're always looking for the guilty party. But blaming one parent or the other for a child's deafness is horrible for the child. It shouldn't happen. They still don't know why I'm deaf and never will and it's probably better that way.

My mother says she didn't know what to do with me. She would look at me but couldn't come up with any activities to create a bond between us. Sometimes she couldn't even bring herself to play with me. She stopped talking to me. What was going through her head was, "I can't even tell her I love her any more because she can't hear."

She was in a state of shock, stunned. She couldn't think rationally.

I have strange memories of my early childhood. It's just chaos in my head, a series of completely unrelated images, like film sequences edited together with long strips of blank film, giant lost spaces.

My life up to age seven is full of gaps. I only have visual memories, like flashbacks, images whose time-frame I can't place. I believe there was no sense whatsoever of time progression in my mind during that period. Past, future, everything was on the same time-space line. Mother would say *yesterday,* but I didn't understand where or what *yesterday* was. *Tomorrow* had no meaning either. And I couldn't ask what they meant. I was helpless, completely unaware of time passing. There was daylight and the darkness of night, and that was it.

I still can't assign dates to things during the period from my birth to age seven, or arrange what I did in chronological order. Time was in a holding pattern. I just experienced things as they happened. Maybe there are memories buried in my head, but I don't know in what order they happened or how old I was. I can't place them. As for events—or I should say situations or scenes because everything was visual—I lived each as an isolated experience, in the present. That's why, in trying to reassemble the puzzle of my early childhood so I could write about it, I found only fragments of images.

Other perceptions dwell in a turmoil that is out of memory's reach. They're locked in that period of solitude, behind that wall of silence, when words were mysterious and language was absent. And yet I was able to manage. I don't know how, but I did.

"Sitting up in your bed," my mother tells me, "you'd see me disappear and come back, to your amazement. You didn't know where I'd gone. To the kitchen, perhaps. I was two distinct images, Mommy disappearing and Mommy coming back. And there was no link between the two."

Dolls Don't Talk

I started learning how to communicate with a speech therapist, using the Borel-Maisonny method. She was an extraordinary woman who was receptive to my mother's tale of woe and put up with her anger and tears. She played dolls and water games with me, and we had tea parties. She showed my mother it was possible to have a relationship with me, to make me laugh, so I could go on living as I had before she knew about my deafness.

I learned to pronounce the letters of the alphabet. They taught me the letters using mouth movements and hand gestures.

My mother sat in on the sessions, which ultimately became a way for her to assume her maternal role. By identifying with the therapist, my mother learned to talk to me again. Our way of communicating was instinctive, animal-like. What I call "umbilical." It revolved around simple things like eating, drinking, and sleeping. My mother didn't stop me from gesturing. She didn't have the heart to, even though that's what they recommended. We also had signs that were our very own, completely made up.

"You tried everything under the sun to communicate with me," my mother remembers, "and it made me laugh so hard it brought tears to my eyes! I'd turn your face towards mine so you could try to make out simple words, and you'd imitate me as I went along. It was so cute."

I don't know how many times she drew my face close to hers in a mother-child encounter that was both fascinating and terrifying, and that functioned as our language.

From that moment on, there was hardly any room left for my father. It was even harder when he came home from work. I wasn't spending much time with him and we didn't have an "umbilical" code. I would utter a few words but he almost never understood. It hurt him to see my mother communicating with me in a language whose intimacy was beyond his reach. He felt excluded. And naturally he was, because it wasn't a language that could be shared by all three of us, or with anyone else. He wanted to communicate directly with me and being excluded bothered him. When he came home in the evening, we had nothing to say to each other. I often went up to my mother and pulled on her arm for her to tell me what he was saying. I wanted so much to "talk" with him and know more about him.

I started saying a few words. Like all deaf children, I wore a hearing aid and more or less put up with it. It channeled noises into my head but they were all the same. It was impossible to differentiate between them or use them in any way. It was more tiring than anything else. But the therapists said I had to wear it! I don't know how many times the ear piece fell into my soup. My mother says the family would find consolation in trite statements like:

"She may be deaf but she's so cute!"
"She'll just be that much smarter!"

Flashback:

> *I have a fabulous doll collection. I'm not sure how many, but dolls I have! How old am I? I don't know, but I'm at the doll age. It's my doll phase. When it's time to go to sleep, I have to arrange them so they're all lined up in a row. I tuck them in. Their hands have to be outside the covers. Then I close their eyes. I spend a long time arranging them before I go to bed. I probably talk to them. I'm sure I do, using the same code as with my mother, making the sign for sleep. Once all the doll people are in bed, I can go to bed, too.*

It's strange that I arranged my dolls so methodically while everything in my head was completely muddled, vague, and mixed-up. I'm still trying to figure out why I used to do it, why I spent an eternity arranging my dolls. My parents always hurried me along so they could put me to bed. It got on my father's nerves. It got on everybody's nerves. But I couldn't sleep if my dolls weren't all in place. They had to be perfectly lined up, eyes closed, the blanket pulled up exactly to where it should be with their arms on top. It all had to be fiendishly precise even though everything in my head was disorganized. Maybe it was my way of putting all the mixed-up experiences I'd had during the day in order before going to sleep. Maybe I was going through the motions of tidying up the day's disorder. During the day, my life was total disorder. At night, I slept neatly tucked away like my dolls, in complete quiet. Dolls don't talk.

I lived in silence because I wasn't communicating. I guess that's what real silence must be like—the total darkness of what can't be communicated. Everyone was dark silence for me except my parents, especially my mother.

Silence therefore had a special meaning for me—the absence of communication. But from another perspective, I've never lived in complete silence. I have my own noises that are inexplicable to hearing people. I have my imagination and it has its noises in image form. I imagine sounds in terms of colors. My own personal silence has colors. It's never black and white.

I perceive hearing people's noises in images too, as sensations. The tranquil waves that gently roll up on the beach evoke a sensation of serenity and calm. Waves that bristle and gallop while arching their backs evoke anger. The wind means my hair floating in the air, freshness and softness on my skin.

Light was important. I liked the day, not the night.

I used to sleep on a sofa in the living room of my parents' tiny apartment. My father was a medical student and my mother, a school teacher. She took time off from her studies to raise me. We weren't very rich, and the apartment was small. I was unaware of all that since I had no idea at the time how society and the hearing world were structured. At night, I slept alone on the sofa. I can still see that yellow and orange sofa. I see a brown wooden table. I see the dining room table with its white frame. The sounds I imagined were always linked to colors, but I couldn't say that a specific sound was blue, green, or red. It's that colors and light played a part in the way I imagined sounds and perceived every situation.

In the light, I could monitor everything with my eyes. Darkness was synonymous with non-communication and, therefore, silence. Absence of light meant panic. Later on, I didn't mind turning out the light before going to sleep.

I have a memory about the darkness of night and how it affected me when I was little: I'm in the living room, lying on my bed, and I see the reflection of headlights shining through the window onto the wall. All those lights that keep coming and going frighten me. I still see them in my mind. There's no wall between the living room and my parents' room. It's a big open space with no door. There's an armchair, a bed, and the large cushion-covered sofa where I sleep. I see myself there as a child, but I don't know how old I am. I'm scared. I was always scared of the cars' headlights at night, those images that came and went on the wall.

Sometimes my parents would tell me they were going out. But did I actually understand what "going out" meant? I thought I was being abandoned, deserted. My perception was that my parents disappeared and then reappeared. Were they going to reappear, though? And when? The notion of "when" was unknown to me. I didn't have the words to express my apprehension to them. I didn't have a language. I couldn't tell them. It was horrible.

I think I could probably guess from their nervous behavior that they were going to "disappear," but their departure always ended up taking me by surprise because I became conscious of it at night. They fed me dinner, put me to bed, and waited till I was sound asleep. They thought they could leave and I wouldn't know. But I would wake up all alone. Maybe I'd wake up because they had left. And I was afraid of the ghostly headlights on the wall.

I was incapable of expressing or explaining that fear. My parents must have thought that nothing could wake me up since I was deaf! But the lights were strange, scary night sounds to me and they alarmed me tremendously. If I had been able to make myself understood, my parents wouldn't have left me all alone. A deaf child has to have somebody there at night. Has to.

I can recall a nightmare I had, too: I'm in the backseat of a car and my mother is driving. I call out to her. I want to ask her something. I want her to answer me. I call her but she doesn't turn around. I keep on calling, and when she finally turns to answer me, we have an accident. The car ends up in a ravine and then in the ocean. I see water all around me. It's horrible. Unbearable. The accident is my fault and I wake up in a state of complete anxiety.

I used to call out to my mother all day long so we could talk. I always wanted to know what was going on, to be in on things. It was a genuine need. She was the only one who truly understood me because of the language we had invented together—that animal-like, "umbilical" language, our special, instinctive code, comprised of mime and gestures. I needed her all the time because there were so many things all mixed-up in my head, so many questions. My great apprehension at that age was crystallized in that nightmare where she didn't turn to look at me.

It's different for children who learn sign language when they're very young or who have deaf parents. They make remarkable strides. I'm astounded by their development. I was really behind because I only learned to sign at seven. Before then I must have been a little like a "retard" or a wild animal.

Now that I look back, I find it incredible. How did I manage before I knew how to sign? I didn't have a language. How could I develop as an individual? How did I understand things? Get people's attention? Ask for things? I remember gesturing a lot.

Was I capable of thinking? Of course, but what did I think about? About my inexhaustible desire to truly communicate. About the sensation I had of being locked behind a huge door that I couldn't open to make people understand me.

I tugged at my mother's sleeve or dress. I pointed to objects, tons of things. She would understand and answer me.

I was slowly making headway and starting to imitate words. *Water,* for example, was the first word I learned to pronounce. I copied what I saw on my mother's lips. I couldn't hear myself, but I rounded my lips to make the sound. The vibrations I felt in my throat created a distinct sound for my mother. And so these words became special for her and me, words that no one else could understand. Mother wanted me to force myself to speak, and I tried for her sake, but what I really wanted to do was point and show. When I had to go to the bathroom, I would point in that direction. To eat, I pointed to the food I wanted and then put my hand to my mouth.

Before I was seven, there were no words, no sentences in my head. Only images. When I tugged at my mother to tell her something, I didn't want her to look away, but rather at me. She should be looking at my face and nothing else. I remember that. That means I was capable of thinking; I was "thinking" communication. And I wanted it.

I remember some unusual situations. Family get-togethers, for example, when there were loads of people around. Their mouths moved a lot and it all bored me. I would go into another room and look at objects, things. I'd pick them up to really look at them. Then I'd go back to the room full of people and tug at my mother. Tugging at her was my way of calling her so she'd look at me and pay attention to me. It was hard when there were people around. I lost contact with her. I was alone on my planet and I wanted her to come back. She was my only link with the world. My father would look at us. He still didn't understand a thing.

I can remember seeing him very angry, with a particular expression on his face. I imitated his anger as if to ask, "Is something wrong?"

Then he would say, "No, no. It's okay!"

Sometimes I used to go tug at my mother so she could translate because I wanted to know more. I wanted to know what was going on. Why, why had I seen anger on my father's face? But she couldn't translate all the time. When she couldn't, I was left in dark silence.

When there were people around, I stared at their faces. I observed all their facial tics and quirks. Some people didn't look at the person they were talking to at the dinner table. They played with their place setting or ran their fingers through their hair. They just looked like images doing things. I couldn't say what I felt. But I could see. I saw if they were happy or not. I saw if they were irritated or if they weren't listening. I had my eyes for listening, but that was not enough. I could see they were using their mouths to communicate with each other. "That must be how I'm different. They make noise with their mouths," I thought. I didn't know what noise was, or silence for that matter. The two words didn't have any meaning.

But it wasn't really silent inside me. I could hear very high-pitched whistling sounds. I used to think they were coming from somewhere else, from outside me. But no. They were my noises. I was the only one who heard them. Was I noise on the inside and silence on the outside?

They must have fitted me with a hearing aid at nine months. Little deaf children often have hearing aids with two earphones connected by a cord in the shape of a **Y** and a microphone on their stomach. It's a monophonic device. I don't remember hearing things with it. Noises maybe. But they were noises that I heard anyway, like vibrations from cars going by or music. The device made them unbearably loud. But could I hear the sounds children hear? No, my toys were mute.

The noises were too loud. They had no meaning. They brought me nothing and just tired me out. I used to take my hearing aid off to sleep because the noise made me nervous. Loud, nameless, disconnected noises were stressful.

"The speech therapist told us not to worry," my mother remembers. "They said you would eventually be able to speak. They gave us hope. With speech therapy and hearing aids you'd become 'hearing.' Of course you'd be behind for your age, but you'd manage. Although it was completely illogical, we hoped that you would end up actually being able to hear someday, as if by magic. It was so hard to accept the fact that you had been born into a world that was different from ours."

Stomachs and Music

After they fitted me with a hearing aid, I began to make the distinction between hearing and deaf people (but I'm not sure exactly when). Hearing people simply didn't wear hearing aids. There were those with and those without. It was a simple distinction.

I wanted to say things, lots of things, but that wall was still there. And it saddened me. I could see that my mother and father were sad, too. I really felt sadness, but wanted my parents to smile and be cheerful. I wanted to make them happy. But I didn't know how. I asked myself, "What's wrong with me? Why do I make them sad?" I still hadn't understood that I was deaf. I only knew I was different.

My first recollection? I have no first or last childhood memory because of the disorganization of my mind at that time. There were only sensations, and eyes and a body to take in those sensations.

I remember stomachs.

Flashback:

> *My mother is pregnant with my little sister and I feel the vibrations very strongly. I sense that something's happening. With my face buried in my mother's belly, I can "hear" life. I have trouble imagining there's a baby in Mommy's tummy. That seems impossible to me. I see a person. And there's supposed to be another person inside of that same person? I say it isn't true. It's a joke. But I like my mother's belly and the sound of life inside it.*

I also like my father's stomach, in the evening when he's discussing things with friends or my mother. When I'm tired, I lie down beside him with my head on his stomach, and I can feel his voice. It goes through his stomach and I can feel the vibrations. It soothes and reassures me. It's like a lullaby. I fall asleep to the vibrations, like a nursery rhyme in my head.

My perception of conflict was physical, too, but it was different: My mother is giving me a spanking. She goes away afterwards. Her hands are sore and so is my behind. Both of us are crying. I can still remember that spanking. I must have understood why she was spanking me, but I don't remember now. My parents never hit me, so I think she was really mad. But I don't know why. That's my only recollection of being punished.

Conflicts with my mother could get complicated. For example, when I didn't want to eat something, Mother would say, "You have to finish your plate."

"I don't want to."

So she plays airplane with the tiny spoon. A spoonful for Daddy, one for Grandma... I see what her game is... a spoonful for me. I open my mouth and swallow. But sometimes I don't want to eat. Period. I tell Mommy off. The little seagull is angry. And when I'm tired of it all, I leave the table. They all think I'm joking, but I'm not. I'm really mad and want to leave. I pack my suitcase with my dolls.

It's a doll's suitcase, so I don't put my coat in it. I put the doll's coats in along with the dolls. I don't know why. Maybe because the dolls are me and I want to show that I'm the one leaving. I go out to the street. My mother panics and comes after me. That's what I do when we argue and I'm really mad. I'm a person, too. I can't always obey. I'm always supposed to agree with my mother, but I want to be independent. Emmanuelle is different. Mommy and I are different from each other.

My father and I used to play together. We had fun and laughed a lot, but I don't know if we were really communicating. Neither did he at the time. And he felt bad about that. As soon as he found out I was deaf, the first thing he wondered was how I would ever hear music. When I was very little, he took me to concerts as a way of passing his love of music on to me. Or maybe he was refusing to face the fact that I was deaf. Anyway, I thought it was fantastic. And it's still fantastic that he didn't put up a barrier between music and me. I was happy to be with him. And I'm convinced I perceived the music intensely. Not with my ears, but with my body. For a long time my father harbored the hope that I would one day wake up, as if from a long sleep. Like Sleeping Beauty. He was sure that music would work that magic. Since he was wild about all kinds of music—classical, jazz, the Beatles—and since I'd always sway to the beat, my father took me to concerts. I grew up believing I could share everything with him.

One evening, my Uncle Fifou, who was a musician, was playing the guitar. I can see him now. The image is clear in my mind. The whole family is listening. He wants to make me experience the guitar, so he tells me to bite the neck of the instrument. As I do, he begins to play. I keep on biting for hours. I can feel every vibration in my body, both high and low notes. The music enters my body and takes up residence there. It begins to play inside me. Mother looks at me completely astounded. She tries to do the same thing but doesn't like it. She says it echoes in her head. To this day my uncle's guitar still bears my teeth marks.

I was lucky to have music when I was a child. Some parents of deaf children think it's pointless, so they deprive their children of music. And some deaf children make fun of music. I love it. I feel its vibrations. The visual spectacle of the concert has an impact on me, too. The people in the concert hall, the lighting effects, the atmosphere are all part of the vibrations. I can sense that everybody's gathered together at the concert for the same thing. It's fantastic: the sparkling golden saxophone, the trumpet players with their cheeks puffed out, the basses. I feel with my feet, or my whole body if I'm stretched out on the floor. And I can imagine the sounds. I've always imagined them. I perceive music through my body, with my bare feet on the floor, latching onto the vibrations. The piano, electric guitar, African drums, percussion instruments, all have colors and I sway along with them. That's how I see it, in color. But the difference between the guitar and the violin is hard for me to recognize. I can't get the violin. I can't feel it with my feet. The violin flies away. It must be high-pitched, like a bird. Like a bird's song, it's uncatchable. Its music is upward, reaching for the sky, not down towards the earth. Sounds in the air must be high; sounds at earth level, low-pitched. The tom-tom makes music that comes up from the earth. I just love African music. I feel it with my feet, my head, my whole body. But I have trouble with classical music. It's so high in the air I can't catch it.

Music is a rainbow of vibrant colors. It's a language beyond words. It's universal. The most beautiful form of art that exists. It's capable of making the human body physically vibrate. Suppose I came from another planet and ran into humans all speaking different languages. I'm sure I would be able to understand them because I'd sense what they were feeling. That's what happens with music. Notes begin to dance inside my body like flames in a fireplace. The fire sets the rhythm: small, big, small, faster, slower—vibrations, emotions, and colors swirl to a magical beat. The field of music is very wide. It's immense and I often get lost in it.

The sound of singing voices remains a mystery to me. Just once, the mystery was broken. I don't know how old I was, but I was still living only in the present.

Flashback:

> *Maria Callas is on TV. My parents are watching and I'm sitting with them in front of the set. I see a powerful-looking woman. She seems to have a strong personality. Suddenly, there's a close-up and at that moment I feel her voice. As I stare at her intently, I realize what her voice must be like. I get the impression that the song she's singing isn't a very happy one. I see that her voice is coming from deep within, from far away, that she's singing from her stomach, from her guts. It has a tremendous effect on me.*

Did I really hear her voice? I have no idea. But I truly felt emotion. Nothing like that ever happened, before or after. Maria callas had touched me. That's the only time in my life that I felt or imagined a voice singing.

Other singers leave me cold. When I watch video clips of them on TV, I sense a lot of violence, lots of images, one after the other. It's impossible to understand anything. They're all so fast, I can't even begin to imagine the music that goes along with them. But the words of some singers like Carole Laure, Jacques Brel, and Jean-Jacques Goldman really move me.

And then there's Michael Jackson! When I see him dance, it looks like he has an electric body. The beat is electrifying. I associate it with an electric image. I feel the electricity.

Dance is something that permeates your body. When I was a teenager, I used to like to go to nightclubs with my deaf friends. It was the only place where the music could be blaring full-blast and not bother anybody. I danced all night with my body pressed against the wall, swaying to the rhythm. The others (the hearing people there) looked at me in astonishment. They must have thought I was crazy.

White Cat, Black Cat

My father used to take me to kindergarten. I liked going with him, but when I got there I would always end up alone in a corner, drawing. In the evening, my mother and I would draw some more. I loved it when she drew a picture and I was supposed to add an eye or a nose. There were drawings everywhere. We used to play a game called Battle, too. Each player had a special color.

I also remember a room with a strange revolving disc. We would put a piece of paper on it, then my mother and I would spurt different colors of paint onto the paper. The colors spread out randomly with the speed of the disc. I didn't know how it worked but it was beautiful.

Another thing we did was watch cartoons on TV or at the movies. After fifteen minutes of Tweety and Sylvester, I was crying, sniveling, and gasping so much my mother got worried. I saw the other kids laughing at Sylvester's blunders, but couldn't figure out why they thought it was funny. It was cruel and it made me feel bad. It wasn't fair that Sylvester always got caught and flattened up against a wall. That's how I saw it. Maybe I was too sensitive. Besides, I really liked cats.

I had a white cat. As far as I knew, it didn't have a name but I was so glad to have it. I used to make it jump in the air and play airplane with it. I'd play helicopter with it and pull it by the tail. I'm sure it was hell for the cat, but it loved me just the same. I did nothing but badger it and it still loved me!

One day, we found the cat with its stomach split open. I don't know how or when it happened. We were in the country. My father was a medical student at the time and tried to save it by sewing its stomach back up. But the operation failed and the cat died. I asked what had happened and my father said, "It's over." For me that meant the cat had disappeared. It was gone. I wouldn't see it any more.

I didn't know the meaning of death. For days I asked where the cat was. They kept explaining that it was over and that I'd never ever see it again. I didn't understand *never,* or *dead.* All I understood was that *dead* meant it was over, *finished.* I thought big people were immortal. They went away and came back. Therefore, they would never be finished.

But it wasn't the same for me. I was going to "go away" like the cat. I couldn't see myself growing up. I thought I'd always be little, all my life. I thought I was limited to my present state. And above all, I thought I was unique, the only one like me in the world. Emmanuelle is deaf and no one else is. Emmanuelle is different. Emmanuelle will never grow up.

Since I couldn't communicate like other people, I couldn't be like them, like grown-ups who can hear. So I was going to be "finished." Sometimes it was impossible to communicate with people. I couldn't ask about all the things I wanted to know and understand. Or people just didn't answer me. That's when I thought about death. I was afraid, and now I know why: I had never seen a deaf adult. I had only seen deaf children in the special education class at my kindergarten. So, in my mind, deaf children never grew up. We were all going to die as little children. I even think I was unaware that hearing people had once been children! There was no possible point of reference for me.

When I saw that the cat wasn't around any more, that it had "gone away," I tried with all my might to understand what had happened. I really wanted to see the cat again, to understand. I wanted to see it because I could only understand things with my eyes. My parents didn't show me the dead cat so I was left with the idea of "gone away." It was all too confusing.

When my little sister was born, we got another cat. A black one this time. His name was Bobbin. My father chose the name, in deference to Freud's *Fort-Da,** he said. The cat always used to play with bobbins of thread. He knew I was deaf, and I knew he knew. It was obvious. When Bobbin was hungry, he would follow my mother around and meow at her. He'd run circles around her. Naturally, she could hear him even though she couldn't see him. When we first got him, he tried that with me but soon realized I wasn't reacting and that ticked him off. So he'd plunk himself down right in front of my head and meow in my face. It was obvious: he knew that to be "heard" he had to stare with his

---

* Translators' note: Freud speaks of a case in which a child played a game that involved repeatedly spinning a bobbin to make it disappear (*fort*) and reappear (*da*). According to Freud, the child was unknowingly mastering his feelings of displeasure caused by his mother's absences.

beautiful green eyes deep into mine. Sometimes when I was lying on my bed, he would grab at my feet to play. I wanted to communicate with him and let him know he was being a pain. I tried using gestures to tell him, "Stop it, you're bugging me." But he didn't get the message. I knew when he was angry because he didn't respond. He turned into a sort of cat statue.

When I saw Tweety and Sylvester, and all the violence heaped on that poor cat, I hated Tweety. He teased Sylvester and never got flustered. The poor kitty didn't have a clue about what was going on and always took a beating. He may have been naive, but that Tweety was really rotten!

I was striving for a difficult kind of independence in a difficult world. I even had trouble pronouncing the word difficult. I used to say, "It's tifikul."

It was "tifikul" to say "tifikul."

It was "tifikul" for me to have an existence independent of my mother. I tried doing things without the help of my "umbilical cord." All alone, for a change of pace, as an adventure. I remember one instance in particular. How old was I? Was it before or after the cat died? I don't know, but I said, "I'm going to go to the bathroom by myself."

I didn't actually say that to my mother. I only said the words in my mind. Usually, when I had to go, I'd call my mother. But that time, we were at some friends' house and she was busy chatting. She wasn't paying attention to me, so I decided I was going to manage all alone.

I went into the bathroom and locked the door like a big person. But then I couldn't get out! I must have jammed the lock or done something to it. I began screaming and screaming and banging on the door. Being locked inside and not being able to get out was torture. My mother was on the other side of the door and could hear the banging. But of course I didn't know that. Suddenly all communication was cut off. There was literally a wall between my mother and me. It was frightening.

I'm sure my mother tried to reassure me. She probably said, "Don't worry, stay calm." But at the time, I couldn't hear her, since I couldn't see her. I thought she was still talking with her friend and that I was all alone. I was terrified. I thought I'd spend the rest of my life in that little room screaming in silence!

Finally I saw a piece of paper being slipped under the door. My mother had made a drawing, because I didn't know how to read yet. It was a picture of a child crying that had been crossed out. Next to it was a picture of a child laughing. I realized that she was on the other side of the door telling me to smile and that everything would be okay. But she didn't make a drawing to show that she would open the door. She was just telling me to laugh, and not cry. So I was still panic-stricken. I could feel myself screaming. I felt my vocal chords vibrating. When I let out high-pitched sounds, my vocal chords don't vibrate at all. But if I make low-pitched sounds, if I yell, I feel the vibrations. That day, I made my vocal chords vibrate till I was out of breath.

I must have cried a long time, like an angry seagull in a storm, before a locksmith came and opened the door, that wall separating me from my mother.

It's "Tifikul"

Everything was difficult. What would have been the simplest of things for a hearing child was hard for me.

They put me in a mainstream kindergarten class for deaf children, and I started making friends with the other kids. That's actually where my social life began.

The speech therapist was able to get me to pronounce a few audible words. In the beginning, I expressed myself with my own particular blend of speech and gesture. "Up to the age of two," my mother says, "you went to a speech therapy center upstairs from a venereal disease clinic. That got me mad. Was deafness a disease to be ashamed of? Then we put you in the neighborhood kindergarten. One day when I came to get you, the teacher was telling the children stories to develop their language skills. You were sitting all by yourself, drawing at a table in a corner, completely oblivious to what was going on. You didn't look very happy."

I don't remember much about that phase of my life. I do remember, though, that I drew a lot. Drawings were important to me. They replaced communication. Through them, I could express part of the unanswered questions that filled my head. But as for that kindergarten with its so-called mainstream class, I've forgotten about it. Or rather, I'd like to forget about it. All those kids sitting in a circle around a teacher telling stories—is that really mainstreaming?

What was I doing there all alone sitting in front of my drawings or jumping rope on the playground? What were they teaching me? Nothing, as far as I'm concerned. What was the point? Who was benefiting from it?

I have a few mental images from that period of my life. One in particular stands out. My father came to get me when I was in the middle of washing my hands at the playground faucet. "Hurry up. We're leaving," he said.

I don't know how he said that or what he did to communicate the fact that I had to hurry so we could leave, but I felt it. He must have prodded me a bit. He probably looked rushed and anxious. Anyway, I got the message from his behavior: "We don't have much time." But I wanted to make him understand another message: "I haven't finished washing my hands." Then, all of a sudden, he wasn't there any more and I started crying my eyes out. There had been a misunderstanding. We hadn't understood each other. He was gone. He had vanished. And there I was all alone, crying. Was I crying about our misunderstanding or because I was alone? Or was it because he had disappeared? I think it was probably about the misunderstanding.

That scene is symbolic of the almost constant breakdown in communication between them and us, the hearing and the deaf. The only way I can understand a piece of information is by visualizing it. I think of it as a scene where I mix physical sensations with a sharpness of observation typical of a mime artist. If something is expressed quickly, it's hard for me to be sure I've understood. But I try to respond at the same pace. That day, when I was washing my hands at the faucet, my father hadn't understood what I wanted to say. Or maybe I was the one who hadn't understood him. And the penalty for that misunderstanding was that he left!

Naturally he came back to get me after a while. I have no idea how long it was, but I remember I was lonely and desperate. I couldn't explain the reason for my tears to him because everything used to get so complicated when there was a misunderstanding like that. Another situation would always ensue that was even harder to understand than the first.

I don't know if the strange scene I just described is a real memory or if I imagined it. In any case, it's strikingly symbolic of the difficulty I had communicating with my father at that time.

Tifikul is a child's word born of that difficulty. One day, when I must have been older, he and I were home alone. He was cooking steaks and wanted to know if I wanted mine well-done or rare. I could see he was trying to show me the difference between raw and cooked. He used the radiator to explain hot and cold. I understood hot and cold, but not raw and cooked. It went on for a long time, till finally he got mad and cooked both steaks the same.

Another time, he was watching a movie on TV. The name of one of the characters was Laborie, like ours except with an *e*. He kept trying to show me the difference between the *t* in our name and the *e* in the character's name on bits of paper. I just couldn't get it, and I kept telling him over and over, "It's tifikul. It's tifikul."

He didn't understand what I was trying to say. We were both exhausted, so we gave up and waited till my mother got home. He asked her what I meant and she burst out laughing, "It's difficult!"

But it was as "tifikul" for him as it was for me, and that was tough on him. Actually, it was tough on me, too. Deaf children are even more vulnerable and sensitive than others. I know I often used to swing back and forth between anger and laughter.

Anger, for example, would set in when nobody could be bothered to talk to me at mealtime. I would pound on the table furiously. I wanted to "talk," to understand what people were saying. I was sick and tired of being held prisoner of a silence they made no attempt to break. I was always trying hard, but they weren't doing enough. Hearing people didn't make much of an effort and I begrudged them that.

I remember one question that stuck in my mind: How did they understand each other with their backs turned? It was "tifikul" for me to realize that people could talk to each other even if they weren't face to face. I could only understand someone if we were both looking at each other. The only way I could get people's attention was by tugging at them—on a sleeve, the hem of a skirt, or a pant leg. That meant, "Look at me. Show me your face, your eyes, so I can understand you."

Seeing. If I couldn't see, I was lost. I needed the help of facial expressions and mouth movements.

I used my voice, too. I would call out to my father when he played the piano. I yelled "Daddy, Daddy" till he finally looked at me. But what did I want to tell him? I really don't know.

And I banged on things. I poked my mother and took her head in my hands to force her to look right at me.

When the doctor came, he would hunt for the spot where I hurt by poking me till I screamed. As a child, that was my way of talking to doctors when I was sick.

I did a lot of things on the sly. Basically, they were my little experiments.

I loved cough syrup. I secretly polished off every bottle I could find and then, of course, got sick. Nobody had told me cough syrup was bad. How could I know that? It was sweet. It tasted good. And it was supposed to make you better because the doctor prescribed it.

I loved "talami," too. That was my word for dried salami. It was like candy to me when I was little. I would steal it and hide it in the closet between piles of clothes or anywhere I could. But the smell of well-chewed bits always tipped my mother off.

When I was around five or six, I was going to school with deaf children and didn't feel isolated any more. The teacher knew I was deaf. I learned how to count with dominoes, and I learned the alphabet and how to paint. Now, going to school was fun.

I had a little deaf friend who came to my house to play. They would put us in a room together. Communicating was easier between us because we had our own signs and gestures.

We played with fire and candles because we weren't supposed to. I loved experimenting with whatever was off limits.

We watched *Goldorak* cartoons and then acted them out. We played with dolls, fought, and jumped around.

I spent a lot of time watching my parents and when I played, I tried recreating what I had seen. I was the mother in charge of the house, tea parties, and cooking. My little friend's job was to look after the children—the dolls. We pretended he was just coming home from work and then we playacted:

"Okay, you do this. I'll do that."

"No. I'll do it."

Then we would argue some more, and that's how the game went.

Understanding the difference between a man and a woman was also "tifikul." I could clearly see that my mother had breasts and my father didn't. My parents dressed differently. One was Mommy and one was Daddy. But besides that? I wanted to know the difference between my little friend and me, too.

Once, when we were on vacation in the south of France, he and I were playing in the water together. Since we were little, we weren't wearing bathing suits so the difference between him and me was apparent. I thought it was funny, and so simple. I understood. We were both deaf children, but we weren't completely identical.

I was like my mother, except that she could hear and I couldn't. She was a big person, but I would never get big. My little friend and I would soon be "finished." That was the period of my life when we still hadn't seen any deaf adults yet and so we couldn't imagine that you could grow up and be deaf, too. There was no point of reference or comparison to make us see that. So we were going to "leave" soon, be "finished"; in other words, die.

And I thought that when I died, my soul would pass into the body of another baby. But this time, the baby would be hearing. I can't explain that strange transformation. How did I know I had a soul? And, at that age, what did I mean by a soul?

I figured it out in my own way after watching a cartoon on TV. It was a story about a little girl. You didn't see her parents for a long time. So to me, that meant they had gone, just like the white cat. To leave was the same as to die. So I thought they were dead. Then the little girl found her parents again. Naturally, they were the same people as at the beginning of the story. It was just that she had been separated from them. But I concocted another story from it: Her parents had come back from the dead and entered other bodies. That's what I called a soul, "leaving and coming back." A soul was something you had or were, and that would leave and come back. In trying to understand death, I must have combined my white cat's disappearance and the cartoon.

At five or six, it's difficult enough for a hearing child to learn concepts. For me, the process was entirely dependent on visual images. The consequence was that I thought that when I was "finished," when it was my turn to leave along with my little friend, our souls would come back in the bodies of other babies. But those babies would be hearing. Maybe I thought the child who was going to take my place would be able to hear because being deaf made life hard for me. Because I didn't have a language to liberate me yet.

It's "tifikul" to understand the world, but you deal with it as best you can. I don't think asking my little friend to show me his private parts at the beach so I could tell the difference between mommies and daddies was much different from what hearing children do.

I believe the major distinguishing characteristic of the way I perceived things before I knew sign language hinged on two things: the absolute necessity of seeing something to be able to understand it, and, having seen it, the momentary impossibility of seeing it differently. That two possible situations might arise out of a single visual element was hard to fathom. For example, I love my maternal grandparents. Conversing with them wasn't easy, but they took care of me a lot when I was kindergarten age. And when I try to recall a visual memory of them, the first thing I see is a dog!

That's because the dog is linked to a situation that I associate with my grandparents and with having to understand a concept for which hearing people had two definitions but, in my mind, was wordless.

First situation: The dog is with his master. It's a big, friendly Doberman type, and they let me pet him.

Second situation: The dog's master is off at work and the dog is alone in a car. I walk up to the car and open the door. The dog barks in my face and bears his teeth at me. I'm terrified. Before, he let me pet him. Now he wants to bite me! I can't imagine two different types of behavior from the same animal image. In the first situation, no one explained the concepts of "friendly" and "vicious" as they related to dogs.

I sense danger. I run away and the dog darts after me. He bites me on the shoulder and I fall. My father comes running and the dog dashes off.

My father wants to give me a shot, but I don't want one. Needles terrify me. My mother realizes that I'm afraid of needles and does her best to comfort me. There they are, the two of them gesticulating above my head, one trying to give me a shot, the other reassuring me. The only thing I can gather from their discussion is the threat of that horrible needle. I want to run to my grandparents' house. They represent total protection, a refuge I love. And I want to go there. But I get the shot instead.

I always had that reflex to run away when people tried to force something on me or when I didn't understand. Whether it was finishing my soup, getting a shot, or submitting to any kind of constraint, I reacted the only way I could because I was unable to talk. Action was a substitute for discourse. In all truthfulness, I should say that my instinct to flee meshed with my personal character when it came to taking orders. I'm by nature independent, determined, and stubborn. Maybe the loneliness of silence accentuated those traits. It's "tifikul" to say.

My Name Is "I"

They taught me how to say my name at school. Emmanuelle. But Emmanuelle was a little like someone detached from me, a double. When I referred to myself, I would say,

"Emmanuelle can't hear you . . ."

"Emmanuelle did this or that . . ."

I carried within me a deaf girl named Emmanuelle, and I would try to speak for her, as though we were two separate people.

I knew how to say other words. I could pronounce some of them fairly well and others, not so well. The speech therapy method involved placing my hand on the therapist's throat to feel the vibrations as the therapist vocalized. We learned the letter *r*. It vibrated like "ra." Then we learned *f* and *sh* sounds. *Sh* was a problem for me. It never came out right. We went from consonants to vowels (with more emphasis on consonants), and then on to entire words. We repeated the same word for hours. I would imitate what I saw on the therapist's lips, with my hand on her neck, copying her like a little monkey.

Each time we pronounced a word, a sound frequency would register on the screen of a machine. Little green lines, like the ones on an electrocardiogram in hospitals, danced before my eyes. You were supposed to follow the little lines that would rise and fall, level out, jump up, and dip back down.

What was a word on that screen to me? It was the amount of energy I had to put out so that my little green line would go as high as the therapist's. It was tiring and I repeated word after word without understanding what they meant. It was nothing but a throat exercise, a kind of parroting.

Deaf people can't all learn to speak and it's a lie to say otherwise. Even for those who do, their capacity for oral expression remains limited.

I was going to be seven years old at the beginning of the next school year, and I was still at the kindergarten level. But my life and the confined universe in which I was evolving, mostly in silence, were both about to change dramatically.

My father heard something on the radio. That something was a miracle in the making. I couldn't even have begun to imagine it. I considered the radio a mysterious object that talked to hearing people. I didn't pay much attention to it. But that day my father said a deaf person was talking on the program *France-Culture!* It was Alfredo Corrado, an actor and director. My father explained to my mother that he was speaking silently through sign language. It was a real language based on movements of the hands and body, and facial expressions, too! An interpreter, American like Corrado, was translating orally into French for the listeners.

Corrado said he had founded the International Visual Theater (IVT), the deaf theater in Vincennes, in 1976. He worked in the United States. There was a university in Washington, D.C., called Gallaudet University that had been created for the deaf, and he had studied there.

My father was stunned. Deaf people capable of going to college! Here in France, they could barely get through the sixth grade!

He was both ecstatic and angered.

He was angered because, as a doctor, he had trusted his colleagues. The pediatricians, ear-nose-throat specialists, speech therapists, and educators had all told him the only way to help get me out of my isolation was to have me learn spoken language. But no one had given him any information about sign language. It was the first time he had heard of it, and what's more, he heard it from a deaf person!

He was ecstatic because in Vincennes, just outside Paris, maybe there was—surely there was—a solution for me! He wanted to take me there. He was ready to give it a try because he suffered so much from not being able to talk with me.

Mother said she didn't want to go with him. She was afraid of being traumatized and maybe disappointed, too. Since she was about to give birth, she decided to let my father take me to Vincennes.

She sensed that the baby she was carrying wasn't deaf. She could tell the difference between the child still nestled in her womb and me. That baby moved around and reacted to exterior noises. I, on the other hand, had slept all too quietly, sheltered from the racket. For the time being, her first concern was the arrival of the family's second child, almost seven years after me. She needed peace and quiet, time for herself. I can understand how the emotions sparked by this new ray of hope might have been too overwhelming for her. She was afraid of being disappointed again. And besides, we had our own system of communicating, what I call the "umbilical" method. We had gotten used to it. But my father had nothing. He realized I was a natural for communicating with others. It was something I was always trying to do. So he was excited by the new prospect that had miraculously come his way via the radio.

I think that when he gave me the priceless gift of sign language, it was the first time he truly accepted my deafness. It was a gift to himself too, since he wanted desperately to be able to talk to me.

Of course I didn't understand a thing and had no idea what was going on. My father looked perplexed. That's the only memory I have of that day that was so very moving for him and so incredibly fantastic for me: the radio and his face. The next day, he took me to Vincennes.

I can still see some of the visual imprints of that day: We're going up some stairs. We enter a large room. My father is talking to two hearing people—two adults who aren't wearing hearing aids. Therefore, I assume they aren't deaf. At this stage of my life, I recognize deaf people only because of their hearing aids. But, as it turns out, one is deaf and the other isn't. One is Alfredo Corrado and the other Bill Moody, a hearing sign language interpreter.

I see Alfredo and Bill signing to each other. I see that my father can understand Bill because Bill is speaking. But the signs mean nothing to me. They're quick, strange, complicated. I've never seen anything like it before. The simplistic code I invented with my mother was based on mime and a few orally pronounced words. I look at the two men in amazement. Their hands and fingers are moving, their bodies too, and they're making facial expressions. It's beautiful and mesmerizing.

Who's deaf and who's hearing? There's no way to tell. Then I realize, "Hey, that's a hearing person talking with his hands!"

Alfredo Corrado is a tall, handsome, Italian-looking man—thin with very dark hair. He has a mustache and rather sharp features. Bill has straight, medium-length hair, blue eyes, and a cheerful face. He's friendly and open. They both seem around the same age as my father.

Jean Gremion, the founder and head of the deaf social and cultural center, is there, too. He greets us.

Alfredo comes up to me and says, "I'm deaf, like you, and I sign. That's my language."

I mime my response, "Why aren't you wearing a hearing aid?"

He smiles. It's obvious that he thinks deaf people don't need hearing aids. But for me, hearing aids are a visible point of reference.

So Alfredo is deaf, but doesn't wear a hearing aid. What's more, he's an adult. I think it took me awhile to grasp that threefold oddity.

What I did realize right away, however, was that I wasn't alone in the world. It was a startling revelation. And a bewildering one because, up till then, I had thought, as do so many deaf children, that I was unique and predestined to die as a child. I discovered that I could have a future since Alfredo was a deaf adult!

That cruel logic about early death persists as long as deaf children haven't encountered a deaf adult. They need to be able to identify with an adult. It's crucial. Parents of deaf children should be made aware of the importance of having their children come in contact with deaf adults as soon as possible, right after birth. The two worlds need to blend—the world of sound and the world of silence. A deaf child's psychological development will be quicker and much better, and the child will grow up free of the pain of being alone in the world with no constructed thought patterns and no future.

Imagine that you had a kitten and never showed it a full-grown cat. It might spend its entire life thinking it was a kitten. Or imagine that the little cat only lived with dogs. It would think it was the only cat in the world and wear itself out trying to communicate in dog language. The cat might succeed at getting a few basic things across to the dogs through motions—eating, drinking, fear, affection, submission or aggressiveness. But it would be so much happier and more well-balanced among its own kind, young and old, speaking cat!

With the oral technique that had been imposed on my parents from the beginning, I had no chance of meeting deaf adults who could serve as role models for me because my parents had been advised against it. I only had contact with hearing people.

I don't have a precise recollection of that first, stupefying visit to Vincennes when I watched in awe as all those hands whirled about. I don't know what my father and the two men said to each other. I just remember my astonishment at seeing my father understand what Alfredo's hands and Bill's mouth were saying. At the time, I still didn't know that because of those men I was going to acquire a language. What stuck in my mind, though, was the stupendous revelation that Emmanuelle would be able to grow up! That was something I had seen now with my very own eyes.

The following week, my father took me back to Vincennes. They were having a parent-child communication workshop. There were lots of parents. Alfredo had the children gather in a circle around him and began working with them. He demonstrated some signs. The parents watched so they could learn, too. They were simple signs, I remember, like "house," "eat," "drink," "sleep," "table."

He drew a house on a flipboard and showed us the corresponding sign. Then he drew a picture of an adult and said, "This is your daddy. You are your daddy's daughter. This is your mommy. You are your mommy's daughter."

He also showed us someone looking for something, first through mime, next using sign. Then he asked, "Where's Mommy?"

I signed, "Mommy is somewhere else."

Then he corrected me.

"Where's Mommy? Mommy is at home. Make the sign for 'Mommy' and 'house.' "

A complete sentence: "Mommy is at home." Finally at the age of seven, I was signing with both hands to identify my mother and designate where she was!

Elated, with my eyes fixed on Alfredo's, I used both hands to repeat, "Mommy is at home."

The first few times I was there, I learned everyday words and then people's names. He was Alfredo, I was Emmanuelle. A sign for him and a sign for me.

Emmanuelle: "Sun-Coming-from-the-Heart." "Emmanuelle" was my name to hearing people, "Sun-Coming-from-the-Heart" was my name to deaf people.

That was the first time I realized you could give people names. That, too, was fantastic. Except for Mommy and Daddy, I didn't know that people in our family had names. I used to meet people, friends of my parents or members of the family, but, in my mind, they didn't have names. There was no way to define them. I was so surprised to learn that his name was Alfredo and the other man was Bill. And me, especially me, Emmanuelle. I finally understood that I had an identity. I, Emmanuelle.

Until then, when I talked about myself, it was like talking about somebody else. Somebody who wasn't "I." People would always say, "Emmanuelle is deaf." It was always "She can't hear you, she can't hear you." There was no "I." I was "she."

People who have had their name in their head practically from birth, a name that Mommy and Daddy repeated, might find that hard to understand. They're used to turning their head when their name is called. Their identity is given to them at birth. They don't have to think about it or ask themselves questions about who they are. They're "I" or "me." It's natural and effortless. They know who they are. They can identify themselves, introduce themselves to people with a symbol that stands for them. But the deaf Emmanuelle didn't know that she was "I," that she was "me." She discovered it with sign language, and now she knew. Emmanuelle could say, "My name is Emmanuelle."

It was a joy to make that discovery. Emmanuelle was no longer that double whose needs, desires, dislikes, and woes I had to painfully explain. I had discovered the world around me and myself in the midst of it.

It was also at that time, when I started seeing deaf adults on a regular basis, that I stopped being afraid of dying. I never thought about it again. And I had my father to thank for that.

It was like being born again. My life was just beginning. The first barrier had fallen. There were still others around me, but an initial opening had been made in my prison wall. I was going to understand the world with my eyes and hands. I could already sense it and I was so eager!

There before me stood the marvelous man who was teaching me about the world, and the names of people and things. There was a sign for Bill, one for Alfredo, one for Jacques (my father), one for my mother, my sister, the house, the table, the cat...I was going to live! And I had so many questions to ask. So many! I was voracious, starved for answers because now people could answer me!

In the beginning, I mixed up all the different communication methods: signs and mime and words that came out orally. I was a bit unsettled, confused. Sign language had happened so suddenly. I was seven years old and had to get things straight in my mind, sort out all the information I was taking in. And there was a good deal of it. You really become a communicating individual, capable of developing, when, for example, you're finally able to use correctly constructed language to say things like, "My name is Emmanuelle. I'm hungry. Mommy is at home, Daddy is with me. My friend's name is Jules, my cat's name is Bobbin."

I didn't learn everything all at once, of course. At home, I continued using a little of the code my mother and I had made up, but started mixing in some sign. I remember they understood me, but I don't recall my first complete signed sentence that they comprehended.

Little by little, I straightened things out in my head and began to construct ideas and organize thoughts. Most importantly, I started communicating with my father.

Then my mother joined us in Vincennes. She, too, was about to emerge from the tunnel of erroneous information and false hopes my parents had been trapped in ever since I was born. She was totally surprised to see that there was a meeting place for the deaf. It was a vibrant, creative place, where they were being taught. It was a place to get to know parents trying to cope with the same problems, to meet professionals specializing in deafness who were rethinking the practices of the medical profession and the information it was disseminating. They had made the decision to teach a language. Sign language. Not a code or jargon, but a real language.

"I was terribly frightened," says my mother in recalling her first visit to Vincennes. "I was face to face with reality. It was like a second diagnosis. Everyone was friendly, but as I listened to the deaf people tell of their suffering as children, of the horrible isolation they had lived in before, of their problems as adults and their ongoing struggle, I was sick. I had been wrong. I had been misled by people who had told me, 'With speech therapy and a hearing aid, she'll be able to speak.' "

"After you were born," my father says, "I could practically hear them say, or at least I wanted to hear them say, 'One day, she WILL HEAR.' "

Vincennes was another world, the real deaf world, devoid of needless patronizing. But it was also a world of hope for the deaf. Sure, deaf people manage to talk, more or less, yet for many of us who are profoundly deaf, it's never more than partially effective. Now, with sign language, plus speech, and my all-consuming desire to communicate, I was going to make tremendous strides.

After seven years of existence, I had just taken a huge step forward. My name is "I."

Marie, Marie

When my little sister was born, I asked what her name was. Marie.

Marie, Marie. I had trouble remembering it. I decided to write it down on paper, over and over, like practicing words at school. I kept going back to my mother to ask her what my little sister's name was. I wanted to be sure. And I would repeat it: "Ma-rie, Ma-rie, Ma-rie . . ."

I'm Emmanuelle. She's Marie.

Marie, Marie, Marie . . .

"What's her name again?"

I wrote it more than a hundred times, letter by letter, to be able to remember it visually. But it was still too hard to pronounce. I had to really work at saying her name.

My father took me to the hospital to see my little sister. I hated hospitals. When Mother was pregnant, I saw her having blood samples taken. I was so afraid, I hid under the bed. Even today, I can't stand the sight of blood. I loathe needles. *Hospital* means needles and blood. *Hospital* means threatening place.

My sister was in an incubator. She wasn't premature, but since the hospital wasn't heated, they put her in there with a few other babies to keep warm.

I don't know if I was happy when I saw her. What I saw mystified me—the incubator and a tiny little thing inside. It was hard to imagine anything about her, there behind the plastic. I can't really remember, but my feelings at that moment weren't very clear. I wondered to myself, "Are both of us the same?"

Contributors

H-Dirksen L. Bauman is Professor of Deaf Studies at Gaulaudet University where he directs the graduate program in Deaf Studies. He is co-editor of *Signing the Body Poetic: Essays in American Sign Language Literature* (University of California Press, 2006), and executive producer of the documentary film *Audism Unveiled*.

Douglas Baynton is Associate Professor of History and American Sign Language at the University of Iowa. The author of *Forbidden Signs: American Culture and the Campaign Against Sign Language* (University of Chicago Press, 1996), he is currently writing a book on the history of the concept of "defective persons" in American immigration policy.

Chris Bell's essays and articles have appeared in *Positively Aware, On the Move: Mobility and Identity, Culture and the Condom*, and *The Faces of AIDS: Living in the Heartland*. He is a PhD student in English at Nottingham Trent University where his research examines cultural responses to the AIDS crisis.

Lerita Coleman Brown is Chair of the Department and Professor of Psychology at Agnes Scott College in Atlanta, Georgia. She is currently completing a manuscript about surviving and living happily with the disabilities associated with having heart and kidney transplants.

Brenda Brueggemann is Professor of English, Women's Studies, and Comparative Studies at Ohio State University where she directs the American Sign Language program and coordinates the Disability Studies undergraduate minor and graduate interdisciplinary specialization. She is author, co-author, editor, or co-editor of the following books: *Lend Me Your Ear: Rhetorical Constructions of Deafness* (Gallaudet UP, 1999); *Disability Studies: Enabling the Humanities* (MLA, 2002): *Literacy and Deaf People: Cultural and Contextual Perspectives* (Gallaudet UP, 2004); *Rhetorical Visions: Reading and Writing in a Visual Culture* (Prentice-Hall, forthcoming); *Teaching, Disability, and Writing: A Critical Sourcebook* (Bedford/St. Martin's, forthcoming); *Double Vision(s): Multidisciplinary Approaches to Women and Deafness* (Gallaudet UP, forthcoming); *Deaf Places: Identities, Institutions, and Issues in Modern Deaf-World* (NYU Press, forthcoming).

James Charlton is a longtime political activist. He helped found Access Living, one of the country's leading centers for independent living in 1979. He has taught social theory and political economy classes for graduate students in Disability Studies at the University of Illinois since 2000. His most recent book *Nothing About Us Without Us: Disability Oppression and Empowerment* (University of California Press) was published in 1998.

G. Thomas Couser is Professor of English and Director of Disability Studies at Hofstra University. His most recent books are *Recovering Bodies: Illness, Disability, and Life Writing* (Wisconsin, 1997) and *Vulnerable Subjects: Ethics and Life Writing* (Cornell, 2004).

Michael Davidson is Professor of Literature at the University of California, San Diego. He has written extensively on disability issues, most recently "Hearing Things: The Scandal of Speech in Deaf

435

Performance," in *Disability Studies: Enabling the Humanities*, Ed. Sharon Snyder, et al. (Modern Language Association, 2002), "Phantom Limbs: Film Noir and the Disabled Body," *GLQ* 9:1-2 (2003), and "Strange Blood: Hemophobia and the Unexplored Boundaries of Queer Nation," in *Beyond the Boundary: Reconstructing Cultural Identity in a Multicultural Context*, edited by Timothy Powell (Rutgers UP, 1999). He is completing a book on disability and cultural studies in an age of globalization.

Lennard J. Davis is Professor of Disability and Human Development, English, and Medical Education at the University of Illinois at Chicago. He is the author of among other works *Enforcing Normalcy: Disability, Deafness, and the Body* (Verso 1995); *Bending Over Backwards: Disability, Dismodernism, and Other Difficult Positions* (New York UP); and *My Sense of Silence: Memoirs of a Childhood with Deafness.* He edited *Shall I Say A Kiss: The Courtship Letters of a Deaf Couple, 1936–1938.* He is currently the director of Project Biocultures (http://www.biocultures.org). His current projects are a book on obsession and another on artificial insemination.

Anne Finger is the author of a memoir, *Past Due: A Story of Disability, Pregnancy and Birth* (Seal Press) as well as the novel, *Bone Truth* (Coffeehouse Press).

Kenny Fries is the author of *Body, Remember: A Memoir* (Dutton, 1997; new edition, University of Wisconsin Press, 2003) and editor of *Staring Back: The Disability Experience from the Inside Out* (Plume, 1997). His books of poems include *Desert Walking* (The Advocado Press) and *Anesthesia* (The Advocado Press). He teaches in the MFA in Creative Writing Program at Goddard College and at Fordham University at Lincoln Center. His new book is *The History of My Shoes and the Evolution of Darwin's Theory.*

Rosemarie Garland-Thomson is Associate Professor of Women's Studies at Emory University in Atlanta, Georgia. Her fields of study are feminist theory, American literature, and disability studies. She is the author of *Extraordinary Bodies: Figuring Physical Disability in American Literature and Culture* (Columbia UP), editor of *Freakery: Cultural Spectacles of the Extraordinary Body* (New York UP), and co-editor of *Disability Studies: Enabling the Humanities* (MLA Press). She is currently writing a book on the dynamics of staring and one on the cultural logic of euthanasia.

Erving Goffman was Professor of Sociology at the University of California at Berkeley and University of Pennsylvania. He was the author of numerous books on social interaction including *The Presentation of Self in Everyday Life* (Anchor) and *Stigma.*

David Hevey is a director, scriptwriter, and photographer. He directed over ten films for the BBC and now directs as a freelancer; his latest film, *The Bells*, has played at several U.S. film festivals, including those held in Denver and Dallas. As a photographer, he shot for LA Movieline, Time Life, and others. He is currently running London-based Hevey-Balcombe Films, with his business partner and co-writer, Bet Balcombe.

Ruth Hubbard is Professor Emerita of Biology at Harvard University. Her work in the fields of biology, biochemistry and photochemistry has focused on the relationship between biology and women and the relevant issues of disability. She is the author of *The Politics of Women's Biology* (Rutger's UP) and co-author with Elijah Wald of *Exploding the Gene Myth: How Genetic Information Is Produced and Manipulated by Scientists, Physicians, Employers, Insurance Companies, Educators, and Law Enforcers* (Beacon Press).

Tom Humphries is Associate Professor in the Department of Communications at the University of California, San Diego. He is the co-author, with Carol A. Padden, of *Inside Deaf Culture* (Harvard UP).

Georgina Kleege, the author of *Sights Unseen* (Yale UP), is an author, translator, and essayist. She has taught writing and literature courses at Ohio State University and University of Oklahoma.

Emmanuelle Laborit, the author of *Cry of the Gull* (Gallaudet UP) is the recipient of the Moliere award for best actress in *Beyond Silence*.

Harlan Lane is University Distinguished Professor in the Department of Psychology at Northeastern University. He is the recipient of the International Social Merit Award of the World Federation of the Deaf as well as numerous other honors. He is the author of numerous books on Deaf history and an internationally recognized advocate for the deaf.

Bradley Lewis is on faculty at New York University's Gallatin School of Individuated Study. He has dual training in interdisciplinary humanities and medicine (specializing in psychiatry). He writes and teaches at the interface of medicine, humanities, science studies, and disability studies. He is cultural studies editor for the *Journal of Medical Humanities* and has written extensively on the cultural dynamics of contemporary psychiatry. He is the author of *Moving Beyond Prozac, DSM, and the New Psychiatry: Birth of Postpsychiatry* and his current book project is a narrative study of sadness.

Simi Linton is President of *Disability/Arts* and the author of *My Body Politic, Claiming Disability: Knowledge and Identity,* as well as numerous articles on disability studies, and disability and the arts. She is Co-director of the University Seminar in Disability Studies at Columbia University.

Robert McRuer is an Associate Professor in the English Department at George Washington University where he teaches disability studies and queer studies. He is the author of *Crip Theory: Cultural Signs of Queerness and Disability* and co-editor, with Abby L. Wilkerson, of "Desiring Disability: Queer Theory Meets Disability Studies," a special issue of *GLQ: A Journal of Lesbian and Gay Studies.*

Nicholas Mirzoeff is Professor of Art and Art Professions at New York University, where he directs the Visual Culture MA/PhD program. His publications include *Silent Poetry: Deafness, Sign and Visual Culture in Modern France* (1995) and *Watching Babylon: The War in Iraq and Global Visual Culture* (2005).

David Mitchell is a faculty member in the Disability Studies program at the University of Illinois, Chicago. To date he has edited three books on disability culture and history including *The Body and Physical Difference* (1997). He has also co-written two books including *Narrative Prosthesis* (2000). He is co-editor of *Encyclopedia of Disability* (2006). He has served as president of the Society for Disability Studies and was a founding member of both the Committee on Disability and the Disability Studies Discussion Group for the Modern Languages Association. Currently he is serving as principal organizer of the Chicago Festival of Disability Arts and Culture.

Anna Mollow is a Ph.D. candidate in English at the University of California, Berkeley, where she is writing a dissertation on literature and medicine. Her work in disability studies has appeared in *MELUS* and *Michigan Quarterly Review.*

Carol Padden is professor in the Department of Communication at UC, San Diego. In addition to *Inside Deaf Culture*, she and Tom Humphries are also the authors of *Deaf in America: Voices from a Culture.*

M. Lynn Rose is Associate Professor of History at Truman State University in Kirksville, Missouri. She is the author of *The Staff of Oedipus: Transforming Disability in Ancient Greece* (University of Michigan Press). Her area of research is disability in the ancient world.

Marsha Saxton is the executive director of the Project on Women and Disability at the Massachusetts Office of Disability. She is a trainer, consultant, and organizer in peer counseling for disabled people. She is the editor of *With Wings: An Anthology of Literature By and About Women With Disabilities* (Feminist Press).

David Serlin is Associate Professor of Communication and Science Studies at the University of California at San Diego. He is the author of *Replaceable You: Engineering the Body in Postwar America* (University of Chicago Press, 2004), and the coeditor of *Artificial Parts, Practical Lives: Modern Histories of Prosthetics* (NYU Press, 2002). He is currently working on a book project about the relationship between disability and architecture.

Tom Shakespeare is principal research associate in sociology, University of Newcastle. His books include *The Sexual Politics of Disability* and *Genetic Politics: from Eugenics to Genome*. He writes and broadcasts widely on disability and genetics and he is a member of Arts Council England.

Tobin Siebers is V. L. Parrington Collegiate Professor and Director of Comparative Literature at the University of Michigan. He has published essays on disability in *American Literary History, Cultural Critique, Literature and Medicine, Michigan Quarterly Review, PMLA,* and the MLA volume on disability studies. He is currently completing two books, *Disability Theory* and *Disability Aesthetics.*

Marquard Smith is Director of Postgraduate Studies and Course Convenor of the MA in Art History in the School of Art and Design History, Kingston University, London. A founder of the cultural studies journal *parallax* (Routledge) and a founder and the editor-in-chief of *journal of visual culture* (Sage Publications), he is most recently editor of *Stelarc: The Monograph* (The MIT Press) and co-editor of *The Prosthetic Impulse: From a Posthuman Present to a Biocultural Present* (The MIT Press). Marq is an Affiliated Member of Project Biocultures, and is completing a book entitled *Moving Bodies: Perverse Visions of Prosthetic Culture.*

Sharon Snyder is on faculty in the Department of Disability and Human Development at the University of Illinois, Chicago. She is the co-author of two books including *Cultural Locations of Disability* (2005), and co-editor of three collections including *Eugenics in America* (2005) and *Disability Studies: Enabling the Humanities* (2003) and *Encyclopedia of Disability* (2006). As founder of the independent production company, Brace Yourselves Productions, she is also an award-winning documentary filmmaker whose work includes, *Self-Preservation: the Art of Riva Lehrer* (2004), *Disability Takes on the Arts* (2005), *A World Without Bodies* (2002), and *Vital Signs: Crip Culture Talks Back* (1996).

Susan Sontag was the author of four novels, five books of essays, and several plays, among them *On Photography* (Picador), *Against Interpretation: And Other Essays* (Picador), *Illness as Metaphor* (Vintage).

Shelley Tremain was the 1997–1998 Ed Roberts Post-doctoral fellow at UC-Berkeley and The World Institute on Disability. From 1999-2001, Tremain was employed as a Research Associate and Co-Principal Investigator at Canada's national policy research institute to promote the human rights of disabled people. She has published widely on disability and is the editor of *Foucault and the Government of Disability* (University of Michigan Press, 2005).

Cheryl Marie Wade is a poet, playwright, videomaker, and performer. She is the editor of *Gnarlybone News*, a free online "cut and paste" disability culture newsletter. Her performance video "Body Talk", received an Award of Achievement from Superfest XXI. She is the recipient of the 1994 National Endowment for the Arts Solo Theater Artist's Fellowship and the CeCe Robinson Award for disability writing and performing.

Susan Wendell is Professor Emerita of Women's Studies at Simon Fraser University. She is the author of *The Rejected Body: Feminist Philosophical Reflections on Disability* (Routledge) and is currently writing a book on the value of suffering and the ethics of disability.

James C. Wilson, Professor of English at the University of Cincinnati, is co-editor of *Embodied Rhetorics: Disability in Language and Culture*. He has disability related essays in *Cultural Critique*, *Rhetoric Review, Disability Studies Quarterly*, and *TCQ*, as well as the MLA collection, *Disability Studies: Enabling the Humanities*.

Index